STARK LIBRARY   JUL   2021

JOBS FOR SKILLED WORKERS

Skilled Jobs in
HEALTH CARE

Cherese Cartlidge

San Diego, CA

© 2021 ReferencePoint Press, Inc.
Printed in the United States

For more information, contact:
ReferencePoint Press, Inc.
PO Box 27779
San Diego, CA 92198
www.ReferencePointPress.com

ALL RIGHTS RESERVED.
No part of this work covered by the copyright hereon may be reproduced or used in any form or by any means—graphic, electronic, or mechanical, including photocopying, recording, taping, web distribution, or information storage retrieval systems—without the written permission of the publisher.

LIBRARY OF CONGRESS CATALOGING-IN-PUBLICATION DATA

Names: Cartlidge, Cherese, author.
Title: Skilled Jobs in Health Care/Cherese Cartlidge.
Description: San Diego, CA: ReferencePoint Press, Inc., 2020. | Series: Jobs for Skilled Workers | Includes bibliographical references and index.
Identifiers: LCCN 2019049319 (print) | LCCN 2019049320 (ebook) | ISBN 9781682828236 (library binding) | ISBN 9781682828243 (ebook)
Subjects: LCSH: Medical personnel—Vocational guidance.
Classification: LCC R690 .C386 2020 (print) | LCC R690 (ebook) | DDC 610.69—dc23
LC record available at https://lccn.loc.gov/2019049319
LC ebook record available at https://lccn.loc.gov/2019049320

Contents

Caring Careers	4
Dental Hygienist	7
Diagnostic Medical Sonographer	15
Emergency Medical Technician	23
Licensed Practical Nurse	30
Massage Therapist	37
Pharmacy Technician	44
Phlebotomist	52
Physical Therapist Assistant	60
Source Notes	68
Interview with a Dental Hygienist	71
Other Jobs in Health Care	74
Index	75
Picture Credits	79
About the Author	80

Caring Careers

When Erin Hendrickson was only a baby, her four-year-old sister was diagnosed with medulloblastoma—a cancerous brain tumor. It was removed, and subsequent chemotherapy cured the cancer but left Hendrickson's sister with long-term side effects, including a lowered IQ. Hendrickson accompanied her parents and sister on a lot of the doctor visits and helped care for her sister throughout their childhood and adolescence. This experience, as well as her sister's eventual death at age twenty-five, had a profound effect on Hendrickson. "I developed a strong sense of compassion and desire to help people," she says. "I knew from this experience a career in healthcare was one that suited me well. My sister was my motivation for choosing radiation therapy."[1]

While she was in high school, Hendrickson started taking steps toward a career in her chosen field. She shadowed radiation therapists at a few local hospitals and eventually gained early acceptance to a hospital-based training program when she was a high school senior. Today Hendrickson says she finds her career as a radiation therapist especially rewarding. "Every patient has a different story to tell and each one is meaningful. We as therapists are with a patient every day throughout their course of treatment and relationships are formed. . . . The joy in seeing patients come back after follow-up cured from their diagnosis or in remission and how happy they are to be done [with] their treatments is one of the best parts of the job."[2]

Choices Galore

Young people who are in interested in health care can select from an incredible array of careers. They may work as dental assistants, doctors, or dieticians. Or they may lean toward exercise physiology, speech pathology, massage therapy, or medical transcription. Psychiatric technicians work for the health care industry, as do pharmacists, phlebotomists, respiratory therapists, athletic trainers, medical secretaries, and home health aides—the list goes on and on. People employed by the health care industry work in all kinds of locations, including hospitals, health practitioner offices, nursing and residential care facilities, private homes, and laboratories.

The amount of education needed for a particular job is often a factor in one's decision to pursue a career in health care. Those who have long dreamed of becoming doctors can anticipate spending eight years in college and medical school, then another three to seven years in internship and residency programs. But not all health care careers require such long, intensive education—in fact, most do not. Health care consultant and recruiter Andrea Clement Santiago writes, "Whether you have a GED [general equivalency diploma] or a Ph.D., there's a healthcare career available to you."[3]

Santiago cites two examples of health care jobs that may require only a high school diploma: patient care coordinator and pharmacy technician. A wide variety of health care jobs require no more than a two-year associate's degree, including dental hygienist, registered nurse, radiation therapist, physical therapy assistant, and respiratory therapist, just to name a few. Those who want to work in nursing but prefer to spend as little time as possible in a classroom might consider becoming a licensed practical nurse (LPN). This job usually requires one to complete a state-approved training program that can be finished in as little as twelve months. "Most LPNs I have spoken with agree that it is the course length that attracted them,"[4] says Tina Johnson, a veteran LPN who serves as president of the National Federation of Licensed Practical Nurses.

An Awesome Future Outlook

Along with the extraordinary variety of jobs, another factor that makes health care careers so attractive is how bright their future looks. According to the Bureau of Labor Statistics (BLS), the health care industry is projected to grow 18 percent through

2026, which is much faster than the 5 percent to 8 percent average for all occupations. This growth will add about 2.4 million new jobs to the workforce—more than any other occupational group. The BLS says that the health care industry has been growing steadily for years, and since 2017 it has been the largest source of jobs in the United States.

Although there are various reasons for the projected future growth in health care careers, the biggest factor is the aging population. According to the US Population Reference Bureau, the number of Americans aged sixty-five and older will nearly double between 2018 and 2060. This increase in older people will lead to a greater demand for health care services—and many more health care professionals. Other factors in the expected surge in health care jobs are improvements in medicine and technology, which will increase demand for services and the professionals who provide them.

With such promising growth, a mind-boggling array of job choices, and large variations in required education, the health care field offers tremendous potential for the future. Although working in health care may not be for everyone, for those who are passionate about helping others and making a difference in people's lives, says Santiago, "working in healthcare can be one of the most rewarding career choices there is."[5]

Dental Hygienist

A Few Facts

Number of Jobs
About 215,150 in 2018

Pay
About $51,930 to $101,820

Educational Requirements
Associate's degree

Certification and Licensing
Dental hygienist license

Personal Qualities
Stamina, dexterity, attention to detail, good interpersonal skills

Work Settings
Dental and orthodontic offices

Future Job Outlook
Growth of 20 percent through 2026

What Does a Dental Hygienist Do?

Dental hygienists work under the direct supervision of a dentist. They are responsible for cleaning patients' teeth, using dental instruments to remove plaque, tartar, and stains from the teeth and beneath the gum line. They also provide fluoride treatments and apply preventive sealants where needed.

Dental hygienists, however, do more than just clean teeth and apply fluoride or sealants. Although the responsibilities of this profession vary from state to state, most hygienists take and interpret dental X-rays to look for cavities or other problems. These professionals examine patients' mouths for signs of oral diseases such as gingivitis, and they may also feel the lymph nodes in the neck to check for swelling or tenderness, which could be a sign of oral cancer. They also educate patients on ways to improve and maintain good oral health, such as proper brushing and flossing techniques. They may also advise patients on selecting toothbrushes and other oral care devices.

Most dental hygienists find it very fulfilling to help people improve and maintain their oral health. A dental hygienist named Anabel J. says, "I like the rewarding feeling when a patient leaves your office feeling not only their teeth cleaned, but also the health education they receive from visiting me, and every time they come back to see me they want to learn more and do more to care for their oral health and overall health in general."[6]

A Typical Workday

Most dental hygienists begin their workday about a half hour before their first patient arrives. This allows them to review charts and dental histories and prepare for the treatments patients will need that day, such as fillings or X-rays. Hygienists must conduct a full assessment of new patients, which includes reading their medical history, taking X-rays, and analyzing their oral health. For existing patients, hygienists begin by asking about any health changes or new medications a patient may be taking.

Most of a typical patient visit is spent cleaning and examining the patient's teeth. Dental hygienists use many tools to do this. They clean the teeth using hand, power, and ultrasonic tools, and sometimes they also use lasers. They remove stains with an air-polishing tool that sprays a combination of water, air, and baking soda. Hygienists polish teeth with a power tool that spins like an electric toothbrush. They use X-ray machines to check for any problems with the teeth or jaw. They also use a tool called a periodontal probe to measure the depth of the gum pockets around each tooth.

In addition to cleaning, polishing, and examining the teeth, dental hygienists may apply a fluoride treatment to help strengthen the surface of the teeth. Once all of these procedures are completed, hygienists provide a diagnosis to the dentist, reporting any problems or issues they have found. The dentist will then make a formal diagnosis and decide on the appropriate treatment, such as a filling, sealants, or a root canal. The hygienist will then explain the treatment to the patient as well as give instructions to help

> ### Changing Lives
>
> "When I entered dental hygiene, I knew I'd finally found my niche. I immediately felt a great sense of satisfaction in knowing that I was helping my patients keep their smiles for a lifetime. . . . Being a dental hygienist gives me a chance to change lives for the better. I'm given an opportunity to treat people with empathy and caring in order to build a foundation of trust. I can help scared patients become more relaxed in the dental office, and my ultimate success is when I have a patient who can't wait to come back."
>
> —Amber Metro-Sanchez, dental hygienist
>
> Amber Metro-Sanchez, "Why I Would Choose Dental Hygiene All Over Again," *RDH*, February 21, 2017. www.rdhmag.com.

improve the patient's oral health, such as flossing more often or using a softer toothbrush.

After the patient leaves, the dental hygienist cleans and disinfects the room and all instruments to prepare for the next patient. And then the whole process begins again and repeats until the end of the hygienist's workday. A full-time dental hygienist will see eight to ten patients a day.

Education and Training

All states require dental hygienists to be licensed, although the requirements vary by state. To be licensed, most states require an associate's degree from an accredited dental hygiene program. The Commission on Dental Accreditation, which is part of the American Dental Association, is responsible for accrediting dental hygiene programs. Such programs are offered at community colleges, technical schools, and universities, and they usually take two to three years to complete. The programs provide both laboratory and classroom instruction, and students study areas such as anatomy, nutrition, medical ethics,

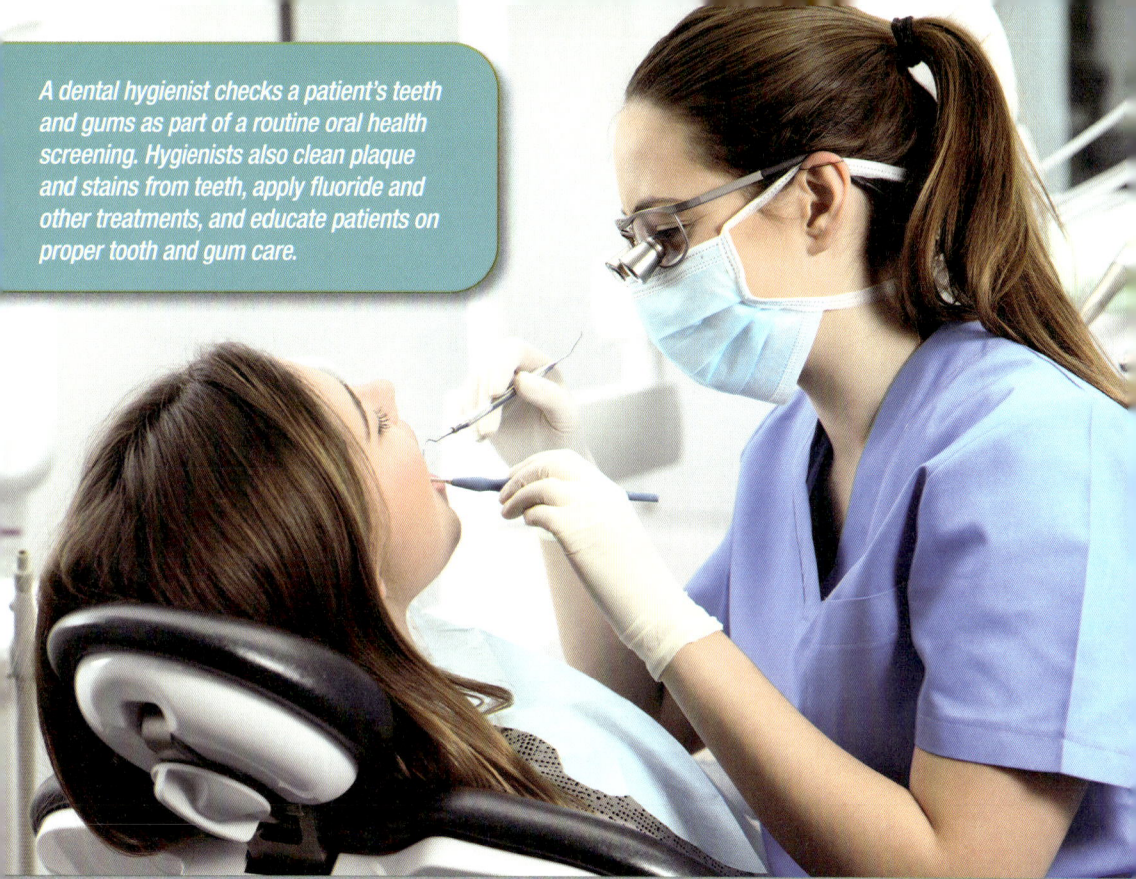

A dental hygienist checks a patient's teeth and gums as part of a routine oral health screening. Hygienists also clean plaque and stains from teeth, apply fluoride and other treatments, and educate patients on proper tooth and gum care.

and periodontics (gum disease). High school students who are interested in a career in this field should take classes in biology, chemistry, and math to help prepare for the rigorous course work involved in these programs. Anastasia Turchetta, a dental hygienist, describes her training: "We took sociology, we took psychology and we took English. We took microbiology, nutrition. . . . Then we took biology, we took radiology, periodontology, pharmacology. . . . Then we had to do public health. . . . You were always busy, and it was almost overwhelming. Yet, the community of students and instructors are amazing."[7]

In addition to graduating from an accredited program, prospective dental hygienists must take a national written exam and a state or regional clinical examination. A passing score on these tests is needed to obtain the registered dental hygienist credential. Cardiopulmonary resuscitation certification may also be required in some areas. And in order to maintain licensure, hygienists must complete continuing education courses.

Skills and Personality

Dental hygienists work closely with dentists and with patients, so excellent interpersonal skills are a must. Many people are nervous about having dental work done or may be in pain, so hygienists need to be patient, understanding, sensitive, and able to explain each step of the treatment. A positive, friendly attitude will also help put patients at ease.

Good communication skills are important as well. A dental hygienist must discuss a patient's care with the dentist and report any problems or issues the hygienist has discovered during a visit, such as cavities, mouth sores, or receding gums. Part of the hygienist's job is to explain oral hygiene care to patients and, if needed, clearly describe any dental issues or necessary treatments.

Dental hygienists need good critical-thinking and problem-solving skills in order to assess patients' needs and help develop care plans so they can maintain or improve their oral health. Being detail oriented helps with this; hygienists must pay careful attention to their work and follow specific steps and procedures that help the dentist diagnose and treat patients. Dexterity is also an important skill to possess. Hygienists need excellent fine-motor skills to use their tools and instruments inside a person's mouth, which is a very small space.

Passion and commitment are also vital skills for hygienists. Turchetta says it takes dedication to be good at this job: "If you cannot find it in you to continually fuel the passion for why you got into this, and how you can literally save someone's life from oral cancer, for example, then it's not for you. To me, that separates someone who's great, or not. It's dedication, it's commitment, it's never-ending."[8]

Working Conditions

About half of dental hygienists work full-time and about half part-time. Some work only a few days a week and may work for more than one dentist. Full-time hygienists typically spend about seven to eight hours with patients, with an hour off for lunch. Most hygienists work under the direct supervision of a dentist, but depending on the state, they may work more independently. The tasks a hygienist performs will also vary by state; some states allow hygienists to diagnose certain issues without the oversight of a dentist.

Because hygienists come in contact with bodily fluids, they must wear protective gear to shield themselves and patients from infectious diseases. This includes gloves, safety glasses or goggles, and surgical face masks. Hygienists must also wash their hands frequently to avoid spreading germs. In addition, when taking X-rays, hygienists must follow safety procedures to reduce the risk that they or their patients will be exposed to radiation. Finally, dental hygienists spend a lot of time bending over patients and performing repetitive actions such as scraping to remove tartar. As a result, many must take care of their own bodies to avoid experiencing back, neck, and shoulder pain.

Employers and Pay

Dental hygienists work in a variety of settings. Most work in dental and orthodontic offices, but some may work in schools, hospitals, public health clinics, or long-term care facilities. They may provide health education at schools or dental health clinics to teach the importance of maintaining good oral health.

According to the Bureau of Labor Statistics (BLS), the median pay for dental hygienists in 2018 was $74,820 per year for those working full-time. The lowest-paid 10 percent earned less than $51,930, and the highest-paid 10 percent earned more than $101,820. Benefits such as vacation pay, sick leave, and retirement contributions may also be available, depending on the employer, but may be offered only to full-time hygienists.

What Is the Future Outlook for Dental Hygienists?

The BLS predicts that employment for dental hygienists will grow by 20 percent through 2026, which is much faster than the average for all occupations. Part of the reason for this growing demand is the large aging population, coupled with the fact that people today

> ### Rebuilding Smiles
>
> "The most rewarding part of being a dental hygienist is helping people rebuild from the ground up. I come from a rural area where we see a lot of oral health issues. . . . I have had the blessing of being a part of so many cases where we go from over a dozen broken teeth to a dazzling smile full of genuine joy. True, legitimate smiles from these patients are the ultimate blessing. I don't know how anyone wouldn't want to do this job if they experience that."
>
> —Carly Scala, dental hygienist
>
> Quoted in DentalPost, "Featured Hygienist of the Week: Carly Scala," October 3, 2017. www.dentalpost.net.

not only live longer but tend to keep more of their original teeth than in the past. The demand for dental care is especially high in rural areas, where people may have less access to it; so job prospects for dental hygienists who want to live in these areas will be strong.

Find Out More

American Dental Association (ADA)
website: www.ada.org

The ADA has advocated for dental hygienists, the dental profession, and public health for more than 150 years. The "Students" section of the ADA website features information about licensing, testing, careers in dentistry, and student debt management.

American Dental Education Association (ADEA)
website: www.adea.org

The mission of the ADEA is to inform dental educators on current issues in education, research, and oral health care. The organization achieves this through research, advocacy, and meetings, and it publishes the *Journal of Dental Education* as well as provides application services to dental schools.

American Dental Hygienist Association (ADHA)

website: www.adha.org

The ADHA, founded in 1923, is the largest organization for dental hygienists nationwide. Its website includes links to career resources, current research and advocacy initiatives, and information about continuing education, scholarships, grants, and industry events.

National Dental Hygienists' Association (NDHA)

website: www.ndhaonline.org

The goal of the NDHA is to address problems faced by African American dental hygienists as well as to increase access to dental care in underserved communities. The NDHA website provides information about scholarships, continuing education, professional development and employment opportunities, and mentoring.

Diagnostic Medical Sonographer

A Few Facts

Number of Jobs
About 71,130 in 2018

Pay
About $29,340 to $93,100

Educational Requirements
Associate's degree

Certification and Licensing
Certification required by most employers

Personal Qualities
Stamina, good interpersonal skills, critical-thinking skills

Work Settings
Hospitals, doctors' offices, medical and diagnostic laboratories

Future Job Outlook
Growth of 17 percent through 2026

What Does a Diagnostic Medical Sonographer Do?

Diagnostic medical sonographers operate imaging equipment such as ultrasound, sonogram, or echocardiogram devices that use high-frequency sound waves to create images of a patient's internal organs or conduct tests on the person. Sonographers are not licensed to assess the images or use them to diagnose patients, but the images they take are used by physicians to diagnose medical conditions. Diagnostic medical sonographers are also called ultrasound technicians, which is just a different title for the same job.

There are many types of diagnostic medical sonographers, including abdominal sonographers, who specialize in imaging the abdominal cavity and nearby organs; cardiac sonographers, who specialize in imaging the heart; and pediatric sonographers, who work with children and infants. The type that is probably most familiar to people is obstetric and gynecologic sonographers, who specialize in imaging pregnant women to track the fetus's growth and health and to detect congenital birth defects.

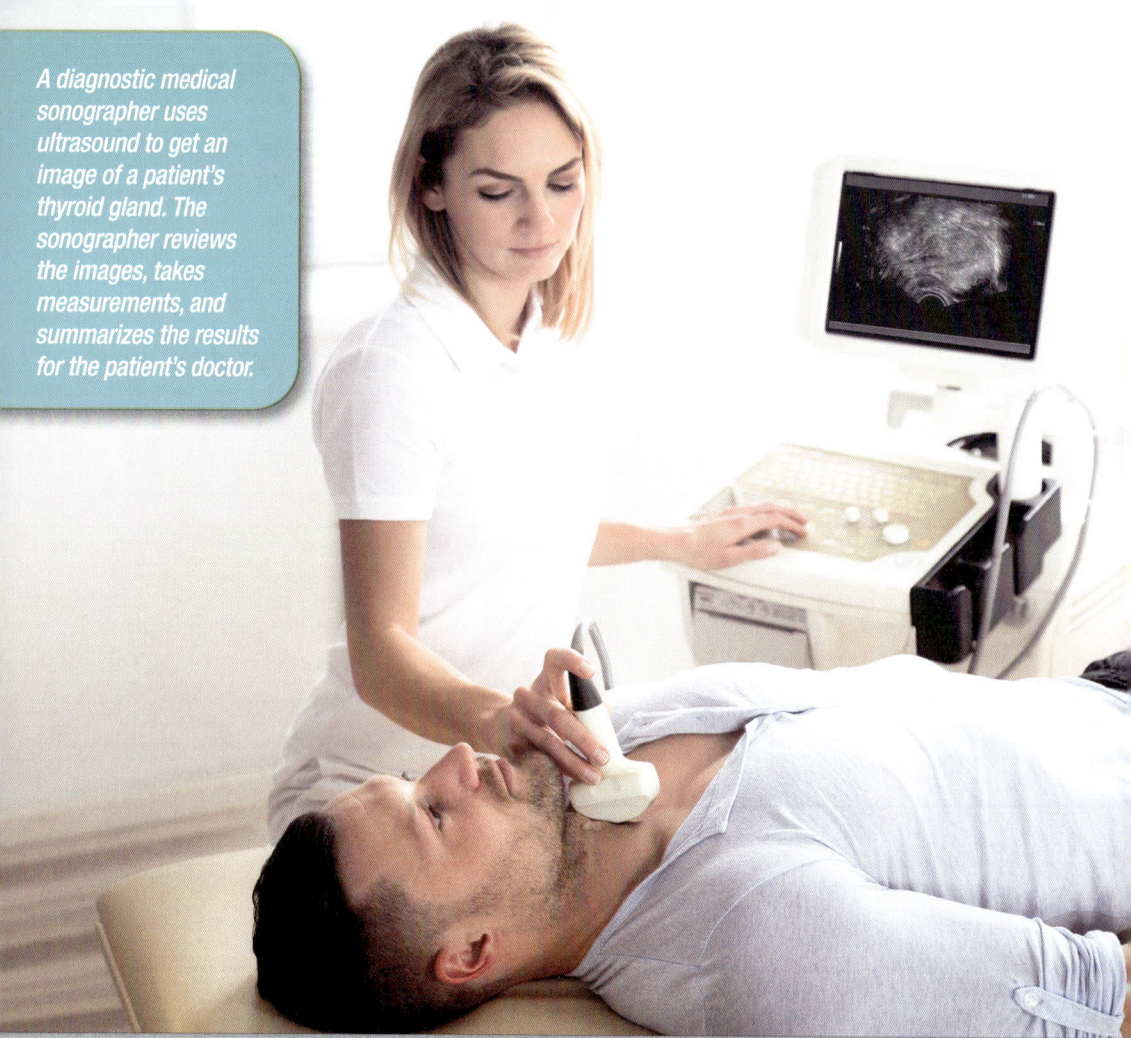

A diagnostic medical sonographer uses ultrasound to get an image of a patient's thyroid gland. The sonographer reviews the images, takes measurements, and summarizes the results for the patient's doctor.

Whatever their specialty, sonographers often work closely with doctors and surgeons before, during, and after medical procedures to help monitor patients. Sonographers report any abnormalities they spot in a patient's scan to the doctors. Shanna, a sonographer at Woodlands Medical Specialists in Florida, says she enjoys being part of a team that helps figure out what is causing a patient's symptoms. But, she says,

> that can also be the worst part of my job. . . . I often get very young patients, and I'm the first to know for sure—not suspect, but to know for sure—that there is really something wrong. For example, you have a seventeen-year-old male

patient come in with right side scrotal pain, and you do the ultrasound and find out he has testicular cancer, and he's seventeen years old. And that can be very difficult.[9]

A Typical Workday

Sonographers usually begin their workday with a morning check-in to discuss the day's procedures with facility staff and review medical charts. Before seeing their first patient, sonographers check the equipment to ensure it is functioning properly. They must document the condition of the equipment, including any failure they find. They then prepare the exam room, gathering ultrasound gel and all other necessary supplies.

Once the room is prepared, the sonographer has the first patient come in and lie on the exam table. The sonographer answers any questions the patient has about the procedure. Then the sonographer spreads gel on the area where the scan will be performed. The gel allows high-frequency sound waves to be transmitted below the surface of the skin. These sound waves are then transmitted through a transducer, which is a hand-held device that the sonographer passes over the area being scanned. The sound waves are reflected by the scanned area and are then sent to a computer, where they are translated into an image displayed on a monitor. The sonographer watches the monitor and makes any necessary adjustments to the equipment during the scan.

After the scan, the sonographer reviews the images to ensure the area has been clearly and adequately documented. He or she selects the best images, takes measurements, and may even evaluate the preliminary results of the scan. Then the sonographer writes a summary for the doctor, including any abnormalities he or she notes in the scan. After cleaning the room and equipment, the sonographer is ready for the next patient. Shanna, the sonographer in Florida, says that in a typical eight-hour workday, she sees eight to seventeen patients.

Education and Training

Sonographers can enter the field with an associate's degree in ultrasound technology or diagnostic medical sonography, which typically takes two years at an accredited community college or university. Many colleges, technical institutes, and some hospitals offer accredited one-year certification programs. The Commission on Accreditation of Allied Health Education Programs accredits diagnostic medical sonography educational programs in the United States.

High school students who are interested in this career should take classes in anatomy, computer science, math, physics, and physiology, which will help prepare them for a sonography training program. Such programs typically include courses in anatomy, applied sciences, medical terminology, and pathology—the study of diseases and their causes. Sonography training programs also include classes related to procedures in a student's particular field, such as abdominal sonography or gynecologic sonography.

In addition to course work, most programs include hands-on training. Students practice scanning one another in order to learn how to identify internal organs and spot any abnormalities. In addition to practicing on each other, students earn credit while working under an experienced sonographer in a doctor's office, hospital, or diagnostic laboratory. They usually rotate through different facilities in order to get a broad range of experience. Kristy Le, a student in the diagnostic medical sonography program at Montgomery College in Maryland, describes her first day of hands-on training doing sonography scans: "It was pretty cool. I got to do a few scans on my own; it was pretty exciting. I saw new scans that I'd never seen before, such as the thyroid. . . . So, yeah, it was a pretty good day."[10]

There is no national requirement for sonographers to be certified, but some states and most employers do require professional certification. To become a registered diagnostic medical sonographer after graduating from an accredited program, a candidate must pass an exam covering general sonography principles and

> **Advice from a Sonographer**
>
> "If you are considering a career in sonography, do your research. Find out if you are suited for this profession. Get into a sonography department and walk a mile in a sonographer's shoes. Make the effort to ensure you are entering a field you desire because it is not without its daily challenges and frustrations. Enjoying this profession for what it is makes the day-to-day issues seem more like speed bumps rather than mountains."
>
> —Samantha Sawyer, sonographer
>
> Quoted in Ultrasound Schools Info, "Interview with Sonographer Samantha Sawyer," 2019. www.ultrasoundschoolsinfo.com.

instruments, an exam covering a specialty area of the candidate's choice, and a physics exam. The American Registry for Diagnostic Medical Sonography administers the exam and awards certification. Many employers also require sonographers to have cardiopulmonary resuscitation certification as well.

Skills and Personality

Because diagnostic medical sonographers work directly with patients and doctors, they need strong interpersonal skills. Some patients may be in pain or be nervous about what the scan will reveal, so sonographers should be prepared to calm and reassure patients. Sonographers should be empathetic and enjoy working with and helping people. "I chose sonography because I love the patient interaction, and as cliché as it sounds, I love caring and helping people and getting to be a part of saving their lives,"[11] explains Naomi, a student in the sonography program at Kettering College in Ohio.

Sonographers also need excellent communication skills to be able to explain the procedure to patients and discuss the images with the doctor. Being detail oriented and having excellent

A Stimulating Job

"I'm an ultrasound tech and I do like my job. But, be prepared to get a little dirty working closely with sick people. There can be high stress with the level of disease and abnormal exams you encounter. But, the day flies by, never are you bored. You are always learning, bettering your skills and highly stimulated."

—Diane, ultrasound technician

Quoted in American Institute of Medical Sciences & Education, "20 Reasons Why Being an Ultrasound Tech Rocks," *AIMS Blog*, June 19, 2019. www.aimseducation.edu.

critical-thinking skills are also a must, as is a passion for figuring out solutions to problems. "My professors often say that if you love mysteries and getting to the bottom of things, then you'll love sonography,"[12] says Naomi.

Sonographers need to be in good physical shape and have good manual dexterity. The job requires them to be on their feet much of the day, so physical stamina is a must. In addition, sonographers sometimes need to lift or reposition patients who need assistance, which requires upper-body strength.

Working Conditions

Most diagnostic medical sonographers work a five-day, forty-hour week and keep regular hours. Some sonographers may work evenings, weekends, or overnight because they are employed in facilities that are open around the clock. Those who work in a hospital typically must be on call once or twice a week, available to show up night or day to perform an emergency scan.

Sonographers spend their days in dimly lit rooms using diagnostic imaging machines and computers. They may also perform sonography scans at the bedside of a hospital patient who cannot be transported. They are on their feet most of the day and sometimes must lean or bend over patients to help reposition them for a scan, which sometimes can lead to muscular pain or repetitive motion injuries on the job. Using proper techniques for these tasks, however, can help minimize the risk of pain or injuries on the job.

Employers and Pay

Most diagnostic medical sonographers are employed by hospitals and doctors' offices, but some also work at outpatient care centers or medical and diagnostic laboratories. According to the Bureau of Labor Statistics (BLS), the average wage for full-time sonographers was about $56,850 per year in 2018. The lowest-paid 10 percent earned less than $29,340, and the highest-paid 10 percent earned more than $93,100. Salaries for sonographers vary based on their education, certifications, area of expertise, and years of experience. Depending on the employer, full-time sonographers may also receive benefits such as vacation pay, sick leave, and retirement contributions.

What Is the Future Outlook for Diagnostic Medical Sonographers?

The BLS predicts that employment for diagnostic medical sonographers will grow by 17 percent through 2026, which is much faster than the average for all occupations. Part of this growth is due to the large and aging baby boomer population, which will increase the need for imaging scans to diagnose medical conditions such as blood clots and heart disease. There will continue to be a nationwide demand for sonographers for the foreseeable future, and those who are skilled in more than one specialty will have an even greater job outlook.

Find Out More

American Institute of Ultrasound in Medicine (AIUM)
website: www.aium.org

The AIUM is a multidisciplinary organization of more than nine thousand health care providers (including diagnostic medical sonographers), researchers, and students. Its mission is to promote the safe use of ultrasound in medicine. The AIUM website includes resources on continuing education, a career center, and information about accreditation.

American Registry for Diagnostic Medical Sonography (ARDMS)

website: www.ardms.org

The ARDMS provides examinations and certification for diagnostic medical sonographers. Its website provides information about the examination process, possible careers for sonography students, and information about other professional organizations for diagnostic medical sonographers.

Society of Diagnostic Medical Sonographers

website: www.sdms.org

This organization is the largest association for diagnostic medical sonographers and sonography students worldwide, boasting more than twenty-eight thousand members. It holds an annual conference and also provides access to current research in sonography. The society's website includes continuing education, a job board, and information about certification and licensing.

Ultrasound Schools Info

website: www.ultrasoundschoolsinfo.com

This website is a leading guide to schools offering degrees and certifications in sonography and provides information about a career in diagnostic medical sonography. It also includes a link to sonography schools by state and interviews with diagnostic medical sonographers.

Emergency Medical Technician

A Few Facts

Number of Jobs
About 257,210 in 2018*

Pay
About $22,760 to $58,640

Educational Requirements
High school diploma or equivalent plus approved training program

Certification and Licensing
National certification required

Personal Qualities
Interpersonal skills, compassion, attention to detail

Work Settings
Ambulances and emergency rooms

Future Job Outlook
Growth of 15 percent through 2026

* Includes both emergency medical technicians and paramedics.

What Does an Emergency Medical Technician Do?

Emergency medical technicians (EMTs) care for sick or injured people in emergency rooms, ambulances, and other emergency medical environments. EMTs respond to emergency calls, providing medical assistance such as first aid and life support for sick or injured people. They must have a basic knowledge of many medical conditions in order to assess a patient's condition and determine what treatment is needed. EMTs also transport patients in an ambulance to a hospital or other medical facility, where they inform the health care staff of any conditions observed and treatment provided. When transporting patients, it is common for one EMT to drive the ambulance while another EMT monitors and provides care to the patient.

An EMT's job does not end once the patient has been safely transported to a hospital. EMTs must take inventory and replace supplies in the ambulance, and they are responsible for cleaning and sanitizing all equipment, which is especially important anytime they treat a patient with a contagious disease.

The specific responsibilities of EMTs vary by state, as do the medical procedures they

A Way of Life

"Being an EMT is one of the most complex and high stress jobs there is. From jumping awake when the pager goes off to dropping everything as you hear those sirens, it is not just a job, it is a lifestyle. No matter what the call, you are there. I believe that with this job comes a great responsibility. The exciting part is not waiting for someone to have a bad day, it is being able to be there when someone does have a bad day, sometimes the worst in their life."

—Kayla Buffam, EMT

Kayla Buffam, "Why I Love Being an EMT," Odyssey, October 3, 2016. www.theodyssey online.com.

perform. Emergency medical technicians are frequently referred to interchangeably as emergency medical responders (EMRs) or paramedics, but these are actually different jobs. Although all provide emergency medical care and their jobs are quite similar, EMRs, EMTs, and paramedics have different levels of training and certification. The highest level of certification is paramedic, and many EMTs go on to become paramedics. And many doctors, nurses, and other health care professionals gained valuable experience by working as an EMT. Kyle Curtis, who worked as an EMT before becoming a medical student, found his job as an EMT very rewarding. "Nothing quite beats the feeling of riding in the back of an ambulance with its sirens blazing heading toward the worst day of someone's life, knowing that you have the knowledge, skills, and dedicated team members to help that person,"[13] says Curtis.

The Workday

The unpredictable nature of emergencies means that no two days are alike for EMTs. Typically, a 911 operator dispatches EMTs to the scene of an incident, such as a car crash, natural disaster, or act of violence. EMTs work alongside police officers and firefighters on the scene. Emergency medical personnel can be summoned to a wide variety of places, including homes, businesses, and even a street or alleyway. EMTs might respond to everything from life-threatening gunshot wounds to minor emergencies involving sprained ankles. They may be called to transport a patient by ambulance from one facility to another, such as a newborn baby to a neonatal intensive care unit at a different hospital. Eric Mailman, a paramedic and operations coordinator at Northern Light Health's medical transport and emergency care in Bangor, Maine, says that on any given day, EMTs may answer anywhere from four to seventeen calls, each different from the last.

An EMT's workday is highly variable, as EMT Kayla Buffam can attest. She explains that calls do not always turn out as anticipated. "You could be called out on a routine call that is so basic such as an older person who fell down, but then you notice that they have internal bleeding," Buffam says. "One thing I have learned is to expect the unexpected, and no call is ever just a normal call."[14]

Education and Training

EMTs must have a high school diploma or equivalent, and they typically need to have a cardiopulmonary resuscitation (CPR) certification to be eligible to enter a certified program in emergency medical technology. Although requirements vary by state, such programs usually take one to two years to complete. A typical program includes both classroom instruction and hands-on training in hospital or ambulance settings. Instruction covers topics such as assessing patients, clearing obstructed airways, dealing with trauma and cardiac emergencies, and using medical equipment such as stretchers and oxygen delivery systems. In addition, because ambulances are typically driven by EMTs or paramedics, most prospective EMTs take an eight-hour course on ambulance driving. High school students who are interested in a career as an EMT should take classes in anatomy and physiology; becoming certified in CPR is also helpful.

After successfully completing a training program, EMTs must pass a national exam to gain certification from the National Registry of Emergency Medical Technicians (NREMT). This exam consists of both written sections and practical demonstrations. All states require EMTs to have NREMT certification in order to be licensed as an EMT; some states also require a separate state exam in order to be licensed. Most states require EMTs to have CPR certification. Many states also require a background check and will not allow anyone with a criminal record to be licensed as an EMT.

Skills and Personality

Because EMTs care for people who are sick or injured and may be frightened and in pain, EMTs need excellent interpersonal skills. They also must be good listeners to accurately help patients, and they must be good communicators in order to relay information to other health care workers. Physical fitness is also a necessity because EMTs must lift, bend over, or kneel alongside patients during treatment. Another essential trait for EMTs is to have assessment skills—being able to review things like a patient's vital signs, consciousness level, and wound severity in order to determine the appropriate treatment.

Because EMTs often interact with patients and their family members in stressful and emotional situations, these professionals must be able to remain cool under pressure. EMTs must be able to take control of what can be a chaotic scene and keep patients and onlookers calm. And it is vital that EMTs remain emotionally strong and continue working even in the midst of upsetting and traumatic situations.

Perhaps the most important personal quality an EMT needs is compassion. "You're in a profession where you care for people on an atypical day, and probably the worst of their lives for some," says EMT Arden Heath. EMTs must be able to provide emotional support to people at these times, especially patients who are facing a life-threatening emergency or are in extreme distress and need to be comforted. "I've come to find over time that I knew I was in the right place when I almost cried the first time a patient asked to hold my hand,"[15] says Heath.

Working Conditions

Most EMTs work full-time, with almost a third working more than forty hours per week. It is common for EMTs to work a twelve- or

> ### An EMT's Senses at Work
>
> "You're going to experience all kinds of events, but nothing can prepare you for traumatic ones. There are events you're going to experience with all of your senses, especially working in the ambulance. You're almost always the first ones on scene, so you'll usually see the brunt of things. You probably won't forget the first time you hear something explode on scene or people cry for their loved ones involved, hold a completely broken body part as it may fall limp in your hands, feel the radiating heat from a burning car, and so much more."
>
> —Arden Heath, EMT
>
> Arden Heath, "16 Things I Wish I Knew Before I Became an EMT," Odyssey, August 11, 2016. www.theodysseyonline.com.

even twenty-four-hour shift. Whereas part-time EMTs may work two to four twelve-hour shifts per month, full-time EMTs may work fifteen twelve-hour shifts per month. Because EMTs must respond to emergencies, many work overnight and on weekends. Anytime they are on duty, EMTs must be available to react at a moment's notice.

EMTs work both indoors and outdoors, in all kinds of weather. Some work with search and rescue crews, which can take them to remote or rough terrain. EMTs usually work in an ambulance, but some work as part of a helicopter or airplane emergency medical crew, transporting seriously ill or injured patients to the hospital or from one medical facility to another.

The job of an EMT is physically strenuous, requiring long shifts and lots of climbing, stooping, lifting, or performing CPR, all of which can be exhausting. And EMTs have one of the highest rates of injuries of all occupations. In addition to injuries sustained while treating patients, EMTs are sometimes injured by patients who become combative or violent. EMTs also have one of the highest rates of illnesses of all professions; on the job, they may be exposed to contagious diseases and viruses such as hepatitis B and HIV. To minimize the risk of injuries and illnesses, EMTs follow safety procedures such as waiting for police to defuse violent situations and wearing gloves while working with patients.

Employers and Pay

EMTs work in emergency rooms, ambulances, and other urgent care environments. Some EMTs work for fire departments or other rescue services, but most are employed by hospitals and emergency medical clinics. Some EMTs may work on college campuses to provide health care services to students.

According to the Bureau of Labor Statistics (BLS), the median annual wage for full-time EMTs and paramedics was about $34,320 in 2018. The lowest-paid 10 percent earned less than $22,760, and the highest-paid 10 percent earned more than $58,640. The salary range can vary widely depending on the state, the employer, and the number of years on the job.

What Is the Future Outlook for Emergency Medical Technicians?

The BLS predicts that employment for EMTs will grow by 15 percent through 2026, which is much faster than the average for all occupations. This job growth is due in part to the rapidly expanding aging population, which will require more emergency services. More aging people will mean an increase in health emergencies related to age, such as strokes and heart attacks, which will contribute to the greater demand for EMTs. More specialized health care facilities are also likely to be needed, which in turn will require more EMTs to help transport patients to these facilities for treatment.

Find Out More

American Academy of Emergency Medicine (AAEM)
website: www.aaem.org

The AAEM is dedicated to the field of emergency medicine and to supporting EMTs in providing the best care possible. The organization also provides test prep courses for board certification, and the "Resources" section of its website offers information about common issues EMTs face, publications, a podcast, and more.

Commission on Accreditation of Allied Health Education Programs (CAAHEP)

website: www.caahep.org

The CAAHEP website has a list of accredited programs for EMTs by state. In the "Students" section, users can find information about the profession as well as a list of frequently asked questions. The website also features a blog and a calendar for industry events.

National Association of Emergency Medical Technicians (NAEMT)

website: www.naemt.org

The NAEMT website provides a wealth of information about becoming an EMT, including an overview of the profession, careers and degrees in the field, and a job board. The NAEMT also hosts industry events, promotes advocacy and continuing education for EMTs, and releases several publications about the field.

National Registry of Emergency Medical Technicians (NREMT)

website: www.nremt.org

The NREMT website provides information about careers in the emergency medical field, including EMTs. It also provides volunteer opportunities as well as certification for EMTs. The website's "Resources" section provides links to organizations and information for EMTs.

Licensed Practical Nurse

A Few Facts

Number of Jobs
About 701,690 in 2018

Pay
About $33,680 to $62,160

Educational Requirements
High school diploma or equivalent plus approved training program

Certification and Licensing
Licensing required

Personal Qualities
Stamina, good interpersonal skills, compassion

Work Settings
Nursing and residential care facilities, hospitals, clinics, doctors' offices

Future Job Outlook
Growth of 12 percent through 2026

What Does a Licensed Practical Nurse Do?

Licensed practical nurses (LPNs) work under the direction of registered nurses and doctors to provide basic care for sick, injured, or disabled patients in hospitals and other health care settings. Licensed practical nurses are also called licensed vocational nurses in some states, and the specific duties they are allowed to perform can vary; for example, in some states, LPNs can give medications and set up intravenous drips, but not everywhere.

In general, an LPN's duties include checking vital signs (such as blood pressure), drawing blood, collecting urine samples, performing routine laboratory tests, checking bandages, inserting and removing catheters, and helping patients bathe and dress. Some LPNs help deliver, care for, and feed infants. LPNs also maintain patient records and report on each patient's status to doctors and registered nurses. They may also be responsible for taking inventory and ordering medical supplies or collecting information for insurance paperwork. In some states, an experienced LPN may be in charge of supervising and directing other LPNs.

Sarah-Zoe Pichette, who works as an LPN at St. Paul's Hospital in Vancouver, British Columbia, notes that patients may wind up spending more time with an LPN than with any other member of the health care team. "I am the first stop and the last stop when you come into the hospital," says Pichette. "I explain the procedure that's going to happen to you, the little things that you can expect during your hospitalization."[16] In addition to communicating such information to patients, LPNs are also tasked with discussing a patient's care with family members, answering their questions, and relaying any concerns to the doctor or registered nurse.

The Workday

Because of the unpredictable nature of health care, LPNs must be prepared for the unexpected. Nicole Miller is an LPN at the Arc of Monroe, a facility for people with intellectual and/or developmental disabilities in Penfield, New York. Miller never quite knows what her workday will look like. "It's never the same thing day to day, your mornings may start the same but . . . you're not just in one place all day, and then next day will be something completely different."[17]

Although the typical workday for LPNs can vary widely, certain aspects of the job are routine. At the beginning of a shift, LPNs typically meet with the medical staff of their facility to review patient charts and get a list of the duties and procedures they will be performing that day. Their duties vary depending on the type of medical facility in which they work. LPNs who work in a doctor's office or medical clinic call patients into an exam room, where they record their medical history, known allergies, height, weight, temperature, blood pressure, pulse, and breathing rate. LPNs may also gather blood, urine, or other specimens and deliver them to the lab for routine testing.

LPNs who work in a hospital or long-term care facility do rounds to visit each patient. Depending on what each patient needs, LPNs may administer medication, check vital signs, or

Comfort, Support, and Understanding

"My job as a [licensed practical] nurse is so rewarding. Knowing that you're supporting someone and ensuring that their health and safety needs are being taken care of, and seeing the appreciation that they have for it. I enjoy comforting someone when they don't feel well, helping them through a tough appointment or diagnosis. . . . You need to be understanding. The people we support are going to have good and bad days and you have to learn how they cope with those bad days in order to support them."

—Nicole Miller, LPN

Nicole Miller, "Being a Licensed Practical Nurse," Arc of Monroe, June 14, 2019. https://arcmonroe.org.

help feed and bathe the patient. They monitor each patient's condition throughout the course of their shift—this is especially important for patients who have had surgery, have been seriously injured, or are receiving new medication. LPNs notify registered nurses and doctors immediately when any patient experiences complications or has an adverse reaction to a medication.

Whatever setting they work in, LPNs must keep detailed records of everything they do—for example, documenting medication time and dosages in a patient's chart. They also clean and sanitize exam rooms and equipment between patients and restock supplies such as bandages, gloves, and specimen containers.

Education and Training

LPNs need a high school diploma or equivalent and must complete a state-approved educational program leading to a certificate or diploma. Such programs can be found at technical schools, universities, community colleges, high schools, and hospitals. Most of these programs take about one year to complete, but some are longer, depending on the state. Programs include course work in subjects such as biology, nursing, and pharmacology as well as supervised clinical experience. High school students who are interested in a career as an LPN should take classes in anatomy, biology, chemistry, and math.

All fifty states require LPNs to be licensed. After completing a program and earning their certificate, LPNs must pass the National Council Licensure Examination. This rigorous computer-based test is administered by the National Council of State Boards of Nursing. Some employers may also require LPNs to have a cardiopulmonary resuscitation certificate. Once licensed, LPNs must renew their license; the length of time a license is valid and the requirements for renewing it vary from state to state. In some states LPNs must only pay a fee, but in others they must undergo continuing education in order to renew.

Skills and Personality

Since LPNs work closely with patients, they need strong interpersonal skills. LPNs must be compassionate, kind, and caring

A licensed practical nurse (LPN) does a blood pressure screening during an in-home visit with a patient. In addition to checking vital signs, LPNs sometimes do routine lab tests, insert and remove catheters, and help maintain patient records.

Helping Others

"I get to talk to patients all day long, helping them out with simple things like telling them their appointment date and time, along with trying to make them feel better when they are feeling under the weather. It can get crazy with a lot of calls coming in, but spending the time to help patients with whatever they need can make that person feel better and making a person feel even a little bit better makes my day."

—Kristy Christy, LPN

Quoted in UPMC, "I Love My Job," 2019. http://mycareer.upmc.com.

toward their patients, who may be in pain or nervous about a procedure. These professionals also need excellent communication skills. "You have to be comfortable enough to speak with people," says Pichette. "You need to glean information from them, talking to them and making them feel comfortable and trust you with their personal information."[18] Strong communication skills are also vital because LPNs must be able to clearly describe any changes in a patient's condition to the doctors and nurses on their team.

LPNs must be detail oriented since even a small mistake on the job can have serious consequences for a patient; this is especially true when administering medication. Having strong problem-solving skills is also essential in order for LPNs to recognize and solve problems that come up during the day. Because LPNs work collaboratively with other health care professionals, they need strong teamwork skills. Physical stamina is also vital since LPNs spend a lot of time standing or performing tasks that require them to bend over patients or lift patients with limited mobility.

Working Conditions

Most LPNs work full-time. Depending on where they work, they may have an eight- to twelve-hour shift and may work a day shift, night shift, or even a split shift—in which they work two or more separate periods in the same day. Because medical care is needed around the clock, many LPNs work weekends and holidays.

LPNs work in clean, well-lit facilities. Most wear scrubs to work, and because they are on their feet much of the day, comfortable shoes are a must. Likewise, LPNs wear face masks and gloves when appropriate to avoid exposure to bodily fluids, infectious diseases, and chemicals on the job. Like all health care workers, frequent handwashing is important for LPNs.

LPNs may have to lift or assist patients who have difficulty standing, walking, or getting out of bed. As a result, they are vulnerable to back injuries. Their jobs can be emotionally stressful as well because they are often dealing with ill and injured people who are anxious or who may take their frustrations out on an LPN.

Employers and Pay

LPNs can be found in many settings. Most work in nursing homes and extended care facilities. LPNs also find employment in hospitals, clinics, doctors' offices, outpatient surgery centers, and home health care services. Some provide care in schools, the military, and correctional facilities.

According to the Bureau of Labor Statistics (BLS), full-time LPNs earned an average of about $46,240 per year in 2018. The lowest-paid 10 percent earned less than $33,680, and the highest-paid 10 percent earned more than $62,160. Salary ranges for LPNs can vary widely depending on education, certifications, years on the job, and additional skills. Benefits such as vacation pay, sick leave, and retirement contributions may also be available, depending on the employer, but they may be offered only to full-time LPNs.

What Is the Future Outlook for Licensed Practical Nurses?

According to the BLS, employment for LPNs will grow by 12 percent through 2026, which is faster than the average for all occupations. One factor that drives this growing demand is the large population of aging people, which will increase the need for LPNs in nursing homes, extended care facilities, and rehabilitation centers. In addition, many procedures that formerly could only be done in hospitals are now being performed in outpatient facilities, which rely on LPNs to help care for patients during short stays. There is a strong need for LPNs in rural and medically underserved areas, so job prospects for those who want to live in these areas will be favorable.

Find Out More

American Nurses Association (ANA)
website: www.nursingworld.org

The ANA is a leading organization representing LPNs. Its website is an excellent resource for certification, continuing education, and advocacy for LPNs. The ANA also sponsors National Nurses Week and Certified Nurses Day, and it publishes the journal *American Nurse Today*.

National Association of Licensed Professional Nurses (NALPN)
website: https://nalpn.org

The NALPN fosters quality professional development for LPNs, with a special focus on public health. It accomplishes this by providing education (including a partnership with Walden University), certification, and an annual conference.

National Council of State Boards of Nursing (NCSBN)
website: www.ncsbn.org

The NCSBN strives to advance research and inform public policy in the nursing field. Its website includes a practice exam, news about the latest research and legislation, and a wealth of online courses and webinars for LPNs.

Nurse Journal
website: https://nursejournal.org

This website provides information for LPNs at all career levels, including degree programs and information about scholarships and financial aid. The "Nursing Careers & Jobs" section provides a list of careers in nursing, including educational requirements and salary information.

Massage Therapist

A Few Facts

Number of Jobs
About 105,160 in 2018

Pay
About $21,340 to $78,280

Educational Requirements
High school diploma or equivalent plus approved training program

Certification and Licensing
License may be required, depending on state

Personal Qualities
Interpersonal skills, compassion, physical stamina

Work Settings
Spas, health care settings, massage franchises, hospitals, and nursing homes

Future Job Outlook
Growth of 26 percent through 2026

What Does a Massage Therapist Do?

Massage therapists are health care workers who use touch to manipulate the muscles and other soft tissues of the body. They use their hands, forearms, elbows, fingers, and sometimes feet to knead clients' muscles. Most people enjoy a good massage, but massage can do more than just promote relaxation and reduce stress. It can also relieve pain and tension, help heal injuries, improve circulation, reduce the effects of cancer treatments, ease childbirth, and improve general wellness. Massage therapists may also give clients guidance on stretching, exercising, and improving their posture as well as teach them stress management and relaxation techniques.

Most massage therapists are skilled in several types of massage techniques, but some specialize in specific styles, such as sports, Swedish, deep tissue, and shiatsu massage. Certain types of massage are given to only one type of client, such as prenatal massage for pregnant women. Some massage therapists specialize in treating certain age groups, such as children or the elderly, and others branch out into alternative therapies, such as acupuncture.

Whether they specialize or offer a choice of techniques, most therapists enjoy helping others and find their career very rewarding. "Being a massage therapist means you can make a real difference in people's lives," says Barbara Alcaraz, a licensed massage therapist. "Knowing that your job makes other people's lives better is immensely rewarding and leads to great job satisfaction."[19]

A Typical Workday

Because massage therapists work by appointment, their schedule and the number of clients they see vary from day to day. Most full-time therapists will see an average of five clients a day. The length of a massage appointment is also variable and can last anywhere from only five or ten minutes to more than an hour, but sixty to ninety minutes is most typical. A massage therapist begins by talking with clients about their needs to determine the type of massage and any areas of the client's body that need special attention, such as the neck or back. For new patients, the therapist will also take a health history.

Clients may lie on a table or sit in a special massage chair during the session. Massage therapists often use lotions, gels, and oils to help their hands glide smoothly over the client's skin. It is also common for therapists to use soft lighting, soothing music, and even aromatherapy to help clients relax, although a massage for a client rehabilitating from an injury may take place in a well-lit room instead. Margaret, a licensed massage therapist, says that her days are typically very active and do not require a lot of time sitting at a desk. "There's very little sitting in massage therapy when you're working with a client," she explains. "You're usually on your feet, working, stretching different ways. Sometimes you're kneeling, sometimes you're sitting on your chair or your little stool, depending on what kind of work you're doing."[20]

After the massage, the therapist typically asks how the client is feeling and how any problem areas are doing. The thera-

> ### Helping People Recover
>
> "I get to help people feel better internally, emotionally, and spiritually. There are very few jobs out there that allow you to do this, and massage therapy is one of them. People come to me with all different types of issues and from all walks of life. Some people have recently been through a divorce, are extremely stressed with work and kids, or are recovering from surgery. Whatever it is, I get to help them through it and put them on the path to a successful recovery."
>
> —Rachael Summers, massage therapist
>
> Rachael Summers, "5 Reasons Why I Love Being a Massage Therapist," *Rachael Summers Blog*, April 12, 2016. www.rachaelsummers.com.

pist may give suggestions for how to manage stress or pain after the session ends. He or she may also outline a treatment plan that includes follow-up appointments, especially for clients with a specific problem or injury. The massage therapist must keep careful records on clients, including the type of massage given and the client's condition and progress. And self-employed therapists must handle their own business operations, including billing, checking inventory, and washing linens.

Education and Training

Education and training for massage therapists vary, but most states require a high school diploma plus an approved massage therapy program. Such programs require five hundred to one thousand hours of training, and they usually take one to two years to complete. Massage therapy programs are typically offered in trade schools, community colleges, and universities and can result in a certificate or an associate's degree in massage therapy. There are several bodies that accredit programs, including the Commission on Massage Therapy Accreditation and the Accrediting Bureau of Health Education Schools.

Training programs cover subjects such as anatomy and physiology; kinesiology, which is the study of motion and body mechan-

Reducing Pain

"I had a client who had been told by three different professionals that the only option left to her (for hand issues around her thumb) was surgery. No other choice. But the surgery was going to require a long recovery and she didn't want to interrupt her life at that time. We were able to keep her functional and greatly reduce her pain for 18 months with just 15 minutes a week. . . . We did not *fix* her issue, but we were able to keep her pain at a manageable level."

—Kathryn Roux Dickerson, massage therapist

Kathryn Roux Dickerson, comment on Quora, "What Is Being a Massage Therapist Like?," March 3, 2017. www.quora.com.

---

ics; pathology, or the study of disease; business management; and ethics. High school students who are interested in a career as a massage therapist can prepare themselves by taking classes in biology, anatomy, physiology, and business. In addition to the course work required, students gain hands-on experience by giving massages under the supervision of a licensed massage therapist.

After successfully completing their training program, aspiring massage therapists must pass an exam such as the Massage and Bodywork Licensing Examination (MBLEx). The MBLEx is administered by the Federation of State Massage Therapy Boards, which regulates the industry. Massage therapists may also be required to have liability insurance, pass a background check, and be certified in first aid and cardiopulmonary resuscitation. In most states, massage therapists must take continuing education classes in order to renew their license.

Skills and Personality

Massage therapists work very closely with people, so they must have excellent interpersonal skills. This includes strong listening and communication skills in order to understand clients' goals and preferences. Therapists must also have empathy toward others because clients are often dealing with painful conditions or injuries. Patience and compassion are also vital skills to build trust with clients and make them feel comfortable. "This is a very personal job. There are often times that you're not only their massage therapist, you're simply their therapist," explains licensed massage therapist Spencer Harwood. "Clients are going to tell you their life story . . . and you have to be able to talk to them about that."[21] Massage therapists not only hear personal details about their clients' lives, but they also have access to confidential information such as medical histories. Therefore, integrity and confidentiality are essential in this profession.

Massage therapists also need physical skills. Since they may give numerous massages and be on their feet most of the day, therapists must have excellent physical stamina. Therapists squeeze and knead muscles for hours at a time, which requires a great deal of strength in the hands and fingers. They also need good dexterity to exert the right amount of pressure when giving a massage.

Skills such as good time-management and decision-making abilities are also necessary. Therapists must use their time wisely during each appointment in order to help clients accomplish their goals for the session. And they must evaluate each client's needs and recommend a treatment plan, so decisiveness is essential. Business skills such as bookkeeping, scheduling, and marketing are especially important for massage therapists who are self-employed.

Working Conditions

Massage therapists may work in a clinic, spa, or massage chain. Some commute to clients' homes or offices for appointments. Self-employed therapists may work out of their own home. Massage therapists' hours tend to be flexible—especially for those who are self-employed—because they schedule their own appointments. But even those who are employed in a spa or massage franchise book their own clients and basically set their own hours; they can also pick up fewer or more shifts as desired. Because of the strength and endurance it takes to give a massage, many therapists only work part-time. According to the American Massage Therapy Association, massage therapists work an average of seventeen hours a week, and about half practice massage as a second job.

Due to the strenuous nature of their job, massage therapists are at risk of injuring themselves. "This job is very demanding, both on your physical and mental skill," Harwood explains. "We're normally working six-hour days where we're constantly pushing. We're also constantly bent in weird positions. Our wrists and joints are doing repetitive, stressful movements. . . . All these things wear and tear on your body."[22] As a result, fatigue and repetitive-motion injuries are common. Massage therapists can minimize their risk of injuries by using proper massage techniques and practicing good self-care, including leaving enough time in between appointments, eating a healthy diet, and exercising—as well as getting regular massages themselves.

Employers and Pay

Many massage therapists are self-employed. They may work out of their own home or travel to clients' homes or offices to give massages. Others work in a variety of settings, including hospitals, spas, fitness centers, resorts, massage franchises, nursing homes, and health care providers' offices.

According to the Bureau of Labor Statistics (BLS), the average wage for full-time massage therapists was about $41,420 per year in 2018. The lowest-paid 10 percent earned less than $21,340, and the highest-paid 10 percent earned more than $78,280. Salaries can depend on many factors, including education, certifications, additional skills, number of years in the profession, employer, and whether the therapist works full- or part-time.

What Is the Future Outlook for Massage Therapists?

According to the BLS, employment for massage therapists is expected to grow by 26 percent through 2026, which is much faster than the average for all occupations. There are several reasons for this rapid growth, including the increasing number of elderly people in the population. Massage franchises have also become more popular, meaning that massage has become available to a wider range of people. The growing need for massage therapists is also thanks to more and more health care professionals prescribing massage as therapy for injuries and chronic pain.

Find Out More

American Massage Therapy Association (AMTA)

website: www.amtamassage.org

The AMTA is a nonprofit organization dedicated to serving massage therapists, massage schools, and massage students. Its website features news articles, online courses, and a school directory.

Associated Bodyworks and Massage Professionals (ABMP)

website: www.abmp.com

The ABMP is a leading provider of liability insurance for massage therapists. In the "Students" section of its website, users can find resources for test prep, developing skills, networking, and more.

Commission on Massage Therapy Accreditation

website: www.comta.org

This organization accredits educational programs for massage therapists and aestheticians. Its website includes a member directory of schools. In the "Massage Therapy Training" section, users can access information about the process of selecting a school, curriculum requirements, and scholarships.

Massage Therapy Foundation

website: http://massagetherapyfoundation.org

This nonprofit is dedicated to education, research, and advocacy for massage therapists. Its website includes information about current research and obtaining grants, volunteer opportunities, and a blog. The "Resources" section provides a wealth of e-books, research infographics, and other tools for massage therapy students.

Pharmacy Technician

A Few Facts

Number of Jobs
About 417,860 in 2018

Pay
About $22,740 to $48,010

Educational Requirements
High school diploma or equivalent plus approved training program or associate's degree

Certification and Licensing
Required by the majority of states

Personal Qualities
Strong interpersonal skills, good listening skills, sharp mind

Work Settings
Pharmacies

Future Job Outlook
Growth of 12 percent through 2026

What Does a Pharmacy Technician Do?

Pharmacy technicians help pharmacists dispense prescription medication to customers or health professionals. Pharmacy technicians do not prescribe medication, but they must know how to measure medications, determine correct dosages, and be familiar with drug names and purposes. "A pharmacy technician is there to serve the pharmacist," says Randy Brown, who has worked in the field for more than ten years. "You can do just about everything a pharmacist does from start to finish as long as you're supervised by the pharmacist."[23]

The tasks a pharmacy technician is allowed to perform vary by state, but they typically include preparing and labeling prescriptions, accepting payment for prescriptions, processing insurance claims, organizing inventory and alerting the pharmacist if there are any shortages of medications or supplies, and answering customers' common questions about medications, such as dosage instructions. The technician also arranges for customers to ask the pharmacist questions about their medications or other health concerns when appropriate. Pharmacy technicians help look out for potential drug interactions and report any suspicious usage patterns that might indicate drug abuse. They must follow strict security protocols to prevent theft or trafficking of medications.

In most states, pharmacy technicians can request refill authorizations from doctors and can mix or compound some medications. They may also operate dispensing equipment to fill prescription orders. In all states, the pharmacist must review prescriptions before they are given to customers.

A Typical Workday

Pharmacy technicians begin their day by gathering and reviewing prescriptions that need to be filled. They may receive written prescription requests or may process requests that have been sent electronically or phoned in by a doctor's office. Prescription refills may also be requested by customers, and the pharmacy technician may need to call the doctor to authorize the refill. Gina, who works as a pharmacy technician, explains this aspect of her job: "If the nurse is calling in for a prescription, we have to give it to the pharmacist to take the order. Once the pharmacist takes that order, then we type it in [the computer] under the patient's name, bill their insurance, and if it goes through the insurance, we fill it; if it rejects, then we call to find out what's going on and why."[24]

After collecting the information needed to fill a prescription, the technician prints the label, locates the medication in the pharmacy, and attaches the label to the medicine bottle or box. If the medicine is not prepackaged, he or she may need to calculate dosage, mix a compound, or count out pills.

Pharmacy technicians have a variety of other responsibilities during their workday. They spend a lot of time on the phone with insurance companies, customers, and doctors' offices. A large part of their time is spent providing customer service, such as answering questions about dosage or helping customers locate over-the-counter medications and other items. Technicians who

Precision and Accuracy

"Pharmacy technicians do much more than 'just count pills!' Depending on the area we work, we may interact directly with patients or be the person behind the scenes getting patients their prescribed medications quickly. We may prepare complex IV [intravenous] products, make oral suspensions, prepare topical creams from scratch, (or) work with radioactive material. We do this with great precision and attention to detail to ensure accuracy so our patients get just what was ordered."

—Kevin, pharmacy technician

Quoted in UW Health, "An Interview with a Pharmacy Technician," 2019. www.uwhealth.org.

work in hospitals may make rounds to deliver medications to patients. Pharmacy technicians also wait on customers, handle the cash register, check inventory, and keep detailed records of the medications in the pharmacy. At the end of the day, pharmacy technicians are often the ones responsible for cleaning and tidying up the pharmacy as well.

Education and Training

In most states, pharmacy technicians must have a high school diploma or equivalent and complete an accredited training program that leads to a certificate in pharmacy technology. Such programs are available at vocational schools, community colleges, and hospitals, and they typically last one year. The American Society of Health-System Pharmacists accredits pharmacy technician programs. Alternatively, students can complete a two-year program at a community college or university to obtain an associate's degree in pharmacy technology.

Whichever program they pursue, prospective pharmacy technicians typically study ways to dispense medications; the names, uses, and doses of medications; over-the-counter drugs; arithmetic needed for mixing or compounding medications; record-keeping; and pharmacy-related laws and ethics. In addition to the course work, these programs usually include some type of clinical experience to provide a student with hands-on practice working in a pharmacy. High school students who are interested in this career should prepare by taking classes in chemistry, biology, computer literacy, and math.

In addition to training, the majority of states require pharmacy technicians to pass a certification exam and register with the state's board of pharmacy. A criminal background check may also be required. Even in states where certification is not mandatory, obtaining a certificate will increase a pharmacy technician's chances of employment. Continuing education courses are typically required in order to maintain the pharmacy technician certification.

Skills and Personality

Because their job involves a lot of human interaction, pharmacy technicians need strong interpersonal skills. It is important to have

A pharmacy technician checks inventory. Technicians have to be familiar with various drugs and their uses in addition to knowing how to measure medications and determine correct dosages.

> **The Good and the Bad**
>
> "I've been a tech for about 3 years. . . . Best team of people I've had at any job. There's a lot of different things that can make the job good or bad, including your ability to deal with different types of customers. It won't always be sunshine and daisies, but you just have to know the rules and stand firm. Don't let patients push you around. Overall I've really enjoyed being a tech."
>
> —Luke Walton, pharmacy technician
>
> Luke Walton (lukeswalton), comment on TreeFrogy, "Pharmacy Technicians, Do You Like Your Job?," Reddit, 2014. www.reddit.com.

good listening skills, be courteous, and to show compassion. "You have to have a general liking for the public," says Brown. "When you're working in retail pharmacy, you have to deal with patients all day long."[25] Strong speaking skills are also important since pharmacy technicians need to communicate effectively with customers, pharmacists, and doctors.

In order to be successful, pharmacy technicians must also have a sharp mind. They need to understand written orders, so strong reading skills are crucial. Attention to detail is also vital when preparing labels and filling prescriptions. Pharmacy technicians must be able to distinguish between medications that look similar or have similar names. A sharp mind is also needed to stay organized while moving from one task to another, such as answering phones, speaking with customers, and compounding medications. Likewise, strong math skills are beneficial, as Brown explains: "Being science and math oriented is a plus, since that's the bulk of what we deal with. You need to be able to do simple multiplication and division in your head."[26]

Physically, pharmacy technicians need good stamina. They spend most of their day on their feet and may also need to climb ladders to reach or stock medications on shelves. They also need to lift moderate loads in order to receive and stock inventory.

Lastly, it is vital for pharmacy technicians to be ethical people. In the majority of states, they must pass a criminal background check and maintain a clean record—especially in terms of drug-related offenses. Pharmacy technicians must have very high standards when it comes to dealing with controlled substances, many of which are not only addictive but also very valuable on the street, so pharmacy technicians must be able to resist any temptation when it comes to these medications. They must also follow a strict code of conduct that protects customers' privacy and sensitive information.

Working Conditions

Pharmacy technicians work in clean, organized, well-lit, and well-ventilated facilities. Most work full-time, but many work part-time. Those who work at twenty-four-hour pharmacies will have a broader work schedule to choose from; they may work days, evenings, overnight, and/or weekends.

Pharmacy technicians spend a lot of time on their feet; therefore, it is recommended that they wear comfortable shoes and clothing to work. They may need to lift heavy boxes or use a stool or stepladder to reach supplies on high shelves. At times, the job can be very fast paced, hectic, and even stressful. "The pharmacy is a very busy environment," says Viki, a pharmacy technician in Arizona. "If you are not good at multitasking, if you are not good in stressful situations, this is not the job for you."[27]

Pharmacy technicians face several on-the-job risks, including exposure to illness, spilled liquid medications, and hazardous vapors. According to the Occupational Safety and Health Administration, technicians may have allergic reactions to some drugs, and medications that kill cancer and bacteria may be hazardous for technicians to handle. It is important that anyone who works in a pharmacy wears protective gear such as gloves and a mask when mixing dangerous compounds.

Employers and Pay

Most pharmacy technicians are employed in pharmacies, including those found in drugstores, grocery stores, and hospitals.

Some also work at pharmacies in hospitals, nursing homes, extended care centers, and correctional facilities. In short, pharmacy technicians can be found anywhere medications are dispensed.

According to the Bureau of Labor Statistics (BLS), the median annual pay for full-time pharmacy technicians was about $32,700 in 2018. The lowest-paid 10 percent earned less than $22,740, and the highest-paid 10 percent earned more than $48,010. The salary varies widely, depending on factors such as education, certifications, additional skills, years of experience, and geographic location.

What Is the Future Outlook for Pharmacy Technicians?

According to the BLS, employment for pharmacy technicians will grow by 12 percent through 2026, which is faster than the average for all occupations. This job growth is being driven by an increased need for prescription medications due to the large aging population and higher rates among all age groups of chronic diseases such as diabetes. Furthermore, advances in medical research will lead to more prescription medications being used to fight diseases, which will also increase the demand for pharmacy services. In addition, because pharmacists are taking on more duties, including giving flu shots and other vaccines, technicians will be in greater demand to take over tasks formerly performed by pharmacists, such as collecting customer information and preparing medications.

Find Out More

American Association of Pharmacy Technicians (AAPT)
website: www.pharmacytechnician.com

The AAPT is the first organization serving the interests of pharmacy technicians. Its website includes continuing education courses, a career center, and information about scholarship opportunities. The AAPT also hosts an annual convention for pharmacy technicians.

American Society of Health-System Pharmacists (ASHP)
website: www.ashp.org

The ASHP represents pharmacy technicians who work in emergency settings. Its website includes numerous resources for pharmacy technicians, including information about policies, professional development and certification, continuing education, and more. The ASHP also hosts several conferences throughout the year.

National Association of Boards of Pharmacy (NABP)
website: https://nabp.pharmacy

The NABP is the leading organization for accreditation and certification for pharmacy technicians. This nonprofit publishes research reports as well as a free weekly electronic newsletter.

Pharmacy Technician Certification Board (PTCB)
website: www.ptcb.org

The PTCB certifies pharmacy technicians. Its website contains resources about the career of pharmacy technician, including job descriptions and outlook. The PTCB is also involved with numerous events and conferences for pharmacy technicians throughout the year.

Phlebotomist

A Few Facts

Number of Jobs
About 125,280 in 2018

Pay
About $25,020 to $49,060

Educational Requirements
High school diploma or equivalent plus approved training program

Certification and Licensing
Professional certification may be required; varies by state

Personal Qualities
People skills, empathy, listening skills, steady hands

Work Settings
Hospitals, doctors' offices, laboratories, blood donor centers

Future Job Outlook
Growth of 25 percent through 2026

What Does a Phlebotomist Do?

Phlebotomists draw blood from patients and donors by using a needle to puncture a vein. The samples they collect are used for various types of laboratory medical testing—for example, to determine whether a patient is anemic. Phlebotomists also draw blood to be used for transfusions, donations, and research. In addition to drawing blood, phlebotomists label the samples; enter information into a database; assemble and maintain instruments such as needles, test tubes, and blood vials; and keep all equipment and work areas clean and sanitary.

Phlebotomists explain their work to patients and provide assistance if patients have an adverse reaction to having their blood drawn, such as feeling faint. "I have a reaction every time I have blood drawn," explains patient Dave Duit. "Hearing goes, sweating, light headed, yawning, see dark spots in my vision, feel like throwing up. I now tell my phlebotomist about my reaction and they take all the necessary precautions to lessen my reaction, and it helps tremendously."[28]

A Typical Workday

The typical day in the life of a phlebotomist will vary depending on where he or she works. In general, though, most start their workday very early—some as early as 5:00 a.m. This is because blood test results are more accurate if blood is drawn before patients have eaten or exercised, so starting early is key to getting a good sample. Phlebotomists begin their workday by reviewing the orders for the day. Before drawing blood from a patient, phlebotomists double-check the patient's identity, date of birth, and medical record.

Whereas phlebotomists who work in a hospital may visit patients in their rooms, those who work in a laboratory or blood donation center will call patients back to their work area. The phlebotomist will talk to a nervous patient or donor to put him or her at ease. The phlebotomist begins a blood draw—or stick, as it is often called—by applying a tourniquet and selecting an appropriate vein. Then he or she cleans the skin and inserts the needle to collect a blood sample. In some cases, such as with very young children, a nurse or medical assistant may provide extra help.

Once the blood is drawn, the phlebotomist must handle it carefully so it does not become contaminated. The phlebotomist must label each vial of blood drawn and enter its corresponding information into a database. He or she may also transport samples to a laboratory for analysis. The phlebotomist must also clean and sanitize the lab area after each patient to prevent the spread of infections or diseases, and she or he must safely dispose of all needles and used bandages. Then the phlebotomist checks and restocks supplies before moving on to the next patient. In a typical day, a phlebotomist may draw blood from all types of patients, including newborn babies, pregnant women, postoperative patients, and senior citizens.

An important aspect of this job is to stay alert to signs that patients are feeling faint. This is a pretty common response to having one's blood drawn, and care must be taken so patients do not further injure themselves in a fall. Phlebotomists care for woozy patients by applying a cool cloth to the forehead, loosening restrictive clothing, helping the patient relax and breathe normally, and providing juice or a soft drink and a small snack, which can bring their blood sugar levels up and help them feel better. "Also, you want to request that the patient remain in the area until they have fully recovered," explains phlebotomist Crystal Crys. "You don't just say, 'Okay, thank you, Mr. Johnson, I'll see you later.' No, have them sit in your chair for a minute or in the waiting area where you can keep an eye on him or her."[29]

Education and Training

Phlebotomists must have a high school diploma or equivalent and have completed a training program. They may need professional certification, depending on the state and/or employer. Some phlebotomists are trained on the job, but the majority go through formal training and seek certification because most employers prefer this route. Some phlebotomists continue their education and go on to become licensed practical nurses and registered nurses.

Phlebotomy training programs typically last a year or less and can be taken at community colleges, vocational schools, technical schools, and teaching hospitals. Course work includes anatomy, physiology, psychology, and medical terminology. Phlebotomy training also includes instruction on collection techniques, laboratory procedures, related laws and regulations, office management, and laboratory technology such as the science of testing human blood. Students who are interested in this career can prepare themselves by taking high school classes in anatomy, biology, and math.

In addition to course instruction, these programs offer students hands-on practice in a laboratory. Typically, phlebotomy students will first learn to insert a needle on a model of a hand. Next they practice drawing blood from one another. This can be nerve-racking, as one phlebotomy student explains on the Student Doctor Network website: "Just started a Phlebotomy class,

> ### An Exhilarating Job
>
> "The non-routine patient interaction is why the job can be very exhilarating. Sticking a sick 8 month old that is dehydrated, screaming, kicking, with sleep deprived parents will get your heart racing and make you feel like you're the biggest jerk in the world. However, there is nothing like the feeling of victory when you get that tiny vial of blood, when others have failed. The lab gets information back to the floor and the kid gets to go home with the proper medication, and you helped make that happen."
>
> —Todd Reese, a phlebotomist and lab technician
>
> Todd Reese, comment on Quora, "What's It Like to Be a Phlebotomist?," March 21, 2018. www.quora.com.

it was exciting and fun, but there was a bit of [a] downside. I was scared to puncture or get skin punctured by other students. . . . Although I did carry out the skin puncture, and able to do more afterwards, but damn, I was very nervous that I was going to mess up the procedure."[30]

California, Louisiana, Nevada, and Washington require phlebotomists to be certified, but even in states where certification is not mandatory, most phlebotomists get certified because it is strongly preferred by employers. Candidates for certification must pass a written exam; a practical demonstration of their blood-drawing skills may also be required. A number of organizations offer certification, including the American Society for Clinical Pathology and the National Phlebotomy Association. Certified phlebotomists must take continuing education classes to maintain their credentials.

Skills and Personality

Because many people are nervous about having their blood drawn, phlebotomists must have excellent people skills. They often explain the procedure to patients to help calm them, so strong speaking and listening skills are a must. Empathy and compassion are also vital. "Honestly, we don't like hurting you," explains phlebotomist Katherine L. Wornek.

> If we tell you to look the other way, take a deep breath or chit chat your ear off without giving you warning that we are about to poke you, it's because we are trying to distract you from any pain and anxiety you may have toward getting your blood drawn. Trust me, we hear multiple times a day about how nervous needles make people feel—we don't expect you to be excited to have a sharp object penetrating your body.[31]

Phlebotomists need good critical-thinking skills and attention to detail in order to choose an appropriate puncture site, draw blood safely, and accurately label and process blood specimens. They must also keep track of a constant flow of patients and document all procedures, so strong organizational skills and an ability to multitask are a plus. Likewise, having solid reading and computer skills are important so they can understand medical documents and record information in a database.

Phlebotomy Anxiety

"Anxiety in the first couple of days or weeks in phlebotomy [training] is pretty normal! I thought I wasn't nervous but when I went for my first stick I completely pulled the needle right back out after going in and my poor classmate bled all over their arm, but after a couple of more tries it became less scary! There's something a little strange about puncturing the skin of another the first time but trust me, once you've done it 50 times, the scare factor/thrill wears off!"

—A phlebotomy student who goes by the screen name aharr157

aharr157, comment on Geo16, "Phlebotomy Scare—Is This Normal?," Student Doctor Network, April 19, 2017. https://forums.studentdoctor.net.

Steady hands, skilled fingers, and good hand-eye coordination are also critical skills for phlebotomists; they need to be able to draw blood successfully on the first attempt to minimize discomfort and anxiety for patients.

Patience is an extremely important skill for phlebotomists to possess. Most people are not excited about having their blood drawn—particularly children—and some patients can be uncooperative. Some blood draws are quite difficult to perform, and a phlebotomist may have to insert the needle multiple times. When encountering such difficulties, it is important to stay calm, focused, and steady.

Working Conditions

The majority of phlebotomists work full-time. Depending on where they work, they may have a regular day shift, although those who work in hospitals and labs—as the majority of phlebotomists do—may be required to occasionally work nights, weekends, and holidays. Some may work a few day shifts, then have a day or two off, and then work a few night shifts. Some work part-time or are on call as needed.

Phlebotomists work in clean, well-lit facilities. They may be on their feet for long periods, so comfortable shoes are a must. And because they are at increased risk for blood-borne diseases such as HIV and hepatitis, it is vital that phlebotomists wear gloves, follow safety procedures, and handle needles and medical waste safely. Like all health care professionals, phlebotomists must wash their hands frequently.

Employers and Pay

Phlebotomists work mainly in hospitals, medical and diagnostic laboratories, nursing homes, blood donor centers, doctors' offices, and outpatient care centers. In fact, phlebotomists can be found in virtually every setting in which medical treatments are performed.

According to the Bureau of Labor Statistics (BLS), the median annual pay for full-time phlebotomists was about $34,480 in 2018. The lowest-paid 10 percent earned less than $25,020, and the highest-paid 10 percent earned more than $49,060. Salaries vary based on employer, training and certification, and number of years on the job. Wages also vary significantly based on location—pay is highest in Alaska and along the West Coast and the East Coast.

What Is the Future Outlook for Phlebotomists?

According to the BLS, employment for phlebotomists is expected to grow by 25 percent through 2026, which is much faster than the average for all occupations. Reasons for this growth include the expanding elderly population and the increase in the number of people with chronic conditions that require blood work for analysis and diagnosis, such as diabetes. Job prospects will be greatest for those phlebotomists who hold certification from an organization such as the National Phlebotomy Association.

Find Out More

American Medical Technologists (AMT)
website: www.americanmedtech.org

The AMT is an internationally recognized certification agency for medical technology professionals, including phlebotomists. In addition to providing study materials and certification exams on its website, the AMT provides webinars and information about applying to schools and hosts an annual meeting for medical technology professionals.

Center for Phlebotomy Education
website: www.phlebotomy.com

The Center for Phlebotomy Education supports comprehensive training for phlebotomists. It achieves this through resources such as a YouTube channel, continuing education courses, and an online newsletter. The center's website even includes an informational video for patients.

National Phlebotomy Association (NPA)
website: www.nationalphlebotomy.org

The NPA is dedicated to expanding phlebotomy education and training, particularly in the area of health and safety. The organization offers certification and an annual conference, and its website contains a job board.

Phlebotomy Careers
website: www.phlebotomycareers.net

This website provides up-to-date information about careers in phlebotomy. It posts articles with general information about the career, schools with accredited phlebotomy programs, training and certification, and more.

Physical Therapist Assistant

A Few Facts

Number of Jobs
About 191,870 in 2018

Pay
About $33,780 to $79,810

Educational Requirements
Associate's degree

Certification and Licensing
Required in all states

Personal Qualities
Excellent people skills, good listening skills, empathy, physical stamina

Work Settings
Physical therapy offices, hospitals, clinics, nursing homes

Future Job Outlook
Growth of 31 percent through 2026

What Does a Physical Therapist Assistant Do?

Physical therapist assistants (PTAs) work under the direction and supervision of licensed physical therapists to help patients who are recovering from injuries and illnesses regain movement and manage pain. They are directly involved with treating patients, following the treatment plan set up by the physical therapist. They also keep track of changes in patients' physical performance and report regularly to the supervising physical therapist about patients' progress. PTAs may also perform clerical duties such as answering phones, scheduling patients, and filling out insurance forms.

The duties of PTAs vary depending on each patient's needs. These professionals often teach patients exercises that promote strength and mobility and show them how to properly walk on crutches or with a cane. They may also teach patients aquatic (water) exercises. With some patients, PTAs may perform electrotherapy, such as ultrasound and electrical stimulation, which helps reduce certain kinds of pain. For other patients, massage or heat treatment may be given.

PTAs work with patients of all ages, from newborns to the elderly, and they help patients who have a wide variety of issues. Todd Bedward, a PTA in Long Beach, California, explains, "I work with people who have balance problems stemming from inner ear disturbances, knee or hip injuries, and brain injuries. We also see people with Parkinson's, Alzheimer's and Lou Gehrig's disease." Like most PTAs, Bedward finds immense satisfaction in helping improve the lives of others. "I love that I can help people almost instantly. I love the fact that when we're done with them, they're fine. They're back to their lives."[32]

The Workday

The types of tasks a PTA is allowed to perform vary by state and setting. For example, PTAs who work in an outpatient facility will have a very different daily experience than those who work in a hospital. Most PTAs are responsible for setting up the treatment area before each patient arrives. Once treatment equipment is ready, the PTA will call the patient back, but she or he may need to help patients with limited mobility get to and from a therapy area. During therapy, the PTA may assist patients with stretches and exercise, teach them how to use a particular piece of equipment, and tell them how many repetitions to perform. The PTA observes patients before, during, and after each session and reports their status to the physical therapist.

PTAs may spend a lot of time educating patients and family members about what to do after treatment, such as how to follow a specific exercise regimen at home. Between each patient and at the end of the day, PTAs are responsible for cleaning the area, including washing and replacing linens where needed. PTAs also keep the treatment area organized and may be required to track inventory and order supplies. Antonio Sanson, a PTA, says, "I have a lot of fun with it. I love working with people. It's a blast for me to go into work every day and to help someone with some exercises, to show someone how to get out of back pain."[33]

A physical therapist assistant (PTA) helps a patient with arm exercises. The PTA works with patients who are recovering from injuries and illnesses regain movement and manage pain.

Education and Training

Individuals must have an associate's degree to work as a PTA. This degree typically takes two years and can be completed at an accredited community college, technical college, or university. The Commission on Accreditation in Physical Therapy Education (CAPTE) oversees and certifies schools that train PTAs. Training programs include classes in algebra, anatomy, physiology, psychology, and English. Because admission to PTA programs is somewhat competitive, teens who are interested in a career in this field will benefit from taking similar classes in high school. PTA training programs also include classroom and lab training in kinesiology (the study of how the body moves), therapy methods (such as using heat, cold, massage, and hydrotherapy), assessment, and basic pharmacology.

In addition to their course work, PTA students gain hands-on clinical experience. This involves shadowing physical therapists and licensed PTAs. Near the end of their training program, prospective PTAs will do an internship under the supervision of a trained mentor, typically for sixteen weeks. During this time, PTA internees will care for real-life patients, practicing assessment, basic care skills, various therapies, and safety precautions.

In addition to graduating from a CAPTE-accredited program, licensure or certification is required in all states as well as in the District of Columbia, Puerto Rico, and the US Virgin Islands. To become certified, prospective PTAs must take and pass the National Physical Therapy Exam, which is administered by the Federation of State Boards of Physical Therapy. Individuals must graduate from a CAPTE-accredited program in order to be eligible to take this exam. Some states also require PTAs to undergo a criminal background check. Once certified, PTAs may also need to take continuing education courses to renew their certification, though this varies by state. And, although not required, many PTAs also earn certification in basic life support, cardiopulmonary resuscitation, and other first aid skills, which helps make them more employable.

Skills and Personality

PTAs work very closely with patients, their families, and other health care professionals, so having excellent interpersonal skills is a must. PTAs need good active listening skills so they can understand patients' questions or concerns about their treatment. PTAs also need good verbal communication skills to correctly give patients instructions regarding their treatment and clearly describe exercises to do at home.

Empathy is also extremely important in this career. Patients are often in pain and can sometimes get discouraged, particularly those who are recovering from a catastrophic injury. So PTAs need to be caring and compassionate, and they need to have a strong desire to help patients—and their family members—cope with these difficulties. Matthew Kelly, a PTA, explains this aspect of his job: "I like [being a PTA] because for a period of time in people's lives, when they otherwise could be dealing with something that's really bad, you get to be a person who could contribute to that otherwise bad experience and make it a little more fun, a little bit more easy on them and their families as well."[34]

In addition to interpersonal skills, PTAs need to be clearheaded and skilled in critical thinking. They often need to solve problems and make decisions about the best course of action during therapy, so they need to be able to weigh options and choose the best one. A keen eye for detail helps PTAs with this task, and it comes in handy when PTAs record details about a patient's therapy session. Good writing skills are also a requirement since PTAs must document aspects of the therapy in patients' medical records. Similarly, good reading comprehension skills are also vital for understanding written instructions from doctors or the supervising physical therapist.

Physically, PTAs should be strong and in good shape because they are often on their feet and their job can be physically demanding. PTAs must often kneel, bend, stoop, and stand for long periods. Some patients may need assistance moving around the therapy area or may even need to be lifted or repositioned. Stamina and strength are also useful when PTAs set up equipment and prepare treatment areas. And because PTAs may need to provide manual therapy—moving, bending, and stretching a patient's legs, for example—dexterity is also a vital skill.

Working Conditions

Most PTAs work a typical day shift from 8:00 a.m. to 5:00 p.m., but some may provide physical therapy services during the early morning or early evening. For example, a PTA may work from 6:00 a.m. to 2:00 p.m. or from 10:00 a.m. to 6:00

> **A Positive Impact**
>
> "[My favorite part about being a PTA is] seeing people achieve functional goals and knowing I played a big part in keeping an EMT [emergency medical technician] on the job, a police officer on the beat, a high school athlete in the game. Just today, I heard from a past patient who was training for the Madison Ironman and was unable to run six weeks out from the race due to pain. He finished pain-free . . . and couldn't be happier. I was so proud. I'm proud of the results my patients can achieve, and I'm happy I've had such a positive impact on my patients' lives."
>
> —Daniel Timm, PTA
>
> Quoted in Charlotte Bohnett, "The Story of a PTA (Interview)," *WebPT Blog*, October 7, 2013. www.webpt.com.

p.m. in order to accommodate patients' work schedules. PTAs who work in hospitals and nursing homes may sometimes be required to work on weekends and holidays. Those who work in a school setting will have the same schedule as teachers. Most PTAs work full-time.

Because of the physical nature of their work, PTAs are susceptible to aches and pains. They are particularly vulnerable to back injuries since they must often lift and move patients who have mobility problems. PTAs can minimize aches and their risk of injury by using proper techniques when assisting patients. "You learn in school about proper body mechanics and the proper way to work to keep both you and your patients safe," says Becky, a PTA in North Highlands, California. "However, there are times that you can be in a difficult position. I would be less than truthful if I didn't tell you that yes I do come home with a back ache every so often."[35]

Employers and Pay

Most PTAs work in physical therapists' offices or in hospitals. PTAs are employed in a variety of other settings as well, including

Saying Goodbye

"On occasion, a patient presents with something that cannot be changed, but managed, and that is difficult. Yet, I am so fortunate to be able to utilize my skill set to help them live the highest quality of physical life possible for their individual situation. Also, in this profession we spend several hours per week with our patients so although I am always thrilled when they are better, sometimes it is hard to say goodbye."

—Beth Crowley, PTA

Beth Crowley, "Why I Love My Job: Beth Crowley, PTA," *Atlanta Journal-Constitution*, October 31, 2013. www.ajc.com.

---

outpatient and inpatient clinics, home health agencies, schools, sports and fitness facilities, and nursing homes.

According to the Bureau of Labor Statistics (BLS), the median annual pay for full-time PTAs was about $58,040 in 2018. The lowest-paid 10 percent earned less than $33,780, and the highest-paid 10 percent earned more than $79,810. Salaries vary based on employer, training and certification, and number of years on the job.

What Is the Future Outlook for Physical Therapist Assistants?

The BLS predicts that employment for PTAs will grow by 31 percent through 2026, which is much faster than the average for all occupations. Part of what is driving this demand is a response to the aging baby-boom generation; baby boomers are staying active later in life than previous generations, which puts them at risk of injury. Likewise, the rise in chronic medical conditions, such as diabetes and obesity, means that more PTAs will be needed to help patients maintain mobility. In addition, physical therapists are increasingly using PTAs to help lower the cost of physical therapy services.

Find Out More

American Council of Academic Physical Therapy (ACAPT)
website: www.acapt.org

The ACAPT, part of the American Physical Therapy Association, is dedicated to the education and professional development of PTAs. It achieves this through research, an online newsletter, and numerous educational events throughout the year.

American Physical Therapy Association (APTA)
website: www.apta.org

The APTA represents more than one hundred thousand physical therapists, PTAs, and physical therapy students. Under its website's "Careers & Education" section, users can find upcoming courses and conferences, a job board, and information about career development, including for PTAs.

Commission on Accreditation in Physical Therapy Education (CAPTE)
website: www.capteonline.org

The CAPTE accredits physical therapy schools. Its website has a list of schools offering accredited programs as well as annual educational workshops for physical therapists and PTAs.

Federation of State Boards of Physical Therapy (FSBPT)
website: www.fsbpt.org

The FSBPT awards licenses to physical therapists and PTAs. Its website has information about state licensing requirements and about the National Physical Therapy Exam under the "Exam Candidates" section. Users can also find volunteer opportunities on the website.

Source Notes

Caring Careers

1. Erin Hendrickson, "Why I Chose to Become a Radiation Therapist," *O-Pro Blog*, OncoLink, March 27, 2013. www.oncolink.org.
2. Hendrickson, "Why I Chose to Become a Radiation Therapist."
3. Andrea Clement Santiago, "Reasons to Work in the Healthcare Field," Verywell Mind, March 30, 2019. www.verywellmind.com.
4. Quoted in Callie Malvik, "LPN or RN: The Advantages of Being an LPN," Rasmussen College, August 30, 2016. www.rasmussen.edu.
5. Santiago, "Reasons to Work in the Healthcare Field."

Dental Hygienist

6. Quoted in DentalPost, "Why Do Dental Hygienists Love Their Jobs?," October 23, 2018. www.dentalpost.net.
7. Quoted in ValuePenguin, "What's It Like Being a Dental Hygienist?," 2019. www.valuepenguin.com.
8. Quoted in ValuePenguin, "What's It Like Being a Dental Hygienist?"

Diagnostic Medical Sonographer

9. Quoted in DrKitVideos, "Ultrasound Technologist," YouTube, December 30, 2012. www.youtube.com.
10. Kristy Le, "A Day in the Life: Sonography Student," YouTube, November 25, 2017. www.youtube.com.
11. Quoted in Premed Takeovers, "A Day in the Life of a Sonography Student," YouTube, November 22, 2017. www.youtube.com.

12. Quoted in Premed Takeovers, "A Day in the Life of a Sonography Student."

Emergency Medical Technician

13. Quoted in Association of American Medical Colleges, "What It's Like to Be an Emergency Medical Technician (EMT)." https://students-residents.aamc.org.
14. Kayla Buffam, "Why I Love Being an EMT," Odyssey, October 3, 2016. www.theodysseyonline.com.
15. Arden Heath, "16 Things I Wish I Knew Before I Became an EMT," Odyssey, August 11, 2016. www.theodysseyonline.com.

Licensed Practical Nurse

16. Quoted in WorkBC's Career Trek, "Licensed Practical Nurse (Episode 101)," YouTube, March 23, 2017. www.youtube.com.
17. Nicole Miller, "Being a Licensed Practical Nurse," Arc of Monroe, June 14, 2019. https://arcmonroe.org.
18. Quoted in WorkBC's Career Trek, "Licensed Practical Nurse (Episode 101)."

Massage Therapist

19. Barbara Alcaraz, "4 Great Reasons to Choose Massage Therapy as a Career," *Northwest Career College Blog*, October 15, 2018. www.northwestcareercollege.edu.
20. Margaret LMT, "Pros and Cons of Being a Massage Therapist," YouTube, May 27, 2018. www.youtube.com.
21. Spencer Harwood (HM Massage), "5 Things I Wish I Knew Before Going into Massage Therapy," YouTube, February 19, 2018. www.youtube.com.
22. Harwood, "5 Things I Wish I Knew Before Going into Massage Therapy."

Pharmacy Technician

23. Quoted in All Allied Health Schools, "Profile: Certified Pharmacy Technician." www.allalliedhealthschools.com.

24. Quoted in Carrington College, "A Day in the Life of a Pharmacy Technician," YouTube, April 27, 2016. www.youtube.com.
25. Quoted in All Allied Health Schools, "Profile."
26. Quoted in All Allied Health Schools, "Profile."
27. Viki, "Becoming & Working as a Pharmacy Technician," YouTube, August 22, 2018. www.youtube.com.

Phlebotomist

28. Dave Duit, comment on Crystal Crys (Crystatic Jewels), "Phlebotomy: Fainting/Patients DO Faint," YouTube, April 24, 2014. www.youtube.com.
29. Crys, "Phlebotomy."
30. Geo16, "Phlebotomy Scare—Is This Normal?," Student Doctor Network, April 19, 2017. https://forums.studentdoctor.net.
31. Katherine L. Wornek, "Tips from a Phlebotomist," *Idaho State Journal*, September 8, 2018. www.idahostatejournal.com.

Physical Therapist Assistant

32. Quoted in All Allied Health Schools, "Profile: Physical Therapy Assistant." www.allalliedhealthschools.com.
33. Antonio Sanson, "Physical Therapy Assistant Day in the Life," YouTube, February 24, 2018. www.youtube.com.
34. Quoted in TherapyJobs.com, "Why I Love My Physical Therapy Assistant Job," 2019. www.therapyjobs.com.
35. Becky, reply to Vallon, "Is There a True Demand for Physical Therapy Assistants? What Are the Pros and Cons of This Profession?," Indeed, 2019. www.indeed.com.

Interview with a Dental Hygienist

Patty Ledgerwood is a dental hygienist who works in San Diego, California. She has worked as a hygienist for thirty-four years. Although she earned a bachelor's degree, one can enter the field with an associate's degree. She answered questions about her career by email.

Q: Why did you become a dental hygienist?

A: When I was in high school I worked as a dental assistant and I really enjoyed working in the dental field. At the time I was considering becoming a teacher. I soon learned that my work as a hygienist is about teaching people about their health. I was also attracted to this field due to the flexibility of the career. It was a great opportunity to work as much or as little as I wanted to and I felt this would be great for raising kids or pursuing other interests as well as my career.

Q: How did you train for your career? What did you find most challenging and/or most surprising about the course work, training, and exams?

A: I attended a four-year university and earned a bachelor's degree of science in dental hygiene. I was surprised by how much chemistry we needed to take. It is important however, to have this background because we are administering anesthesia. There is also a lot of biology-based classes, which is to be expected in a medical field. Even with all the course work, I feel the most challenging are the state board exams. These are timed practical exams where we find our own patients and clean their teeth and then get checked and graded on these. While this is a very stressful process there is a good percentage of people who pass.

Q: Can you describe your typical workday?

A: I typically see about eight patients a day on an hourly schedule. In that time frame we review their medical history, do an oral cancer evaluation, check their periodontal condition, clean and scale their teeth, polish their teeth, educate about oral hygiene, take X-rays if needed, identify any pathology going on in the mouth (i.e., cavities, fillings that are failing, crowns that are leaking, bite issues, jaw concerns, or any complaints the patient may have), take photos if needed, then have the dentist come in and examine their mouths.

Q: What do you like most about your job?

A: I enjoy educating people about the health of their mouth and how it relates to the health of their bodies. I enjoy seeing how far the dental field has progressed with all the new technology, and I am always learning new things. I also enjoy meeting a lot of different people from different backgrounds with different interests.

Q: Can you give an example or two of how new technologies have altered the way you do your job?

A: Technology moves very fast in the dental field. One of the great innovations has been digital X-rays. No more developing film and dealing with fixer and developer solutions and machines that break down. Digital also means you can adjust the contrast or magnify areas to see better. These can also be emailed to any specialist needing the information. Other great technology is newer ultrasonic tips to make debris removal easier. Another one is placement of antibiotics directly in the periodontal pockets which is a great help in eliminating inflammation. A fantastic new development which doesn't directly affect the hygienist but is a great example of how quickly technology is moving in the dental field is the ability to create crowns in one day, right in the office using CAD CAM [computer-aided design and manufacturing] systems. These use scanning technology, and impressions are no longer required. All these fantastic things are helping to improve the dental professional's role and make the experience better for the patients. I'm very excited to see what else the future holds.

Q: What do you like least about your job?

A: The time constraints. Not everyone has the same mouth or the same problems. Sometimes people come in with certain issues going on or sometimes they have very difficult mouths to clean and it takes longer than I have time for. It causes me to run behind, thus putting things in a very stressful situation because people are not always understanding.

Q: What personal qualities do you find most valuable for this type of work?

A: Someone who is a very people oriented person and has a desire to help people. Also a very detail oriented person. Someone who has a passion to help people improve their health.

Q: What advice do you have for students who are interested in this career?

A: This is an excellent career. You can have the flexibility to work as much or as little as you need to. You can make a nice salary but you really need to enjoy doing it for the career and professional aspects. To prepare, it helps to have a good background in science classes.

Other Jobs in Health Care

- Cardiovascular technologist
- Clinical laboratory technician
- Clinical laboratory technologist
- Dental assistant
- Dental laboratory technician
- Dispensing optician
- Health information technician
- Home health aide
- Laboratory animal caretaker
- Magnetic resonance imaging technologist
- Medical assistant
- Medical equipment preparer
- Medical laboratory technician
- Medical records technician
- Medical transcriptionist
- Nuclear medicine technologist
- Nursing assistant
- Occupational therapy assistant
- Optician
- Orderly
- Paramedic
- Personal care aide
- Physical therapist aide
- Psychiatric aide
- Radiation therapist
- Radiologic technologist
- Respiratory therapist
- Surgical technologist
- Vascular technologist
- Veterinary assistant
- Veterinary technician

Editor's note: The online *Occupational Outlook Handbook* of the US Department of Labor's Bureau of Labor Statistics is an excellent source of information on jobs in hundreds of career fields, including many of those listed here. The *Occupational Outlook Handbook* may be accessed online at www.bls.gov/ooh.

Index

Note: Boldface page numbers indicate illustrations.

Accrediting Bureau of Health Education Schools, 39
Alcaraz, Barbara, 38
American Academy of Emergency Medicine (AAEM), 28–29
American Association of Pharmacy Technicians (AAPT), 50–51
American Council of Academic Physical Therapy (ACAPT), 67
American Dental Association (ADA), 9, 13
American Dental Education Association (ADEA), 13
American Dental Hygienist Association (ADHA), 14
American Institute of Ultrasound in Medicine (AIUM), 21–22
American Massage Therapy Association (AMTA), 43
American Medical Technologists (AMT), 58
American Nurses Association (ANA), 36
American Physical Therapy Association (APTA), 67
American Registry for Diagnostic Medical Sonography (ARDMS), 22
American Society for Clinical Pathology, 55
American Society of Health-System Pharmacists (ASHP), 46, 51
Associated Bodyworks and Massage Professionals (ABMP), 43

Brown, Randy, 44, 48
Buffam, Kayla, 24, 25
Bureau of Labor Statistics (BLS)
  on dental hygienist, 12
  on diagnostic medical sonographer, 21
  on emergency medical technician, 28
  on growth in health care industry, 5–6
  on licensed practical nurse, 35
  on massage therapist, 42
  on pharmacy technician, 50
  on phlebotomist, 58
  on physical therapist assistant, 66

Center for Phlebotomy Education, 58–59
Christy, Kristy, 34
Commission on Accreditation in Physical Therapy Education (CAPTE), 62, 67

Commission on Accreditation of Allied Health Education Programs (CAAHEP), 18, 29
Commission on Dental Accreditation, 9
Commission on Massage Therapy Accreditation, 39, 43
Crowley, Beth, 66
Crys, Crystal, 54
Curtis, Kyle, 24

dental hygienist, **10**
  certification/licensing, 7
  educational requirements, 7, 9–10
  employers of, 12
  future job outlook, 7, 12–13
  information resources, 13–14
  interview with, 71–73
  number of jobs, 7
  role of, 7–8
  salary/earnings, 7, 12
  skills/personal qualities, 7, 11
  typical workday, 8–9
  working conditions, 11–12
  work settings, 7
diagnostic medical sonographer, **16**
  certification/licensing, 15
  educational requirements, 15, 18–19
  employers of, 21
  future job outlook, 15, 21
  information resources, 21–22
  number of jobs, 15
  role of, 15–17
  salary/earnings, 15, 21
  skills/personal qualities, 15, 19–20
  typical workday, 17
  working conditions, 20–21
  work settings, 15
Dickerson, Kathryn Roux, 40

emergency medical technician (EMT)
  certification/licensing, 23
  educational requirements, 23, 25–26
  employers of, 28
  future job outlook, 23, 28
  information resources, 28–29
  number of jobs, 23
  role of, 23–24
  salary/earnings, 23, 28
  skills/personal qualities, 23, 26
  typical workday, 24–25
  working conditions, 26–28
  work settings, 23

Federation of State Boards of Physical Therapy (FSBPT), 63, 67

Harwood, Spencer, 41, 42
health care industry
  growth in, 5–6
  other jobs in, 74
  possible careers, 4–5
Heath, Arden, 26, 27
Hendrickson, Erin, 4

Johnson, Tina, 5

Kelly, Matthew, 64

Ledgerwood, Patty, 71–73
licensed practical nurse (LPN), **33**

certification/licensing, 30
educational requirements, 30, 32–33
employers of, 35
future job outlook, 30, 35–36
information resources, 36
number of jobs, 30
role of, 30–31
salary/earnings, 30, 35
skills/personal qualities, 30, 33–34
typical workday, 30–32
working conditions, 34–35
work settings, 30

Mailman, Eric, 25
Massage and Bodywork Licensing Examination (MBLEx), 40
massage therapist
certification/licensing, 37
educational requirements, 37, 39–40
employers of, 42
future job outlook, 37, 42–43
information resources, 43
number of jobs, 37
role of, 37–38
salary/earnings, 37, 42
skills/personal qualities, 37, 40–41
typical workday, 38–39
working conditions, 41–42
work settings, 37
Massage Therapy Foundation, 43
Metro-Sanchez, Amber, 9
Miller, Nicole, 31, 32

National Association of Boards of Pharmacy (NABP), 51
National Association of Emergency Medical Technicians (NAEMT), 29
National Association of Licensed Professional Nurses (NALPN), 36
National Council Licensure Examination, 33
National Council of State Boards of Nursing (NCSBN), 36
National Dental Hygienists' Association (NDHA), 14
National Phlebotomy Association (NPA), 55, 59
National Physical Therapy Exam, 63
National Registry of Emergency Medical Technicians (NREMT), 25–26, 29
Nurse Journal (website), 36

Occupational Outlook Handbook (Bureau of Labor Statistics), 74

pharmacy technician, **47**
certification/licensing, 44
educational requirements, 44, 46–47
employers of, 49–50
future job outlook, 44, 50
information resources, 50–51
number of jobs, 44
role of, 44–45
salary/earnings, 44, 50
skills/personal qualities, 44, 47–49

typical workday, 45–46
   working conditions, 49
   work settings, 44
Pharmacy Technician
   Certification Board (PTCB),
   51
phlebotomist
   certification/licensing, 52
   educational requirements, 52,
      54–55
   employers of, 57
   future job outlook, 52, 58
   information resources, 58–59
   number of jobs, 52
   role of, 52
   salary/earnings, 52, 58
   skills/personal qualities, 52,
      55–57
   typical workday, 53–54
   working conditions, 57
   work settings, 52
Phlebotomy Careers, 59
physical therapist assistant, **62**
   certification/licensing, 60
   educational requirements, 60,
      62–63
   employers of, 65–66
   future job outlook, 60, 66
   information resources, 67
   number of jobs, 60
   role of, 60–61
   salary/earnings, 60, 66
   skills/personal qualities, 60,
      63–64
   typical workday, 61
   working conditions, 64–65
   work settings, 60
Pichette, Sarah-Zoe, 31, 34
Population Reference Bureau,
   US, 6

Reese, Todd, 55

Santiago, Andrea Clement, 5,
   6
Sawyer, Samantha, 19
Scala, Carly, 13
Society of Diagnostic Medical
   Sonographers, 22
sonographer. *See* diagnostic
   medical sonographer
Student Doctor Network
   (website), 54–55
Summers, Rachael, 39

Timm, Daniel, 65
Turchetta, Anastasia, 10, 11

Ultrasound Schools Info, 22

Walton, Luke, 48
Wornek, Katherine L., 56

Picture Credits

Cover: Tyler Olson/Shutterstock

10: iStock Images
16: Andrey Popov/Depositphotos
33: Drazen Zigic/Shutterstock.com
47: SofikoS/Shutterstock
62: SDI Productions/iStock

About the Author

Cherese Cartlidge holds a bachelor's degree in psychology and a master's degree in education. She is a freelance editor and the author of more than twenty books for children and young adults.

Library of
Davidson College

STUDIEN ZUR DEUTSCHEN LITERATUR

Band 92

Herausgegeben von Wilfried Barner, Richard Brinkmann und Conrad Wiedemann

Mark William Roche

Dynamic Stillness

Philosophical Conceptions of *Ruhe*
in Schiller, Hölderlin, Büchner, and Heine

Max Niemeyer Verlag Tübingen 1987

The publication of this book was supported by the College of Humanities and the Graduate School of Ohio State University.

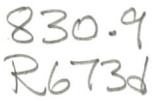

CIP-Kurztitelaufnahme der Deutschen Bibliothek

Roche, Mark William:
Dynamic stillness : philos. conceptions of ›Ruhe‹ in Schiller, Hölderlin, Büchner, and Heine / Mark William Roche. – Tübingen : Niemeyer, 1987.
  (Studien zur deutschen Literatur ; Bd. 92)
NE: GT

ISBN 3-484-18092-7   ISSN 0081-7236

© Max Niemeyer Verlag Tübingen 1987
Alle Rechte vorbehalten. Ohne Genehmigung des Verlages ist es nicht gestattet, dieses Buch oder Teile daraus photomechanisch zu vervielfältigen.
Printed in Germany.
Satz und Druck: Druckerei Maisch + Queck, 7016 Gerlingen
Einband: Heinrich Koch, Tübingen

Contents

Preface IX

Abbreviations XI

PART I – DYNAMIC STILLNESS   1

1. The Synthesis of Perfection and Becoming in Schiller's *Über naive und Sentimentalische Dichtung*. A Reevaluation of the Category "Idyllic" 4

   The Naive and the Sentimental as Philosophical Principles 4
      Schiller's Application of the Terms beyond the Aesthetic Sphere 4
      The Naive and the Sentimental in the Context of Contemporary Philosophy 6
         The Naive and the Concept of Intellectual Intuition 7
         The Sentimental and the Concept of Infinite Approximation 9
   The Unity of the Naive and the Sentimental 19
      The Self-cancellation of the Naive 21
      The Self-cancellation of the Sentimental 23
      Contradiction and Resolution 25
      Schiller's Desire for Unity 28
   Ambiguities in the Category "Idyllic" 32
      The Conflicting Definitions 32
         The Idyll as an Elegiac Subcategory 33
         The Idyll as a Sentimental Subcategory 34
         The Idyll as a False Synthesis of the Naive and the Sentimental 35
         The Idyll as a Valid Synthesis of the Naive and the Sentimental 37
      Interpreting the Idyllic 40
      The Idyllic as Synthesis 46
   Dynamic Stillness and German *Klassik* 47
      Schiller's Theoretical Essays 47

	Schiller's Drama	50
	Schiller's Poetry	55
	Goethe	57
	Hegel	60

2. Narration and *Ruhe* in Hölderlin's *Hyperion*. A Reinterpretation of the Novel's Conclusion ... 63

Narrative Levels and Conceptions of *Ruhe* ... 63
    The Early Ideal of Static Stillness ... 63
    H1 and H2. Patterns of Development and Narrative Reflections ... 64
    The *Schiksaalslied* ... 70
    Pain and Repose ... 72
    The Final Ideal of Dynamic Stillness. Hyperion's Reevaluations . 75
    Diotima's Eloquence and Hyperion's Accountability ... 77
The Reinterpretation of the Novel's Conclusion. *Ruhe* and the *Scheltrede* ... 80
    The *Scheltrede* ... 82
    The Linguistic Argument. Tense and Address ... 84
    The Organic Argument I. *Ruhe* in the Novel as a Whole ... 86
    The Argument by Analogy I. Schiller's *Über naive und sentimentalische Dichtung* ... 89
    Excursus. Hölderlin's *Hyperion* and Spinoza's *Ethics* ... 93
    The Argument by Analogy II. Sophocles' *Oedipus at Colonus* .. 96
    Excursus. The Reader in the Text ... 98
    The Organic Argument II. Hölderlin's Metaphysics ... 100
    Excursus. A Stroke of Incompletion ... 106
Making Sense of Narrative Levels at the Novel's Conclusion ... 107
Hyperion in the Context of Hölderlin's Life and Work ... 113
    The Concept of *Ruhe* in Hölderlin's Work ... 114
    The Initial Fulfillment of Synthesis and Eventual Loss of Repose ... 116

PART II – DEFICIENT STILLNESS   121

3. The Threefold Inversion of Traditional Notions of *Ruhe* in Büchner's *Lenz* ... 124

The Inversion of Aesthetic Stillness ... 126
    The Tradition of Aesthetic Stillness ... 132
    Büchner and the Tradition of Aesthetic Stillness ... 133

    The Inversion of Religious Stillness 134
        The Tradition of Religious Stillness 139
        Büchner and the Tradition of Religious Stillness 150
    The Inversion of Psychological-Moral Stillness and the Struggle
    with Idealism 151
        The Tradition of Psychological-Moral Stillness 163
        Büchner and the Tradition of Psychological-Moral Stillness ... 171
        Repose, Suffering, Apathy 173
    Büchner's *Lenz* in the Context of the Historical Lenz's
    Philosophical Anthropology 175

4. **HEINE AND THE POLITICAL CONNOTATIONS OF *RUHE*** 178

    The Politics of Aesthetic Stillness 178
        Goethe's Statues 178
        From Repose to Revolution 182
    Heine's God of Motion 184
        Political Repression and Indifference in the Context of
        Religious Quietude 186
        Heine's Inversion of Religious Stillness 189
    German Somnolence 190
        Dormant Regeneration: Herder, Hölderlin, Menzel 190
        Dreaming, Sleeping, Death: German Romanticism 193
        Dreaming, Thinking, Acting: German Idealism 194
        Lullabies, Lethargy, and Listlessness: Heine's Contemporaries
        on *Ruhe* 195
        The German Michel 198
    Political Quietude and Aesthetic Motion in Heine's *Zeitgeschichte* .. 202
        „Doktrin" 203
        „Wartet nur" 204
        „Bei des Nachtwächters Ankunft zu Paris" 206
        „Zur Beruhigung" 212
        Irony and Motion 216
    The Critique of German *Ruhe* in *Deutschland. Ein Wintermärchen* .. 217
        A Travelling Narrator in a Stagnant Land 220
        Barbarossa: Germany's Hibernating Hero 223
        Hammonia's Reading of Germany 225
        Negativity in the *Wintermärchen* 227
    Heine's Concept of Political Quietude in its Intellectual-Historical
    Context 229
        Lessing's *Emilia Galotti* 229
        Pastoral *Ruhe* 232

    Heine and Pastoral *Ruhe* 235
    Oppressive *Ruhe* 236
        Excursus. The Politics of *Ruhe* in the Wake of Heine: Tucholsky,
        Brecht, and Handke 240

5. CONCLUSION 245

WORKS CITED 261

INDEX OF NAMES 283

INDEX OF SUBJECTS 289

Preface

For centuries the German word *Ruhe* has had almost magical associations.[1] Religious thinkers considered repose a principal attribute of God, poets wrote odes to stillness, and heroes strove for a goal of tranquillity and composure. Through a study of *Ruhe* one can recognize the evolution of several distinct traditions in German intellectual history. Drawing upon a large number of primary texts and the few secondary works which address the topic, I differentiate in this study four kinds of *Ruhe*. First, religious: In the mystic-pietistic tradition in Germany stillness is considered not only a characteristic of divinity but also a necessary precondition of man's oneness with God. Second, aesthetic: In the eighteenth century Winckelmann, who considered sculpture the highest of aesthetic forms, argued that stillness is a facet of all great art. Third, psychological-moral: From Stoic texts such as Seneca's *De tranquillitate animi* and later writings such as Spinoza's highly popular *Ethics* many a German sought to achieve the *Gemütsruhe* of a life in harmony with the laws of the cosmos. Fourth, political: At least since the *Allgemeines Landrecht für die preußischen Staaten* of 1794 Germans have associated political stabilization with *Ruhe*. According to this influential document the citizen is obliged to preserve „Ruhe und Ordnung"; the state in turn guarantees „Ruhe und Sicherheit".

Besides analyzing *Ruhe* according to the spheres in which it functions, one can make a distinction, as Hölderlin does, between a „lebendige" and a „leere Ruhe", what I call dynamic and deficient stillness. In the first half of this study I analyze the eighteenth-century concept of dynamic stillness; here I offer new readings of Schiller's essay *Über naive und sentimentalische Dichtung* and Hölderlin's novel, *Hyperion*. In the second half I analyze Büchner's story *Lenz*, in particular its inversion of the traditionally positive associations of *Ruhe*, and I consider Heine's *Zeitgedichte* and his satire *Deutschland. Ein Wintermärchen* in the context of the increasingly pejorative association of *Ruhe* with political quietude.

---

[1] I often resist translating the word „Ruhe" so as not to lose its multiple associations. Possible English translations cover a wide range and include such diverse words as quiet, calm, peace, detachment, death, harmony, sleep, collectedness, inactivity, serenity, order, resignation, composure, equanimity, stillness, repose, tranquillity, silence, and rest.

IX

Ruhe is a prominent term that enters into a remarkable number of literary works from Meister Eckhart's sermons to Peter Handke's *Kaspar*.[2] I have focused on four authors whose works occupy significant positions in the development of the concept. While I view the works within their specific intellectual-historical contexts, I focus on the texts themselves. In each chapter the reader will find new interpretations. These range from major reinterpretations, like the reevaluation of the category "idyllic" in *Über naive und sentimentalische Dichtung,* the rereading of the conclusion of *Hyperion* and of the discourse on art in *Lenz,* to a more modest introduction of new dimensions to our understanding of the works in question, for example, the relation of the naive and sentimental to the philosophical discourse of the late eighteenth century, the significance of allusions in *Hyperion* to Sophocles' *Oedipus at Colonus* and Schiller's *Über naive und sentimentalische Dichtung,* and the importance of dormant regeneration for an understanding of Heine's *Zeitgedichte.*

Rather than burden the reader with a schematic history of the concept at the outset of this study, I have tried to allow both a conceptual and historical description of *Ruhe* to emerge simultaneously from my discussion of the individual texts. Dynamic stillness is analyzed in chapters one and two, deficient stillness in chapters three and four. The traditions of aesthetic, religious, and psychological-moral stillness are discussed in the context of Büchner's inversion of these traditions, and the politics of *Ruhe* is viewed together with Heine's critique of political quietude. In each case a central text or set of texts presents us with the starting point for a consideration of the philosophical and historical dimensions of *Ruhe*. By analyzing the works not only in their intellectual-historical contexts but as aesthetic constructs, I have tried to avoid the commonest danger of intellectual-historical studies – treating texts merely as documentary proof of a particular historical development. Competing discourses, narrative levels, rhetorical language, and other „intrinsic" features occupy prominent positions in my analyses.

Finally, besides attempting to combine close textual readings with an awareness of intellectual-historical context, I have found it useful to adopt a proleptic approach, particularly in the first two chapters, where my readings challenge both traditional and poststructuralist interpretations.

---

[2] A list of authors who wrote odes and hymns to stillness becomes quite long, even if one limits it to a time span of one generation. In the late eighteenth century alone one thinks of Friedrich Leopold Stolberg („Die Ruhe" 1772), Gotthold Friedrich Stäudlin („An die Ruhe" 1784), Friedrich Matthison („An die Stille" 1787), Christian Ludwig Neuffer („An die Ruhe" 1791, „Die Ruhe. Eine allegorische Hymne" 1800, „Hymne an die Ruhe" 1805), Heusinger („An die Ruhe" 1797), and Hölderlin („Die Stille" 1788, „An die Ruhe" 1789, „An die Stille" 1790).

Abbreviations

Primary texts are cited simply by volume and page number wherever the context clearly reveals the author of the quote and the bibliography lists only one work or edition by that author. Works conventionally referred to by section or line number are so cited here.

References to the secondary literature are given simply with the author's name, followed by the year of his or her study and then the pertinent page numbers. Wherever two works by the same author bear the same date, I list an abbreviated title.

Complete bibliographical information for the following abbreviations can be located at the back of this study.

A/B	Kant. *Werke in zwölf Bänden*. A or B precedes the page number of the first [A] or second [B] edition of the work cited, that is, the *Kritik der reinen Vernunft* [KrV], the *Kritik der praktischen Vernunft* [KpV], or the *Kritik der Urteilskraft* [KdU].
B	Heine. *Sämtliche Schriften*. Ed. Klaus Briegleb.
Bihlmeyer	Seuse. *Deutsche Schriften*. Ed. Karl Bihlmeyer.
De tranq	Seneca's *De tranquillitate animi* as cited in his *Moral Essays*.
DHA	Heine. *Historisch-kritische Gesamtausgabe der Werke. Düsseldorfer Ausgabe*. Ed. Manfred Windfuhr et al.
DW	Meister Eckhart. *Die deutschen Werke*.
E	The *Ethics* of Spinoza as quoted in: *Opera*. Ed. Carl Gebhardt. Or: *Works of Spinoza*. Trans. R. H. M. Elwes.
Ep	Seneca. *Ad Lucilium Epistolae Morales*.
Fichte	*Fichtes sämmtliche Werke*. Ed. I. H. Fichte.
HA	*Goethes Werke*. Ed. Erich Trunz.
Hegel	*Werke in zwanzig Bänden*. Ed. Eva Moldenhauer and Karl Markus Michel.
HSA	Heine. *Säkularausgabe*.
Jonas	*Schillers Briefe. Kritische Gesamtausgabe*. Ed. Fritz Jonas.
KA	*Kritische Friedrich-Schlegel-Ausgabe*. Ed. Ernst Behler et al.
L	Büchner. *Sämtliche Werke und Briefe. Historisch-kritische Ausgabe mit Kommentar*. Ed. Werner R. Lehmann.
LM	*Gotthold Ephraim Lessings sämtliche Schriften*. Ed. Karl Lachmann.
LW	Meister Eckhart. *Die lateinischen Werke*.
NA	*Schillers Werke. Nationalausgabe*. Ed. Julius Peterson and Hermann Schneider.
SA	*Schillers sämtliche Werke. Säkularausgabe in 16 Bänden*.
Schlechta	Nietzsche. *Werke*. Ed. Karl Schlechta.
Schulz	Fichte. *Briefwechsel. Kritische Gesamtausgabe*. Ed. Hans Schulz.
StA	Hölderlin. *Sämtliche Werke. Große Stuttgarter Ausgabe*. Ed. Friedrich Beißner.
Suphan	Herder. *Sämtliche Werke*. Ed. Bernhard Suphan.
WA	*Goethes Werke*. Hrsg. im Auftrage der Großherzogin Sophie von Sachsen.
WL	Hegel. *Wissenschaft der Logik*. Ed. Georg Lasson.

PART I

Dynamic Stillness

absolutes motus est quies est deus.   (Cusanus)

As children we spun tops and were fascinated with the seeming stillness in the spinning motion of the top. The faster the top would rotate, the more it would seem at rest. Imagine that a top is being moved as fast as possible, that it is spinning not just fast enough that it appears still, but at absolute velocity. The cardinal in Cusanus' *De possest* argues that it would then be completely motionless, at perfect rest. He illustrates his argument by describing a circle, *b c*, which rotates about a point *a* as would the upper circle of a top; he then diagrams the spinning top together with a fixed circle, *d e*.

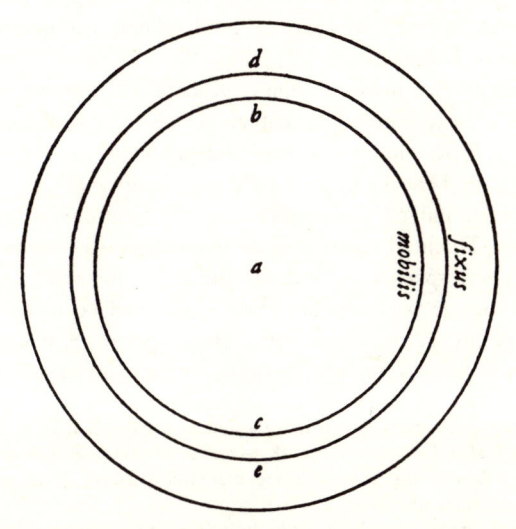

If the circle *b c* were moving at infinite velocity, it would be completely motionless:[1]

---

[1] "Quando motus foret in fine velocitatis, *b* et *c* puncta in eodem puncto temporis forent cum *d* puncto circuli fixi sine eo, quod alter punctus scilicet *b* prius tempore fuisset quam *c,* aliter non esset maximus et infinitus motus, et tamen non esset motus sed quies, quia nullo tempore illa puncta de *d* fixo recederent" (*De possest*, 19, 7–12). For another significant passage on the coincidence of motion and stillness in Cusanus see *De coniecturis,* I, 8.

Wenn die Bewegung die äußerste Grenze der Geschwindigkeit erreicht hätte, dann wären die Punkte *b* und *c* in dem selben Zeit-punkt wie der Punkt *d* des festen Kreises, ohne daß der eine Punkt, z. B. *b*, früher wäre als *c;* sonst wäre es nicht die größte und unendliche Bewegung. Trotzdem wäre es nicht Bewegung, sondern Ruhe, weil sich jene beiden Punkte niemals von *d,* dem festen, entfernten.

Infinite motion would at the same time be no motion, perfect repose, for the whole of the circle *b c* would at every instant be simultaneously present at point *d* and not only at *d* but at every other point of the circle *d e*. For Cusanus this perfect unity of motion and repose is divine.[2]

Cusanus' synthesis it meaningful for us insofar as it illustrates an idea that is also central to the period of German *Klassik.*[3] Goethe, Schiller, and Hölderlin were fascinated with the concept of dynamic repose.[4] For Schiller and Hölderlin such repose embodies perfection:[5] Schiller speaks of a „Ruhe der Vollendung" (NA XX, 472), Hölderlin of a „Vollendungsruhe" (StA III, 126).[6] The association of stillness with perfection makes sense in part genetically. Repose had highly positive associations not only in Christianity, but as far back as antiquity and as recent as the late eighteenth century. It is also conceptually coherent. These writers use the concept in such a way that it includes itself and its own opposite, both stillness *and* motion; it is in no way deficient or lacking.

The history of dynamic stillness reaches an apex during the late eighteenth and early nineteenth century. There were two reasons for this development. First, the widespread reception of the Stoics, Spinoza, Winckelmann, and the Pietists brought the significance of psychological-moral, aesthetic, and religious stillness to the forefront of contemporary consciousness. The ideal status of *Ruhe* was experienced in several increasingly overlapping spheres. Second, the late eighteenth and early nineteenth century was an age of synthesis. Philosophers and poets strove to unify competing traditions, ideas, and forms. Hegel's writings, which bear many structural similarities to those of Cusanus, are the most heralded example of

---

[2] See *De docta ignorantia* II, 10, where the motto for this half of the study can be located. See also *De possest,* esp. 18, 1–24, 22. In this context one might recall Augustine's statement in the *Confessions* that God is always active, yet ever at rest: "semper agens, semper quietus" (I, 4).

[3] The unity of rest and motion is a significant theme for other synthetic thinkers in the history of philosophy. See Plato, *Parmenides* 145e–146a and *Sophist* 248a–259d; Proclus, *The Elements of Theology,* props. 26–27; Pseudo-Dionysius, *Divine Names,* IX, 8–9 = 916B–D; XI, 1–5 = 948C–955B; Hegel 3: 33–39, 46–47.

[4] Herder, too, could be included in this list. See esp. *Kalligone* (Suphan XXII: 48–53, 171, 294).

[5] Cf. Herder, who writes „Vollkommenheit ist Ruhe" (Suphan VIII, 65), and Jean Paul, who speaks of a „Ruhe der Vollendung" (V, 78).

[6] See also StA II, 253.

this, but the drive for synthesis was shared no less by his immediate predecessors in philosophy and by contemporaries in the field of literature, among them most notably Goethe, Schiller, and Hölderlin.

My study of the ways in which Schiller and Hölderlin focus on contradiction and its overcoming – particularly the seeming contradiction of the unity of motion and rest – leads to new interpretations of Schiller's *Über naive und sentimentalische Dichtung* and Hölderlin's *Hyperion*. In my study of Schiller I focus on his conflicting definitions of the category "idyllic" and argue that the most coherent reading of his essay would consider the idyll not a subcategory of the sentimental but rather the synthesis of naive equanimity and sentimental striving. In his final and lengthiest definition Schiller does in fact speak of the idyll as a „Ruhe der Vollendung" that includes „Streben". In my study of *Hyperion* I have tried to show that Hyperion's development as a narrator is reflected in his increasing stillness; moreover, as Hyperion reaches a state of composure he modulates his former ideal of static stillness to include a dynamic element. This leads him to reevaluate his previous attitudes toward Nature and the gods, childhood and history, and also Diotima. With a series of arguments, one of which is based on a proper understanding of the role of *Ruhe* in the novel, I argue for a reinterpretation of the novel's conclusion: Hyperion's criticism of the Germans in his penultimate letter is not an insignificant reminiscence but rather the pinnacle of his present activity as narrator. Hölderlin, like Schiller, admits into his conception of *Ruhe* privileged moments of intense activity.

1. The Synthesis of Perfection and Becoming in Schiller's *Über naive und sentimentalische Dichtung*. A Reevaluation of the Category "Idyllic"

> Ruhe wäre also der herrschende Eindruck dieser Dichtungsart, aber Ruhe der Vollendung, nicht der Trägheit; eine Ruhe, die aus dem Gleichgewicht nicht aus dem Stillstand der Kräfte, die aus der Fülle nicht aus der Leerheit fließt und von dem Gefühl eines unendlichen Vermögens begleitet wird [...] Das Gemüth muß befriedigt werden, aber ohne daß das Streben darum aufhöre. (Schiller)

Schiller's distinction between naive and sentimental poetry is common knowledge to most students of German intellectual and literary history. In its simplest form the thesis states that the naive poet remains in an original state of oneness with Nature; the sentimental poet, having lost this initial unity, strives to regain it. Throughout his essay Schiller rephrases and elaborates on this dualism. He tells us that while the naive poet creates artistic works without any great struggle, the sentimental poet labors over his products. The naive poet simply imitates the real; the sentimental poet, on the other hand, portrays ideas, yet he never fulfills the task of conveying the absolute idea or the ideal. He is locked into an eternal state of becoming. The naive poet, in contrast, never leaves an enclosed sphere of perfection. His goals, however limited, are never left unfulfilled.

The Naive and the Sentimental as Philosophical Principles

Schiller's Application of the Terms beyond the Aesthetic Sphere

Most interpreters of Schiller's essay concentrate on this specifically poetic dichotomy. Critics have placed the naive in the context of eighteenth-century aesthetic discussions of the term,[1] and they have treated the senti-

---

[1] Schiller was familiar with the definitions of the naive in Moses Mendelssohn's *Über das Erhabene und Naive in den schönen Wissenschaften*, Johann Georg Sulzer's *Allgemeine Theorie der schönen Künste*, Christoph Martin Wieland's *Abhandlung vom Naiven*, Kant's *Kritik der Urteilskraft* (§ 54), and probably also Diderot's *Encyclopédie, ou Dictionnaire raisonné des sciences*. See Hermand (1964) and Koopmann (1969), 68–69. For an extensive discussion of eighteenth-century notions of the naive see Jäger (1975).

mental as Schiller's attempt to legitimize his own poetry in the face of Goethe's naive genius.[2] While these approaches illuminate the contextual origins and poetic significance of Schiller's terms, they in no way exhaust their meaning. There is, in fact, no inherent reason to restrict one's understanding of the naive and sentimental to their poetic function. These categories form a basic dualism valid beyond their specific application to the creative process or the work of art. Schiller himself frequently applies his categories beyond the sphere of poetics. For example, he terms certain actions and dispositions naive or sentimental. In the beginning of his essay – in a section originally entitled not „Über naive Dichtung" but simply and generally „Über das Naive"[3] – Schiller explicates „das Naive der Überraschung" and „das Naive der Gesinnung" (418).[4] The naive of surprise occurs when one's emotions overrule the dictates of one's intellect and an inner nature suddenly reveals itself from behind all facades.[5] The consistent and unsophisticated genuineness of an individual in an artificial environment is what Schiller understands by the naive of temperament.[6] At one juncture in his essay Schiller applies the terms naive and sentimental to a discussion of the philosophy of history, suggesting that man must pass from the naive to the sentimental both as a being and an individual (438). Here the naive and sentimental correspond to „zwey verschiedenen Formen der Menschheit" (439). In the final section of his essay Schiller discusses naive and sentimental individuals minus any poetic qualities (492). Schiller considers the naive individual a realist, the sentimental an idealist. Among Schiller's many lucid distinctions are the following. The realist is content with the world. He easily fulfills his utilitarian and eudemonic goals. The idealist, on the other hand, is discontent; he strives for unrealizable and absolute ideals. In the political

---

[2] Of the many critics who discuss Schiller's essay in the light of his relationship to Goethe I mention here: Knippel (1909), 40; Meng (1936), 110; Szondi (1972), 182–84, 190–91, 196–98; Wentzlaff-Eggebert (1949), 216–25; and Witte (1949), 53. Goethe himself commented on this aspect of the essay. See his conversation with Eckermann from March 21, 1830 (Eckermann, 405–06).
[3] Schiller's essay was originally published in three installments, in the eleventh and twelfth issues of *Die Horen* in 1795 and in the first issue of the following year. The titles of the respective issues were: „Über das Naive"; „Die sentimentalischen Dichter"; and „Beschluß der Abhandlung über naive und sentimentalische Dichter, nebst einigen Bemerkungen einen charakteristischen Unterschied unter den Menschen betreffend."
[4] Quotations from *Über naive und sentimentalische Dichtung* are taken from volume XX of the *Nationalausgabe* and are followed in this chapter simply by page number.
[5] Hermann Weigand's illustration of the naive of surprise by way of Act III, scene 4 of *Maria Stuart* is illuminating.
[6] For the naive of temperament one might think of the young Parzival (esp. book III) or the young Simplicissimus (book I, esp. ch. 8). See Simons (1981), 30.

sphere the realist is mainly concerned with prosperity for all. The idealist, in contrast, directs his efforts towards the ideal of freedom, and he bases his moral rigorism on a postulate of freedom (492): „Er [nimmt] seine Bestimmungsgründe [...] aus reiner Vernunft" (496).[7] The realist meanwhile bases his moral judgments on purely empirical grounds: his previous experience and the desire for happiness. While the realist is consistent in his relationships with others, the idealist wavers between generosity (Since his concern with the whole prevents him from being obsessed with his own self.) and inequity (Since this same concern often blinds him to the individuality of others.) With this sketch of just a few of Schiller's distinctions one sees that his discourse opens into the fields of psychology, sociology, politics, and ethics. Even when Schiller discusses the naive and sentimental as genres of composition, he places the emphasis not on what is usually understood by aesthetic form but rather on modes of perception or general attitudes of mind, what he calls „Empfindungsarten" (442) or „Empfindungsweisen" (466):

> Daß ich die Benennungen Satyre, Elegie und Idylle in einem weitern Sinne gebrauche, als gewöhnlich geschieht, werde ich bey Lesern, die tiefer in die Sache dringen, kaum zu verantworten brauchen. Meine Absicht dabey ist keinesweges die Grenzen zu verrücken, welche der bisherige Observanz sowohl der Satyre und Elegie als der Idylle mit gutem Grunde gesteckt hat; ich sehe bloß auf die in diesen Dichtungsarten herrschende *Empfindungsweise,* und es ist ja bekannt genug, daß diese sich keineswegs in jene engen Grenzen einschließen läßt. (449)

The Naive and the Sentimental in the Context of Contemporary Philosophy

Schiller's application of the naive and sentimental to so many diverse spheres suggests that these categories are not just poetic markers, but rather general structures of thought and being.[8] It therefore makes sense to view these categories beyond their specifically poetic context. Moreover, the naive and the sentimental correspond to central concepts in the philosophy of the late eighteenth and early nineteenth centuries. Before I draw these parallels in detail, it will be necessary to look more closely at the sets of terms Schiller associates with his two main categories, beginning with the naive.

---

[7] The allusion of course is to Kant's *Kritik der praktischen Vernunft.*
[8] Two previous critics have suggested that Schiller's supposedly aesthetic categories represent general principles. See Binder (1959), 268–69; Binder (1960), 141–45; and Havenstein (1938), 242, 249. Their entire argument overlaps with the first half of mine: Schiller's own application of the terms beyond the poetic sphere. I will add a second argument: the parallels between Schiller's conceptual definitions of the naive and the sentimental and major issues in contemporaneous philosophy.

The Naive and the Concept of Intellectual Intuition

Towards the beginning of *Über naive und sentimentalische Dichtung* Schiller suggests that we are attracted to naive objects insofar as they represent a particular set of ideas:

> Es sind nicht diese Gegenstände, es ist eine durch sie dargestellte Idee, was wir in ihnen lieben. Wir lieben in ihnen das stille schaffende Leben, das ruhige Wirken aus sich selbst, das Daseyn nach eignen Gesetzen, die innere Nothwendigkeit, die ewige Einheit mit sich selbst. (414)

Schiller associates with the naive the notion of „das stille [...] Leben" and „das ruhige Wirken". He also speaks of a „ruhige Haltung" (427), a „ruhige Nothwendigkeit" (429), the „große Ruhe" of Nature (428), and „das ruhige Naturglück" (428). Naive works of art, he tells us, leave with us an impression of serenity and repose (441). In addition Schiller associates with the naive the concept of self-sufficiency: „das Dasein nach eignen Gesetzen, die innere Nothwendigkeit". The naive contains perfection: Schiller attributes to it „Vollendung" (415) and „Vollkommenheit" (414, 438). The naive is „in jedem Moment ein selbständiges und vollendetes Ganze" (473). Being a self-sufficient and perfect totality, it knows no lacks, no tensions: the naive „Gemüth" is always „ruhig, aufgelöst, einig mit sich selbst und vollkommen befriedigt" (474). The naive is free of negation, wholly positive, thus a single and stable whole, what Schiller calls „eine ungetheilte Einheit" (473).

Schiller's concept of the naive has been interpreted not only in the context of contemporary aesthetic discussions of the naive, but also in the light of Biblical notions of paradise, the fall, and redemption,[9] the contemporary notion of a Grecian ideal,[10] the Rousseauian concept of a return to Nature,[11] and the eighteenth-century *Querelle des Anciens et des Modernes*.[12] One might, however, consider the naive on a more abstract level. Schiller's conception of the naive can be seen in the context of attempts by German Idealists to deal with the notion of undifferentiated unity. Kant, for example, in his *Kritik der reinen Vernunft*, sets out to distinguish man's capacity for knowledge from that of a divinity or „Urwesen"; specifically, he argues that man is not capable of „intellektuelle Anschauung" (B 68–72, B 307–12), that is, of any original or immediate sense of unity. Man knows objects only as mediated through sensory perception and the categories of understanding.

---

[9] See, for example, Abrams (1973), 213–17; Binder (1960), 153; and Rüdiger (1959), 238–41.
[10] See Butler (1935), 182–84 and Hatfield (1964), 133–35.
[11] On Rousseau's role in *Über naive und sentimentalische Dichtung* see Eggli (1927), I: 38, 42–47; Liepe (1963); and Meng (1936), 88.
[12] See Jauß (1974).

A concern with undifferentiated unity is evident throughout German Idealism. In rewriting Kantian philosophy Fichte suggests that man *is* capable of intellectual intuition or an intuitive perception of pure identity, „das Subjektive und Objektive in einem" (Fichte I, 528). Indeed he considers this concept of original unity the foundation of his and all philosophy: „Diese intellectuelle Anschauung ist der einzige feste Standpunct für alle Philosophie" (Fichte I, 466). Schelling as well considers the principle of undifferentiated unity the foundation of philosophy. He, too, begins with „das absolute Identische" or „die intellektuelle Anschauung" (III, 625). For Schelling, however, the first principle, „das Absolute" (IV, 115), is found not in the activity of the Fichtean absolute ego but rather in „Natur" (II, 610) or „Vernunft" (IV, 114),[13] whereby both terms are to be understood in not an everyday but rather a speculative sense, as „totale Indifferenz des Subjektiven und Objektiven" (IV, 114). Schleiermacher expresses the contemporary interest in absolute unity as well. Without referring specifically to the concept of intellectual intuition he defines religion as a oneness with the universe, a sense of totality, „Anschauen des Universums" (31). Like Schiller and Schelling before him, Schleiermacher considers Nature the symbol for this totality: „Die Religion lebt ihr ganzes Leben auch in der Natur, aber in der unendlichen Natur des Ganzen, des Einen und Allen" (29). Even Hegel thematizes what Schiller calls the naive when he proposes beginning his *Wissenschaft der Logik* with „reines Sein".[14] With splendid harmony of form and content he defines the undifferentiated and undefinable without really defining it, that is, by purposely avoiding a predicate. Without formulating a complete sentence Hegel begins: „Sein, reines Sein, – ohne alle weitere Bestimmung" (WL I, 66).

Important differences in these thinkers' descriptions and evaluations of undifferentiated unity spring to the mind of any student of German Idealism. In this discussion of nondifferentiation, however, the differences seem less important than the suggestion of similarity, of unity and nondifferentiation. Without complication one can readily place Schiller's concept of the naive into this philosophical context. *Any restriction of the naive to a solely aesthetic realm is cancelled then not only on the basis of Schiller's own application of the term to other spheres but also because of its correspondence with one of the central philosophical topics of the period.* A comparison of Schiller's definition of the

---

[13] The first quotation is taken from Schelling's *System des transcendentalen Idealismus*, the second from his *Darstellung meines Systems der Philosophie*.

[14] Hegel does not in fact *begin* with pure being. Since pure being has no predicates, since it is *bestimmungslos*, it is not yet a category, a *Denkbestimmung*. It is a „leere Abstraktion" (Hegel 8, 192). The first category therefore is „Werden", what Hegel calls „der erste Begriff" (Hegel 8, 192). It might be added that Hegel is a vehement critic of „intellektuelle Anschauung". See esp. WL I: 55 and 63.

sentimental with contemporary notions of infinite approximation will reveal a second set of parallels.[15]

The Sentimental and the Concept of Infinite Approximation

The sentimental, in contrast to the naive, encompasses the sphere of the negative, the realm of dualisms. It is characterized by consciousness, by an awareness of the other as other. Where the naive individual is perfectly content, the sentimental individual is forever „unglücklich" (431); he suffers from the gap between what is and what ought to be. While the naive individual is at one with himself and totally calm, the sentimental individual is divided; he is in constant „Unruhe" (430) and „Bewegung" (474).

Schiller divides the sentimental into two subcategories, the satiric and the elegiac. Each is concerned with two conflicting spheres, „mit der Wirklichkeit als Grenze und mit seiner Idee als dem Unendlichen" (441). Schiller distinguishes between the two sentimental modes on the basis of which of the two spheres dominates. If the sentimental individual concentrates on the real and criticizes it against his consciousness of the ideal, then he is satiric. While the satirist emphasizes the weaknesses of reality, the elegiac individual turns away from reality and concentrates on the ideal. In correspondence with his sentimental consciousness the elegiac individual locates his ideal not in the present but in the distant past or future. Schiller expresses his distinction between the satiric and elegiac as follows:

> Denn nun entsteht die Frage, ob er mehr bey der Wirklichkeit, ob er mehr bey dem Ideale verweilen – ob er jene als einen Gegenstand der Abneigung, ob er dieses als einen Gegenstand der Zuneigung ausführen will. Seine Darstellung wird also entweder *satyrisch*, oder sie wird [...] *elegisch* sein. (441)

Whether satiric or elegiac, the sentimental individual can never achieve a synthesis of the real and the ideal. His never-ceasing attempt to bridge the two realms makes for his infinite striving. The condition of infinite striving is in fact so central that Schiller defines the sentimental as „die Kunst des Unendlichen" (440).[16]

"Sentimental" infinity plays a significant role in German philosophy from the period of Lessing to the time of Hegel. A critic might be expected to mention *Lessing* in the context of *Über naive und sentimentalische Dichtung* either to elaborate on Schiller's suggestion that *Nathan der Weise* is a near

---

[15] To my knowledge only one critic has suggested parallels between Schiller's notion of the sentimental and contemporary philosophy. Lovejoy implies, without filling in the details, that one could draw analogies between Kant's ethics, Fichte's metaphysics, and Schiller's idea of infinite striving. See Lovejoy (1920), 4–5, 139.

[16] Schiller discusses the infinity of the sentimental again and again. See, for example, 415, 438, 440, 457, and 489.

comedy (446) or to trace Schiller's notion that ontogeny recapitulates phylogeny back to *Die Erziehung des Menschengeschlechts*.[17] Yet, one might note another aspect of Lessing's writings in the context of Schiller's essay, for Lessing, like many Enlightenment and Storm and Stress thinkers,[18] valorized infinite striving and criticized stasis or *Ruhe*. Lessing, one might say, helped prepare the way for Schiller's introduction of the concept of sentimental infinity. Lessing asserts in his „Duplik" that he would prefer to strive for, rather than attain, truth:

> Wenn Gott in seiner Rechten alle Wahrheit, und in seiner Linken den einzigen immer regen Trieb nach Wahrheit, obschon mit dem Zusatze, mich immer und ewig zu irren, verschlossen hielte, und spräche zu mir: wähle! Ich fiele ihm mit Demut in seine Linke, und sagte: Vater gieb! die reine Wahrheit ist ja doch nur für dich allein! (LM XIII, 24)

This seemingly reverent act of setting aside truth for God alone might also be taken as a criticism of divinity, for Lessing argues in the previous paragraph that the utmost value of humanity, the expansion of man's „Kräfte", is made possible through man's longing for truth; the possession of truth, on the other hand, would lead to stasis, an undesirable state implicitly associated with the divine:

> Nicht die Wahrheit, in deren Besitz ein Mensch ist, oder zu seyn vermeynet, sondern die aufrichtige Mühe, die er angewandt hat, hinter die Wahrheit zu kommen, macht den Werth des Menschen. Denn nicht durch den Besitz, sondern durch die Nachforschung der Wahrheit erweitern sich seine Kräfte, worinn allein seine immer wachsende Vollkommenheit bestehet. Der Besitz macht ruhig, träge, stolz. (LM XIII, 23–24)

Lessing contrasts the stasis of possession with the dynamism of an „immer wachsende Vollkommenheit". Here Lessing's preference for striving originates not from the pious claim that God alone should possess truth, but rather from the statement that truth, if possessed, is itself undesirable. Such a truth would lack dynamism and vitality. It is of course possible that *Ruhe* and possession are negative categories only for man and not also for God, but the passage can be read either way. In fact, the interpretation of this passage as an *absolute* criticism of stasis receives support from another text in which Lessing associates with the idea of a divine being „in dem unveränderlichen

---

[17] „Was die Erziehung bey dem einzeln Menschen ist, ist die Offenbarung bey dem ganzen Menschengeschlechte" (LM XIII, 415). Analogies between the development of the individual and mankind occur throughout this period. Besides Lessing and Schiller (Note, by the way, also nos. 24 and 25 of the *Ästhetische Briefe:* NA XX: 338 and 394.) see the opening paragraph of Hölderlin's preface to the penultimate version of *Hyperion* (StA III, 163) and Hegel's preface to his *Phänomenologie des Geistes* (Hegel 3, 32).

[18] One thinks, for example, of Lenz's *Versuch über das erste Principium der Moral*.

Genuße seiner allerhöchsten Vollkommenheit [...] die Vorstellung von unendlicher Langeweile".[19]

In all three of his critiques, the first of which was completed the year Lessing died, Kant discusses various notions of infinity.[20] In fact, Kant states in a letter to Christian Garve that the antinomies of pure reason, which revolve around the categories of finitude and infinitude, were the starting point for his entire critical philosophy.[21] Kant's first two antimonies illustrate in a conceptual fashion the problems inherent in any "sentimental" attempt to reach the unconditioned.[22] The thesis of the first antinomy states that the world is spatially and temporally finite: if the reverse were true, an eternity would have had to have passed before the present moment were reached, and this is impossible. The antithesis considers the world both spatially and temporally infinite: before the origin of the world, there would have had to have been empty time or nothingness, but out of such nothingness nothing can originate. The thesis of the second antinomy argues the existence of simple parts: if there were no simple parts, there could be no composite parts since these consist of simple parts; therefore nothing could exist. The antithesis suggests that everything is composite and argues that the thesis tries to supply us with a „leeres Gedankending" that cannot be known (B 475). Each conflicting view is thus proven. Kant suggests that because the world cannot itself be contradictory, the contradictions must have arisen from our faculties of cognition. Kant's argument is that reason leads to contradictions whenever it exceeds the limits of possible experience.

The importance of these first two or mathematical antinomies for our understanding of Schiller's arguments concerning the sentimental is that the thesis of each antinomy, much like sentimental consciousness, argues for a transition to the unlimited. The ideas associated with the theses are „nichts

---

[19] The passage, which is from „F. H. Jacobi über seine Gespräche mit Lessing", can be found in Lessing's *Werke,* VIII, 572.
[20] The one critique not discussed in this context, *Kritik der Urteilskraft,* contains a lengthy discussion of infinity within the „Analytik des Erhabenen".
[21] In his letter to Garve of September, 21, 1798, Kant writes: „Die Antinomie der r. V. [...] diese war es, welche mich aus dem dogmatischen Schlummer zuerst aufweckte und zur Kritik der Vernunft selbst hintrieb, um das Skandal des scheinbaren Widerspruchs der Vernunft mit ihr selbst zu heben" (*Kant's Briefe,* 780).
[22] Schiller's essay has often been interpreted in the context of Kant's popular philosophy, e. g., his *Idee zu einer allgemeinen Geschichte in weltbürgerlicher Absicht* and his *Mutmaßlicher Anfang der Menschengeschichte.* I'm suggesting that one can view *Über naive und sentimentalische Dichtung* in the context of Kant's philosophically rigorous writings, the critiques. Until now references to the critiques have been restricted to Kant's discussion of triadically structured categories in §11 of *Kritik der reinen Vernunft* (see esp. Szondi [1972], 200–04) and his discussion of the naive in §54 of *Kritik der Urteilskraft.*

als bis zum Unbedingten erweiterte Kategorien" (B 436). The unlimited, however, is unattainable in experience: „Das Schlechthinunbedingte wird in der Erfahrung gar nicht angetroffen" (B 538). The ideas therefore can tell us only what *should* happen in any transition from the conditioned to the entire series of all conditions and finally to the origin of the conditioned, the unconditioned, not what really *is* the case with the object itself. Kant therefore proposes the following solution to the first antinomy: we should refrain from stating that the world is either finite or infinite but nevertheless search indefinitely for the totality of conditions that would constitute the finitude of the world if it were indeed finite.[23] The totality of conditions is not given („gegeben"); nonetheless, the search for the totality of conditions, i. e., the unconditioned, is assigned („aufgegeben") to us as a task that must be performed indefinitely (B 526). This indefinite process („ein Rückgang in unbestimmte Weite (in indefinitum)" B 540–41) is a regulative idea:

> Diese Regel aber sagt nichts mehr, als daß, so weit wir auch in der Reihe der empirischen Bedingungen gekommen sein mögen, wir nirgend eine absolute Grenze annehmen sollen, sondern jede Erscheinung, als bedingt, einer andern, als ihrer Bedingung, unterordnen, zu dieser also ferner fortschreiten müssen, welches der regressus in indefinitum ist, der, weil er keine Größe im Objekt bestimmt, von dem in infinitum deutlich genug zu unterscheiden ist. (B 547–48)

A progression "in infinitum" would imply that the object itself is infinite. The progression "in indefinitum" weights our *experience* of the object. One can speak here of an epistemological process with no definite end. Any application of the terms "finite" or "infinite" to the objects themselves is denied: „So ist daraus klar, daß wir die Weltgröße weder als endlich, noch unendlich annehmen können, weil der Regressus (dadurch jene vorgestellt wird) keines von beiden zuläßt" (B 546). Neither the thesis nor the antithesis is true. Kant offers a parallel solution to the second antinomy whereby once again our experience dictates that we cannot reach the unlimited. A body „ist also ins Unendliche teilbar, ohne doch darum aus unendlich viel Teilen zu bestehen" (B 553).

The theses of the third and fourth or dynamic antinomies, like the first two, maintain a speculative interest in the unlimited. Thus the third and fourth theses, which argue for freedom and the existence of a necessary being, are based on the transition from the conditioned to the unconditioned. Accordingly, Kant takes recourse in the fourth antinomy to the cosmological proof of God's existence. The antitheses argue that there is no freedom (third antinomy) and that all is contingent (fourth antinomy), once again accusing the theses of presenting mere „Gedankendinge" as knowable objects. Kant

---

[23] Kant wants to say nothing about the „Weltgröße an sich" (B 547), since according to his theory no knowledge of an absolute limit is possible.

suggests that all the theses and antitheses of the dynamic antinomies could be valid in their respective realms, the theses in the realm of noumena, the antitheses in the sphere of phenomena. There is no real contradiction as long as the two realms are separate: „sie" „können" „beiderseits wahr sein" (B 590).

The speculative hypothesis of freedom from the third antinomy becomes in Kant's second critique a practical postulate:[24] freedom is a condition for the possibility of the moral law. Kant understands freedom both in a negative sense (as independence from all external conditions or goals) and in a positive sense (as knowledge of the moral law). The law itself – that you should act such that the maxim of your will could always hold at the same time as a principle establishing universal law – is valid for all rational beings, including God (A 57; A 146). For God the moral law is „ein Gesetz der Heiligkeit" (A 146). Kant defines holiness as „die völlige Angemessenheit des Willens [...] zum moralischen Gesetze" (A 220). This fitness of the will to the moral law is „eine Vollkommenheit, deren kein vernünftiges Wesen der Sinnenwelt, in keinem Zeitpunkte seines Daseins, fähig ist" (A 220). Man can adhere to the moral law only in infinite approximation, „in einem ins Unendliche gehenden Progressus" (A 220).[25] Kant's morality then is sentimental not only because it is free of finite, utilitarian goals, but also because it leads to an infinite or sentimental progression.

Kant's ideas of indefinite progression in the epistemological sphere and infinite progression in the moral sphere are adopted by *Fichte* in both his theoretical and practical philosophy.[26] While the desire to eradicate the Kantian thing-in-itself and ground freedom philosophically motivated Fichte to write his *Wissenschaftslehre*,[27] the structure of his central argument, that of the relationship between the infinitude and finitude of the ego,[28] owes much to Kant's arguments in the antinomy of pure reason, as Fichte himself readily

---

[24] „Ein *Bedürfnis* der reinen Vernunft in ihrem spekulativen Gebrauche führt nur auf *Hypothesen*, das der reinen praktischen Vernunft aber zu Postulaten" (KpV, A 255–56).

[25] See also A 58, A 149, and A 231.

[26] The following lengthy excursus on Fichte serves two purposes: first, it suggests a philosophical, rather than simply aesthetic, context for Schiller's concept of the sentimental; second, it introduces a number of ideas and arguments that will later help us understand Schiller's concept of the idyllic as a synthesis of perfection and becoming.

[27] See Fichte's sketch of a letter to Baggesen from April 1795 in Schulz I, 499. Note also his comment in a letter to Reinhold of January 8, 1800: „Mein System ist vom Anfange bis zu Ende nur eine Analyse des Begriffs der Freiheit" (Schulz II, 206). In this context see also his *Erste Einleitung in die Wissenschaftslehre* and his *Zweite Einleitung in die Wissenschaftslehre*, esp. I, 491–515.

[28] See Fichte I: 115, 117, 156, 213–17, 245–46, 254–92, and 316.

admits (I, 246). Fichte's starting point is the absolute ego or undifferentiated identity, in Schiller's terminology, a wholly "naive" state. In order for the absolute ego to become more than pure undifferentiated unity, it must posit a limit upon itself, i.e., a non-ego. This limit is the transcendental condition of the ego's activity and consciousness. The ego has its being (It is no longer pure and undifferentiated nothingness: „Nichts.") and its limit (It is no longer pure and undifferentiated totality: „Alles.") in its negation (I, 264).

The ego itself is infinite and unconditioned insofar as all that is, is posited by the ego: „Insofern das Ich absolut ist, ist es *unendlich* und unbeschränkt. Alles, was es ist, setzt es; und was es nicht setzt, ist nicht" (I, 254–55). Yet, insofar as the ego posits a non-ego it imposes limits upon itself and is finite: „Insofern das Ich sich ein Nicht-Ich entgegensetzt, setzt es nothwendig *Schranken* [...] und sich selbst in diese Schranken" (I, 255). The activity then of positing the non-ego marks the finitude as well as the infinitude of the ego. The ego is limited by the other but sets these limits itself: „Das Ich ist demnach abhängig seinem Daseyn nach; aber es ist schlechthin unabhängig in den Bestimmungen dieses seines Daseyns" (I, 279). The ego has the capacity to reestablish its limits into infinity; indeed, whenever the limits would be surpassed, the ego can establish new limits, „die es in die Unendlichkeit hinaus erweitern kann, weil diese Erweiterung lediglich von ihm abhängt" (I, 269). This ability of the ego to establish itself and its limits into infinity, however, is possible only at the cost of suffering at every moment a limit.

The ego's striving to overcome an object[29] is dependent on the existence of the object as a limit; the cessation of striving would imply the cancellation of this limit and with it the cancellation of the object: „Dieses unendliche Streben ist ins unendliche [sic] hinaus die *Bedingung der Möglichkeit alles Objects:* kein Streben, kein Object" (I, 261–62). Sentimental striving is the condition for the possibility of the object. This object is the ideal towards which one strives as well as that which prevents the fulfillment of one's striving. Just as there is no object without striving, so is there no striving without an object or a limit. *One should overcome the limit only insofar as one cannot.* In other words, a limit is necessary for striving. Or to rephrase this again, infinite striving is inherently finite. Schiller applies the same logic to his own discussion of the sentimental in his letter to Humboldt of December 25, 1795: „Die sentimentalische Poesie ist zwar Conditio sine qua non von dem poetischen *Ideale,* aber sie ist auch eine ewige *Hinderniß* desselben" (NA XXVIII, 145).

---

[29] Throughout this paragraph the word "object" means both *Ziel* and *Gegenstand,* for in the Fichtean model of practical activity the object (or goal) of one's striving is the elimination of the object (or non-ego).

If one were to overcome the limit, striving would cease and one would return to the unseparateness, the pure nothingness, of the absolute ego:

> Wäre das Ich mehr als strebend [...] so wäre es kein Ich, es setzte sich nicht selbst, und wäre demnach Nichts. Hätte es dieses unendliche Streben nicht, so könnte es abermals nicht sich selbst setzen, denn es könnte sich nichts entgegensetzen; es wäre demnach auch kein Ich, und mithin Nichts. (Fichte I, 270)

To cancel the non-ego, to attain the goal of one's striving, would be to annihilate the ego and transform it into nothingness.

The ego suffers then from two conflicting drives: the drive to cancel the other and the drive to preserve itself. While the "practical" drive of the ego is to surpass the non-ego, fill out infinity, and obliterate all limits,[30] its "theoretical" drive is to achieve consciousness, which is possible only on the basis of limits.[31] Insofar as the ego is conscious of itself, it is conscious of its limits and is finite. In knowledge of this finitude it tries to expand itself into infinity. The ego becomes active and tries to overcome the non-ego; however, insofar as the ego remains active, it does not overcome its limits. More precisely, it sets further limits on itself, for consciousness and the continuation of practical activity demand such limits. Thus, there is in the ego a constant oscillation of mutually dependent forces, one „centrifugal in die Unendlichkeit hinaus" and one „centripetal", returning into itself by means of limits (I, 274). This attempt both to overcome limits and to forever reset them generates the „stete Erweiterung unserer Schranken in das Unendliche fort" (I, 278).

In Fichte's practical philosophy infinity plays an equally dominant role; here, as in his theoretical writings, Fichte refers back to Kant. In the first of his lectures *Über die Bestimmung des Gelehrten* Fichte makes explicit reference to the Kantian notion of „das höchste Gut" from the antinomy of practical reason. With Kant, Fichte argues that the complete correspondence of "is" with "ought" is unattainable in this life; it can only be infinitely approximated.[32] One year before the publication of Schiller's *Über naive und sentimentalische Dichtung* Fichte defines in a nutshell sentimental infinity:[33]

---

[30] „Das Ich fordert, dass es alle Realität in sich fasse, und die Unendlichkeit erfülle" (Fichte I, 277).

[31] „Das Ich soll demnach die Unendlichkeit nicht ausfüllen [...] *wenn* ein wirkliches Bewusstseyn möglich seyn soll" (Fichte I, 275).

[32] The Kantian postulate of the immortality of the soul, which solves the antinomy of practical reason, guarantees the self the supreme good („das Oberste"), which is the unity of the highest good („das Höchste"), namely virtue, and the perfect good („das Vollendete"), happiness. Beyond the world of experience, in infinite existence, virtue must bring forth happiness (A 198–215).

[33] The importance of Fichte's *Wissenschaftslehre* for the theory of drives in Schiller's *Ästhetische Briefe* has long been recognized (see Koopmann [1969], II, 63), and their exchange of letters in the summer of 1795 has also received much attention (see

> Es liegt im Begriffe des Menschen, dass sein letztes Ziel unerreichbar, sein Weg zu demselben unendlich seyn muss. Mithin ist es nicht die Bestimmung des Menschen, dieses Ziel zu erreichen. Aber er kann und soll diesem Ziele immer näher kommen: und daher ist die *Annäherung ins unendliche zu diesem Ziele* seine wahre Bestimmung als *Mensch*. (VI, 300)

Unlike Schiller, however, Fichte considers infinite approximation a universal, not just a "sentimental", condition. „*Vollkommenheit*" is man's highest, yet unattainable, goal: „das höchste unerreichbare Ziel des Menschen" (VI, 300). Fichte writes: „*Vervollkommnung ins unendliche* aber ist seine Bestimmung" (VI, 300). According to Fichte, perfection is not only impossible; it is inappropriate. If man were perfect, he would become a God and cease to strive: man's final goal „muss […] ewig unerreichbar bleiben […] wenn der Mensch nicht aufhören soll, Mensch zu seyn, und wenn er nicht Gott werden soll" (VI, 299–300). In his second lecture Fichte adds: „Könnten alle Menschen vollkommen werden, könnten sie ihr höchstes Ziel erreichen, so wären sie alle einander völlig gleich; sie wären nur Eins" (VI, 310). All diversity would be swallowed up into a single identity. So, although Fichte is adamant that such unity is man's goal, he is also aware of it as a goal never in danger of being realized. Fichte seems more than content with the unrealizability of this final goal and with the condition („Bestimmung") of infinite striving. He concludes his cycle of lectures with the sentences: „Lassen Sie uns froh seyn über den Anblick des weiten Feldes, das wir zu bearbeiten haben! Lassen Sie uns froh seyn, dass wir Kraft in uns fühlen, und dass unsere Aufgabe unendlich ist!" (VI, 346).

In order to distinguish Idealism from Dogmatism, *Schelling* appropriates in one of his earliest writings Fichte's idea of infinite striving. In his *Philosophische Briefe über Dogmatismus und Kriticismus,* published the same year as Schiller's essay on naive and sentimental poetry, Schelling suggests that Idealism or Criticism is marked by an infinite approximation towards goals, while Dogmatism believes these goals realizable: „Der Kriticismus [muß] das letzte Ziel nur als Gegenstand einer unendlichen Aufgabe betrachten; er wird selbst nothwendig zum Dogmatismus, sobald er das letzte Ziel als realisirt (in einem Objekt) oder als realisirbar (in irgend einem einzelnen Zeitpunkte) aufstellt" (I, 331). If the goal is realized, total unity is reestablished, and the subject loses itself in the object: „Für das endliche Subjekt bleibt nichts übrig, als sich selbst als Subjekt zu vernichten, um durch

---

NA XXVII, 221), but the importance of Fichte for an understanding of sentimental consciousness has gone virtually unnoticed. Schiller was familiar with not only Kant's works but also Fichte's *Grundlage der gesammten Wirtschaftslehre* and his *Einige Vorlesungen über die Bestimmung des Gelehrten*. See Schiller's notes in letters 4 and 13 of his *Ästhetische Briefe*. See also his letters to Körner of October 9, 1794 (Jonas IV, 39) and to Friedrich von Hoven of November 21, 1794 (Jonas IV, 69).

Selbstvernichtung mit jenem Objekt identisch zu werden" (I, 332). To avoid such a dogmatic turn, Schelling prefers „das ewige Streben" (I, 315) to the „Erreichung des letzten Ziels" (I, 331).[34] Perfection becomes for him an intolerable concept: „In dem Augenblicke, da er [the philosopher] selbst sein System vollendet zu haben glaubte, würde er sich selbst unerträglich werden" (I, 306).[35]

Schelling's notion of eternal striving is based, much like Fichte's concept of infinite approximation, on the idea of a limitless extension of limits. In fact, in the „Allgemeine Deduktion des transcendentalen Idealismus" of his *System des transcendentalen Idealismus* Schelling explicitly deduces the concept of an „unendliches Werden" from the limitless ability of the self to set, cancel, and reset its own limits: „Damit es [das Ich] ein Werden sey, muß es beschränkt seyn. Damit es ein unendliches Werden sey, muß die Schranke aufgehoben werden" (III, 383). If the self does not surpass its limits, then it is not active, not in a state of becoming. On the other hand, if the self surpasses its limits and completes its goals, its becoming is not infinite: „Die Schranke soll also aufgehoben werden und zugleich nicht aufgehoben werden. Aufgehoben, damit das Werden ein unendliches, nicht aufgehoben, damit es nie aufhöre, ein Werden zu seyn" (III, 383). Schelling solves the problem of a simultaneous cancellation and noncancellation of limits by introducing the Fichtean notion of an "unendliche Erweiterung der Schranke" (Schelling III, 384). The self can and must forever reset its own limits. In other philosophical essays of this period, for example in the *Erster Entwurf eines Systems der Naturphilosophie,* Schelling applies this Fichtean logic of infinite activity to Nature itself. For Schelling the physical universe takes on the character of an active self. Nature consists not only of naive unity but also of sentimental duplicity, what he calls „Duplizität in der Identität" (III, 251). Schelling suggests, „daß also auch in der Ruhe der Natur Bewegung sey" (III, 274–75). Nature, „das unendlich Werdende", is „nie vollendet" (III, 15); it has the power once associated with the Fichtean ego to limit itself into infinity: „Ist die Natur absolute Thätigkeit, so muß diese Thätigkeit als ins Unendliche gehemmt erscheinen. (Der ursprüngliche Grund dieser

---

[34] In the later stages of his philosophy Schelling held to the basic insight that *actual* unity obliterates striving. The *desire* for unity or stillness, on the other hand, generates striving. „Wäre nur Einheit und alles im Frieden, dann fürwahr würde sich nichts rühren wollen, und alles in Verdrossenheit versinken, da es jetzt eifrig hervor strebt, um aus der Unruhe in die Ruhe zu gelangen" (VIII, 321). The quotation is from *Die Weltalter.*

[35] In his eighth letter Schelling cites Lessing's equation of divinity and boredom: „Vielleicht erinnerte ich Sie an Lessing's Bekenntniß, daß er mit der Idee eines unendlichen Wesens eine Vorstellung von unendlicher *Langeweile* verbinde, bei der ihm angst und wehe werde – oder auch an jenen (blasphemischen) Ausruf: Ich möchte um alles in der Welt nicht selig werden!" (I, 326).

Hemmung aber muß, da die Natur *schlechthin* thätig ist, doch nur wieder *in ihr selbst* gesucht werden)" (III, 16). Schelling's Nature, like the Fichtean ego, is „die absolute Thätigkeit" that „immer *wird* und nie *ist*" (Schelling III, 16). In his *Stuttgarter Privatvorlesungen* of 1810, Schelling, still concerned with the philosophy of becoming, associates the principle of dynamic contrareity with God and writes, „daß in ihm [Gott] neben dem ewigen Seyn auch ein ewiges Werden ist" (VII, 432).

Keenly aware of the importance of infinite becoming, infinite approximation, and the break between "is" and "ought" in the philosophies of his predecessors, Hegel writes in his *Wissenschaft der Logik*: „Das Sollen hat neuerlich eine große Rolle in der Philosophie [...] gespielt" (WL I, 121). Hegel is thinking here of „das perennierende Sollen" or the abstract infinity of infinite approximation (WL I, 131).[36] Concepts of infinity fascinated Hegel just as they did his contemporaries. In fact Hegel discusses infinity in almost all his writings. The common element throughout – from his discussion of the „zweite übersinnliche Welt" in the *Phänomenologie des Geistes* (Hegel, 3, 128)[37] to his lectures on the philosophy of religion – is his rejection of the principle of infinite approximation. In the preface to his *Philosophie des Rechts,* for example, Hegel expresses his disapproval of the „Halbheit, die das Erkennen in eine *Annäherung* zur Wahrheit setzt" (Hegel 7, 27). In the *Wissenschaft der Logik* his criticism is stronger still: „Aber die Annäherung ist ohnehin für sich eine nichts sagende und nichts begriflich machende Kategorie [...] und unendlich nahe heißt selbst die Negation des Naheseins und des Annäherns" (WL I, 274). For Hegel the idea of infinite approximation is a „schlechte Unendlichkeit" (WL I, 131): it is "bad", not primarily in a moral but rather, in a logical sense. "Bad" for Hegel is whatever does not function „seinem Begriff oder seiner Bestimmung [...] gemäß" (Hegel 8, 369), whatever is logically incoherent, such as the concept of infinite approximation. In his *Logik* Hegel shows why this concept of infinite approximation cannot be defended logically; here as well he offers his most rigorous defense of the true or logically coherent infinite. This true or all-inclusive infinite, which is not limited – as is the "bad" infinite – by having its ends external to itself, provides a key to Hegel's entire philosophy; Hegel

---

[36] „Die Kantische und die Fichtesche Philosophie sind rücksichtlich des Ethischen auf diesem Standpunkt des Sollens stehengeblieben. Die perennierende Annäherung an das Vernunftgesetz ist das Äußerste, wozu man auf diesem Wege gelangt" (Hegel 8, 200).

[37] „So hat die übersinnliche Welt, welche die verkehrte ist, über die andere zugleich übergegriffen und [hat] sie an sich selbst; sie ist für sich die verkehrte, d.h. die verkehrte ihrer selbst; sie ist sie selbst und ihre entgegengesetzte in *einer* Einheit. Nur so ist sie der Unterschied als innerer oder Unterschied *an sich selbst* oder ist als *Unendlichkeit*" (Hegel 3, 131).

himself calls it „der Grundbegriff der Philosophie" (Hegel 8, 203), and he grounds much of his later philosophy on the discussion of finitude and infinitude in the *Logik*.[38] The quantity and vehemence of Hegel's polemics against the concept of a sentimental or bad infinite is perhaps as good an index as any of its importance for his immediate predecessors.

This widespread prominence suggests that *Schiller's concept of the sentimental grew out of a more than simply aesthetic context and that this category, by association, has itself significance beyond the aesthetic sphere.*

The Unity of the Naive and the Sentimental

I have tried to establish that the naive and the sentimental are more than simply aesthetic categories:[39] first, supported by Schiller's own wide-ranging application of the terms; second, on the basis of parallels between Schiller's categories and ideas in contemporary philosophy. The abstract and conceptual definitions Schiller assigns to his terms only reinforce this thesis; the categories have more than simply aesthetic import. Schiller enriches his essential dichotomy of naive oneness and sentimental longing through an intricate series of dualisms. One can list the terms of each major opposition:

---

[38] Hegel bases, for example, his discussion of the cosmological, teleological, and ontological proofs of God's existence on „Kategorien, die in dem Felde der logischen Betrachtung zu Hause sind" (17, 419), in particular the categories of finitude and infinitude (17, 442). See also 17, 480.

[39] Georg Lukács (1964) sees Schiller's distinction between the naive and sentimental as essentially historical (154, 160). There are several problems with Lukács' proposition. First, in establishing his hierarchy Lukács considers only the aesthetic and historical significance of Schiller's categories (160). But Schiller applies his dualism to other spheres as well; therefore, even if Lukács could defend his thesis of the primacy of the historical over the aesthetic, he would also have to defend its primacy over other spheres, in particular the logical. Second, the idea of a strict historical dualism is itself problematic. The Greeks are not just naive, and the modern world is not just sentimental. Third, Lukács acknowledges that Schiller is striving for a future unity of the naive and the sentimental (161), but such a unity makes no sense in terms of a revival of the actual and *historical* Greek society; Schiller refers here to the revival of *conceptual* terms such as unity, which one associates not only with the Greek past but also with childhood or the naive poet. The emphasis Lukács places on economic conditions in the sentimental sphere (see esp. 147–48, 156–57) is valuable and enhances the reader's understanding of Schiller's essay; it is, however, not of exclusive or primary importance. Finally, Lukács cannot coherently argue that the validity of philosophical positions can be reduced to the historical conditions out of which they originate (primacy of history over ideas), for this would invalidate his own position. By his own admission he is writing before the advent of a Utopian society.

NAIVE	SENTIMENTAL[40]
undifferentiated unity	desire for unity (436, 473)
totality	partiality (436, 473, 474)
unseparateness	separation (427, 431, 436, 473)
unrelatedness	necessary relationship to another (413, 414, 427, 441, 473)
perfection	desire for perfection (417, 427, 428, 438)
finitude	infinitude (440)
finite goals	infinite goals (438, 474)
achievement of goals	infinite approximation toward goals (415, 438, 474)
absolute portrayal	portrayal of an absolute (470)
reality	possibility (481)
imitation of reality	portrayal of ideality (437)
necessity	freedom (415, 476, 482, 492)
life and action	repose and contemplation (490)
constancy	change (415)
stasis	progress (415, 474)
stillness	motion (414, 428, 429, 441, 474)
equivalence of is and ought	dualism of is and ought (414, 437)
harmony and resolution	tension, conflict, strife (428, 436, 474)
happiness and contentment	dissatisfaction (427, 428, 431, 474)
self-sufficient	points toward a goal beyond itself (473, 474)
dependent on nature and reality	posits ideas out of its own self (473, 476, 478)
capable of direct representation, even vulgarity	capable of the arbitrary use of phantasy (486)
danger of indolence	danger of overexcitement (481)
realism	idealism (491–503)
„immer zu Hause"	[„immer nach Hause"] (428)

Such dualisms mark a sentimental world-view, and Schiller's essay has often been considered sentimental;[41] but the question arises, whether Schiller's dualisms are ultimately coherent, whether the terms he introduces can be placed in absolute opposition to one another. And, if a strict separation of the naive and sentimental is impossible, then the question must be asked, whether Schiller was portraying in his essay something other than the strict dichotomy between naive perfection and sentimental becoming. Before answering this far-reaching question, we must first consider the tenability of the dualisms themselves.[42]

---

[40] The two terms near the end of the list, realism and idealism, could be subdivided to generate yet another twenty or thirty major oppositions. Concerning the final dualism: Novalis' lines – „Wo gehn wir denn hin?" „Immer nach Hause." – are often quoted (I, 325). No one seems to have noticed in this context Schiller's definition of the naive as a condition where the individual is „immer zu Hause" (428). Novalis was of course familiar with Schiller's work.

[41] See most recently Bahti (1980).

[42] If the arguments that follow break certain "common sense" expectations, then this should not surprise the reader, for Schiller's terms are "speculative". *They are not*

The Self-cancellation of the Naive

Schiller considers the naive self-sufficient: „ein selbständiges [...] Ganze" (473). He disassociates it from the sphere of „Nothdurft" (419) or „Bedürftigkeit" (463), and he tells us that the naive has no lacks. But Schiller also states that the naive does not stand by itself, that it depends on reality. The naive „steht [...] in einer Abhängigkeit von der Erfahrung" (476). „Das naive Dichtergenie bedarf [...] eines Beystandes von aussen" (476). In fact the naive is doubly limited, since Nature, upon which the naive is dependent, is in a major sense itself „abhängig und bedürftig" (482).[43] The supposedly self-sufficient naive requires something beyond itself for its own existence; it therefore takes on a characteristic most often associated with the sentimental, dependence on another.[44]

Other attempts to fix the naive seem equally elusive. The naive, an „ungetheilte Einheit" (473) would exclude differentiation; yet its very exclusion of differentiation is a mark of differentiation. The naive is undifferentiated only insofar as it negates differentiation; in its negation and onesidedness it itself becomes differentiated. Its unseparateness is separate from separateness and is therefore itself separate. Taken to its logical conclusion, the undifferentiated is itself differentiated, thus not naive, but sentimental, dualistic.

Similar to this untenable concept of naive unseparateness is the idea that the naive is an independent term, „ein selbständiges [...] Ganze" (473), „ein Ganzes in sich selbst" (474). The naive would present itself as simply and unproblematically itself without any relation to another. It exists only „durch sich selbst" (413). But every seemingly simple term – let us call it any something – is also not something else. This something else – let us call it another – limits the original essence (by making it not the other) and creates the conditions for its being (in not being other it can be itself). The something is thus other than another. While every something is necessarily

---

directed towards our everyday sense of the disjunctive; rather, they point us in the direction of a hidden synthesis. The arguments might also appear out of place in a study of Schiller, but this is only because they contrast with a common approach to his works that tends to shy away from theoretical or logical analyses of individual concepts and relies instead on biographical and genetic analyses or simple paraphrase. For evidence of the expanse of such Schiller criticism and a critique of the same see Ellis (1969), 12–46. Finally, the informed reader will note the strongly Hegelian tone of the arguments introduced in this chapter. The justification for using Hegelian arguments in an analysis of Schiller's dualisms is that the Hegelian solution is not just Hegelian, a whim of Hegel's as it were, but rather lies in the very terms of the dualisms themselves and should be applied to the terms insofar as they appear already in Schiller's essay.

[43] See also 493 and 494.
[44] The other on which the sentimental depends is its external goal.

also another (it is an other to every other something), every other (or second term), is, of course, to itself a something (or a first term). Every something therefore is also another and every other is a something, but insofar as the other becomes a something it, too, becomes another. One could say then that the truth of the something is something else or another. Expressed in a different way, every seemingly simple term is involved in and defined by its relation to otherness. In fact, when Schiller defines the naive not simply as nature but as nature when viewed in contrast to art („daß die Natur mit der Kunst im Kontraste stehe" 413) and when he suggests that the naive is not childlikeness but rather childlikeness where it is no longer expected („eine Kindlichkeit wo sie nicht mehr erwartet wird" 419), he seems to be aware of the fact that the naive is determined by its relationship to otherness.[45] The logical structure which suggests that every something is the negation of another should belong only in a sentimental world, yet it belongs to the naive as well. The naive is behind its own back sentimental.

Another category associated with the naive is perfection, „Vollkommenheit" (414). Schiller tells his readers early in the essay that the naive portrays „unsere höchste Vollendung im Ideale" (414); yet one paragraph later he claims that the ideal is possible only as a synthesis of the naive and sentimental: „Aber nur, wenn beydes sich mit einander verbindet [...] geht das Göttliche oder das Ideal hervor" (415). The naive, supposedly a whole unto itself, excludes the sentimental from its own being and is, therefore, not a whole but only part of a larger whole that includes both the naive and the sentimental. The exclusion of the sentimental or the unlimited makes the naive limited and not whole. The naive, insofar as it excludes sentimental elements that Schiller openly admires – e.g., freedom, motion, and reflection – cannot be considered perfect. The naive, being limited in this way, does not fulfill the task of portraying the absolute.[46] The naive is thus not perfect, but imperfect. Imperfection, we remember, is a sentimental characteristic.

Central to Schiller's concept of the naive is its finitude. Schiller speaks of the naive as „die Kunst der Begrenzung" (440). Specifically, the naive artist orients himself toward the finite and particular; in general, as I have shown above, the naive is limited by the sentimental, by what it is not. The naive presents itself as perfect or absolute, and yet it is essentially finite; in fact it is absolute in its finitude, which is to suggest, paradoxically, that even its finitude is not absolute but finite. The finitude of the finite requires that it pass over into an other which is not itself finite; otherwise the finite would be

---

[45] On this point see Szondi (1972), 194–95.
[46] „Das Absolute [...] ist seine Aufgabe und seine Sphäre. Wir haben gesehen, daß das naive Genie zwar nicht in Gefahr ist, diese Sphäre zu überschreiten, wohl aber *sie nicht ganz zu erfüllen*" (481).

absolutized. It would be no longer finite. Naive finitude must pass over into sentimental infinity if it is to remain itself finite and not absolute. Here again the naive logically leads to the sentimental; it contains its other as a moment within itself.

In these few paragraphs I have been able to discuss only a selection of the major categories Schiller associates with the naive: self-sufficiency, unseparateness, unrelatedness, perfection, and finitude; but I would argue that the remaining categories are equally unstable and likewise pass over into the sphere of the sentimental. The categories Schiller assigns to the sentimental are subject to an analogous process of self-cancellation. Each attribute, whether it be freedom, change, ideality, or infinity, is in truth not just sentimental but also naive.

The Self-cancellation of the Sentimental

While the naive individual follows necessity, the sentimental individual or idealist is free.[47] He is free in an absolute sense: he is free even to impose his will upon others. Any restrictions on such use of his freedom would of course limit his freedom such that it would be no longer absolute. Absolute freedom then includes this moment of arbitrary willfulness. This imposition of one will upon another, however, is not freedom, but necessity; indeed, such necessity is clearly inherent in the idea of absolute freedom. As soon as freedom is absolutized it can easily turn into despotism, as the actions of Marquis Posa in Schiller's *Don Carlos* show[48] and as was evident to Schiller as an observer of developments in the French Revolution.[49]

Although Schiller frequently tells us that the naive is the sphere of necessity (e.g., 415, 492), he does in one passage define it as „das freiwillige Daseyn" (413). This makes sense since freedom and necessity are interchangeable insofar as each is taken to imply a sense of proportion. One would not want to be free to do anything which is not itself in harmony with the laws of nature. Moreover, one can best utilize one's freedom by knowing

---

[47] „Wir sind frey und sie sind nothwendig" (415).
[48] See Act IV, scenes 12–17 of *Don Carlos* as well as Schiller's description of Posa as a near despot in no. 11 of his *Briefe über Don Carlos*.
[49] The transition from absolute freedom to tyranny in the French Revolution, an important development for most German intellectuals of the day, is thematized by Hegel in the chapter „Die absolute Freiheit und der Schrecken" of his *Phänomenologie des Geistes*. Note also Hegel's later and somewhat related reflection: „Ebenso ist es bekannt, wie im Politischen die Extreme der Anarchie und des Despotismus einander gegenseitig herbeizuführen pflegen" (8, 175). As Hegel implies, the thought is not new. Schiller might well have been acquainted with it, directly or indirectly, from books 8 and 9 of *The Republic*, where Plato discusses the transition from anarchy to tyranny. See esp. 562c–64b and 574d–75d.

the laws of nature. Kant's ethics – which unite freedom and knowledge of the moral law – would have been for Schiller the major contemporary example of such a synthesis. Schiller himself implies that freedom and necessity can be united when he tells us in the *Kallias-Briefe* that the perfect order and harmony of an English dance is an excellent image for the idea of social freedom.[50] In his *Ästhetische Briefe* Schiller explicitly states that true freedom is „nicht Gesetzlosigkeit, sondern Harmonie von Gesetzen, nicht Willkührlichkeit, sondern höchste innere Nothwendigkeit" (NA XX, 367). While absolute freedom is nothing other than the terror of necessity, true freedom can only operate in harmony with an order or necessity that is both recognized and affirmed. However defined, sentimental freedom easily slides into the sphere of (naive) necessity.

Schiller considers the naive the realm of constancy, the sentimental that of change: „wir wechseln, sie bleiben eins" (415). Yet this sentimental immersion in a state of change is itself permanent. While the superficial details of any series of changes may vary, the essential structure of change remains. Changing constantly, the sentimental is locked into the sameness of change. Such permanency is in fact the mark of a naive state.

An essential aspect of the sentimental is its striving for an ideal. The ideal after which the sentimental strives, however, is just a postulate, „ein unendliches [...] das er niemals erreicht" (438); it is in a strongly Kantian sense that which should be, but isn't. One can strive for, but never attain, this ideal (474). Supposedly beyond all limits, it is limited by its exclusion of the present, its lack of reality.[51] An ideal excluded from reality, from existence, is a finite ideal; more appropriately expressed, it is no longer an ideal at all, for the ideal, in order to be itself ideal (and not lacking), must also be real. The limitations associated with the ideal locate it no longer in the sentimental sphere, but rather in the naive realm of finitude.

The sentimental individual can hope only to approach his goal in an endless progress, „in einem unendlichen Fortschritte" (415). He strives to supersede all limits and negate his finitude, but whenever a specific boundary is eliminated, new limits are set. The transcendence of boundaries remains forever incomplete; further, this state of limited transcendence is itself never transcended, such that the so-called infinite process is just as finite as it is infinite.

Schiller conceives of the sentimental as infinite, „ein unendliches" [sic] (474), but insofar as sentimental infinity is the negation of naive finitude, the infinite has a limit, that is, an other which it is not; further, the existence of

---

[50] Letter to Körner of February 23, 1793 (Jonas III, 285).
[51] The sentimental artist does of course exist, but he exists as sentimental only insofar as he posits a goal that does not exist.

such a limit is the mark not of the infinite but of the finite. The infinite, as soon as it is considered the opposite of the finite, is no longer its opposite: the infinite, like the finite, becomes a limited essence; it too is something opposed to something else, it too has a limit. Such opposition to another is, of course, the definition of finitude. The infinite and the finite are in this sense not different, but the same: both are finite. Sentimental infinity is a would-be infinity. In truth, it is finite, that is, naive.

Contradiction and Resolution

The arguments presented above suggest that a strict dualism between the naive and the sentimental is untenable: the naive is essentially also sentimental, and the sentimental contains the naive as a moment within itself.[52] But

---

[52] Two critics, Peter Szondi and Timothy Bahti, have argued before me that the naive is sentimental. There are, however, several important differences among our positions. Szondi (1972) bases much of his argument on Schiller's letter to Goethe of August 23, 1794, and argues that the modern poet can become as the Greeks were, i.e., naive, only by means of reflection and effort, i.e., by sentimental means (184). Here Szondi makes no mention of a universal or necessary connection between the naive and sentimental. The central passage in *Über naive und sentimentalische Dichtung* for Szondi's thesis is a footnote in which Schiller states that the sentimental, when viewed in its fullest form, contains the naive and is therefore no longer antithetical to it. Although Szondi finds in this statement support for a conceptual and not merely historical coupling of the naive and sentimental he offers no philosophical arguments for their connectedness; he simply rephrases Schiller's own statement that a unity is both desirable and possible. For Bahti (1980) the fact that the naive is sentimental means that the naive is "always already artistic in its construction" (278). The naive is idyllic in Bahti's analysis, which is to say that it is a fiction, in particular a "fiction of an origin" (286), conceived from an elegiac standpoint. The seemingly historical and genuine past is distorted by our own subjective view of it. It is something "artfully-produced", nongenuine (281). According to Bahti, this dialectic "denies the possibility of any historicism that would pretend to account for any thing ‚durch sich selbst' [...] or, in Ranke's phrase, ‚wie es eigentlich gewesen wäre [sic]'" (281). Neither Bahti nor Szondi escape a one-sided dialectic. They begin with the naive and end with the sentimental. They do not notice that the sentimental is just as naive as the naive is sentimental and that both terms are united in a higher category, namely the idyllic. For each critic the idyllic remains a subgenre of the sentimental. Bahti's essay, moreover, despite providing several individual insights, suffers from a typically *deconstructionist* weakness. The framework that supports his claims contains a series of internal contradictions. Bahti suggests that Schiller's essay shows "reading itself – even 'simply' as an activity that might result in some determinable and transportable understanding – is repeatedly negated in its efforts toward accuracy and conclusion" (295). Yet Bahti himself does not hesitate in considering specific definitions "more accurate" than others or in viewing a particular reading as "obvious" (282). Moreover, if Bahti's theory that no reading is accurate is itself accurate, then his theory is wrong, for the claim of accuracy would contradict the

such an analysis does not result in the "deconstruction" of Schiller's claims. One need not draw the conclusion that Schiller's invalid dualisms are the mark of a weak thinker,[53] nor is it necessary to conclude that all possible conceptual distinctions are untenable, mere metaphors that don't quite work. These conclusions remove the responsibility for contradictions from the sphere of the object and place blame upon either the author or language itself. One might call these solutions neo-Kantian: the responsibility for contradictions on the level of concepts cannot lie in the objects to which these concepts correspond, for the objects of the world cannot possibly be contradictory.[54] But to quote from Hegel's criticism of Kant:[55]

> Es ist dies eine zu große Zärtlichkeit für die Welt, von ihr den Widerspruch zu entfernen, ihn dagegen in den Geist, in die Vernunft zu verlegen und darin unaufgelöst bestehen zu lassen. In der Tat ist es der Geist, der so stark ist, den Widerspruch ertragen zu können, aber er ist es auch, der ihn aufzulösen weiß. (WL I, 236)

The world is full of oppositions. Objects are inherently contradictory, but not just contradictory. Where Kant places the blame for the four antinomies on man's limited knowledge, Hegel argues that the antinomies resolve themselves as soon as they are thought through to their own conclusion.[56]

---

theory of necessary inaccuracy. On the other hand, if his theory is inaccurate, as it must be, given the structure of his theory, it follows that the thesis of necessary inaccuracy is itself inaccurate and as such implies a self-cancellation. The theory of necessary misreading is itself a misreading and must pass over into another theory, but not another inaccurate theory, for that would only confirm the truth of the theory of necessary inaccuracy, necessary misreading, but the truth of this theory is not the theory of necessary misreading but the inaccuracy of this theory and so the necessary reestablishment of the possibility of accurate and coherent readings. Finally, Bahti's general argument against logic (271, 278, 281) must be considered either arbitrary, in which case his argument, on its own terms, need not be taken seriously, need not be taken as an argument at all, or it is logical, in which case his argument against logic refutes itself.

[53] A critic who does reproach Schiller for invalid reasoning is Wells (1967–68), esp. 186–87.

[54] Schiller's *Die Braut von Messina* provides us with an example of a contradiction for which the neo-Kantian solution proves wholly inadequate. I am thinking of the prophecies that Beatrice will unite and also destroy her brothers (1299–1357, 2326–75). Isabella claims that the contradictory oracles are both wrong, but the action of the play demonstrates that they can be resolved.

[55] Hegel uses this image repeatedly. See, for example, 8, 126–29 and 20, 359.

[56] For Hegel's detailed criticisms of individual antinomies see WL I: 90ff., 183ff; WL II: 143ff., 387ff. The same Kantian-Hegelian dichotomy can be observed in their views towards the supersensible. Hegel suggests in the third chapter of the *Phänomenologie des Geistes* that we have no knowledge of „das übersinnliche Jenseits" not because human reason is „zu kurzsichtig oder beschränkt", as Kant claims, but rather because in pure emptiness there is nothing to be known (Hegel 3, 117–18).

And while the law of noncontradiction is of course still valid for Hegel's philosophy, he is able to find many contradictions that philosophers before him never noticed. In fact he is struck by the fact that Kant discusses only four antinomies and suggests that one can find a contradiction in every concept:[57]

> Die Hauptsache, die zu bemerken ist, ist, daß nicht nur in den vier besonderen, aus der Kosmologie genommenen Gegenständen die Antinomie sich befindet, sondern vielmehr in *allen* Gegenständen aller Gattungen, in *allen* Vorstellungen, Begriffen und Ideen. (Hegel 8, 127–28)

The contradictions in Schiller's text do not discredit his essay. Quite the contrary, Schiller's insights into the interrelatedness of the naive and sentimental and the untenability of their isolation form the first step towards substantiating his own claim that a synthesis of the naive and sentimental is both desirable and possible. We have seen that the two terms, however Schiller defines them, are interrelated. A unity is implicit in the individual, self-cancelling categories of Schiller's dualism; they need only be thought through to their conclusion before their resolution in a higher unity is revealed.[58] Each category in its highest form includes, rather than excludes, its other. I am suggesting not that Schiller was aware of the arguments I have been introducing to support these claims, but that the arguments do apply to Schiller's categories and can be used to show that his belief in unity was justified. What seem like lapses in Schiller's descriptions of the categories, e.g., his ascription of the sentimental category of freedom to the naive, can be reinterpreted as insights into the interrelatedness of the categories. Although the *sentimental* dualism of the naive and the sentimental breaks down, this does not result in the pure identity of the naive and the sentimental, the obliteration of all distinctions, for this would mean a return to the untenable simplicity of the *naive*. The synthesis is not one of pure identity; the two terms form a differentiated unity.[59]

---

[57] See Hegel 20, 356.
[58] Meng (1936) would deny any such unity: „Zwischen Einssein und Gespaltensein, Identität mit der Natur und Getrenntsein von ihr [...] kein Sowohl-Alsauch (keine Synthese!), sondern nur das klare Entweder-Oder" (108). At another point he writes: „Eine wirkliche Verschmelzung beider Dichtercharaktere ist undenkbar: der eine entsteht durch die Aufhebung des andern" (176).
[59] A more detailed philosophical argument for the *differentiated unity* of the naive or finite and the sentimental or infinite would function as follows. It is the self-referential condition of the finite to be itself finite, to cancel itself and pass over into its other; it contains its negation, the infinite, within itself. Here the unity of the two terms is apparent. The finite passes over into the infinite. The infinite, however, lies in a sphere beyond the finite. Here the separation of the two terms manifests itself. The infinite, however, has itself a limit. Thus it, too, contains its

Schiller's Desire for Unity

The establishment of such a synthesis seems to have been one of the major goals of Schiller's essay. In fact the reason Schiller emphasizes the poetic aspects of the naive and sentimental is that for him poetry is the realm of unity,[60] and it is the unity of the naive and sentimental that interests him:[61]

---

negation (the finite) within itself. Once again one sees the unity of the two terms. The limit upon the infinite makes it not infinite but finite. The infinite vanishes and its other, the finite, takes its place. Once again the separation of the two terms becomes clear. In this process the unity and the separation of the finite and the infinite pass one another by. The two terms are unified, then separated, then unified, and then separated again. Unity and separation are juxtaposed but not themselves unified. One need simply consider the finite and the infinite first in *relation* to one another and then as *separate* to discover that they are in either case indeed *unified*. Observed together, each category contains its other. The finite passes over into the infinite; its truth is its own negation. The infinite must become finite; otherwise it excludes its other. Observed in isolation, the two categories are again revealed in their essential unity. The infinite is the other; it is only one side, thus not infinite, not a whole, but finite. The finite, taken in isolation, is not finite or dependent on another, but a whole without an other outside itself. It becomes the whole that the other should be. It is infinite. Even in their isolation the terms are unified. Each contains the other as a moment in itself. Each is itself and its own opposite; thus each is the unity of both, and since both are found in each, they are essentially the same; thus there is one unity, not two. The truth is the falsity of the isolation of either. Both the finite, the naive, and the infinite, the sentimental, are negated in their isolation. Each is what it is by way of the other or, more precisely, by way of the negation of the other as other. The finite is the finite as opposed to the infinite as well as the finite that passes over into the infinite; the finite is itself, then, essentially, infinite. The infinite is the other of the finite and simultaneously the whole that recognizes itself as both infinite and finite. Any strict either-or is false. The naive is at once the naive as opposed to the sentimental and the naive reestablished in a unity with the sentimental. The sentimental is the sentimental as the negation of the naive as well as itself in union with the naive. To ask whether a term is purely naive or sentimental is to commit – if one might use a modern term here – a "category-mistake". The separation not the union is what appears as incoherent. Indeed, from this perspective one of the central philosophical and aesthetic questions of the day, the question of how to make the infinite finite, which both Schelling and Schlegel considered the most central problem of all philosophy (Schelling I, 313; KA XII, 38), is solved simply by dissolving the question. It is not so much a question of how the infinite becomes finite but rather how one ever thought of them as separate in the first place. On this solution to the problem see WL I, 142–44. The most popular recent argument against a synthesis of finitude and infinitude stems from Charles Taylor's book on Hegel. See Taylor (1975), 235–44, 346–49. In order to avoid here a lengthy excursus on Taylor's argument I simply refer the interested reader to Stanley Rosen's defense against Taylor's argument in his review of Taylor's book. See Rosen (1977), esp. 248.

[60] Schiller's view of poetry as a unifying force pervades almost all his writings, not only here and in the *Ästhetische Briefe* but also, for example, in his lecture „Was

> Zwar solange man beyde Charaktere biß zum *dichterischen* exaltirt, wie wir sie auch bißher betrachtet haben, verliert sich vieles von den ihnen adhärirenden Schranken und auch ihr Gegensatz wird immer weniger merklich, in einem je höhern Grade sie poetisch werden; denn die poetische Stimmung ist ein selbständiges Ganze, in welchem alle Unterschiede und alle Mängel verschwinden. (491)

In his analysis of the realists and idealists, that is, naive and sentimental individuals minus any poetic qualities, the one-sidedness of each type becomes clearer and the need for synthesis more apparent. Here the ideal is split in two. Schiller writes, „daß das Ideal menschlicher Natur unter beyde verteilt, von keinem aber völlig erreicht ist" (500).

Schiller does not argue for the unambiguous superiority of the sentimental over the naive. While critics sometimes stress the preeminence of the sentimental insofar as it is beyond or after the naive and thus closer to the ideal,[62] one could argue the priority of the naive, for where the sentimental represents an advance in consciousness, it suffers a loss of unity. Division marks the sphere of the sentimental; unity characterizes the naive. Insofar as Schiller's ideal consists of the unity of the naive and the sentimental or the *unity* of unity and duplicity, the ideal itself reveals the preeminence of unity. One could therefore say – in this one respect at least – that the ideal indicates a preeminence of the naive. In another sense as well the sentimental falls behind the naive: the sentimental, unlike the naive, individual does not uniformly adhere to any specific moral code: „Bey dem Idealisten [...] [wird man] weit weniger moralische Gleichförmigkeit im Ganzen finden" (496). To be sure, the sentimental individual or idealist is more advanced insofar as

---

kann eine gute Schaubühne eigentlich wirken?" (NA XX, 100) and his critique „Über Bürgers Gedichte" (NA XXII, 245).

[61] I am suggesting that a conceptual analysis of the terms can also generate the unity Schiller desires and can show, as Schiller puts it in the *Ästhetische Briefe*, „daß das Leiden die Thätigkeit [...] daß die Beschränkung die Unendlichkeit keineswegs ausschließe" (NA XX, 397).

[62] Critics who view the sentimental as a superior category include Bauch (1903), 500–01, 508; Rüdiger (1959), 242; von Wiese (1963), 98; von Wiese (1965), 177; and von Wiese (1969), 44. This hierarchy would seem to find support from a statement in Schiller's letter to Humboldt of November 30, 1795, where he writes that by bringing „Bewegung" into the sphere of the gods and writing „eine Idylle in meinem Sinne" he hopes „dadurch mit der sentimentalischen Poesie über die naive triumphiert zu haben". But I would interpret this to mean that the sentimental triumphs over the naive only by including it as a moment in itself. Moreover, in *Über naive und sentimentalische Dichtung* Schiller repeatedly states that each of his two main categories has its individual advantages and faults. See esp. 558–59, 560, 585, 590–91. Cf. Korff (1930) II, 510–12. I would thus also disagree with a critic like Havenstein (1938) who argues that the naive is the higher, more valuable category (249).

he, unlike the naive figure,[63] has the capacity to ground his morality in unconditional reason and could defend it from the attacks of any sceptics.[64] The idealist takes the grounds of his determinations from pure reason.[65] Nonetheless, the sentimental individual is incapable of following his morality with the immediacy or consistency of a naive consciousness: „So geschieht es denn nicht selten, daß er über dem unbegrenzten Ideale den begrenzten Fall der Anwendung übersiehet" (496). The sentimental individual is more often capable of error and capable of greater error than his naive counterpart (496–97). Moreover, he suffers the temptation to destroy through critical distance the innately good morality of the naive consciousness before reestablishing a morality of his own on a higher plane.[66]

---

[63] The naive, which strictly speaking lacks both the ability to relate itself to something outside itself and any capacity for self-reflexivity, could never argue for its superiority over another position, nor could it ever thematize itself as a tenable position in its own right. In fact, even if the naive were able to thematize itself, it still could not ground itself as absolute, since it purports to base all its knowledge on experience: „Auf alles, was bedingungsweise existirt, erstreckt sich der Kreis seines Wissens und Wirkens, aber nie bringt er es auch weiter als zu bedingten Erkenntnissen und die Regeln, die er sich aus einzelnen Erfahrungen bildet, gelten, in ihrer ganzen Strenge genommen, auch nur Einmal" (493). The naive could never coherently argue for the validity of its own position, i.e., that all knowledge is based on experience, for the unconditionality of the claim could not itself be based on experience, which is always conditioned. The claim would thus cancel itself. This self-cancellation illustrates the idealism that Schiller viewed as inherent in any attempt to go beyond individual phenomena to laws, even a law that seems realistic or materialistic, e.g., „Naturnothwendigkeit" (500).

[64] „Nicht mit Erkenntnissen zufrieden, die bloß unter bestimmten Voraussetzungen gültig sind, sucht er biß zu Wahrheiten zu dringen, die nichts mehr voraussetzen und die Voraussetzung von allem andern sind. Ihn befriedigt nur die philosophische Einsicht, welche alles bedingte Wissen auf ein Unbedingtes zurückführt" (495).

[65] „Da er nur in so fern Idealist heißt, als er aus reiner Vernunft seine Bestimmungsgründe nimmt […]" (496).

[66] Schiller's categories apply to historical developments, but not in quite the way he imagined, for the transition from naive to sentimental morality and indeed even to a synthesis of the two had already taken place in Greece. The aged Cephalus, for example, must give way in *Republic I* to the destructive and power-positivistic views of the young Thrasymachus. Thrasymachus in turn must relent to Socrates, who combines in his morality both his naive *daimōn* and an intellectual rigor that demands an unconditional or sentimental code of ethics. Recent philosophical criticism has shown that such cycles were repeated several times in the history of philosophy (see Hösle [Wahrheit/1984]): this speaks for the accuracy of Schiller's sequence of categories as well as against his application of them to just one great cycle. Critics have long since recognized errors in Schiller's interpretation of the Greek world. See, for example, Basch (1911), 221–36, 345–46. Butler (1935) has criticized Schiller's assumption that the Greek tragic writers were naive (183). Wells (1966) has attacked Schiller's interpretation of Homer (500–02). One might

Naive goodness and sentimental consciousness must, according to Schiller, be united:

> Ich bemerke, um jeder Mißdeutung vorzubeugen, daß es bey dieser Einteilung ganz und gar nicht darauf abgesehen ist, eine Wahl zwischen beyden, folglich eine Begünstigung des einen mit Ausschließung des andern zu veranlassen. Gerade diese *Ausschließung,* welche sich in der Erfahrung findet, bekämpfe ich; und das Resultat der gegenwärtigen Betrachtungen wird der Beweis seyn, daß nur durch die vollkommen gleiche *Einschließung* beyder dem Vernunftbegriffe der Menschheit kann Genüge geleistet werden. (492–93)

Even earlier in the essay the call for a synthesis of dualisms dominates. In the very first pages Schiller expresses his desire for a synthesis of necessity and freedom, stillness and motion:

> Wir sind frey, und sie sind nothwendig; wir wechseln, sie bleiben eins. Aber nur, wenn beydes sich miteinander verbindet – wenn der Wille das Gesetz der Nothwendigkeit frey befolgt und bey allem Wechsel der Phantasie die Vernunft ihre Regel behauptet, geht das Göttliche oder das Ideal hervor. (415)

Schiller consistently refers to the need for unity. He suggests, for example, that the naive and sentimental can and should be unified „unter einem gemeinschaftlichen höhern Begriff" (439). In another passage he speaks yet again of this „höhern Begriff, der sie beide unter sich faßt" (437). For Schiller the excellence of Goethe's *Die Leiden des jungen Werther* derives in part from its unification of naive and sentimental characteristics (438). Finally, Schiller's preference for unity manifests itself by way of negation. He devotes several pages to the faults of the categories insofar as each is taken in isolation: the naive is a „Gegenstand ohne Geist", the sentimental a „Geistesspiel ohne Gegenstand" (482). Each is in its own way empty and deficient. In particular, the naive is capable of producing „die plattesten und schmutzigsten Abdrücke gemeiner Natur" (486), while the sentimental taken to its extreme can easily generate „ein zahlreiches Heer phantastischer Produktionen" (486). Even the traditional concept of art as a recreational (naive) and educative (sentimental) force generates extremes:

> Dem Begriff der *Erholung,* welche die Poesie zu gewähren habe, werden, wie wir gesehen, gewöhnlich viel zu enge Grenzen gesetzt, weil man ihn zu einseitig auf das bloße Bedürfniß der Sinnlichkeit zu beziehen pflegt. Gerade umgekehrt wird

---

as well add to the list Schiller's erroneous assumption that the Greek comedy writers were naive since comedy, even in Schiller's view, appeals not to the passions but to the intellect and plays upon the distance between hero and audience (446). In Schiller's defense it can only be stated that he does on occasion waver regarding the direct correspondence of naive and ancient, sentimental and modern. On the latter point see most recently Jones (1984).

dem Begriff der *Veredlung,* welche der Dichter beabsichtigen soll, gewöhnlich ein viel zu weiter Umfang gegeben, weil man ihn zu einseitig nach der bloßen Idee bestimmt. (489)

Schiller calls upon his readers to avoid such extremes and to reveal in themselves „das schöne Ganze menschlicher Natur" (490). Such totality, Schiller insists, is possible only through the union of the naive and sentimental: „Denn endlich müssen wir es doch gestehen, daß weder der naive noch der sentimentalische Charakter, für sich allein betrachtet, das Ideal schöner Menschlichkeit ganz erschöpfen, das nur aus der innigen Verbindung beyder hervorgehen kann" (491).

Ambiguities in the Category "Idyllic"

The Conflicting Definitions

In this next section I would like to suggest that the unity of the naive and the sentimental is to be equated with Schiller's notion of the idyllic.[67] Early in *Über naive und sentimentalische Dichtung* before offering a thorough analysis of the idyll, Schiller makes an anticipatory appeal to this term and suggests that the sentimental should regain the virtues of the naive without sacrificing its own advantages:

> Strebe nach Ruhe, aber durch das Gleichgewicht nicht durch den Stillstand deiner Thätigkeit. Jene Natur, die du dem Vernunftlosen beneidest, ist keiner Achtung, keiner Sehnsucht werth. Sie liegt hinter dir, sie muß ewig hinter dir liegen. (428)

Nonetheless, naive perfection should act as a model:

> Aber wenn du über das verlorene *Glück* der Natur getröstet bist, so laß ihre *Vollkommenheit* deinem Herzen zum Muster dienen. Trittst du heraus zu ihr aus deinem künstlichen Kreis, steht sie vor dir in ihrer großen Ruhe, in ihrer naiven Schönheit, in ihrer kindlichen Unschuld und Einfalt; dann verweile bey diesem Bilde, pflege dieses Gefühl, es ist deiner herrlichsten Menschheit würdig. Laß dir nicht mehr einfallen, mit ihr *tauschen* zu wollen, aber nimm sie in dich auf und strebe, ihren unendlichen Vorzug mit deinem eigenen unendlichen Prärogativ zu vermählen, und aus beydem das Göttliche zu erzeugen. Sie umgebe dich wie eine liebliche *Idylle.* (428–29)

---

[67] Perhaps the major difference between Schiller's two great essays is that in *Über die ästhetische Erziehung des Menschen* he quite clearly conceives of the need for a synthesis and unambiguously terms it the „Spieltrieb"; in *Über naive und sentimentalische Dichtung* Schiller slowly moves toward a synthesis, all the while shifting his view of the idyllic, so that it is necessary for an interpreter to point out that the idyll has indeed become the synthetic term in this essay.

Schiller's detailed account of the idyllic, his portrayal of it as a synthesis of a naive „Ruhe der Vollendung" and sentimental „Streben", comes much later in the essay. Between these passages Schiller offers several different definitions of the idyllic, making its exact location in his table of categories highly problematic.[68] Schiller calls the idyll variously: a subcategory of the elegy; one of three subcategories of the sentimental along with the satire and the elegy; a false or merely attempted synthesis of the naive and sentimental; and finally, the true or successful synthesis of the naive and sentimental.

The Idyll as an Elegiac Subcategory

Schiller first calls the idyll a subcategory of the elegy. The elegy, itself a subspecies of the sentimental, exhibits a dualism between the real and ideal. Unlike satire, which concerns itself with the problems of the real, the elegy focuses on the ideal. Schiller divides the elegy, like the satire, into two kinds:

> Entweder ist die Natur und das Ideal ein Gegenstand der Trauer, wenn jene als verloren, dieses als unerreicht dargestellt wird. Oder beyde sind ein Gegenstand der Freude, indem sie als wirklich vorgestellt werden. Das erste gibt die *Elegie* in engerer, das andere die *Idylle* in weitester Bedeutung. (448-49)

Although the idyll portrays the existence of a perfect state, such perfection cannot exist for a sentimental consciousness. Therefore, whenever the sentimental artist portrays „das Gemählde der unverdorbenen Natur oder des erfüllten Ideales", he cannot hide the fact that the ideal only *appears* real; the genuine opposition of the ideal and real discloses itself „in jedem Pinselstrich" (449).

At this point in his essay Schiller insists that the idyll is a subset of the elegy and that there are only two subspecies of the sentimental: the satiric and the elegiac. After introducing the two world-views, he writes: „an eine von diesen beyden Empfindungsarten wird jeder sentimentalische Dichter sich halten" (441-42). The categories Schiller introduces until this point must be broken down as follows:[69]

---

[68] Olive Sayce (1962) has shown the usefulness of a close study of individual categories in Schiller's writings. Although she does not mention the idyllic, her general statement at the conclusion of her essay bears repetition as a motto for the next few pages of my study: „Es ist unmöglich, Schiller zu verstehen, ohne die ihm so eigentümliche Vieldeutigkeit und Bedeutungsschwankung in Betracht zu ziehen. Ziel einer sprachlichen Untersuchung muß es sein, die verschiedenen Bedeutungen eines Worts aufzudecken, nicht um Schiller der Inkonsequenz zu beschuldigen, sondern als Vorbedingung für ein tieferes Verständnis" (176).
[69] Schiller subdivides satire into two kinds: the playful and the pathetic. The distinction is not central to my argument here and can be passed over. I will reintroduce it when I discuss satiric elements in *Hyperion*.

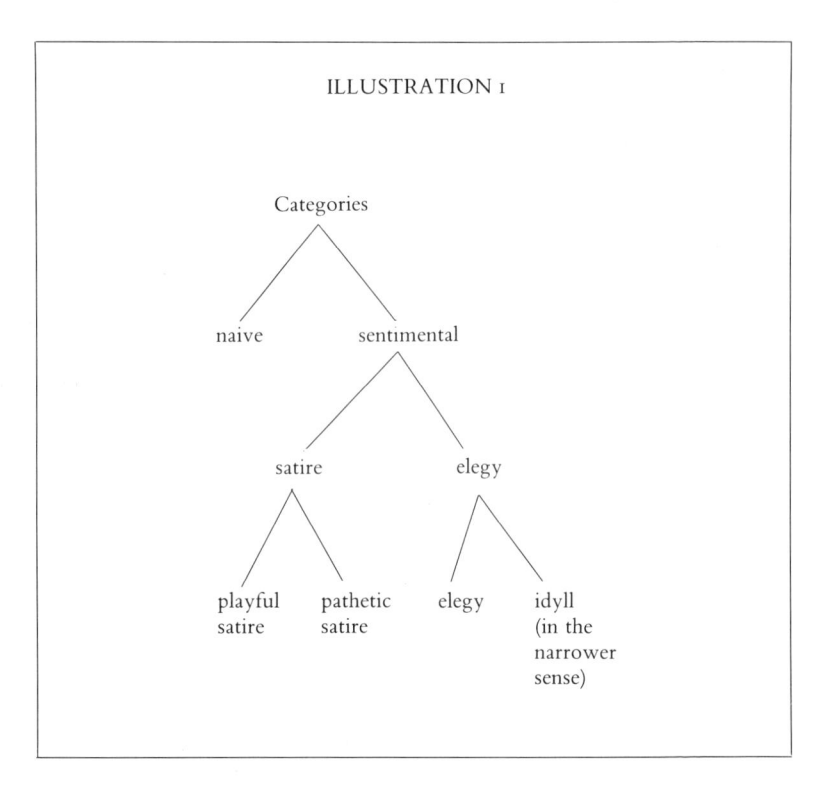

```
                        ILLUSTRATION 1


                           Categories
                          /         \
                         /           \
                      naive        sentimental
                                   /         \
                                  /           \
                               satire         elegy
                               /    \         /    \
                              /      \       /      \
                          playful  pathetic elegy   idyll
                          satire   satire           (in the
                                                    narrower
                                                    sense)
```

The Idyll as a Sentimental Subcategory

Later in the essay Schiller shifts his understanding of the idyll and calls it a „dritte Species sentimentalischer Dichtung" (466). The idyll, now a direct subcategory of the sentimental, is on the same level with the satire and the elegy. „Die Satyre, Elegie und Idylle" are for Schiller at this juncture in the essay „die drey einzig möglichen Arten sentimentalischer Poesie" (466). The chart of the categories must now read as in Illustration 2.

In a lengthy footnote Schiller compares the three sentimental modes. He writes that sentimental poetry must always deal simultaneously

> mit zwey streitenden Objekten, mit dem Ideale nehmlich und mit der Erfahrung [...] zwischen welchen sich weder mehr noch weniger als gerade die drey folgenden Verhältnisse denken lassen. Entweder ist es der *Widerspruch* des wirklichen Zustandes oder es ist die *Übereinstimmung* desselben mit dem Ideal, welche vorzugsweise das Gemüth beschäftigt; oder dieses ist zwischen beyden getheilt. In dem ersten Falle wird es durch die Kraft des innern Streits, *durch die energische Bewegung,* in dem andern wird es durch die Harmonie des innern Lebens, *durch die energische Ruhe* befriedigt; in dem dritten *wechselt* Streit mit Harmonie, wechselt Ruhe mit Bewegung. (466)

ILLUSTRATION 2

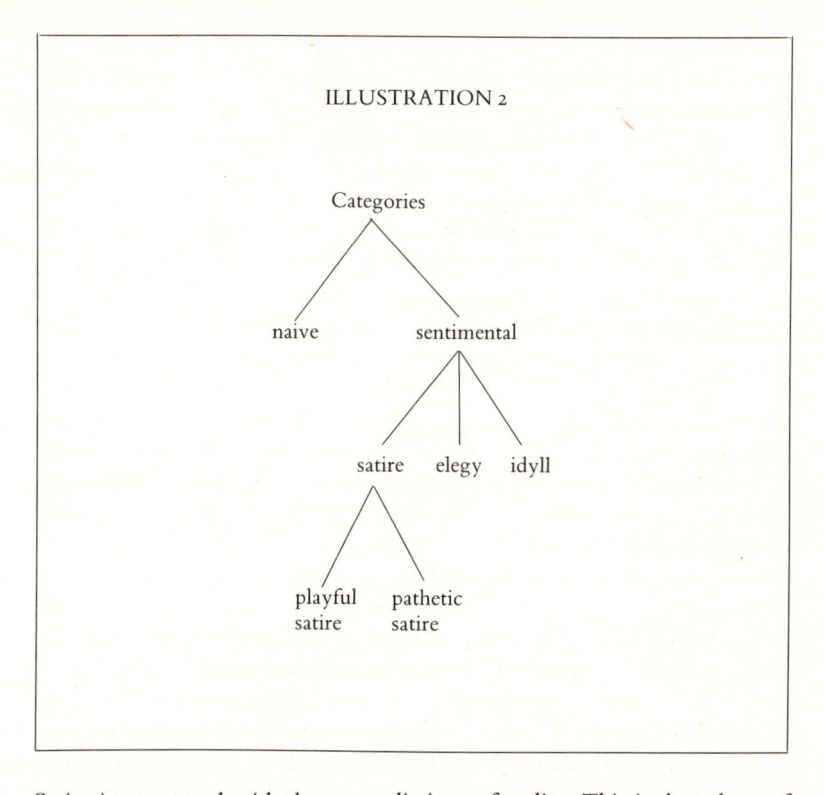

```
                    Categories
                    /        \
                 naive      sentimental
                             /    |    \
                         satire elegy  idyll
                          /   \
                    playful  pathetic
                    satire    satire
```

Satire is concerned with the contradictions of reality. This is the sphere of inner struggle, of „energische Bewegung". Schiller suggests that the elegy shifts back and forth between „Ruhe" and „Bewegung", between the harmony of the ideal and the real and the dualism of the ideal and the real. This seems at first an odd definition, since Schiller had just definded the elegy as the tension of the ideal and the real and the dualism of the ideal and the real; nonetheless, the meta-tension of which Schiller speaks remains dualistic. Further, the highest pole remains the ideal, for the ideal, when thought through to its conclusion, is nothing other than the ideal made real. The tension and the focus thus remain elegiac in nature. The idyllic signals the harmony of inner life, of the real with the ideal. Schiller calls this „energische Ruhe".

The Idyll as a False Synthesis of the Naive and the Sentimental

According to these first two definitions, the idyll is unequivocally of a sentimental type. But when Schiller discusses the idyll in detail, he distinguishes two more kinds, one of which is not just sentimental. One could call Schiller's final two terms the false and the true idyll in analogy to his distinction between a false and a true realism (502).[70] Each form of the idyll attempts to synthesize the naive and the sentimental. Schiller first speaks of the „Schäfer-" or „Hirtenidylle" (469), which involves the retreat into a past paradise or golden age.[71] Such an idyll represents the past as present. Schiller writes: „Sie stellen unglücklicherweise das Ziel *hinter* uns, dem sie uns doch *entgegen führen* sollten, und können uns daher bloß das traurige Gefühl eines Verlustes, nicht das fröhliche der Hoffnung einflößen" (469). This sentimental idyll invokes a „Ruhe" that replaces but does not include „Bewegung". It can only pacify („besänftigen"), not also rejuvenate („beleben"): „Wir können sie daher nur lieben und aufsuchen, wenn wir der Ruhe bedürftig sind, nicht wenn unsre Kräfte nach Bewegung und Thätigkeit streben" (469). Schiller does offer limited praise of this idyll, namely, for its attempt to synthesize the naive and the sentimental (471), but in simply portraying naive content from a sentimental vantage point the sentimental idyll fails to achieve a valid synthesis. Unlike the naive proper, which is internally consistent, this false depiction of a naive state suffers from the contradiction between present consciousness and the desired state of past simplicity. It remains dualistic; moreover, it sacrifices many of the advantages of the sentimental, such as the portrayal of higher ideals. According to Schiller the idyllic poet turns to the past because he does not find the ideal realized in the present. In this way the ideal is never real-ized; it remains distant. There is no genuine unity. Each pole is, as Schiller says (471), only half itself rather than – as will be the case with the true idyll – fully itself and partly also its other. Schiller argues that until one is „am Ziel der Vollkommenheit" one must choose between „Idealität" and „Individualität" (471). The true idyll, which does reach this goal of perfection, is not only ideal, but also real, manifest, and individual. Here individuality is not opposed to ideality; it is, rather, its fullest expression.

---

[70] My suggestion to call Schiller's coherent, if somewhat unorthodox, notion of the idyllic "the true idyll" should not be confused with Moses Mendelssohn's use of the term „wahre Idylle" in the eighty-sixth of his *Briefe, die neueste Literatur betreffend,* where he refers to the idylls of Theocritus, Vergil and Geßner. See Mendelssohn, IV/2, 23.

[71] A discussion of Schiller's concept of the idyll in relationship to other eighteenth-century theories from Gottsched onwards lies beyond the central argument of my chapter. The most recent review of the major theories with references to much of the secondary literature can be found in „Idyllen-begriff und Idyllentheorie im 18. Jahrhundert" in Rockwell (1980), 25–38. It will become clear that Schiller's theory shares very little with the traditional concept of the idyll: Schiller has superimposed on the primary eighteenth-century genre of harmony his own willfully different set of terms and relations.

The Idyll as a Valid Synthesis of the Naive and the Sentimental

Schiller calls for an idyll that would lead man, „der nun einmal nicht mehr nach *Arkadien* zurückkann, bis nach *Elisium*" (472).[72] Critics often distinguish between an Arcadian and Elysian idyll, suggesting in particular that the Elysian idyll is future-directed and Utopian. They have also drawn parallels between Schiller's Elysian idyll and Ernst Bloch's concept of art as the realm of possibility, the not-yet.[73] The idyll then is seen first of all as a projection into the *future* and second as an *aesthetic* portrayal in the present of this future condition.[74] I will argue that the first position overlooks the extent to which the idyllic is not just sentimental but also naive or present. The interpretation of the idyll as a merely aesthetic projection, meanwhile, ignores the fact that Schiller's categories are general principles: they are not just aesthetic, but also, for example, psychological and political categories; they apply to all realms of reality.[75] The idyll, as we will see in detail, is not an aesthetic means to a moral or political end. It is, rather, in each realm to which the concept applies, a means and an end simultaneously.

Insofar as one terms the idyll a future ideal, one transforms it back into a subset of the elegy: while the so-called Utopian idyll does not place the ideal in the past (one particular aspect of the elegiac), it does project the ideal into the future (another definitely elegiac trait). The idyll, defined as a nonpresent ideal, is not a synthesis of the naive and the sentimental; it is merely sentimental, specifically elegiac. However, the next few paragraphs of Schiller's essay contradict this reading of the idyllic as a purely sentimental category. Schiller writes:

> Der Begriff dieser Idylle ist der Begriff eines völlig aufgelösten Kampfes sowohl in dem einzelnen Menschen, als in der Gesellschaft, einer freyen Vereinigung der Neigungen mit dem Gesetze, einer zur höchsten sittlichen Würde hinaufgeläuter-

---

[72] Schiller rephrases this appeal at one point, suggesting that the true idyll leads us from „Ruhe" and „Schlaf" „vorwärts zu unserer Mündigkeit" (472). This allusion to „Mündigkeit" would seem to be a direct reference to at least one of the ideals invoked by Kant in his famous essay on Enlightenment, „Beantwortung der Frage: Was ist Aufklärung?" The essay begins: „*Aufklärung ist der Ausgang des Menschen aus seiner selbst verschuldeten Unmündigkeit*" (XI, 53). On Schiller's reception of this essay in another context see Meyer (1963), 340–49.

[73] Siekmann (1980), for example, makes the connection to Ernst Bloch (27). Cf. Berghahn (1982).

[74] See among other: Geißler (1961), 278; Habel (1975), 79, 81; Janke (1977), 284; Rüdiger (1959), 239, 241; Sautermeister (1971), 18, 20; Siekmann (1980), 27, 34; Wertheim (1959), 122; von Wiese (1959), 545–46; and von Wiese (1965), 172, 180–82.

[75] Although the suggestion that art is not "real", may be true in a given sense, it is not in this case valid as an objection to my interpretation of the idyllic, for I do not view the idyllic as a simply aesthetic category, as a genre within the realm of poetry.

ten Natur, kurz, er ist kein andrer als das Ideal der Schönheit auf das wirkliche Leben angewendet. Ihr Charakter besteht also darinn, daß *aller Gegensatz der Wirklichkeit mit dem Ideale,* der den Stoff zu der satyrischen und elegischen Dichtung hergegeben hatte, vollkommen aufgehoben sey, und mit demselben auch aller Streit der Empfindungen aufhöre. (472)

The true idyll is not just sentimental; it represents a „Vereinigung" of sentimental characteristics (*Kampf, Gesetz, Würde, Ideal*) and naive properties (*Auflösung, Neigungen, Natur, das wirkliche Leben*). In fact the dominant tone of this supposedly sentimental idyll is „Ruhe", a distinctly naive concept:[76]

> *Ruhe* wäre also der herrschende Eindruck dieser Dichtungsart, aber Ruhe der Vollendung, nicht der Trägheit; eine Ruhe, die aus dem Gleichgewicht nicht aus dem Stillstand der Kräfte, die aus der Fülle nicht aus der Leerheit fließt, und von dem Gefühl eines unendlichen Vermögens begleitet wird. (472–73)

The true idyll is naive insofar as it contains the elements of repose and perfection: „Ruhe der Vollendung". A purely sentimental mode would strive for but never achieve *Ruhe*; its constant state of dualisms would exclude the possibility of naive perfection and stillness. In fact Schiller mentions Ewald von Kleist's „Sehnsucht nach Ruhe" as an example of sentimental poetry (454). Also, in the often quoted letter to Humboldt of December 25, 1795, Schiller says of the sentimental: „Die sentimentalische wird von mir als nach dem Ideal strebend vorgestellt" (NA XXVIII, 144). Of the introduction of perfection into this sentimental mode Schiller writes: „Hat sie sich aber vollendet, so ist sie nicht mehr sentimentalisch" (NA XXVIII, 144). Since the idyll is perfect, it is not just sentimental but also naive. Moreover, the idyll is not just naive but naive in a wholly positive way, for it eschews the typically naive dangers of „Trägheit", „Stillstand", and „Leerheit". By avoiding such dangers the naive becomes equally sentimental. It contains the *Kraft, Fülle,* and *unendliches Vermögen* associated with this mode. Finally, the idyll contains the dynamism of motion and striving, a clearly sentimental characteristic. Schiller continues: „Aber eben darum, weil aller Widerstand hinwegfällt, so wird es hier ungleich schwüriger als in den zwey vorigen Dichtungsarten, die *Bewegung* hervorzubringen, ohne welche doch überall keine poetische Wirkung sich denken läßt" (473). Although motion is difficult to generate, it is indeed contained within the idyll. The motion is not self-evident, since the idyll itself is not just sentimental, not just in *Unruhe,* as are the „zwey vorige Dichtungsarten", namely the satire and the elegy. The idyll is unified, like

---

[76] Most interpreters of Schiller's essay quote this passage, which asserts that *Ruhe* is the dominant tone of the idyll, but no one has interpreted the passage in detail. Despite a promising title, „Energische Ruhe. Über Schillers Plan zu einer Idylle", Helmerking's brief article (1959), like the individual paragraphs of many other interpretations, consists simply of a series of quotations from Schiller's text and his letters to Humboldt without extensive commentary or analysis.

the naive, though not undifferentiated; it encompasses sentimental „Mannichfaltigkeit". It is „befriedigt", as the naive was, yet its contentment does not exclude striving: „Die höchste Einheit muß seyn, aber sie darf der Mannichfaltigkeit nichts nehmen; das Gemüth muß befriedigt werden, aber ohne daß das Streben darum aufhöre" (473).

The confusion as to where to locate the idyll stems from its synthetic character. The idyll contains naive oneness and repose, it is concerned with reality as is the satiric, and it contains the motion inherent in elegiac striving; yet no one of these categories can by itself exhaust the idyll. Schiller's multiplicity of definitions stands in correlation to the very meaning of the term "idyllic". Just as the idyll is at odds with itself thematically, both at rest and in motion, so is Schiller's description of it. The idyll is naive yet not just naive. It is sentimental yet not just sentimental. Insofar as the idyll is unlike any one of these two or unlike any particular subcategory of the sentimental, it passes over into its other and can be said to be in *motion*. Insofar as the idyll is, however, both naive and sentimental at once, it is a whole concept that need not pass over into another. It is stable and remains *still*. The idyll then is both thematically and formally at once still and in motion. An appropriate chart for this elusive category might look as follows:

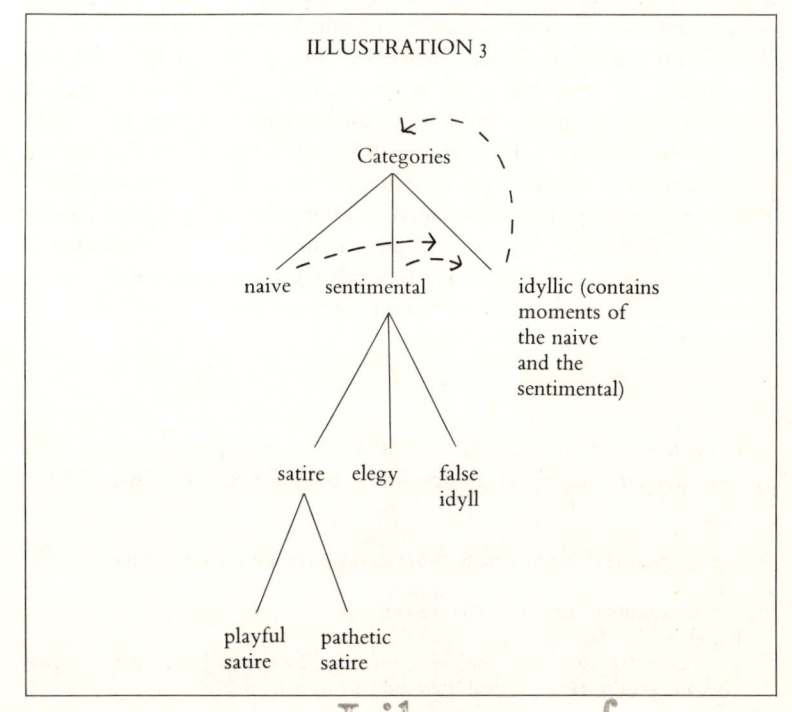

ILLUSTRATION 3

Categories

naive   sentimental   idyllic (contains moments of the naive and the sentimental)

satire   elegy   false idyll

playful satire   pathetic satire

Schiller raises the true idyll above not only the elegy, the satire, and the false idyll, but also the naive and the sentimental insofar as these are taken in isolation from one another. The true idyll negates all of these categories in their one-sidedness, while simultaneously recognizing and sublating the moment of truth contained in each. Two external factors highlight the significance of the idyll within the essay and reinforce its priviliged status.[77] First, in his final version of the essay Schiller gives only the idyll its own section heading (466). Second, Schiller writes that he plans in the future to give a more detailed exposition of this one particular category (466). The idyll alone seems worthy of further study.

Interpreting the Idyllic

Schiller's equivocations on the idyll and the shifting importance of this category have confused readers of his essay, and much of the critical discourse has only added to this confusion. Scholars speak of the idyll as though it were an unambiguous concept;[78] yet, as I have shown, Schiller defines the concept in several different ways. Even the term "sentimental idyll" is polyvalent; Schiller's definitions of the idyll as a subcategory of the elegy and as a sentimental category on an equal level with the elegy and the satire could each be construed as the so-called sentimental idyll; yet it is important to note the differences in Schiller's two definitions. In the scholarship on Schiller's essay the term "sentimental idyll" has two other and, in fact, conflicting meanings. Some critics use the term "sentimental idyll" to refer to what I have called the false idyll, the return to Arcadia;[79] others use the same term to designate the so-called Elysian or future-directed idyll.[80] The term "sentimental idyll" is, moreover, not only confusing, it is erroneous. By ascribing the attribute "sentimental" to Schiller's final definition of the idyll, critics suggest that this idyll is solely sentimental and not also naive. In order to clarify some of the confusions inherent in the one term "idyllic", I suggest the following distinctions:

idyll 0

I use this term to refer to the naive idyll. Schiller originally presents the idyll as a sentimental category, yet he does at one point conceive of a "naive idyll".

---

[77] Meng (1936: 148) and Siekmann (1980: 17–18) have noted these two points before me.
[78] See, for example, Simons (1981), 32–33.
[79] For example, Meng (1936), 511.
[80] See Gerhard (1950), 310; Rüdiger (1959), 239; Siekmann (1980), 25; Hermann Weigand (1954), 167; and Paul Weigand (1949), 105.

He writes: „Was ich hier an der Schäferidylle tadle, gilt übrigens nur von der sentimentalischen; denn der naiven kann es nie an Gehalt fehlen, da er hier *in der Form selbst* schon erhalten ist" (469). In its traditional generic meaning the idyll does overlap with the naive. In fact the idyll originated in the supposedly naive world of the Greeks, with Theocritus. Several critics, especially interpreters of Schiller's dramas,[81] use the general term "idyll" when they mean only the naive idyll, idyll o.

idyll 1

I refer here to Schiller's first explicit definition of the idyll as a subcategory of the elegy.

idyll 2

This term corresponds to Schiller's second definition of the idyll, his rendering of it as a direct subset of the sentimental on an equal level with the elegy and the satire.

idyll 3

Schiller's third specific description of the idyll is that of the Arcadian or false idyll; here sentimental consciousness attempts to return to a naive state.

idyll 4

This refers to the idyll as the synthesis of a naive „Ruhe der Vollendung" and sentimental „Streben". It corresponds to Schiller's lengthiest and final definition of the idyll, but also to the first occurence of the term early in the essay (429). I prefer to use the numerical representation (idyll 4) or the concept of the true idyll rather than the term Elysian idyll.[82] Unfortunately, critics have already adopted Schiller's term "Elysian" to refer to an idyll that is unreal, incomplete, a future projection. I have been arguing that such an interpretation fails to do justice to the sense of present fulfillment Schiller associates with an "Elysian idyll". To prevent confusion between my definition and the definitions of other critics I have purposely avoided the term "Elysian".

Interpreters of Schiller's essay tend not to accept this synthetic description of the idyll. Most of them insist that the idyllic remains a sentimental cate-

---

[81] See Field (1950) and Sautermeister (1971).
[82] When I use the term idyll without any specification in this chapter, I am referring to idyll 4, the true idyll.

gory.[83] But the sentimental is characterized by lack of unity, imperfection, and restlessness, while the idyll is unified, perfect, and calm; for this reason alone the idyll cannot be said to belong to the sentimental species. Moreover, Schiller had written in an early section of the essay that part of the essence of the *sentimental* is the opposition of the ideal and the real, „daß [...] das Ideal der Wirklichkeit *entgegengesetzt werde*" (449). Yet in his lengthy definition of the *idyllic* he suggests that this opposition has been superseded: „Ihr Charakter besteht also darin, daß *aller Gegensatz der Wirklichkeit mit dem Ideale* [...] vollkommen aufgehoben sey" (472).[84] If the idyllic were just an idea and not also real and existent, it could safely be called sentimental; but this is not the case. The idyll is characterized by the naive traits of perfection and presence as much as by the sentimental status of the longed-for ideal. Further, in Swabian usage and for Schiller in particular „Wirklichkeit" means not just reality in general, but present reality. „Wirklich" can be rewritten as „gegenwärtig". Ursula Wertheim (1959) brings this particularly Swabian meaning

---

[83] Critics who see the idyll as a subcategory of the sentimental are correct insofar as they rely solely on Schiller's first two definitions. These critics, however, overlook the naive aspects of Schiller's later, more elaborate definition of the term. A list of the critics who do consider the idyll a sentimental category would include, for example: Anderegg (1964), 93–96; Bahti (1980), 278; Böschenstein-Schäfer (1967), 83; Cysarz (1959), 590; Dierse (1971), 194–95; Gerhard (1950), 310, 403–04; Grimm (1982), 314–15; Janke (1977), 283; Jauß (1974), 101–02; Lukács (1964), 146–47, 151; Middell (1980), 264; Müller (1959), 191; Rüdiger (1959), 238–39, 241, 247; Siekmann (1980), 17, 25; Simons (1981), 32–34; and Szondi (1972), 189. Some critics have suggested in passing that the idyll might be seen as a synthesis of the naive and the sentimental, for example: Homann (1977), 92; Kraft (1968), 209; Mainland (1951), xxvi–xxvii; Marleyn (1955–56), 241; Sautermeister (1971), 25–26; and von Wiese (1959), 545–46. None of these critics, however, have noted the specifically naive and sentimental elements in Schiller's actual description of the idyll. Helmut Koopmann and Benno von Wiese in their notes to the *National-Ausgabe* suggest that the idyll *would* consist of a synthesis of the naive and the sentimental (NA, XXI 298, 307). They suggest, however, that such a synthesis is „unerreichbar" (NA XXI, 308) and thus unwittingly relegate the idyll to an exclusively sentimental status. One critic has explicitly denied that Schiller even desired a unity. See Wessell (1971), 197–98.

[84] To my knowledge only one other critic has noted this point. Knippel (1909) writes: „Wenn Schiller sagt, daß die sentimentale Poesie diejenige sei, welche nach dem *Ideal strebt,* d.h. die, welche nach der *Übereinstimmung von Ideal und Wirklichkeit strebt,* und wenn er nun die Idylle definiert als *Darstellung der Übereinstimmung von Ideal und Wirklichkeit,* kann er sie dann noch zur sentimentalen Dichtungsgattung rechnen? Wohl nicht" (41). I would adjust Knippel's conclusion somewhat and suggest that the contradiction tells us only that the idyll is not solely sentimental. Knippel's conclusion that the idyll is not at all sentimental can be based only on the assumption that a harmony of the ideal and the real would exclude dynamism and motion. Schiller does not share this assumption.

of „wirklich" to our attention in an article on Schiller's interpretation of Heracles. She writes:

> Wenn das Begriffspaar „Ideal und Wirklichkeit" antithetisch gebraucht wird, so heißt Wirklichkeit bei Schiller nicht bloß Realität schlechthin, sondern *gegenwärtige* Wirklichkeit. Das hat seinen Grund im schwäbischen Sprachgebrauch Schillers, in dem das Wort „wirklich" stets in einer doppelten Bedeutung angewandt werden kann: einmal im Sinn von „tatsächlich", zum zweiten aber im Sinn von „jetzt, gegenwärtig", eine Nuance, die dem Norddeutschen unbekannt ist. (117)

To illustrate her point Wertheim cites several passages of Schiller that are quoted in the *Schwäbisches Wörterbuch*.[85] Schiller's use of the term „Wirklichkeit" to signify present reality and not any "ideal" concept of reality can be verified in *Über naive und sentimentalische Dichtung* where he writes: „In der Satyre wird die Wirklichkeit als Mangel, dem Ideal als der höchsten Realität gegenüber gestellt" (442). Strangely enough, Wertheim overlooks this meaning of „wirklich" when interpreting Schiller's concept of the idyllic. Schiller writes that in the idyll the ideal is applied to „das wirkliche Leben" and, to repeat the central phrase here, engenders a condition in which „*aller Gegensatz der Wirklichkeit mit dem Ideale* [...] vollkommen aufgehoben sey" (472). Like other critics Wertheim interprets the idyll as a future or potential reality; she speaks of an „Idylle der Zukunft" (120).

Another group of interpreters overstresses or misinterprets the naive aspects of the idyll, its stillness and perfection. These critics argue that idyllic perfection must be static and that in this perfection the sentimental process must cease.[86] Perfection would seem comprehensible only as a static condition, yet such perfection is itself deficient: it lacks the positive dynamism of the sentimental. The idyllic, Schiller's highest state, becomes displaced into a world without motion or change, a world beyond history and life. This interpretation transforms the idyll into a wholly naive category, but such a return could hardly have been Schiller's goal. Schiller after all affirms the transition from the naive to the sentimental. To conceive of the idyllic as a static category is to eliminate the extent to which it contains the sentimental

---

[85] VI/I, 874. As additional evidence for her thesis, Wertheim quotes a passage from an early sketch of „Das Reich der Schatten" (122): „Aber laßt die Wirklichkeit zurücke, / Reißt euch los vom Augenblicke etc." Taken from Schiller's letter to Humboldt of September 7, 1795 (NA XXVIII, 45).

[86] For example: Binder (1960), 152–56; Knippel (1909), 41, 72; Rockwell (1980), 50–51; and von Wiese (1965), 180. Oellers can be included in this group, although he suggests that Schiller's exclusion of history from the idyll becomes clear only through a study of *Wallenstein* and *Die Jungfrau von Orleans*. See Oellers (1982), esp. 129. These misreadings arise not so much from the critics one-sidedness as from the shifts of meaning within Schiller's essay. Only a comprehensive account of these changes can do justice to the "true" synthetic nature of the idyllic.

as a moment in itself. Schiller was too much of a Fichtean not to have noticed that the cessation of infinite striving would signify a return to pure nothingness. If one eliminates all opposition, one is left with emptiness. For this reason Schiller emphasizes that idyllic perfection does not and cannot, if it is to remain truly perfect, exclude sentimental striving.[87]

The most prolific and influential writer on the problem of the idyll in German *Klassik* is Gerhard Kaiser.[88] Kaiser notes that Schiller's idyll is characterized by both infinite approximation and perfection, yet Kaiser sees these two moments as disparate. For Kaiser the idyll consists of sentimental longing for a Utopian ideal that can be attained only through death.[89] The idyllic becomes sentimental or naive depending on which moment is stressed: unfulfilled striving or perfection in death. But Schiller does not argue that the idyll represents a sentimental striving which passes over into unity only upon the cessation of striving; such a view contains two separate and unmediated moments; it is not synthetic, but dualistic.[90] Kaiser's rendering of the idyll reads much like the Schillerian elegy in which motion *alternates* with stillness. Kaiser does not recognize in the idyll the synthesis, the dynamic calm or „energische Ruhe", Schiller ascribes to it but rather a „Ruhe *nach* dem Kampf".[91]

---

[87] My discussion of the true idyll suggests that perfection and becoming are not opposed terms. This is different from the Romantic opposition of these categories. Despite the many surface similarities between Schiller and Friedrich Schlegel, the latter argues that the essence of Romantic poetry is that „sie ewig nur werden, nie vollendet sein kann" („Athenäums"-Fragment no. 116 = KA II, 183). For a full account of the Schiller-Schlegel relationship see Brinkmann (1958); Eichner (1955); Jauß (1974); Lovejoy (1920); Meng (1936), 157–60; and Wessell (1971).

[88] The conciseste formulation of Kaiser's views can be found in the chapter „Vergötterung und Tod. Die thematische Einheit von Schillers Werk" in Kaiser (1978), 11–44. But see also 137–38, 165–66, 209 and Kaiser (1977), 90, 93, 105. Kaiser's importance for recent interpretations of Schiller's conception of the idyll can be seen in Gethmann-Siefert's contribution (1980), which consists of a lengthy *Auseinandersetzung* with Kaiser in an attempt to reestablish the Utopian aspect of Schiller's idyll.

[89] Kaiser equates Schiller's concept of idyllic perfection with death, that is, with the cessation of striving and consciousness, but Schiller himself includes in his concept of idyllic perfection a moment of striving („das Gemüth muß befriedigt werden, aber ohne daß das Streben darum aufhöre" 473). See Kaiser (1978), 14, 20, 29, 33.

[90] For Kaiser, the idyll contains *either* motion *or* stillness; the terms are external to one another. Conceptually, his idyll does not differ from a *Flucht in die Ruhe,* in which flight and repose are both considered but simply juxtaposed and not at all mediated.

[91] Kaiser (1978), 29. Emphasis added. Kaiser's misreading of the distinction between the elegy and the idyll is evident when he writes: „und so entrückt die Elegie wie die große Idylle das Ideal an die Todesschwelle, die eine in die Vergangenheit, als

Essentially Kaiser brings to his notion of the idyll two moments, striving and perfection, neither of which in isolation represents a tenable definition of the idyll. Insofar as Kaiser includes both moments, his thesis could be said to represent an advance over previous one-sided interpretations. Yet Kaiser merely juxtaposes the two elements; he does not synthesize them. One could therefore also say that his theory is doubly false. It contains not one but two mistaken views.[92] Schiller himself describes the idyll as a synthesis. The idyll does contain motion and striving but not just these moments;[93] otherwise, it would be solely sentimental. And it does have unity and stillness, but not just these characteristics; otherwise it would be purely naive. The idyll contains both characteristics at once. Its perfection is not, as Kaiser would have it, „ein Ziel jenseits des Weges."[94] Perfection is found in the process. The idyll is circular, complete within itself. It represents real fulfillment in the present, yet this fulfillment or realization does not exhaust itself in the present, for it contains within itself the concept of further striving. As such it is, on the level of symbols, as much a line as a circle; it is both a line that returns into itself and a circle that opens into the future. It is a genuine *coincidentia oppositorum* or in the rhetoric of German Idealism an *Aufhebung*.[95]

---

verlorenes Ideal, die andere in die Zukunft, als zu erzielendes" (Kaiser [1978], 35). But Schiller defines both of these concepts, the past as well as the future ideal, as elegiac, and he specifically differentiates them from the idyll. The elegy, taken in its narrower sense, exhibits either „die Natur" insofar as it is „verloren" or „das Ideal" insofar as it is „unerreicht" (448). David Miles would also restrict Schiller's elegy to a longing for the past. See Miles (1971), 111.

[92] Kaiser's misinterpretation of the concept "idyllic" colors his interpretations of Schiller's dramas. Given the *dynamism* of Schiller's concept of the idyllic, Kaiser's argument that the idyll cannot be realized at the end of *Wilhelm Tell* because „die Geschichte weitergeht" is highly problematic. See Kaiser (1978), 215.

[93] Schiller speaks of infinite approximation not only in *Über naive und sentimentalische Dichtung* but also in his other writings, for example, *Philosophie der Physiologie* (NA XX, 10), *Anmut und Würde* (NA XX, 289), and *Ästhetische Briefe* (NA XX, 343, 353). In the context of Schiller's reflections on the idyllic it is clear that the emphasis on infinite striving does not exclude the possibility of perfection or repose; it merely counters the idea that perfection could be *exhausted* in the present.

[94] Kaiser (1978), 40. In his description of Schiller's idyll Kaiser inexplicably speaks of „der Sprung zwischen Idee und Wirklichkeit" (Kaiser [1978], 196) and contrasts Schiller with Hegel, but, as we have seen, Schiller explicitly states that in the idyll, „aller Gegensatz der Wirklichkeit mit dem Ideale [...] vollkommen aufgehoben sey" (472).

[95] Schiller uses the verb *aufheben* to mean both to preserve and to cancel already in his *Ästhetische Briefe*. See NA XX: 366 and 375. The term also occurs in *Über naive und sentimentalische Dichtung* (472); moreover, the idea that this term evokes is evident in other expressions as well. See, for example, 429. For Hegel's later reflections on the word he made famous, see WL I, 93–95.

The Idyllic as Synthesis

Schiller's idyll then is not a simple return to a past golden age, a sentimental approximation into infinity, an aesthetic anticipation of a future condition, the attainment of a final stage that excludes motion and striving, nor even the transition point between infinite striving and fulfillment in death. Instead, the idyll is an infinite process that is complete or finite at every moment. In keeping with Schiller's preference for organic over mechanistic metaphors,[96] one might in an attempt to reformulate our understanding of the idyllic think of it metaphorically as an organic object: one cannot determine when such an object, say a tree, is complete, for it is complete at all stages and yet it continues to grow. The perfection of the idyll clearly differs, on the other hand, from an artificial object, say a building, which is at any given moment either finished or unfinished. The idyll is fulfillment and extension simultaneously.

Insofar as the idyll synthesizes elements divergent in realism and idealism, one might, to once again reformulate our grasp of this concept, suggest that it consists of the idealist's sense of the whole without sacrificing the realist's attention to detail. The idyllic individual does not, as does the idealist, divorce himself from the world of realization, nor does he restrict himself to fixed and limited ends, as does the realist. The idyll is neither the mere possibility of the idealist nor the mere reality of the realist: rather, it is possibility made real, another *possest,* or in Schiller's description of the divine, „absolute Verkündigung des Vermögens, Wirklichkeit alles Möglichen" (NA XX, 343). *In the idyllic sphere, as in the naive, one actualizes one's possibilities but, as in the sentimental, one also actualizes the possibility of having possibilities not yet realized.* Naive perfection is real or present at all moments in the idyll, yet the present is not a final or static state, for it contains its other, the sentimental moment of becoming, as a part of itself. To argue that if the process is complete there can be no striving, or that if there is striving there can be no completion, is to misunderstand the synthesis. Schiller's essay attempts to overcome not only the false and restrictive oneness of the naive, which the German intellectuals of the period associated with Rousseau's return to nature, it also attempts to eliminate the dissatisfaction and discontent his contemporaries associated with modern striving.

Sentimental pain and the suffering associated with striving are embraced in the idyll not only as conditions for the path to perfection but as themselves a part of perfection itself. *One understands that there ought to be sentimental breaks between what is and what ought to be, so that from a higher vantage point everything*

---

[96] See *Über die nothwendigen Grenzen beim Gebrauch schöner Formen*, NA XXI, 9.

indeed is as it ought to be. Here one might recall Schiller's affirmation of suffering and the is-ought dualism in his essay *Über den Grund des Vergnügens an tragischen Gegenständen*:

> So scheint es eine Zweckwidrigkeit in der Natur zu seyn, daß der Mensch leidet, der doch nicht zum Leiden bestimmt ist, und diese Zweckwidrigkeit thut uns wehe. Aber dieses *Wehethun* der Zweckwidrigkeit ist zweckmäßig für unsere vernünftige Natur überhaupt und, in so fern es uns zur Thätigkeit auffordert, zweckmäßig für die menschliche Gesellschaft. Wir müssen also über die Unlust selbst, welche das Zweckwidrige in uns erregt, nothwendig Lust empfinden, weil jene Unlust zweckmäßig ist. (NA XX, 138)

A psychology based on Schiller's concept of the idyllic would teach that one can be at once content, calm, reconciled to the present and also dissatisfied, in motion, and desirous of more.[97] One is calm, but not static, critical, but not unfulfilled. Conceptually, one could not want more of perfection than a perfection of becoming (thus the reconciliation and the repose); yet knowing that a part of perfection is this becoming, this desire to work towards better conditions in a particular context, one cannot confuse the calm with stasis.

Dynamic Stillness and German Klassik

Schiller's Theoretical Essays

Not only in *Über naive und sentimentalische Dichtung* but in other theoretical writings as well Schiller criticizes a false or static stillness. In one of his earliest essays, „Die Tugend in ihren Folgen betrachtet", Schiller considers „Ruhe der Seele in allen Stürmen des Schiksals" the primary effect of virtue (NA XX, 35). The stillness Schiller values originates not from a denial of worldly concerns but rather from clarity of thought amidst external strife and inner pain. Schiller develops this theme further in his second dissertation, *Versuch über den Zusammenhang der thierischen Natur des Menschen mit seiner Geistigen,* where he writes of Gaius Mucius Scaevola's heroism in convincing the Etruscan king Lars Porsena to make peace with the Romans and withdraw his forces from Rome. Schiller attributes Mucius' endurance of pain to his ability to live „beständig in hellen deutlichen Ideen":

> Nicht Mangel der Empfindung war es, nicht Vernichtung derselben, daß Mucius, die Hand in lohen Flammen bratend, den Feind mit dem römischen Blik der stolzen Ruhe anstarren konnte, sondern der Gedanke des grossen, ihn bewundern-

---

[97] In the language of Fichte's drives one is „zugleich befriedigt und nicht befriedigt" (Fichte I, 291). True contentment does not deny the necessity of that activity which tries to limit dissatisfaction, but nor does it deny dissatisfaction, for it recognizes dissatisfaction as a necessary condition of the possibility of consciousness and of the advancement over nothingness.

den Roms, der in seiner Seele herrschte, hielt sie gleichsam innerhalb ihrer selbst gefangen, daß der heftige Reiz des thierischen Übels zu wenig war sie aus dem Gleichgewicht zu heben. Aber darum war der Schmerz des Römers nicht geringer als der des weichsten Wollüstlings. (NA XX, 46)

Here again Schiller describes not stillness in place of turmoil or activity but rather stillness in the midst of suffering.

Schiller criticizes any concept of *Ruhe* that excludes dynamic involvement. In the short dialogue „Der Jüngling und der Greis", of which Schiller seems to have been a coauthor,[98] Selim, the younger figure, states: „Ruhe ist nicht die Bestimmung unserer Natur [...] Unaufhaltsames Streben ist das Element der Seele." After Selim implies that striving is more fulfilling and enjoyable than stasis, Almar, the elder partner in conversation, responds with a pertinent question: „Du sprichst so viel von Wünschen und Streben, wo bleibt dann dein Genuß? Nach deinen Paradoxen wird dessen Fülle wohl ein Unglück sein." Selim responds: „Allerdings, wenn sie anhaltend wäre." Almar asks if Selim is pursuing a goal he would be afraid to attain. Selim replies: „Ich fürchte es nicht, aber die Seele hört auf zu glühen, die Schwingen der Imagination sinken am Ziele; der Zauber verschwindet [...] Ich fürchte es nicht, Almar, weil neue erhabnere Ziele mir wieder entgegenwinken, meine Laufbahn ist die Ewigkeit." This early text shows remarkable insight into what Schiller will later describe as the tension between naive fulfillment and sentimental striving. Already in 1782 Schiller recognizes that stagnation commences as soon as one's goals are exhausted. In *Über naive und sentimentalische Dichtung* Schiller advances his position to suggest that there is enjoyment, even perfection, in this nonattainment of a final goal, so that one's goal is in effect no longer the exhaustion of one's original goal, but rather, paradoxically, the nonexhaustion of this goal or unceasing activity. That Schiller, with his dynamic and dramatic world-view, would invoke *Ruhe* as an absolute in *Über naive und sentimentalische Dichtung* speaks for the highly positive associations of the word at that time in German history. It is also evidence of the contemporary tendency to use *Ruhe* as a synthetic term. Idyllic *Ruhe* means everything but simple repose.

The affirmation of dynamism in Schiller's theoretical writings shows significant parallels to Fichte, as I have suggested earlier. Schiller had read Fichte's deliberations on the ego and the non-ego. He was familiar with Fichte's argument that the ego is itself active only insofar as it is confronted by the limiting activity of the non-ego. This activity (*Thätigkeit*) of the non-ego upon the ego places the ego in a position of passivity (*Leiden*). The metaphysical discourse in which Fichte discusses the passivity (*Leiden*) or activity of the ego is different from the traditional discourse of a philosophy

---

[98] See NA XXII, 371. The entire text can be found in NA XXII, 79–81.

of the passions (*Philosophie der Affekte*) in which suffering (*Leiden*) plays a dominant role. The same word „Leiden" has two very different meanings for two distinct branches of philosophy. Yet, during the period of German Idealism and shortly thereafter, these two discourses seem to melt into one, so that Schiller, for example, thinks of the actual passion of suffering, not the metaphysical principle of passivity or relationship to otherness, as the force that generates the ego's striving and activity. Schiller displays his familiarity with Fichte's metaphysical discourse on the reciprocal relationship of passivity and activity in the ego and non-ego when he writes in the *Kallias-Briefe*:[99]

> Wir verhalten uns gegen die Natur (als Erscheinung) entweder *leidend* oder *thätig,* oder leidend und thätig *zugleich.* / *leidend:* wenn wir ihre Wirkungen bloß *empfinden; thätig:* wenn wir ihre Wirkungen bestimmen; beides *zugleich,* wenn wir sie uns *vorstellen.*

In a passage from the nineteenth of his *Ästhetische Briefe* Schiller again makes this Fichtean point: „Der endliche Geist ist derjenige, der nicht anders, als durch Leiden thätig wird, nur durch Schranken zum Absoluten gelangt, nur insofern er Stoff empfängt, handelt und bildet" (NA XX, 371). Yet in his essay *Über den Grund des Vergnügens an tragischen Gegenständen* Schiller suggests that it is actual suffering, i. e., „Leiden" or „Wehetun", not passivity, that inspires „Thätigkeit" (NA XX, 138).

Suffering is a central concept in all of Schiller's essays on dignity, tragedy, and the sublime. In *Über das Pathetische* Schiller writes that the depiction of suffering is the means to the end of art, which he defines as portrayal of the supersensible or man's stillness in suffering (NA XX, 196). Schiller raises this idea to a formula when he writes:[100] „Das erste Gesetz der tragischen Kunst war Darstellung der leidenden Natur. Das zweyte ist Darstellung des moralischen Widerstandes gegen das Leiden" (NA XX, 199). As in Schiller's earliest writings, the dominant idea is one not of avoidance but of endurance of pain, not escape from suffering but immersion in it:

> Die Helden sind für alle Leiden der Menschheit so gut empfindlich als andere, und eben das macht sie zu Helden, daß sie das Leiden stark und innig fühlen, und doch nicht davon überwältigt werden [...] Nirgends sucht der Grieche in der Abstumpfung und Gleichgültigkeit gegen das Leiden seinen Ruhm, sondern in *Ertragung* desselben bey allem Gefühl für dasselbe. (NA XX, 198)

Schiller's affirmation of suffering and in particular of stillness in suffering helps explain his attraction to Laocoon, whom he mentions not only in *Über das Pathetische* (NA XX, 197) but also in strophes twelve and thirteen of „Das Ideal und das Leben" and already in *Über Anmuth und Würde,* where Schiller, following Winckelmann's lead, describes how in Laocoon „Züge der Ruhe

---

[99] Letter to Körner of February 8, 1793 (Jonas III, 240).
[100] Cf. NA XX, 192–95.

unter die Züge des Schmerzes gemischt sind". Schiller states, it is this „*Ruhe im Leiden,* als worinn die Würde eigentlich besteht" (NA XX, 296). In *Über das Erhabene* Schiller suggests that one can overcome the dominance of the physical world over consciousness, that one can transform suffering into understood necessity or freedom:

> Kann er also den physischen Kräften keine verhältnißmäßige physische Kraft mehr entgegen setzen, so bleibt ihm, um keine Gewalt zu erleiden, nichts anderes übrig, als: *ein Verhältniß,* welches ihm so nachtheilig ist, *ganz und gar aufzuheben,* und eine Gewalt, die er der That nach erleiden muß, *dem Begriff nach zu vernichten.* Eine Gewalt dem Begriffe nach vernichten, heißt aber nichts anders, als sich derselben freywillig unterwerfen. (NA XXI, 39).

Schiller's notion of *stillness in suffering* coupled with his affirmation of that very *engagement* which leads man inevitably into *suffering* brings us back to the idyllic notion of a synthesis of stillness and motion. Schiller's concept of the idyllic in *Über naive und sentimentalische Dichtung* need not be seen in isolation from his other theoretical essays.

Schiller's Drama

In his dramas Schiller attacks any social peace or *Ruhe* achieved through either oppression from above or apathy from below.[101] In a short footnote on freedom and culture in his *Universalhistorische Übersicht* Schiller writes:

> Ruhe ist die Bedingung der Kultur, aber nichts ist der Freiheit gefährlicher als Ruhe. Alle verfeinerte Nationen des Altertums haben die Blüte ihrer Kultur mit ihrer Freiheit erkauft, *weil sie ihre Ruhe von der Unterdrückung erhielten.* (SA XIII, 118)

Ruhe, although necessary for culture, is invalid if attained through oppression. *Don Carlos,* which contains Schiller's most famous polemic for freedom,[102] depicts despotic *Ruhe* in the empire of King Philipp II. When the activist Posa arrives, Elisabeth greets him with the words: „Ich zweifle sehr, ob Sie / Sich werden können in Madrid gefallen. / Man ist sehr – ruhig in

---

[101] In this study I do not attempt to isolate naive, sentimental, or idyllic moments in Schiller's dramas. For recent studies along these lines see Frye (1984), Hinderer (1981), Kaiser (1978), Martini (1972), Sautermeister (1971), Siekmann (1980), and Völker (1976). Instead I focus on the critique in his dramas of a false idyll. I will, however, in my second chapter provide a detailed illustration of Schiller's concept of the idyllic, for Hölderlin's *Hyperion* is both an example and a modulation of Schiller's true idyll.

[102] Seidlin (1960) relates the interesting story that viewers of *Don Carlos* in Hamburg during the first years of Hitler's reign applauded when Posa was supposed to deliver the famous line „Geben Sie Gedankenfreiheit!", even though the line was censored (31). The audience knew exactly where the line belonged, even when it was left unspoken.

Madrid" (519–21). In the famous exchange between King Philipp and Posa in Act III, scene 10, the King praises this very *Ruhe*. Posa, however, calls it the tranquillity of a graveyard:

> König. […] Sehet
> In meinem Spanien Euch um. Hier blüht
> Des Bürgers Glück in nie bewölktem Frieden;
> Und *diese Ruhe* gönn' ich den Flamändern.
> Marquis. (schnell)
> Die Ruhe eines Kirchhofs!
> (3158–62)

In his critique of political quietude Schiller targets not only the ruler who forces quietude upon his people but also the subjects who are idle, unaware, asleep.[103] In his dramas he thematizes the desire of the hero or heroine to *withdraw* from society and enter into an apolitical way of life, as in *Die Räuber, Die Verschwörung des Fiesco zu Genua, Kabale und Liebe,* and *Don Carlos*,[104] as well as the possibility of *continuing* to live a self-contained existence independent of any major social or civic responsibilities, as in *Die Jungfrau von Orleans* or *Wilhelm Tell*.

In *Die Räuber* Karl Moor experiences the temptation to return to a limited but peaceful existence together with his beloved: „Im Schatten meiner väterlichen Haine, in den Armen meiner Amalia lockt mich ein edler Vergnügen" (I, 2). He later laments his inability to return to such a pastoral existence: „O ihr Tage des Friedens! […] O all ihr Elysiumszenen meiner Kindheit! – Werdet ihr nimmer zurückkehren – […] Dahin! Dahin! unwiederbringlich!"[105] Moor's loss enables him to enter a sphere in which the ideals of freedom and brotherhood are invoked, yet it also forces him into a reality of destruction and injustice.

Schiller's second drama, *Fiesco,* also portrays the conflict of the private sphere of withdrawal and quietude with the social sphere of ideals and politics. The central confrontation takes place in Act IV, scene 14. Leonore perceives an either-or tension between her private relationship with Fiesco and his role in the public arena, as a potential duke: „Mein Gemahl ist hin,

---

[103] In his letter to Herzog von Augustenburg on July 13, 1793, Schiller terms „Erschlaffung" one of the two great evils of his day: „was für ein Bild ist das, das sich im Spiegel der jetzigen Zeit uns darstellt? Hier die empörendste Verwilderung, dort das entgegengesetzte Extrem der Erschlaffung: die zwey traurigsten Verirrungen, in die der Menschenkarakter versinken kann, in Einer Epoche vereint!" (Jonas III, 333). Throughout the final version of the *Ästhetische Briefe* Schiller criticizes passivity, unawareness, and quietude in the form of *Ruhe* or „Erschlaffung". See esp. nos. 5, 10, and 17.
[104] I do not discuss *Wallenstein* in this particular section, but note the opportunity Max gives Wallenstein to leave the stage of history and politics (*Wallensteins Tod,* II, 2)
[105] III, 2. See also IV, 1.

wenn ich den Herzog umarme." On a more abstract level she defines the schism as one between „Liebe" and „Herrschsucht"; she elaborates: „*Liebe* hat *Tränen* und kann Tränen *verstehen; Herrschsucht* hat eherne Augen, worin ewig nie die Empfindung perlt [...] *Herrschsucht* zerträmmert die Welt in ein rasselndes Kettenhaus, *Liebe* träumt sich in jede Wüste Elysium." Leonore would be willing to sacrifice „Liebe" and „Ruhe" if only Fiesco would remain unchanged, but she senses that love and peace will remain forever in conflict with his political ambitions: „Ich würde sagen, opfre die *Liebe* der Größe, opfre die *Ruhe* – wenn nur Fiesco noch bleibt – Gott! Das ist Radstoß!" So Leonore must call upon Fiesco to leave the political sphere altogether: „Laß uns fliehen." Leonore's appeal clearly disturbs Fiesco; the stage directions describe him as „durch und durch erschüttert". But Fiesco chooses politics over love; unwittingly and dramatically slaying Leonore, Fiesco kills himself as a lover as well. Leonore's apolitical stance would seem to rank higher than Fiesco's political demagogery (Verrina calls him „Genuas gefährlichsten Tyrann" (III, 2), yet her position of total withdrawal seems spurious as well. She restricts love to a wholly private sphere: „*Liebe* hat nur *ein* Gut, tut Verzicht auf die ganze übrige Schöpfung." Leonore's view contrasts with Schiller's own interpretation of love as a force that transcends isolation and unites all creation:

> Egoismus errichtet seinen Mittelpunkt in sich selber; Liebe pflanzt ihn außerhalb ihrer in die Achse des ewigen Ganzen. Liebe zielt nach Einheit, Egoismus ist Einsamkeit. Liebe ist die mitherrschende Bürgerin eines blühenden Freistaats, Egoismus ein Despot in einer verwüsteten Schöpfung. (NA XX, 123)

Here in the *Philosophische Briefe* love is not restrictive, but expansive: „Begierde nach fremder Glükseligkeit nennen wir Wohlwollen, *Liebe*" (NA XX, 119). Schiller's corpus relativizes then not only Fiesco's drive for power but also Leonore's vision of isolation.

The possibility of withdrawal arises in *Kabale und Liebe* as well, in particular in Act III, scene 4, where Ferdinand, in a call reminiscent of Leonore's, asks Luise to flee with him into a private sphere of love: „*Du, Luise, und ich* und die *Liebe*! – Liegt nicht in diesem Zirkel der ganze Himmel? oder brauchst du noch etwas Viertes dazu?" Here, too, love is strangely restrictive, a set number, a closed circle. Such love limits Ferdinand's view of the state; his country becomes nothing more than a private relationship: „Mein Vaterland ist, wo mich Luise liebt." In Ferdinand's eyes his most sacred duty is to secure Luise's „Ruhe". But Luise refuses to flee into the tranquil existence Ferdinand envisages. She speaks of her own and also of his commitments to her father, to Ferdinand's father, indeed to the global order itself. She is willing to renounce a union, „das die Fugen der Bürgerwelt auseinandertreiben und die allgemeine ewige Ordnung zugrund stürzen würde." Her concern corresponds to the outward love defined in the

Philosophische Briefe, not the restrictive love we see in Ferdinand and Leonore. In the final act Ferdinand does attain „Ruhe", but not for Luise, rather for himself, and not the pastoral „Ruhe" he originally desired, but the empty stillness that follows total destruction: „Ich bin ja ruhig – ruhig, sagt man ja, ist auch der schaudernde Strich Landes, worüber die Pest ging – ich bins" (V, 2).

Private love and social responsibility conflict as well for the title figure of Schiller's next play, *Don Carlos*. Carlos' wish for a relationship with Elisabeth, his love for her, or as Marquis Posa puts it, his love for himself, prevents him from fulfilling the political task of working with Posa for the freedom of Flanders. Posa attacks Carlos for his restrictive love:

> Einst war's ganz anders. Da warst du so reich,
> So warm, so reich! Ein ganzer Weltkreis hatte
> In deinem weiten Busen Raum. Das alles
> Ist nun dahin, von *einer* Leidenschaft,
> Von einem kleinen Eigennutz verschlungen.
> Dein Herz ist ausgestorben. Keine Träne
> Dem ungeheurn Schicksal der Provinzen,
> Nicht einmal eine Träne mehr – O Karl,
> Wie arm bist du, wie bettelarm geworden,
> Seitdem du niemand liebst als dich! (2415–23)

Earlier Elisabeth had inspired Carlos to sacrifice his love of her for the love of mankind. While a tension between individual love and political action was evident, individual love seemed capable of inspiring political activity. The Queen had told Carlos:

> Die Liebe ist Ihr großes Amt [...]
> [...] Elisabeth
> War Ihre erste Liebe. Ihre zwote
> Sei Spanien! Wie gerne, guter Karl,
> Will ich der besseren Geliebten weichen! (787–94)

Carlos had thereupon told Posa: „Ich bin entschlossen. Flandern sei gerettet. / Sie will es – das ist mir genug" (901–02). Carlos' relationship to the Queen parallels Posa's relationship to Carlos. With Carlos the process takes much longer, and he suffers several setbacks, but in the end he transforms his love of an individual into love of mankind. What applies to Posa also applies in the end to Carlos: „An die Stelle eines Individuums tritt bei ihm jetzt das ganze Geschlecht; ein vorübergehender jugendlicher Affekt erweitert sich in eine allumfassende unendliche Philanthropie."[106] Carlos' insight, which he expresses to the Queen, is too late: „Mutter, endlich seh ich ein, / Es gibt ein höher, wünschenswerter Gut, / Als dich besitzen" (5320–22). Nonetheless,

---

[106] *Briefe über Don Carlos,* no. 3.

the development is evident: he would sacrifice his enclosure in a false and restrictive idyll for political activity.

Johanna, too, must leave a private existence in order to become an important figure in the public arena. In the prologue to *Die Jungfrau von Orleans* she announces her departure: „Ihr traulich stillen Täler lebet wohl! / [...] / Ihr Pläzte all meiner stillen Freuden, / Euch lass' ich hinter mir auf immerdar." (384; 393–94). In order to carry out her vast goals, she must not only leave her original, naive existence but also refrain from entering into any restrictive and binding relationship with a particular individual.[107] As a vehement critic of „müß'ge Ruh",[108] she stands in sharp contrast to other village members. Thibaut, her father, prefers to stay away from political conflict:

> [...] Wir
> Sind friedliche Landleute [...]
> [...] Laßt uns still gehorchen harren,
> Wen uns der Sieg zum König wird.
> [...] Und denke jeder
> Nur an das Nächste! Lassen wir die Großen,
> Der Erde Fürsten um die Erde losen;
> Wir können ruhig die Zerstörung schauen,
> Denn sturmfest steht der Boden, den wir bauen. (366–78)

King Karl, a figure satirized for sitting „in tatenloser Ruhe" while Orleans is threatened (441), contrasts with Johanna as well. He envisages a return to the medieval notion of love: „Er will die alten Zeiten wieder bringen, / Wo zarte Minne herrschte" (517–18). Dunois corrects his vision of *pastoral* love: „Wie ich / Aus jenen alten Büchern mir gelesen, / War Liebe stets mit hoher Rittertat / Gepaart, und Helden, hat man mich gelehrt, / Nicht Schäfer saßen an der Tafelrunde" (539–43). Johanna moves so far beyond her idyllic origins that she not only fights, but falls in love with, the enemy. In her love for Lionel she would overcome not only a false or restrictive idyll but also a limiting heroism (III, 10; IV, 1).

The development of the hero in Schiller's final completed drama, *Wilhelm Tell*, parallels that of Johanna, insofar as he, too, must leave an originally restrictive sphere associated with *Ruhe* and take on civic responsibilities. In Tell's first public words to his fellow village-members, he preaches withdrawal and individualism: „Ein jeder lebe still bei sich daheim, / Dem Friedlichen gewährt man gern den Frieden" (427–28). But in the face of clear conflict Tell relinquishes his restrictive existence, his praise of „Geduld und Schweigen" (420), for social responsibility: „Es kann der Frömmste nicht im Frieden bleiben, / Wenn es dem bösen Nachbar nicht gefällt" (2683–84).

---

[107] Prologue 4; I, 10; III, 4.
[108] III, 3; III, 4.

Here, as at the end of Lessing's *Emilia Galotti* and in Act III of *Maria Stuart*,[109] tolerance reaches its own limits. Stauffacher had asked early in the play: „Soll man ertragen, was unleidlich ist?" (421).[110] Attinghausen develops this theme of the limits of tolerance and suggests later: „Sie sollen kommen, uns ein Joch aufzwingen, / Das wir entschlossen sind, *nicht* zu ertragen!" (912–13). Tell's and his friends' awakening to suffering and to the limits of suffering as well as Tell's own advancement to the sphere of intersubjectivity help make possible both a life of higher freedom and an overcoming of internal tensions.

These brief comments on Schiller's critique of quietude through oppression, withdrawal into a restrictive idyllic sphere, and apathy, substantiate the thesis that for Schiller *Ruhe* is positive only insofar as it contains within itself action, involvement, dynamism.

Schiller's Poetry

An idyllic synthesis of sentimental motion and naive stillness can also be found in Schiller's lyrical writings. Walter Silz (1959) has suggested that in Schiller's poetry the sentimental play of oppositions tends to dominate over naive simplicity. Besides the antithetical structure of most of his poems one can also observe a sentimental content. In the „Sprüche des Konfuzius", for example, one hears:

> Rastlos vorwärts mußt du streben,
> Nie ermüdet stille stehn,
> Willst du die Vollendung sehn. (SA I, 213)

Such moments of motion are often superseded by a higher form of stillness. A couplet of „Die Worte des Glaubens" reads:

> Und ob alles in ewigem Wechsel kreist,
> Es beharret im Wechsel ein ruhiger Geist. (SA I, 164)

Unfortunately, critics have spoken of the idyllic in Schiller's poetry only with reference to Schiller's plan, first announced in his letter to Humboldt of November 29, 1795, to write an idyll depicting the marriage of Heracles and Hebe, the „Übertritt des Menschen in den Gott" (NA XXVIII, 119). Schiller's supposed inability to successfully carry out this project has been taken as evidence of the impossibility of writing or of even conceiving of an

---

[109] When Maria Stuart reaches the bounds of her tolerance, she expresses pride in the face of Elisabeth's power: „Mäßigung! ich habe / Ertragen, was ein Mensch ertragen kann. / Fahr hin, lammherzige Gelassenheit, / Zum Himmel fliehe, leidende Geduld, / Spreng' endlich deine Bande, tritt hervor / Aus deiner Höhle, langverhaltner Groll" (2436–40).

[110] See also I, 4 and II, 2.

idyll.[111] But there is no reason to restrict the idyllic to this one motif.[112] Indeed, Schiller's pathos-ridden evocation of the idyll in this letter – his wish to eliminate both sentimental striving and naive reality – conflicts with his own definition of the idyll in *Über naive und sentimentalische Dichtung*. In his essay Schiller wanted to synthesize the ideal and the real, sentimental striving and naive contentment. In the letter to Humboldt he gleefully writes of an empty condition absolved of striving and reality: „alles Sterbliche ausgelöscht, lauter Licht, lauter Freyheit, lauter Vermögen – keinen Schatten, keine Schranke, nichts von dem allen mehr zu sehen" (NA XXVIII, 120). These external reflections should hardly be taken as Schiller's most analytic or credible statement on the category of the idyllic. For illustrations of the idyllic, one should focus not on the one motif of Hercules and Hebe but on the widespread synthesis of motion and rest throughout Schiller's writings.[113] Schiller's elegy „Der Tanz" (SA I, 120–21), for example, portrays the idyllic synthesis of stillness and motion and was written the same year as *Über naive und sentimentalische Dichtung*. Here the poet describes a dance; in particular he focuses his attention on the seeming dissolution and clear resolution of harmony in the dancers' motions. The poet then draws an analogy between the harmony of the dance and the cosmos:[114]

> Ewig zerstört, es erzeugt sich ewig die drehende Schöpfung,
> Und ein stilles Gesetz lenkt der Verwandlungen Spiel.

Explicitly the poet tells us: „Die Ruhe besteht in der bewegten Gestalt." The synthesis of stillness and motion in the aesthetic sphere, „im Spiele", as well as in the cosmos is taken in the last line of the poem as a model for social action. The „du" in the poem recognizes the harmony of the dance, but not „die Harmonien des Weltalls".[115] A criticism of this blindness is implicit in the poem's conclusion:

> Das du im Spiele doch ehrst, fliehst du im Handeln das Maß.

Dynamic stillness is not simply an aesthetic ideal, confined to the realm of dance or play; it is an ethical ideal as well.

---

[111] See the discussion following the essay by Habel (1975) on Heracles, esp. 84.
[112] For a *heros* who successfully incorporates the idyllic synthesis of negativity and repose one might think not of Heracles in his marriage with Hebe but of Oedipus in the last hours of his life, as he becomes reconciled with the gods – more on this later.
[113] Concerning the idyllic aspects of *Wilhelm Tell* Wertheim (1959) has written: „‚Wilhelm Tell' hat die geplante Idylle von Herakles im Olymp verdrängt" (134). She also makes the interesting suggestion that the transference of the idyll from Olympia to Switzerland was Schiller's way of stressing reality over transcendence.
[114] For an analysis see Düsing (1969), 213–15.
[115] The notion of the „Harmonien des Weltalls" harks back to the Pythagorean idea of a *harmonia* of the heavens, a music of the spheres.

The idyllic synthesis of stillness and motion has an overarching presence throughout Schiller's theoretical, dramatic, and lyrical writings, even if the critics' inflated discussion of the Heracles–Hebe project might tempt one to think otherwise.

Goethe

The synthesis of stillness and fluidity is central to not only Schiller's but Goethe's writings as well. As Peter Szondi (1972) has argued, Schiller saw in Goethe an exemplary synthesis of naive and sentimental characteristics. Thus, it is no surprise to find throughout Goethe's works the concept of dynamic stillness. In *Faust* Goethe emphasizes sentimental dynamism. The character Faust equates stillness with the loss of life's meaning.

> Werd' ich beruhigt je mich auf ein Faulbett legen,
> So sei es gleich um mich getan! (1692–93)

Not only Faust, but the Lord, too, notes the dangers of a deficient stillness:

> Des Menschen Tätigkeit kann allzuleicht erschlaffen,
> Er liebt sich bald die unbedingte Ruh;
> Drum geb' ich gern ihm den Gesellen zu,
> Der reizt und wirkt und muß als Teufel schaffen. (340–43)

The greatest sin in this Lord's universe would seem to be rest, stasis, acceptance of the status quo; he invokes a principle of negativity, a „Geist des Widerspruchs" (4030), to drive man forward. Hegel, who was fond of Goethe's writings and openly expressed his indebtedness to him,[116] also spoke of the driving force of contradiction, calling it „die Wurzel aller Bewegung und Lebendigkeit; nur insofern etwas in sich selbst einen Widerspruch hat, bewegt es sich, hat Trieb und Tätigkeit" (WL II, 58).[117] Goethe himself discusses this topic with Eckermann on March 28, 1827, and states: „Das Gleiche läßt uns in Ruhe; aber der Widerspruch ist es, der uns produktiv macht" (Eckermann, 601). Sentimental negativity and infinite

---

[116] See Hegel's letter to Goethe of April 24, 1825, in which he writes: „wenn ich den Gang meiner geistigen Entwicklung übersehe, sehe ich Sie überall darein verflochten und mag mich einen Ihrer Söhne nennen" (*Briefe von und an Hegel,* III, 83). See also Goethe's letters to Knebel of November 14, 1827, and to Zelter of March 11, 1832 (*Goethes Briefe,* III, 260; IV, 477).

[117] Schelling, too, suggests that the transition from stasis to motion takes place by way of contradiction. He writes in *Die Weltalter:* „Die Menschen zeigen im Leben sich keiner Sache abgeneigter als dem Widerspruch, der sie zu handeln zwingt und aus ihrer behaglichen Ruhe nöthigt [...] was schlechthin nicht verstattet nicht zu wirken, was zum Handeln treibt, ja zwingt, ist allein der Widerspruch. Ohne Widerspruch also wäre keine Bewegung, kein Leben, kein Fortschritt, sondern ewiger Stillstand, ein Todesschlummer aller Kräfte" (VIII, 219).

activity dominate in *Faust*. Even when Faust contemplates suicide, he desires ultimately to enter into „neuen Sphären reiner Tätigkeit" (705).

In a conversation with Eckermann on February 4, 1829, Goethe suggests that continuous striving guarantees immortality. This notion of eternal activity finds poetic expression in the poem „Eins und Alles" (HA I, 369):

Und umzuschaffen das Geschaffne,
Damit sich's nicht zum Starren waffne.
Wirkt ewiges lebendiges Tun.
Und was nicht war, nun will es werden,
Zu reinen Sonnen, farbigen Erden,
In keinem Falle darf es ruhn.

While Goethe never tired of portraying constant motion[118] or stressing its virtues, from his early poem „Rastlose Liebe" to his later „Sprüche",[119] he never identified with Faustian dissatisfaction.[120] Goethe lashes out against what he calls the „Lazarettpoesie" of his contemporaries who speak only of „dem Leiden und dem Jammer der Erde [...] Das ist ein wahrer Mißbrauch der Poesie, die uns doch eigentlich dazu gegeben ist, um die kleinen Zwiste des Lebens auszugleichen und den Menschen mit der Welt und seinem Zustand zufrieden zu machen."[121] Goethe is of course beyond Faust when he exclaims in „Vermächtnis": „Der Augenblick ist Ewigkeit" (HA I, 370). Faust, but not Goethe, is:

Der Unmensch ohne Zweck und Ruh'
Der wie ein Wassersturz von Fels zu Felsen brauste
Begierig wütend nach dem Abgrund zu. (3349–51)

In killing Philemon und Baucis, Faust destroys a potential part of himself, a moment of repose that Goethe himself was not willing to relinquish. In Goethe's world-view Faust's extreme restlessness is complemented by the tranquillity of Iphigenie and her sense of moderation.[122] Moments of repose and moderation can be located elsewhere in Goethe's writings as well: in the

---

[118] Butler (1935) has written that Goethe's lyrical poetry "is more dynamic than that of any other poet in the world" (69).
[119] See, for example, the following two „Sprüche" (HA I, 305–06):
Die endliche Ruhe wird nur verspürt,
Sobald der Pol den Pol berührt.
Drum danket Gott, ihr Söhne der Zeit,
Daß er die Pole für ewig entzweit.
[120] See Kaufmann's discussion of this in his essays "Goethe and the History of Ideas" and "Goethe's Faith and Faust's Redemption" in Kaufmann (1960), 51–76.
[121] Eckermann, 268 (September 24, 1827).
[122] Schiller by the way speaks of the „Ruhe" embodied in *Iphigenie*: „Man kann dieses Stück nicht lesen, ohne sich von einem gewissen Geiste des Altertums angeweht zu fühlen, der für eine bloße, auch die gelungenste Nachahmung viel zu wahr, viel zu lebendig ist. Man findet hier die imponierende große *Ruhe*, die jede Antike so unerreichbar macht" (NA XXII, 212). More than a decade after writing this

„schöne Seele" episode of *Wilhelm Meisters Lehrjahre*,[123] for example, or in the description of „ein ruhig Volk in stillem Fleiße" in the poem „Illmenau" (HA I, 112).

In much of Goethe's late poetry the two moments of naive tranquillity and sentimental activity take on still greater prominence and are united in the same work. Goethe's „Dauer im Wechsel" unites motion and permanency, the latter being attained through art („die Gunst der Musen"), love („Gehalt"), or reason („Form") (HA I, 248). The sonnet „Mächtiges Überraschen" opens with the image of a river racing to the ocean. The river then reaches a mountain wall that limits its passage. The third stanza of the poem describes the resulting condition:

> Die Welle sprüht und staunt zurück und weichet
> Und schwillt bergan, sich immer selbst zu trinken;
> Gehemmt ist nun zum Vater hin das Streben. (HA I, 294)

The final stanza describes the sudden stillness of the stream as itself the beginning of a new form of life, one symbolic of divinity on earth. The heavens are reflected not in the fast moving stream but in the still lake:

> Sie schwankt und ruht, zum See zurückgedeichet;
> Gestirne, spiegelnd sich, beschaun das Blinken
> Des Wellenschlags am Fels, ein neues Leben.

Finally, the poem „Wenn im Unendlichen" opens with a description of infinite flux and motion, pure sentimental dynamism:

> Wenn im Unendlichen dasselbe
> Sich wiederholend ewig fließt,
> Das tausendfältige Gewölbe
> Sich kräftig ineinander schließt,
> Strömt Lebenslust aus allen Dingen,
> Dem kleinsten wie dem größten Stern,

---

review, Schiller still noted the stillness of Goethe's play, yet here, in his letter to Körner from January 21, 1802, he criticizes this stillness insofar as it excludes dynamism: „Ich habe mich sehr gewundert, daß sie auf mich den günstigen Eindruck nicht mehr gemacht hat, wie sonst [...] die sinnliche Kraft, das Leben, die Bewegung und alles, was ein Werk zu einem ächten dramatischen specificirt, geht ihr sehr ab" (Jonas VI, 335).

[123] The Goethe-Schiller correspondence on *Wilhelm Meister* originated simultaneously with Schiller's study of the naive and the sentimental. Schiller's own experience of Goethe's novel reflects a happy conflation of repose and unrest: „Ich bin beunruhigt und bin befriedigt, Verlangen und Ruhe sind wunderbar vermischt" (NA XXVIII, 232). Moreover, the hero of the novel synthesizes idealism and realism. Schiller writes to Goethe: „er tritt von einem leeren und unbestimmten Ideal in ein bestimmtes thätiges Leben, aber ohne die idealisierende Kraft dabey einzubüßen" (NA XXVIII, 254). For further discussion of *Wilhelm Meister* as a unity of the naive and the sentimental see Barner (1983), 90–93, 108, and Borchmeyer (1978), 313–14.

The poem closes, however, with a sense of the stillness of the whole, located in God, reminiscent in fact of Schiller's „Die Worte des Glaubens", if not also of the Aristotelian concept of an unmoved mover:

> Und alles Drängen, alles Ringen
> Ist ewige Ruh in Gott dem Herrn. (HA I, 367)

Hegel

The synthesis of stillness and motion, clearly important for Goethe and Schiller, is equally central for Hegel, whom one might want to call the philosopher of German *Klassik*.[124] For Hegel the absolute is not a "naive" state of „bewegungslose Sichselbstgleichheit" (WL I, 138) as with the early Schelling, nor is it the pure approximation of an infinitely distant goal as with Kant and Fichte. Hegel reverses the assumptions of sentimental consciousness, according to which „das Absolute müsse weit jenseits liegen", and argues that it is „das ganz Gegenwärtige" (Hegel 8, 85). The Hegelian infinite is present: „Es ist und ist da, präsent, gegenwärtig" (WL I, 138).[125] In affirming the present and particular, Hegel likes to quote from Goethe's poetry[126] and even uses a poetic image himself in one passage where he attacks the "sentimental" ethics of Kant: „Die Lorbeeren des bloßen Wollens sind trockene Blätter, die niemals gegrünt haben" (Hegel 7, 236).

Both becoming and perfection, motion and stillness, play major roles in Hegel's philosophy. Like few philosophers before or since, Hegel stresses the concepts of becoming and motion. One thinks of the shifts of consciousness in the *Phänomenologie des Geistes,* the transitions of categories in the *Wissen-*

---

[124] The difference between *Klassik* and Romanticism in Germany is not one between „Vollendung" or „Ruhe" on the one side and „Unendlichkeit" or „Bewegung" on the other. See Fritz Strich's famous contrast (1924), esp. 1–15. Such a view clearly does injustice to Faustian moments in Goethe and dramatic elements in Schiller.

[125] Many similarities exist between Schiller's notion of the "idyll" and Hegel's concept of a "true infinite". Hegel's attacks on the genre of the idyll in his *Vorlesungen über die Ästhetik"* (Hegel 13: 250, 335–36; 15: 390–92, 414) should not be confused with a critique of Schiller's speculative concept of the idyll, for Schiller's definition likewise includes a critique of the traditional idyll. Von Wiese (1965) loses sight of this when pointing out differences between Hegel and Schiller (182). Several articles on the relationship between Schiller and Hegel have appeared in the past two decades. See also Böhler (1972), Rohrmoser (1959), and esp. Hoffheimer (1985), who notes that Hegel subscribed to *Die Horen* when he was in Bern and therefore would have received the three installments of *Über naive und sentimentalische Dichtung.* In this context see also Hegel's statement in his *Ästhetik* that Schiller was the first thinker to overcome Kant's dualisms (Hegel 13, 89).

[126] See Hegel 7, 65 and 8, 170. See also Kaufmann's suggestion that Goethe's views on striving "probably helped to inspire [...] Hegel's contrast between the 'good' and the 'bad' infinite" (1960: 56).

schaft der Logik, and the stages in the Hegelian understanding of history or of the history of philosophy.[127] For Hegel everything finite is unstable and must pass over into its other. It falls prey to its own „Unruhe" (WL I, 115). Yet Hegel is also the philosopher of the whole, a whole that sees the culmination of history at each present stage and grasps this present in its stillness and perfection. Motion without stillness is nothing other than the Hegelian "bad infinite". Slightly reminiscent of Schiller's dance as a synthesis of stillness and motion is the Hegelian concept of a bacchanalian revel:

> Das Wahre ist so der bacchantische Taumel, an dem kein Glied nicht trunken ist; und weil jedes, indem es sich absondert, ebenso unmittelbar [sich] auflöst, ist er ebenso die durchsichtige und einfache Ruhe. In dem Gerichte jener Bewegung bestehen zwar die einzelnen Gestalten des Geistes wie die bestimmten Gedanken nicht, aber sie sind so sehr auch positive notwendige Momente, als sie negativ und verschwindend sind. – In dem *Ganzen* der Bewegung, es als Ruhe aufgefaßt, ist dasjenige, was sich in ihr unterscheidet und besonderes Dasein gibt, als ein solches, das sich *erinnert,* aufbewahrt, dessen Dasein das Wissen von sich selbst ist, wie dieses ebenso unmittelbar Dasein ist. (Hegel 3, 46–47)

The differences between Hegel, Schiller, and Goethe of course cannot be overlooked and are obvious to the knowledgeable reader. One thinks, for example, of Schiller's triad of Nature-Art-Ideal (NA XX, 558) as opposed to the Hegelian triad of Idea-Nature-Spirit, also of the aesthetic means Schiller would engage in delineating and achieving an absolute synthesis as opposed to the Hegelian emphasis on logic and philosophical rigor[128] or Goethe's general mistrust of philosophical systems and his emphasis on experience and ocular knowing. But despite these and numerous other differences the sense of a synthesis of stillness and motion seems common to all three writers.[129] Another figure of this classical period who tried to bridge the

---

[127] Note, for example, the following passage from the *Vorlesungen über die Geschichte der Philosophie:* „Denn die Idee, in ihrer Ruhe gedacht, ist wohl zeitlos; sie in ihrer Ruhe denken ist, sie in Gestalt der Unmittelbarkeit festhalten, ist gleichbedeutend mit der *inneren* Anschauung derselben. Aber die Idee ist als konkret, als Einheit Unterschiedener, wie oben angeführt ist, wesentlich nicht Ruhe und ihr Dasein wesentlich nicht Anschauung, sondern als Unterscheidung in sich und damit Entwicklung tritt sie in ihr selbst ins Dasein und in die Äußerlichkeit im Elemente des Denkens; und so erscheint im Denken die reine Philosophie als eine in der Zeit fortschreitende Existenz" (Hegel 18, 51–52).

[128] Not only do Schiller and Hegel posit different moments in their triads, their methodological frameworks for developing these differ as well. Hegel develops his antitheses out of the process of thinking each thesis through to its own conclusion. The thesis thus generates the antithesis. See Hegel 3, 27; 8, 188; 10, 14; 18, 460. Schiller, it seems, simply looks for whatever oppositions occur to him, then posits them as polarities.

[129] Of course within the idea of a synthesis of stillness and motion differences are still apparent. Schiller tends to reveal his sense of synthesis by targeting the *inadequacies*

dualisms of his age and who identified his ultimate synthesis with a notion of dynamic stillness or „lebendige Ruhe" is Hölderlin.[130] His novel, *Hyperion*, which both appropriates and develops Schiller's concepts of the elegiac, satiric, and idyllic, forms the subject of the next chapter of this study.

---

of either pure stillness or pure motion. We see this in his critique of the false idyll, his caricatures of the realist and idealist, and his insistence on the need for synthesis. Goethe, on the other hand, expresses his love of synthesis by praising the *strengths* of each pole; he seems able to identify with the virtues of Faust's striving as well as Iphigenie's tranquil piety. Hegel, finally, offers the idea that motion and stillness, when thought through to their conclusion, are really *not opposed* at all. A synthesis is achieved by understanding the logical structure of the two terms involved.

[130] The three poets I discuss under the rubric of dynamic stillness are Goethe, Schiller, and Hölderlin. Commentary on Goethe and Schiller is almost limitless and need not be listed here. Recent comparative studies of Schiller and Hölderlin include Miller (1970); Mommsen (1965); Strack (1976), 236–44; and Yom (1972). Only a few critics offer information on the connections between Goethe and Hölderlin. See esp. Mason (1975) and Requadt (1966).

2. Narration and Ruhe in Hölderlins *Hyperion*. A Reinterpretation of the Novel's Conclusion

> Denn alsdann sammelt sich der Mensch bei ihr [der Poesie], und sie giebt ihm Ruhe, nicht die leere, sondern die lebendige Ruhe, wo alle Kräfte regsam sind, und nur wegen ihrer innigen Harmonie nicht als thätig erkannt werden. (Hölderlin)

Narrative Levels and Conceptions of *Ruhe*

The Early Ideal of Static Stillness

In his early stages Hyperion projects a concept of ideal *Ruhe* onto three different kinds of beings: first, Nature or God; second, past stages of the individual or of mankind, namely, childhood and Periclean Athens; and third, ideal persons, most significantly Diotima. In each of his first four letters Hyperion speaks of the oneness and stillness of *Nature*. He expresses the desire to depart from the human sphere and return „in die Arme der Natur, der wandellosen, stillen und schönen" (I, 9).[1] Again and again Hyperion thematizes the „Vollendungsruhe" of Nature: „die seelige Natur war wandellos in ihrer Schöne geblieben" (II, 63). Plants and trees offer Hyperion *Ruhe* and solace: „ich will hinausgehn unter die Pflanzen und Bäume, und unter sie hin mich legen und beten, daß die Natur zu solcher Ruhe mich bringe" (I, 132). But not just individual parts of Nature, rather Nature in its entirety, *natura naturans,* soothes and mediates Hyperion's fragmented existence:

> Eines zu seyn mit Allem, was lebt, in seeliger Selbstvergessenheit wiederzukehren in's All der Natur, das ist der Gipfel der Gedanken und Freuden, das ist die heilige Bergeshöhe, der Ort der ewigen Ruhe. (I, 10)

Hyperion also invokes the unity and *Ruhe* of *childhood*. Diotima describes the spring as „voll unaufhörlichen Wachstums und doch auch so mühelos, so seeligruhig, wie ein Kind, das vor sich hin spielt, und nicht weiter denkt" (II, 4). In the hymnic third letter Hyperion cries out: „Ruhe der Kindheit! himmlische Ruhe! wie oft steh' ich stille vor dir in liebender Betrachtung" (I, 12). *Ruhe* and childhood are often juxtaposed: „Mit einer wunderbaren Ruhe, recht, wie ein Kind, das nichts vom nächsten Augenblike weiß, lag ich

---

[1] In this chapter quotations from *Hyperion* are given with volume and page number of the original edition.

so da" (I, 65). Hyperion dreams of returning to the tranquillity of childhood: „Daß man werden kann, wie die Kinder, daß noch die goldne Zeit der Unschuld wiederkehrt, die Zeit des Friedens und der Freiheit, daß doch Eine Freude ist, Eine Ruhestätte auf Erden" (I, 91). The peacefulness Hyperion sees in Nature and childhood he also finds in *Diotima*. Hyperion speaks of her „Kinderstille" (II, 78). Like Nature Diotima is „wandellos" (I, 103). She is even divine: „göttlich ruhig" (I, 90). Hyperion adds: „O Bellarmin! das war Freude, Stille des Lebens, Götterruhe" (I, 121). Hyperion contrasts his own „wilde Widersprüche" with her „wandellose Schönheit" und „lächelnde Vollendung" and writes: „Wie die Wooge des Oceans das Gestade seeliger Inseln, so umfluthete mein ruheloses Herz den Frieden des himmlischen Mädchens" (I, 103). The presence of Diotima's „stille Seele" (I, 104), much like Nature, serves to make Hyperion more peaceful: „Schon lange war unter Diotimas Einfluß mehr Gleichgewicht in meine Seele gekommen" (I, 137). Such moments of stillness and harmony represent „große Stunden im Leben" (I, 136). They can be reached through Nature, through contact with congenial people such as Diotima or Adamas,[2] or by remembering childhood or a childlike nation, undisturbed and pure, such as *Athens*: „So lag vor uns Athen [...] / Hier, sagte Diotima, lernt man stille seyn über sein eigen Schiksaal, es seye gut oder böse. / Hier lernt man stille seyn über Alles, fuhr ich fort" (I, 151–52).

Such experiences of *Ruhe* are for Hyperion as momentary as they are monumental. Soon after identifying with the *Ruhe* of another person or object, Hyperion reflects and loses his unity: „Auf dieser Höhe steh' ich oft, mein Bellarmin! Aber ein Moment des Besinnens wirft mich herab" (I, 11). The course of Hyperion's development will lead him to overcome such instantaneous *Begeisterung* for the more stable *Ruhe* of reflection. Through retrospection Hyperion loses his initial oneness, yet through this same capacity he gains a more conscious and complex unity. The same faculty of reflection that earlier deprived Hyperion of unity later guarantees his harmony. By observing the narrator's thoughts we will see Hyperion advance toward a reflective as well as dynamic conception of *Ruhe*.

H1 and H2. Patterns of Development and Narrative Reflections

Hyperion's initial reason for relating the story of his life is external and simple. In his third letter Hyperion states that he writes about the past

---

[2] Adamas, who embodies both „Ruhe und Stärke" (I, 18), likewise brings Hyperion closer to a state of equilibrium and repose. See I, 20–21. In the „Fragment von Hyperion" Hölderlin terms this reorientation to one's center „Zurechtweisung" (StA III, 163), a term that plays a prominent role in Schiller's *Über naive und sentimentalische Dichtung* as well. See NA XX, 484.

because Bellarmin has requested him to: „Ich danke dir, daß du mich bittest, dir von mir zu erzählen, daß du die vorigen Zeiten mir ins Gedächtniß bringst" (I, 12). In his fifth letter Hyperion tells Bellarmin that he retreats into the past to find *Ruhe:* „Wie ein Geist, der keine Ruhe am Acheron findet, kehr' ich zurük in die verlassnen Gegenden meines Lebens" (I, 27). His present discontent leads him to seek an escape in the past. The reason for writing is negative, and the *Ruhe* he seeks is static.

In the final letter of the first book of the first volume Hyperion relates his abject experience of nothingness (I, 78) and concludes his reflections with the sentences: „So dacht' ich. Wie das alles in mich kam, begreif ich noch nicht" (I, 80). The second book then opens with Hyperion's first lengthy narrative excursus: „Ich lebe jezt auf der Insel des Ajax, der theuern Salamis" (I, 83).[3] The „jezt" of his present existence contrasts with the pastness of his previous depression. Hyperion the narrator relates his love for Greece, his fishing and his reading, and then refers to his act of remembering:

> Oder schau' ich auf's Meer hinaus und überdenke mein Leben, sein Steigen und Sinken, seine Seeligkeit und seine Trauer und meine Vergangenheit lautet mir oft, wie ein Saitenspiel, wo der Meister alle Töne durchläuft, und Streit und Einklang mit verborgener Ordnung untereinanderwirft. (I, 84)

The narrator's reflections on the harmonic *Saitenspiel* contrast with Hyperion's comments on his past condition in the following letter: „Wie war denn ich? war ich nicht wie ein zerrissen Saitenspiel? Ein wenig tönt ich noch, aber es waren Todestöne" (I, 92). As one can see from such juxtapositions, the narrating Hyperion (H2) begins to distance himself from the events of his past and the previous reflections of the experiencing Hyperion (H1).[4]

In the second letter of the second book of volume one Hyperion tells Bellarmin that he is strong enough to write: „Nun bin ich stark genug; nun laß mich dir erzählen" (I, 85). This ability to encounter the past and formulate the experience in words requires strength, which is itself increased through writing:

> Ich will die Brust an den Freuden der Vergangenheit versuchen, bis sie, wie Stahl, wird, ich will mich üben an ihnen, bis ich unüberwindlich bin. / Ha! fallen sie doch, wie ein Schwerdtschlag, oft mir auf die Seele, aber ich spiele mit dem Schwerdte, bis ich es gewohnt bin, ich halte die Hand in's Feuer, bis ich es ertrage, wie Wasser. / Ich will nicht zagen; ja! ich will stark seyn! (I, 122)

---

[3] Binder (1970/Namen) suggests there may be „ein geheimer sprachlicher Zusammenhang" between the concept „Ruhe" and Hyperion's place of residence, Salamis. In an earlier fragment Hölderlin calls Salamis the „Insel der Ruhe" (StA III, 256). Binder writes: „Könnte Hölderlin nicht an das arabische salám (Salem, hebr. schalom) denken, das Frieden, Ruhe und Heil bedeutet?" (225).

[4] It is essential for an understanding of the novel that one distinguish Hyperion the narrator (H2) from Hyperion the character in the narrative (H1). Aspetsberger first introduced this particular terminology. See (1968), 24–25 and (1971), 80–81.

Hyperion's cultivation of strength, however, is not a smooth process, not even for the narrator Hyperion. Just as the character Hyperion experiences moments of eccentricity and centeredness, so does the narrator in his path toward harmonic consciousness suffer *setbacks*. The narrator Hyperion tells Bellarmin in another excursus of the same volume that he immerses himself in the past in order to escape the present. He writes as a hermit who has removed himself from the chaos of the world: „Ich baue meinem Herzen ein Grab, damit es ruhen möge; ich spinne mich ein, weil überall es Winter ist; in seeligen Erinnerungen hüll ich vor dem Sturme mich ein" (I, 110). Hyperion suggests at the beginning of the second book of volume one that he can see the hidden order of his life, but he loses this clarity of vision a few letters later as he remembers his loss of Diotima:

> O ich wär' ein glüklicher, ein treflicher Mensch geworden mit ihr! / Mit ihr! aber das ist mislungen, und nun irr' ich herum in dem, was vor und in mir ist, und drüber hinaus, und weiß nicht, was ich machen soll aus mir und andern Dingen. (I, 105)

In his twenty-ninth letter the "narrating" Hyperion himself "experiences" a loss of direction and loses control over his writing. He senses his failure to master and properly order his previous experiences, and he encounters the fear of destruction through narration. In trying to relate his fate he must retell and relive his earlier agonies, but he is not always prepared for the task. He writes in the present:[5] „Ich seh', ich sehe, wie das enden muß. Das Steuer ist in die Wooge gefallen und das Schiff wird, wie an den Füßen ein Kind, ergriffen und an den Felsen geschleudert" (I, 136). Hyperion is not immediately hardened to his fate. He develops the strength to encounter his previous pain only after arduous practice in writing. By the end of his narration Hyperion does gain direction over his writing, he does accept his fate, and he no longer views his writing as a mode of hibernation. As a writer he is neither disoriented nor apathetic.

Clearly Hyperion's path to powerful as well as socially engaged writing is not direct. Nor does it suddenly begin with the act of narration, with the appearance of H2. At the end of his development the narrating Hyperion has become increasingly reflective, he has gained repose, and he has learned to accept suffering. But already the experiencing narrator reflects on his past: „ich überdachte stiller mein Schiksaal" (I, 64). In Smyrna Hyperion remembers Adamas (I, 38–39), and in Tina he reflects on his life with Alabanda (I, 76). Hyperion the character experiences moments of tranquillity as well.[6] The narrator will later affirm suffering and criticize the „Leidensfreien" (I, 68), but the character Hyperion already writes Diotima: „Der ächte

---

[5] See Gaskill (1981).
[6] See, for example, I, 26 and I, 43.

Schmerz begeistert. Wer auf sein Elend tritt, steht höher. Und das ist herrlich, daß wir erst im Leiden recht der Seele Freiheit fühlen" (II, 50). The character Hyperion also affirms pain in an earlier moment of insight when he states: „Das Leiden, das ich gerne verläugnet hätte, wurde mir lieb, und ich legt' es, wie ein Kind, mir an die Brust" (I, 115). The experiencing Hyperion stretches the existence of suffering even onto Nature and thus anticipates a high point of the novel; in accepting his initial departure from Diotima he states that he and Diotima, in their love for one another, are like „göttliche Natur [...] voll Leidens und doch gut" (II, 17). Hyperion the character thus anticipates many of the mature positions of Hyperion the narrator. Moreover, the narrator sometimes identifies with the experiences of his earlier self in such a way that the reader has difficulties apportioning voices. One wonders whether Hyperion is simply relating previous thoughts or actually identifying with them in the present.

Despite the overlapping traits of character and narrator, one can in most cases easily distinguish the speaker. When Hyperion copies his correspondence with Diotima or his previous conversations with Alabanda, he quotes a Hyperion of the past, H1. When Hyperion reflects on the act of writing and tells the reader that his present perceptions and moods differ from his earlier ones, the reader listens to the voice of the narrator, H2. Moreover, it is fair to say that the experiencing Hyperion is predominantly „heimathlos und ohne Ruhestätte" (II, 51), or in another phrase „ruhelos und ohne Ziel" (II, 79); the narrator, on the other hand, becomes increasingly tranquil. He writes to Bellarmin: „du solltest sogar meinen Briefen es ansehn, wie meine Seele täglich stiller wird und stiller" (II, 21).

In fact some of the arguments introduced to support the assertion that H1 does have an advanced consciousness must be relativized. The suffering that the experiencing Hyperion had placed closely against his breast shallows in comparison with the agony he experiences at Alabanda's betrayal:

> Mir war, wie einer Braut, wenn sie erfährt, daß ihr Geliebter insgeheim mit einer Dirne lebe. / O es war der Schmerz nicht, den man hegen mag, den man am Herzen trägt, wie ein Kind, und in Schlummer singt mit Tönen der Nachtigall! (I, 60)

Although the character Hyperion tries to allay his various pains and does now and again become "still", he can hold on to his stillness only for „wenige Augenblike" (I, 60). H1 does at times ponder his past, but in his final rumination he desires to return to childhood in order to free himself from the burdens of thought. Although the character Hyperion has been taught to accept pain, his departure from Adamas, expressed in the following lines, differs strikingly from the later Hyperion's meditations on the final departures of Alabanda and Diotima: „Ich habe den Schmerz ertragen gelernt, aber für solch' ein Scheiden hab' ich keine Kraft in mir" (I, 26).

Although H1 exhibits features we later recognize as characteristic of H2, we can distinguish two Hyperions, and we can speak of H2's specific development as narrator as well as of the overarching development from the early phases of H1 to the later stages of H2.[7]

---

[7] Given contemporary trends in literary criticism it seems no longer a trivial assumption that Hyperion goes through a process of development or *Bildung*. Several German critics have questioned the extent to which Hyperion develops, and one might anticipate a flurry of similar positions from the *deconstructionist* wing of literary criticism. One argument already voiced by Ingeborg Gerlach (1973) and Gisbert Lepper (1968) suggests that Hyperion the narrator does not differ from Hyperion the hero. In their view one cannot argue that Hyperion distances himself from his earlier actions, that he criticizes them, or that he advances in consciousness (see Gerlach 70, 73, 82, 84, 98 and Lepper 194). This reading however, misses a major shift in Hyperion's consciousness, for Hyperion clearly reevaluates, during the course of his writing, several earlier positions, for example, his desire to return to a static and undifferentiated unity with Nature or to revert to the simplicity and ignorance of childhood. It is no surprise, therefore, to see that Gerlach has overlooked the change in Hyperion's attitude toward *Ruhe*. She sees *Ruhe* as, not dynamic but, static: „In Wahrheit bedeutet sie [die Ruhe] das Eingehen in die Natur, in das unbewegte Sein" (185). After having established the distinctions between H1 and H2, one should still anticipate the argument that the more reflective and later statements of Hyperion are not necessarily more mature or richer than his earlier ones: although there may be a chronology of early and late, this does not correspond, necessarily, to a hierarchy of false and true. One obvious, if external, counterargument to this position is Hölderlin's own explicit intention to portray in his novel the education of an individual to „Vernunft" (StA VI, 137/ no. 88). Next one might call attention to Hyperion's own insight that through letter writing he is becoming more stable, „stiller [...] und stiller" (II, 21). One might point as well to the fact that early in the novel a single moment of reflection could abruptly destroy Hyperion's harmony; he is later able to remain in a state of harmony despite, as well as because of, his ability to reflect. There is, of course, no passage in the novel which questions the validity of a sustained harmony or harmony in the midst of strife, something Hyperion obtains only in his later, more reflective period. In addition, one could argue for the psychological insight or logical validity of Hyperion's later reflections, for example, that gods or perfect beings are not to be equated with children or nonsuffering, nonthinking beings. One more seeming obstacle to the proposition of Hyperion's development would be the suggestion that each view presented in *Hyperion* is equal to every other: there is no hierarchy whatsoever; the novel offers its readers a panorama of experiences, all equally valid and equally erroneous (see Gerlach 82, 84, and 103). This view would take its support primarily from the preface. Hölderlin seems to warn us not to make a system out of the novel, not to see in it a *fabula docet* (see Gerlach 81). But close textual readings of the preface, such as Ulrich Gaier (1978–79: 89–95) and Howard Gaskill (1984: 27–31) have undertaken, show that Hölderlin does not ask us to relativize all lessons of the novel in endless play. Instead Hölderlin tells us neither to take the novel too lightly nor to interpret it without any regard for its aesthetic worth. We should not read the novel *just* („blos") as a *fabula docet*, but we can and indeed should read it for its intellectual content as well as enjoy it for its poetic force and beauty. Another potential source

The narrator Hyperion opens one of his central self-reflexive passages after relating his first departure from Diotima. At that time he was restless and disoriented. The following narrative excursus begins with a markedly different and confident tone:

> Warum erzähl' ich dir und wiederhole mein Leiden und rege die ruhelose Jugend wieder auf in mir? Ists nicht genug, Einmal das Sterbliche durchwandert zu haben? warum bleib' ich im Frieden meines Geistes nicht stille? / Darum, mein Bellarmin! weil jeder Athemzug des Lebens unserm Herzen werth bleibt, weil alle Verwandlungen der reinen Natur auch mit zu ihrer Schöne gehören. Unsre Seele, wenn sie die sterblichen Erfahrungen ablegt und allein nur lebt in heiliger Ruhe, ist sie nicht, wie ein unbelaubter Baum? wie ein Haupt ohne Loken? Lieber Bellarmin! ich habe eine Weile geruht; wie ein Kind, hab' ich unter den stillen Hügeln von Salamis gelebt, vergessen des Schiksaals und des Strebens der Menschen. Seitdem ist manches anders in meinem Auge geworden, und ich habe nun so viel Frieden in mir, um ruhig zu bleiben, bei jedem Blik ins menschliche Leben. (II, 20–21)

---

of support for the thesis of a relativization of all views would be the footnote in volume 1, book 1, where a series of Hyperion's comments are characterized as „bloße Phänomene des menschlichen Gemüths" (I, 16). One might argue that this statement applies to all of Hyperion's views, that the novel itself establishes no hierarchy; instead the work simply allows various views of Hyperion to pass before us. But the suggestion that all of the novel's statements can be reduced to mere „Phänomene des menschlichen Gemüths" and are presented without hierarchy cancels itself insofar as it would grant the statement that all appearances are equivalent and merely „Phänomene des menschlichen Gemüths" a nonequivalent and privileged status. It would establish this position as the first in a hierarchy. Finally, any meta-argument that would grant this footnote a higher and more stable status than the rest of the text because it stems not from Hyperion but from a different and arguably wiser speaker would ignore the fact that the footnote refers to one particular passage that questions God's transcendence and would have been inserted not to undercut the novel's structure but as a guard against censorship and a defense against potential attacks on the author's religious views. One must remember that Hölderlin was always aware of the tension between his mother and himself on matters of religious concern. See letters 9, 41, 45, 82, 91, 134, 170, and 173. The footnote to the *Hyperion* passage closely resembles Hölderlin's statement to his mother in 1799 that she should not take every passage in his works literally: „Das Gedichtchen [„An die Parzen"] hätte Sie nicht beunruhigen sollen, theuerste Mutter! [...] Überhaupt, liebste Mutter! muß ich Sie bitten, nicht alles für strengen Ernst zu nehmen, was Sie von mir lesen. Der Dichter muß, wenn er seine kleine Welt darstellen will, die Schöpfung nachahmen, wo nicht jedes Einzelne vollkommen ist, und wo Gott reegnen läßt auf Gute und Böse und Gerechte und Ungerechte; er muß oft etwas Unwahres und Widersprechendes sagen, das sich aber natürlich im Ganzen, worinn es als etwas Vergängliches gesagt ist, in Wahrheit und Harmonie auflösen muß, und so wie der Reegenbogen nur schön ist nach dem Gewitter, so tritt auch im Gedichte das Wahre und Harmonische aus dem Falschen und aus dem Irrtum und Leiden nur desto schöner und erfreulicher hervor" (StA VI, 344/no. 185). In addition, one must remember that the age in general was not tolerant of atheistic views. The first volume of *Hyperion* had just appeared as the debates in Weimar and Jena on Fichte's and Forberg's alleged atheism were getting under way.

Of special importance in this passage is Hyperion's justification of his writing. He writes because he sees that all transformations, all moments of his life, are part of its general beauty. In order to encounter the past, Hyperion relinquishes an initial tranquillity of mind. To ignore the events of the past and to live in isolation, not only from others but also from his own history, would be to enter into a „sacred" stillness that he compares to a tree without foliage. Hyperion sacrifices this childlike stillness of forgetfulness for a stillness that contains negativity. He is now strong enough to remember his entire past. Moreover, where Hyperion began writing simply in response to Bellarmin's request, he now recognizes that this external appeal corresponded to an inner need, a need to articulate his thoughts and reflect on his self and his relationship to the world, a need which, though awakened, was not yet conscious. Hyperion's process of writing validates this very need. Hyperion does not just relate past occurrences, he tells us how he reacted to these events at the time. More importantly, he tells us how he reacts to them now and, to take this one step further, how he reacts in the present to his present act of reacting to the past, a process of reflection that Wolfgang Binder has appropriately termed „ein Bewußtsein des Bewußtseins vom Bewußtsein".[8]

The *Schiksaalslied*

At the beginning of the second book of volume two, immediately after Hyperion relates a moment of extreme despair, the narrator again reflects on his writing. He tells us that he had just written Diotima of his plan to commit suicide in battle. The narrator alludes to this low point and suggests that such negative moments are not absolute:

> Ich war in einem holden Traume, da ich die Briefe, die ich einst gewechselt, für dich abschrieb. Nun schreib' ich wieder dir, mein Bellarmin! und führe weiter dich hinab, hinab bis in die tiefste Tiefe meiner Laiden, und dann, du lezter meiner Lieben! komm mit mir heraus zur Stelle, wo ein neuer Tag uns anglänzt. (II, 59)

The affirmative view of the world to which this passage alludes can be found in Hyperion's fifty-eighth letter. This prominent narrative excursus, like previous ones, is placed alongside earlier moments of negativity. Shortly before this excursus Hyperion relates, with utter despondency, his departure from Alabanda: „Ich hatte solches Weh im Leben nie erfahren" (II, 89). Hyperion then sings a „Schiksaalslied" that laments the blind, purposeless, meaningless fate of man:

---

[8] Binder (1970/Idealismus), 16.

> Ihr wandelt droben im Licht
>   Auf weichem Boden, seelige Genien!
>   Glänzende Götterlüfte
>   Rühren euch leicht,
>   Wie die Finger der Künstlerin
>   Heilige Saiten.
>
> Schiksaallos, wie der schlafende
>   Säugling, athmen die Himmlischen;
>   Keusch bewahrt
>   In bescheidener Knospe,
>   Blühet ewig
>   Ihnen der Geist,
>   Und die seeligen Augen
>   Bliken in stiller
>   Ewiger Klarheit.
>
> Doch uns ist gegeben,
>   Auf keiner Stätte zu ruhn,
>   Es schwinden, es fallen
>   Die leidenden Menschen
>   Blindlings von einer
>   Stunde zur andern,
>   Wie Wasser von Klippe
>   Zu Klippe geworfen,
>   Jahr lang ins Ungewisse hinab.
>   (II, 94–95)

In this song of fate the poet draws a Homeric contrast between the gods (strophes 1 and 2) and man (strophe 3).[9] The gods are secure and tranquil; man, meanwhile, rests nowhere. The verse enjambments of the third strophe, where one long sentence races forward from line to line, enhance this image. The concentration of verbs of motion in this stanza („schwinden", „fallen", „geworfen") adds to the effect as well. While the gods are twice related to eternity („ewig": lines 11 and 15), man's existence is in time. The references here are „von einer / Stunde zur anderen" as well as the forceful, spondaic phrase, „Jahr lang". While the gods remain „auf weichem Boden", man rests „auf keiner Stätte". The poet has also set up a contrast between the two metaphors. While the divine breezes are said to softly touch the gods as the fingers of the (female) artist touch the sacred strings of a harp, the poet compares man to water being thrown from cliff to cliff forever down into the unknown. Where in the tradition a cliff often symbolizes the heroic imperviousness and resistance of a strong self,[10] here, in a striking

---

[9] For a discussion of this Homeric dualism see the chapter „Die elend und die leicht Lebenden" in Schrade (1952), 175–82. A selection of the more explicit passages on man's misery might include *The Iliad* 17, 446–47; 24, 525–26; and *The Odyssey* 18, 130–31. For passages on the gods who live at ease (*rheia zōontes*) see *The Iliad* 6, 138; and *The Odyssey* 4, 805; 5, 122; 6, 42–45.

[10] See Schöne (1964), 100–01, 112–13, 133–34, 210–11.

reversal, the self likens not the cliff but the water which is thrown against this hard surface. The stationary and exalted „droben" of the first line contrasts with the final word of the poem, „hinab". An interesting clash also exists between the pronouns of the first lines of each part of the poem: „Ihr" is the subject of an *active* sentence; „uns", because it is the object of a *passive* sentence, helps display man's inability to control his own destiny. Man also lacks insight; „Blindlings" contrasts with a plethora of words associated with vision and wisdom on the part of the gods: „im Licht", „glänzend", „die seeligen Augen", „bliken", and „Klarheit". Where the poet places the gods in a sphere of *light* and eternal truth, he associates man with the impermanence of *water*.

Pain and Repose

After singing this devastatingly pessimistic song of fate Hyperion receives Diotima's final letter and Notara's confirmation of her death. Hyperion's resulting hopelessness is documented in his written response to Notara. Hyperion writes: „mit mir ists aus" (II, 109). He again contemplates suicide and concludes: „es kann der Mensch nichts ändern und das Licht des Lebens kommt und scheidet wie es will" (II, 112). Embedded in the narrative between two moments of ultimate despair, Hyperion's singing of the song of misery after Alabanda's final departure and Hyperion's desperate response to Notara's announcement of Diotima's death, are the mediated reflections of the narrator, reflections that represent for most critics the climax of the novel. Hyperion writes:

> So schrieb Notara; und du fragst, mein Bellarmin! wie jezt mir ist, indem ich diß erzähle? / Bester! ich bin ruhig, denn ich will nichts bessers haben, als die Götter. Muß nicht alles leiden? Und je trefflicher es ist, je tiefer! Leidet nicht die heilige Natur? O meine Gottheit! daß du trauern könntest, wie du seelig bist, das konnt' ich lange nicht fassen. Aber die Wonne, die nicht leidet, ist Schlaf, und ohne Tod ist kein Leben. Solltest du ewig seyn, wie ein Kind und schlummern, dem Nichts gleich? den Sieg entbehren? nicht die Vollendungen alle durchlaufen? Ja! ja! werth ist der Schmerz, am Herzen der Menschen zu liegen, und dein Vertrauter zu seyn, o Natur! Denn er nur führt von einer Wonne zur andern, und es ist kein andrer Gefährte, denn er. (II, 106–07)

The narrator's comments, his affirmation of suffering[11] and acceptance of Diotima's death, contrast with his previous unrest at her departure (II, 16) and his unstable reaction to her death.

Central to this passage is the consequent fashion with which Hyperion

---

[11] Walter Kaufmann's assertion that a "joyous affirmation of life with all its pain [...] is not found in German literature before" Nietzsche must be revised in the light of this passage. See Kaufmann (1960), 230–31.

revokes the pessimism of the *Schiksaalslied*.[12] Hyperion's statement, „das konnte ich lange nicht fassen", refers to his previous despondency, specifically to the views expressed in the *Schiksaalslied*. The dualism of ideal and real posited in the *Schiksaalslied,* in which there are only „leidende Menschen" transforms into a monism where even „die Götter [...] leiden." The gods are no longer otherworldly or „droben", no longer nontemporal or „ewig". Gods who are „schiksaallos, wie der schlafende / Säugling" are unfulfilled beings: „Solltest du ewig sein, wie ein Kind und schlummern, dem Nichts gleich?" Pure being without differentiation is pure nothingness. The ideal of pure being against which reality was lamented in the *Schiksaalslied* is itself viewed as not real; lacking reality, it is no longer ideal, no longer a desired state.[13] Hyperion criticizes the supposedly ideal status of the gods and affirms the flux of reality, the flux of man. „Die Vollendungen alle durchlaufen" is a positive condition. The Hyperion who in the *Schiksaalslied* was allowed „auf keiner Stätte zu ruhen" is now „ruhig". His blindness is replaced by a clear consciousness, and he is content with a life of transformation and motion.[14]

---

[12] Not only does H2 take back the *Schiksaalslied* point by point in the passage just quoted, he also revokes it in the thirteenth letter, where he writes of the appearance of divinity in the figure of Diotima: „Ich hab' es heilig bewahrt! wie ein Palladium, hab' ich es in mir getragen, das Göttliche, das mir erschien! und wenn hinfort mich das Schicksaal ergreift und von einem Abgrund in den andern mich wirft, und alle Kräfte ertränkt in mir und alle Gedanken, so soll diß Einzige doch mich selber überleben in mir, und leuchten in mir und herrschen, in ewiger, unzerstörbarer Klarheit!" (I, 90). Here on the narrative level Hyperion stresses the unity of the seemingly opposed worlds of the divine and the human. The cross reference to the *Schiksaalslied* is apparent in the reflections on fate and the abyss, the water or drowning metaphor, the idea of being thrown downwards, and finally, the evocation of eternal clarity. Cf. Schuffels (1977), 110–12.

[13] The ideal, insofar as it is not real, is not ideal (or perfect), for it lacks something, namely reality. Hölderlin would have been acquainted with this argument from his study of Spinoza. See letter 41. In his *Ethics* Spinoza reproduces a form of the ontological argument. See the proofs and the note to EI, Prop. 11.

[14] Passages in *Hyperion* must be understood contextually, as Eppelsheimer (1962) and Ryan (1965) have shown. This is especially evident with regard to the *Schiksaalslied*. Drayton Miller (1970) quotes the final stanza of the *Schiksaalslied* and writes: "In the second half of *Hyperion* Hölderlin becomes increasingly pessimistic and his conception of fate assumes utterly desperate and negativistic proportions" (158). Miller apparently does not see that the *Schiksaalslied* is a quote from the past that Hyperion overcomes on the narrative level. Miller quotes other isolated passages from the novel as well and presents them as Hölderlin's views. He consistently cites, for example, the refrain „Eines zu sein mit allem" as evidence of Hölderlin's desire for pantheistic and mystical nondifferentiation, thus overlooking its relative position in the novel (64, 67, 86). David Miles (1971) misunderstands the significance of both the *Schiksaalslied* and the novel's closing vision of all-unity as well. He writes: „Hölderlin's final stage of *Bildung* is curiously unselfconscious, as if one

The juxtaposition of Hyperion's restlessness, desperation, and renunciation of life, with his calm, his joy, and his affirmation of suffering, is aesthetically inspired. The contrast works powerfully upon the reader. More importantly, the juxtaposition is thematically inspired. *Hyperion is calmest when one would expect him to be most disoriented.* He affirms suffering when suffering is greatest, i.e., when he reflects on the loss of Alabanda and Diotima. Earlier Hyperion was hesitant to relate his past; here it becomes clear that these events no longer threaten his stability. Hyperion can accept suffering because he knows that it is the condition of his humanity and development. Pain alone „führt von einer Wonne zur andern, und es ist kein andrer Gefährte, denn er [der Schmerz]". Pain is to be not eliminated, but embraced. With remarkable insight into paradox and synthesis Hyperion suggests that suffering and lack of harmony are intrinsic elements of harmony.[15] Pain does not impurify the wholeness of life; on the contrary, as a condition for passage from the emptiness of nonconsciousness it makes wholeness possible.[16] Hyperion reproves the „leidensfreie Ruhe der Götter" (StA III, 201), and with this the idea of an ideal man free of suffering. Hyperion rebukes the opposite extreme as well, that is, those whose being is only in suffering, those who are unable to envisage harmony. For Hyperion pain is necessary for and thus ultimately conducive to harmony; the two are not exclusive. Hyperion's own grand comprehensive view of the world is marked by a stable tranquillity, a philosophic calm, which is secure because it cannot be overturned by motion, suffering, or disharmony. These have no

---

were placed in the Garden once again, and yet this time near the Tree of Life, far removed from the Tree of Knowledge (like the gods, ‚keusch bewahrt in bescheidener Knospe')" (103). Miles seems not to realize that the unselfconsciousness of the gods, as portrayed in the *Schiksaalslied,* does not represent the goal of Hyperion's development, also that the undifferentiated totality evoked in the quotation of the final letter is overcome in the course of writing and is replaced with a conscious and differentiated unity. One might add that for Hölderlin the Tree of Knowledge and the Tree of Life are not mutually exclusive. On the contrary, one thinks, for example, of the lines from the short ode „Sokrates und Alcibiades": „Wer das Tiefste gedacht, liebt das Lebendigste" (StA I, 260).

[15] Even in his personal life Hölderlin saw suffering as a positive and educative force. This is observable from his earliest letters onward. See letters 3, 87, 96, 123, 136, 150, and 180. In a letter to his brother from July 4, 1798, Hölderlin quotes from *Hyperion* on the topic of pain: „Es bleibt uns überall noch eine Freude. Der ächte Schmerz begeistert" (StA VI, 277–78/no. 162). Two critics, Binder and Prignitz, have been especially attentive to the topic of suffering in Hölderlin. See Binder (1970/Abschied) and Prignitz (1976), 211–26.

[16] Hölderlin is thus able to state in *Hyperions Jugend:* „daß der Adel deines Wesens im Schmerze nur sich offenbaren kann!" He adds the following paradoxical and Fichtean formulation: „Das ist die Herrlichkeit des Menschen, daß ihm ewig nichts genügt" (StA III, 204). For an analysis of Hölderlin's understanding of finitude in the context of his reception of Fichte see Barnouw (1972).

power over Hyperion's repose, for they are not outside his repose but rather elements of that repose itself. One is reminded of an aphorism of Hölderlin's wherein he speaks of the necessity of error but also of the sublation of error in a system of truth:

> Nur das ist die wahrste Wahrheit, in der auch der Irrtum, weil sie ihn im ganzen ihres Systems, in seine Zeit und seine Stelle sezt, zur Wahrheit wird. Sie ist das Licht, das sich selber und auch die Nacht erleuchtet [...] Das ist ewige Heiterkeit, ist Gottesfreude, daß man alles Einzelne in die Stelle des Ganzen sezt, wohin es gehört. (StA IV, 234–35)

The Final Ideal of Dynamic Stillness. Hyperion's Reevaluations

The god-man dualism of the *Schiksaalslied,* essentially a dualism of nonsuffering and suffering, of stillness and motion, of the ideal and real, is undercut at the novel's conclusion.[17] Suffering is integrated into the ideal; stillness and motion are no longer viewed as exclusive concepts; and the visualization of an otherworldly and ideal realm is unmasked as simple illusion. These insights are reflected in Hyperion's view of the beings (God, Nature, and Diotima) as well as the period of man (childhood) and of history (Periclean Athens) into which he had projected an unalterable stillness.

Hyperion reads each manifestation of static Ruhe as deficient and affirms the emergence of dynamism within each essence. In his second letter Hyperion had called his ecstatic union with nature „Leben der Gottheit [...] heilige Bergeshöhe" (I, 10). But this *divinity,* like that of the gods in the *Schiksaalslied,* is characterized by a lack of individuation and consciousness („Alle Gedanken schwinden vor dem Bilde der ewigeinigen Welt" I, 11). At the end of his narrative development Hyperion no longer considers such pure and undifferentiated bliss divine. He realizes that the nonsuffering, nonconscious gods of the *Schiksaalslied* are empty, and he returns to his earlier, insightful definition of divinity as „das Eine in sich selber unterschiedene" (I, 145).[18]

---

[17] This *Schiksaalslied* is not Hyperion's ultimate song of fate; thus, the title generally ascribed to the poem, „Hyperions Schiksaalslied" (StA I, 265), is misleading. The song does not originate with Hyperion; it was taught to him by Adamas, and it is introduced not with a possessive adjective, viz. *mein,* but with the indefinite article „ein". In fact it is ironic to ascribe the song to Hyperion, since he, a human, carries a divine name and thus represents a synthesis of the divine and human rather than the dualism of the two as portrayed in the *Schiksaalslied.* Diotima's statement to Hyperion, „Dein Nahmensbruder, der herrliche Hyperion des Himmels ist in dir" (I, 130), adds support to this argument as do the novel's numerous references to the idea of the „Gott in uns". (e.g., I, 27, I, 48, II, 76).

[18] Strictly speaking, *hen diapheron eauto* is the essence of beauty, but beauty and divinity overlap in the important sentences: „Der Mensch ist aber ein Gott, so bald er Mensch ist. Und ist er ein Gott, so ist er schön" (I, 141).

The gods do suffer and are thus, in the contemporary Fichtean model, self-differentiated. Previously Hyperion had also thought that „die Natur leidet keinen Verlust in sich" (I, 102–03). In the central passage on *Ruhe* Hyperion writes that *Nature,* like the gods, must suffer. Indeed, Hyperion views Nature and God in a Spinozistic sense as one:[19] „Leidet nicht die heilige Natur? O meine Gottheit!" The *childhood* to which the character Hyperion would return in his final letter („Wär ich so gerne doch zum Kinde geworden" II, 121) and which the early narrator idealizes in the hymnic third letter is criticized as a spurious *Ruhe,* an undifferentiated unity, „dem nichts gleich". Hyperion no longer prefers to return to a state in which he knew nothing („nichts wußte" I, 13); he no longer states as he did in his letter of praise to childhood: „War ich da nicht mehr als jezt" (I, 13). He has overcome his idolization of the nonconscious. The child's passage to consciousness is its fulfillment, not its loss. At the beginning of his narrative Hyperion thought unhistorically; indeed he despised history or any notion of the fall. As he progresses toward a fuller understanding of the child's passage to consciousness, he also gains insight into the temporality of *Athens.* He recognizes that the ideal state did exist („das ganze war da [...] das Unendlicheinige war" I, 145), but he sees it in the context of history and change; the possibility of its passage from time is the condition of its existence in time. Hyperion sees even *Diotima* in this way. Her appearance in time bespeaks her temporality and thus the inevitability of her death. Initially Hyperion wanted Diotima to preserve her *Ruhe:* „Laß dich in deiner Ruhe nicht stören [...] Laß in den Kümmernissen der Erde deine Schöne nicht altern" (I, 115). But this state of *Ruhe,* linked incessantly with Diotima's lack of desires and needs (She is introduced as „göttlichgenügsam" and „bedürfnißlos" I, 103.), reminds one of Hyperion's own empty stillness after his fight with Alabanda, when he lived without concerns, without cares, without any commitments whatsoever. At that time Hyperion lived „sehr still, sehr anspruchslos" (I, 69), and his narrative commentary on this existence, his criticism of his own apathetic stillness, prepares the reader for Diotima's advancement from self-sufficient stillness, from her state of being „anspruchlos" (I, 97), to her own self-awareness and concern for Hyperion.[20] Hyperion tells Bellarmin:

---

[19] Spinoza does not differentiate between God and Nature. He uses the phrase *Deus sive Natura* almost as a proper name in itself.

[20] My comparison between Diotima's and Hyperion's *Anspruchslosigkeit* will surprise most readers, but it is justified at least in part: Diotima in her self-sufficiency and Hyperion in his apathy are both empty of striving. The tenability of such a parallel underscores Diotima's complexity. H1 viewed her as perfect, but the later Hyperion recognizes that she incorporates only one side of the ideal. Alabanda provides what Diotima lacks: heroic striving. H2's recognition of Diotima's one-sidedness undercuts her divinity – as it had been conceived by H1 – but Diotima's

Denke, daß es besser ist zu sterben, weil man lebte, als zu leben, weil man nie gelebt! Neide die Leidensfreien nicht, die Gözen von Holz, denen nichts mangelt, weil ihre Seele so arm ist, die nichts fragen nach Regen und Sonnenschein, weil sie nichts haben, was der Pflege bedürfte. (I, 68)

Diotima's self-sufficient and ahistorical *Ruhe* is disturbed in the course of her relationship with Hyperion. She becomes mortal. Hyperion acknowledges: „auch das Göttliche" „muß" „sich demüthigen" „und die Sterblichkeit mit allem Sterblichen theilen" (II, 5). Just as a child must enter the world of suffering in order to fulfill itself, so too must Diotima enter the temporal world: „Man kannte fast das seelige Kind nicht mehr, so erhaben und so leidend war sie geworden" (II, 11). This suffering is at once the death of the divine[21] (It must pass out of existence.) as well as its fulfillment (Such temporality is the condition for its appearance in history.).[22] Hyperion's impassioned acceptance of Diotima's death is thus one with his affirmation of her divinity. As much as Hyperion becomes quiet through contact with Diotima, so does Diotima become *bewegt* through contact with Hyperion. Diotima is „das sanfte Mädchen nicht mehr" (II, 72). She has played with Hyperion's dangerous flame: „kindischfurchtlos spielt' ich um deine gefährliche Flamme" (II, 69). In her letter of departure she repeats this image:[23] „Dein Feuer lebt' in mir, dein Geist war in mich übergegangen" (II, 100). In symbolic affirmation of the fire of temporality, she wills, „daß sie lieber möcht' im Feuer von der Erde scheiden" (II, 104). Her death is the immanent result of her appearance in history and her contact with human striving.

Diotima's Eloquence and Hyperion's Accountability

Diotima's death is functional as well. She dies to free Hyperion for his role as hermit, poet, and educator. To become the kind of artist he desires to be,

---

singular virtue becomes transformed into an integral part of the harmonious whole of Hyperion's personality; in this way Diotima takes part in the divinity of Hyperion and so remains divine herself.

[21] One might want to undercut Diotima's divinity by emphasizing her domestic traits – a god who cooks? But Hyperion has already reevaluated the divine so as to include in his concept of divinity just such capabilities. He even anticipates this potential criticism: „Tausendmal hab' ich in meiner Herzensfreude gelacht über die Menschen, die sich einbilden, ein erhabner Geist könne unmöglich wissen, wie man ein Gemüße bereitet" (I, 100). Such a goddess is not transposed into a transcendent and distant world; she is not excluded from the everyday. She is, in Hölderlin's phrase, „heilignüchtern" (StA II, 117).

[22] See II, 5 and II, 106.

[23] See also II, 96: „Dein Mädchen ist verwelkt, seitdem du fort bist, ein Feuer in mir hat mälig mich verzehrt, und nur ein kleiner Rest ist übrig" (II, 96). The association of Diotima with fire is developed throughout the second volume. Besides the passages quoted see II: 11, 43, 78, and 99.

Hyperion believes that he must distance himself from any immediate political activities as well as any relationship that might distract him from his global concerns. Diotima announces the necessity of his relinquishing „Thatenlust" and „Liebe" (II, 22). In her final letter she tells him: „Dir ist dein Lorbeer nicht gereift und deine Myrthen verblühten, denn Priester sollst du seyn der göttlichen Natur" (II, 104). In transcending all particularity Hyperion will be able to fulfill Hölderlin's concept of poetic totality. In the one italicized sentence of the entire novel Diotima writes that Hyperion „*ruht nicht mehr in einzelner Freude*" (II, 68). He acts out the symbolism of his name: Hyper-ion.[24] In a scene at sunrise on Delos, the island of the sungod, and to be sure on Cynthus, the hill of Apollo, Adamas points to the sun and says to Hyperion: „Sei, wie dieser!" (I, 24). Moreover, Diotima states: „Dein Nahmensbruder, der herrliche Hyperion des Himmels ist in dir" (I, 130). After gaining insight into the historicity of Periclean Athens, Hyperion recognizes his mission. He sees that what was once present can now be regained. After the conversation on Athens Diotima calls Hyperion the „Erzieher unsers Volks" (I, 159) and argues that as a sun he must not love her alone:[25]

> Willst du dich verschließen in den Himmel deiner Liebe, und die Welt, die deiner bedürfte, verdorren und erkalten lassen unter dir? Du mußt, wie der Lichtstral, herab, wie der allerfrischende Regen, mußt du nieder in's Land der Sterblichkeit, du mußt erleuchten, wie Apoll, erschüttern, beleben, wie Jupiter, sonst bist du deines Himmels nicht werth. (I, 157)

After Diotima abandons the possibility of idyllic withdrawal and after Hyperion fails in his impatient attempts at revolution through battle, he recognizes that he can fulfill his mission best as a „Künstler" (I, 159). As a writer Hyperion will not be a passive hermit waiting for the „Regen vom Himmel" (I, 54); instead he will himself become an active spiritual source.[26] After Diotima's death Hyperion loses sight of this social task. The narrator

---

[24] Binder (1970/Namen) discusses the symbolism of the name „Hyperion" (180–92). See esp. 183: „Hyperion wäre also der Drüber-hingehende, der Transzendierende und darin dem Sonnengott ähnlich."
[25] Hyperion is the Greek god of the sun. See *The Iliad,* 8, 480.
[26] The comparison between Hyperion and the sun sheds light on Hyperion as an embodiment of stillness and motion. We know that Hyperion has attained stillness; yet he is also compared to the sun, a ball of fire and heat, itself in motion and creating motion – the extreme movement of the sun's particles dissolves cold and stillness. In this context we should remember Hyperion's earlier reflections on Adamas and note to what extent they now apply to Hyperion's own role in relationship to his readers: „Wie oft warst du mir nahe, da du längst mir ferne warst, verklärtest mich mit deinem Lichte, und wärmtest mich, daß mein erstarrtes Herz sich wieder bewegte, wie der verhärtete Quell, wenn der Stral des Himmels ihn berührt!" (I, 18).

exclaims in his second letter: „Mein Geschäft auf Erden ist aus" (I, 9).[27] In truth Hyperion's act of writing this sentence is part of his very task of showing the reader how such disorientation can be redirected toward a life of harmony. Diotima's death disorients him, but it also frees him for his writing, through which he is able to manifest his social consciousness. Removed from all particular attachments Hyperion gains a wider consciousness and acts out his role as writer and educator. As a hermit Hyperion no longer depends on other persons to reach his goal of repose. The earlier *Ruhe* that Hyperion had attained in the presence of Adamas or with Diotima was the result of their strength of personality rather than Hyperion's own ability to find stillness or his knowledge of tranquillity as a proper goal of development.[28] He was dependent on others much as he termed progress within the state dependent on sustenance from above, on „Regen vom Himmel" (I, 54). Hyperion's later view of the state will allow for moments of individuation and action. Likewise with *Ruhe,* Hyperion attains repose at the

---

[27] This is reminiscent of Don Carlos' „Mein Geschäft ist aus" (1237). In fact the general conflict between love of an individual and concern for a group is common to both *Hyperion* and *Don Carlos.* Two passages from *Hyperion* will serve to remind us of Hyperion's "Don-Carlos-conflict": first, Hyperion's conversation with Diotima when she chastises him for his parochialism: „‚O so bist du ja mir Alles,' rief ich! / ‚Alles? böser Heuchler und die Menschheit, die du doch am Ende einzig liebst?'" (I, 121); second, Hyperion's isolationist statement: „Was kümmert mich der Schiffbruch der Welt, ich weiß von nichts, als meiner seeligen Insel" (I, 156). Just as Elisabeth sacrifices her love for Don Carlos (791–93), so does Diotima relinquish her love for Hyperion. Don Carlos feels throughout the play the tension between his love of Elisabeth and his responsibility to the ideals he shares with Marquis Posa. The conflict is reconciled when finally her love motivates his political action (901–02; 5320–22). Diotima is Hyperion's muse too. The influence of *Don Carlos* on *Hyperion* is further revealed in one of the two letters in which Hölderlin expresses his admiration for Schiller's play (see also letter 194). Hölderlin writes of his own tension between individual love and concern for the whole, almost as if he were arguing for the necessity of Hyperion's departure from Diotima: „Ich hange nicht mer so warm an einzelnen Menschen. Meine Liebe ist das Menschengeschlecht [...] Ich möchte ins Allgemeine wirken, das Allgemeine läßt uns das Einzelne nicht gerade hintansezen, aber doch leben wir nicht so mit ganzer Seele für das Einzelne, wenn das Allgemeine einmal ein Gegenstand unserer Wünsche und Bestrebungen geworden ist" (StA VI, 92–93/no. 65). The „Don-Carlos-conflict" by the way plays a central role in many of Schiller's works, for example, in *Die Jungfrau von Orleans,* where Johanna must relinquish individual „Männerliebe" (411) in order to reach her wider goals: „Eine reine Jungfrau / Vollbringt jedwedes Herrliche auf Erden, / Wenn sie der irdischen Liebe widersteht" (1087–89; see also 1620–22 and 2201–04).

[28] As long as one depends on others, repose easily slips into emptiness or unrest, as is clear from *Hyperions Jugend:* „Ich hatte mich gewöhnt, Ruh' und Freude aus fremder Hand zu erwarten, und war nun dürftiger geworden, als zuvor" (StA III, 213). We will see a similar pattern in Büchner's *Lenz.*

end of the novel not only through the presence of Diotima or immersion in Nature but through his own reflection. He has relinquished the love of an individual person for the love of wisdom and for life as an artist and educator.[29] In Diotima's last few sentences she prophesies: „die dichterischen Tage keimen dir schon" (II, 104). Diotima's prophecy moves her beyond the original realm of stillness; no longer the silent person to whom we were introduced, Diotima concludes her life with what is one of the longest letters of the novel. She states herself: „Stille war mein Leben; mein Tod ist beredt" (II, 101). Diotima overcomes her passive „Stille" by entering the sphere of prophecy; Hyperion, too, integrates into his *Ruhe* an oratorical element. He communicates the polemical speech against the Germans.

The Reinterpretation of the Novel's Conclusion. *Ruhe* and the *Scheltrede*

Hyperion's state of *Ruhe* in the fifty-eighth letter does not form, as previous critics have believed, the goal of Hyperion's development.[30] Hyperion continues to develop after the *Ruhe* passage.[31] The same Hyperion who

---

[29] In discussing Hyperion's „Don-Carlos-conflict", his juxtaposition of solitude and universality, I have followed the positions Hölderlin presents to us. From an external perspective, a critique seems in order. Since the novel concludes with a synthesis of the universal and particular, a point soon to be elaborated, the view implicit here – that global concerns and individual relations are mutually exclusive – seems misguided. Moreover, the destruction of all concrete intersubjective relations makes Hyperion's eventual synthesis unequivocally abstract. While the departure of Alabanda and the death of Diotima derive from their one-sidedness and function to prepare us for Hyperion's independence and his overcoming of suffering, the rhetoric that suggests the necessity of sacrificing individual relations for an initially vague generality is hardly convincing. Hölderlin's later loss of synthesis might be read with this in mind.

[30] Lawrence Ryan (1970) suggests that Hyperion's reflections on his tranquillity represent „den Standpunkt des Erzählers zum letzten Mal" (196). They contain „sein letztes Wort" (1965), 198. See also (1965), 221 and (1970), 199. Among the many critics who follow Ryan on this point are Harrison (1975), 80–81; Hauschild (1977), 146; Prignitz (1976), 210; and Thurmair (1981), 80. My contention with Ryan on this point should not obscure my debt to him in many other respects.

[31] Ryan, too, conceives of a development of the hero after his reflections on *Ruhe*, but Ryan sees it occurring beyond the novel itself; he speaks of the development of a Hyperion-Hölderlin. See Ryan (1965), 7, 228 and (1970), 197. Although Kurz (1975) objects to Ryan's classification of Hyperion as a poet (arguing that „dichterisch" (I, 104) refers to „schöpferisches Handeln überhaupt" 161), he too perceives Hyperion's creative activity as lying beyond the novel, beyond his existence as a hermit; he thus misses the significance of the *Scheltrede*.

articulates the reflections on *Ruhe* presents his readers with the polemical attack on the Germans.[32] Five arguments support this claim. The first and strongest is based on a close reading of the novel's language, particularly in the passage in question: the *Scheltrede* is spoken in the present tense and is addressed directly to Bellarmin; this indicates its origin in Hyperion the narrator (H 2). The second argument is based on the assumption, verified through the details of this analysis, that *Hyperion* is a coherent and internally consistent work of art: the novel as a whole thematizes the concept of dynamic repose and demands such dynamism at its conclusion. The third and fourth reasons draw on allusions in the novel to other works that contain analogous, if not exactly similar, structures. Hölderlin's allusions encourage the interpreter to read the novel in the light of these works. The third argument draws attention to the fact that the categories Schiller developed in *Über naive und sentimentalische Dichtung* strongly influenced Hölderlin's composition of *Hyperion*. In the preface Hölderlin explicitly states that Hyperion has „elegischen Karakter" (I, 4). An analysis of Hölderlin's reception of Schiller's categories makes clear Hölderlin's awareness of the dynamism and force inherent in Schiller's "idyllic" *Ruhe* and shows why the "idyllic" mode of the fifty-eighth letter passes over into the "satiric" mode of the *Scheltrede*. The fourth argument for my reinterpretation draws upon the allusion to *Oedipus at Colonus* that Hyperion places in his introduction to the *Scheltrede*. Sophocles' final drama proposes the coherency of reconciliation and tranquil composure with passioned criticism and bitter cursing, a coherency which Hölderlin worked into the conclusion of *Hyperion* as well. Finally, if one assumes that *Hyperion* proposes ideas consistent with Hölderlin's general world-view the validity of my reinterpretation can be confirmed by an appeal to parallel structures in Hölderlin's metaphysics. In the theoretical treatises of the period immediately following *Hyperion* Hölderlin argues that totality and repose fulfill themselves in their relationship to history; one might thus expect Hyperion's comprehensive consciousness and repose to be followed by a reference to the particular and historical.

---

[32] Since first developing my thesis that the *Scheltrede* stems from H 2, I have come across one critic, Klaus Schuffels (1977), a student of Pierre Bertaux', who arrives at the same conclusion (108). Schuffels offers a political argument: Throughout the novel Hyperion believes in the possibility of social and political reform. Despite certain setbacks, e. g., his brief consideration of suicide, no evidence suggests that Hyperion relinquishes his belief in man's ability to overcome fate or injustice. Since we can assume Hyperion is steadfast in this goal, we can envisage the *Scheltrede* as the pinnacle of his desire for renewal. Hyperion tries to shake the Germans out of their present condition and show them that they can overcome „Schiksaal".

The *Scheltrede*

In the *Scheltrede* itself Hyperion turns to the historical present and rebukes the Germans for their disharmony, narrow-mindedness, and indigence. Although many thematic parallels can be drawn to other writers of this period, notably Rousseau,[33] Herder,[34] and Schiller, Hölderlin's reproaches are unique in their intensity and specificity. The *Scheltrede* begins with Hyperion censuring the Germans for their lack of unity and harmony. The well-known lines tell us: „Ich kann kein Volk mir denken, das zerrissner wäre, wie die Deutschen, Handwerker siehst du, aber keine Menschen, Denker, aber keine Menschen, Priester, aber keine Menschen, Herrn und Knechte, Jungen und gesezte Leute, aber keine Menschen" (II, 112–13). Hyperion criticizes the Germans insofar as they are not whole persons, not well-rounded individuals, but persons with one virtue at the expense of others, specialists in this or that area of knowledge, unaware of what lies beyond their limited vision. They are their vocation and nothing more: handworker, thinker, priest. A similar criticism of the myopic vision of specialists can be seen in the sixth of Schiller's *Ästhetische Briefe,* where he writes, not specifically of the Germans but, of modern man in general that he is merely an „Abdruck seines Geschäfts, seiner Wissenschaft" (NA XX, 323). Hyperion criticizes the Germans as „allberechenden Barbaren" (II, 114). Schiller had defined a barbarian as one who destroys his feelings („Gefühle") because of his principles („Grundsätze"): „Der Mensch kann sich aber auf eine doppelte Weise entgegen gesetzt seyn: entweder als Wilder, wenn seine Gefühle über seine Grundsätze herrschen; oder als Barbar, wenn seine Grundsätze seine Gefühle zerstören" (NA XX, 318). Clearly this influence is apparent in Hyperion's statement that the Germans are „Barbaren [...] tief-unfähig jedes göttlichen Gefühls" (II, 112).

The second major criticism of the Germans can be brought under the concept of narrowness. Just as Schiller in his *Ästhetische Briefe* speaks of one-

---

[33] See Stierle (1980–81), 51, who quotes from Rousseau's *Discours sur les sciences et les arts:* «Nous avons des Physiciens, des Géometres, des Chymistes, des Astronomes, des Poëtes, des Musiciens, des Peintres; nous n'avons plus de citoyens; ou s'il nous en reste encore, dispersés dans nos campagnes abandonnées, ils y périssent indigens et méprisés» (III, 26).

[34] According to Herder man now lives in an age, „wo Alles getrennt ist, jeder nur mit Einer Kraft oder Einem Kräftlein seiner Seele dienen soll, und übrigens unter einem Elenden Mechanismus seufzet [...] kein einzelnes Glied nimmt mehr am Ganzen Theil [...] Und so gibts denn jene Menge trockner oder fauler Auswüchse, [...] zusammengeworfne Haufen Austerschaalen [...] Spekulanten ohne Hand und Auge, Schwätzer ohne Gefühl, Regelngeber ohn' alle Kunst und Übung, Papageien, Raben und Kunstrichter, elende Halbdenker und Halbempfinder" (Suphan VIII, 217–18). Cited by Nickel (1963), 151–53, and taken from Herder's „Vom Erkennen und Empfinden".

sided and limited spheres (NA XX, 323), so does Hyperion argue that the Germans are narrow-minded, blind to whatever is new, other, or different. This theme is as visible in Hölderlin's own correspondence as in the actual passages in *Hyperion*.[35] Hölderlin criticizes the Germans' „ängstlich enge Sphäre" (StA VI, 303/no. 172). He believes, „daß sich die gewöhnlichsten Tugenden und Mängel der Deutschen auf eine ziemlich bornirte Häuslichkeit reduziren. Sie sind überall *glebae addicti* und die meisten sind auf irgend eine Art, wörtlich oder metaphorisch, an ihre Erdscholle gefesselt" (StA VI, 303/no. 172). Hölderlin criticizes this overinvolvement with one's own finite sphere, for it counters his (and Hyperion's) insistence on „Allgemeinsinn" and religious and poetic openness (StA VI, 304/no. 172). Hölderlin sees German philosophy – although it is by itself far too concerned with infinite, and thus unfulfilled, striving – as an appropriate antidote to the contemporary overemphasis on finitude and the resultant complacency among the Germans:

> Da nun gröstentheils die Deutschen in diesem ängstlich bornirten Zustande sich befanden, so konnten sie keinen heilsameren Einfluß erfahren, als den der neuen Philosophie, die bis zum Extrem auf Allgemeinheit des Interesses dringt, und das unendliche Streben in der Brust des Menschen aufdekt, und wenn sie schon sich zu einseitig an die große Selbstthätigkeit der Menschennatur hält, so ist sie doch, als Philosophie der Zeit, die einzig mögliche. (StA VI, 304/no. 172)

A third theme pervades the *Scheltrede,* namely indigence. Like Schiller, who attacks the idol of necessity and the notion of a „Nothstaat" in his *Ästhetische Briefe*,[36] Hyperion chastises the Germans for acting only according to a principle of utility. Because the Germans remain „gerne beim Nothwendigsten [...] darum ist bei ihnen auch so viele Stümperarbeit und so wenig Freies, Aechterfreuliches" (II, 113). Hyperion undercuts even the virtues of the Germans: „Die Tugenden der Deutschen aber sind ein glänzend Uebel und nichts weiter; denn Nothwerk sind sie nur, aus feiger Angst, mit Sclavenmühe, dem wüsten Herzen abgedrungen" (II, 114). The Germans act out of a lifeless image of duty and are ignorant of beauty, festivity, love, whatever does not serve a particular purpose.

Hyperion's criticisms are unmistakeably clear and demand little analysis. What the *Scheltrede* does ask of the interpreter, however, is a justification of its position within the novel. We turn now to arguments that legitimize the

---

[35] Hölderlin's strongest criticisms of the Germans are found in letters 172 and 179, but see also 121 (StA VI, 208) and 170 (StA VI, 297). Scharfschwerdt (1971) analyzes these criticisms in their historical context. See esp. 206–26. For a general overview of Hölderlin's attitudes towards the Germans see Beck (1982).

[36] Schiller writes: „Der *Nutzen* ist das große Idol der Zeit" (NA XX, 311). His conception and criticism of a „Nothstaat" or „Staat der Noth" are especially prominent in letters 3 and 4.

position of the *Scheltrede* aesthetically and substantiate the thesis that Hyperion the narrator voices these criticisms at the very pinnacle of his development.

The Linguistic Argument. Tense and Address

First and foremost, technical evidence supports the thesis that the *Scheltrede* (beginning with the words: „Es ist ein hartes Wort" II, 112) stems from the narrator Hyperion (H2). The following criteria apply when distinguishing H2 from H1. Statements originating from the character Hyperion are always either rendered in quotations or spoken in the past tense or explicitly designated as past (for example, Hyperion's letters to Diotima or countless statements preceded by such phrases as „sagt ich" or „rief ich"). Several times long series of statements are followed with the distancing reflection of H2: „So dacht' ich."[37] Statements from the narrator are spoken in the present tense and are often accompanied by words such as „jezt" or „nun" as opposed to „um diese Zeit", „dann", „oft", „oftmals", or „damals".[38] The narrative digressions are usually self-referential; Hyperion will often ponder over his own act of writing.[39] When not reflecting in general terms on his narration, Hyperion sometimes simply states: „ich" „sprech'" „davon" (I, 23) or „ich" „sage" „dir" (I, 69) or „ich" „schreib'" „dir" (II, 59). The narrative digressions might also include apothegms or reflections on how Hyperion's present behavior and attitudes differ from previous ones. A direct address in the second person is usually indicative of a narrative reflection,[40] and an address such as „Lieber Bellarmin" or „mein Bellarmin" or „Bellarmin" or simply „Lieber" indicates twenty out of twenty-six times that the speaker of the surrounding reflections is the narrator.[41]

The fifty-ninth letter of *Hyperion*, which contains the *Scheltrede*, begins, „So kam ich unter die Deutschen" (II, 112). For three short paragraphs Hyperion uses the past tense; he then switches to the present: „Es ist ein

---

[37] I, 67; I, 80; II, 124. See Ryan (1965), 96 and (1970), 187.
[38] „Jezt": I, 7; I, 83; I, 85; II, 106. „Nun": I, 85; I, 105; I, 107; II, 59. „Um diese Zeit": I, 113. „Dann": II, 121. „Oft": I, 14; I, 15; I, 30; I, 70; I, 104. „Oftmals": I, 29. „Damals": I, 24; II, 107.
[39] For example, I, 122 and II, 20–21.
[40] For example, I, 12 and I, 67.
[41] Ryan (1970) writes correctly, though with less precision: „so ist die unmittelbare Anrede an den Briefempfänger sehr oft ein Zeichen für das Sprechen aus der Gegenwartssituation des Erzählers" (181). See also (1965), 58, 96. The passages are: H1: I, 121; II, 16; II, 59; II, 89; II, 112; II, 119. H2: I, 8; I, 22; I, 27; I, 37; I, 67; I, 89; I, 91; I, 93; I, 102; I, 107; I, 113; I, 123; I, 132; I, 136; II, 5; II, 20; II, 59; II, 106; II, 118 (twice).

hartes Wort" (II, 112). Hyperion continues in the present tense for six pages.[42] These pages display the criteria used to characterize the narrating, not the experiencing, Hyperion. Besides the slightly ambiguous use of „O Bellarmin" and the unambiguous use of the present tense, Hyperion uses the second person throughout and states explicitly: „sag' ichs"; „ich sag' es"; „ich sage dir".

The letter ends with a potentially perplexing statement: „Genug! du kennst mich, wirst es gut aufnehmen, Bellarmin! Ich sprach in deinem Nahmen auch, ich sprach für alle, die in diesem Lande sind und leiden, wie ich dort gelitten" (II, 118). The past tense – usually employed by Hyperion to distance himself from a previous statement – would seem at first glance to indicate that H2 appears on the scene to break any immediate identification with H1. However, the phrase „ich sprach" does not signal the writer's act of distancing himself from thoughts or statements of the past, as is the case with the phrase „so dacht' ich". The phrase „ich sprach" refers to the immediate act of letter writing and serves, rather, to emphasize Hyperion's present awareness of the power of language. Where he had earlier doubted the value of language, i.e., in the presence of Diotima (I, 95), he now affirms both its necessity and utility.[43] Hyperion's use of „ich sprach" – as opposed to „so

---

[42] Aspetsberger (1971) speaks of a „merkwürdige Verschmelzung der Ebenen H1 und H2 in der Rede über die Deutschen" (133). Prill (1983) writes similarly: „beide Erzählebenen verschmelzen miteinander" (38). The distinction, however, is clear. Hyperion begins the letter narrating the *past* event of his trip to Germany. This simply sets the stage for his *present* statements on the Germans, which follow until the end of the letter. In arguing that the *Scheltrede* represents a low point in Hyperion's development, Aspetsberger (1971) makes evident his misunderstanding of Hyperion's revised notion of dynamic stillness. For Aspetsberger Hyperion's vision of ahistorical *Ruhe* in the first letter supersedes his reflections on history in the *Scheltrede* (112–13).

[43] In *Hyperion* language is considered inadequate for expression; Hyperion cannot, for example, fully capture Diotima's essence (I, 105–06). Much of the positive evaluation of language stems from its metaphoric use; Hyperion views Diotima's silence, for example, as a kind of language (II, 52–53). The issue is complex, however, for Hyperion's letters, the very forum in which language is relativized or questioned, consist of language; even the questioning of language obtains its legitimacy only through the validity of its own language. In the course of his reflections Hyperion begins to value writing as a means toward fuller self-understanding. Here language is affirmed as a source of strength and communication. Even the goddess of silence, Diotima, finds that she is able to move from suffering to joy through writing (II, 34). The increasing value she attaches to language can also be seen in the tremendous length of her final letters. For an admirable portrayal of the complexity of Hyperion's „Ambivalenz in der Wertung der Sprache" see Aspetsberger (1971), esp. 165–97. In this context note Hölderlin's personal evaluation of language in letter 231, where he expresses his consciousness of its difficulties but also notes its irreplaceable and genuine value (StA VI, 420).

dacht' ich" – helps us grasp not only that Hyperion is speaking in the present tense, it also indicates that he has shifted the focus of his concerns from pure subjectivity, i.e., thinking and consciousness, to intersubjectivity, i.e., communication and mediation. Hyperion does not rest within himself.

The Organic Argument I. *Ruhe* in the Novel as a Whole

My second argument for suggesting that the narrator's comments do not culminate in a stage of simple quietude stems from an understanding of the role of repose in the novel. Although one of the most significant positive terms in *Hyperion,* „Ruhe" is not unambiguous. I have suggested that the novel criticizes a concept of static stillness. A few new examples will suffice to render this theme present. The pejorative term „Todtenstille" is introduced three times, most importantly after Alabanda's final departure (II, 93).[44] In describing one of Alabanda's thugs, Hyperion uses a negative image: „Die Stille seiner Züge war die Stille eines Schlachtfelds" (I, 55). At another point Hyperion views „still" and „leer" as compatible adjectives (I, 126). In addition, Hyperion forsakes living with Diotima in a private sphere, „in stillem Glüke" (II, 79). Finally, the most significant passages for a concept of deficient stillness come in the last four letters of the first book of the first volume, where Hyperion relates his departure from the world: „Geduldig nahm ich nach und nach von allem Abschied" (I, 72).[45] Hyperion becomes so sensitive to others that he says: „Ich hatte Stunden, wo ich das Lachen eines Kindes fürchtete [...] Dabei war ich meist sehr still" (I, 77). Throughout these pages Hyperion describes himself as „still" and „an-

---

[44] See also I, 92 and I, 120.
[45] This experience of empty stillness is introduced by Hyperion's desire, skillfully depicted in his departure from Smyrna, to withdraw from the world: „Ein frischer Bergwind trieb mich aus dem Hafen von Smyrna. Mit einer wunderbaren Ruhe, recht, wie ein Kind, das nichts vom nächsten Augenblike weiß, lag ich so da auf meinem Schiffe, und sah die Bäume und Moskeen dieser Stadt an [...] das sah ich an, und ließ es weiter gehn und immer weiter; wie ich aber nun auf's hohe Meer hinauskam, und alles nach und nach hinabsank, wie ein Sarg in's Grab, da mit einmal war es auch, als wäre mein Herz gebrochen" (I, 65–66). As Hyperion, in his self-indulgence and inner death, begins to lose consciousness of the physical world and sees it disappearing on the horizon like a coffin into a grave, he rushes to retrieve it: „O Himmel! schrie ich, und alles Leben in mir erwacht' und rang, die fliehende Gegenwart zu halten, aber sie war dahin, dahin!" (I, 66). The entire experience anticipates a major moment in the life of Büchner's Danton: „Man hat mir von einer Krankheit erzählt, die einem das Gedächtniß verlieren mache. Der Tod soll etwas davon haben. Dann kommt mir manchmal die Hoffnung, daß er vielleicht noch kräftiger wirke und einem *Alles* verlieren mache. Wenn das wäre! – Dann lief ich wie ein Christ, um einen Feind, d.h. mein Gedächtniß, zu retten" (L I, 39).

spruchslos" (I, 69). He had become utterly passive: „Ich ließ nun jedem gerne seine Meinung, seine Unart. Ich war bekehrt, ich wollte niemand mehr bekehren" (I, 69). He adds:

> Ich war nun ruhig geworden. Nun trieb mich nichts mehr auf um Mitternacht. Nun sengt' ich mich in meiner eignen Flamme nicht mehr. / Ich sah nun still und einsam vor mich hin, und schweift' in die Vergangenheit und in die Zukunft mit dem Auge nicht. Nun drängte Fernes und Nahes sich in meinem Sinne nicht mehr; die Menschen, wenn sie mich nicht zwangen, sie zu sehen, sah ich nicht. (I, 73)

Here Hyperion incorporates the *Ruhe* of apathy. It is a simple tranquillity, devoid of desire and bordering on nihilism.[46]

The later Hyperion criticizes *leere Ruhe,* for it neglects and negates „süße Unruhe" (I, 87). Hyperion writes to Diotima: „stille zu stehn, ist schlimmer, wie alles" (II, 44). Repose is positive only insofar as it does not exclude motion. In a moment of dynamic centeredness Hyperion writes: „Wie der Sternenhimmel, bin ich still und bewegt" (I, 85). In another passage Diotima tells Hyperion: „etwas stiller mußt du mir werden" (I, 131). Hyperion responds that, yes, he must become *ruhig* so as to see the *motion* of beauty: „Du hast recht [...] sonst seh ich ja im Meere der Schönheit seine leisen lieblichen Bewegungen nicht" (I, 131).

Hyperion's idols, Diotima and Alabanda, incorporate, according to Gregor Thurmair, the two poles of *Ruhe* and *Streben*.[47] Each represents a particular virtue in a one-sided manner. The early Hyperion oscillates between the two modes of existence, just as he fluctuates between allegiance to Diotima and Alabanda. Alabanda awakens in Hyperion the spirit of action and becoming. When Hyperion is with Diotima he experiences stillness; she quiets his eccentricity and discontent: „Wie oft hab' ich meine Klagen vor diesem Bilde gestillt! wie oft hat sich das übermüthige Leben und der strebende Geist besänftigt" (I, 104).

The early Hyperion oscillates between the poles of eccentric striving and static repose; the later Hyperion, however, gains a sense of the unity of the

---

[46] See Hyperion's comments just a few pages later: „Wenn ich hinsehe in's Leben, was ist das lezte von allem? Nichts. Wenn ich aufsteige im Geiste, was ist das Höchste von allem? Nichts" (I, 79).

[47] See Thurmair (1980), 67–91. He writes: „Zwischen den beiden Extremen Diotimas und Alabandes – Ruhe hier, unendliches Streben da – steht Hyperion" (72–73). Thurmair's analysis is, I think, fundamentally correct. It is weakened, however, by the fact that he is forced to overlook the several references to Alabanda's *Ruhe*. Hyperion cries out, for example: „O Diotima! o Alabanda! edle, ruhiggroße Wesen!" (II, 30). Concerning Alabanda Hyperion writes: „wie er, ohne ein Wort, mit seiner großen Ruhe mich lehrte, den freien Lauf der Welt neidlos und männlich zu verstehen!" (II, 62). See also I: 43, 52, and 62. Despite his interest in the idyllic, Thurmair does not note the connection between Schiller's notion of the idyllic and Hyperion's *Ruhe* on Salamis.

two positions.[48] In an early conversation with Alabanda Hyperion laments the fact that man can hold „nichts fest" and that he suffers „das wandelnde Schiksaal" (I, 50). Hyperion wishes that man could be as peaceful as the stars: „O wer ihm nur so still und sinnend, wie dem Gange der Sterne, zusehn könnte!" (I, 50). In her last few sentences Diotima provides a contrast to the star imagery of this earlier passage. She writes: „Beständigkeit haben die Sterne gewählt, in stiller Lebensfülle wallen sie stets und kennen das Alter nicht. Wir stellen im Wechsel das Vollendete dar" (II, 103). The early Hyperion suffers from an oscillation of moods. He shifts from the negativity of despair to utter enthusiasm and back again. Both change and perfection occur in this eccentric course, but the early Hyperion is unable to mediate the two. The higher term is *Wechsel*. As the later Hyperion achieves a dynamic stillness, he still experiences moments of change and negativity, but here negativity is not other to his perfection; it is a part of perfection itself, a moment within the whole. The higher term is no longer *Wechsel,* but *Vollendung.* Hyperion's dynamic stillness is not a modulation that incorporates moments of perfection but rather a perfection that embraces modulation.

In his final reflections on *Ruhe* Hyperion embraces just such a notion of dynamic perfection. Earlier he notes that perfection can be present: „Die Vollendung, die wir über die Sterne hinauf entfernen, die wir hinausschieben bis an's Ende der Zeit, die hab' ich gegenwärtig gefühlt" (I, 93). To emphasize that this experience of divinity is not restricted to his own personal and subjective feelings, he adds: „Es war da, das Höchste, in diesem Kreise der Menschennatur und der Dinge war es da!" (I, 93). In reevaluating his ideal of *Ruhe* Hyperion learns that perfection or divinity fulfills itself in temporality. Instead of seeing perfection as infinitely distant (like the stars) or realized (in childhood, for example) and then forever lost, Hyperion reevaluates perfection such that his goal is not distant, but present, not static, but in motion. Infinite striving toward an unreachable goal and static *Ruhe* or complacency are superseded in Hyperion's later notion that his goal is both at hand and in motion. It is forever being realized and realizing itself. An otherworldy perfection would *lack* presence; a static perfection would *lack*

---

[48] The intricate structure of the work reflects Hyperion's increasing sense of unity. In volume I, book I Hyperion is with Alabanda, not Diotima. In volume I, book II he is with Diotima. The two figures, though they themselves never meet (I take this to be a reflection of their one-sidedness.) are then united in the individual books of volume II. In volume II, book I Hyperion spends time with both Diotima and Alabanda; and while he is with Alabanda, he writes to Diotima. In the second book of the second volume he relates his departure from Alabanda and the death of Diotima in one breath; he then follows this with his philosophical, yet energetic, calm, thus showing in his own person the unity of the principles that these two figures represent.

motion. The "final" *Ruhe* of Hyperion will not halt this process of perfection; rather, it will generate the *Scheltrede*.

The Argument by Analogy I. Schiller's *Über naive und sentimentalische Dichtung*

Hyperion's attack on the Germans has been criticized as not fitting into the structure of the work aesthetically.[49] This critique is misguided. Far from being an anomalous letter, the *Scheltrede* is the climax of the novel. The structural significance of this letter can best be seen by studying Hölderlin's appropriation of Schiller's categories from *Über naive und sentimentalische Dichtung*.[50] The unconscious mystical unity with Nature experienced passively by Hyperion – and related in his final and second letters – is vaguely reminiscent of Schiller's suggestion that naive unity does not originate from any personal „Verdienst" (NA XX, 414); it is rather a „*Gunst der Natur*" (NA XX, 475).[51] Schiller's view, „daß die Reflexion keinen Antheil daran habe" (NA XX, 475), applies to Hyperion's experience as well. More importantly, Hölderlin states in his preface that Hyperion has „elegischen Karakter" (I, 4). As we saw in our first chapter, Schiller divides his concept of sentimental poetry into two groups: "elegiac" and "satiric". We remember that for Schiller the sentimental poet has lost his oneness with Nature. Harmony for him is not an experience but an idea. Hyperion relates this well: „Ideal ist, was Natur war" (I, 112).[52] The sentimental poet strives to regain unity. He

---

[49] Walter Silz (1969) speaks of "the artistic indefensibility of this sudden outburst, the inappropriateness of injecting it at this place in the hero's development and the novel's structure" (90). He adds: "None of those who have extolled the perfect structure of *Hyperion* has ever demonstrated the structural necessity of this letter. It makes no helpful contribution to plot and character. In the economy of the novel it can only be called a divagation, an excrescence, a blemish; one can try to explain it, but it cannot be justified on artistic grounds" (85).
[50] Wolfgang Binder (1970/Namen) first noted the parallel to Schiller's notion of the elegiac (139–40). Lawrence Ryan (1965) repeats Binder's insight (60). Ulrich Gaier (1978–79: 142) and Jochen Schmidt (1979: 204–06) extend the analogy by drawing attention to the satiric tone of the *Scheltrede*. I would advance the analogy still further by arguing that the *Ruhe* on Salamis corresponds to Schiller's notion of the idyllic and that this *Ruhe* – in Schiller's words a „Ruhe" that contains „Streben" – leads directly to the satiric tone of the *Scheltrede*.
[51] This is not to deny that additional sources exist as well, e.g., Pietism or Goethe's *Die Leiden des jungen Werthers*.
[52] For a discussion of this sentence see Pott (1980–81). One could draw countless parallels between Schiller's definition of the sentimental and Hyperion's earliest experiences. I mention just one example. According to Schiller the sentimental individual will often condemn his capacity for reason as „einen Fluch oder […] ein Übel" (NA XX, 427). Here one thinks of Hyperion's condemnation of reason in his first few letters.

views the world in one of two basic ways: either he perceives the idea as perfection, as infinitude, or he observes reality as a limit, as finite. In Schiller's system a character is either elegiac or satiric, depending on which view of the world dominates. The perception that feels itself drawn to the ideal is elegiac. Schiller calls the mirror perception, which is repelled by reality, satiric. Both the elegiac and satiric sentiments thematize distance from Nature and the ideal. The primary tone of *Hyperion* is elegiac. One thinks, to name just one specific example, of Hyperion's desire to return to childhood in his third and last letters. In general Hyperion's life is characterized by the two fundamental sentiments of the elegiac, mourning for the past and striving for the ideal. The elegiac finds its purest formulation in the conversation on Athens at the end of volume one; at the corresponding position of the second volume the satiric mode is presented. An emphasis on ideality (the elegiac) shifts to an emphasis on reality (the satiric).[53]

The prominent passage on *Ruhe* incorporates Schiller's concept of the idyllic[54] and realizes the „Auflösung der Dissonanzen" spoken of in the preface.[55] Schiller, we remember, defines the idyllic mode, a mode pervaded by *Ruhe*, as involving „einen völlig aufgelösten Kampf" (NA XX, 472). Moreover, Schiller writes concerning the idyllic:

> Ihr Charakter besteht also darinn, daß *aller Gegensatz der Wirklichkeit mit dem Ideale*, der den Stoff zu der satyrischen und elegischen Dichtung hergegeben hatte, vollkommen aufgehoben sey, und mit demselben auch aller Streit der Empfindungen aufhöre. (NA XX, 472)

Schiller then speaks of the dynamic stillness intrinsic to the idyllic mode:

> Ruhe wäre also der herrschende Eindruck dieser Dichtungsart, aber Ruhe der Vollendung, nicht der Trägheit; eine *Ruhe,* die aus dem *Gleichgewicht* nicht aus dem Stillstand der *Kräfte,* die aus der Fülle nicht aus der *Leerheit* fließt [...] das Gemüth muß befriedigt werden, aber ohne daß das *Streben* darum aufhöre. (NA XX, 472-73) (emphasis added)

Schiller's definition of idyllic *Ruhe* corresponds almost word for word to the „lebendige Ruhe" that Hölderlin affirms in the letter to his brother of January 1, 1799:[56]

---

[53] Behind this structural contrast lies a hidden symmetry. Reflections on the stillness of Athens stand out in the final letter of volume I; these then pass over into a critique of Northerners and, by implication, the Germans. In volume II Hyperion's final reflections on stillness precede the *Scheltrede,* the hero's clearest condemnation of the Germans.
[54] Hermann Weigand (1954) has noted perceptively: „The one, the only name that comes to mind among Schiller's contemporaries as the exponent of the ultimate sentimental idyll is Hölderlin" (168). Weigand mentions a selection of Hölderlin's later hymns; he does not consider *Hyperion.*
[55] See Ryan (1965), 225.
[56] There is a similar image in *Hyperions Jugend,* where Hölderlin writes of „diese

> Denn alsdann sammelt sich der Mensch bei ihr [der Poesie], und sie giebt ihm *Ruhe,* nicht die *leere,* sondern die lebendige Ruhe, wo alle *Kräfte* regsam sind, und nur wegen ihrer innigen *Harmonie* nicht als *thätig* erkannt werden. (StA VI, 305/ no. 172) (emphasis added)

Ruhe allows for, indeed demands, motion and direction. Remarkable in this comparison are not just the similarities but also the differences. For Schiller the idyllic is a synthetic term. His sequence of categories is: first, the naive; second, the elegiac or satiric; and third, the idyllic. Hölderlin's sequence differs. After the naive comes the elegiac, but this is followed by the idyllic, which in turn precedes the satiric. In order to emphasize the dynamism of the idyllic, Hölderlin reverses Schiller's order of categories. He places satire after the idyll but only to show it as a moment within the idyll. In voicing his critique of the Germans, Hyperion develops, he does not lose, his repose. Idyllic stillness encompasses satiric motion. Hölderlin's use of "pathetic satire" even enhances the effect of dynamism, since this kind of satire is linked with the sublime and thus extreme motion; Schiller associates playful satire, on the other hand, with beauty and stillness.[57]

Just as idyllic stillness contains the motion of satire, so does idyllic wholeness include the particularity of satire.[58] While Hyperion harmonizes the dissonances of consciousness, he still acknowledges the existence of incongruities in reality. According to the preface the „Dissonanzen" are resolved „in einem gewissen Karakter", not in the world. The ecstatic oneness with Nature experienced by „Kinder des Augenbliks" (I, 79) momentarily and mystically covers all incongruities such that they return, uncontrollably, upon „ein Moment des Besinnens" (I, 11). Repose involves a form of consciousness that affirms dissonance as necessary to the world. Hyperion still recognizes the existence of pain, even if he also sees it in its proper perspective and understands its importance. In still recognizing the inadequacies of the world Hyperion overcomes a purely subjective and impotent reconciliation of mind which suggests that with an understanding of the necessity and pattern of dissonance one need not concern oneself with the removal of actual evils in the world, with real change.[59] Hyperion's

---

Ruhe und Regsamkeit, wo alle Kräfte ineinander spielen, wie die stillen Farben am Bogen des Friedens" (StA III, 207). See also its final form in I, 144.

[57] See NA XX: 442 and 444.

[58] By integrating the particular into his sense of the whole, Hyperion avoids the dangers that both Hölderlin and Schiller find in the idealist, who, „indem er den Geist des Ganzen fühle, das Einzelne zu wenig ins Auge fasse" (StA IV, 226). The passage is from *Ein Wort über die Iliade.* Cf. NA XX, 495.

[59] Hyperion has achieved a comprehensive and stable consciousness, yet he still has the power to envisage the particular and argue for change. Unlike Hegel, who on occasion was concerned with reestablishing unity only on the level of thought, Hölderlin never accepted a quietistic tone of resignation. See Hegel's preface to his

tranquil reconciliation is not his final moment. His idyllic harmony or *Ruhe* fulfills itself in its relation to history. Totality is total only when it does not exclude history. The harmonic oneness of the poet with the All and his turn toward negative reality are related. The satiric moment of the *Scheltrede* is not only a complement of the elegiac but an extension, or more precisely the fulfillment, of the idyllic. While idyllic fullness *passes over* into the particularity of the satiric, this very passage is itself the *fulfillment* of idyllic wholeness. The *Scheltrede* is not artificially pasted onto the text; it is, rather, aesthetically and thematically integrated.[60]

The fulfillment of the hermit's total consciousness is his act of becoming an educator.[61] He responds to history, not merely his own, but rather a

---

Grundlinien der Philosophie des Rechts, esp. 8, 26–28, as well as his comment in the introduction to his *Vorlesungen über die Geschichte der Philosophie:* „Die Philosophie fängt an mit dem Untergange einer reellen Welt; wenn sie auftritt mit ihren Abstraktionen, grau in grau malend, so ist die Frische der Jugend, der Lebendigkeit schon fort, und es ist ihre Versöhnung eine Versöhnung nicht in der Wirklichkeit, sondern in der ideellen Welt" (18, 71–72). For Hölderlin's explicit criticism of „Quietismus" see StA IV, 213.

[60] *Hyperion* is related not only to *Über naive und sentimentalische Dichtung* but also to Schiller's general concept of aesthetic education. In the letter of his brother of January 1, 1799, Hölderlin writes that „die philosophisch politische Bildung [...] die Menschen zu den wesentlichen, unumgänglich nothwendigen Verhältnissen, zu Pflicht und Recht, zusammenknüpft," but he adds that a more perfect *Bildung* would also demand „Menschenharmonie", this in turn could arise only through aesthetic education (StA VI, 306–07/no. 172). Indigence, lack of harmony, and narrowness, the vices Hyperion criticizes in the *Scheltrede,* could all be eliminated, according to Hölderlin, through aesthetic education. In his letter to Niethammer of February 24, 1796, Hölderlin announces his desire to write the „Neue Briefe über die ästhetische Erziehung des Menschen" (StA VI, 203/no. 117). In *Hyperion*, which one could term a series of *letters* on the theme of *aesthetic education*, Hölderlin attempts to act out the Schillerian concept that mind can determine being. Schiller speaks in his *Ästhetische Briefe* of man's need for „eine totale Revolution in seiner ganzen Empfindungsweise" (NA XX, 405); Hölderlin in turn writes of the need for „die Umkehr aller Vorstellungsarten und Formen" (StA V, 271). Hyperion's paradigmatic education should act as a model for such transformations of consciousness.

[61] The *Scheltrede* accords with Hölderlin's own highest ideas of effectiveness: it is both satirical and oratorical. Hölderlin writes to his brother of satire: „Ich bitte Dich, das, was Du mir von der ernsten Satyre schreibst, ja nicht aufzugeben. Schiller sagt auch, man müsse jezt das Publikum recht in Indignation sezen, um darauf zu wirken" (StA VI, 152/no. 93). He also writes to him of the effectiveness of oratory: „Ist es Dein Ernst, als Schriftsteller auf den deutschen Karakter zu wirken und diß ungeheure Brachfeld umzuakern und anzusäen, so wollt' ich Dir rathen, es lieber in *oratorischen,* als poëtischen Versuchen zu thun. Du würdest schneller und sicherer zum Zweke gelangen. Ich wunderte mich schon oft, daß unsere guten Köpfe nicht häufiger darauf gerathen, eine kraftvolle Rede zu schreiben, z. B. über den Mangel an Natursinn bei den Gelehrten und Geschäftsleuten" (StA VI, 263/no. 152).

general, more expansive history, the history of a nation. Because of their emphasis on and despite their criticism of reality, the satiric lines are characterized by a definite reference to history. After having reached a state of strength and harmony Hyperion is able to confront the negativity of reality. He is „ruhig [...] bei jedem Blik ins menschliche Leben" (II, 21). Hyperion views the world with a harmonic consciousness that makes him capable of confronting pain by knowing its constitutive activity.

Excursus. Hölderlin's *Hyperion* and Spinoza's *Ethics*

In *Hyperion* Hölderlin portrays a hero who understands and affirms pain by virtue of his education to reason. In his novel Hölderlin wanted to portray „der große Übergang aus der Jugend in das Wesen des Mannes, vom Affecte zur Vernunft" (StA VI, 137/no. 88). Interesting parallels can be drawn here between *Hyperion* and *The Ethics* of Spinoza. In fact, during the composition of *Hyperion* Hölderlin had been reading Spinoza.[62] In his *Ethics* Spinoza teaches that man is ruled by fate, driven about by external causes and tossed "to and fro like waves of the sea driven by contrary winds",[63] insofar as his ideas are confused, insofar as he does not understand the order and harmony of the universe. Through a clear understanding of causality and necessity, emotions or affects such as pain can be mitigated: "In so far as we understand the causes of pain, it to that extent ceases to be a passion, that is, it ceases to be pain."[64] Also in his fifth book Spinoza writes: "The mind has greater power over the emotions and is less subject thereto, in so far as it understands all things as necessary."[65] One reconciles oneself to pain to such an extent that pain passes over into "the intellectual love of God" or the philosophical affirmation of existence. A person who reaches such a state is serene; no longer disturbed by his fate, he sees it as necessary and possesses "true acquiesence".[66] Just as *Ruhe,* a constant motif in *Hyperion,* represents the

---

[62] Hölderlin's acquaintance with Spinoza reaches back to Tübingen. See the letter of February, 1791, to his mother as well as his excerpts from Jacobi's *Briefe über die Lehre des Spinoza* (StA IV, 207–10). In a letter to Hegel Hölderlin writes that he had jotted down his criticism of Fichte „unmittelbar nach der Lectüre des Spinoza" (StA VI, 156/no. 94). This was also during the early stages of his work on *Hyperion.*
[63] "Ex quibus apparet, nos à causis externis multis modis agitari, nosque, perinde ut maris undæ, à contrariis ventis agitatæ, fluctuari, nostri eventûs, atque fati inscios" (E III, Prop. 59, Schol.).
[64] "Quòd quatenus Tristitiæ causas intelligimus, eatenus [...] ipsa definit esse passio, hoc est [...] eatenus definit esse Tristitia" (E V, Prop. 18, Schol.).
[65] "Quatenus Mens res omnes, ut necessarias intelligit, eatenus majorem in affectûs potentiam habet, seu minùs ab iisdem patitur" (E V, Prop. 6).
[66] In the final note of the entire work Spinoza writes: "Sapiens [...] vix animo movetur [...] sed semper verâ animi acquiescentiâ potitur" (E V, Prop. 42, Schol.).

pinnacle of the hero's development,[67] so is peace of mind or acquiescence of spirit a central theme from the end of book II to the conclusion of Spinoza's *Ethics*.[68] Indeed, at the very conclusion of his text Spinoza tells us that whoever has the third or highest level of knowledge,[69] that is, knowledge of God, has reached the summit of human perfection, which Spinoza equates with acquiescence of spirit: "From this third kind of knowledge arises the highest possible mental acquiescence [...] consequently, he who knows things by this kind of knowledge passes to the summit of human perfection."[70] Hyperion, too, affirms pain through his education to reason and his insight into necessity. Like the wise man in Spinoza's *Ethics* Hyperion is aware of the whole and his place within that whole. Hyperion's earlier life was characterized by inconstancy and vacillation. He was tossed about like water – „wie Wasser von Klippe / Zu Klippe geworfen" – almost in imitation of Spinoza's doctrine of *fluctatio* (EIII). But Hyperion rises from the sphere of confused ideas, where the mind cannot comprehend the order of the world and the individual's life is inconstant because he does not judge with reason or by reference to the whole. The later Hyperion is no longer prey to his emotions. Instead of deriding them, he understands them and thus gains power over them.[71] Hyperion makes the transition to freedom by

---

[67] Note Hölderlin's own explicit praise of the virtues of *Ruhe*. In a letter in which he writes, „Mich beschäftigt jezt beinahe einzig mein Roman," Hölderlin also states, very much in the spirit of Spinoza: „Friedsames inneres Leben ist doch das Höchste, was der Mensch haben kan" (StA VI, 109–10/no. 75). See also StA VI, 271/no. 157).

[68] Already in book II, Spinoza writes that proper knowledge "completely tranquilizes our spirit" (EII, Prop. 49, Schol.). In book IV he writes: "Est reverâ Acquiescentia in se ipso summum, quod sperare possumus" (EIV, Prop. 52, Schol.). Towards the close of the same book he tells us: "Beatitudo nihil aliud est, quàm ipsa animi acquiescentia" (EIV, App, Caput 4). Other important passages in the *Ethics* that treat the Latin equivalent of a *Gemütsruhe* and are not quoted elsewhere in this study include: EIV, App, Caput 32; and in EV: Prop. 10, Schol; Prop. 27; Prop. 32, Dem; Prop. 36, Schol; Prop. 38, Schol. Included in this list are passages where Spinoza speaks of an "animi acquiescentia", a "mentis acquiescentia", and the related concept of an "acquiescentia in se ipso".

[69] On Spinoza's distinction between three kinds of knowledge see EII, Prop. 40, Schol. 2.

[70] "Ex hôc tertio cognitionis genere summa, quae dari potest, Mentis acquiescentia oritur [...] adeóque qui res hôc cognitionis genere cognoscit, is ad summam humanam perfectionem transit" (EV, Prop. 27; EV, Prop. 27, Dem.).

[71] My comparison between Hölderlin and Spinoza should not overshadow their many differences. I note here one central distinction. In contrast to the wise man of Spinoza's *Ethics* Hölderlin's Hyperion knows not only to overcome pain but also to affirm its constitutive character. Spinoza's monism did not allow him to see the dialectical importance of pain. In Spinoza's system pain has no positive role; it is to be forgotten or eliminated. In *Hyperion* pain is superseded only as it becomes an

developing adequate, rather than confused, ideas, that is, by grasping the order of the world. Hyperion's act of overcoming the strict contrast between the gods and the world, evident in his reflections on *Ruhe,* is also Spinozistic: first, insofar as it shows that Hyperion no longer "lies at the mercy of fortune" (IV, Praef.); and second, insofar as it indicates the attainment of unity. The parallel extends still further. For Spinoza God is all of Being; thus, the love of God is the love of total existence. The *Ruhe* of Spinoza, like the *Ruhe* of the mature Hyperion, differs from the apathetic *Ruhe* of Hyperion's seventh, eighth, and ninth letters and the „Herzenshärte" of Alabanda's thugs (I, 56); Spinoza's *Ruhe,* like that of the narrator Hyperion, calls for a relationship to the other. The other is seen not as wholly other but as a mutual part of the whole. One realizes that one is "in God", not separate (EV, Prop. 30). Spinoza writes: "This love towards God [...] is the more fostered, in proportion as we conceive a greater number of men to be joined to God by the same bond of love."[72] The connection to Spinoza[73] provides further support for the view that Hyperion does not conclude his life with a turn away from the world, a turn to the merely contemplative. The hermit Hyperion, who had distanced himself from all particularity in order to grasp totality, turns back to the world, with which he is one, and acts out his role as artist and educator, trying to bring insight to a greater number of men.

---

integral part of the character's development. For Hölderlin the negativity of pain fulfills a positive, formative function; it generates *Bildung,* which might itself be viewed as the negation of the negation. Spinoza's and Hölderlin's differing attitudes toward negativity are also reflected in their views as to whether or not the divine can suffer. For Spinoza the answer is clearly no (EV, Prop. 17); for the mature Hyperion, who might be said to represent Hölderlin's views on the subject, the answer is yes: the gods do suffer (II, 106).

[72] "Hic erga Deum Amor, neque Invidiæ, neque Zelotypiæ affectu inquinari potest; sed eò magis fovetur, quò plures homines eodem Amoris vinculo cum Deo junctos imaginamur" (EV, Prop. 20).

[73] Although a comprehensive study of Spinoza's influence on Hölderlin has yet to be written, the literature does offer isolated references to the topic. See esp. Bachmaier (1979), 91–94; Mieth (1978); Mommsen (1974); Nickel (1963), 61–66; and Prill (1983), 120–26. Mommsen's article from 1974 is particularly important in the context of this study. After completing this chapter, I received Mommsen's essay through interlibrary loan and found that he, too, notes the importance of the *animi acquiescentia* for Spinoza (82) and relates this to Hölderlin's portrayal of Hyperion. Mommsen's reference, however, is limited to two general sentences: „In Hölderlins *Hyperion* bietet die schwankende Haltung des Helden – im Gegensatz zur Götterruhe Diotimas – ein typisches Beispiel für Spinozas Fluctuatio. Die innere Handlung des Romans beruht darauf, daß ein Ausgleich hergestellt wird: mehr und mehr beruhigt sich Hyperions Fluctuatio, er nähert sich dem Vorbild der Acquiescentia, das er in Diotima sieht" (84–85). In a footnote to this passage Mommsen promises to develop the topic sometime in the future (88).

The Argument by Analogy II. Sophocles' *Oedipus at Colonus*

While the connection to Spinoza's *Ethics* is only implicit, the novel includes more than one direct reference to Sophocles' *Oedipus at Colonus*.[74] It might seem that Hyperion's agitation as he voices the *Scheltrede* stands in contradistinction to the composure he attained in the course of his narration; but I would suggest that Hyperion's directed execration and his repose are not incompatible.[75] The allusion to Sophocles' *Oedipus at Colonus* at the start of the *Scheltrede* gives us further evidence for this conclusion. Hyperion writes: „Demüthig kam ich, wie der heimathlose blinde Oedipus zum Thore von Athen, wo ihn der Götterhain empfieng, und schöne Seelen ihm begegneten – / Wie anders gieng es mir!" The irony of Hyperion's lines is that Oedipus' reception outside Athens was, if one includes his initial collision with the chorus and his encounters with Creon and Polyneices, not that different from Hyperion's reception in Germany. Hyperion acknowledges the few Germans who do cultivate the good and the beautiful, the counterparts of Theseus in Sophocles' play. But the others, whom Hyperion feels deserve his wrath, are cursed and condemned. It is significant that Oedipus, who in his last days achieves peace of mind and finds himself reconciled with the gods, is moved to unrelenting anger as well. Oedipus expresses his vengeance against the scheming Creon. Moreover, he is merciless in his curse against his disloyal son, Polyneices; he calls him a "scoundrel" (1354), his "murderer" (1361), and "no son" of his (1369). In short, Oedipus' curse is as strong as Hyperion's. The significance of the parallel lies not in the mutual expression of harsh emotions but in the exact location of *thumos* in relationship to the respective hero's achievement of composure.[76] Both heroes have suffered, both have achieved repose, yet each expresses his wrath in the midst of the greatest calm. It is well-known that Sophocles alters the epic source for

---

[74] The importance of *Oedipus at Colonus* for Hölderlin is evident in his partial translation of the play (StA V, 275–76) and in the motto for the second volume of *Hyperion*. The studies on Hölderlin and Sophocles with which I am familiar (Benn (1958–59) and Binder (1969–70)) have not tried to interpret the reference in the *Scheltrede*.

[75] One might object, along with Aspetsberger (1971: 306), to my suggestion that in the *Scheltrede* Hyperion does not lose his *Ruhe*. But this objection is valid only if one defines *Ruhe* as a condition that excludes motion.

[76] A reintroduction of extreme negativity into an already established stance of affirmation and composure provides an interesting aesthetic contrast, but it also establishes the strength of the composure; not even the greatest amount of negativity can upset it. Despite innumerable differences in detail, this basic aesthetic and logical structure is common to *Oedipus at Colonus*, *Hyperion*, and even Rilke's *Duiniser Elegien*. In his eighth elegy, Rilke reintroduces negativity, thus making clear that the affirmation of the seventh cannot be shaken; on the contrary, it is reasserted and advanced in the ninth elegy.

his play,[77] transferring the curse from Thebes to Colonus and postponing it to the last hours of Oedipus' life. In having Oedipus voice his brutal curse just previous to his harmonious death, Sophocles shows us that his hero is able to remain calm amidst the most fervent passion. His condemnation originates not during a period of disorientation or of the arbitrary and chaotic flow of emotions but from a position of strength (Oedipus is in a position of almost divine power during his last hours and is in a sense carrying out justice.),[78] of insight (reflected in the ability of this blind man to lead Theseus to "the place where I must die" "without a soul to guide me" (1520f.), also in his prophecies (1425, 1428)), and of repose (Oedipus' growing contentment is not shattered by his encounters with Creon and Polyneices but reaches new heights in his final hour (1663ff.)). Hyperion's critique, too, arises out of repose and the height of reflection. Able to remain calm while recalling the departure of Alabanda and death of Diotima and while condemning the Germans, Hyperion enjoys a repose that is of an enduring nature.

That Hölderlin cites not Oedipus' repose but the pessimistic outcry of the chorus as a motto for the second volume of *Hyperion* is yet another example of the complexity of Hölderlin's work and of the importance of reading all passages contextually. The passage – "Not to be born surpasses thought and speech. / The second best is to have seen the light / And then to go back quickly whence we came" – has a position in Sophocles' play analogous to that in Hyperion's novel.[79] The lines surface as a statement of negativity undermined by the hero's development. In Sophocles' play they are spoken by the chorus or elders, a group that demonstrates its mediocrity, superficiality and unreliability on more than one occasion.[80] In the beginning of the play the elders lure Oedipus out of the sacred grove with a promise of safety (176–77); they then break that promise, stating that he should be exiled from the country (226). Later, they reopen Oedipus' wounds with a malevolent curiosity (510ff.). After Oedipus curses Polyneices, the chorus awaits, in fear and despair, still more terror and suffering (1447ff.; 1463ff.), yet Oedipus is justly confident of his reconciliation (1472ff.). The thunder that brings panic

---

[77] See Bowra (1944), 324–25. Others have noted this in the wake of Bowra. See, for example, Whitman (1951), 211.
[78] See Bowra (1944), 310ff. and Knox (1964), 147f., 160.
[79] These lines (1224ff.) have their corollary in Eccl. 4, 2–3 (see also Job 3, 1–23) and are cited by Heine twice in his later years. See B VI/1: 189 and 333.
[80] The chorus normally represents in Sophocles' plays „das kleine, gewöhnliche Denken" (Egermann (1979), 10). See also Whitman (1951), who writes, "the most explicit moral statements are made by the chorus, as a rule, and therefore tend rather to bear out those formulae which must be particularly rejected as unfitting to the whole" (18).

and disarray to the chorus is for Oedipus the summons he has been awaiting (94–95). Moreover, in the very speech from which Hölderlin's motto derives, the chorus blindly echoes tradition, lamenting the isolation and wretchedness of old age:[81] "And in the end he comes to strengthless age, / Abhorred by all men, without company, / Unfriended in that uttermost twilight / Where he must live with every bitter thing" (1235–38). Here the chorus fails to see that Oedipus moves in a sphere of intersubjectivity and reconciliation, beginning (even before these lines are spoken) with his love for his daughter(s), and passing on, thereafter, to his friendship with Theseus, his new home in Athens, and his ultimate union with the gods.[82] Finally, the motto is a quotation not only for Hölderlin but – as Hölderlin would surely have known – for Sophocles too: the passage is frequent in Greek literature and can be found, for example, in Theognis, Herodotus, and Euripides.[83] It is a moment that the synthetic poet Sophocles includes in his play but also overcomes, just as Hölderlin has Hyperion experience and then transcend his earlier abnegation of life. By introducing the second half of the novel with this passage, Hölderlin brings the reader, too, through pessimism and negativity before letting him/her recognize that this moment and others like it are ultimately superseded by a greater and more logical whole.

At least two aesthetic models exist, then, by which we can comprehend the structural and aesthetic significance of the *Scheltrede* and in which we can discern the seeds for Hyperion's coupling of dynamism and repose: Schiller's categories of the elegiac, the satiric, and the idyllic in *Über naive und sentimentalische Dichtung* and Oedipus' ability to unite composure and anger in Sophocles' *Oedipus at Colonus*.

Excursus. The Reader in the Text

Recent interpretations of *Hyperion* have concentrated on the development of a specifically poetic consciousness.[84] Without denying Hyperion's specific vocation, I would like to deemphasize it for a moment and stress the wider

---

[81] See *The Iliad*, 19, 336; *The Odyssey*, 24, 250; and Hesiod's *Theogony*, 225.
[82] See Hösle (1984/Vollendung), 152–53, 158–59, 165–67.
[83] See Theognis, 425–28; Herodotus, I, 31; V, 4; and Euripides, fr. 285, 449, 452, 908 in *Tragicorum Graecorum Fragmenta* (For Latin translations see nos. 285, 454, 461, and 963 of *Euripidis perditarum fabularum fragmenta*.). See also *Homeri et Hesiodi Certamen*, 70–74 and Bacchylides, 5, 160–62. Cf. Cicero, *Tusculan Disputations*, I, 48 (115); Dio Chrysostom, XXIII, 2; Plutarch, *Consolatio ad Apollonium*, 27 D–E and *De audiendis poetis*, 36 F; Sextus Empiricus, III, 230–32; and Diogenes Laertius, X, 126 (Epicurus).
[84] The topic is already implicit in the subtitle of Ryan's monograph (1965): „Exzentrische Bahn und Dichterberuf."

appeal of Hyperion's development, his philosophic calm. Hyperion's consciousness enables him to be more than just a function of fluctuating moods. The interconnection between consciousness and stability of selfhood is reflected in Hyperion's juxtaposition: „Hab' ich ein Bewustseyn? Hab' ich ein Bleiben in mir?" (II, 8). Insofar as Hyperion extends his consciousness of himself, he is tranquil and stable. His goal is a lasting unity such as Socrates attains at the end of Plato's *Symposium* and in Hölderlin's own „Rheinhymne":[85]

> Ein Weiser aber vermocht es
> Vom Mittag bis in die Mitternacht,
> Und bis der Morgen erglänzte,
> Beim Gastmahl helle zu bleiben. (StA II, 148)

Through his reflection and in his repose Hyperion achieves not only stability and clarity of insight but also the capacity to educate others. Hyperion's education to composure through narration is something that his readers can imitate. In a letter to his brother Hölderlin notes not only the central importance of repose but also the fact that it can be reached through insight and practice:

> Der ruhige Verstand ist die heilige Aegide, die im Kriege der Welt das Herz vor giftigen Pfeilen bewahrt. Und ich glaube [...] daß dieser ruhige Verstand, mehr als irgend eine Tugend der Seele, durch die Einsicht seines Werths und gutwillige beharrliche Übung kann erworben werden. (StA VI, 302/no. 172)

Hyperion's own role as educator is carried out, indirectly, through his model education and his paradigmatic achievement of *Ruhe* and, directly, by his criticism of the narrowness and complacency of the Germans.

One might at first wonder why one of Hyperion's first acts as an educator, his voicing of the *Scheltrede,* is directed not against his own countrymen, the Greeks, but rather against the Germans. Several reasons come to mind. The first is historical and somewhat external to the text. Greece was under Turkish domination not only at the time of the events of the novel but also during the novel's publication in 1797 and 1799; it would have been factually impossible for Hyperion (or Hölderlin for that matter) to chastise the Greeks for the *inner* disharmony Hyperion finds among the Germans. The second reason leads us to the novel's definition of beauty as a unity differentiated in two, that is, to the secret identity of Greece and Germany. According to Hölderlin's analysis of the movement of history in his odes „An die Deutschen" and „Gesang des Deutschen" and his hymns „Am Quell der Donau" and „Germanien", the Germans were destined to carry on the Greek tradition. The final reason relates to the explicit and implicit readership of Hyperion's letters. The recipient of Hyperion's wis-

---

[85] Cf. Ryan (1965), 63.

dom and insight is not a Greek but a German, Bellarmin. Bellarmin means the beautiful German,[86] and in its overarching ethical and social significance the name refers to those readers potentially capable of insight and harmonious existence.[87] The readers of the novel are, of course, primarily Germans and the reader – if he or she has followed Hyperion's *Bildung* – is, like Hyperion, prepared to be confronted with negativity. Not only can the *Scheltrede* be expressed at the end of Hyperion's development in the novel, so too can it be understood.

The Organic Argument II. Hölderlin's Metaphysics

In his final reflections on *Ruhe* Hyperion accepts his fate and orders his life. I have suggested that this repose is neither ahistorical nor quietistic. I would like to buttress my reading with one final argument. To do so I will draw upon Hölderlin's metaphysics of the whole and the particular, the one and the many, as it is reflected in *Hyperion,* Hölderlin's philosophical essays, and his personal correspondence.

The references in the novel to Hyperion's status as poet, his transcendence of particularity, and his orientation towards the whole suggest that he has „jene ungewöhnliche Tendenz zur Allgemeinheit" characteristic of the Hölderlinian poet (StA IV, 156). Like Empedocles Hyperion has „jene ruhige Betrachtung, jene Vollständigkeit und durchgängige Bestimmtheit des Bewußtseyns [...] womit der Dichter auf ein *Ganzes* blikt" (StA IV, 156). The totality toward which Hyperion casts his gaze is not undifferentiated. For Hölderlin the whole realizes itself by breaking its pristine totality and recognizing a relationship within itself. Hyperion's turn back to the particular and historical, his voicing of the *Scheltrede,* is consistent with this idea.

In the programmatic final letter of the first volume of the novel Hyperion defines *beauty* as "hen deapheron eauto" or „das Eine in sich selber unterschiedne" (I, 145). Hyperion argues that originally no distinction could be made between the gods and man: „Im Anfang war der Mensch und seine Götter Eins" (I, 142). With this lack of distinction, however, comes a lack of consciousness. Beauty or the gods or man (All three were undifferentiated, thus interchangeable, and not at all themselves.) were „sich selber unbekannt" (I, 142). Beauty is essentially beauty only when it becomes differentiated or, in the cosmic analogy, when man is separated from the gods. This

---

[86] See Binder (1970/Namen), 210–13.
[87] Bellarmin is a non-character and we learn little about him, not because he is the non-ego against whom Hyperion defines his own self, but because he is an open character with whom the reader can and should identify. The reader is invited to place himself in Bellarmin's role as recipient of the story of Hyperion's path to wisdom and reconciliation.

disengagement is as much a fulfillment as a fall. Beauty, being of both divine and human origin, demands the original nondifferentiation of god (and man) as well as human consciousness in its difference. The original and undifferentiated being desires to come into consciousness, „will sich selber fühlen". Thus, Hyperion tells us, „der Mensch" „gab" „sich seine Götter" (I, 141). As Ryan (1965) points out in his analysis of this passage (136), this does not mean that the gods can be reduced to a projection of the human mind, for they, like man, are grounded in initial oneness. Since man and the gods originally form one undifferentiated unity, it is misleading to say either that the gods created man or that man invented the gods. One can only say that this unity, in order to manifest itself, must become differentiated. Hyperion calls this self-differentiation of an original unity beauty.

The close relationship between consciousness, finitude, and beauty reaches back to earlier stages of the composition of the novel. In the *metrische Fassung* we hear: „Also da, als die schöne Welt für uns anfieng, da wir zum Bewußtsein kamen, da wurden wir endlich" (StA III, 192). Although this and another related passage from the first chapter of *Hyperions Jugend* allude to Diotima's allegorical narration of the birth of love in the *Symposium* (203 b), the concepts employed remind the reader of Fichte's *Wissenschaftslehre*:[88]

> [...] als der Überfluß mit der Armuth sich gattete, da ward die Liebe. Das geschah am Tage, da Aphrodite geboren ward. Am Tage, da die schöne Welt für uns begann, begann für uns die Dürftigkeit des Lebens. Wären wir einst mangellos und frei von aller Schranke gewesen, umsonst hätten wir doch nicht die Allgenügsamkeit verloren, das Vorrecht reiner Geister. Wir tauschten das Gefühl des Lebens, das lichte Bewußtseyn für die leidensfreie Ruhe der Götter ein. Denke, wenn es möglich ist, den reinen Geist! Er befaßt sich mit dem Stoffe nicht; drum lebt auch kein Welt für ihn; für ihn geht keine Sonne auf und unter; er ist alles, und darum ist er nichts für sich. (StA III, 201–02)

Hyperion's first insight into the necessary passage from the undifferentiated to the separated, from „die leidensfreie Ruhe der Götter" to a world in which even „die Götter [...] leiden" (StA II, 106), stems from his reading of Fichte. Already in 1795, in the fragment *Urtheil und Seyn* (StA IV, 216–17), Hölderlin makes clear his understanding of this basic idea. He defines „Seyn" as „die Verbindung des Subjects und Objects":

> Wo Subject und Object schlechthin, nicht nur zum Theil vereiniget ist, mithin so vereiniget, daß gar keine Theilung vorgenommen werden kan, ohne das Wesen desjenigen, was getrennt werden soll, zu verlezen, da und sonst nirgends kann von einem Seyn schlechthin die Rede seyn, wie es bei der intellectualen Anschauung der Fall ist.

„Urtheil" is „die ursprüngliche Trennung des in der intellectualen Anschauung innigst vereinigten Objects und Subjects, diejenige Trennung, wodurch

---

[88] Cf. Düsing (1981), 104–05.

erst Object und Subject möglich wird, die Ur=Theilung". Hölderlin argues that Fichte's absolute ego is an example of „Ur=Theilung", not „Seyn":

> Aber dieses Seyn muß nicht mit der Identität verwechselt werden. Wenn ich sage: Ich bin Ich, so ist das Subject (Ich) und das Object (Ich) so vereiniget, daß gar keine Trennung vorgenommen werden kann, ohne, das Wesen desjenigen, was getrennt werden soll, zu verlezen; im Gegenteil das Ich ist nur durch diese Trennung des Ichs vom Ich möglich. Wie kann ich sagen: Ich! ohne Selbstbewußtseyn? Wie ist aber Selbstbewußtseyn möglich? Dadurch daß ich mich mir selbst entgegenseze, mich von mir selbst trenne, aber ungeachtet dieser Trennung mich im entgegengesezten als dasselbe erkenne. Aber in wieferne als dasselbe? Ich kann, ich muß so fragen; denn in einer andern Rüksicht ist es sich entgegengesezt. Also ist die Identität keine Vereinigung des Objects und Subjects, die schlechthin stattfände, also ist die Identität nicht = dem absoluten Seyn.

The Fichtean concept of intellectual intuition, because it includes a relationship between subject and object, is not *pure* being; correspondingly, pure being cannot be called an "ego" or a self, since a self is itself only insofar as it knows itself in relationship to itself. Pure being („Seyn schlechthin") does not allow for any such internal relationship. Hölderlin makes a similar attempt to criticize Fichte in his letter to Hegel of January 26, 1795, where he writes:

> Sein absolutes Ich (= Spinozas Substanz) enthält alle Realität; es ist alles, u. außer ihm ist nichts; es giebt also für dieses abs. Ich kein Object, denn sonst wäre nicht alle Realität in ihm; ein Bewußtsein ohne Object ist aber nicht denkbar, und wenn ich selbst dieses Object bin, so bin ich als solches notwendig beschränkt, sollte es auch nur in der Zeit seyn, also nicht absolut; also ist in dem absoluten Ich kein Bewußtsein denkbar, als absolutes Ich hab ich kein Bewußtsein, und insofern ich kein Bewußtsein habe, insofern bin ich (für mich) nichts, also das absolute Ich ist (für mich) Nichts. (StA VI, 155/no. 94)

Our primary concern in these passages is not the validity of Hölderlin's critique[89] but the fact that Hölderlin, in his attempt to criticize Fichte, is using

---

[89] Hölderlin's critique tells us only that the absolute ego lacks consciousness, which is of course what Fichte himself suggested when he postulated the separation of the absolute ego. The critique is directed not against the logical validity of a pure being but rather against its designation as an ego. In comparison with Hegel, Hölderlin remains quite Fichtean: for Hölderlin Being or Unity is privileged logically and chronologically, even though it requires its other pole in order for itself to become „fühlbar". Dieter Henrich (1975) has written: „Auch im steten Bezug des Wechsels kann Hölderlin also die gründende Einheit nicht entbehren, wenn er auch den Weg in die Trennung als endgültig und die innige Ursprungseinheit als verloren, und zwar glücklich verloren anerkennt" (33). Henrich contrasts Hölderlin (and Fichte) in this respect with Hegel: „Und dies ist nun Hegels eigentümlicher Gedanke: daß die Relata in der Entgegensetzung zwar aus einem Ganzen verstanden werden müssen, daß dieses Ganze ihnen aber nicht vorausgeht als Sein oder als intellektuale Anschauung, – sondern daß es nur der entwickelte Begriff der Relation selber ist" (36).

Fichte's own insight: the separation of an original totality is a transcendental condition of the possibility of consciousness. We find this idea in Hölderlin's correspondence as well,[90] for example, in a letter Hölderlin writes to Isaak von Sinclair:[91]

> Es ist auch gut, und sogar die erste Bedingung alles Lebens und aller Organisation, daß keine Kraft monarchisch ist im Himmel und auf Erden. Die absolute Monarchie hebt sich überall selbst auf, denn sie ist objectlos; es hat auch im strengen Sinne niemals eine gegeben. Alles greift ineinander und leidet, so wie es thätig ist. (StA VI, 300/no. 171)

The idea that any monistic principle necessarily cancels itself is revealed more fully in Hölderlin's general theory of the modulation of tones and his specific conception of tragedy. In *Die Verfahrungsweise des poetischen Geistes* Hölderlin grounds his theory of tones philosophically (StA IV, 241–65). His theory contains two major poles: stationary and undifferentiated unity, termed at various points in the essay, „das Zugleichsein", „das Verweilen des Geistes", „ruhiger Gehalt", or „die Einigkeit", and differentiation and modulation, termed „Fortschritt", „Fortstreben des Geistes", „wechselnde Form", or „das Leben". Each pole, when taken in isolation, cancels itself. The pole of unity lacks distinction. As „ein Ununterscheidbares" it is empty, what Hölderlin calls a „*leere* Unendlichkeit" (StA IV, 615). It can be likened to the initial emptiness of Fichte's absolute ego which, we remember, Hölderlin equates with nonbeing.[92] Modulation, taken in isolation from unity, when it is „nichts Ganzes und Einiges mehr", is an infinity of isolated moments, „eine Unendlichkeit isolirter Momente" (StA IV, 615); as such it lacks unity.[93] Each pole, the first representative of Eleatic or Spinozistic oneness, the second representing the philosophical position of Anaxagoras and the Atomists as well as that of Leibniz, lacks the character of an absolute. But Hölderlin does not suggest that the absolute resides in the simple emanation of the one or in the unity of the many; rather he equates it with the *unity* of emanation and unification. „Das Harmonischentgegengesetzte", likely Hölderlin's translation for the Greek *hen diapheron eauto*,[94] is to be seen „weder als Einiges entgegengesezt, noch als Entgegengesetztes vereinigt, sondern als beedes in *Einem*" (StA IV, 251). True unity „ist also nie blos Entgegensezung des Einigen, auch nie blos Beziehung Vereinigung des Entgegengesezten und Wechselnden, Entgegengesetztes und Einiges ist in ihr unzertrennlich" (StA

---

[90] Besides the passage quoted below, see StA VI, 290–91/no. 167.
[91] Hölderlin's use of *Leiden* and *Thätigkeit* in this passage reminds us that the source of these reflections can be found in Fichte.
[92] Letter to Hegel of January 26, 1795 (StA VI, 155/no. 94).
[93] This metaphysical state has in Hölderlin a strong political corollary, viz., German parochialism. See the *Scheltrede* and letters 172 and 179.
[94] See Konrad (1967), 33.

IV, 251). The process by which the whole differentiates itself is the same process through which the parts are able to take part in the whole. Differentiation and unification constitute one another reciprocally. What interests us in the context of *Hyperion* is the idea that the original unity becomes itself a unity only through differentiation.[95]

Drawing upon Fichte's insight into the separation of the whole as a free act, Spinoza's understanding of the reciprocity of freedom and necessity in the divine,[96] as well as the Platonic image of Zeus as a first cause,[97] Hölderlin calls this act of emanation and unification the „nothwendiger *Willkür* des Zeus" (StA IV, 269). The unity must differentiate itself in order to become conscious of itself, to become, in Hölderlin's phrase, „fühlbar".[98] Otherwise, unity is indistinguishable from pure nothingness. The absolute is thus subject to a freely undertaken necessity. The differentiation is free, for the divine is not constrained or determined by something external to itself; its action is determined by itself alone. It is necessary, because the differentiation follows inescapably from divine nature.

One can find this idea of a dynamic and differentiated unity throughout Hölderlin's later poetry. The gods, in part symbolic for oneness and wholeness, fulfill themselves in history; they enter man's consciousness and are thus able to manifest themselves, to become truly total beings, no longer excluded from history. In „Der Rhein" the poet states:

> [...] Denn weil
> Die Seeligsten nichts fühlen von selbst,
> Muß wohl, wenn solches zu sagen
> Erlaubt ist, in der Götter Nahmen
> Theilnehmend fühlen ein Andrer,
> Den brauchen sie. (StA II, 145)

Here, too, the poet employs the language of necessity („muß wohl"; „brauchen"). The verb „fühlen" is Hölderlin's expression for becoming conscious. We see it again in „Der Ister", where the gods require earthly reflection in order to gain consciousness:

---

[95] The basic idea in Hölderlin's „Wechsel der Töne", namely, that the one freely manifests itself through self-differentiation, is again reminiscent of Fichte's insight into the self-differentiation of the absolute ego. Even the language is similar. Fichte's absolute ego manifests itself through „den Trieb nach Wechsel" (Fichte I, 321) or „den Trieb nach Wechselbestimmung" (Fichte I, 326). The self-differentiation of the absolute ego is, moreover, for Fichte as well as for Hölderlin an activity. See Fichte I, 160 and elsewhere. On the last point see Bachmaier (1979), 97–98.
[96] See EI, Def. 7: "Ea res libera dicitur, quae ex sola suae naturae necessitate existit."
[97] See *Philebus* 30D. Cf. Kurz (1975), 171.
[98] StA IV, 241. See also StA IV: 243 and 249–50.

> [...] Ein Zeichen braucht es
> Nichts anderes, schlecht und recht, damit es Sonn
> Und Mond trag' im Gemüth, untrennbar,
> Und fortgeh, Tag und Nacht auch, und
> Die Himmlischen warm sich fühlen aneinander.
> Darum sind jene [the rivers] auch
> Die Freude des Höchsten. Denn wie käm er
> Herunter? Und wie Hertha grün
> Sind sie die Kinder des Himmels.
>
> (StA II, 191)

The rivers are quite literally children of heaven insofar as they have nourished themselves through the rain from above. „Der Höchste" manifests himself through the rivers insofar as the river, acting as a mirror, brings the heavens to the earth. Each sphere depends on the other for its own manifestation. „Der Archipelagus" offers a third example of the god's dependence on man:

> Immer bedürfen ja, wie Heroën den Kranz, die geweihten
> Elemente zum Ruhme das Herz der fühlenden Menschen.
>
> (StA II, 104)

The goal of poetry according to Hölderlin is the manifestation of the divine in the particular. Through the intricate modulation of tones „der Geist" becomes „in seiner Unendlichkeit fühlbar" (StA IV, 249–50).

The structure of tragedy illuminates this idea best. Tragedy, with a "basic tone" and an "effect" that is "ideal" and an "artistic effect" that is "heroic", manifests unity through its portrayal of separation.[99] In his *Anmerkungen zum Oedipus* Hölderlin writes: „Die Darstellung des Tragischen beruht vorzüglich darauf [...] daß das gränzenlose Eineswerden durch gränzenloses Scheiden sich reiniget."[100] In *Die Verfahrungsweise des poetischen Geistes* we see yet again the theme that has now become familiar to us: „Die Fühlbarkeit des Ganzen schreitet also in eben dem Grade und Verhältnisse fort, in welchem die Trennung in den Theilen und in ihrem Centrum, worin die Theile und das Ganze am fühlbarsten sind, fortschreitet" (StA IV, 269).

The parallel I would like to draw between these metaphysical reflections and the conclusion of *Hyperion* is as follows: While totality or the divine fulfills itself through separation and its relationship to the particular, Hype-

---

[99] It would not serve my particular argument to discuss here the thematic and syntactic characteristics of Hölderlin's three tones, the naive, heroic, and ideal, or to list the possible combinations of tones. Corssen (1951) and Ryan (1960) offer introductions to this topic. Readers interested in the Schiller-Hölderlin relationship might want to consult the critics' diverse attempts to correlate Schiller's categories in *Über naive und sentimentalische Dichtung* with Hölderlin's tones. See esp. Binder (1960), 145 and Szondi (1977), 163–69.
[100] StA V, 201. See also the brief essay *Die Bedeutung der Tragödien* (StA IV, 274).

rion's pinnacle of stillness, his consciousness of the whole, fulfills itself in the particularity of the *Scheltrede*. The ideal orientation of the passage on *Ruhe* with its philosophical rhetoric passes over into the heroic tone of the *Scheltrede* with its mood of struggle. As in Hölderlin's general model, here in *Hyperion*, unity manifests itself through dynamic separation, through its relationship to the particular or historical.

Excursus. A Stroke of Incompletion

While the divine requires man's articulation, man does not, according to Hölderlin, exhaust the divine. In Hölderlin's view the gods must be kept separate from the sphere of man; otherwise, each would be reduced to the emptiness of nondifferentiation. Hölderlin asserts the separation of gods and man in *Der Tod des Empedokles,* where (in the first version) Empedocles is termed guilty for having forgotten this distinction: „Weil er des Unterschieds zu sehr vergaß" (StA IV, 11).[101] The idea is also evident in the later hymns, for example, in „Germanien", where the eagle speaks to the priestess Germania of sacred meaning:

> Dreifach umschreibe du es,
> Doch ungesprochen auch, wie es da ist,
> Unschuldige, muß es bleiben.
> (StA II, 152)

One thinks also of the late sketch „... Der Vatikan..." where Hölderlin writes: „Gott rein und mit Unterscheidung / Bewahren, das ist uns vertrauet" (StA II, 252). Hölderlin's statement „Unterschiedenes ist / gut" (StA II, 327) belongs in this context as well.[102]

This central Hölderlinian theme of the fulfillment, yet *nonexhaustion,* of totality in history is present in Hyperion's last letters. Hyperion attains a seemingly complete consciousness in his reflections on *Ruhe,* but the novel ends with a stroke of incompletion or nonexhaustion: „So dacht ich. Nächstens mehr." Critics have universally interpreted this final phrase to imply Hölderlin's acceptance of the Kantian-Fichtean doctrine of infinite approximation.[103] But the passage on *Ruhe* indicates that there is no dualism between the real and the ideal. What ideal condition would one infinitely approximate? Surely not a condition without suffering, for that is itself „dem

---

[101] See also the extreme differentiation of divine and human spheres for which Hermocrates calls in response to Empedocles' hybris (StA IV: 91, 97).
[102] For a fuller discussion of this topic see the chapter „Unterschiedene Einheit. Eine Grundstruktur im Spätwerk Hölderlins" in Lüders (1968), 19–77.
[103] See, for example, Ryan (1965), 50, 56, 236 and (1970), 205, 208, also Prignitz (1976), 212.

Nichts gleich". The divine, it is said, fulfills itself in suffering: „Muß nicht alles leiden? Und je treflicher es ist, je tiefer! [...] Ja! ja! werth ist der Schmerz" (II, 106–07). The „Nächstens mehr", which refers to the future of H2,[104] is a gesture of limitation or humility (Hyperion's process of *Bildung* is not complete; Hyperion is not yet what he wants to be.) but also a sign of strength (Hyperion does have the desire to move forward; his repose is not static.). While „Nächstens mehr" does imply an infinite process, it does not suggest that the goal lies beyond the process (as in the notion of infinite approximation). Perfection lies not „droben" (II, 94) but rather in the process of history itself („Wir stellen im Wechsel das Vollendete dar" II, 103). Perfection is present in history, and yet, with his concluding remark, Hyperion implies that it is not complete. *To use the paradoxical language of which Hölderlin, like all synthetic thinkers, was so fond, it is a completion so complete as to contain within it incompletion.*

Making Sense of Narrative Levels at the Novel's Conclusion

Juxtaposed between the *Ruhe* passage and the critique of the Germans, then again between the critique and the narrator's final words („So dacht' ich. Nächstens mehr."), lie several pages of narration of past events and quoted statements from the past. Their position near the text's conclusion invites further inquiry. Why does Hölderlin place statements originating from H1 after the supposed climax of the novel, the last lengthy excursus of H2?[105]

To answer this question we can turn to the first sentence that follows the quoted vision of Nature: „So dacht' ich" (II, 124).[106] As at earlier points in the

---

[104] I see „Nächstens mehr" as a sign of further activity in the life of Hyperion. Some early critics, Böhlendorff and Emerich for example, interpreted these lines to mean that Hölderlin planned to write a third volume. See StA III, 318. Note also Mason's basic agreement with this position (1958–60: 133ff.). The aesthetic-interpretive and historical-literal interpretations of the phrase are not mutually exclusive.

[105] This is an important question that recent criticism has posed, if not answered. Böschenstein-Schäfer (1980–81) asks, if the novel reaches its high point with Hyperion's developed consciousness, why does it conclude with the mystical vision of nature: „Warum aber hat dann der Dichter an eine so ausgezeichnete Stelle wie den Schluß die große Vision der von der Natur gestifteten Einheit alles Seienden gesetzt? [...] Die Spannung zwischen dem ‚logischen' und dem poetisch strukturellen Schlußpunkt müßte ebenso reflektiert werden wie die Relativierung beider durch die zwei abschließenden Sätze" (394–95).

[106] Although I offer immanent reasons for the anticlimactic conclusion of *Hyperion*, one might want to go beyond the novel and consider the influence of Pindar on Hölderlin. Benn (1962) suggests that one of the major influences of Pindar "on the compositional structure of Hölderlin's poetry" is "quiet endings" (121). For Pindar

novel, the narrator uses this weighty phrase to distance himself from his earlier views.[107] At such moments the pastness of the past is evident. The sentence must be read: „So *dacht'* ich." The Hyperion who writes this is a different Hyperion with a different set of values.[108] Yet the actual statement from which Hyperion seems to distance himself here at the novel's conclusion is one of unity:

---

and Hölderlin a fading ending can be as appropriate as a climactic one. Benn notes in his discussion of this point Hölderlin's own observation that the poet need not think, „daß er nur im *crescendo* von Schwächern zum Stärkern sich selber übertreffen könne" (126).

[107] Aspetsberger sees Hyperion's final vision as H2's reconstruction of the thoughts of H1. See Aspetsberger (1971), 102, 132–39. While this argument allows him to overturn Ryan's thesis – that Hyperion becomes a writer only after finishing his letters – and to suggest, instead, that Hyperion's letters are themselves a work of art, it tells us very little about the final vision. After all, H2 has reconstructed all of H1's reflections with the possible exception of the quoted letters. Moreover, we assume that the letters reproduce more or less accurately H1's earlier positions. In terms of content then the author would be H1. On this point see Hamlin (1973), 152.

[108] I cannot agree with Aspetsberger (1971), who sees no major development in the course of Hyperion's writing, no fundamental changes in his world-view, only „*eine geistige Anreicherung*" (326). See also 300, 315, 339, and 342. Aspetsberger's main argument rests on the fact that H1 envisages world-unity in the last letter of the novel, before H2 begins to write: „Eine Entwicklung des Erzählers erscheint von vornherein insofern relativiert, als Hyperion von Anfang an die Welteinheit weiß und von ihr her darstellt" (300). According to Aspetsberger, then, Hyperion has his most important insight before he becomes a narrator, but this initial insight into unity lacks differentiation. Aspetsberger argues that because a narrator mediates the vision, it is not undifferentiated. But one must note, first, that the speaker at the end of the novel does not identify with, but rather distances himself from, this earlier quotation; second, that the content of the letter is filled with explicit praise of nondifferentiation. In narrating his life Hyperion develops a consciousness of differentiation without losing his initial intuitive grasp of unity. More importantly, Hyperion not only achieves a higher consciousness and becomes more stable, he revises his earlier ideals. In his first letter Hyperion wishes away his previous life and desires to return to a motionless Nature. Later he regrets nothing in his life, affirming it all as necessary, and he reinterprets Nature as a dynamic force. In his second letter Hyperion considers a consciousless immersion in Nature divine; he explicitly states that he would prefer to have no consciousness rather than to experience pain. Later he sees that even the gods fulfill themselves in consciousness and suffering. In his second letter Hyperion curses thinking and differentiation; he wishes he'd never learned anything. At the peak of his development he achieves a clarity of thought reminiscent of the Stoics or Spinoza. In his third letter Hyperion writes that he was happier as a child, without knowledge of self or world; later he suggests that such painless bliss is not greater than sleep, and he equates the ignorant child with nothingness. In these later reflections Hyperion (H2) reevaluates not only the experiences of H1 but also earlier standpoints and perspectives of H2.

„Wie der Zwist der Liebenden, sind die Dissonanzen der Welt. Versöhnung ist mitten im Streit und alles Getrennte findet sich wieder. / Es scheiden und kehren im Herzen die Adern und einiges, ewiges, glühendes Leben ist Alles." (II, 124)

One might read Hyperion's final reflection with this theme in mind and note therein the *unity* of H1 and H2. One would then read the sentence: „So dacht' ich."[109] It is, to be sure, the same self who has and speaks of the vision. The narrator attains unity on the level of reflection and recognizes that the character Hyperion anticipates this unity on an intuitive level. H1 mystically experiences unity; he cannot, however, reflect upon it. The act of reflection is reserved for H2, yet the subject of the narrator's reflections is one with the primary experience of his earlier self, unity. Where both character and narrator envisage unity, the two selves can be said to merge into one. Departure point and telos, H1 and H2, conjoin.[110] The real unity of the novel's conclusion is not the earlier, undifferentiated vision of unity but the fulfillment of this in the constitution of a unified self, manifest in the sentence „So dacht' *ich.*" Hyperion has united not only Diotima's *Ruhe* and Alabanda's *Streben* but also Diotima's closing vision of all-unity and Alabanda's final image of individuality and selfhood. Hyperion is a self who is both different from and at one with his previous self. This self-differentiated unity corresponds to the novel's definition of beauty as „das Eine in sich selber unterschiedne" (I, 145). Hyperion mirrors this concept in his development. As he narrates, he distances himself from his earlier self, but he is also able to affirm his identity with this self; in so relinquishing and embracing his earlier self, he comes to a new selfhood and yet remains himself. The unity is manifest even in the details of time reference. In his last two sentences Hyperion writes in the present, but the theme of his *present* reflections is at once the *past* („So dacht' ich") and the *future* („Nächstens mehr").

The self-differentiated unity of Hyperion the individual is also the self-differentiated unity of *Hyperion* the novel. A consideration of Hyperion's definition of beauty as well as its embodiment in his development will help guide us in establishing why such a seemingly strange juxtaposition of narrative levels occurs even at the novel's conclusion. First, the poet wanted to emphasize the *difference* between the early and late Hyperion. At the end of the novel Hyperion attains not a unity of undifferentiated oneness or a dissolution of the self in the wholeness of Nature but a conscious unity that recognizes difference and affirms its value. This unity is not only differentiated within itself, it is different from the earlier unity. To emphasize this

---

[109] Ryan (1965: 226) notes only the act of distancing involved in the sentence „So dacht' ich" not also the unity implicit in the idea that it is in a major sense the same Hyperion who thought then and who thinks now.
[110] Cf. Hamlin (1973), 152.

contrast Hölderlin juxtaposes the final passages. Hyperion presents his attainment of *Ruhe* with the time reference „jezt" (II, 106); he introduces the following pages – which contain quotations from the letter Hyperion had written to Notara immediately after Diotima's death – with the word „damals" (II, 107). Hyperion's contemplation of suicide (II, 109) and his impotency („es kann der Mensch nichts ändern" II, 112) thus contrast with his affirmation of suffering and his strong sense of self. So too, the mystical vision of Nature at the end of the novel forms a contrast with the reflective *Ruhe* of Hyperion's more mature period. Contrasts between the character's nihilism and the narrator's affirmation or between ecstatic emotion and deliberation are visible throughout the novel and serve to accentuate the narrator's advancement over his previous condition. Second, Hölderlin employs such juxtapositions in order to stress *unity*. The inclusion of H1's position at the end of the text creates a circular structure for the novel.[111] The story concludes with his trip to Germany (last letter). The story of H2 begins thereafter with his return to Greece (first letter). The final letter of the novel thus leads into the first.[112] This circular structure is also symbolic of the unity

---

[111] Abrams and Brown place the circuitous journey of Hyperion in the context of European Romanticism. See Abrams (1973), 199–252, esp. 237–44 and Brown (1979), 167–69. The novel is, of course, not just circular but also progressive. Consider both Hyperion's development and the concluding remark „Nächstens mehr". With Hegel we can say that the return to the origin is also an advance: „Zugleich ist diese Rückkehr zum Anfang ein Fortgang" (Hegel 8, 393). Although I do not find the concept of an „exzentrische Bahn" (StA III, 236) – which is lifted from the penultimate, not the final, version of the novel – as helpful a guide to reading and analysis as most interpreters of the novel, I should note here that some critics do see in the elliptical and progressive movement of the *Bahn* a spiral image. See, for example, Doppler (1968), 112. For other interpretations of the „exzentrische Bahn" see Brown (1978), Gaier (1978–79), 109–16, Miles (1971), Ryan (1965), esp. 11–12, Schadewaldt (1952), and Strack (1976), 179–220. I tend to agree with Ryan (1965), who suggests that Hyperion moves beyond the eccentric path insofar as he overcomes the dissonances ascribed to his eccentricity by recognizing them as a necessary and integral part of perfection (228, 236). I myself would propose that *Hyperion discarded this astronomical image from his final version insofar as he wanted to stress not the elliptical orbit of Hyperion around two centers, each of which is of course the sun, but rather the centeredness of Hyperion; after all, in the final version Hyperion is linked not to any particular course of orbit around the sun but to the sun itself.*

[112] While Hölderlin's concept of *Ruhe* is displayed in the novel's broad circular structure, it also manifests itself in the minutest details of syntax. Walter Silz (1969) has noted that Hölderlin tends to retard the personal pronouns in *Hyperion* (84), in particular the reflexives, as for example in the sentences: „schrökt ja aus meinen Träumen mich auf (I, 8) or „die wilden Ranken breiteten richtungslos über dem Boden sich aus" (I, 18). Hölderlin's unorthodox syntax requires the reader to move from the finite verb to the reflexive and back again. This halts the general flow of reading and creates an effect of *Ruhe,* but it also brings movement into the sentence. It establishes the need to rush forward and complete what has only been

of subject (H2) and object (H1), of he who reflects and that upon which is being reflected, as would be evident to any reader of Fichte.[113] Moreover, the experience of oneness with Nature in the final letter anticipates many prominent themes found in the mature Hyperion. The sense of equality evident in Hyperion's mystical oneness („Frei sind wir, gleichen uns nicht ängstig von außen [...] wir lieben den Aether doch all' und innigst im Innersten gleichen wir uns" II, 123) takes on political significance in the context of Hyperion's later goals as educator. Hyperion would raise his people to a level of harmony and equality. Hyperion's early experience of oneness foreshadows the totality of his poetic consciousness and the non-exclusive nature of his existence as a "hermit". Mystical oneness becomes itself a major stage in Hyperion's education to poetic consciousness. As is stated at the conclusion of volume I, book II, philosophical and poetic differentiation build on the original oneness of beauty, a beauty initiated by Nature, not consciousness. One can formulate thoughts that harmonize contradictions only insofar as one has an intuitive sense of unity.[114]

Hyperion's earlier statement that the gods are as men finds a counterpoint in the final letter. Hölderlin introduces a sense of man's dependence on Nature or, one might say, the gods. Implicit in this is a criticism of *Fichte*. Where Hyperion had earlier demonstrated the power of mind over Nature, he now grants Nature a role in determining mind. Hölderlin does not share the Fichtean thesis of an autonomous self voiced by Alabanda: „Ich fühl' in mir ein Leben, das kein Gott geschaffen, und kein Sterblicher gezeugt. Ich glaube, daß wir durch uns selber sind, und nur aus freier Lust so innig mit dem All verbunden" (II, 90).[115] For Hölderlin the self, and especially the poet, is not wholly autonomous. While human activity can develop and refine

---

begun. This dynamic stillness, with the corresponding spatial image of a movement forward and a return, parallels the general structure of the novel. Also, as Benjamin Bennett suggested to me, it could be seen as a critical gesture directed against Lessing's stress in *Laokoon* on purely linear and progressive reading.

[113] Hegel, too, equates the subject-object unity with the image of a circle. See Hegel 10, 216–17 and 18, 46.

[114] There is a connection here to the Platonic notion of *anamnēsis* as described for example in *Meno*.

[115] On this concept of autonomy see Fichte II, 249: „Es ist in mir ein Trieb zu absoluter, unabhängiger Selbstthätigkeit. Nichts ist mir unausstehlicher, als nur an einem anderen, für ein anderes, und durch ein anderes zu seyn." On the subject's dominance of Nature, another view that Hyperion criticizes in his final letter, see Fichte II, 192–93: „Ich will der Herr der Natur seyn, und sie soll mein Diener seyn; ich will einen meiner Kraft gemäßen Einfluß auf sie haben, sie aber soll keinen haben auf mich." A final criticism of Fichte is evident in Hölderlin's ultimately negative portrayal of Alabanda's „Thatenlust". This serves in part as a critique of Fichte's dictum: „Handeln! Handeln! das ist es, wozu wir da sind" (VI, 345). On this last point see Prignitz (1976), 158–59.

„schaffende Kraft", „die Kraft selbst ist ewig und nicht der Menschenhände Werk" (StA VI, 329–30/no. 179). This anti-Fichtean notion of the self is understandably close to Schelling. For Schelling the „Eindruck allbelebender, allwaltender Naturkräfte" generates a work of art. Poetry is „das reine Geschenk der Natur". Artistic activity is „keine Eigenschaft, kein Vermögen".[116] For Hölderlin, too, poetry does not stem from the power of the poet alone. He is dependent on discontinuous moments of inspiration, on intellectual intuition or a mystical experience of oneness with Nature.[117] Poetry is a matter of chance, of happy inspiration or *Glück* („Der Gesang [...] glükt").[118]

The positioning of a moment of mystical oneness with Nature at the end of the novel and at a turning point in Hyperion's development emphasizes the dependence of consciousness on original unity. Further, it descredits any one-sided glorification of the power of consciousness to distinguish and differentiate. On the other hand, Hyperion's advancement over this original unity indicates that inspiration or the experience of pure unity does not alone lead to poetry. Poetry demands the kind of struggle with language and expression one finds in Hyperion's letters. For Hölderlin, too, it is clear that poetry requires reflection and workmanship. One thinks here of art as *téchnē*, of Hölderlin's intricate theory of tones, or of his image of a poetic „Werkstatt" in the ode „An die Deutschen" (StA II, 9). While distinctions depend on unity, so does unity depend on distinctions. In his essay *Die Verfahrungsweise des poetischen Geistes* Hölderlin tells us that the divine is

> weder bloßes Bewußtseyn, bloße Reflexion (subjective, oder objective,) mit Verlust des innern und äußern Lebens noch bloßes Streben (subjectiv oder objectiv bestimmtes) mit Verlust der innern und äußern Harmonie, noch bloße Harmonie, wie die intellectuale Anschauung und ihr mythisches bildliches Subject, Object, mit Verlust des Bewußtseyns, und der Einheit, sondern [...] alles diß zugleich. (StA IV, 259)

---

[116] *Über das Verhältnis der bildenden Künste zur Natur* (VII: 306, 312, 324).
[117] Hölderlin defines intellectual intuition as „jene Einigkeit mit allem, was lebt" (StA IV, 267). For a study of the concept of intellectual intuition during this period with references to both Hölderlin and Spinoza see Neubauer (1972).
[118] „Wie wenn am Feiertage..." (StA II, 119). Despite Hölderlin's emphasis on the portrayal of ideas in poetry, his rigorous rewriting of earlier drafts of his lyrics, and the difficulties he often had in achieving poetic inspiration, he does embody one major aspect of the "naive" poet. Schiller terms „die naive Dichtung" „ein glücklicher Wurf" (NA XX, 473). For the naive poet as well as for Hölderlin poetic inspiration is a gift that cannot be forced by will or reflection; for Hölderlin alone, however – and this brings him back into the sphere of the sentimental – such moments of inspiration are wholly discontinuous. In one fine passage Hölderlin combines a sentimental with a naive image and speaks of himself as a „verunglükter Poët" (StA VI, 289/no. 167).

While Hyperion's harmonic consciousness supersedes his mystical oneness with Nature, his development toward consciousness depends on such moments of inspiration no less than the gods depend on man.

Hyperion in the Context of Hölderlin's Life and Work

The synthesis in *Hyperion* for which I have argued would seem to be at odds with much of what one understands as particularly Hölderlinian. One is inclined to equate Hölderlin with the „unglückliches Bewußtsein" of Hegel's *Phänomenologie des Geistes* (Hegel 3, 163–77) rather than to suggest that he might himself be the creator of an Hegelian-like synthesis.[119] In fact with so much attention paid to the disharmony and dissonance of the late Hölderlin it is not surprising that one critic recently suggested we probe *Hyperion* for early intimations of Hölderlin's broken synthesis.[120] In anticipation then of the objection that a synthetic reading of *Hyperion* is at odds with what we understand by the mature Hölderlin, I would like to place my reading of the novel in the context of Hölderlin's larger corpus. First, I would like to stress the extent to which *Ruhe* is a central concept throughout Hölderlin's works.[121] Second, I will suggest that the work of the late Hölderlin does not represent a break from *Hyperion* but rather follows the pattern of the novel itself.

---

[119] One common argument against drawing analogies between Hölderlin and Hegel rests on the view that in any Hegelian synthesis history is totally overcome; there is no openness, only closure. See, for example, Ryan (1961–62), 37–38. Recent interpretations of Hegel have shown the falsity of this view: Hans Brockard (1970), in discussing Hegel's philosophy of history, writes, „Im Abschlußcharakter liegt Eröffnungstendenz," and he cites a wealth of literature to suggest that the abstruse assertion, „Hegel habe sich bzw. seine Philosophie für das Ende der Geschichte gehalten [...] darf heute im großen und ganzen als ausdiskutiert und widerlegt gelten" (51). James Ogilvy (1975), writing on the history of criticism and the philosophy of interpretation, argues: "Like the true infinite the true absolute must answer to demands for both openness and closure, both *Unendlichkeit* and determinateness" (527). For a more precise discussion of this problem see Hösle and Wandschneider (1983).
[120] See Böschenstein-Schäfer (1980–81), 394.
[121] Interpreters of Hölderlin have long since noticed the importance of *Ruhe* in Hölderlin, beginning with Kampe's handwritten dissertation from the year 1902. Of the books and articles written on Hölderlin in the latter half of this century perhaps as many as twenty mention in passing the concept of *Ruhe*. Of these I note only the more extensive and revealing studies; de Man (1965), esp. 161–65; Mojašević (1963–64); Jochen Schmidt (1978), 165–66; and Thurmair (1980).

The Concept of *Ruhe* in Hölderlin's Work

Hölderlin's praise of *Ruhe* begins early. „Die Stille", „An die Ruhe", and „An die Stille" were all written when Hölderlin was twenty years old or younger. His interest in *Ruhe* continues through his latest works and permeates his personal correspondence.[122] One could locate every passage on *Ruhe* in the poetry after 1800 by using the Böschenstein-*Konkordanz* or throughout Hölderlin's poetry by consulting the *Wörterbuch zu Friedrich Hölderlin*. But these aids are not as helpful as they might seem, for Hölderlin wrote scarcely a poem in which the concept „Ruhe" does not play a role. For a study of this particular concept such aids are about as useful as an index to the idea of "the good" in Plato.

Of Hölderlin's early poems on stillness the most interesting is „An die Ruhe" (StA I, 92–93). In a work of the same period, „Zornige Sehnsucht", the poet criticizes the deficiencies of a static stillness: „Ruhe beglükt mich nicht" (StA I, 90). This is not the *Ruhe* of the ode „An die Ruhe", for here Hölderlin emphasizes the positive dynamism inherent in stillness: *Ruhe* bestows „Riesenkraft" and generates a „Götterwerk". The poem is partly influenced by Friedrich Stolberg,[123] but the central figure is the poet Rousseau, to whom reference is made in the closing strophe and whom Lenz, Schiller, and Fichte chastise for his *empty* stillness.[124] In fact in *Über naive und sentimentalische Dichtung* Schiller criticizes Rousseau not only for his „Bedürfniß nach physischer Ruhe" and his desire to return „zu der geistlosen Einförmigkeit des ersten Standes" but also for the contradiction between his „leidenschaftliche Empfindlichkeit" and the rigorous „Denkkraft" that

---

[122] The letters in which Hölderlin expresses his desire for *Ruhe* are almost countless. He writes to Hegel: „Du bist mer mit Dir selbst im Reinen, als ich. Dir ists gut, irgend einen Lärm in der Nähe zu haben; ich brauche Stille" (StA VI, 127/no. 84). To Neuffer he writes: „Doch hast Du Ruhe. Und ohne sie ist alles Leben so gut, wie der Tod. Ich möchte sie auch haben, mein Lieber" (StA VI, 243/no. 140). To his mother he writes: „Freiheit und Ruhe ist das einzige, was ich suche, und brauche, und das hoff ich zu finden" (StA VI, 248/no. 143). He writes to his brother: „Ich suche Ruhe, mein Bruder! [...] ich suche nur Ruhe" (StA VI, 263/no. 152). He writes to his sister: „Ich habe in mir ein so tiefes dringendes Bedürfniß nach Ruhe und Stille – mehr als Du mir ansehn kannst, und ansehn sollst" (StA VI, 404/no. 219). But Hölderlin is not always without *Ruhe*. See, for example, letters 136 and 137. Other letters in which Hölderlin expresses his desire for or appreciation of *Ruhe* are nos. 43, 72, 75, 80, 86, 87, 96, 112, 116, 117, 125, 138, 142, 146, 153, 157, 167, 169, 172, 175, 185, 197, 199, 204, 205, 210, 217, 223, 228, and 229.

[123] See Stolberg's essay „Über die Ruhe nach dem Genuß und über den Zustand des Dichters in dieser Ruhe" as well as Beck's discussion of Stolberg's influence on Hölderlin (1944), esp. 99–100.

[124] See Lenz I, 492–93; Schiller NA XX, 451–52; Fichte VI: 341, 344–45.

spawned his political writings.[125] Hölderlin, before Schiller's words were ever written, insists on the coherence of *Ruhe* and political action in Rousseau and in general. The beginning and center of this ode to stillness are marked by a strong heroic tone:

> Erquiklich, wie die heimische Ruhebank
>   Im fernen Schlachtgetümmel dem Krieger deucht,
>   Wenn die zerfleischten Arme sinken,
>   Und der geschmetterte Stahl im Blut liegt –
> So bist du, Ruhe! freundliche Trösterin!
>   Du schenkst Riesenkraft dem Verachteten;
>   Er höhnet Dominikgesichtern,
>   Höhnet der zischenden Natterzunge.

Hölderlin integrates in action a necessary element of repose and in repose a clear moment of action. The poem is infused with social awareness and criticism. It contains two references to vanity and conceit at the court („Dominikgesichtern", v. 10 and „Dünkel", v. 20)[126] and expresses concern for the socially oppressed (the „Verachteten" of v. 10). Throughout, the poet sees *Ruhe* in the context not of eternity but of temporality. The poem opens with the „Gruß des Hahns" and closes with „die / Scheidende Sonne". The first part of the poem stresses the activities *Ruhe* generates, and the poem closes with a reflection on what *Ruhe* has accomplished; throughout, repose is a dynamic, engendering concept. In a later poem „Die Muße" (StA I, 237) Hölderlin again speaks of the synthesis of repose and activity: the „Geist der Ruh" and the „Geist der Unruh" are „aus Einem Schoose geboren".

Hölderlin never relinquishes his ideal of dynamic stillness; he even warns against any absolutization of *Ruhe* that would exclude necessary unrest. The first version of „Stimme des Volks" concludes with the strophe:[127]

> Drum weil sie fromm ist, ehr' ich den Himmlischen
>   Zu lieb des Volkes Stimme, die ruhige,
>   Doch um der Götter und der Menschen
>   Willen, sie ruhe zu gern nicht immer!
> (StA II, 7)

For Hölderlin *Ruhe* is primarily a synthetic term, and his philosophical predilection for synthesis manifests itself in a stylistic preference for oxymorons. One thinks of examples such as the following: „traurigfroh" (StA II, 14), „heilignüchtern" (StA II, 117), „seeligbescheiden" (StA II, 146), „freundlichernst" (StA III, 534), and „zärtliche Waffen" (StA III, 537). Often

---

[125] NA XX, 451–52. See de Man (1965), esp. 159–60.
[126] See Alewyn (1963–64).
[127] StA II, 50. For an interpretation of this strophe see Hof (1954), 334–38 and Ryan (1960), 174.

the oxymorons are related in one way or another to concepts of stillness: „stillebegeisternd" (StA II, 73), „stillhinwandelnd" (StA II, 73), „stillegehend" (StA II, 237), „in Eile zögernd" (StA II, 50), „stilltönend" (StA II, 232), „still vereint im freieren Lied" (StA II, 110–11), „still in dämmriger Luft ertönen geläutete Gloken" (StA II, 90), „still wiederklingend" (StA III, 533), „ruhigwandelne Töne" (StA III, 533), and „der stille Gott der Zeit" (StA III, 536). I have taken the last three examples from „Friedensfeier" (StA III, 531–38), a hymn that represents a second pinnacle of Hölderlin's reflections on stillness.[128] In a unique coinage the poet speaks here of Christ as a „Ruhigmächtiger".[129] The entire hymn celebrates peace and unity; all the gods are called together in a great adjuration of stillness.[130] The poem considers not only the union of divine beings but also the harmony of the divine and the human and the reconciliation of man with man. The political implications are clear: „Und einer, der nicht Fluth noch Flamme gescheuet, / Erstaunet, da es stille worden, umsonst nicht, jezt, / Da Herrschaft nirgends ist zu sehn bei Geistern und Menschen."

The Initial Fulfillment of Synthesis and Eventual Loss of Repose

In my analysis of the novel I showed that Hyperion passes from undifferentiation to differentiation and consciousness, from unconscious ecstasy to historical awareness and responsibility. This movement remains an essential structure in Hölderlin's thought even after his completion of the novel. The character Empedocles, for example, passed through a similar transformation as Hölderlin revised his conception of the drama. The first version of *Der Tod des Empedokles* portrays Empedocles' hybris and obliteration of all distinctions; his desire for death meanwhile corresponds to a personal need. In the *Grund zum Empedokles* and the third version of the play his death expresses political sacrifice. The *Grund zum Empedokles* also introduces Empedocles',,Gegner", who unites distinctions in a more differentiated way than Empedocles.[131] Hölderlin reworked his earlier odes according to a similar structure of development. Jochen Schmidt (1978) sees in the later

---

[128] Of the many interpreters of „Friedensfeier" Binder (1970/Friedensfeier), Jochen Schmidt (1965–66), and Szondi (1977) are most attentive to the topic of stillness.

[129] The term has arisen in part out of Hölderlin's unique mythology. The „Ruhigmächtiger" is a synthesis of Saturn's „Frieden" and Jupiter's „Macht". We recall the lines from the ode „Natur und Kunst oder Saturn und Jupiter" (StA II, 37–38): „aus Saturnus / Frieden ist jegliche Macht erwachsen".

[130] Another later poem of Hölderlin's, „Der Archipelagus" (StA II, 103–12), is similarly an adjuration of a divine centering force characterized by its stillness. See Walser (1962), esp. 93 and 173.

[131] StA IV, 162. Cf. Lüders (1968), esp. 6–11.

odes a „Wendung vom eigenen Erlebensgenuß zur geschichtlichen Verantwortung" (178). He notes that this movement is not final but must be reconstituted again and again; he writes, „daß [...] der Übergang nicht ein für allemal vollzogen ist, sondern daß er sich auch später immer wieder neu vollzieht" (179). Finally, Schmidt suggests that this transition first takes place during Hölderlin's work on *Empedokles*:

> Am Anfang steht das geniale, seinem eigenen Daseinsgefühl hingegebende Individuum und sein individuelles Glück; dann aber, in der Spätfassung, rückt die geschichtliche Verantwortung in den Mittelpunkt. Während der Arbeit am „Empedokles", von 1799 bis 1801, findet dieser entscheidende Übergang zum ersten Mal statt. (179)

But *Hyperion*, which was completed before *Empedokles*, also contains this basic structure. One can say, therefore, that *Hyperion* is not revoked in Hölderlin's later period but, metaphorically speaking, reworked. Though shifts in Hölderlin's later period are apparent, the basic idea of a transition from ecstasy to consciousness and responsibility remains. The comparison between the movement within *Hyperion* and in the transitions between the versions of *Empedokles* is strengthened by the thought that Hyperion resists a suicide motivated by personal frustration and eventually moves toward his historical task. Moreover, Hyperion, like Empedocles after him,[132] unites dissonances in his own individual character. Each figure recognizes that as long as the solution remains private, harmony is restricted. Correspondingly, the Empedocles of the third version dissolves his individuality for a more enduring harmony that extends to the people of Agrigento.[133] Hyperion, too, moves beyond his private self in order to ensure a greater participation in harmony.

Hölderlin's turn to the particular and historical, which I have suggested is already evident in *Hyperion*, is not originally a denial of synthesis but an awareness of that element within the synthesis which requires more emphasis; it is thus a fulfillment of synthesis. *Since a comprehensive consciousness and an understanding of harmony have already been achieved, the only mode of advancement is in the realm of the particular.* Hölderlin's view that the gods need man in order to appear suggests that any correspondence of ideal and real depends in part on the work of man. Specific tasks must be accomplished. In his later years Hölderlin reflects increasingly on his own historical mission as a poet,[134] and he begins writing hymns whose content „unmittelbar das

---

[132] See StA IV, 154–55.
[133] StA IV, 156–57.
[134] See „Gesang des Deutschen", „An die Deutschen", „Dichterberuf", „Wie wenn am Feiertage...", „Brod und Wein", „Germanien", „Andenken", and numerous other examples. Hölderlin's personal occupation as poet is not the only valid one. See, for example, his view of the hero in „An Eduard" (StA II, 41–42).

Vaterland angehn soll oder die Zeit" (StA VI, 345/no. 242). While Hölderlin's hymns will never be confused with Heine's satirical *Zeitgedichte,* his later poetry does evidence a turn to the historical and to the poet's role within history.

One of the poet's major tasks is to undertake a critique of the present age.[135] Hölderlin turns his eyes to the motion within stillness, to the need for and particularities of change. His criticisms in the ode „Der Frieden" provide us with an example of this:

> Zu lang, zu lang schon treten die Sterblichen
> Sich gern aufs Haupt, und zanken um Herrschaft sich,
> Den Nachbar fürchtend, und es hat auf
> Eigenem Boden der Mann nicht Seegen.
>
> Und unstät wehn und irren, dem Chaos gleich,
> Dem gährenden Geschlechte die Wünsche noch
> Umher und wild ist und verzagt und kalt von
> Sorgen das Leben der Armen immer. (StA II, 7)

Hölderlin's attention to the shortcomings of his age may well have helped engender his final sense of despondency. With his vision focused on the particular he risks the danger of losing sight of the overarching harmony within which individual inadequacies necessarily exist. Hölderlin's immersion in the turmoil of the world, his overexposure to what he terms in one letter „die zerstörende Wirklichkeit" (StA VI, 262/no. 152), might well have generated his desire to retreat to a private idyll, a possibility that Hyperion had considered and rejected. Evidence of such a drive is clear in the opening stanzas of „Der Zeitgeist":

> Zu lang schon waltest über dem Haupte mir
> Du in der dunkeln Wolke, du Gott der Zeit!
> Zu wild, zu bang ist's ringsum, und es
> Trümmert und wankt ja, wohin ich blike.
>
> Ach! wie ein Knabe, seh' ich zu Boden oft,
> Such' in der Höhle Rettung von dir, und möcht'
> Ich Blöder, eine Stelle finden,
> Alleserschütt'rer! wo du nicht wärest (StA I, 300)

Lines such as these or the moment in „Mnemosyne" („Vorwärts aber und rückwarts wollen wir / Nicht sehn. Uns wiegen lassen, wie / Auf schwankem Kahne der See" StA II, 197) remind one of Hölderlin's early poem „Da ich ein Knabe war", a poem that Hölderlin had overcome, indirectly, through his hero's, Hyperion's, reevaluation of childhood and the gods. Hölderlin's emphasis on present inadequacies leads not only to retreat and withdrawal,[136] it also engenders doubt about the ability of the poet to help

---

[135] See Thurmair (1980), 159–213, esp. 159–60 and 167–74.
[136] From such a retreat one might nonetheless still quietly prepare for renewal. See Thurmair (1980), 195.

generate renewal and about the possibility of regeneration altogether. Such doubt and despair overcome the late Hölderlin.

Hölderlin reacts to the synthesis of *Hyperion* in a multifaceted and complex manner. His conception of idyllic withdrawal and most especially his doubt, as reflected in his letters and later poetry, have attracted much critical attention, but his initial reaction to synthesis, the acquisition of a particular task and his critique of the present social and political world, two elements already present in *Hyperion,* in the form of the *Scheltrede,* deserve our consideration as well, not only for their own intrinsic value, but also because they are not arbitrary reactions to or denials of synthetic thought but rather its fulfillment and advancement.

PART II

Deficient Stillness

> JAKOB, HEINRICH, JOE
> Wunderbar ist das Heraufkommen des Abends
> Und schön sind die Gespräche der Männer unter sich!
> PAUL
> Aber etwas fehlt.
> JAKOB, HEINRICH, JOE
> Schön ist die Ruhe und der Frieden
> Und beglückend ist die Eintracht.
> PAUL
> Aber etwas fehlt.
> JAKOB, HEINRICH, JOE
> Herrlich ist das einfache Leben
> Und ohnegleichen ist die Größe der Natur.
> PAUL
> Aber etwas fehlt.   (Brecht)

For the writers of dynamic stillness *Ruhe* is a synthetic term that includes itself and its opposite. For Büchner, Heine, and other nineteenth-century writers this privileging of stillness is suspect. The concept „Ruhe" is for them deficient. It lacks activity, dynamism, motion. In the words of Paul from Brecht's *Aufstieg und Fall der Stadt Mahagonny* „etwas fehlt" (scene 8). To say that *Ruhe* is deficient is to suggest that it is one-sided, not synthetic or complete enough. What I implied with regard to the late Hölderlin I would like to suggest here as well, namely, that the focus on the particular, the concrete, the historical should be seen not as a denial but as the fulfillment of synthesis, the stress on motion not a negation of, but a complement to, stillness. If structural perfection was achieved in German Idealism material perfection was not. Synthesis will pass over into negativity wherever the particular is insufficiently treated or satisfied in the whole. Without regard for the integration of the particular into the whole, one can focus on the particular qua particular. This is the project of Büchner and Heine – even if, in their own eyes, the entire system of structural perfection seems misguided. Büchner und Heine are critical of synthetic thinkers, of poets of harmony and the whole; by turning their eyes away from the whole, they can see, criticize, and develop the particular more freely. This turn to the particular is, however, dialectical; in essence it fulfills the whole as it had never been fulfilled before. It brings the particular into the whole and thus advances, rather than negates, synthesis. What Büchner and Heine negate in word they develop in practice.

The stress on the particular is especially evident in Heine. Where Goethe attempts to convey the eternal within the moment, Heine is interested in the moment qua moment. His thinking is not systematic but associative and passes from part to part with regard only for aesthetic, not philosophical, unity. Heine shares with many of his contemporaries a loss of interest in global, synthetic forms and a predelication for smaller works that treat particular themes.[1] In these works Heine undercuts ideal images and draws attention to deficiencies. He desires not the appearance of reconciliation but its reality. Instead of seeing the world *sub specie aeternitatis,* as do the Idealists, Heine prefers to see it *sub specie ironiae.*

While synthetic writers emphasize organic concepts such as dynamic centeredness, differentiated harmony, and vibrant tranquillity of mind, writers critical of stillness foreground the associations of *Ruhe* with emptiness, indifference, death, and sleep. Büchner and Heine systematically invert the positive associations of *Ruhe*. Büchner's inversion in *Lenz* is threefold. First, the character Lenz, in his conversation on art, explicitly attacks the ideal of aesthetic stillness. Second, *Ruhe* no longer signifies proximity to God, as in the mystic-pietistic tradition; rather, it is linked to Lenz's atheism. Third, as Lenz becomes ever more tranquil he becomes impassive; eventually he goes insane. This inverts a traditional association of *Ruhe* with peace of mind and life in harmony with society. Büchner's explicit preference for activity places him in the company of the historical Lenz, who heatedly attacks *Ruhe* in his *Versuch über das erste Principium der Moral*. Heine, too, finds fault with the ideal of *Ruhe*. In his *Zeitgedichte* and in *Deutschland. Ein Wintermärchen* he reproaches the Germans for their quietude. He criticizes their naive faith in Germany's slow and inner evolution towards freedom and their passive acceptance of present inequities. Heine's inversions, like Büchner's, span aesthetics, religion, and morality, but the focus of his critique is political, and in my analysis of Heine I will seek to establish the political dimensions of *Ruhe*. Heine does not see in *Ruhe* underlying activity; quite the contrary, to the extent that the German people are *ruhig,* they are asleep.

In conjunction with their critique of stillness, nineteenth-century writers exhibit increasing interest in categories such as time, progress, and motion. The Romantics had valorized motion, both in their theoretical texts – one thinks of Schlegel's *Athenäums-Fragmente* – and in their poetry. The ubiquitous *Wanderer*-motif, with its religious origins and aesthetic implications, can be found in Romantic prose and poetry from Tieck to Eichendorff. In his

---

[1] See Sengle (1971–80), esp. I, 48–63; II, 1002–07. It is natural, therefore, that in the chapter on Heine we will look at numerous smaller works rather than one magnum opus.

critique of sculpture as an aesthetic ideal, Büchner's Lenz takes this stress on motion to the nth degree and argues for an art that is fluid, nonfixated, beyond itself. Heine revises the Romantic idea of motion as well. In contrast to the Romantics, the goal of Heine's travels, both literal and metaphoric, is not the unconditional but the particular, the historical, the temporal.[2] Heine writes poems about and for the present, *Zeitgedichte*. No longer interested in joyful repose *(euthymia)*, Heine's contemporaries Ludwig Börne and Theodor Mundt speak of „freudige Bewegung" and „Freude der Bewegung".[3] Adolph Krapf in Leopold Feldmann's political comedy *Der deutsche Michel* states clearly: „Nicht die Ruhe ist es, sondern die Bewegung, nach der ich mich sehne" (214). Eighteenth-century poets composed odes to stillness; nineteenth-century authors write hymns to motion. It is not the tranquil individuals, content with themselves, who move history forward, but rather the „Bewegungsmänner" or „Männer der Bewegung", as Heine and others suggest.[4] Mundt opens his *Madonna*, published the same year as Büchner's *Dantons Tod*, with a paean to motion (3–6). He ascribes motion to literature, history, love, virtually anything that is positive. He calls *Madonna* „ein *Buch der Bewegung*" and adds that „alle Schriften, die unter der Atmosphäre dieser Zeit geboren werden, wie Reisebücher, Wanderbücher, Bewegungsbücher aussehen" (434). Motion is literal for Mundt and for Heine, in whose steps Mundt's travel pictures are conceived, but it is also metaphorical. The age itself is underway: „Die Zeit befindet sich auf Reisen, sie hat große Wanderungen vor, und holt aus, als wollte sie noch unermeßliche Berge überschreiten, ehe sie wieder Hütten bauen wird in der Ruhe eines glücklichen Thals" (434). For Mundt the eternal is no longer still, it is in motion. Insofar as history moves forward, whatever is still, passes away; whatever is in motion, is eternal. In his article „Über Bewegungsparteien in der Literatur" he writes: „Wer *stehen bleibt*, kann nicht *bestehen*. Wer *bestehen* will, muß sich *bewegen*" (1). Shortly thereafter in *Madonna* he adds: „was sich bewegt, das ist ewig! Und was ewig ist, bewegt sich" (5).

---

[2] Cf. Novalis: „Wir suchen überall das Unbedingte" (II, 413).
[3] Börne III, 419; Mundt, *Madonna*, 21.
[4] B III, 396; Gutzkow V, 210; Mundt, *Madonna*, 361; Wienbarg, *Zur neuesten Literatur*, 4.

3. The Threefold Inversion of Traditional Notions of Ruhe in Büchner's *Lenz*

> Philippeau: Was willst du denn?
> Danton: Ruhe.
> Philippeau: Die ist in Gott.
> Danton: Im Nichts. Versenke dich in was Ruhigers, als das Nichts und wenn die höchste Ruhe Gott ist, ist nicht das Nichts Gott?
> (Büchner)

The connotations of *Ruhe* in Büchner's *Lenz*[1] range from self-fulfillment, orientation in society, and oneness with God to emptiness, indifference, and atheism.[2] Although Büchner intermingles these diverse associations throughout, the positive import of the word predominates early in the story; the negative associations gain in turn toward the story's conclusion. Recognizing the division of *Lenz* into five parts,[3] I note the following general development of the concept „Ruhe".

---

[1] References to *Lenz* are from the Reclam edition edited by Hubert Gersch and are followed simply by page number. This superior edition is based on the original printing of *Lenz* by Karl Gutzkow. It should be noted, however, that the differences between Gersch's edition and the previous standard edition edited by Lehmann are not as revolutionary as the tone in the introduction to the Reclam edition or in Gersch (1983) would imply.

[2] It is not uncommon to find two kinds of *Ruhe* in the same author or the same work. In Goethe and Kleist one finds a duplicity within individual passages. Tasso speaks of the inactivity that disturbs his peace of mind: „Mir läßt die Ruh / Am mindsten Ruhe" (3066–67). Kleist writes in his letter to Wilhelmine von Zenge of July 21, 1801, that he left Berlin, „weil ich mich vor der Ruhe fürchtete, in welcher ich Ruhe grade am wenigsten fand" (II, 667).

[3] See Fellmann (1963). The five parts include the prologue (5, 1–6, 32), Lenz's time *with* Oberlin (6, 32–13, 24), his time *without* Oberlin (13, 25–23, 4), his time *beside* Oberlin (23, 5–30, 23), and the epilogue (30, 24–31, 12). According to Fellmann's structural analysis the beginning of each major section coincides with the arrival of a specific figure, in sequence, Lenz, Kaufmann, and Oberlin (16). Although the second part begins with Kaufmann's arrival on page 13, line 25, Oberlin does not leave until page 17, line 6. Fellmann's designations, however helpful, are not precise: it is only part way through the second section that Lenz is literally "without" Oberlin. Neuse (1970) and Henry Schmidt (1977) offer more elaborate structural analyses of *Lenz* with emphasis on contrapuntal opposition. Despite the fact that some of the most recent critical studies on *Lenz* consider the text a fragment (e.g., Gersch [1983], 16 and Spiess [1983], 35), the story is, even in its present, unfinished form, remarkable both for its structure and meaning. Fragment or not *Lenz* invites sophisticated inquiry.

The Prologue: In the prologue Lenz wavers between simple indifference and eccentric fits of imagination. The narrator marks Lenz's moments of apathy by describing him as „ruhig" (7).

First Part: As Lenz enters the village, sees lights, and encounters friendly faces, he becomes happily „ruhig" (7). During this period with Oberlin a *Ruhe* of contentment, integration, and activity dominates. Lenz achieves repose by helping Oberlin with his ministerial duties and by leading a vigorous existence:

> Lenz fortwährend sein Begleiter, bald in Gespräch, bald tätig am Geschäft, bald in die Natur versunken. Es wirkte alles wohltätig und beruhigend auf ihn [...] Je mehr er sich in das Leben hineinlebte, ward er ruhiger, er unterstützte Oberlin, zeichnete, las die Bibel. (9–10)

Reminiscent of the classical ideal of dynamic stillness, Lenz's *Ruhe* exists in harmony with meaningful activity: „Lenz ging vergnügt auf sein Zimmer, er dachte auf einen Text zum Predigen und verfiel in Sinnen, und seine Nächte wurden ruhig" (11). Although references to Lenz's happy *Ruhe* abound in this section, negative moments of unrest and empty stillness do surface. Alone in his room on his first night in Waldbach, Lenz regains the *Ruhe* of sleep only after much turmoil and a nocturnal swim in the cold well. After his sermon, when he feels isolated and depressed, Lenz again experiences an empty stillness.

Second Part: Kaufmann's arrival disrupts Lenz's idyllic enclosure, thus threatening his already somewhat unstable *Ruhe*; Kaufmann reminds Lenz of his ill-fated past and his present obligations:

> Um diese Zeit kam Kaufmann mit seiner Braut ins Steintal. Lenzen war anfangs das Zusammentreffen unangenehm, er hatte sich so ein Plätzchen zurechtgemacht, das bißchen Ruhe war ihn so kostbar und jetzt kam ihm jemand entgegen, der ihn an so vieles erinnerte, mit dem er sprechen, reden mußte, der seine Verhältnisse kannte. (13)

When, after the discourse on art, Kaufmann commands Lenz to return home, support his father, and set goals for himself, Lenz calls out in despair for the precious repose that has already begun to elude him: „Laßt mich doch in Ruhe! Nur ein bißchen Ruhe, jetzt wo es mir ein wenig wohl wird! Weg? Ich verstehe das nicht, mit den zwei Worten ist die Welt verhunzt" (16). Lenz can grasp this disappearing stillness only in memory; he recalls his beloved: „ich war immer ruhig, wenn ich sie ansah, oder sie so den Kopf an mich lehnte und Gott! Gott – Ich war schon lange nicht mehr ruhig" (20–21). In the present Lenz does once again achieve *Ruhe*, but here – in his isolation from God and other people – it takes on the dramatically different meaning of emptiness: „Der Atheismus [...] faßte ihn ganz sicher und ruhig und fest. Er wußte nicht mehr, was ihn vorhin so bewegt hatte, es fror ihn" (22).

Third Part: Upon Oberlin's return Lenz feels the heated unrest of disorientation, yet this soon passes over into the stillness of boredom and indifference: „er lag im Bett ruhig und unbeweglich" (24). Lenz has forever lost his earlier, positive repose: „alles was er an Ruhe aus der Nähe Oberlins und aus der Stille des Tals geschöpft hatte, war weg" (27). As *Ruhe* eludes Lenz, he only reiterates his intense desire for it: „ich will ja nichts als Ruhe, Ruhe, nur ein wenig Ruhe und schlafen können" (29). But positive repose is unattainable for him even in death (29).

Epilogue: At the story's conclusion the narrator describes Lenz's apathetic stillness. Where in the prologue Lenz walked into town and suffered only brief moments of indifference, here Lenz is driven away. His apathy is final:

> Er saß mit kalter Resignation im Wagen, wie sie das Tal hervor nach Westen fuhren. Es war ihm einerlei, wohin man ihn führte; mehrmals wo der Wagen bei dem schlechten Wege in Gefahr geriet, blieb er ganz ruhig sitzen; er war vollkommen gleichgültig. (30)

This sketch of the modulation of *Ruhe* in the story, in particular its strong change from an ideal to a negative condition, helps us understand the basic development of the story. It also gives us the necessary background to look at aspects of Lenz's *Ruhe* in greater detail, specifically the relation of his negative *Ruhe* to the traditionally positive and dominant associations of the concept in aesthetics, religion, psychology, and morality.

The Inversion of Aesthetic Stillness

In the discourse on art in section one, Lenz seems to be at the height of his intellectual powers. He speaks eloquently, where he will later spout broken sentences. He is alert and excited about his topic, where he will later become apathetic. And he expounds upon a subject he knows well: „er war auf seinem Gebiete" (14). In the discourse Lenz argues against aesthetic idealism. He criticizes, first, artists who claim to portray reality as it is (but don't really know what it's like) and, second, artists who falsely idealize reality:[4] „Die Dichter, von denen man sage, sie geben die Wirklichkeit, hätten auch keine Ahnung davon, doch seien sie immer noch erträglicher, als die, welche die Wirklichkeit verklären wollten" (14). Lenz does not discuss the first group in any detail. It would seem to consist of artists who try to portray reality

---

[4] The term "idealist period", insofar as it would refer to Kant, Schiller, and Hegel, must be read anachronistically, as Mayer (1954: 146) and Hauser (1974: 55) have suggested. Yet, if one considers Winckelmann the forerunner of aesthetic idealism, then the narrator's comment, „die idealistische Periode fing damals an" (14), presents no difficulties.

without paying attention to seemingly insignificant persons or without a sense of vitality or feeling. Lenz directs his lengthiest and most vehement polemic against the idealists. First, he criticizes their *mode of selection*. They portray ideal figures who are supposedly better and greater than real persons. Lenz argues that these figures are less beautiful and significant than nature itself. For Lenz the world already *is* as it *ought* to be; it does not need artists to raise it to a supposedly higher level: „Der liebe Gott hat die Welt wohl gemacht wie sie sein soll, und wir können wohl nicht was Besseres klecksen, unser einziges Bestreben soll sein, ihm ein wenig nachzuschaffen" (14). The idealists refuse to recognize the validity of the present world and of the individuals in it: „Dieser Idealismus ist die schmählichste Verachtung der menschlichen Natur" (14). Moreover, their „idealistische Gestalten" leave the viewer cold. Idealist artists create „Holzpuppen" that produce an effect of emptiness, stillness, lifelessness (14). Rather than raising life to a higher level, such art falls below life. For the character Lenz, unlike Winckelmann or Goethe,[5] life stands higher than art.

Lenz contests the claim that the pinnacle of art lies in beauty. He argues instead for vitality and the possibility of existence:

> Ich verlange in allem Leben, Möglichkeit des Daseins, und dann ist's gut; wir haben dann nicht zu fragen, ob es schön, ob es häßlich ist, das Gefühl, daß was geschaffen sei, Leben habe, stehe über diesen beiden, und sei das einzige Kriterium in Kunstsachen. (14)

In his presentation Lenz uses the term "beauty" in two distinct ways. In contrasting the beautiful and the ugly he argues that the artist should portray more than what is simply "beautiful". One should sketch whatever has life, whatever is, in Lenz's new terminology, part of „unendliche Schönheit" (15). Infinite beauty contains the traditionally ugly as well as the traditionally beautiful. The social dimension of Lenz's critique of idealism shines through in his call for a sympathetic art that is capable of portraying the underprivileged and the "ugly":[6]

> Man versuche es einmal und senke sich in das Leben des Geringsten und gebe es wieder, in den Zuckungen, den Andeutungen, dem ganzen feinen, kaum bemerkten Mienenspiel [...]. Man muß die Menschheit lieben, um in das eigentümliche Wesen jedes einzudringen, es darf einem keiner zu gering, keiner zu häßlich sein, erst dann kann man sie verstehen; das unbedeutendste Gesicht macht einen tiefern Eindruck als die bloße Empfindung des Schönen, und man kann die Gestalten aus sich heraustreten lassen, ohne etwas vom Äußern hineinzukopieren, wo einem kein Leben, keine Muskeln, kein Puls entgegen schwillt und pocht. (14–15)

---

[5] Se HA XII, 102–04.
[6] For a discussion of the role of *Mitleid* in Lenz's aesthetics and a comparison with Schopenhauer see Schings (1980), 78–84.

Lenz does not argue simply for the reproduction of reality with an emphasis on the ugly and the downtrodden. He is concerned not with technical reproduction but rather with sympathetic identification. More specifically, he asks the artist to imitate not the world but God („*ihm* ein wenig nachzuschaffen" 14).[7] Much like Schelling in his critique of Winckelmann from 1806, Büchner's character Lenz asks the poet to imitate not nature but the process and dynamism of creation itself.[8] The artist should not reproduce a particular scene of life and then freeze it; rather, he should create and, like the original creator, watch his creation pass from one form into another.

This brings us to the second focus of Lenz's critique: *selection in general*.[9] Lenz believes that beauty continuously passes from one scene of life into another. The artist who selects a picture and turns it to stone freezes this Protean process. While Lenz feels this temptation himself, he resists it, and he notes that from the disturbance and dissolution of this picture, from motion, a new beauty arises:

> Wie ich gestern neben am Tal hinaufging, sah ich auf einem Steine zwei Mädchen sitzen, die eine band ihre Haare auf, die andre half ihr; und das goldne Haar hing herab, und ein ernstes bleiches Gesicht, und doch so jung, und die schwarze Tracht und die andre so sorgsam bemüht. Die schönsten, innigsten Bilder der altdeutschen Schule geben kaum eine Ahnung davon. Man möchte manchmal ein Medusenhaupt sein, um so eine Gruppe in Stein verwandeln zu können, und den Leuten zurufen. Sie standen auf, die schöne Gruppe war zerstört; aber wie sie so hinabstiegen, zwischen den Felsen war es wieder ein anderes Bild. Die schönsten Bilder, die schwellendsten Töne, gruppieren, lösen sich auf. Nur eins bleibt, eine unendliche Schönheit, die aus einer Form in die andre tritt, ewig aufgeblättert, verändert, man kann sie aber freilich nicht immer festhalten und in Museen stellen und auf Noten ziehen und dann alt und jung herbeirufen, und die Buben und Alten darüber radotieren und sich entzücken lassen. (14–15)

Because a particular scene can be so precious, one does feel the temptation to transform it into stone and call others to come view it; but as soon as one freezes the picture, it loses its vitality. When the picture is destroyed, another takes its place, and true beauty is formed. The most beautiful pictures cannot

---

[7] Emphasis added. Thorn-Prikker (1978) mistakenly understands Lenz to be advocating „eine Reproduktion der Wirklichkeit" (61). Holub (1985), too, speaks of Lenz's call for "fidelity to reality" (120).
[8] In *Über das Verhältnis der bildenden Künste zur Natur* Schelling argues that Winckelmann's „idealische Formen" are cold, sterile, and empty of life. Instead of copying the works of antiquity (or of nature) the artist should imitate the creative force that produced (or in the case of nature continues to produce) these works. See VII, 294–98.
[9] In his detailed discussions of Büchner's aesthetics Benn, like other interpreters, mentions only Büchner's revolt against a particular type of selection, namely idealization, not also his more radical critique of selection in general. See Benn (1969) and (1976), 84–99.

be fixed; they dissolve themselves: „Die schönsten Bilder [...] lösen sich auf." Beauty passes „aus einer Form in die andere [...] ewig aufgeblättert, verändert". If a scene is to reveal „Leben, Möglichkeit des Daseins", it cannot be immortalized, it cannot be captured.[10] In fact, when Lenz sees that the picture of the two girls, which he had frozen in his own mind, becomes dissolved in real life, he sees in this dissolution, this life process, the greater virtue of „unendliche Schönheit". Infinite beauty is not the timelessness of an arrested image but continuous change, endless destruction and regeneration. Where classical aesthetics tries to give life duration through art,[11] Lenz argues that such permanence does not preserve life; the very attempt at preservation destroys and transfigures life such that it is no longer recognizable as such. To select and fixate a moment would be to deny life's eternal flow and flux. In addition, the artist, in following the principle of selection, does injustice to those moments he must necessarily overlook as he selects. The artist cannot possibly portray the world as it is, for he is compelled by the very nature of selection and the particularity of the work of art to eliminate certain vital elements from whatever scene he creates. In effect Lenz is arguing against art in general, for art had always involved selection rather than totality, particularity of space rather than total environment, fixation rather than dissolution, permanence in stone or script rather than constant flux and dissolution. The only way to avoid these seemingly necessary conditions would be to redefine art as a continuous process, a series of events. Lenz's attack on sculpture as the highest form and stillness as the highest principle of art anticipates a movement in the plastic arts that did not surface until the second half of the twentieth century.[12]

---

[10] Knapp (1973) conceives the Medusa head as an image for the ideal artist (74–75). Hauser (1974) misreads the passage as well: "The Medusa's head, with its power to turn living beings into stone, obviously is meant as a symbol for the highest aspirations of the artist. Perfection in art is represented by an exact but frozen image of life" (57). Most recently, Holub (1985) repeats these mistakes, asserting that each "individual segment of reality" is "aesthetically sufficient unto itself" (118). Lenz places his emphasis "on the slice (out) of life, the snap shot of the external world" (119). His realism calls for "a cessation of motion, a removal of a scene from its temporal sequence" (118). See also Benn (1976), 94–95. In misinterpreting Lenz's tentative desire to freeze a scene as his final wish, critics miss the significance of the following sentences which are introduced by the contrastive „aber" and affirm endless metamorphosis. Far from being the image of the ideal artist, the Medusa head freezes and negates life.

[11] Cf HA XII, 102–04.

[12] Where Büchner's modernity has previously been seen in the Kafkaesque aspects of his narrative, his refined understanding of schizophrenia, his development of open drama, and his advanced social consciousness, the most contemporary aspect of his work may well lie in Lenz's theory of art, which advances Romantic thought beyond recognition and approximates the contemporary concept of art as a

Despite its modernity, Lenz's aesthetic theory has numerous problems. In fact the theory cancels itself on several levels.[13] Lenz proposes an *ideal* aesthetic law that does not correspond to the way art already *is*, yet art as it is, does form a part of reality and, according to the very same law, should be affirmed. Further, Lenz argues for a universal and timelessly valid program of artistic excellence, thus contradicting his emphasis on historicity and change as well as his attempted refutation of the classical ideal, in which art concerns itself with the eternal values inherent in life. An additional contradiction lies in Lenz's ranking of some art works as better than others while at the same time proposing a theory of beauty that renders art, beauty, and indeed itself obsolete. Insofar as Lenz's arguments imply the impossibility of art, it cannot surprise the reader that after this discourse Lenz does not write any more dramas. After arguing for the self-cancellation of art, Lenz can himself no longer fulfill his role as an artist.[14] The fact, however, that Lenz's

---

"happening". Lenz does not of course propose any "happenings"; he does not suggest, for example, that one try to recreate the scene with the two girls. Nonetheless, Lenz's abstract views on art and beauty overlap in several significant ways with the *theory* behind Allan Kaprow's view of art as a "happening". Both Lenz and Kaprow wish to abandon stability and permanence as principles of art; they stress "constant metamorphosis" and discard the concept of the finished product (Kaprow/1966: 169). Kaprow even advocates – very much in the spirit of Lenz's statements – the incorporation of perishable materials in his art. Like Lenz, Kaprow argues that "the line between art and life should be kept as fluid, and perhaps indistinct, as possible" (1966: 188–89). Consequently, art should be continuous with the observer. The spectator, no longer passive or quiet, should be involved in the action. According to Kaprow, "audiences should be eliminated entirely" (1966: 195). Lenz argues that one cannot always hold art fast and put it into museums „und dann alt und jung herbeirufen [...]" (15). Insofar as art becomes an autonomous object viewed by an audience, it becomes artificial, divorced from life. According to both Lenz and Kaprow one should not construct a self-contained entity, but rather let the entire environment become the aesthetic realm – as for example with the two girls in Lenz's narrative, who stand up and move within the environment. Kaprow praises Jackson Pollock insofar as his works "cease to become paintings and become *environments*" (1958: 56). Finally, where Lenz would return art to the everyday world, to real-life figures, Kaprow's art is equally preoccupied with the people, space, and objects of everyday experience.

[13] After this chapter was virtually completed, Holub's article on the paradoxes of the *Kunstgespräch* appeared. While we share an interest in contradictions, our readings of the *Kunstgespräch* differ, as do, in most cases, our senses of what its contradictions are.

[14] King (1974) argues that Lenz loses his creativity insofar as he is pressured into fulfilling "society's expectations" (153), but Lenz's crisis seems more fundamental and intrinsic. It goes beyond the Romantic contrast of artist and society. On his own terms, as he develops them in his discourse on art, Lenz can no longer function as an artist. Since literature is no longer art, the logical, if also self-

implicit argument against art is embedded in Büchner's artwork should caution the reader from identifying Lenz's theories with Büchner's, as has become almost universal practice.[15]

While Lenz seems to have rejected art, he nonetheless praises two Dutch paintings. Here he demonstrates through examples his preference for art that portrays suffering and humility. Where classical aesthetics had argued for stillness in suffering (Winckelmann and Schiller), Lenz argues for simple suffering and gives his discourse on aesthetics a religious tone. He describes „Christus und die Jünger von Emmaus": „da erkennen sie ihn, in einfachmenschlicher Art, und die göttlich-leidenden Züge reden ihnen deutlich" (16). Here Lenz attempts to resolve the tension between his (implicit) thesis of the impossibility of art and his admiration of two actual paintings. Instead of praising the paintings themselves or the fixed moments depicted in them, Lenz transforms the paintings into occurrences in time,[16] into stories with change and development. He reads action into the stillness and ignores the captured moment. With the help of the appropriate Biblical passage Lenz creates an entire narrative around „Christus und die Jünger von Emmaus":[17] „Es ist ein trüber, dämmernder Abend, ein einförmiger roter Streifen am Horizont, halbfinster auf der Straße, da kommt ein Unbekannter zu ihnen, sie sprechen, er bricht das Brot [...]" (15–16). For his description of the second painting, Lenz invents a series of circumstances to surround the moment depicted, and he sets the picture in this context:

> Die Frau hat nicht zur Kirche gekonnt, und sie verrichtet die Andacht zu Haus, das Fenster ist offen, sie sitzt darnach hingewandt, und es ist als schwebten zu dem Fenster über die weite ebne Landschaft die Glockentöne von dem Dorfe herein und verhallet der Sang der nahen Gemeinde aus der Kirche her, und die Frau liest den Text nach. (16)

Lenz's attacks on cold, impassive heroes, the tranquil response to art, and, most especially, sculpture and stillness as aesthetic ideals represent a direct polemic against what must be considered one of the most important aesthetic categories of the eighteenth and early nineteenth century: *Ruhe*. The follow-

---

destructive, consequence of this theory is that Lenz no longer write. Critics have traditionally viewed Lenz's discourse on art as the moment of his greatest sanity. See, for example, Adolph (1978), 108; Jansen (1975); and von Wiese (1963). But a close look at Lenz's seemingly coherent discourse reveals that the ideas expressed there lead – by way of the dissolution of art and of ideals – to his insanity.

[15] See most recently Buck (1981: 18, 21) and Horn (1982: 223–24).
[16] In general Lenz describes or misdescribes the paintings so as to subsume them under his specific program of aesthetics. For a discussion of his nonrecognition of the supernatural female head (probably Maria Magdalena) and the "Verklärung" of Christ's face in the actual model for the first painting, see Requadt (1974), 109.
[17] Luke 24, 13–24, 53.

ing excursus will show the extent of the revolutionary inversion Büchner makes on behalf of his character Lenz.

The Tradition of Aesthetic Stillness

The concept „Ruhe" plays a significant role in several distinct areas of German aesthetics of the late eighteenth and early nineteenth century: the medium of presentation (One thinks of Winckelmann's valorization of sculpture.), the preferred objects of portrayal (Laocoon, for example, in his "stillness"), the most general of generic types (the beautiful defined as equanimity, the sublime as stillness in suffering), the creative process (stillness as a condition of inspiration), and the reception of the work of art (repose as the optimal response for the viewer of an aesthetic object).

Most of these aesthetic categories of stillness originate with Winckelmann. He argues not only for sculpture as the highest of aesthetic forms but also for heroes, eternal mythological figures, whom the artist can capture in a moment of internal repose:

> Das allgemeine vorzügliche Kennzeichen der griechischen Meisterstücke ist endlich eine edle Einfalt, und eine stille Größe, sowohl in der Stellung als im Ausdrucke. So wie die Tiefe des Meers allezeit ruhig bleibt, die Oberfläche mag noch so wüten, ebenso zeiget der Ausdruck in den Figuren der Griechen bei allen Leidenschaften eine große und gesetzte Seele. [...] Je ruhiger der Stand des Körpers ist, desto geschickter ist er, den wahren Charakter der Seele zu schildern: in allen Stellungen, die von dem Stande der Ruhe zu sehr abweichen, befindet sich die Seele nicht in dem Zustande, der ihr der eigentlichste ist, sondern in einem gewaltsamen und erzwungenen Zustande. Kenntlicher und bezeichnender wird die Seele in heftigen Leidenschaften; groß aber und edel ist sie in dem Stande der Einheit, in dem Stande der Ruhe. (20–21)[18]

Winckelmann's conception of aesthetic stillness influenced almost every writer of the period. Goethe, well aware of repose as only one side of aesthetic beauty, writes: „Man sieht also, daß bei der Schönheit *Ruhe* mit *Kraft*, *Untätigkeit* mit *Vermögen* eigentlich in Anschlag komme" (HA XII, 22). According to Kant's analysis of aesthetic judgment the beautiful object appears to us in a state of equilibrium and repose (KdU B80, B98). While motion and incongruity characterize the Kantian sublime – whether

---

[18] Winckelmann, like Goethe, Schiller, and Hölderlin after him, considers repose a dynamic category: „Aber in dieser Ruhe muß die Seele durch Züge, die ihr und keiner andern Seele eigen sind, bezeichnet werden, um sie zu ruhig, aber zugleich wirksam, stille, aber nicht gleichgültig oder schläfrig zu bilden" (21). The dynamism of Winckelmann's Laocoon concept is also evident in the sculpture itself: Laocoon is full of passion and motion. Büchner's character Lenz would seem to overlook such aspects in order to make a rhetorically more effective case for pure dynamism.

mathematical or dynamic – (KdU B 80), Schiller reconstitutes the sublime with a moment of stillness („Ruhe im Leiden" NA XX, 296), thus showing as much indebtedness to Winckelmann as to Kant. However much the artist may want to express suffering or happiness, his external product, according to Schelling, must be still and harmonious: „Der äußere Ausdruck des Kunstwerks ist also der Ausdruck der Ruhe, und der stillen Größe, selbst da, wo die höchste Spannung des Schmerzes oder der Freude ausgedrückt werden soll" (III, 620). Hölderlin's early hymn „An die Vollendung" contains a reminder of Winckelmann's theory as well: „Voll hoher Einfalt / Einfältig still und groß / Rangen des Siegs gewiß / Rangen dir [der Vollendung] zu die Väter" (StA I, 75). Even the Romantics knew of Winckelmann's ideas. Schlegel writes in *Lucinde*: „Größe in Ruhe, sagen die Meister, sei der höchste Gegenstand der bildenden Kunst" (V, 26). Novalis contrasts heroes and poets in chapter six of *Heinrich von Ofterdingen* and cites „Ruhe" as a main attribute of the latter group. Finally, when Jean Paul discusses antiquity in his *Vorschule der Ästhetik*, he considers „heitere Ruhe" one of the four central characteristics of Greek art (V, 77).

According to the numerous German artists and philosophers of the late eighteenth century who equated the problem of inspiration with the question of how to make the infinite finite, the divine human, both the creator and the recipient of the aesthetic object are ideally still. The stillness of a pool of water as it reflects the heavens mirrors the process of artistic inspiration.[19] The poet, like a still lake, can receive the divine if he/she is in utter repose. Goethe uses such images in *Die Leiden des jungen Werthers* (HA VI, 9) and in his later poem „Mächtiges Überraschen" (HA I, 294). In „Zueignung" he relates how the poet takes „mit stiller Seele [...] / Der Dichtung Schleier aus der Hand der Wahrheit" (HA I, 152). Hölderlin employs the image of reflecting water as a metaphor for poetic inspiration in passages quoted above from his hymns „Der Rhein" and „Der Ister", and Wackenroder alludes to this idea in his *Herzensergießungen eines kunstliebenden Klosterbruders* (71). For Wackenroder stillness characterizes not only the creation, but also the reception of an art work: „Der echte Genuß erfordert eine stille und ruhige Fassung des Gemüts und äußert sich nicht durch Ausrufungen und Zusammenschlagen der Hände, sondern allein durch innere Bewegungen" (74).

Büchner and the Tradition of Aesthetic Stillness

Lenz's explicit rejection of sculpture as an ideal, his praise of suffering rather than stillness in suffering, his view of proper creativity as originating in not

---

[19] The image is taken in part from the mystic tradition. See Langen (1940), 270–73; Langen (1959), 126; Langen (1968), 182.

repose or withdrawal but rather direct immersion in „das Leben des Geringsten" (14), his praise of art as an agitating, emotional force,[20] and finally, his definition of beauty as activity, dissolution, and motion stand in direct contrast to the traditional conception of the equivalence of beauty and stillness. While one cannot determine whether Büchner had read Winckelmann,[21] the prevalence and multifaceted nature of aesthetic stillness during Büchner's life lead one to conclude that the idea of beauty which Büchner voices through Lenz is directed at least in part against the ideal of aesthetic stillness I have just sketched.

The Inversion of Religious Stillness

Although Lenz rejects aesthetic stillness, he affirms an ideal of existential tranquillity. In the first section of the story Lenz's repose originates in part from his religious encounters. Lenz works closely with Oberlin as his host performs his ministerial duties (9), and he reads the Bible: „Doch je mehr er sich in das Leben hineinlebte, ward er ruhiger, er unterstützte Oberlin, zeichnete, las die Bibel" (9–10).[22] Lenz experiences the proximity of God in an almost mystical way: „wie Gott so ganz bei ihm eingekehrt [...] dieser Glaube, dieser ewige Himmel im Leben, dies Sein in Gott; jetzt erst ging ihm die Heilige Schrift auf" (10). A sense of adjustment and being-at-home, symbolized in the appearance of his mother, accompanies Lenz's pious reception of divinity:

> Alles so still [...] Es wurde ihm heimlich nach und nach [...] ein heimliches Weihnachtsgefühl beschlich ihn, er meinte manchmal seine Mutter müsse hinter einem Baume hervortreten [...] wie er hinunterging, sah er, daß um seinen Schatten sich ein Regenbogen von Strahlen legte, es wurde ihm, als hätte ihn was an der Stirn berührt, das Wesen sprach ihn an. (10)

Not only does his mother appear to him, an essence seems to touch him on the forehead and speak to him. The rainbow, symbolic of the bridge between God and man,[23] implies that the essence is divine. This religious experience

---

[20] Where classical aesthetics considered tranquillity the proper response to an aesthetic work, Lenz appeals to the „Gefühlsader" (14): „Der Dichter und Bildende ist mir der liebste, der mir die Natur am wirklichsten gibt, so daß ich über seinem Gebild fühle" (15).

[21] In another context Benn (1976) has written that one is inclined to suspect that Büchner had read Winckelmann (79–80). The question is, in any case, not as central as it might seem for, as I have shown, Winckelmann's concept of aesthetic stillness had become commonplace in the early nineteenth century.

[22] Just before Kaufmann's arrival, we hear again: „er [...] las viel in der Bibel" (13).

[23] Cf. Gen. 9, 13: "I set my bow in the cloud, and it shall be a sign of the covenant between me and the earth."

134

moves Lenz to ask Oberlin for the opportunity to deliver a homily. As he prepares his sermon, Lenz experiences the repose traditionally associated with piety: „Lenz ging vergnügt auf sein Zimmer, er dachte auf einen Text zum Predigen und verfiel in Sinnen, und seine Nächte wurden ruhig" (11). In his discourse on art Lenz had argued that sympathy is a condition of aesthetic vitality. In his sermon he seems to suggest that it leads to religious intensity as well:

> Sein ganzer Schmerz wachte jetzt auf, und legte sich in sein Herz. Ein süßes Gefühl unendlichen Wohls beschlich ihn. Er sprach einfach mit den Leuten, sie litten alle mit ihm, und es war ihm ein Trost, wenn er über einige müdgeweinte Augen Schlaf, und gequälten Herzen Ruhe bringen, wenn er über dieses von materiellen Bedürfnissen gequälte Sein, diese dumpfen Leiden gen Himmel leiten konnte. (11)

Through suffering Lenz experiences a sense of well-being („ein süßes Gefühl unendlichen Wohls") and community („sie litten alle mit ihm"). Suffering paves a path towards heaven.[24] The parishoners sing: „Laß in mir die heil'gen Schmerzen, / Tiefe Bronnen ganz aufbrechen; / Leiden sei all' mein Gewinst, / Leiden sei mein Gottesdienst" (11). Lenz does experience intense pain („er fühlte tiefen unnennbaren Schmerz" 12), but this pain brings forth another mystical union, one that combines piety with eroticism: „Jetzt, ein anderes Sein, göttliche, zuckende Lippen bückten sich über ihm aus, und sogen sich an seine Lippen [...] es war ihm als müsse er sich auflösen, er konnte kein Ende finden der Wollust" (12). After his sermon Lenz's communal suffering is drawn inward. Not stretching outward toward God or other people, his suffering is transformed into self-pity („ein leises tiefes Mitleid in sich selbst" 12). The narrator alludes to Lenz's empty stillness and his impending lunacy: „Alles war ruhig und still und kalt, und der Mond schien die ganze Nacht und stand über den Bergen" (12). While Lenz's *Ruhe* of exhaustion does finally free him from suffering, it is accompanied by isolation and loss of piety.

---

[24] Thorn-Prikker (1978: 63) interprets Lenz's sermon, in particular his wish to direct these weighty afflictions toward heaven („diese dumpfen Leiden gen Himmel leiten"), as a call for the elimination of suffering, not an affirmation of suffering as a path towards God. Thorn-Prikker overlooks the narrator's previous assertion that Lenz's pain had awakened in him a sweet feeling of endless well-being as well as the fact that Lenz's intense grief actually engenders an experience of mystical unity. Kobel (1974: 152–53) offers a positive evaluation of suffering in Lenz's sermon as does Wittkowski (1978/Europäische: 265). Wittkowski, however, sees throughout Büchner's writings only an affirmation of suffering, a pietistic „Religion des Leidens" (1976: 386). See Wittkowski (1973), Wittkowski (1978/Europäische), and Wittkowski (1978/Georg Büchner: 157–58). Hinderer (1981), more attentive to the ambiguity of Büchner's works, sees suffering „als Fels des Glaubens *und* als Fels des Atheismus" (176). Emphasis added. In this context see also Stern (1964).

In the very next episode Lenz awakens to tell Oberlin that he is calm, and he relates the dream of his mother's death: „sie sei gewiß tot; er sei ganz ruhig darüber" (12). Earlier the appearance of Lenz's mother had symbolized a sense of being-at-home, and the narrator had presented it as a mystical experience. Her death here would seem to symbolize not only the loss of Lenz's sense of comfort but also the cessation of his mystical experiences.[25] Lenz's *Ruhe* is not the repose of someone willing to accept pain and affirm death; instead, it signifies a release from the struggles and tensions of mystical experiences. As such it is a *Ruhe* of loss. In fact, after this vision of death Lenz's mystical experiences cease entirely. A faint glimmer of Lenz's piety shimmers through at the end of the first section of the story when, in the discourse on art, he speaks of the excellence of God's creation: „Der liebe Gott hat die Welt wohl gemacht wie sie sein soll, und wir können wohl nicht was Besseres klecksen" (14). The repetition of „wohl" in this brief utterance raises some doubt, however, about Lenz's allegiance to his own statement and might even be said to contain the seeds of his later reversal, his scornful belief that the world should indeed be different (29).

Lenz's „religiöse Quälereien" become fully manifest during the second part of the story, when Oberlin is away (21). Although Lenz continues to pray, he does so unsuccessfully (19, 26–27). No longer sure of his own position in the world („er verzweifelte an sich selbst" 21) or of God's love, he calls out twice for a concrete sign of God's presence: „Dann flehete er, Gott möge ein Zeichen an ihm tun [...] er betete mit allem Jammer der Verzweiflung [...] daß Gott ein Zeichen an ihm tue" (21–22). Art has failed Lenz, and he must now search for meaning in religion, but salvation eludes him here as well. No sign comes to him. Despite Lenz's pleas, God does not revive the dead child, who in Lehmann's edition carries the same first name as Friederike Brion, the woman with whom Lenz associates happiness and repose (L I, 93). Lenz can revive neither the child nor the happiness he associates with the name Friederike. In desperation Lenz decides that he himself will assume the role left vacant by this silent God. He utters Christ's words:[26] „Stehe auf und wandle!" (22). The failure of Lenz's attempt drives him into rage and near insanity („da stürzte er halb wahnsinnig nieder" 22). With no sign from heaven Lenz listens to the voice of hell in his breast: „In seiner Brust war ein Triumph-Gesang der Hölle" (22). The inversion of divine and human roles continues. Lenz imagines himself omnipotent and

---

[25] See also Fellmann (1963), 42–43.
[26] Matt. 2, 9. Comparisons with Christ are common for figures in Büchner's works. Cf., for example, the analogies with Robespierre and Danton in *Dantons Tod* (I, 6 and II, 5). Such analogies would seem to indicate that man must fill roles left vacant by the absence or silence of God.

God impotent;[27] he would grind the world into pieces with his teeth and spit it into the face of the creator:

> es war ihm, als könne er eine ungeheure Faust hinauf in den Himmel ballen und Gott herbeireißen und zwischen seinen Wolken schleifen; als könnte er die Welt mit den Zähnen zermalmen und sie dem Schöpfer ins Gesicht speien; er schwur, er lästerte. (22)

Lenz then laughs satanically: „Lenz mußte laut lachen, und mit dem Lachen griff der Atheismus in ihn und faßte ihn ganz sicher und ruhig und fest. Er wußte nicht mehr, was ihn vorhin so bewegt hatte, es fror ihn" (22). Lenz's laughter is impassioned, cold, likened to ice.[28] Here Lenz is „ruhig", but his stillness – as we see here for the first time – is linked with atheism, not piety.

Lenz suffers these religious torments during Oberlin's absence. When Oberlin returns, the minister is unable to successfully redirect Lenz toward God and religious contentment. Not only has Lenz reached depths of doubt and impiety, such that chances for a reversal seem slim, but Oberlin too has changed. He now sides with Kaufmann's view that Lenz should return home and enter a profession: „Dabei erzählte er von Pfeffel, das Leben eines Landgeistlichen glücklich preisend. Dabei ermahnte er ihn, sich in den Wunsch seines Vaters zu fügen, seinem Berufe gemäß zu leben, heimzukehren" (23). No longer sympathizing with Lenz as an individual, Oberlin approaches him with commands and formulas;[29] thereupon Lenz loses what little tranquillity he still possessed: „Er sagte ihm: Ehre Vater und Mutter u. dgl. m. Über dem Gespräch geriet Lenz in heftige Unruhe [...] er sprach abgebrochen. Ja, ich halt' es aber nicht aus; wollen Sie mich verstoßen? [...] Ich bin abgefallen, verdammt in Ewigkeit, ich bin der Ewige Jude" (23).

Lenz's sense of his own restlessness and impiety is evident in this comparison with the Eternal Jew, who was doomed to roam the earth through eternity. This analogy, like the later abstract reference to Lenz's „Wahnsinn durch die Ewigkeit" (28), demonstrates that the story operates

---

[27] Lenz's feeling of omnipotence is symptomatic of schizophrenia (see Ueding [1976], 125–26), but it also reflects deeper layers within the story, for example, the reversal of divine and human roles and Lenz's increasing impiety.
[28] Cf. also 20: „Er [...] erhob sich kalt und gleichgültig, seine Tränen waren ihm dann wie Eis, er mußte lachen."
[29] Oberlin's inability to deal with the individuality of Lenz's suffering has often been noted. Oberlin is simple and cannot grasp Lenz's complicated tensions and needs. During the philosophical discourse on art he is silent. When Lenz reflects on the differences between higher and lower forms of life, Oberlin cuts him off: „Oberlin brach es ab, es führte ihn zu weit von seiner einfachen Art ab" (13). On this point see also Hinderer (1983: 286); King (1974: 151–52); Kobel (1974: 158–79, 210); Lindenberger (1964: 73); Parker (1967–68: 108–09); and Richards (1977: 137). Müller-Seidel (1968) has suggested that the act of sympathy which Oberlin fails to perform is accomplished by the narrator.

on a level more global that the pathological; Lenz's suffering has religious and philosophical dimensions. The Eternal Jew might have been a perfect subject for Lenz's aesthetics of motion. One could almost imagine Lenz presenting Ahasuerus as a counter ideal to the still and stable figures privileged in idealist texts. As the story unfolds, however, we see Lenz's religious desires refute his aesthetic precepts. Lenz does not seek the motion of the Wandering Jew; he desires, instead, stability, centeredness, repose, and sleep.

Lenz's suffering and the suffering he sees in the world no longer lead to mystical and religious experiences as he had wished in his pietistically inspired sermon. Ultimately pain drives him away from God, and he must imagine himself a devil: „er sei das ewig Verdammte, der Satan" (28). Just as in trying to revive the child, Lenz had usurped Christ's role, so does he again boldly imagine himself as God. Here he announces that he would be different from the present Lord; he would eliminate suffering:

> Oberlin sprach ihm von Gott. Lenz wand sich ruhig los und sah ihn mit einem Ausdruck unendlichen Leidens an, und sagte endlich: aber ich, wär' ich allmächtig, sehen Sie, wenn ich so wäre, und ich könnte das Leiden nicht ertragen, ich würde retten, retten. (29)

While Lenz continues to experience intermittent moments of torturous unrest, a mood of indifference predominates at the story's conclusion. Lenz is not so much restless as he is „ruhig" and empty (29, 30, 31). Oberlin comes to Lenz's room and finds him impassive: „er lag im Bett ruhig und unbeweglich"(24). Lenz ridicules Oberlin's profession as „einen [...] behaglichen Zeitvertreib" to which one turns „aus Müßiggang" (25). Prayer, too, originates only in boredom (25). Lenz's emptiness, listlessness, and passivity are accompanied in a dissonant way by their opposites: anguish and unrest. This juxtaposition is persuasively illustrated in the paradox towards the end of the story:

> Sehn Sie, Herr Pfarrer, wenn ich das nur nicht mehr hören müßte mir wäre geholfen. „Was denn, mein Lieber?" Hören Sie denn nichts, hören Sie denn nicht die entsetzliche Stimme, die um den ganzen Horizont schreit, und die man gewöhnlich die Stille heißt, seit ich in dem stillen Tal bin, hör' ich's immer, es läßt mich nicht schlafen, ja Herr Pfarrer, wenn ich wieder einmal schlafen könnte. Er ging dann kopfschüttelnd weiter. (30)

Earlier, when the narrator had called Lenz an atheist, he explicitly described him as „ruhig" (22). Now in a combined state of religious apathy and torment, Lenz is overwhelmed by stillness. *Ruhe* and *Stille*, traditionally the conditions of intense religious experience and symbols of proximity to God, become in Büchner's story the reverse: they mark Lenz's atheism, his utter distance from God.

By associating *Ruhe* with atheism rather than piety, Büchner inverts a prominent tradition. In the following excursus I trace the concept of religious stillness in its major stages from antiquity to the early nineteenth century, emphasizing writers who might have influenced Büchner's understanding of *Ruhe*, either directly or indirectly, that is, writers with whom Büchner was familiar, such as Lucretius and Christian Friedrich Richter, or writers who had a strong influence on German conceptions of religious stillness in general, for example, Meister Eckhart and Angelus Silesius.

The Tradition of Religious Stillness

The concept of religious stillness reaches beyond Christianity to antiquity and can be found in philosophers such as Aristotle and Epicurus, with whom Büchner was quite familiar.[30] In the final book of his *Nicomachean Ethics* Aristotle argues that true happiness exists only in repose and contemplation, in "self-sufficiency, leisureliness, and unweariedness" (1177b). Aristotle thereupon relates this definition of happiness to his understanding of the gods. All actions seem "trivial and unworthy of gods. Still, every one supposes that they *live* and therefore that they are active." Aristotle solves this puzzle by suggesting that, if you take away from a living being action, all that remains is "contemplation". "Therefore the activity of God, which surpasses all others in blessedness, must be contemplative" (1178b). The perfect activity of God is eternal contemplative repose. Aristotle reinforces this association of repose with divinity in his discussion of the unmoved mover in Book 8 of his *Physics* and Book 12 of his *Metaphysics*. Aristotle calls the pure thinking being that sets in motion the activity of the world and is itself at rest God (1072b). In his excerpts on Aristotle's *Physics* from Wilhelm Gottlieb Tennemann's *Geschichte der Philosophie* Büchner discusses this Aristotelian concept of the unmoved mover (L II, 387–88). In addition, in his notes on Aristotle's theology Büchner reflects specifically on God's immutability:

> Die Gottheit ist ohne alle Veränderung. Gott ist das seligste Wesen. Seine Seligkeit besteht einzig und allein in seinem unwandelbaren, harmonischen Denken [...] Gott ist der Ursprung und das Ziel aller Bewegung. Die absolute Ursache berührt das Bewegte, ohne von ihm wieder berührt zu werden. (L II, 395–96)

Another major philosopher of antiquity to speak of divine repose, Epicurus, was equally familiar to Büchner. Büchner concludes his excerpts from Tennemann with a discussion of Epicurus and Lucretius; here Büchner

---

[30] The most comprehensive study of religious stillness in antiquity is Klaus Schneider (1966). On the topic of religious stillness in general see Gustav Mensching (1926).

specifically mentions the concept of divine inactivity and repose.[31] Epicurus' view of the gods as tranquil beings is evident from his own brief fragments[32] as well as from statements made about him by opponents and followers alike.[33] In his polemic against Epicurus in *De ira dei* Lactantius blames Epicurus for attributing God's happiness to his eternal repose. "'Ideo' inquit 'incorruptus est ac beatus, quia semper quietas.'"[34] Epicurus' most devoted follower, Lucretius, shares his teacher's view of the gods. In his address to Epicurus at the opening of the third book of *De rerum natura* Lucretius writes of the gods' "peaceful abodes" and suggests that nothing can disturb "the quiet of their minds" (3: 18–24). In the first and second books of his poem, Lucretius twice presents his readers with the same vivid statement on the gods' eternal repose. The gods live in the deepest peace, far removed and separated from our troubles; they are without pain or danger, in no need of man, and untouched by wrath:[35]

> omnis enim per se divom natura necessest
> inmortali aevo summa cum pace fruatur
> semota ab nostris rebus seiunctaque longe;
> nam privata dolore omni, privata periclis,
> ipsa suis pollens opibus, nil indiga nostri,
> nec bene promeritis capitur neque tangitur ira.

Even more significant for Büchner's understanding of religious stillness is the role it plays in the Judaeo-Christian tradition. Büchner, whose works contain numerous Biblical allusions, would probably have known the words "God in peace"[36] or the expression "Peace be with you", with which Christ greeted his disciples after his resurrection.[37] Surely Büchner would have been familiar with the famous statement in Genesis that God rested on the seventh day.[38] The scriptures characterize the kingdom of God above all by peace.

---

[31] „Die Seeligkeit schließt alle Thätigkeit aus" (L II, 408). Büchner's familiarity with Epicureanism is documented in *Dantons Tod* as well.

[32] See "Letter to Herodotus" (77), "Letter to Menoeceus" (123), and "Principal Doctrines" (I).

[33] For references besides those noted below see the section "de vita deorum beata" in *Epicurea*, 241–44.

[34] 17, 2. In arguing for the Old Testament conception of God's wrath Lactantius must attempt to refute Epicurus, the major defender of God's inactivity and tranquillity.

[35] 1:44–49 = 2:646–51. Cf. 2:1093; 5:165–74.

[36] Mark 5, 25–34; Luke 7, 50.

[37] John 20, 19–26. Cf. John 14, 27 and Matt. 11, 28–29.

[38] The statement in Genesis (2, 2–3) that God rested on the seventh day is an important reference point for praise of religious stillness from early Christianity to Pietism. See, for example, Richter, 85–87. Augustine's interpretation of this passage is surely the most influential. In the last chapter of his *De civitate dei* he speaks of the perpetual Sabbath when we shall know God perfectly: "Hoc perfecte tunc sciemus, quando perfecte vacabimus, et perfecte videbimus quia ipse est Deus

Isaiah, for example, speaks of the future transformation of all creation into a world of peace: "Then justice will dwell in the wilderness, and righteousness abide in the fruitful field. / And the effect of righteousness will be peace, and the result of righteousness, quietness and trust for ever. / My people will abide in a peaceful habitation, in secure dwellings, and in quiet resting places."[39] Most importantly, peace is ascribed to Christ,[40] a figure with whom Lenz, however, can identify only in moments of pure restlessness. In the first paragraph of each of his twelve letters Paul expresses his wish that through Christ his readers will find repose.[41]

The individual who wants to receive the divine in his soul must be "still before the Lord, and wait patiently for him".[42] Repose is both a condition of and a reward for piety.[43] Restlessness meanwhile is the unmistakeable consequence of impiety: "But the wicked are like the tossing sea; for it cannot rest, and its waters toss up mire and dirt. There is no peace, says my God, for the wicked."[44] In the New Testament one finds increasing emphasis on peace not as the cessation of worldly battle but as a spiritual and inner condition that manifests itself independently of external circumstances: "I have said this to you, that in me you may have peace. In the world you have tribulation; but be of good cheer, I have overcome the world" (John 16, 33).

Büchner would probably not have had any familiarity with the concept of religious stillness in the patristic literature of early Christianity,[45] but he did have some acquaintance with mysticism.[46] In his sermon "In omnibus

---

[...]. Ibi vacabimus et videbimus, videbimus et amabimus, amabimus et laudabimus" (XXII, 30). In general Augustine considers repose an essential goal of religious life and argues that with God such rest is assured. In the *Confessions* we hear, for example: "quies est apud te valde et vita imperturbalis" (II, 10); "requiescite in eo et quieti eritis" (IV, 12).

[39] Isa. 32, 16–18. See also Isa: 2, 4; 9, 6; 11, 1–9; 60, 17–18; Zech: 8, 12; 9, 9–10; Luke: 1, 79; 19, 38; Rom. 14, 17–19; Heb. 3, 11.

[40] See esp. Luke 2, 14, but also Eph: 2, 2–22; 6, 15; Phil. 4, 7; and 2 Thess. 3, 16. Note also Paul's references to a "God of peace" in Rom. 15, 33 and Phil. 4, 9.

[41] See also Acts 10, 36 and the reference to the "peace of Christ" in Colo. 3, 15.

[42] Ps. 37, 7. See also Ps. 62, 1; Isa. 30, 15; Lam. 3, 26.

[43] See Eccles. 3, 7; Isa: 41, 1; 53, 7; Hab. 2, 20; Zech. 2, 13. In the New Testament see Luke: 2, 19; 2, 51; 9, 36; Jas: 1, 19–21; 3, 1–18.

[44] Isa. 57, 20–21. See also Ps. 35, 20; Isa. 48, 22; Jer. 6, 16. For a differentiation of Old Testament ideas on peace see Caspari (1910). For the New Testament view of peace as the consequence of virtue see Matt: 5, 9; 11, 29; 2 Tim. 2, 22; Heb. 12, 4; Jas. 3, 18.

[45] Gregory of Nyssa is one of the most interesting figures in this tradition, for he speaks, in his *Life of Moses*, not only of the virtues of quiet contemplation but also of a kind of dynamic stillness, as for example when he argues that physical stillness is a necessary condition of spiritual progress (II, 243).

[46] See L II, 269.

requiem quaesivi" the mystic Meister Eckhart suggests that the trinity, the human soul, indeed all creatures, have as their goal stillness:

> Vrâgete man mich, daz ich endelîche berihten sölte, waz der schepfer gemeinet haete, daz er alle crêatûren geschaffen haete, ich spraeche: ‚ruowe'. Vrâgete man mich ze dem andern mâle, waz diu heilige drîvalticheit suochte zemâle an allen irn werken, ich spraeche: ‚ruowe'. Vrâgete man mich ze dem dritten mâle, waz diu sêle suochte an allen irn bewegungen, ich spraeche: ‚ruowe'. Vrâgete man mich ze dem vierden mâle, waz alle crêatûren suochten an irn natiurlîchen begerungen und bewegungen, ich spraeche: ‚ruowe'. (DW III, 11–12)

The goal of God's creation and therefore of all creatures, including man, is stillness. Insofar as man is capable of reaching this goal he is capable of becoming like God, for „niht enist gote sô glîch an allen crêatûren als ruowe" (DW III, 16). This concept of the parallel structure of divine essence and human soul[47] is central to Eckhart's theology.[48] The two ends of Eckhart's analogy are, first, the Godhead, and second, the „vünkelîn der sêle".[49] The goal of man's striving is the unity and stillness of the Godhead, which is even more essential than the trinity:

> Dirre vunke [...] wil in den einvaltigen grunt, in die stillen wüeste, dâ nie underscheit îngeluogete weder vater noch sun noch heiliger geist [...] dirre grunt ist ein einvaltic stille, diu in ir selben unbewegelich ist, und von dirre unbewegelicheit werdent beweget alliu dinc.[50]

Man does not rest until he reaches this goal; but when he does, his repose is divine: „Wan si des éinen niht enhât, dar umbe geruowet diu sêle niemer, ez enwerde allez ein in gote. Got ist ein; daz ist der sêle sælicheit und ir gezierde und ir ruowe" (DW I, 369–70).

---

[47] The concept that man must become like God in order to receive or mirror his virtues can also be found in antiquity. In the *Republic* it is the divine element in us by which we grasp divinity, our sunlike eye which allows us to see the sun (508). Lucretius introduces the specific element of stillness to this idea of identifying intuition: to receive the divine, man must himself possess a tranquillity of spirit (5:1198–1203; 6:43–78).
[48] The analogy is actually quite complex for, according to Eckhart, nothing is so similar and dissimilar simultaneously as creator and the created: "nihil tam dissimile quam creator et quaelibet creatura [...] nihil tam simile quam creator et creatura quaelibet [...] nihil tam dissimile pariter et simile alteri cuiquam, quam deus et creatura quaelibet sunt et dissimilia et similia pariter" (LW II, 110).
[49] For the expression „vünkelîn der sêle" see DW I: 331, 10–11; 332, 3; 343, 6; and esp. 380, 8–381, 2: „diz vünkelîn ist gote alsô sippe, daz ez ist ein einic ein ungescheiden und daz bilde in sich treget aller crêatûren, bilde sunder bilde und bilde über bilde."
[50] DW II, 419–21. The echoes of the Aristotelian concept of the unmoved mover are obvious in this passage. The link between Aristotelian and Christian ideas of divinity had been made explicit by Aquinas in his first argument for the existence of God, i. e., the argument from physical motion. See Aquinas, *Summa Theologiae* I, 2, 3; *Summa Contra Gentiles* I, 13; and *Compendium Theologiae* I, 3.

In his sermons Eckhart tells his listeners how to attain stillness and avoid the dangers of restlessness.[51] Above all, one should not search for peace in external things:

> Die liute, die vride suochent in ûzwendigen dingen, ez sî an steten oder an wîsen oder an liuten oder an werken oder daz ellende oder diu armuot oder smâcheit, swie grôz diu sî oder swaz daz sî, daz ist dennoch allez nihtes noch engibet keinen vride. (DW V, 193–94)

Inner peace is more easily reached as one relinquishes one's needs and achieves a state of disinterested withdrawal: „Der mensche ist der beste, der des enbern kan, des er keine nôt enhât. Dar umbe, der allermeist kan enbern und versmæhen, der hât allermeist gelâzen" (DW V, 300). In order to enter the soul, God does not require man's active help; he simply needs *Ruhe*.[52] In a free translation and revision of Anselm, Eckhart makes it clear that fasting and even prayer run counter to the „ruowe" necessary for God to enter the soul.[53] One must negate one's individuality and relinquish one's will: „Niemer enstât ein unvride in dir ûf, ez enkome von eigenem willen [...]. Dar umbe hebe an dir selber an ze dem êrsten und lâz dich" (DW V, 192–93). In short, rest is found neither in the external world nor through one's own acts of exertion. Peace is found in and through God alone: „Wan als vil bist dû in gote, als vil dû bist in vride, und als vil ûz gote, als vil dû bist ûz vride. Ist iht einez in gote, daz selbe hât vride. Als vil in gote, als vil in vride."[54]

According to Eckhart one should be prepared to receive God whether one is in rest or unrest:

> nement sie got in dem vride und in der ruowe, sô suln sie in ouch nemen in dem unvride und in der unruowe, sô ist im zemâle reht; mêr: nement sie in minner in dem unvride und in der unruowe dan in der ruowe und in dem vride, sô ist im unreht. (DW II, 81–82)

In fact for Eckhart stillness is most admirable amidst turmoil, for here one exhibits the greatest inner strength: „Daz ein mensche ein ruowic leben habe, daz ist guot; mêr: daz ein mensche ein pînlich leben habe mit gedult, daz ist bezzer; mêr: daz man dennne ruowe habe in dem pînlîchen lebene, daz ist daz beste" (DW III, 145). According to Eckhart fleeing from one situation to another leads nowhere; one must find an inner peace, an inner solitude, independent of all external conditions: „Der mensche [...] muoz ein innerlich einœde lernen, swâ oder bî swem er ist" (DW V, 207).

---

[51] See esp. DW III, 18, 1–21, 6.
[52] In this stillness God speaks to man: „In der stille und in der ruowe [...] da sprichet got in die sêle und sprichet sich alzemâle in die sêle" (DW I, 317). See also LW IV, 228: "ibi est quies et silentium, ubi pater loquitur verbum." In addition see DW III, 266. Cf. Tauler, 10–12.
[53] See Völker (1964), 121.
[54] DW V, 308. Cf. DW I, 118.

We see in Eckhart a metaphysical stillness (God is *ruhig*.), an epistemological stillness (Man "sees" God most clearly when he is *ruhig*.), and finally a literary stillness, whereby the proper response to mystical union is „stilleswîgen".[55] Each of these concepts is ideally coupled with an inner dynamism. Eckhart uses and even invents verbs of dynamism to convey the motion inherent in the stillness of mystical union.[56] In such stillness Christ *enters* the human soul; he is born there. To stress the dynamism inherent in proper stillness Eckhart presents his listeners with a highly imaginative rendering of the Biblical passage "Go in peace": „Waz ûz gote geborn ist, daz suochet vride und loufet in vride. Dar umbe sprach er: ‚vade in pace, louf in den vride'. Der mensche, der in einem loufe ist und in einem stæten loufe ist und daz in vride ist, der ist ein himelischer mensche" (DW I, 118).

It is ironic, although understandable, that Eckhart, with his fondness for paradox, should come under the inquisition not only for his mystical ideas but also for his concept of divine transcendence. While he seemed to reduce God to man in his descriptions of mystical union, he also appeared to attack God's goodness when, in trying to preserve his otherness, he suggested that we cannot apply any finite predicates to him: not even good, better, or best.[57] According to Eckhart God is for us nothing, „ein niht".[58] Suso, a defender of Eckhart[59] and along with Tauler one of the other great German mystics, reinforces this idea of the Godhead as nothingness: „Daz selb vernúnftig wa, da von geseit ist [...] mag man nemmen die istigen namlosen nihtekeit; und da kumt der geist uf daz niht der einikeit. Und dú einikeit heisset dar umb ein niht, wan der geist enkan enkein zitlich wise finden, waz es sie" (Bihlmeyer 187). For Tauler, too, God escapes human categorization:

> Got enist alles des nút das du von im genemmen kanst: er ist úber wise, úber wesen, úber gût, und alles des nút das du von im bekennen oder genemmen kanst: do ist er fúrbas úber denne dehein verstentnisse begriffen kan, noch hoch noch nider, sus noch so, verre úber alle wise, dis noch das. (204)

For the mystics God's otherness is an element of his divinity, but for the character Lenz, as he searches for an immediate sign from God, this otherness

---

[55] DW I, 312. Cf. Quint (1953), 53. These three concepts by the way capture the essence of William James's definition of mysticism as noetic, passive, and ineffable. See James (1958).
[56] Cf. Quint (1928), 701.
[57] Cf. Clark (1949), 17–19.
[58] For Eckhart's view of God as nothingness see esp. DW III, 222, 11–229, 5.
[59] Suso's first book – "The Little Book on Truth" – defended Eckhart against charges made against him under the inquisition. In Suso's biography Eckhart appears to Suso in a vision and tells him that he has been brought to heaven and is now in the presence of God: „Von dem meister ward er bewiset, daz er waz in überswenker grůnlichi, in die sin sele blos vergôtet waz in gote" (Bihlmeyer 23).

becomes the catalyst for his atheistic outbursts. God is silent, he is nothing, and, most importantly, he is unable to help us.

Suso, Tauler, and later mystics followed Eckhart in many of his basic ideas, including the general praise of interiority and repose.[60] Suso writes: „Nu wol uf, sel minú, samen dich genzlich von aller usserkeit in ein stilles swigen rehter inrkeit" (Bihlmeyer 211). The title of the ninth entry of Suso's *Briefbüchlein* reads: „Wie ein mensch ze rŵwe sines herzen in got súl komen" (Bihlmeyer 387). Here Suso meditates on Aristotle's unmoved mover:

> Ach hier umbe so vellet mir iez ein spruch in, den las ich in der schule der natúrlichen kunst; ich las in und verstŵnd sin aber do nit. Der hoh meister [i.e., Aristotle] der sprichet also: der alliche fúrst, einvaltig wesende, der bewegt ellú ding und ist er unbeweglich. Er bewegt als ein begirliches minnekliches lieb sol tŵn: er git den herzen ilen und begirden lofen, und ist er stille as ein unbeweglich zil, dez ellú wesen varent und begerent. (Bihlmeyer 388)

Suso, like Eckhart, reflects on the Biblical passage "In omnibus requiem quaesivi".[61] Tauler, too, has a sermon with this motto, wherein he writes: „alles do der mensche sine rŵwe sŵcht, das nút luter Got enist, das ist alles wurmstichig" (203).

The Baroque mystic Angelus Silesius, whose collection of verse, *Der cherubinische Wandersmann,* has been described by one critic as „eine Neuauflage Eckeharts im 17. Jahrhundert",[62] was equally immersed in ideas of religious stillness. In 24 of the 302 poems that constitute the first book of the *Cherubinischer Wandersmann,* Silesius invokes the concept of repose.[63] Silesius, whose work provides an important link between medieval mysticism and the Pietism of the seventeenth and eighteenth century,[64] shares with Eckhart the view that man must pass beyond God to the Godhead („Jch muß noch über GOtt in eine wŵste ziehn" I, 7) as well as the idea of God's dependence

---

[60] Despite Suso's and Tauler's inheritance from Eckhart their conceptions of *Ruhe* differ slightly from Eckhart's. For Suso, and even more so for Tauler, *ruowe* and *gelâzenheit* become increasingly psychological terms, whereby the abnegation of the world receives less emphasis than simple internal equanimity of spirit. On this point see Völker (1972).
[61] Bihlmeyer 387–89 (*Briefbüchlein* IX) = Bihlmeyer 468–70 (*Großes Briefbuch* XXI).
[62] Karrer (1926), 55.
[63] The references are nos. 2, 37, 38, 49, 51, 53, 58, 76, 130, 136, 167, 169, 171, 189, 214, 217, 224, 227, 239, 240, 243, 277, 294, and 299. This amounts to almost one of every twelve.
[64] Through Abraham von Franckenberg, Silesius became acquainted with Böhme's thought and the writings of the German mystics. See Sammons (1967), 21–24. Gottfried Arnold, an important Pietist, particularly as far as religious stillness is concerned, republished the *Cherubinischer Wandersmann* with an introduction in 1701.

on man and, specifically, Christ's birth in the human soul.[65] In one of his Alexandrine couplets Silesius describes stillness as the highest good: „Ruh ist das höchste Gutt" (I, 49). Correspondingly, he attributes such stillness to God: „GOtt ist die Ewge Ruh / weil Er nichts sucht noch wil: / Wiltu ingleichem nichts / so bistu eben vil" (I, 76). Silesius calls on his readers to imitate this model of stillness (II, 119) so that they might become one with God: „Die Ruhe deß Gemütts besteht in dem allein / Daß es Vollkömmlich ist mit GOtt ein einges Ein" (V, 321). Silesius' rhymed couplets are often full of contrast and paradox. Silesius makes use of rhetorical chiasmus as, for example, when he writes: „So viel die Seel in GOtt / so viel ruht GOtt in jhr: / Nichts minder oder mehr / Mensch glaub es / wird er dir" (I, 167). Jeffrey Sammons (1967) has suggested that "the scattershot technique of short, often startling verses, which are thrust upon the reader without any apparent order [...] radiates nervousness and lack of inner peace and equilibrium instead of mystical abandonment, struggle instead of quietude, and, ultimately, doubt instead of certainty" (99–100). Despite this latent turmoil and unnrest, stillness remains Silesius' manifest goal; he conceives of an ideal quietude that would result when one sets no goals, when one completely relinquishes one's own will. This ideal quietude often borders on indifference. Silesius writes: „Wenn du die Dinge nimbst ohn allen unterscheid; / So bleibstu still und gleich in Lieb und auch in Leyd" (I, 38). He sounds like a Stoic with a religious undertone: „Alls gilt dem Weisen gleich; er sitzt in ruh und stille: / Geht es nach seinem nicht / so gehts nach GOttes wille" (V, 136). Where such indifference signifies in Büchner's *Lenz* a loss of divine harmony and presence, for Silesius it indicates proximity to God: „Wer unbeweglich bleibt in Freud / in Leid / in Pein; / Der kan nunmehr nit weit von GOttes Gleichheit seyn" (I, 51). Silesius sees indifference or quietude as the proper expression of reverence for God;[66] silence or stillness is the highest form of prayer: „GOtt ist so überalls daß man nichts sprechen kan: / Drumb bettestu Jhn auch mit schweigen besser an."[67]

---

[65] On God's dependence on man see I, 8; I, 204; I, 224; and II, 3. In one couplet Silesius goes so far as to suggest that *God* finds rest in *man* (I, 277). On Silesius' conception of God's birth in man see II, 103; II, 112; and V, 252.
[66] Another Baroque writer, Grimmelshausen, similarly believed that one serves God best in isolation and repose. Simplicissimus tells the Dutch ship captain in the final chapter of Grimmelshausen's novel: „hier ist [...] ein stille Ruhe, darinnen man dem Allerhöchsten allein dienen, seine Wunder betrachten und ihn loben und preisen kann" (602).
[67] I, 240. See also I, 239; II, 19; II, 68; and IV, 11.

After medieval and Baroque mysticism the next significant stage in religious conceptions of stillness within the German tradition is Pietism.[68] Among the Pietists – frequently called, with reference to Psalm 35, „die Stillen im Lande" – one finds virtually all aspects of religious stillness united: God and especially Christ as models for human stillness; quietude or emptiness as a form of prayer; stillness as a condition of mystical union; mystical oneness as an experience of dynamic repose that results in silence; and finally, tranquillity and centeredness as the primary effects of religious experience. Gottfried Arnold, Gerhard Tersteegen, and Christian Friedrich Richter are the most prolific and important writers in this context.[69]

Already the titles of Arnold's hymns reveal his preoccupation with the topic of religious stillness: „Weg zur Ruhe" (146–47), „Vom göttlichen Frieden" (226–27), and „Aeußere und innere Stille" (271–72). In one of his untitled hymns Arnold praises the eight primary virtues of Christ. Second only to Christ's piety is his stillness:

O stiller Jesu, wie dein Wille,
Dem Willen deines Vaters stille
Und bis zum Tod gehorsam war:
Also mach auch gleichermaßen,
Mein Herz und Willen dir gelassen;
Ach stille meinen Willen gar!

---

[68] In this sketch of the history of the idea of religious stillness, one should note, at least briefly, the seventeenth-century Roman Catholic movement of quietism, which developed independently of German mysticism and exerted considerable influence on Pietist ideas of religious stillness. The primary exponents of quietism were Miguel de Molinos in Spain and Italy and Jeanne Marie Guyon and François Fénelon in France. Quietism is a mode of prayer and inactivity based on belief in the divinity of repose. It calls for willful passivity and self-oblivion. Because the quietists saw action as contrary to perfect repose in God, they suggested that man not seek God's love, but rather wait for God to act upon the soul. For an early and exhaustive account of quietist doctrine see Heppe (1875). On 490ff. Heppe relates the Catholic quietist movement to Pietism. Tersteegen and Arnold, two important Pietists who wrote extensively on religious stillness, had received the quietist movement favorably. Heppel calls Tersteegen „der eigentliche Herold der Frau von Guyon und der quietistischen Mystik im evangelischen Deutschland" (502) and cites besides Tersteegen's explicit praise of Guyon his several editions and translations of French quietist literature (504). Heppe also notes that Gottfried Arnold published a German translation of Molinos' *Geistlicher Wegweiser* (505). A more recent and concise discussion of the background and doctrine of quietism, along with an introduction to the lives and ideas of its more important proponents, can be found in Knox (1950), 231–87. See also Daniel-Rops (1958), I, 424–53.

[69] Although I do not discuss Zinzendorf, his poem „Über die Ruhe des Gemüths" (123–25) is an excellent example of the strong Pietist focus on Christ as a model for human stillness. On this topic cf. Arnold (116, 156, 271) and Tersteegen (p. 16 = I, 69; p. 17 = I, 73; p. 433).

Mach mich dir gleich gesinnt,
Wie ein gehorsam Kind.
   Stille! stille!
Jesu, ei nu, Hilf mir dazu,
Daß ich fein stille sei wie du. (156)

After listing all Christ's virtues, the poet concludes with yet another reference to *Ruhe*: „Jesu, ei nu, Laß mich, wie du, / Und wo du bist, einst finden Ruh!" (158). *Ruhe* can be attained not only, positively, by emulating Christ but also, negatively, by avoiding the external trappings of the world, the cares and dispersions of society, „die Unruh dieser äußern Dinge" (64). One should leave – as Büchner's Lenz would like to – the „Unruh, Streit und Jammer, / Die große Städt und Schlösser haben" (65) as well as relinquish all personal will and simply let God take over: „Ach, wenn doch in der stillen Still / Geschähe willig Gottes Will!" (58).[70]

Gerhard Tersteegen's influential[71] *Geistliches Blumen=Gärtlein* is also filled with praise of religious stillness and tranquillity.[72] According to Tersteegen God himself is ruhig,[73] and through God we come to „Ruhe".[74] „Ruhe" cannot be found in the world,[75] nor can it be reached through the exertion of one's own will:[76]

Gedenck nicht weit hinaus, wilt du GOtt in dir finden; / Was ist, und wird geschehn, laß alles sanft verschwinden, / Und bleibe, wie ein Kind, ohn Sorg, ohn Witz und Will: / Es braucht nicht grosse Kunst: GOtt wohnet in der Still. (p. 3 = I, 10)

In order to find God one must become passive, „Willen-los".[77] Passivity, stillness and silence allow us to hear God, and whenever we hear God we are "still".[78] This stillness is man's most proper and appropriate condition:

Alles am rechten Ort

Ein Stein sich nach der Erde neigt;
Ein Flämmlein in die Höhe steigt;
Ein Fisch will in dem Wasser leben;
Ein Vogel in der Luft muß schweben;
Wann jedes ist da, wo es soll,
So ist es still, und ihm ist wohl:
Mein Geist ist ruhig und vergnüget,
Wann er in GOtt, sein'm Ruh=Punct, lieget.
(p. 10 = I, 40)

---

[70] See also 106–07.
[71] On Tersteegen's influence see Heppe (1875), 503 and Martin Schmidt (1978), 40.
[72] Besides passages cited below see I: 61, 188, 282, and 285.
[73] P. 27 = I, 120; pp. 281, 283.
[74] P. 28 = I, 125; p. 75 = I, 335; p. 91 = I, 413; p. 439.
[75] P. 16 = I, 69; p. 91 = I, 412; pp. 285–86, 437, 440.
[76] See p. 13 = I, 54; p. 52 = I, 232; p. 86 = I, 386; p. 98 = I, 444; pp. 429, 456.
[77] P. 24 = I, 105. See also p. 3 = I, 9; p. 7 = I, 26; p. 11 = I, 46.
[78] Pp. 43–44 = I, 189; p. 79 = I, 354; pp. 32–33 = I, 141.

Tersteegen unites several major themes in the poem „Aeussere und innere Stille": „Wie sûß ists, wann Gedancken, Glieder, Sinnen, / Affecten, Wille, und Begierden stille, sind; / Wann alles schweigt, von aussen und von innen, / Und man im heitern Grund GOtt gegenwârtig findt!" (pp. 23–24 = I, 103). Christian Friedrich Richter's treatise „Von der Ruhe der Seelen" is an especially useful text for an understanding of Pietist conceptions of stillness. According to Richter „Ruhe" is „der Endzweck der Schöpfung".[79] In the tradition of Stoicism, Richter equates unrest with sickness and compares a tranquil soul to a healthy body (222). But unlike the Stoics or Neostoics, the Pietists do not consider wisdom the proper tool for achieving *Ruhe*.[80] Richter devotes an entire chapter to the topic: „Daß es vergeblich sey / Ruhe in der Weisheit und so genannten Tugend der Menschen zu suchen / und Daß die Philosophi von dem wahren Grunde der Gemûths=Ruhe nichts gewußt" (213). Only God can lead us to divine stillness. This theme is overshadowed in Richter's essay only by his emphasis on and colorful depiction of the individual who refuses to follow the path toward sacred tranquillity. At the close of his seventh chapter Richter presents a vivid summary of man's search for *Ruhe* everywhere but with God (211–13). To such a „verlassenes and verirretes Gemûthe" (210) Richter offers the following words of encouragement: „Gewißlich es ist eine ganz unbegreiffliche Langmuth und Gelindigkeit Gottes / daß er noch nicht seinen Eifer wider dich außgeschûttet / und dich elenden Wurm von dem Erdboden vertilget / und gânzlich außgerottet" (109). Richter devotes much attention to the „Unruhe und Unzufriedenheit" suffered by all who deny God (126–27). He constantly rephrases the battle between God and Satan as the struggle between *Ruhe* and *Unruhe*.[81] Just as the religious tradition knows of an inner sanctuary, a God within, so too is an inner hell possible. Richter speaks of „die Hölle in dir" (138), where Büchner will later write of Lenz: „In seiner Brust war ein Triumph-Gesang der Hölle" (22). True peace – „göttliche Ruhe" (95) – is for Richter equally internal. He chastises those who are „stets mit irdischen Dingen occupiret", and he devotes an entire chapter to the attempt to prove: „Daß es vergeblich sey / die Ruhe der Seelen und des Gemûths in der Welt / und in âusserlichen Dingen zu suchen" (165, 185). One should search for „seine Ruhe und Zufriedenheit allein in und durch Gott" (173).

The religious concept of stillness remained prominent beyond Pietism and into the eighteenth and early nineteenth century. The entries for „Ruhe"

---

[79] Richter 87. Cf. Richter 169.
[80] Unlike Silesius, who praises the wise man in *Der cherubinische Wandersmann* (e.g., IV, 109; V, 136) – the Cherubin or second order of angels are characterized of course by their knowledge – Richter and his fellow Pietists are critical of wisdom and the ideal of the wise man.
[81] See esp. 94–106.

and „ruhen" in Zedler's *Großes vollständiges Universal-Lexikon aller Wissenschaften und Künste* from the mid-eighteenth century focus directly on religious stillness; moreover, the lexicon contains special entries for „Ruhe GOttes" (9 pages), „Ruhe des HErrn" (2 pages), and „Ruhe des Meßias" (6 pages). The prominence of the concept for this period can be further demonstrated by pertinent passages in Klopstock, Schiller, Hölderlin, and the Romantics. In Klopstock's „Frühlingsfeyer" the world becomes still at the appearance of God: „Alles ist still vor dir, du Naher! / Rings umher ist Alles still!" (65). The hymn concludes with the poet rejoicing in Jehova's peaceful rather than stormy revelation and in the religious appearance of „der Bogen des Friedens" (67). Following Klopstock, Schiller speaks of „der stille Gott" (SA I, 196), of „Himmelsruh" (SA I, 17), and also of „Gott" as „ein ruhiger Geist" (SA I, 164). In „Die Götter Griechenlands" he refers to the religious stillness of antiquity:[82] Helios' „stille Majestät" (SA I, 157) and „der Götter stille Schar" (SA I, 159). In Hölderlin we encounter such terms as „Himmelsruh" (StA I, 133), „gottgesandte Ruhe" (StA I, 93), and „Götterruhe" (StA IV, 5). In „Abbitte" the poet speaks of „die goldene Götterruhe" (StA I, 244) and in „Der Archipelagus" of „die Himmlischen, sie, die Kräfte der Höhe, die stillen" (StA II, 103). The concept is found in other authors of the period as well. Novalis, for example, writes in *Heinrich von Ofterdingen* of a „heilige Stille" (I, 196) and a „himmlische Ruhe" (I, 267). Schlegel speaks in *Lucinde* of the inactivity of the gods and the „heilige Stille der echten Passivität" (KA V, 26–27).

Büchner and the Tradition of Religious Stillness

Büchner's awareness of the concept of religious stillness reveals itself in many ways.[83] First, Büchner was familiar with the antique concept of religious stillness in Aristotle, Epicurus, and Lucretius. Second, he was a close reader of the *Bible*, as the many allusions in his literary works indicate. Third, Büchner's notes on Spinoza reveal that he had at least some familiarity with mysticism (L II, 269). Fourth, Büchner developed a knowledge of Pietism when he lived in Strasbourg and studied Oberlin, himself a Pietist; moreover, the hymn („Laß in mir die heil'gen Schmerzen [...]") quoted in *Lenz* has its origins in Pietism, specifically with Christian Friedrich Richter,

---

[82] The divine stillness of antiquity was central to Hegel as well. See 13, 210 and 14, 81–86.
[83] If one of Büchner' final reflections can be interpreted on a more than literal level, it too would provide support for his awareness – if not also his acceptance during his troubled last days – of the divine as a source of repose: „Ich fühle keinen Ekel, keinen Überdruß; aber ich bin müde, sehr müde. Der Herr schenke mir Ruhe!" (*Werke und Briefe*, 586).

who also wrote the treatise discussed above, „Von der Ruhe der Seelen". In fact, both the hymn and the treatise were available in the same volume, Richter's *Erbauliche Betrachtungen*. This work was so popular that it went through five editions in the eighteenth century alone.[84] Next, the concept is, as we could see, widespread in the literature of German *Klassik* and German Romanticism, with which Büchner was partly familiar. In his own early religious poem „Die Nacht" Büchner gives *Ruhe* a prominent position among God's gifts to man (L I, 187–88). Then, there is the suggestion in *Lenz* itself that the hero tries to find *Ruhe* through religious vehicles such as homilies and prayer. Most important and indeed overwhelming as evidence for Büchner's cognizance of the concept of religious stillness is the following passage in *Dantons Tod* where Philippeau invites Danton to find *Ruhe* in God:

Philippeau: Was willst du denn?
Danton: Ruhe.
Philippeau: Die ist in Gott.
Danton: Im Nichts. Versenke dich in was Ruhigers, als das Nichts und wenn die höchste Ruhe Gott ist, ist nicht das Nichts Gott? Aber ich bin ein Atheist. (L I, 61)

Philippeau's equation of divinity and repose verifies Büchner's awareness of the tradition he was to invert in *Lenz*. The (non-)definition of God as nothingness is seemingly reminiscent of the mystic tradition; for Danton, however, nothingness alludes not to the wholeness or otherness but to the emptiness of divinity.[85] Danton is an atheist.[86] The *Ruhe* that Büchner's characters ascribe to God is the *Ruhe* of absence (Danton) or boredom (Valerio):

Valerio: Es war vor Erschaffung der Welt –
Hofprediger: Daß –
Valerio: Gott lange Weile hatte – (L I, 132)

Büchner molds Lenz in just such an image of divine repose.

The Inversion of Psychological-Moral Stillness and the Struggle with Idealism

At the story's conclusion Lenz not only turns away from God, he loses his sanity. Already in the prologue Lenz views nature in a way that exposes the

---

[84] See Altmann (1972), 218–20.
[85] Cf. Nietzsche's similar critique of the saints' ascetic ideal as „einen Vorwand zum Winterschlaf, ihre *novissima gloriae cupido*, ihre Ruhe im Nichts („Gott"), ihre Form des Irrsinns" (Schlechta II, 839). Cf. also Schopenhauer 9, 325.
[86] Danton's atheism rests on the fact that he doesn't even believe in the possibility of nothingness.

range of his disorientation. He experiences, first, indifference, then, wild fits of imagination (5). His imagination in turn passes from self-expansion to utter self-contraction (5–6). This tension then subsides and passes back into a pole of strict sobriety: „Aber es waren nur Augenblicke, und dann erhob er sich nüchtern, fest, ruhig als wäre ein Schattenspiel vor ihm vorübergezogen, er wußte von nichts mehr" (6). The series of distorted views culminates in Lenz's feeling of approaching insanity: „Es war [...] als jage der Wahnsinn auf Rossen hinter ihm" (6).

Lenz arrives from his journey to Waldbach with torn clothes (7), in part a reflection of his inner turmoil. His tensions, however, begin to subside as he hears voices, sees the radiance of light, and encounters friendly, quiet faces:

> Endlich hörte er Stimmen, er sah Lichter, es wurde ihm leichter [...] Er ging durch das Dorf, die Lichter schienen durch die Fenster, er sah hinein im Vorbeigehen, Kinder am Tische, alte Weiber, Mädchen, alles ruhige, stille Gesichter, es war ihm als müsse das Licht von ihnen ausstrahlen, es ward ihm leicht. (6–7)

With Oberlin and his family Lenz gains a sense of peace:

> Nach und nach wurde er ruhig, das heimliche Zimmer und die stillen Gesichter, die aus dem Schatten hervortraten, das helle Kindergesicht, auf dem alles Licht zu ruhen schien und das neugierig, vertraulich aufschaute, bis zur Mutter, die hinten im Schatten engelgleich stille saß. (7)[87]

Lenz feels at home in the company of this sympathetic family. In fact he appears like a child, that is, like someone who is at one with himself: „man drängte sich teilnehmend um ihn, er war gleich zu Haus, sein blasses Kindergesicht, das jetzt lächelte, sein lebendiges Erzählen; er wurde ruhig" (7). With Oberlin Lenz finds many moments of centeredness and stillness:

> Er mußte Oberlin oft in die Augen sehen, und die mächtige Ruhe, die uns über der ruhenden Natur, im tiefen Wald, in mondhellen, schmelzenden Sommernächten überfällt, schien ihm noch näher, in diesem ruhigen Auge, diesem ehrwürdigen ernsten Gesicht. (9)

Oberlin's oneness with himself and with society functions in part as a model for Lenz, and as Lenz works together with Oberlin he begins to share in his harmony. Lenz becomes „ruhiger" (10).

Despite Lenz's increasing harmony he cannot completely resolve his inner tensions. During his first night, when it is dark and he is left by himself, Lenz loses his orientation and falls prey to fear: „das Licht war erloschen, die Finsternis verschlang alles; eine unnennbare Angst erfaßte ihn" (7–8). Later during his stay the process recurs: „Aber nur solange das Licht im Tale lag, war es ihm erträglich; gegen Abend befiel ihn eine sonderbare Angst, er hätte

---

[87] The reference to angelic stillness is yet another indication that Büchner knew of the religious implications of *Ruhe*.

der Sonne nachlaufen mögen" (9). For his repose Lenz depends on factors beyond his control: the presence of other people or external images such as light. Because he does not acquire his repose from within, it often slips away and becomes one end of a dichotomy. Throughout the story division characterizes Lenz's existence. He suffers from tensions between not only repose and unrest but also communion and separation, piety and atheism, hybris and inferiority, activity and lethargy. These and other tensions can be grounded in a primary dualism of idealism and anti-idealism.

Lenz encounters idealism in not only an aesthetic but also a societal sphere. It is surely no accident that Kaufmann defends both idealist aesthetics and a societal structure built on sacrifice of the present and longing for future goals. Immediately following the discourse on art the narrator writes:

> Nach dem Essen nahm ihn Kaufmann beiseite. Er hatte Briefe von Lenzens Vater erhalten, sein Sohn sollte zurück, ihn unterstützen. Kaufmann sagte ihm, wie er sein Leben hier verschleudre, unnütz verliere, er solle sich ein Ziel stecken und dergleichen mehr. (16)

Kaufmann upholds a societal order characterized, like idealist aesthetics, by imperatives and external teleology. In our chapter on Schiller we saw to what extent the idealist philosophy of Kant and Fichte is characterized by *das Sollen*, by necessary and continuous striving for unreachable goals. In his discourse on art Lenz terms just such a projection of external goals, with its resulting emphasis on the break between "is" and "ought", idealist. Idealist aesthetics is characterized by its external *teleology* and its imperatives, the idea that the world *should* be different than it is. This particular aesthetic norm corresponds to Kaufmann's expectation that Lenz *should* fulfill a particular role in society, that he begin to act differently, that he set *goals* for himself. *Kaufmann's admonition of Lenz's social behavior thus provides a moral corollary to idealist aesthetics.*[88] Lenz's response to Kaufmann's position in both the aesthetic and social spheres proves disastrous. Lenz's denial of teleology in the aesthetic sphere makes it impossible for him to remain an artist. His refusal to set goals within the social sphere means that he can no longer function in the communal order. In setting overarching goals the idealist sacrifices the present for future rewards. Lenz rejects this kind of denial: „Immer steigen, ringen und so in Ewigkeit alles was der Augenblick gibt,

---

[88] Many critics have discussed the relationship of the discourse on art to the rest of the story. Most do not view the discourse as integral. See, most recently, Richards (1977). Interpreters have completely overlooked the implicit connection between the aesthetic and moral views of the world to which Lenz finds himself in opposition. Each is characterized by external teleology. Critics who have previously linked aesthetics and morality did so only with reference to the criticism of nobility implicit in the discourse on art itself. See esp. Mayer (1954), 148.

153

wegwerfen und immer darben, um einmal zu genießen; dürsten, während einem helle Quellen über den Weg springen" (16–17).[89] During the discourse on art Lenz was able to forget himself. Here Kaufmann reminds him of his place within society and disrupts his simple equanimity. Kaufmann's intrusion into Lenz's life deprives Lenz of all hope of *Ruhe*. In fact the societal obligations represented by Kaufmann stand in direct opposition to Lenz's world of tranquillity.[90] The narrator introduces Kaufmann with the words:

> Um diese Zeit kam Kaufmann mit seiner Braut ins Steintal. Lenzen war anfangs das Zusammentreffen unangenehm, er hatte sich so ein Plätzchen zurechtgemacht, das bißchen Ruhe war ihm so kostbar und jetzt kam ihm jemand entgegen, der ihn an so vieles erinnerte, mit dem er sprechen, reden mußte, der seine Verhältnisse kannte. (13)

Kaufmann knows Lenz's past. His arrival disturbs Lenz, for Lenz had attained repose not by integrating the past into his present condition (as was the case with Hyperion) but by negating it. Kaufmann also refers to Lenz's future („er solle sich ein Ziel stecken" 16). Oberlin does not concern himself with Lenz's past or future („Oberlin wußte von allem nichts" 13). In fact during Lenz's entire visit no one had asked him about his previous mistakes or his future goals: „Niemand frug, woher er gekommen und wohin er gehen werde" (13). As Kaufmann confronts Lenz with his call to duty, Lenz calls out for *Ruhe*. He sees in the words „Hier weg?" and „nach Haus" the destruction of his world: „Laßt mich doch in Ruhe! Nur ein bißchen Ruhe, jetzt wo es mir ein wenig wohl wird! Weg? Ich verstehe das nicht, mit den zwei Worten ist die Welt verhunzt" (16). The worlds which these words conjure up would shake Lenz out of his peace not only because home represents a return to the past, and with it the imposition of societal obligations, but also because a departure from his present environment would deprive Lenz of the conditions that had granted him *Ruhe*. At Kaufmann's departure Lenz again alludes to the disruption of his tranquillity; his final words to Kaufmann are: „Laßt mich in Ruhe" (17). Lenz does not

---

[89] The concept „immer darben, um einmal zu genießen" is also present in *Dantons Tod* (II, 2) and *Leonce und Lena* (II, 1). See, in addition, Büchner's criticism of teleology in his early essay „Über den Selbstmord" (L II, 21) and his lecture „Über Schädelnerven" (L II, 291–92). Armstrong (1981) refers to these passages and writes: „Allen Zitaten ist die Vorstellung gemeinsam, daß die Natur nicht auf die Erreichung von Zielen gerichtet ist und daß das menschliche Leben es nicht sein sollte" (96). The problem implicit in Büchner's analysis and Armstrong's conclusion is that a new *goal* has been posited. Our perspectives *should* be different than they are. The critique of teleology necessarily cancels itself.

[90] In Oberlin's report Kaufmann had sent Lenz to the preacher to find comfort and repose. In Büchner's story Kaufmann's role is reversed: in trying to bring Lenz back to the social order, Kaufmann disrupts Lenz's tranquillity.

return with Kaufmann, nor does he set any specific goals that would lead him back to society; nonetheless, he loses all possibility of inner peace. The narrator's statement that Lenz hiked into the country and „suchte keinen Weg" (18) has symbolic as well as literal significance. Lenz does not set specific goals, yet without a goal he finds himself lost. His lack of purpose, his critique of teleology, and his denial of stability disrupt his existence as much as does his fear of possibly having to set goals.

Lenz, the staunch defender of anti-idealism and critic of the substitution of distant ideals for present reality, is no more at home as an anti-idealist than as an idealist. Despite his avowed this-worldliness Lenz yearns for transcendent meaning, for signs from God. Despite his expressed contentment with the world as it is now, independent of human attempts to improve or manipulate it, Lenz finds himself searching for a mode of orientation not yet available to him and eventually for a new world altogether. In theory Lenz relinquishes idealist philosophy; in practice he continues to search for stability and orientation. Such searching, however, makes Lenz on his own terms an idealist.[91] Lenz suffers from the loss of goals and general orientation inherent in the idealist system. He is a despairing idealist who has lost both his faith and his reason yet still searches for God and meaning.[92] He is an anti-idealist who cannot accept his own theory that the world is as it ought to be. Ultimately Lenz will propose an alternate world, an *ideal* world free of suffering (29).

Lenz's wanderings through nature and his strong attraction to the simple life of Oberlin reflect his desire to replace his spirit with nature, his intellect with simple living. His lack of success in this attempt binds him yet again to the idealist mode. Lenz would release himself from the burdens of thought by sinking into nature, simple living, or even sleep – yet the contradictions and turmoil that arise as he tries to free himself of the idealist inheritance continue to torture him. Nature is transformed into a corollary of Lenz's own spiritual condition;[93] Lenz does not quite fit in with Oberlin and his family; and Oberlin himself is too simple to grasp Lenz's thoughts; finally,

---

[91] The inconsistency between Lenz's disquisition on literature and art and the rest of his behavior has been overlooked. Benn (1976) writes for example: "The views on literature and art which Camille expresses are not particularly appropriate in his mouth [...] In the Novelle there is no such inconsistency. Nothing could be more appropriate than Lenz's speech attacking idealization in art" (205–06).

[92] Even Lenz's seemingly nonsensical immersion in water, his repeated bathing, underscores his continued desire for religious experience (8, 9, 24). Water imagery is commonly used to express man's relationship to God: God is himself a "spring"; his essence "flows" into the soul; the "rain" which comes down from the heavens symbolizes divine grace, etc. See Langen (1954), 319–28.

[93] Cf. Michels (1981), esp. 18.

the oblivion of sleep remains impossible for him. Lenz cannot remain an idealist, but nor can he deny his intellect. Unable to reach his goals – art without stillness, meaning without idealism, an intellectual negation of intellect, and a perfect world void of suffering – Lenz experiences the idealist break between "is" and "ought". That Lenz has himself eliminated the possibility of his being an artist, that his attempts to negate intellect lead only to more intellectual torment, and that the world free of suffering, which he finally attains, is hardly perfect, demonstrate the contradictions inherent in his anti-idealist strivings. Lenz will free himself of his intellectual torment, thus suspending his knowledge of contradiction, only by denying his intellect altogether. Lenz's escape will be his insanity, the total negation of structure, vitality, meaning, and intellect. It is an escape against which a part of his self – that part which seeks consciousness through pain – struggles, albeit in vain.

In addition to Lenz's idealist behavior and his forced and failed attempts to break free of the idealist inheritance, the narrator leaves a series of clues by which we can recognize Lenz's covert idealism. While there are as many definitions of idealism as there are German Idealists,[94] one particular form of German Idealism, the Fichtean philosophy of the subjective origins of the world, is most readily identifiable as "idealist" in the common understanding of the term.[95] The narrator describes Lenz several times as though he were either an adherent of or living proof of Fichtean immaterialism. Lenz views the world as nothing but his own projection. Even the references to the mysterious "was" or "es" that would threaten Lenz and force him to do and see things in a particular way are introduced with modalization; these seemingly external forces originate in Lenz's subjective view of the world.[96] The clearest statement of Lenz's epistemological antirealism comes as Lenz begins to show signs of both atheism and insanity: „Es war ihm dann, als existiere er allein, als bestünde die Welt nur in seiner Einbildung, als sei

---

[94] For a sampling of the diversity of definitions see Kant's refutation of problematic and dogmatic idealism as well as his interpretation of his own philosophy as transcendental or critical idealism (KrV: A 369–80; B 274–75; B 518–24; *Prologommena:* V: 158, 254). See also Schiller's *Briefe über Don Carlos* (esp. nos. 2, 6, and 11) and the conclusion of *Über naive und sentimentalische Dichtung* (NA XX, 492–503). In addition one might look at Hegel's discussion of idealism at the conclusion of the second chapter of the first book of his *Wissenschaft der Logik* (WL I, 145–46) and the condensed version of this in §95 of his *Enzyclopädie* (Hegel 8, 200–03).
[95] Büchner was of course familiar with Fichtean idealism. The spoof on King Peter in *Leonce und Lena* (I, 2) is ample evidence alone, but there is more. See Hinderer (1981: 180), Lehmann (1963: 197–213), and Wittkowski (1976).
[96] See, for example: „Es war als ginge ihm was nach, und als müsse ihn was Entsetzliches erreichen" (6). The narrator uses modalization frequently, esp. in the beginning of the story, where one encounters it two or three times a page.

nichts, als er" (28).[97] Less obvious indications of Lenz's idealism surface early in the story. During Lenz's first night in the schoolhouse, the world seems to him a projection of his own power of imagination, a dream: „es war ihm wie ein Schatten, ein Traum" (7). One can observe Lenz's latent idealism again during his traumatic experience of darkness: „Das Licht war erloschen, die Finsternis verschlang alles; eine unnennbare Angst erfaßte ihn, er sprang auf, er lief durchs Zimmer, die Treppe hinunter, vors Haus; aber umsonst, alles finster, nichts, er war sich selbst ein Traum" (7–8). Lenz tries to bring himself to consciousness by allowing the non-ego to work upon him. As with Schiller and Hölderlin earlier, the passivity *(Leiden)* of the ego in relationship to the non-ego becomes pain *(Leiden)*: „Er konnte sich nicht mehr finden, ein dunkler Instinkt trieb ihn, sich zu retten, er stieß an die Steine, er riß sich mit den Nägeln, der Schmerz fing an, ihm das Bewußtsein wiederzugeben" (8). Later in the story Lenz smashes his head against the wall in an attempt, „sich zu sich selbst zu bringen durch physischen Schmerz" (29).[98] The idealist aspects of Lenz's view of the world alert us to the tensions between his expressed anti-idealism and his latent idealism. Lenz's view of the world as his own projection and his desperate drive to regain consciousness often coincide with an experience of darkness that is symbolic of a loss of meaning. Insofar as idealist meaning disappears, the idealist self is threatened:

---

[97] That this statement can be interpreted psychologically does not rule out its intellectual-historical significance. The story has many levels. Schizophrenia or split-personality has its corollary in the idealist philosophy of self-consciousness. When the narrator writes, „es war als sei er doppelt" (28), the reader thinks of a Fichtean philosophical position as readily as of a psychopathological state.

[98] Hinderer (1981: 179–81) traces the idea that pain awakens consciousness and activity back to Kant. It can also be found in Leibniz' *Nouveaux Essais* (Bk. 2, ch. 21, sec. 36), which Kant of course had read – at some point between its publication in 1765 and his dissertation of 1770. Leibniz proposes, much like Schiller and Hölderlin later, that unrest and striving are conditions of happiness; he also suggests that suffering acts as a spur to stimulate the will: «l'amas de ces petits succès continuels de la nature qui se met de plus en plus à son aise, en tendant au bien et jouissant de son image, ou diminuant le sentiment de la douleur, est déja un plaisir considerable et vaut souvent mieux que la jouissance même du bien; *et bien loin qu'on doive regarder cette inquietude comme une chose incompatible avec la felicité*, je trouve que l'inquietude est essentielle à la felicité des creatures, la quelle ne consiste jamais dans une parfaite possession qui les rendroit insensibles et comme stupides, mais dans un progrés continuel et non interrompu à des plus grands biens, qui ne peut manquer d'estre accompagné d'un desir ou du moins d'une inquietude continuelle, mais telle que je viens d'expliquer, qui ne va pas jusqu'à incommoder, mais qui se borne à ces elemens ou rudimens de la douleur, *inapperceptibles* à part, les quels ne laissent pas d'estre suffisans pour servir d'éguillon, et pour exciter la volonté» (Leibniz VI/6, 189). The concept reaches forward as far as Nietzsche. See the section „Die Begierde nach Leiden" in *Die fröhliche Wissenschaft* (Schlechta II, 74–75).

> Aber nur solange das Licht im Tale lag, war es ihm erträglich; gegen Abend befiel ihn eine sonderbare Angst, er hätte der Sonne nachlaufen mögen; wie die Gegenstände nach und nach schattiger wurden, kam ihm alles so traumartig, so zuwider vor, es kam ihm die Angst an wie Kindern, die im Dunkeln schlafen; es war ihm als sei er blind; jetzt wuchs sie, der Alp des Wahnsinns setzte sich zu seinen Füßen, der rettungslose Gedanke, als sei alles nur sein Traum, öffnete sich vor ihm, er klammerte sich an alle Gegenstände, Gestalten zogen rasch an ihm vorbei, er drängte sich an sie, es waren Schatten, das Leben wich aus ihm und seine Glieder waren ganz starr. (9)

The threatening nature of Lenz's obsession with his self contrasts with the few times when Lenz is free of such idealist concerns and appears content, as when he arrives at Oberlin's house (7) or when he discusses art (14–16).

Although Büchner has been praised for his advanced depiction of schizophrenia,[99] *Lenz's insanity is not just a case study: it symbolizes the loss of meaning and ideals experienced by someone who has tried to relinquish idealism.* In abandoning teleology and idealism Lenz forfeits his place in the social order. He loses all sense of integration and coherence. Lenz's isolation and unconnectedness is further represented in his severed relationship with Friederike and his difficulties in communicating. Lenz's self-expansion, experienced first in the prologue,[100] recurs later in the story in the form of his Fichtean immaterialism, his negation of reality; the other pole of Lenz's unsettling relationship to the world, his self-dilution, also prefigured in the prologue,[101] manifests itself again in Lenz's isolation. This becomes particularly clear through Lenz's loss of Friederike. We first hear of her in a conversation between Lenz and Oberlin's wife:

> Er faßte sich ein Herz, er konnte nicht mehr schweigen, er mußte davon sprechen. „Beste Madame Oberlin, können Sie mir nicht sagen, was das Frauenzimmer macht, dessen Schicksal mir so zentnerschwer auf dem Herzen liegt?" (20)

Lenz remembers the peace he experienced with Friederike: „ich war immer ruhig, wenn ich sie ansah, oder sie so den Kopf an mich lehnte und Gott! Gott – Ich war schon lange nicht mehr ruhig" (20–21). Instead of peace Lenz now feels the isolation and loss of self associated with a loss of love: „Jetzt ist es mir so eng, so eng, sehn Sie, es ist mir manchmal, als stieß' ich mit den Händen an den Himmel; o ich ersticke!" (21). Contraction continues to

---

[99] See Sharp (1981) and Irle (1965) along with their references to numerous earlier treatments of the topic.
[100] „Er meinte, er müsse den Sturm in sich ziehen, alles in sich fassen, er dehnte sich aus und lag über der Erde" (6).
[101] „Er stand still und legte das Haupt ins Moos und schloß die Augen halb, und dann zog es weit von ihm, die Erde wich unter ihm, sie wurde klein wie ein wandelnder Stern und tauchte sich in einen brausenden Strom, der seine klare Flut unter ihm zog" (6).

overcome Lenz and brings with it a sense of *Angst*:[102] „die Landschaft beängstigte ihn, sie war so eng, daß er an alles zu stoßen fürchtete" (26).

The narrator carefully connects the two spheres of Lenz's unconnectedness: interpersonal relations and the use of language. Lenz's unconnected words and incoherent sentences commence specifically at those moments when he attempts to discuss his disastrous love affair. The narrator concludes Lenz's first discussion of Friederike with the comments: „Er sprach später noch oft mit Madame Oberlin davon, aber meist nur in abgebrochenen Sätzen" (21). The second time the topic is raised, Lenz again has trouble communicating. He cannot form even a linguistic unity:

> Er sprach abgebrochen [...]. Dann frug er plötzlich freundlich, was das Frauenzimmer mache. Oberlin sagte, er wisse von nichts, er wolle ihm aber in allem helfen und raten, er müsse ihm aber Ort, Umstände und Person angeben. Er antwortete nichts wie gebrochne Worte: ach sie ist tot! Lebt sie noch? du Engel, sie liebte mich – ich liebte sie, sie war's würdig, o du Engel. Verfluchte Eifersucht, ich habe sie aufgeopfert – sie liebte noch einen andern – ich liebte sie, sie war's würdig – o gute Mutter, auch die liebte mich. Ich bin ein Mörder. (23)

Lenz has destroyed for both his beloved and himself the possibility of finding salvation through a binding relationship. For this reason he imagines himself a murderer. With his use of language Lenz continues to express unconnectedness: he forms broken sentences, questions that elicit no proper response, and thoughts that lack coherent association. Lenz mentions Friederike two more times. When running through the courtyard on his way to the fountain, he yells her name „mit äußerster Schnelle, Verwirrung und Verzweiflung" (24); later, he mentions her in a purely cryptic manner:

> Liebster Herr Pfarrer, das Frauenzimmer, wovon ich Ihnen sagte, ist gestorben, ja gestorben, der Engel. Woher wissen Sie das? – Hieroglyphen, Hieroglyphen – und dann zum Himmel geschaut und wieder: ja gestorben – Hieroglyphen. Es war dann nichts weiter aus ihm zu bringen. (26–27)

The narrator notes Lenz's inability to communicate in yet another passage: „Im Gespräch stockte er oft, eine unbeschreibliche Angst befiel ihn, er hatte das Ende seines Satzes verloren; dann meinte er, er müsse das zuletzt gesprochene Wort behalten und immer sprechen, nur mit großer Anstrengung unterdrückte er diese Gelüste" (27). Toward the end of the story, when Lenz can neither communicate nor view the world coherently, we increasingly see events through the narrator's point of view.[103] Almost as in *Die Leiden des jungen Werthers*, where the objective narrator must replace the

---

[102] „Enge" and „Angst" are of course etymologically related.
[103] As a result Büchner stays closer to the Oberlin report. Cf. Pütz (1965), esp. 17. An instructive discussion of the narrator and narrative technique in *Lenz* can be found in Pascal (1978).

deceased hero, in *Lenz* the narrator, who often adopts the perspective of the hero, eventually distances himself from him, so that, toward the end of the story, we no longer view events from the hero's point of view. Metaphorically speaking, Lenz becomes silent. The less we see of Lenz's internal state, the more we imagine that his consciousness is devoid of meaning, even of conflict. The narrator's portrayal of Lenz's difficulties with language lends support, of course, to the thesis that Büchner was aware of the external effects of psychological disturbances, but the hero's ineffective attempts at communication also symbolize the loss of meaning and coherence in an anti-idealist world. When Lenz finally speaks, his language reveals his inner emptiness: „Er schien ganz vernünftig, sprach mit den Leuten; er tat alles wie es die andern taten, es war aber eine entsetzliche Leere in ihm, er fühlte keine Angst mehr, kein Verlangen; sein Dasein war ihm eine notwendige Last" (31).[104]

Not only do Lenz's failures in communicating reveal his loss of meaning, but so too his final state of boredom.[105] *Langeweile* simply adds a temporal dimension to Lenz's emptiness. When Goethe, who experiences dynamic stillness, writes that the moment is eternity (HA I, 370), his moments are overfull with meaning and vitality. For Büchner's Lenz, suffering from deficient stillness, the eternity of the moment is not that of the „erfüllter Augenblick" but its reverse, *lange Weile*.[106] The first signs of Lenz's boredom and emptiness surface during Oberlin's absence. Lenz searches desperately for an activity that will fill his time with significance: „er zeichnete, malte, las, griff nach jeder Zerstreuung, alles hastig von einem zum andern" (20). He experiences a restless drive to fulfill himself and overcome his present

---

[104] King (1974) argues that because Lenz, a docile and insane being, enters the tread wheel of the world, the emptiness of rational, everyday life is exposed (153). The thesis is not tenable. Lenz „schien [...] vernünftig." He merely *appears* rational. He does not become a full member of society. The passage reveals his emptiness, not necessarily that of the world.

[105] Boredom is a much discussed topic in Büchner scholarship. The other important passages are in *Dantons Tod* (II, 1) and *Leonce und Lena* (I, 1). Beckers (1961), Jancke (1975), and Mosler (1974) have written on the topic. For a more general literary-historical understanding of boredom see Kuhn (1976) and Völker (1975). Kuhn tells the story of the development of *ennui* in Western literature from Sophocles' *Philoctetes* to the present. Völker provides a semantic history of the word *Langeweile* from 1200 to 1800. See also Rehm (1963), who focuses on manifestations of boredom in nineteenth-century philosophy and literature and recognizes a general connection between boredom and the loss of a secure relationship to God.

[106] Into the nineteenth century certain writers, including Heine and Büchner, spell the term with the temporal element in mind: „lange Weile". See B II, 551 and *Leonce und Lena* (III, 3). Büchner's extensive use of the word at this point in the story reinforces the association of Lenz with the Eternal Jew, and thus with the image of long-enduring mental and physical torment.

emptiness: „er hatte keinen Haß, keine Liebe, keine Hoffnung, eine schreckliche Leere und doch eine folternde Unruhe, sie auszufüllen" (27). But the unrest Lenz feels in trying to put meaning into his life leads nowhere. It's expression and outcome are merely physical. Not only does Lenz wander in nature, but the entire story depicts him in the restlessness of travel, a common diversion to boredom, attacked already by the Stoics as an improper means for finding self-fulfillment.[107] Lenz does not progress during his restlessness; his condition remains, in effect, static: „Er hatte *nichts*" (27). All attempts to fill his time with meaning have failed, and his dispersion again passes over into boredom. Oberlin finds Lenz in bed „ruhig und unbeweglich" (24). After some hesitation, Lenz finally responds to Oberlin's presence with a series of reflections on boredom:

> Oberlin mußte lange fragen, ehe er Antwort bekam; endlich sagte er: Ja Herr Pfarrer, sehen Sie, die Langeweile! die Langeweile! o! so langweilig, ich weiß gar nicht mehr, was ich sagen soll, ich habe schon alle Figuren an die Wand gezeichnet. Oberlin sagte ihm, er möge sich zu Gott wenden; da lachte er und sagte: ja wenn ich so glücklich wäre, wie Sie, einen so behaglichen Zeitvertreib aufzufinden, ja man könnte sich die Zeit schon so ausfüllen. Alles aus Müßiggang. Denn die meisten beten aus Langeweile; die andern verlieben sich aus Langeweile, die dritten sind tugendhaft, die vierten lasterhaft und ich gar nichts, gar nichts, ich mag mich nicht einmal umbringen: es ist zu langweilig. (24–25)

The importance of Lenz's apathy and boredom, his empty *Ruhe*,[108] is underscored by the fact that Oberlin's report doesn't even mention it.[109] Instead, Oberlin records Lenz's increasing violence and inner turmoil; he writes for example of Lenz's increasing rage and his attacks on his guards (L I, 474–80). Büchner leaves only one slight trace of unrest in his last paragraph;[110] otherwise, boredom and indifference dominate. Despite his affirmation of involvement and vitality, Lenz eventually finds himself as apa-

---

[107] See Seneca's *Letters*, esp. nos. 2, 28, 54, 55, 56, 104; De tranq II, 10–15; Marcus Aurelius, I, 16; II, 7; IV, 3; XII, 8; and Lipsius, IV, 527–30.

[108] Büchner would have known of the equation of apathy and a negative concept of *Ruhe* from Goethe's *Die Leiden des jungen Werthers*, where Albert is „ruhig" and „gelassen" but also, much to Werther's dismay, „so ohne Teilnehmung" (HA VI: 42, 47, 59, 106).

[109] Thorn-Prikker (1981) has written correctly, if somewhat generally: „An drei Stellen weicht die Erzählung inhaltlich wesentlich von ihrer Vorlage ab: Im Kunstgespräch, in den Szenen mit religiösem Inhalt und in der Krankheitsdarstellung" (188). My analysis covers principally these areas: the inversion of aesthetic stillness in the discourse on art; the abandonment of religious centeredness and stillness; and finally, the portrayal of Lenz's apathy, boredom, and isolation as an inversion of psychological-moral stillness.

[110] „Lenz starrte ruhig hinaus, keine Ahnung, kein Drang; nur wuchs eine dumpfe Angst in ihm, je mehr die Gegenstände sich in der Finsternis verloren. Sie mußten einkehren; da machte er wieder mehrere Versuche, Hand an sich zu legen, war aber zu scharf bewacht" (31).

thetic and cold as the idealist puppets he had attacked in his discourse on art. Where he had earlier called out for sympathy, for „Leben, Möglichkeit des Daseins" (14),[111] he now finds himself suffering from a torpid rest bordering on death („der dumpfen ans Nichtsein grenzenden Ruhe" 29). Lenz has relinquished not only an ordered world but also that element of striving essential to the Fichtean ego or Hegelian spirit; having eliminated opposition and contradiction, Lenz has erased his entire consciousness. He has regressed to nothingness.

A symbol, throughout the story, of Lenz's increasingly negative stillness has been the cold.[112] One measures temperature by the movement of particles, and coldness is the state in which molecules approximate stillness. The narrator demonstrates his awareness of this scientific contrast between motion and coldness in his portrayal of Lenz's frigid emptiness: „er griff nach allem, was sein Blut sonst hatte rascher fließen machen, er versuchte alles, aber kalt, kalt" (9). The narrator makes explicit the connection between coldness and stillness in a passage that is also remarkable for its stylistic stillness, its polysyndeton.[113] The narrator captures Lenz's solitude and self-pity: „alles war ruhig und still und kalt" (12). Later, when Lenz approaches another abyss of meaninglessness, he suddenly gains the strength to laugh, but he laughs out of indifference, and his tears turn to ice: „er lag in den heißesten Tränen, und dann bekam er plötzlich eine Stärke, und erhob sich kalt und gleichgültig, seine Tränen waren ihm dann wie Eis" (19–20). Coldness is also linked to death. After Lenz attempts to revive the body of the dead child, the narrator tells us: „die Leiche blieb kalt" (22). When Lenz himself approaches a kind of lifelessness, he is not only cold but frozen: „Er wußte nicht mehr, was ihn vorhin so bewegt hatte, es fror ihn, er dachte, er wolle jetzt zu Bette gehn, und er ging kalt und unerschütterlich durch das unheimliche Dunkel – es war ihm alles leer und hohl" (22). Lenz, empty of vitality, remains cold and indifferent and still on the last pages of the story:

> Er saß mit kalter Resignation im Wagen, wie sie das Tal hervor nach Westen fuhren. Es war ihm einerlei, wohin man ihn führte; mehrmals wo der Wagen bei dem schlechten Wege in Gefahr geriet, blieb er ganz ruhig sitzen; er war vollkommen gleichgültig. In diesem Zustand legte er den Weg durchs Gebirg zurück. (30)

---

[111] Thorn-Prikker (1978) mistakenly interprets this phrase to mean „die Möglichkeit eines Daseins ohne Leiden" (65), but it is clear from the position Lenz reaches (his indifference without suffering and thus without consciousness) that this is not his goal. Lenz's lack of pain is a mark of inner emptiness, a form of death.

[112] The *Ruhe* of coldness (and also of *Wissenschaft*) is often opposed to the kind of sympathetic understanding Lenz values in his discourse on art. Besides Büchner's *Woyzeck* („Beim Doktor") see, for example, Schiller's *Don Carlos* (4145), Schlegel's *Lucinde* (KA V, 50), Grabbe's *Don Juan und Faust* (I, 3), Heine's *Englische Fragmente* (B II, 550), and Mann's *Doktor Faustus* (630).

[113] See Hasubeck (1969), 52–53.

The stillness of contentment that Lenz had noticed in the valley soon after his arrival in Waldbach (9) becomes transformed at the time of his departure into the stillness of horror (30). The stillness of the *locus terribilis* replaces that of the *locus amoenus*. Lenz is not lulled into contentment by the harmonic tones of nature; he is jarringly tortured by „die entsetzliche Stimme [...] [der] Stille" (30).

Lenz's *Ruhe* of indifference or *Gleichgültigkeit* stands in stark contrast to a traditional conception of *Ruhe* as *Gleichmut*, as cheerful contentment and centeredness. Lenz's pain and subsequent emptiness have replaced the vital concept, prominent from the Stoics and Spinoza into German *Klassik*, of a stillness in suffering. The *Ruhe* of isolation and coldness that Lenz attains at the end of the story is the reverse of the *Ruhe* that, in the tradition, helps the individual to find his or her appropriate role within the state and the cosmos. The following excursus on this traditional concept of repose will prepare us for an understanding of the details and significance of Büchner's inversion.

The Tradition of Psychological-Moral Stillness

The polyvalence of aesthetic stillness together with the secularization of the religious concept of *Ruhe* helped generate a third kind of stillness: the psychological-moral. For Winckelmann *Ruhe* is a psychological as well as an aesthetic ideal.[114] The figures represented in Greek sculpture are divine beings and noble persons capable of displaying stillness in suffering. In the religious tradition man can approximate divine repose insofar as he nears a oneness with God; in *Hyperion*, as we saw, this oneness becomes transformed into a oneness with oneself. *Ruhe* is indicative not of harmony with God but of harmonic self-consciousness or simply peace of mind. In addition, another tradition contributed to the development of psychological stillness and expanded the concept by adding a moral dimension; proponents of psychological-moral stillness suggest that an individual who is at one with himself will also act in harmony with the laws of the state and the cosmos. The self, state, and cosmos are structured in analogous ways and ideally characterized by stillness.[115] Much like religious stillness, the psychological-moral concept of *Gemütsruhe* has its origins in antiquity and is prominent throughout European and, in particular, German intellectual and literary history.

The concept of a tranquillity of mind finds its first major proponents in Stoicism. Three of the primary attributes of the wise man in Stoicism were

---

[114] Cf. Rehm (1951). Rehm's article is the most extensive and useful discussion to date of the history of the idea of *Ruhe*.

[115] The analogies are as old as Plato (*Republic* 368c–369b; *Philebus* 29b–30a; *Timaeus* 30c) and are especially prominent in Stoicism.

apatheia (absence of passion), *ataraxia* (freedom from disturbance), and *autarkeia* (independence).[116] All imply imperviousness to perturbations. The sage achieves these virtues by recognizing what is insignificant and thus harmless to his inner spirit and by knowing the necessity and ultimate harmony of all occurrences. To what extent *apatheia* signified for the Early Stoics such as Zeno and Chrysippus indifference to community and the social order is still a matter of debate,[117] but it is commonly accepted that the Middle Stoic Panaitius placed an unmistakeable emphasis on the social responsibility of the wise man and initiated a movement that found its culmination in the Later Stoa of Seneca, Epictetus, and Marcus Aurelius, as well as the eclectic philosophy of Cicero.[118] Posidonius, a student of Panaitius, also rejected the idea of virtuous apathy and withdrawal; he spoke instead of cosmic sympathy *(sympatheia)*, an organic concept implying the unity and mutual interaction of all parts of the universe.[119]

The concern for man's role within society exhibited in the Middle Stoa is even more prominent in the writings of the Later Stoa. Seneca, Epictetus, and Marcus Aurelius focus their attention not on logic or physics but on ethics and within ethics not on asceticism but on duty. Throughout their discussions of ethics *Ruhe* plays a major role.[120] The importance of this concept for Seneca can be observed not only in his *Letters* but also in his highly influential essay *De tranquillitate animi*. Here Seneca rebukes what he calls "inquietam inertiam" (XII, 3) and offers advice on how to achieve peace of mind: be content with your fate, accept whatever seeming evils might occur, and refrain from desiring what is beyond immediate reach. One becomes tranquil insofar as one shows indifference towards whatever is unimportant; the insight that only what is internal is important enables one to remain quiet amidst all external disturbances. One achieves the peace within a storm which, as we saw in chapter one, Schiller was later to idealize in his theoretical essays. Seneca speaks explicitly of just such a peace: "in media tempestate tranquillitas" (De tranq XIV, 10). Interior tranquillity

---

[116] For a discussion of the wise man in Stoic thought see Pohlenz (1972), 153–58.
[117] See Barth (1946), 136, 178; North (1966), 301; and Pohlenz (1972), I: 139–40, 152, 217; II: 108.
[118] In his treatise on moral goodness and duty, *De officiis*, Cicero admits that he is following the Stoics (I, ii), in particular Panaetius (III, ii). In this essay Cicero integrates Stoic peace of mind with concern for public affairs, as when he suggests that "tranquillitas animi" and "securitas" are essential to the good statesman (I, xxi).
[119] Posidonius' concept of *sympatheia* with its stress on man as a social being was to exert a powerful influence on Marcus Aurelius. See Pohlenz (1972), I: 217–18, 296, 348.
[120] For Epictetus see his *Discourses*, esp. II, I, 21; II, II, 1–26; and III, XIII, 9–17. For Seneca and Marcus Aurelius see below.

plays a guiding role throughout Seneca's letters. A few passages will serve as examples. In his twenty-eighth letter Seneca argues that even amidst the turmoil of a city one can lead a life of peace: "Num quid tam turbidum fieri potest quam forum? Ibi quoque licet quiete vivere, si necesse sit" (28, 6). According to Seneca one's place of residence should not influence peace of mind; it's the spirit that makes everything agreeable to oneself: "Sed non multum ad tranquillitatem locus confert; animus est, qui sibi commendet omnia" (55, 8). A genuine or peaceful stillness is attained only by virtue of reflection and reason: "Nulla placida est quies, nisi qua ratio conposuit" (56, 6).

Seneca equates the virtue of *Ruhe* with Democritus' and Panaitius' concept of *euthymia* or happiness,[121] thus transforming tranquillity into one of the highest of virtues: "Quod desideras autem magnum et summum est deoque vicinum, non concuti. Hanc stabilem animi sedem Graeci euthymian vocant, de qua Democriti volumen egregium est; ego tranquillitatem voco" (De tranq II, 3). The concept of a *happy* tranquillity can be seen throughout Seneca, as for example in his *Letters*, where he writes that the wise man is not only calm and unshaken but also joyful and happy; he lives on a plane with the gods:[122] "Sapiens ille plenus est gaudio, hilaris et placidus, inconcussus; cum dis ex pari vivit" (Ep 59, 14). Marcus Aurelius also knows of the union of "cheerfulness" and "tranquillity" (III, 5). Indeed, the impact of this equation will be felt into the eighteenth century.[123] In the Zedler lexicon the paranthetic translation for „Gemûthsruhe" is nothing other than „Eythymia".

Seneca's *Ruhe* of happiness is neither private nor restricting. In one of his letters he explicitly criticizes the suggestion that the wise man attain tranquillity of mind by removing himself from all contact with the world (9, 1ff.). Repose and service to society are reciprocally beneficial.[124] The individual should find something in which he may be useful to the state ("aliquid, in quo utilis civitati sit" De tranq IV, 2). Seneca stresses not withdrawal but integration and friendship (Ep 9, 1ff.; De tranq VII, 1–4). He

---

[121] See Diogenes Laertius IX, 20 and IX, 45.
[122] See also Ep 23, 4–6 and 92, 3, where Seneca writes: "Quid est beata vita? Securitas et perpetua tranquillitas."
[123] The unity of tranquillity and happiness can be observed through Lipsius, Spinoza, and Pietism into the period of German *Klassik,* where „Freude" and „Ruhe" have a commonly magical significance. See Lipsius' third paradox in his *Manuductionis ad Stoicam philosophiam*, iii, 5 (IV, 759–62), where he argues that the wise man is always happy. See E III, Prop. XI, Schol. and E III, Aff. Def. II, also the *Theologico-Political Treatise* (Gebhardt III, 67). For Pietism see Richter 82, 117 and esp. 114. On the concept of *Freude* in German *Klassik* see Mommsen (1974); Jochen Schmidt (1978), 111–13; and Schultz (1926).
[124] See De tranq III, 1–8; IV, 1–8; XVII, 3.

contrasts Stoic philosophy with Epicureanism and writes: "Non de ea philosophia loquor, quae civem extra patriam posuit, extra mundum deos" (Ep 90, 35). For Seneca the individual should live for the other person: "alteri vivas oportet, si vis tibi vivere" (Ep 48, 2). We see in Seneca's concept of tranquillity the coherence of quietude and responsibility. Harmony should exist on every level.

Next to Seneca's *Letters* one of the most widely read Stoic texts is Marcus Aurelius' *Meditations*. Marcus stresses inner tranquillity, serenity of temper, quietness, equanimity, calm composure, acquiescence, and other such related attributes throughout his *Meditations*.[125] According to Marcus inner tranquillity arises from a knowledge of cosmic harmony. All events in the world follow a logical and necessary sequence. An understanding of this "woven tapestry of causation" enables one "to face many things more calmly" (VII, 75; X, 5). Besides encouraging us to accept every "strand in the tapestry of causation" (V, 9), Marcus tells us that our own actions should conform "to the laws of reason" (III, 6). By affirming our fate and acting rationally we achieve "peace of mind" (III, 6). For Marcus unity is prominent not only in the chain of causality but also in the relationships of men. "All things in the unverse" are "interwoven, and in consequence linked in mutual affection" (VI, 38). In another passage he tells us that the Mind of the universe is social: *ho tou holou nous koinōnikos* (V, 30). Brotherhood is a central concept for Marcus (II, 1), and like Seneca he speaks of a universal or "common citizenship" (IV, 4).[126] For Marcus the world is a single city: *ho kosmos hōsanei polis esti*.[127] In the *Meditations* "sympathy" predominates over "apathy"; a primary condition of "perfection of character" is that the self be "never apathetic".[128]

Two points become clear in this introduction to the Stoic concept of tranquillity. First, the Stoics valued *Ruhe* as a virtue of the wise and happy man. Second, a proper peace of mind enables the self to act in harmony with society. *Tranquillitas animi* leads to integration and responsibility, not isolation or insensitivity.[129]

---

[125] See I, 1; II, 5; III, 5, 6; V, 2; VI, 11, 16, 30; VII, 27, 28, 33, 68; XII, 22 and elsewhere.
[126] Cf. *De vita beata* (XX, 5), where Seneca writes, "Patriam meam esse mundum sciam."
[127] IV, 4. See also VI, 44.
[128] VII, 69. See also I, 8.
[129] The Stoics share the first of these two points with the Epicureans. Velleius, the Epicurean speaker in Cicero's *De natura deorum*, likewise believes that repose is a condition of happiness: "nisi quietum autem nihil beatum est" (I, 20). But the Stoics do not share the Epicurean belief, here again voiced by Velleius, that happiness consists in exemption from duty: "Nos autem beatam vitam in animi securitate et in omnium vacatione munerum ponimus" (I, 20).

Two of the most important figures for the introduction into Germany of this Stoic concept of tranquillity are the sixteenth-century scholar Justus Lipsius and the seventeenth-century philosopher Baruch Spinoza. Lipsius worked until his death on a commentary on Seneca and published an introduction to Stoicism as well as an interpretation of the Stoic philosophy of nature, but his first piece on Stoicism, the early essay *De constantia*, published in 1584 and translated into German in 1599, was his most influential work. The importance of Lipsius' essay lies for us not in his treatment of the relationship of Stoicism to Christianity but rather in the connection between *constantia* and the Stoic idea of a tranquillity of mind.[130] Lipsius defines constancy as a proper strength of spirit that remains unmoved by anything external or accidental: "Constantiam hîc appello, rectum et immotum animi robur, non elati externis aut fortuitis, non depressi" (IV, 530–31). He discusses at length the impediments to constancy, which range from false goods such as money and honor to false evils like sickness or poverty, and he presents several arguments as to why constancy would be beneficial for us. The proximity of constancy and *Ruhe* becomes especially clear in one passage of the German translation where the translator has Lipsius speak of „des Gemüts ruhe und Bestendigkeit" [sic]. *De constantia* went through eighty Latin editions in three centuries and was translated into every major European language.[131] Lipsius' source, Seneca, and in part Lipsius himself influenced the writings of such major Baroque authors as Opitz,[132] Fleming,[133] and Gryphius.[134]

But Spinoza, who himself might well have been familiar with Lipsius,[135] is the more important and influential figure for late eighteenth- and early nineteenth-century conceptions of *Ruhe*. Although Spinoza distances himself from the Stoic view that the mind can govern the emotions absolutely (E V,

---

[130] Lohmeier (1981) distinguishes the two, suggesting that in the German Baroque *constantia* is reserved for heroic defiance of fate, while *tranquillitas animi* is the more gentle and private pastoral state of simple contentment. See 90–107, 250, 260, 435. The distinction is helpful, though not absolute.

[131] See Kirk (1939), 9.

[132] Opitz' poem „Zlatna" carries the subtitle „Von Ruhe des Gemûthes" and argues that „deß Lebens wahre Ruh" is „das Hôchste Gut" (316–17).

[133] Consider Fleming's sonnett „An Sich", which is full of Stoic elements (61).

[134] See Schings (1966), esp. 192–213, 226–34, 236, 279. As Schings notes, one sees the importance of constancy already in the titles of Gryphius' dramas, for example, *Beständige mutter oder die heilige Felicitas* and *Catharina von Georgien oder bewehrete beständigkeit*. The equation, however, between Seneca and Lipsius on the one hand and Gryphius on the other is not exact; Schings discusses important differences. See 234–47 and 254–64. For differences between Stoic and Christian ideas of constancy in general see Welzig (1961), esp. 422.

[135] See Dilthey II, 285.

Praef.), he is indebted to Stoicism for many of his views on moral behavior and psychology, as Dilthey has shown.[136] In his *Tractatus Theologico-Politicus* Spinoza praises the philosopher and wise man for placing true happiness solely in virtue and peace of mind: "qui veram fœlicitatem in sola virtute, et tranquillitate animi constituunt" (Gebhardt III, 88). Spinoza's praise of inner tranquillity is especially prominent in his discussion of Solomon, who teaches that understanding renders man blessed and happy and gives him true peace of mind: "Porro cap. 3. vs. 13. expressissimis verbis docet, intellectum hominem beatum et fœlicem reddere, veramque animi tranquillitatem dare" (Gebhardt III, 67). Spinoza praises Solomon for noting that only the wise live in peace and equanimity: "Soli igitur sapientes ex sententia etiam Salomonis animo pacato et constante vivunt, non ut impii, quorum animus contrariis affectibus fluctuat, adeoque (ut Esaias etiam ait cap. 57. vs. 20) pacem, neque quietem habent" (Gebhardt III, 67). I discussed Spinoza's *Ethics* already in the second chapter of this study and need only mention in this context the two most important thoughts: that *animi acquiescentia* is Spinoza's ideal and that it leads to sympathetic understanding and integration into society. These ideas were well received in Germany at the close of the eighteenth century.

Critics normally attribute Spinoza's notoriety in late eighteenth- and early nineteenth-century Germany to Lessing's, Jacobi's, and Mendelssohn's discussions of his pantheism, but Spinoza's concept of the *animi acquiescentia* played an equally significant role for the philosophers and authors who praised him during this period. Goethe and his contemporaries spoke explicitly of the *Ruhe* embodied in Spinoza's personality and philosophy. In his *Philosophische Briefe* Schelling speaks of „die Ruhe und den ‚Himmel im Verstande' [...] in dem er [Spinoza] so sichtbar lebte und webte" (I, 305). Despite his critique of Spinoza's view of the infinite, Schelling closes his seventh letter with a reflection on the philosopher's admirable stillness: „Lassen Sie uns hier stille stehen, Freund, und die Ruhe bewundern, mit der Spinoza der Vollendung seines Systems entgegenging. Mag er doch jene Ruhe in der *Liebe* des Unendlichen gefunden haben (I, 316). In his Munich lectures on the history of philosophy Schelling lauds at length Spinoza's „beruhigende Wirkung":

Der Spinozismus ist wirklich die das Denken in Ruhestand, in völlige Quiescenz versetzende Lehre, in ihren höchsten Folgerungen das System des vollendeten theoretischen und praktischen Quietismus, der wohlthätig erscheinen kann unter

---

[136] See the section „Spinoza und die stoische Tradition" in *Die Autonomie des Denkens, der konstruktive Rationalismus und der pantheistische Monismus nach ihrem Zusammenhang im 17. Jahrhundert*, in Dilthey II, 283–96. Seneca's *Letters* by the way were among the works left in Spinoza's personal library. See Freudenthal (1899), 163.

den Stürmen des nie ruhenden, immer beweglichen Denkens, wie Lucretius [...] den Zustand einer solchen Ruhe schildert [...] Unstreitig ist es diese Stille und Ruhe des Spinozischen Systems, welche besonders die Vorstellung seiner *Tiefe* hervorbringt, und mit verborgenem, aber unwiderstehlichem Reiz so viele Gemüther angezogen hat. (X, 35)

Schleiermacher indirectly ascribes *Ruhe* to Spinoza when he writes in his *Reden über die Religion* that Spinoza was an astute observer of the infinite and eternal (31) and then tells us: „die wahren Beschauer des Ewigen waren immer ruhige Seelen" (36). Schlegel writes that in Spinoza's system „der höchste Zustand des Menschen [ist] *Ruhe*" (KA XII, 30).[137] Goethe notes Spinoza's influence in books 14 and 16 of *Dichtung und Wahrheit*. He writes in particular of Spinoza's *Ethics*: „ich fand hier eine Beruhigung meiner Leidenschaften" (HA X, 35). He adds: „Die alles ausgleichende Ruhe Spinozas kontrastierte mit meinem alles aufregenden Streben" (HA X, 35). In book 16 he again speaks of the „Beruhigung" and „Friedensluft" he experiences in reading Spinoza and writes: „Mein Zutrauen auf Spinoza ruhte auf der friedlichen Wirkung, die er in mir hervorbrachte" (HA X, 76–78). In his „Studie nach Spinoza" Goethe speaks of the „innere beneidenswerte Ruhe" of those who, like Spinoza, have a sense of the total interconnection of all things (HA XIII, 9). Finally, Heine sees in Spinoza's writings not only stillness but dynamic stillness: „Bei der Lektüre des Spinoza ergreift uns ein Gefühl wie beim Anblick der großen Natur in ihrer lebendigsten Ruhe" (B III, 561).

In their reception of Stoicism[138] and Spinoza contemporaries revived the Stoic analogies between the individual and the cosmos and the individual and the state, whereby stillness characterizes each in its ideal form. In „Die Schöpfung" Herder encourages youth to be still like the cosmos: „Jugend sei / wie dies Weltall still und frei / Und voll reger Gotteskraft, / die im Ruhn hier alles schafft!" (Suphan XXIX, 440). In *Hyperion*, we remember, the hero pictures an ideal state modeled after the stillness of Diotima: „O du, mit deiner Elysiumsstille, könnten wir das schaffen, was du bist!" (StA III, 114). Even in the middle of the nineteenth century, when direct references to the Stoics and Spinoza become scarcer, these analogies remain prominent. One

---

[137] See also KA II, 317.
[138] Not only Spinoza, the Stoics too were read during this period. Schiller mentions Seneca and Marcus Aurelius several times in his early theoretical writings, and his character Kosinsky has not only read Seneca, he has memorized him: „Du hast dich wacker in den Schulen gehalten, du hast deinen Seneca meisterlich auswendig gelernt" (*Die Räuber*, III, 2). Hölderlin owned a copy of Marcus' *Meditations* in the original Greek (see Müller [1944], 22) and integrated many of Marcus' ideas into his ode „Dichtermuth" (see Jochen Schmidt [1978], 104–12). A comprehensive and factual account of the influence of Stoicism on German literature seems to be a gap in the research; nonetheless, Merrifield (1967) sheds some light on the subject.

significant example from the period after the composition of *Lenz* will demonstrate that the Stoic themes had not been exhausted by the time of Büchner's writing. After Heinrich Lee of Gottfried Keller's *Der grüne Heinrich* reads Goethe, he writes almost as Goethe himself had written after reading Spinoza:

> Es war die hingebende Liebe an alles Gewordene und Bestehende, welche das Recht und die Bedeutung jeglichen Dinges ehrt und den Zusammenhang und die Tiefe der Welt empfindet. Diese Liebe steht höher als das künstlerische Herausstehlen des einzelnen zu eigennützigem Zwecke, welches zuletzt immer zu Kleinlichkeit und Laune führt; sie steht auch höher als das Genießen und Absondern nach Stimmungen und romantischen Liebhabereien, und nur sie allein vermag eine gleichmäßige und dauernde Glut zu geben. (I, 391)

The hero alludes not only to a sense of totality but also to stillness, a divine principle and a model for the individual who wants to become an active and integral part of the cosmos:

> Nur die Ruhe in der Bewegung hält die Welt und macht den Mann; die Welt ist innerlich ruhig und still, und so muß es auch der Mann sein, der sie verstehen und als ein wirkender Teil von ihr sie widerspiegeln will. Ruhe zieht das Leben an, Unruhe verscheucht es; Gott hält sich mäuschenstill, darum bewegt sich die Welt um ihn. (I, 391)

This stillness originates from a sense of the whole and – much as with the Stoics and Spinoza – leads to the proper fulfillment of one's civic duties:

> Der ruhige feste Gleichmut, welcher aus solcher Auffassung des Ganzen und Vergleichung des Einzelnen hervorgeht, glücklich gemischt mit lebendigem Gefühl und Feuer für das nächst zu Ergreifende und Selbsterlebte, macht erst den guten und wohlgebildeten Weltbürger aus [...] jene Ruhe [gibt] ihm denjenigen Trost und Halt, ohne welchen kein selbstbewußtes menschliches Wesen denkbar ist und leben kann. (I, 595)

The concept of *Ruhe* in Keller's story „Das verlorene Lachen" contains the traditional associations of cheerfulness and integration. At the story's opening the narrator describes Jukundus as „die Ruhe und Gelassenheit selbst". Moreover, he is „von steter Fröhlichkeit" and „immer [...] teilnehmend [...] und hilfreich" (II, 447).[139] Here too we see the analogy of cosmic and individual stillness:[140] „Wenn sich das Ewige und Unendliche immer so still

---

[139] Although Keller still portrays „Ruhe" as an ideal, he inverts its traditional religious associations. Not the pious Justine or her pastor but rather the widow Frau Ursula and her daughter, Agathchen, who stand demonstrably outside the sphere of the church, attain inner peace and tranquillity. Jukundus finds in them „eine vollkommene Zufriedenheit und Seelenruhe", which they achieve „wo anders her [...] als aus ihrer Kirchenlehre" (II, 522; II, 511).

[140] See also Keller's poem „Stille der Nacht" where the individual feels „wie die Welt so still und gut".

hält und verbirgt, warum sollten wir uns nicht einmal eine Zeit ganz vergnügt und friedlich still halten können?" (II, 529)

With only minor overlap we can speak of three major elements in the tradition of psychological-moral *Ruhe*. First, *Ruhe* is a psychic ideal attained through insight into the world order. Second, psychological stillness or peace of mind leads not to withdrawal but rather to integration into the social order. It engenders a sense of civic responsibility. Finally, through psychic *Ruhe* one achieves a healthiness of mind so that one is secured from the disturbance of pain. Throughout the tradition advocates of psychological-moral stillness have alluded to the rhetoric of medicine. In Hippocratic medicine *hēsychia* or peace is, next to *krasis*, "the most general attribute of health".[141] *Hēsychia* is in fact the earliest empirical characterization of health in Greek society and signifies balance, equilibrium, and quietness of life. While the Stoics profess indifference toward health in a physical sense,[142] they nonetheless refer to themselves in a positive way as physicians of the soul who treat the health of the mind and help the individual gain quietude.[143] Plutarch, who was strongly influenced by the Stoics, in particular Panaetius, uses the very phrase "physician of the soul" *(psychēs iatros)* in his essay on *The Tranquillity of Mind*.[144] Spinoza writes that his *Ethics* provides a "remedy" against the ill-health of the mind.[145] Lipsius opens the final chapter of *De constantia* with the comment that the reader has now heard everything the author wanted to say about and for constancy in the face of pain.[146] From the Stoics to the period of German *Klassik* and beyond, tranquillity serves as a medicine for pain; it is not by chance that Schiller speaks of a „Ruhe im Leiden" (NA XX, 296).

Büchner and the Tradition of Psychological-Moral Stillness

My sketch of the tradition of psychological-moral stillness has shown that Stoic ideas and ideals were widespread in the early nineteenth century. Büchner need not have read Panaitius, Seneca, or Lipsius to become aware of the concept of psychological-moral stillness. Nonetheless, evidence does speak for Büchner's detailed awareness of this tradition. As a student Büchner had immersed himself in philosophy;[147] shortly before his death he

---

[141] Vlastos (1946), 68.
[142] It is morally neutral. See Seneca, Ep 94, 8.
[143] See Seneca, Ep 68, 8; 78, 1–29.
[144] 465 D. Cf. 468 C and 468 F.
[145] E V, Prop. XX, Schol.
[146] "Explicui copias meas omnes et sermonem, Lipsi: et habes quae pro Constantiâ dicenda mihi censui in Dolorem" (IV, 607).
[147] He writes to August Stöber: „Ich werfe mich mit aller Gewalt in die Philosophie" (L II, 421). See also L II: 174 and 186.

had planned to hold lectures in Zürich on the history of philosophy.[148] Büchner's early essays reveal an acquaintance with Stoicism, in particular the concept of „höchste innre Ruhe" and the idea of the sage's invulnerability to pain.[149] In his notes on Epicurus we again see that Büchner is aware of stillness and of the elimination of suffering as psychological goals. Concerning the philosophy of Epicurus Büchner writes:

> Es giebt nämlich zweierlei Arten des Vergnügens, die eine, wenn das Gemüth angenehm afficirt wird, die zweite, wenn die Seele, ohne durch angenehme oder unangenehme Gefühle bewegt zu werden, in dem Zustande der Ruhe oder Zufriedenheit ist [...] Epikur rechnet nun zwar beyde Arten zur Glückseeligkeit, doch so, daß er der zweiten einen Vorrang zugesteht. Der Zustand der Schmerzlosigkeit ist das letzte Ziel alles Bestrebens [...] wird die Begierde gestillt, so entspringt das Vergnügen, und daraus ein Zustand der Ruhe, in welchem die Seele nichts mehr wünschet, also vollkommen beglückt ist. Dieser Zustand ist das Höchste, welches kein Vergnügen übersteigen kann [...] das höchste Gut [...] keinen Schmerz empfinden. (L I, 404).

Most importantly, Büchner had a detailed knowledge of the philosophy of Spinoza. His commentary on Spinoza deals mainly with aspects of the *Ethics* but it also takes into account his *Tractatus Theologico-Politicus*.[150] Like other early nineteenth-century writers Büchner was aware of the importance of stillness in Spinoza's philosophy: „So liegt also schon über den ersten Rissen des Spinozismus eine unendliche Ruhe. Alle Glückseeligkeit ist allein im Anschauen des Ewigen, Unveränderlichen" (L II, 268–69). Büchner's awareness of psychological stillness is evident, finally, in the actions of his characters: Lenz, like Danton, seeks the equilibrium and balance of a healthy repose.

Büchner inverts the tradition of psychological-moral stillness primarily by equating *Ruhe* with not *Gleichmut* but *Gleichgültigkeit*. The inversion can be looked at from other angles as well. Lenz's *Ruhe* carries with it an overcoming of pain but, far from indicating health, it signals emptiness and insanity. *Ruhe* had traditionally signaled integration into society; Lenz, however, is incapable of meaningful activity. Behind Lenz's *Ruhe* is not the coherent and harmonious world order one associates with Stoicism or German Idealism but a mixture of chaos and emptiness. In our last chapter we saw how Hölderlin, partly influenced by Spinoza, had stressed the whole in which suffering has its particular place. After grasping the perfection of the whole (and achieving acquiescence) Hyperion turned to the inadequacies of the particular (and entered the satiric mode of the *Scheltrede*). With Büchner the process differs: In rejecting Spinoza, he sees not the whole but

---

[148] See L II: 454 and 460.
[149] L II, 27. See also L II, 32.
[150] *Dantons Tod* and *Leonce und Lena* also contain allusions to the philosophy of Spinoza.

only the particular. In the particular there is real pain. Such pain must be seen as unjustified, purposeless, and absurd insofar as it is not sublated into a harmonic world-view, not seen from the perspective of the universal order *(sub specie aeternitatis)*. As Büchner's Danton relinquished the guiding principles and teleology that justified the French revolution, he became preoccupied with the absurdity of individual suffering. It no longer served a greater purpose.[151] Lenz, too, has relinquished all goals; he is thus blind to any hidden meaning behind his suffering and disorientation. He can focus only on the particular; without a sense of the universal or eternal, absurdity and emptiness overwhelm him.

Repose, Suffering, Apathy

Throughout the story Lenz had sought repose. The story provided, however, two different kinds, a harmonic and an empty repose. When Lenz is „ruhig" in the positive sense of the word, he is also and equally active, as for example when he assists Oberlin with his ministerial duties or when he composes his homily. Here Lenz is tranquil but not passive. He does not view work as part of an infinite chain of delayed rewards. In this context even suffering assumes positive associations. Suffering and its intersubjective counterpart, sympathy, replace Kant's disinterested contemplation as the conditions that guarantee the communal aspect of aesthetic activity.[152] The principle of sympathy also guides Lenz's reflections in his homily. Suffering has positive connotations even during the early moments of Lenz's empty stillness. Just as Lenz strives for stillness when he suffers from unrest, so does he strive for motion and suffering when he is locked into a state of insensateness. Suffering awakens Lenz to consciousness and activity. In his final state of empty stillness, when he is free of suffering, Lenz loses all sensation. His overcoming of suffering leads only to inner death. Much like his contemporary Schopenhauer, Büchner presents us with the dichotomy of pain or „Noth" and emptiness or „Langeweile".[153]

While Büchner seems to criticize on behalf of Lenz a static stillness, he

---

[151] Cf. Wessell (1972).
[152] According to Kant, „Schön ist das, was ohne Begriff *allgemein* gefällt" (KdU B 32). Emphasis added.
[153] Cf. Schopenhauer: „Der allgemeinste Überblick zeigt uns, als die beiden Feinde des menschlichen Glückes, den Schmerz und die Langeweile. Dazu noch läßt sich bemerken, daß, in dem Maaße, als es uns glückt, vom einen derselben uns zu entfernen, wir dem andern uns nähern, und umgekehrt" (8, 359). See also 1: 218; 2: 390, 392, 394; 8: 364; 9: 318.

also points to the intolerability of pure unrest, pure suffering.[154] In the latter part of the story Lenz experiences not only the emptiness of apathy with its concurrent release of suffering and elimination of meaningful activity but also an overwhelming sense of pain, disorientation, and restlessness. One can chart Lenz's progress as follows:

ILLUSTRATION 4

	Positive Suffering	Negative Suffering	No Suffering
Harmonic Repose	X	Ø	Ø
Restlessness	Ø	X	Ø
Empty Repose	Ø	Ø	X

The symbol Ø signifies that the two elements under question do not occur simultaneously. For example, when Lenz experiences "negative suffering", he does not at the same time reach "harmonic repose". The X's mark Lenz's actual experiences: first, a synthesis of harmonic repose with activity and communal *Mitleid*; next, suffering and unrest, divorced from any sense of harmony; finally, an obliteration of suffering and an apathetic stillness devoid of sensation or meaning. Insofar as repose eludes Lenz, he becomes immersed in suffering and loses sight of its purpose. The very pain that

---

[154] Where *Lenz* focuses on the problems associated with empty repose, *Woyzeck* concentrates on the societal conditions that drive an individual into restlessness. *Lenz* shows us the dangers of someone who finds an empty *Ruhe* outside of society, *Woyzeck* depicts the despair of an individual whom the strings of obligation move about as though he were a marionette. Woyzeck's own statement, „ich hab kei Ruh" (L I, 177), is complemented by numerous other references to his restlessness, especially in his encounters with the Hauptmann (L I: 163–64 and 171–72).

awakens him to consciousness is more than he can endure. When Lenz succeeds in eliminating this seemingly intolerable suffering, he loses consciousness and awareness; he is no longer capable of the passion of sympathy. Unable to recognize a distinction between necessary suffering (without which there would be apathy) and the suffering one must attempt to eliminate (unjust social conditions, for example), Lenz passes from an energetic calm to unrest and suffering and onward to the empty repose of an individual isolated from God, society, and himself.

Büchner's *Lenz* in the Context of the Historical Lenz's Philosophical Anthropology

The character Lenz experiences a tension between his view of suffering as a force that enables both consciousness and action and his desire for release from such suffering. These two views of suffering along with corresponding ideas about man, perfection, and repose were much discussed in the eighteenth and early nineteenth century. The historical Jakob Michael Reinhold Lenz participated in this debate. In his essay *Versuch über das erste Principium der Moral*, which Büchner may well have read while composing his story,[155] Lenz criticizes Rousseau's definition of happiness. Rousseau equates happiness with simple repose or the harmony of desire and capacity. According to Rousseau's analysis in book two of *Émile*, we are happy insofar as we fulfill our desires. Because our human faculties, our ability to fulfill desires, are limited, we should restrict these desires. Insofar as we diminish the excess of the desires over the faculties we become happier. Unhappiness, on the other hand, increases with the awareness of evil and the inevitable desire to eradicate it. We become aware of something in the world that should be changed but also recognize our inability to effect that change. This destroys the harmony of desire and capacity. By restricting our vision to the private sphere and to the present, we could avoid unhappiness. Whatever evil we are unaware of cannot disturb us. As soon as we envisage possible improvements for ourselves or the world, these become necessary; without these improvements we are in misery: «car la misére ne consiśte pas dans la privation des choses, mais dans le besoin qui s'en fait sentir» (IV, 304). An increase in desires and needs only enlarges the intensity of man's unhappi-

---

[155] Hinderer (1977) suggests that the *Versuch über das erste Principium der Moral* might have been among the documents that August Stöber gave Büchner for his work on Oberlin and Lenz (160). Hinderer's thesis derives its probability from two facts: first, August Stöber gave Büchner all his manuscripts on Lenz; second, Stöber was the first to publish this particular essay.

ness: «C'est à force de nous travailler pour augmenter nôtre bonheur que nous le changeons en misére» (IV, 305).

Lenz organizes his polemic against Rousseau by arguing that two basic drives direct all actions: „der Trieb nach Vollkommenheit" and „der Trieb nach Glückseligkeit" (I, 487). The drive for perfection is the desire for ever increasing development of our faculties and capacities: „Der Trieb nach Vollkommenheit ist also das ursprüngliche Verlangen unsers Wesens, sich eines immer größern Umfanges unserer Kräfte und Fähigkeiten bewußt zu werden" (I, 488). The drive for happiness is a drive for that condition most appropriate to our drive for perfection. Lenz's definitions of the two drives become clearer as we look more closely at man's two possible states: repose and motion. Lenz tells us, „daß es in der ganzen Schöpfung nur zween mögliche Zustände gebe, die Ruhe und die Bewegung" (I, 492). Happiness is the condition („Zustand") most appropriate to our property („Eigenschaft") of perfection (I, 491). Our property of perfection, however, is not perfection itself but rather the drive toward perfection; only a god could achieve perfection. The state therefore that best enhances this human drive toward perfection is not stasis but motion: „Wenn also die Frage ist, welcher Zustand für unser Ich das aus Materie und Geist zusammengesetzt ist, der glücklichste sei, so versteht es sich zum voraus, daß wir hier einen Zustand der Bewegung meinen" (I, 492). Lenz writes: „Wir sollen immer weiter gehen und nie stille stehen" (I, 489). In contrast to Rousseau, Lenz argues that we are less happy when in repose, happiest when in motion. Motion is most conducive to *human* perfection („dem Umfange unserer Fähigkeiten am angemessensten" I, 492).

Insofar as Büchner inverts the traditionally positive associations of stillness in aesthetics, religion, psychology, and morality, he seems to be declaring his allegiance to the historical Lenz, in particular Lenz's affirmation of motion over stillness,[156] but Büchner's position is not that simple. Büchner's stance is antithetical, negative; the story's final statement remains unclear. Since the stillness Lenz attains at the story's conclusion is empty (the inversion of religious and psychological-moral stillness), one might think that the work criticizes an ideal of stillness. Yet, Lenz's explicit critique of stillness in the discourse on art cannot be identified with Büchner's own position: Lenz's critique contains internal inconsistencies, contributes to his loss of stabilization and ultimate insanity, and is incompatible with Büchner's artistic construction. Büchner's own position remains unstable and unidentifiable. As Maurice Benn has shown, Büchner was an author of

---

[156] The Storm and Stress movement as a whole was critical of Winckelmann's ideal of stillness. See, for example, Rehm's discussion of Heinse (1951: 117).

revolt, ready to reject rather than accept, criticize rather than appropriate.[157] In *Lenz* we see him rejecting the traditionally positive associations of *Ruhe* on behalf of his character Lenz. Büchner has identified empty stillness as a central target of his critique, but he recognizes pure motion as an equally spurious goal. His character Lenz is happiest, in fact, at those very moments when he achieves an ideal synthesis of dynamic repose.

In his writing, Büchner pays special attention to the particular, the negative, the motion within stillness, but he recognizes that pure motion without stillness is as undesirable a condition as pure stillness itself. Behind Büchner's negativity, directed on the one hand against pure stillness, on the other against pure motion, might well lie a hidden ideal, consisting of a synthesis of stillness and motion. Like Hölderlin, but even more so, Büchner writes in the wake of a harmonic ideal of stillness where he would stress the dynamism that does not cancel but rather makes synthesis possible.

---

[157] Benn (1976), esp. 1–3, 265–70.

4. Heine and the Political Connotations of *Ruhe*

„Nachtwächter mit langen Fortschrittsbeinen,
Du kommst so verstört einhergerannt!
Wie geht es daheim den lieben Meinen,
Ist schon befreit das Vaterland?"
Vortrefflich geht es, der stille Segen,
Er wuchert im sittlich gehüteten Haus,
Und ruhig und sicher auf friedlichen Wegen,
Entwickelt sich Deutschland von innen heraus.
(Heine)

The Politics of Aesthetic Stillness

In a brief survey during the last chapter we saw that the age of Goethe, what Heine called „die Kunstperiode",[1] valued stillness as a constitutive element of outstanding art. Büchner was critical of this concept; his near contemporary Heine was as well,[2] though in a different way. In his important letter of July 28, 1835, Büchner places Goethe above Schiller, for the former created full and lively characters, whereas Schiller produced idealized puppets. Heine's evaluation in *Die romantische Schule* differs; he praises Schiller at the expense of Goethe, for the latter's art works, though outstanding in purely aesthetic terms, are not politically active, not in spirit with ideas of motion and progress. Schiller, meanwhile, „schrieb für die großen Ideen der Revolution, er zerstörte die geistigen Bastillen, er baute an dem Tempel der Freiheit" (III, 393).

Goethe's Statues

Heine's relationship to Goethe was ambivalent. Heine never questioned the excellence of Goethe's craftmanship, his ability to give outstanding aesthetic and material shape to the spiritual, nor was he critical of Goethe's hedonistic-

---

[1] Unless otherwise indicated, references with volume and page number refer in this chapter to Heine's *Sämtliche Schriften*. Ed. Klaus Briegleb, et al. 6 vols. München: Hanser, 1968–76. For the term „Kunstperiode" see esp. *Französische Maler* (1831) and *Die romantische Schule* (1835–36).

[2] Heine was born in 1797, sixteen years before Büchner. But Büchner died already in 1837, nearly twenty years before Heine, and since many of the works discussed in this chapter were written after Büchner's death, I have let this chapter follow my discussion of Büchner. On the relationship of the two writers see Benn (1977); Fischer (1971); Mayer (1982), 104, 130–32, 219–22; and Poschmann (1979). Although philological evidence indicates that Heine directly influenced Büchner, the most significant parallels seem to stem simply from their overlapping continuation and critique of the idealist age.

sensualistic impulses. What did bother Heine was Goethe's ideal of aesthetic stillness and his noncommittal „Gemütsruhe", which exerted „einen quietisierenden Einfluß auf die deutsche Jugend" and hindered the political development of the nation (III, 395–96). In an earlier section on Hölderlin's appropriation of Spinoza, I stressed the dynamism and political import of the latter's pantheism. Goethe's fatalistic indifference stems from his false understanding of pantheism:[3]

> Es ist leider wahr, wir müssen es eingestehn, nicht selten hat der Pantheismus die Menschen zu Indifferentisten gemacht. Sie dachten: wenn alles Gott ist, so mag es gleichgültig sein, womit man sich beschäftigt, ob mit Wolken oder mit antiken Gemmen, ob mit Volksliedern oder mit Affenknochen, ob mit Menschen oder mit Komödianten. Aber da ist eben der Irrtum: Alles ist nicht Gott, sondern Gott ist Alles; Gott manifestiert sich nicht in gleichem Maße in allen Dingen, er manifestiert sich vielmehr nach verschiedenen Graden in den verschiedenen Dingen, und jedes trägt in sich den Drang einen höheren Grad der Göttlichkeit zu erlangen; und das ist das große Gesetz des Fortschrittes in der Natur. (III, 394)

Heine, unlike Goethe, integrates into his pantheistic world-view a progressive concept of marginalism: some things have more of God than others. Goethe's pantheism suggests – in Heine's interpretation at least – that the world is already divine, that what is, is grand. Such pantheism leads to a benign repose, a contentment indifferent to evil and unconcerned with stagnation or regression. For Heine, however, the divine is not static. God is not equally present in all things. The world allows for an order of rank, and God manifests himself through the development of this order. Heine's god is of motion, not repose:

> Gott manifestiert sich in den Dingen mehr oder minder, er lebt in dieser ständigen Manifestation, Gott ist in der Bewegung, in der Handlung, in der Zeit, sein heiliger Odem weht durch die Blätter der Geschichte, letztere ist das eigentliche Buch Gottes. (III, 394–95)

God manifests himself not in Nature but in the development of history.

While in Goethe's *Italienische Reise* one sees little else but „die Ruhe der Natur" (II, 367), in Heine's comparable text, *Die Reise von München nach Genua*, one finds an analysis of Italy's degrading political situation and reflections on emancipation and the political task of the poet.[4] For Heine Goethe's focus on nature and subordinate concern for the issues of the day originate from his false, if also highly influential, pantheism. The Goethean belief that art should have a quietistic influence predominates in Germany. According to Heine the value of German tragedies lies not in the action or revelation of emotions but in the language. In contrast to French tragedies,

---

[3] On Heine's varying uses of the term „Indifferentismus" see Mende (1976). The most recent account of Heine's pantheism is Malsch (1978).
[4] Cf. Windfuhr (1976), 90–96.

which include „jener unaufhörliche Sturm der Gefühle, jener beständige Donner und Blitz, jene ewige Gemütsbewegung" (III, 300), German tragedies do not affect the public. In Germany one finds quiet, patient, dull observers: „Im deutschen Parterre sitzen friedliebende Staatsbürger und Regierungsbeamte, die dort ruhig ihr Sauerkraut verdauen möchten" (III, 300). The French, in contrast, do not seek to be soothed: „Die Unruhe treibt den Franzosen ins Theater, und hier sucht er am allerwenigsten Ruhe" (III, 300).

Heine, like Börne before him,[5] conflates aesthetic stillness and political quietude by describing Goethe's works as statues.[6] Sculpture, the ideal form of aesthetic stillness, is lifeless, in Heine's literalization of the image, infertile.[7] The statues, however beautiful, do not move men to action:

> Man kann sich darin verlieben, aber sie sind unfruchtbar: die Goetheschen Dichtungen bringen nicht die Tat hervor, wie die Schillerschen. Die Tat ist das Kind des Wortes, und die Goetheschen schönen Worte sind kinderlos. (III, 395)

Because Goethe's works are beautiful in a traditional sense, because they embody classical harmony, they pacify the viewer. He/She feels at peace and forgets the dissonances of the world. Coldness, a static state commonly associated with *Ruhe* and indifference, is for Heine an additional attribute of Goethe's works, one that they share with their models from Greek antiquity:

> Diese Antiken mahnten mich an die Goetheschen Dichtungen, die ebenso vollendet, ebenso herrlich, ebenso ruhig sind, und ebenfalls mit Wehmut zu fühlen scheinen, daß ihre Starrheit und Kälte sie von unserem jetzigen bewegt warmen Leben abscheidet, daß sie nicht mit uns leiden und jauchzen können, daß sie keine Menschen sind, sondern unglückliche Mischlinge von Gottheit und Stein. (III, 396)

Goethe's works of stone, like Greek statues, are both aesthetically still and socially indifferent or cold.

As is well known, Heine's comments on Goethe are relativized elsewhere in his writings. In 1840 Heine chastises Börne for not recognizing Goethe's „künstlerische Form":

---

[5] Börne spoke of Goethe's „steinerne Ruhe" (II, 204). For references to other contemporaries who associated Goethe's art, negatively, with sculpture see DHA 11, 419–20; Dietze (1962), 39, 272; and Koopmann (1972), 60.

[6] Heine's critique of Goethe's art – that he creates mere statues – would be from Winckelmann's standpoint pure praise. Heine was opposed to Winckelmann's adoration of sculpture as well as his ideal of aesthetic stillness. In one passage Heine mocks the concept of „edle Einfalt und heitre Ruhe" (II, 163); in another he comments critically that in Germany's „stille Gewässer" one finds „mehr Tiefe als Wellenschlag" (III, 299).

[7] Heine's view of Greek statues is complex. He criticizes them as static and lifeless, but he also portrays them as sensual and vibrant, i.e., as representatives of the Greek gods, who were forced into exile by Christian spiritualism. For a detailed account of Heine's view of sculpture as a symbol of apolitical, ineffective art see Seeba (1976). On the subject of the gods' exile see Sandor (1967).

[...] in seiner subjektiven Befangenheit begriff er nicht die objektive Freiheit, die Goethische Weise, und die künstlerische Form hielt er für Gemütlosigkeit: er glich dem Kinde, welches, ohne den glühenden Sinn einer griechischen Statue zu ahnen, nur die marmornen Formen betastet und über Kälte klagt. (IV, 11–12)[8]

Coldness was a focus of Heine's own critique in *Die romantische Schule*. Heine also objected to Goethe's vision of art as sculpture and to his distance from the present moment. In his polemic against Börne, however, Heine criticizes „knechtische Hingebung an den Moment, als Mangel an Bildnerruhe, an Kunst" (IV, 130). Finally, Heine adopts for himself a position of indifference vis-à-vis Börne's enthusiasm (IV, 98–99, 131). Where Heine criticized Goethe earlier for his poor politics, he praises him now for his outstanding creations. Heine's attitude toward Goethe had always been ambivalent. Here Heine merely shifts the focus of his interest and stresses Goethe's aesthetic talents rather than his political weaknesses. The apparent contradictions arise simply from the vehemence of Heine's various rhetorical positions.

Heine's ambivalent attitude toward Goethe and the categories he associates with him stems from his understanding of the function of art. Heine wanted art, not propaganda. Many passages make this unmistakeably clear.[9] Heine's plea for the autonomy of form in the face of those political poets who subordinate it to content and his unwillingness to accept a party program do not necessarily place him in a Goethean camp.[10] For Heine, the poet should remain political, but that means only, yet sufficiently – and in contrast to Heine's own vision of Goethe – that he focus on the present and be on the brink of the movement we call historical progress. In his *Zeitgedichte* Heine attempts to unite art and politics by substituting intellectual protest and irony for what he took to be Goethe's political stability and aesthetic stillness.[11] Goethe's concern with personal ethics and *Bildung* were for Heine not social and political enough; his day-to-day activities as a politician were supportive of the status quo, of the Restoration. Finally, not only do his works embody aesthetic stillness and have a quietistic influence, Goethe himself incorporated such traits and became everything but a model political activist. Heine speaks of Goethe's „stillsitzende Ruhe" (III, 620). When Fichte was charged with atheism, Goethe – justified or not – did what he, in his stillness and tranquillity, could be expected to do, nothing: „Der deutsche Jupiter blieb ruhig sitzen, und ließ sich ruhig anbeten und beräuchern" (III, 620).

---

[8] Börne had written in his *Briefe aus Paris* that he would reread Goethe's *Natürliche Tochter* „im nächsten Sommer, im Juli, in den Tagen, wo man Gefrornes liebt" (III, 295). See also Börne III, 838–39.
[9] III, 317; IV: 11–12, 41, 45, 501; HSA XXI, 292.
[10] See Fingerhut (1971), 49–50.
[11] Heine's view of Goethe obviously tells us more about Heine than Goethe. Consider Goethe's irony, his occasional satire, and his concept of dynamic stillness.

From Repose to Revolution

Heine is not free of the temptation to enjoy personal quietude and the pure autonomy of art, but in three striking passages, his preface to *Salon I*, the final pages of *Französische Maler*, and the Helgoland letters of *Ludwig Börne. Eine Denkschrift*, he acknowledges the need to overcome such quietistic leanings. In his preface to *Salon I* Heine announces his desire to return

> in das Land der Poesie [...] ich möchte Ruhe haben [...] Und stille Lieder wollte ich dichten, und nur für mich, oder allenfalls um sie irgend einer verborgenen Nachtigall vorzulesen. Es ging auch im Anfang, mein Gemüt ward wieder umfriedet von dem Geiste der Dichtkunst [...] (III, 11)

Heine then narrates how he found himself suddenly in the presence of Germans leaving their homeland. The emigrants complain of the conditions in Germany and ask: „Was sollten wir tun? Sollten wir eine Revolution anfangen?" (III, 13). Heine responds that $\frac{1}{10}$ of what the Germans tolerate would have created 36 revolutions in France. Aware of German quietude and its consequences, Heine abandons his desire for idyllic tranquillity and autonomous art: „Ade Ruhe! Ade stille Träume!" (III, 17). He is ready to adopt an active, polemical stance.

In *Französische Maler* Heine describes the sounds of history outside his window, „den mißtönenden Lärm der Weltgeschichte" (III, 69). The disturbances in the streets of Paris and the cries of protest over the failed revolution in Poland bother him in his withdrawn, journalistic enterprise: „Es wird mir schwer, ruhig am Schreibtische sitzenzubleiben und meinen armen Kunstbericht, meine friedliche Gemäldebeurteilung, zu Ende zu schreiben" (III, 69). To write of aesthetic pleasure and not act in a situation where one hears „das rohe Geräusch des Lebens [...] den Notschrei der erbitterten Armut" requires a Goethean consciousness of indifference: „Es gehört fast ein Goethescher Egoismus dazu, um hier zu einem ungetrübten Kunstgenuß zu gelangen" (III, 70–71). With determination and commitment Heine relinquishes his current idyllic enterprise and speaks of the „neue Kunst", which will not stand in „Widerspruch mit der Gegenwart" nor be separated from „die Politik des Tages" (III, 72). Heine's new art will be part of the movement of time („die Zeitbewegung" III, 72). Again Heine sacrifices his desire for *Ruhe*.

In his essay on Ludwig Börne, Heine invites the reader to identify with his disillusion over the lack of revolution in Germany and adopt his desire for withdrawal as well as his fatalistic, cyclical view of history,[12] but the mood

---

[12] See the following two passages: „Ich selber bin dieses Guerillakrieges müde und sehne mich nach Ruhe, wenigstens nach einem Zustand, wo ich mich meinen natürlichen Neigungen, meiner träumerischen Art und Weise, meinem phantastischen Sinnen und Grübeln, ganz fessellos hingeben kann [...]. Ich bin müde und

quickly changes. After assuming this stance, Heine reveals another side, his enthusiasm for the events of 1830 and his hopes for Germany's future. Ideally, the reader would identify with Heine's escapist and lethargic attitude, then follow him as he awakens to the July revolution:

> Fort ist meine Sehnsucht nach Ruhe. Ich weiß jetzt wieder was ich will, was ich soll, was ich muß... Ich bin der Sohn der Revolution und greife wieder zu den gefeiten Waffen, worüber meine Mutter ihren Zaubersegen ausgesprochen [...] Worte gleich flammenden Sternen die aus der Höhe herabschießen und die Paläste verbrennen und die Hütten erleuchten... Worte gleich blanken Wurfspeeren, die bis in den siebenten Himmel hinaufschwirren und die frommen Heuchler treffen, die sich dort eingeschlichen ins Allerheiligste... Ich bin ganz Freude und Gesang, ganz Schwert und Flamme! (IV, 53)

One wonders to what extent Heine's earlier desire for *Ruhe* is genuine, to what degree it represents a feigned position designed for artistic effect.[13] In any case, the reader, after identifying with Heine's longing for repose, should follow him further by abandoning this position and confronting the issues of the day.

Heine's stress on the present shines through clearly in a short essay on the philosophy of history, posthumously titled „Verschiedenartige Geschichtsauffassung". Here Heine contrasts two modes of perceiving history, the first of which envisages „einen trostlosen Kreislauf" (III, 21). For fatalists of this sort there is never anything new under the sun; thus, they can smile condescendingly at man's attempts to improve the world. Heine includes in this group „die Poeten aus der Wolfgang Goetheschen Kunstperiode", whom he chastises for their „Indifferentismus gegen alle politischen Angelegenheiten des Vaterlandes" (III, 21). Here Heine draws a direct connection between literature and conceptions of history, condemning Goethe's pantheistic art insofar as it teaches that the world is divine and stable, that what is possible is already real.[14] The opposing historical view does recognize progress, but in such a way as to direct all its attention toward the future; like its fatalistic counterpart, this – to use Schiller's category, sentimental – perspective is accompanied by an unwillingness to focus on the present. This linear view of history argues that the possible is not real; further, the unspoken undercurrent of this quasi-progressive theory is that

---

lechze nach Ruhe, Ich werde mir ebenfalls eine deutsche Nachtmütze anschaffen und über die Ohren ziehen" (IV, 35–36). „Die Welt bleibt, nicht im starren Stillstand, aber im erfolglosesten Kreislauf" (IV, 49).

[13] On the specific question of the fictionality and later composition of the Helgoland letters see DHA 11: 251–56 and 455–58. In general one must be sceptical of Heine's autobiographical comments. See esp. Sammons (1969 and 1979) and Fingerhut (1972), 131–89.

[14] This mirrors a moment in Hegel of which Heine was critical during this period. See II, 525 and III, 97.

the possible will never become real. The Romantics, who, in Heine's view, deny reality by striving for the unconditional and infinite, fit this mode, as do the *Tendenzdichter*, insofar as they soar so high in their empty enthusiasm that they lose sight of the earth (IV, 486). In Heine's reading of history the possible is not – as with the fatalists – already real nor is it – as with the quasi-progressives – never to be realized; rather, it might and should become real. Heine would negate the two opposing views of history and integrate his own historical perspective into a new idea of art, in which „die Gegenwart ihren Wert behalte" (III, 22). In a fragment he writes programmatically:[15]

> Unsre lyrike Poesie tritt in eine neue Phase. Die somnanbule Periode des Liedes, der stillen Gemüthsblume, hat ein Ende [...] Es handelt sich jetzt nicht mehr um Zukunftsträume, sondern um die harte Frohn der Wirklichkeit.

With his emphasis on reality and the present, Heine would pass from a somnambulistic art, whose ethical ideal is indifference and whose aesthetic ideal is stillness, to an art that would contribute to the movement of history. On a personal level Heine shares with the readers his own desire for withdrawal, tranquillity, and purely autonomous art; nonetheless, he eventually asserts that the only legitimate activity in the present is to contribute to progress by focusing on the political and social issues of the day.

Heine's God of Motion

One of the central issues in Heine's day was religion. In Heine's view the Christian religion had served four purposes: first, it provided a spiritual counterforce to Roman materialism and Northern barbarism;[16] second, through the example of Christ, it provided comfort to sufferers when solace was especially needed;[17] third, in its medieval stages it offered its followers a tranquil and harmonic world-view; finally, with the Reformation, it introduced freedom of thought to German culture (III, 541). Each of these virtues

---

[15] Quoted in Reeves (1974), 143.
[16] „Keineswegs jedoch leugnen wir hier den Nutzen, den die christkatholische Weltansicht in Europa gestiftet. Sie war notwendig als eine heilsame Reaktion gegen den grauenhaft kolossalen Materialismus, der sich im römischen Reiche entfaltet hatte und alle geistige Herrlichkeit des Menschen zu vernichten drohte" (III, 362–63). „Jener Spiritualismus wirkte heilsam auf die übergesunden Völker des Nordens; die allzuvollblütigen barbarischen Leiber wurden christlich vergeistigt; es begann die europäische Zivilisation. Das ist eine preiswürdige, heilige Seite des Christentums" (III, 363–64).
[17] „Diese Religion [Christianity] war eine Wohltat für die leidende Menschheit während achtzehn Jahrhunderten, sie war providentiell, göttlich, heilig" (III, 519).

has, meanwhile, either been developed to the point where it has passed over into its opposite and become disadvantageous or been surpassed and developed in more positive light by nonreligious forces. First, Christian spiritualism has itself become needy of a corrective. The Christian denial of matter and flesh has led to contemporary man's one-sidedness. In addition, spiritualism and the promise of an afterlife have made hunger, inequality, and injustice seem irrelevant. In Heine's reading, Christians turn their backs on contemporary social problems, including their own, and focus on inner development. Heine's poem „Die Wanderratten" demonstrates the insufficiency of this spiritualist world-view; religion can do nothing to stem hunger and stop everyday problems (VI/1, 307). Second, since Christianity espouses „die Lehre von der Verwerflichkeit aller irdischen Güter" (III, 362), a Christian can rightfully demand neither material rights nor material privileges. Man's just condition becomes suffering. In Heine's view Christ should no longer be praised as the hero with whom human sufferers might identify; instead, he should be condemned as a false example for quietistic souls unaware that the sufferings they endure are of worldly, not divine, origins.[18] Christ's lessons on how to suffer[19] only inhibit progress.[20] Third, the bliss of a „beruhigtes Leben" (II, 215) and „viel ruhiges Glück" (II, 214), which the Catholic value system and medieval way of life had nurtured, must also be seen as anti-progressive. Medieval happiness came at the price of „eine Unterjochung der schlimmsten Art" (II, 215), the subjugation of individuality and reason. Yet, as Heine states: „Der Geist [...] läßt sich [...] nicht einlullen durch Glockengeläute" (II, 214). Luther introduced freedom to the Christian church. Moreover, the heirs to Luther's doctrine of emancipation are to be found outside the church among the philosophers of German Idealism. The revolution of Idealism has led, theoretically at least, to the autonomy of man and to his freedom, not within but, from the church. Christianity has developed beyond itself.

Just as religion develops, so too does God: „Gott ist in der Bewegung, in der Handlung, in der Zeit, sein heiliger Odem weht durch die Blätter der Geschichte" (III, 394–95). This inversion of the traditional concept of a God in repose implies, in the context of Heine's reception of Hegel and the Saint-

---

[18] „Die bisherige spiritualistische Religion war heilsam und nothwendig, solange der größte Theil der Menschen im Elend lebten und sich mit der himmlischen Seligkeit vertrösten mußten. Seit aber, durch die Fortschritte der Industrie und Oeconomie, es möglich geworden die Menschen aus ihrem materiellen Elende herauszuziehen und auf Erden zu beseligen, seitdem – Sie verstehen mich" (HSA XXI, 56).

[19] „Wer seinen Gott leiden sieht, trägt leichter die eignen Schmerzen" (II, 493).

[20] From a different perspective Heine praises Christ as progressive; he is a liberator and a democrat. See II, 499–500 and IV, 605–06.

Simonians,[21] that God is not eternally stable, that he has become flesh, become man. Heine, along with his predecessors, has secularized the Gospel of John. In Hegel's and Heine's reading of the incarnation, God comes to himself through history.[22] God is history, and as man develops, so too does God. With his affirmation of progress Heine predicates God's motion. In addition, he renounces the religion that would deny the law of motion and remain unchanging in its essence, Catholicism. For Heine, like Mundt, the motion within Christianity, which Catholicism never recognized, was the Reformation.[23] Yet, neither the Reformation nor even its successor German Idealism represents a final stage in the development of God in the world; each must give way to the increasingly political liberation of religion.

Political Repression and Indifference in the Context of Religious Quietude

A major focus of Heine's critique of religion is the religious quietude that encourages political oppression. Germany's ruling parties are fond of religion in so far as the pious support the existing regime. Christianity serves the present state in two ways: first, the devout Christian knows how to be obedient before authorities; second, the moral Christian preserves the rights of others to own property. With a combination of humor and social criticism Heine writes that Christianity is necessary for the state, „damit die Untertanen hübsch demütig gehorchen, und auch außerdem nicht zu viel gestohlen [...] wird" (II, 512). The stillness and obedience encouraged by both secular and religious authorities contribute to regressive quietude. Not without

---

[21] In a manuscript variant Heine writes: „Aber Gott ist nicht bloß in der Substanz enthalten, wie die Alten ihn begriffen, sondern Gott ist in dem ‚Prozeß', wie Hegel sich ausgedrückt und wie er auch von den Saint-Simonisten gedacht wird" (III, 866). Literature on Heine's relationship to the Saint-Simonians is extensive. Butler (1926) offers the most thorough but also one of the earliest accounts of their influence on Heine and Young Germany. A shorter, more recent overview is offered by Iggers (1958). The latest debate focuses on the relative influence of Enfantin vis-à-vis Hegel. See Sternberger (1972) and Reeves (1974 and 1980). Literature on Hegel and Heine is voluminous, despite the fact that Heine's understanding and appropriation of Hegel may have been limited, as Sammons has consistently argued (1969, 1979, 1982). The briefest judicious account of Hegel and Heine is Windfuhr (1973), while the most extensive presentation is Krüger (1977). Two other works stand out insofar as they shed unusual light on the subject: Saueracker-Ritter (1974) presents a positivistic collection of information relating to the question of Heine's exact knowledge of Hegel, and Hengst (1973) discusses Heine in relationship to not just the Left but also the Right Hegelians.

[22] See esp. III: 510–11 and 569.

[23] Mundt writes: „Die Bewegung des Katholizismus war schon die Reformation" (*Madonna*, 362).

significance Heine speaks of „das stille sabbatliche Deutschland".[24] One of his striking rhymes captures this conflation as well: „Majestät / Pietät" (VI/ 1, 272).

Heine often speaks of political and religious oppression in the same breath. The highest goal in the present is for him „die Befreiung von den Resten des Feudalismus und Klerikalismus" (II, 380).[25] Both try to instill in the Germans fear of revolution: „Aristokraten und Pfaffen drohen beständig mit den Schreckbildern aus den Zeiten des Terrorismus" (II, 656). In a preface in French to his *Reisebilder* Heine speaks of his tirades against *«prêtrise et aristocratie»* (II, 677). In a letter to Varnhagen from 1830 he writes that the revolution must encompass all social interests but singles out „Adel und Kirche" as „die einzig verbündeten Feinde" (HSA XX, 422). Feudalism and clericalism are mutually supportive. The monarch's power is sanctioned by God according to an established doctrine of absolutism, the divine right of kings, or in Heine's mocking phrase, „das [...] göttliche Recht des Despotismus" (II, 657).[26] Just as religion upholds the power of the state, so does the state support religion. Religious leaders, as long as they teach obedience in the secular sphere, are free to direct the spiritual lives of the populace. The model for two realms, strongly supported by Luther,[27] is as old as the New Testament: "Let every person be subject to the governing authorities. For there is no authority except from God, and those that exist have been instituted by God" (Rom. 13, 1). In 1831 the *Evangelische Kirchen-Zeitung*, edited by Ernst Wilhelm Hengstenberg, a frequent object of Heine's satire, still appeals to this Biblical text in its attacks on liberal theology:[28]

> Früher wurde das Ansehn und die Unverletzlichkeit der Obrigkeit auf die Schrift und auf sie allein gegründet. Das ‚ein Jedermann sey unterthan der Obrigkeit, die Gewalt über ihn hat' u.s.w., war die feste Stütze der Throne. Jeder hatte also ein festes Princip, von dem aus er den Gehorsam gegen die Obrigkeit vor sich selbst und vor Anderen rechtfertigen konnte.

Heine's critique of religion, in particular religious stillness, is directed against not only the aristocracy and clergy but also the *Untertan*. Heine never stops

---

[24] V, 532. See also II, 540.
[25] Admittedly, the prime targets will later shift for Heine as he begins to recognize the power of the aristocracy of wealth.
[26] At least as a negative formula – that the monarch receives his rights from no one else and is responsible to no one else – the theory of the divine right of kings was preserved as long as monarchical government itself. See Boldt (1975), 61. The critique of *Gottesgnadentum* is prominent by the way in *Der hessische Landbote*, where Büchner writes: „Das alles duldet ihr, weil euch Schurken sagen: ‚diese Regierung sey von Gott'. Diese Religion ist nicht von Gott, sondern vom Vater der Lügen" (L II, 46).
[27] See esp. „Von weltlicher Obrigkeit, wie weit man ihr Gehorsam sei" (1523).
[28] Hengstenberg, 36. Cf. Johann Schmidt (1977), 114.

criticizing the Germans for their subservience, obedience, and loyalty vis-à-vis the authorities. *Ruhe* and *Geduld* are for Heine German qualities, but they are also specifically religious: „Der Obrigkeit gehorchen, ist / Die erste Pflicht für Jud und Christ" (VI/1, 230). Religion ist not just an opium *for* the people, instituted by the machinations of clerics and aristocrats and accepted by the pious, it is an opium *of* the people; it functions as necessary, if self-deluding, consolation in the face of economic and political powerlessness.[29] Heine writes concerning the period of French occupation:

> Not lehrt beten, sagt das Sprüchwort, und wahrlich nie war die Not in Deutschland größer, und daher das Volk dem Beten, der Religion, dem Christentum, zugänglicher als damals [...] Die allgemeine Betrübnis fand Trost in der Religion, und es entstand ein pietistisches Hingeben in den Willen Gottes, von welchem allein die Hülfe erwartet wurde. (III, 378)

Whether through the trickery of clerics or the compensatory psychic needs of the people, this submission to the will of God internalized economic and political problems and encouraged ineffective, quietistic passivity. Christianity, in preaching „Hundedemut und Engelsgeduld", became „die erprobteste Stütze des Despotismus" (III, 362).

For Heine religion encourages a form of indifference as dangerous as Goethe's: „Goethe mit seinem Eiapopeia, die Pietisten mit ihrem langweiligen Gebetbücherton, die Mystiker mit ihrem Magnetismus, hatten Deutschland völlig eingeschläfert" (III, 209). The devout Christian should not be concerned with the state's policies, be they just or unjust, a point nicely captured by Heine's contemporary Gottfried Kinkel in „Des Untertanen Glaubensbekenntnis".[30] For Arnold Ruge, the Left Hegelian who claimed to have influenced, together with Marx, Heine's turn to political poetry in the 1840s,[31] indifference is a telling characteristic of religious and political *Ruhe*. The individual who would imitate God sees in the divine being „den indifferenten Zuschauer der Weltereignisse" (190). Just as God is indifferent or still, so too are the pious. The state of course knows the advantages of ruling over such a „bewußtlosen, indifferenten Haufen" (190):

> Er [der Polizeistaat] wünscht, daß die Bürger „ein ruhiges und zufriednes Leben führen in aller Gottseligkeit und Ehrbarkeit", daß sie sich nur für sich und ihrer Seelen Seligkeit, ja nicht für das öffentliche Wesen interessiren, daß sie im Frieden, also nur als Privatpersonen, höchstens mit himmlischen und religiösen Interessen, d.h. ohne Partei für geistige Unterschiede der Wirklichkeit, sind; und nur wenn er

---

[29] See Oesterle (1972), 26. Religion functions as solace in the face of illness and pain as well; one might read Heine's conversion primarily in this light. What changes is not Heine's view of religion as an opiate but his sense of man's need for it. See Spencer (1979), also Lukács (1964), 305.
[30] Reprinted in *Die Achtundvierziger*, 195–96.
[31] *Begegnungen mit Heine*, I, 547.

es befiehlt, etwa zum Behuf eines Krieges, dürfen die Bürger des Polizeistaates oder die Spießbürger Partei ergreifen und ein politisches Interesse haben. (190) Religious *Ruhe*, with its indifference toward political events, only feeds the tyranny of political quietude.

Heine's Inversions of Religious Stillness

In his attacks on religious ideology and the status of the church, Heine makes use of the technique of inversion with which we are familiar from our study of *Lenz*. We have already heard Heine speak of a God in motion as opposed to the traditional concept of a God in repose. In most instances his inversions are still more focused. Heine treats original sin, or in German *Erbsünde* (literally, inherited sin), in a comical and critical manner: whoever believes in inherited sin („Erbsünde") will not revolt against the inherited privileges („Erbprivilegien") enjoyed by the aristocracy of birth (III, 206). In the poem „Erleuchtung" (IV, 430–31) Heine inverts the traditional religious motif of the awakening.[32] In this poem the hero's illumination is not of the merits but of the inadequacies and deceit of religion. The awakening becomes an awakening *from* religious stupor. Heine's inversions often relate to the traditionally sacred connotations of *Ruhe*. He mocks, for example, the sacred seventh day of rest: „Ich arbeite nicht am Sabbat, dem siebenten Tage, wo Gott geruht; ja, aus Vorsicht, da man nicht mehr genau weiß, welcher dieser siebente Ruhetag war, tue ich oft die ganze Woche nichts" (II, 511). The *Ruhe* Heine finds in religion is not the tranquillity of a unified soul or a soul at rest in God but the sleep induced from a bad sermon.[33] He speaks of the „Seelenärzte, die $^1/_{10\,000}$ Vernunft in einem Eimer Moralwasser schütten, und uns damit des Sonntags zur Ruhe predigen" (II, 502). Religious *Ruhe* is unveiled as a *Ruhe* not of dynamic centeredness but of pious resignation and stagnation. „Stiller Franz" in *Atta Troll* stirs only in prayer, not in life: „Er, der nur im Teegeschwätze / Und im Beten sich bewegte!" (IV, 539). Heine writes that during the Restoration religious stillness contributed to Germany's loud snoring: „viele fingen sogar an zu snarchen, sorglos vertrauend auf Gott und die von ihm eingesetzte hohe Obrigkeit, unsere 36 Monarchen" (II, 681). This is the god of sleep, whom Heine would replace with a god of motion.

---

[32] See Isa: 8, 20; 58, 10; and John 8, 12.
[33] The „Ruhe" Lenz gives his parishoners in church might also be read as sleep, but for Lenz – suffering from intellectual restlessness and disorientation – such sleep represents bliss; Heine, concerned with Germany's political stagnation and wretched contentment, attacks and mocks such stillness.

German Somnolence

Heine's concept of German quietude involves a nexus of themes. Throughout his writings Heine associates German *Ruhe* with somnolence. He speaks not only of „das ruhige, stille deutsche Volk" (IV, 77) but also of „unser erschlafftes Volk" (II, 147) and „das Schlafmützentum der Deutschen" (HSA XX, 384). Germany is „das stille Traumland" (III, 209). Sleep functions as a metaphor for political quietude, and dreaming symbolizes apolitical interiority. The Germans, so Heine, substitute for activity in the present a world of dreams that takes them back into the past, viz. the Middle Ages with its feudal tradition, or forward into the future, viz. the Christian heaven, which legitimizes their song of renunciation and disconcern for present inequities. The Germans are „Vor- und Nachdenker, Träumer, die nur in der Vergangenheit und in der Zukunft leben, und keine Gegenwart haben" (II, 535).[34] They are for Heine unaware not only of the significant issues of the day but also of their own servility; as a result, they acquiesce in the status quo.

Dormant Regeneration: Herder, Hölderlin, Menzel

Heine's and Young Germany's conception of sleep as a metaphor for contemporary Germany is not new; new is their criticism of it. In the speculative histories of the late eighteenth and early nineteenth century sleep symbolized regeneration. For Herder sleep was part of the dormant, regenerating process of evolution, which he privileged over the violence of revolution. In *Thiton und Aurora* (1792), Herder denounces clearly, if indirectly, the revolutionary tendencies that were threatening to make their way from France to Germany. Admonishing any demonstration of „Gewaltsamkeit", Herder would prefer that Germany remain „auf dem Wege der heilenden Natur" (Suphan XVI, 117):

> Nicht Revolutionen, sondern *Evolutionen* sind der stille Gang dieser grossen Mutter, dadurch sie schlummernde Kräfte erweckt, Keime entwickelt, das zu frühe Alter verjüngt, und oft den scheinbaren Tod in neues leben verwandelt. (Suphan XVI, 117–18)

In Herder one finds the concept of slow, inner development („Diese Evolutionen gehen langsam, oft unbemerkt fort [...] Immer kommen verborgenere, tieferliegende [Kräfte] zum Vorschein" Suphan XVI, 118), the awakening of dormant qualities („Auf die Nacht des Schlafs folgt der Morgen des Erwachens" Suphan XVI, 118), and the organic imagery of

---

[34] Heine adds mockingly that because the Germans don't live in the present, they need neither freedom nor equality.

natural growth („Die Natur macht Jahrszeiten, sie fördert Kräfte; sie fördert sie auch im Menschengeschlechte" Suphan XVI, 119). For Herder evolutionary regeneration implies the organic development of elements otherwise taken to be without life:

> Nicht Revolution, aber eine glückliche *Evolution der in uns schlummernden, uns neuverjüngenden Kräfte.* Was wir Überleben unsrer selbst, also Tod nennen, ist bei bessern Seelen nur Schlummer zu neuem Erwachen, eine Abspannung des Bogens zu neuem Gebrauche. So ruhet der Acker, damit er desto reicher trage: so erstirbt der Baum im Winter, damit er im Frühling neu sprosse und treibe. (Suphan XVI, 122)

Herder was not without influence in his concept of evolution. Hölderlin, in a letter to Neuffer,[35] copies the very passage quoted above and in several other contexts uses the imagery of nature to suggest that the present contains the seeds for future growth.[36] In *Hyperion*, after refuting Alabanda's revolutionary impulses and appealing to the natural images of spring and youth, Hyperion states: „Der Tod ist ein Bote des Lebens, und daß wir jetzt schlafen in unsern Krankenhäusern, diß zeugt vom nahen gesunden Erwachen" (StA III, 32). Watchfulness at night („wachend zu bleiben bei Nacht") is of course central to the dynamic tranquillity of the poet's voyage and mission as a harbinger of the gods' return in „Brod und Wein".[37] Most importantly in this context, Hölderlin consistently applies the image of dormant regeneration to Germany:[38]

> Ich glaube an eine künftige Revolution der Gesinnungen und Vorstellungsarten, die alles bisherige schaamroth machen wird. Und dazu kann Deutschland vielleicht sehr viel beitragen. Je stiller ein Staat aufwächst, um so herrlicher wird er, wenn er zur Reife kömmt. Deutschland ist still, bescheiden, es wird viel gedacht, viel gearbeitet, und große Bewegungen sind in den Herzen der Jugend, ohne daß sie in Phrasen übergehen wie sonstwo. (StA VI, 229/no. 132)

In celebrating the peace of Lunéville Hölderlin writes to his brother of Germany's silent and natural development:

> daß das deutsche Herz in solchem Klima, unter dem Seegen dieses neuen Friedens erst recht aufgehn, und geräuschlos, wie die wachsende Natur, seine geheimen Kräfte entfalten wird, diß mein' ich, diß seh' und glaub' ich. (StA VI, 407/no. 222)

---

[35] StA VI, 125/no. 83.
[36] StA VI, 93/no. 65; StA VI, 310/no. 173.
[37] StA II/1, 91. See also „Dichterberuf" (StA II/1, 46–48).
[38] Hölderlin, not unlike Heine, does at times question Germany's evolutionary capabilities. In „Gesang des Deutschen" the poet's characterization of Germany as „allduldend, gleich der schweigenden Mutter Erd'", is without praise (StA II/1, 3–4), and in „An die Deutschen" the poet describes his countrymen as „thatenarm und gedankenvoll" and expresses his impatience with their merely internal development (StA II/1, 9–10). „Germanien", which celebrates „die stillste Tochter Gottes […]. Voll süßen Schlummers", speaks more confidently of Germany's dormant regeneration (StA II/1, 149–52).

Herder and Hölderlin advocate organic evolution, a natural development based on hidden capacities. Though their position is not directly acquiescent, their belief in Germany's slow and natural growth, what Heine mockingly calls Germany's „langsamen Schneckengang", makes them vulnerable to the dangers of a quietistic acceptance of injustice (HSA XX, 414).

The classical authors who celebrated dynamic stillness were not the only ones to embrace the concept of inner development. Heine's contemporary Menzel adopted this notion too. While conservatives increasingly employed the concept of dormant regeneration in their attempts to justify Germany's lack of revolution, liberals attacked it, ever more vehemently, as an ideology that supports the status quo. In his *Briefe aus Paris* Börne, one of Menzel's intellectual sparring partners, criticizes the stillness on Germany's streets in the light of revolutionary activities in France (3–4).[39] He mocks Germany's subservience, servility, and patience.[40] His countrymen substitute in place of revolutionary action „stille Gebete" (776), and the entire nation lives under „Schlafmützen und Schlafrock" (24).[41] Finally, Börne quotes with disparagement the phrase that has since become a comic, if nonetheless powerful, formula: „Ruhe ist die erste Bürgerpflicht" (255, 528).[42] As a direct response to this criticism Menzel revived in his *Geschichte der deutschen Literatur* of 1836 the traditional praise of evolutionary and progressive *Ruhe*:

> Die jetzige Stille ist der deutschen Art vollkommen angemessen, die Deutschen befinden sich wohl dabei. Nennt es Börne einen Schlaf, nun so ist es ein gesunder Schlaf, und wohl dem, der ruhig schläft. Ich möchte es einen Pflanzenschlaf nennen, ein stilles gedeihliches Wachsthum [...]. Gewiß ist die Stille, in welcher das deutsche Leben sich jetzt in sich selbst versenkt hat, ein Zeichen seiner innerlichen Fruchtbarkeit, und ich finde sie mehr dem ruhigen Wohlbehagen einer hoffnungsvollen Mutter zu vergleichen, als dem thierischen Winterschlaf eines Bären, wie sie uns Börne darstellt. (IV, 331–33)

Heine, who had his struggles with both Menzel and Börne, was, if not familiar with Herder's or Hölderlin's praise of regenerating slumber, well aware of these passages. In fact, Heine's commentary on Börne's rebuttal in *Menzel der Franzosenfresser*, where Börne quotes and refutes the above passage,[43] is strikingly positive. Moreover, in no less than four passages, two

---

[39] The following quotations are from volume III of Börne's *Sämtliche Schriften*.
[40] See 144, 166, 243, 557, 776, and 786.
[41] See also 528 and 562.
[42] The phrase originated with Count Schulenburg, city commandant of Berlin, who announced in October 1806 after the battle at Jena: „Der König hat eine Bataille verloren. Jetzt ist Ruhe die erste Bürgerpflicht. Ich fordere die Einwohner Berlins dazu auf" (Büchmann [1956], 485).
[43] Börne follows the quote from Menzel with a bitter attack on German quietude: „Diese der ‚Deutschen Literaturgeschichte' des Herrn Menzels ausgezogene Stellen, eine wahre Klatschrosenpredigt und ein Polizei-Eiapopeia, haben so viel

of which address Menzel by name, Heine refers to the German „Pflanzen-schlaf".[44]

Dreaming, Sleeping, Death: German Romanticism

Heine's critique of Germany's slumber, its sleepiness and thoughts of night, is directed against not only the ideology of evolution but also the Romantic escape into otherworldliness. The Romantics provide Heine with an entirely different, if equally suspect, tradition in praise of sleep. Heine, with his stress on the concrete, the particular, the individual, abhorred the Romantic celebration of night and nondifferentiation.[45] For Novalis, whose *Hymnen an die Nacht* represent the pinnacle of this movement, night and sleep are eternal:

> Zugemessen ward dem Lichte seine Zeit; aber zeitlos und raumlos ist der Nacht Herrschaft. – Ewig ist die Dauer des Schlafs. Heiliger Schlaf – beglücke zu selten nicht der Nacht Geweihte in diesem irdischen Tagewerk. (I, 133)

Heine, like Hölderlin, views night as a metaphor for the gods' exile; in Novalis' conception God returns at night. Night is not the preparation for an awakening but itself a sacred and final state: „Die Nacht ward der Offenbarungen mächtiger Schoß – in ihn kehrten die Götter zurück" (I, 145). To see the „Wunderherrlichkeit" (I, 131) opened by night is to overcome one's desire to return to the restlessness of day: „Wer oben stand auf dem Grenzgebürge der Welt, und hinübersah in das neue Land, in der Nacht Wohnsitz – wahrlich der kehrt nicht in das Treiben der Welt zurück, in das Land, wo das Licht in ewiger Unruh hauset" (I, 137). *Ruhe*, for Novalis, becomes death. His „Sehnsucht nach dem Tode" celebrates eternal sleep and the abnegation of life: „Gelobt sei uns die ewge Nacht, / Gelobt der ewge Schlummer" (I, 153).[46]

Angähnendes, Einschläferndes, Nachtmützenartiges und Eintölpelndes, das man, schon schlaftrunken, nach der ersten besten Fronvogtei hintaumeln möchte und dort ehrerbietig stammeln: ‚Wir pausieren zwar beträchtlich, sind nur im stillen fruchtbar, warten geduldig auf unsere Niederkunft […] und schlafen unsern guten deutschen Pflanzenschlaf; doch könnte es geschehen, daß wir einmal im Schlafe ungebührlich mit den Blättern flüstern; darum sperrt uns ein, lieber Herr Vogt, um uns gegen unsere eigene Exaltation sicherzustellen. Tut das, lieber Herr' (III, 893–94).

[44] IV, 110; IV, 429 („Zur Beruhigung"); V, 43; V, 472.

[45] Heine did of course accept to a limited degree the Romantic overcoming of mimetic art through the use of the imagination and, metaphorically speaking, dreaming. Cf. Maier (1969), 62, 68. For additional, more progressive, similarities between Heine and the Romantics see Hohendahl (1973). On Heine's relationship to the Romantics in general see Clasen (1979).

[46] Such blindness to the day is for Heine not ony Romantic but quintessentially German; the enlightened French, meanwhile, scorn such flights of fancy. Heine even remarks, suggestively, that, just as in life, so in drama, dreams play a greater role in Germany than in France (III, 301–03).

In Heine's view „der deutsche Geist" emigrated during the French Revolution into the dream world of German Romanticism, „ins Traumreich des Gedankens und der Romantik" (II, 680). Dreams represent for the Romantics heightened use of the imagination and a poeticized reality that transcends the mundane. For Heine it is clear: in overextending their phantasy and immersing themselves in the otherworldly, the Romantics ignore historical reality. The distinction between dream and world is lost: „Die Welt wird Traum, der Traum wird Welt" (Novalis I, 319).

Heine of course writes dream-poems too. He begins his *Buch der Lieder* with a section of „Traumbilder", and the dream motif recurs throughout his works. For Heine, however, dreams are not just evocative of another world. Heine's dreams end invariably with waking, with a return to reality. The seduction of the dream world serves, primarily, to bring the reader all the more surely back to the everyday world.[47] The reader is confronted with the harshness of reality and the falsity of the dream.[48] Heine's systematic inversion of the Romantic dream image awakens the reader to the status of the dream as dream and thus to his/her own critical consciousness. Romantic dreams are revealed as seductive escapes from reality, momentary, not eternal. In a social and political sense Heine wanted his readers to awaken – via the parallel experience in his poems and travel pictures – to the realities of contemporary Germany.

Dreaming, Thinking, Acting: German Idealism

While Heine directs his criticism of the dream world in part against the darkness of Romanticism, he also criticizes the idealist tradition, which, though rational, remains theoretical rather than practical. Thus Heine can call the German revolution in ideas, i.e., the Idealist and primarily Kantian critique of religion, the dream of the French revolutionary reality. Heine is critical of dreams or pure thought and imagination insofar as they represent an abnegation of reality, yet Heine's view is complex. He also embraces dreams as a sign of Germany's intellectual depth and as potential for eventual transformation into action. While chastising the Germans for their lack of reality, he praises them for their promise.

Heine focuses his discussion of the history of German religion and philosophy on the comparison between German contemplation and French action. The first occurrence of this parallel stems from his polemical *Einleitung zu Kahldorf über den Adel*:

---

[47] Cf. Klussmann (1973), also Siegrist (1965).
[48] For two especially nice examples see I: 92–93 and 227–28.

> Seltsam ist es, daß das praktische Treiben unserer Nachbaren jenseits des Rheins dennoch eine eigne Wahlverwandschaft hatte mit unserem philosophischen Träumen im geruhsamen Deutschland. Man vergleiche nur die Geschichte der französischen Revolution mit der Geschichte der deutschen Philosophie, und man sollte glauben: die Franzosen, denen so viel wirkliche Geschäfte oblagen, wobei sie durchaus wach bleiben mußten, hätten uns Deutsche ersucht unterdessen für sie zu schlafen und zu träumen, und unsre deutsche Philosophie sei nichts anders, als der Traum der französischen Revolution. (II, 655)

In this introduction Heine criticizes the Germans not only for their philosophical dreaming but also for the focus of their speculations. German philosophers do not analyze the everyday, the immediate, the political:

> Nun ja, wir träumten, in unserer deutschen Weise, d. h. wir philosophierten. Zwar nicht über die Dinge, die uns zunächst betrafen, oder zunächst passierten, sondern wir philosophierten über die Realität der Dinge an und für sich, über die letzten Gründe der Dinge. (II, 655)

Either Germany's dream world represents the otherworldliness of pure thought and must be negated as a form of sleep or it contains the analytic structures through which one might study present historical conditions; as such it could help prepare the Germans for revolutionary action. The question for Heine – as for most nineteenth-century students of Hegel – becomes: Does German Idealism represent a twilight, and thus the pure intellectuality of a completed system, or a new dawn, and thus the preparation for political activity?[49] Much as *Ruhe* becomes increasingly political as it reaches its most synthetic moments, so too, for Heine, should philosophy take this course, especially since it has become a complete system; progress remains only in the practical sphere. Heine, a principal forerunner of Left Hegelianism,[50] writes decisively: „In der Philosophie hätten wir also den großen Kreislauf glücklich beschlossen, und es ist natürlich, daß wir jetzt zur Politik übergehen" (II, 656).

Lullabies, Lethargy, and Listlessness: Heine's Contemporaries on *Ruhe*

Heine shared this vision of a politicized Germany and the accompanying criticism of somnolent withdrawal with many of his contemporaries. Börne,

---

[49] Michelet, for example, writes in response to Hegel's preface to the *Philosophie des Rechts* and, as he would have it, in the spirit of true Hegelianism, „daß die Philosophie nicht nur die Eule der Minverva sei, die ihren Flug erst mit der einbrechenden Dämmerung beginne, sondern auch der Hahnenschlag, der die Morgenröthe eines neu anbrechenden Tages verkünde" (398). Cf. Stuke (1963), 63–71.
[50] Cf. Calvié (1973); Reeves (1972–73); Stuke (1963), 58–63; and Windfuhr (1972), 16.

for example, sees himself – not unlike Socrates – as a stinging fly trying to waken the Germans from their sleep:[51]

> Das deutsche Volk […] schläft wie ein Veilchen um Mitternacht, wie ein Kind im Schoße der Mutter; aber wir sind auch unermüdliche Fliegen. Und weckt es unser Stachel nicht auf, so weckt es einst der Donner, und tut es der Donner nicht, so tut es ein Erdbeben. (III, 933)

Menzel had compared the German populace to a sleeping giant and praised it for its patience and endurance, suggesting that when the god of thunder beat it with a hammer, it took this to be merely a leaf that had fallen on its nose. Börne responds indignantly that while normal people sleep only long enough to regenerate themselves, the Germans doze endlessly: „Doch das Riesenvolk der Deutschen schläft Tag und Nacht, und alle Tage, und das ganze Jahr und schon drei Jahrhundert lang!"[52]

Similarly, the Young German Ludolf Wienbarg, in his *Wanderungen durch den Thierkreis* (1835), composes a section on „Die schlafende Freiheit", in which he describes how the Germans had „Jahrhunderte lang in verschiedenen deutschen Staatsgefängnissen, nämlich deutschen Staaten ruhig an der Kette gelegen und geschlummert" (125). German freedom was awakened during the Wars of Liberation but then fell asleep again, owing to the repressive policies of Metternich and the German princes. Much like Heine, however, Wienbarg stresses Germany's former revolutionary spirit, symbolized in Luther, and anticipates a time when Germany, once again awakened from its sleep, might shake the continent with renewed power.

Early in the first volume of his *Bilder und Träume aus Wien* (1836), Adolf Glaßbrenner retells a dream that opens with a nation nestled in „eine ungeheure Wiege" between two mountains.[53] The government official atop one of the mountains sings a lullaby, „damit das Volk schlafe". The allegory continues: the official, with the help of his black-clothed, gruesome-looking men, fights off the light from the stars and the songs of freedom that pass over in dream-like clouds, such that the nation remains „ruhig wie im Grabe". The government's final tactic, after, first, appealing to the nation's naturally quietist disposition and, second, arousing fear in the face of a powerful police force, is the call to religious stillness, to prayer: „sie sollten beten und schlafen, und schlafen und beten, denn solches sei der Wille des

---

[51] *Apology* 30e.
[52] III, 964. Börne recognizes the validity of *Ruhe*, but not in its current deficient form: „Ruhe ist Glück – wenn sie ein *Ausruhen* ist, wenn wir sie gewählt, wenn wir sie gefunden, nachdem wir sie gesucht; aber Ruhe ist kein Glück, wenn, wie in unserm Vaterlande, sie unsere einzige Beschäftigung ist. In Deutschland gehe ich aus, Bewegung zu suchen und finde sie nie" (II, 823).
[53] For this and the following quotes see Glaßbrenner, *Bilder und Träume aus Wien*, I, 31–32.

Herrn, der sie gesendet." The tactics are successfull, and the nation remains asleep in its cradle.

Georg Herwegh mocks Germany's lethargy and inability to keep up with advances outside the country in his poem „Die Deutschen" (124–125). In „Wiegenlied" he parodies Goethe's quietism.[54] The first two stanzas of the six stanza poem read:

> Deutschland – auf weichem Pfühle
> Mach dir den Kopf nicht schwer!
> Im irdischen Gewühle
> Schlafe, was willst du mehr?
>
> Laß jede Freiheit dir rauben,
> Setze dich nicht zur Wehr,
> Du behälst ja den christlichen Glauben:
> Schlafe, was willst du mehr? (123)

Herwegh ironizes here Goethe's „Nachtgesang" (WA I, 88), from which the refrain is taken, as an opiate in the face of reality. Moreover, Goethe's sleeping subject is just an individual; for Herwegh it becomes the entire nation.

Hoffmann von Fallersleben, too, had parodied Goethe's poem with its invitation to sleep and sleep alone.[55] „Schlafe! was willst du mehr?" is the title of one of his *Unpolitische Lieder* (I, 24).[56] In addition, just as Herwegh has a „Wiegenlied", so too does Hoffmann. Hoffmann uses the imagery of sleep primarily to attack the passivity of religious piety.[57] Finally, in keeping with the widespread, contemporary call for an awakening, Hoffmann's „Wächterlied" begins with a watchman attempting to arouse the populace from sleep. Only a few individuals stir, however, and the watchman is killed: „Dem Wächter hieb man ab den Kopf, / Dann aber schlief man weiter fort."[58] The poem concludes with the image of a sleeping nation unable to awaken from its stupor:

---

[54] In keeping with the contemporary critique of German *Ruhe* as somnolence, many poets wrote satirical *Wiegenlieder*. Ernst Ortlepp sketched a „Wiegenlied für Deutschland" (reprinted in Petzet [1903], 420–21). Ludwig Pfau attacked the Prussians in his „Badisches Wiegenlied" (*Die Achtundvierziger*, 234). Glaßbrenner wrote, besides the cradle dream cited above, an allegorical „Wiegenlied" (*Verbotene Lieder*, 16–17). Herwegh, too, wrote more than one „Wiegenlied" (see *Die Achtundvierziger*, 172–73). Finally, Heine's original title for the ballad „Karl I" was „Wiegenlied", a clear sign of political satire.

[55] One can add Heine to the list, though his reception of Goethe's „Nachtgesang" takes place in a love poem (I, 137).

[56] Poems not cited here in which sleep and repose play a role are „Eile mit Weile!" (I, 56), „Langweilig und schlecht" (II, 60), and „Die deutschen Fahnen zu Paris" (II, 130).

[57] *Unpolitische Lieder*, II, 101. Cf. „Fromm", I, 81.

[58] *Unpolitische Lieder*, II, 69.

Wer will noch Hahn und Wächter sein?
Wer wecket uns aus Schlafes Noth
Bald zu der Freiheit Morgenroth?
Wir schlafen in den Tag hinein. (II, 69)

Neither Wienbarg, Glaßbrenner, Herwegh, nor Hoffmann shares the reputation Heine does today. Except for occassional flashes of wit, these authors did not write works of lasting value. Unlike Heine and the other authors in this study, their positions are generally straightforward and simple. They do demonstrate, however, together with Börne, the pervasiveness of the shift from dynamic to deficient stillness. Even authors at odds with one another, such as Heine and Hoffmann von Fallersleben, sense the common importance of German somnolence.[59] All of them criticize Germany for its *Ruhe*. Moreover, like Heine, they collectively view Germany's quietude in the context of aesthetic stillness, religious otherworldliness, and political unawareness.

The German Michel

The image of the drowsy German Michel surfaces frequently in the contemporary condemnation of German stillness.[60] Michel, passive and apolitical, is usually portrayed with his night cap, a symbol of drowsiness and limited intelligence.[61] Discarding an earlier association of Michel with arrogant nationalism, Heine and his contemporaries portray the average German as an ignorant Philistine and lethargic fool who lets himself be pushed about by princes and clerics.[62]

According to the contemporary myth, Michel had awakened in 1813 during the Wars of Liberation; since then he again feel asleep, just as the

---

[59] Hoffmann was the one political poet whom Heine never ceased to criticize. For a differentiation of the so-called *Tendenzdichter* see Hooten (1978).

[60] On the history of Michel, from his first verified appearance in 1541 to the present, see Grote (1967) and Hauffen (1918). Michel appears so frequently in the literature of the period that a book with songs about him was published in 1843, the *Liederbuch des deutschen Michel*. The text was not available to me.

[61] See the article on „Nacht Mûtze" in Zedler's *Großes vollständiges Universal-Lexikon* (XXIII, 281–82).

[62] See esp. Hoffmann von Fallersleben's „Vetter Michel" (*Unpolitische Lieder*, II, 9); „Vetter Michels Vaterland" (*Die Achtundvierziger*, 190); and „Michels Abendlied" (*Schwefeläther*, 33–34); Adolf Glaßbrenner's „Vom kleinen Michel" (*Verbotene Lieder*, 58–62); „Der deutsche Michel beim Fortschritt" (*Verbotene Lieder*, 145–51); „An Michel" (*Unterm Brennglas*, 97); „Der Tod des deutschen Michels" (*Unterm Brennglas*, 249–54); and „Neuer Gesang des deutschen Michels" (*Unterm Brennglas*, 275–78). The Michel poems in Franz Dingelstedt's *Lieder eines kosmopolitischen Nachtwächters* also support this view (85–86, 151–55), as does, to a certain degree, the portrayal of Michel in Leopold Feldmann's *Der deutsche Michel*.

desire for a liberal and unified Germany became dormant. In his essay on Börne, after commenting on his own desire for a dreamy and reflective mode of life, specifically for „Ruhe", Heine writes:

> Welche Ironie des Geschickes, daß ich, der ich mich so gerne auf die Pfühle des stillen beschaulichen Gemütslebens bette, daß eben ich dazu bestimmt war, meine armen Mitdeutschen aus ihrer Behaglichkeit hervorzugeißeln, und in die Bewegung hineinzuhetzen! [...] ich mußte [...] den armen deutschen Michel beständig an der Nase zupfen, daß er aus seinem gesunden Riesenschlaf erwache... Freilich, ich konnte dadurch bei dem schnarchenden Giganten nur ein sanftes Niesen, keineswegs, aber ein Erwachen bewirken... Und riß ich auch heftig an seinem Kopfkissen, so rückte er es sich doch wieder zurecht mit schlaftrunkener Hand... (IV, 35–36)

Heine's efforts to awaken his fatherland are in vain: he can get little more than a gentle sneeze from the snoring giant. Here again Heine associates somnolence with Germany's cerebral tradition. When he tries to set Michel's night cap on fire, it is so wet with the perspiration of thought that it only smokes: „Einst wollte ich aus Verzweiflung seine Nachtmütze in Brand stecken, aber sie war so feucht von Gedankenschweiß, daß sie nur gelinde rauchte... und Michel lächelte im Schlummer" (IV, 36).

In 1848 liberal Germans again portrayed Michel as awake, though his falling asleep follows with the failure of the revolution. In one caricature Michel's doctors comment on their sick patient:[63]

> Du bist sehr krank, guter Michel. In den Märztagen hast du zu viel geschrien, das verursachte dir den Catarrh. Dein Gehirn ist zerrüttet durch republikanische Ideen, es muß heraus. Du mußt Mohn trinken u. 33 Jahre schlafen, dann wird's uns besser werden.

Heine, too, has a rendition of „Michel nach dem März" (VI/1, 207–71). The poet admires Michel for initially confronting his rulers:

> Wie stolz erhob er das blonde Haupt
> Vor seinen Landesvätern!
> Wie sprach er – was doch unerlaubt –
> Von hohen Landesverrätern.

Yet, the admiration lasts only as long as Michel's resolve:

> Doch als die schwarz-rot-goldne Fahn,
> Der altgermanische Plunder,
> Aufs neu erschien, da schwand mein Wahn
> Und die süßen Märchenwunder.

Michel quickly surrenders his revolutionary impulses to the Romanticism and feudalism with which the black-red-gold flag is associated.[64] The

---

[63] „Der deutsche Michel und seine Doktoren". Reproduced in Blum (1898).
[64] In „Vitzliputzli" the flag reminds the poet of the feudal Middle Ages: „Teure Farben! Schwarz-rot-goldgelb! / Diese Affensteißcouleuren / Die erinnern mich mit Wehmut / An das Banner Barbarossas" (VI/1, 58).

German revolution turns into a forum for nationalists who place unity above political freedom and justice:

> Schon sah ich den Arndt, den Vater Jahn –
> Die Helden aus andern Zeiten
> Aus ihren Gräbern wieder nahn
> Und für den Kaiser streiten.

Arndt, the militant herald of German patriotism and poet of the Wars of Liberation, and Jahn, intolerant towards the French and Jews, and the founder of the nationalistic gymnastic movement for youth, represent the interests of the Emperor. Both Arndt and Jahn are alive in 1848; the poet's quip about them rising from their graves is designed to play on their outdated ideas. Once again the hopes for revival are put to sleep, and Germany's feudal tradition is restored:

> Derweil der Michel geduldig und gut
> Begann zu schlafen und schnarchen,
> Und wieder erwachte unter der Hut
> Von vierunddreißig Monarchen.

Michel awakens, but only in a somnambulistic state; any disturbance of quietude is limited to his own snoring. After Heine's death and in the latter half of the nineteenth century, Michel continues to be addressed, at this point especially by nationalists,[65] with the optative: „Michel, wach auf!" or „Michel, erwache!"[66]

One could rewrite Heine's view of the Germans entirely under the rubric of sleeping and waking. During the early phase of the French Revolution scarcely a German intellectual supported the revolution. There was „eine brutale Ruhe in ganz Germanien" (III, 625). „Die bleiern deutscheste Schlafsucht" „lastete auf dem Volke" (III, 625). No protest came from below, nor any reform from above. The princes „hatten sich bequem die friedliche Nachtmütze über die Ohren und die Krone gezogen und gähnten seelen-

---

[65] See Grote (1967), 63. In this context consider Wander's comments after he cites an article from 1849 which argues that no writer is strong enough to wake Michel: „Er [Michel] hat aber 1870 bewiesen, dass alles einmal, auch sein Schlaf und seine Geduld ein Ende habe, er hat gezeigt, dass er, wenn er zur rechten Zeit und auf die rechte Weise geweckt wird, aufzustehen und den ihm gebührenden Platz einzunehmen weiß" (III, 654).

[66] Although the Third Reich consciously replaced Michel with their own Nordic hero, their use of the slogan „Deutschland, erwache!" and their designation of their own party as „Die Bewegung" played upon this long tradition. Despite their stress on motion, the National Socialists did embrace a false ideal of stillness: first, they contrasted Germanic *Ruhe* with the restlessness and rootlessness of the hated Jew; second, silence, obedience, and injustice were essential ingredients of the *Ruhe und Ordnung* of National Socialism. In this context see Ernst Ottwald's anti-free corps novel *Ruhe und Ordnung*.

ruhig" (II, 681)., Here characteristics of the German Michel invade even the realm of rulers. The Germans awakened briefly during the Wars of Liberation, but soon thereafter the lethargic spirit of the Restoration pervaded the air: „überall Stagnation, Lethargie und Gähnen" (II, 678). Even the watchmen were still: „Die Wächter des Volks, ihre goldenen Nachtmützen tief über die Ohren gezogen, und tief eingehüllt in Schlafröcken von Hermelin, saßen auf roten Polsterstühlen, und schliefen ebenfalls, und schnarchten sogar" (III, 209). Heine boasts that during this time his book of travel pictures awakened „den deutschen Geist aus seiner Schlafsucht" (II, 683), but he knows that his claim covers only a limited group of intellectuals. In fact he mocks the many readers who, aware of Heine's politics, ask him not to disturb their tranquillity: „Willst du nicht mit uns träumen, so wecke uns wenigstens nicht aus dem süßen Schlafe" (II, 650). With each wave of revolution Heine's hope for progress is subtley awakened, but his voice is loudest and clearest when he mocks Germany's habitual fall into somnolence, first after the Wars of Liberation, then again after 1830 and 1848.

Heine's critique of German somnolence encompasses three areas. First, Heine is critical of the concept of slow regeneration, which remains prominent from Herder to Menzel. Conservatives employ this ideology of interiority as a subterfuge for repression and indolence. Second, Heine attacks sleeping and dreaming, metaphors for the German flight from political and social consciousness. Goethe, the Romantics, even the Idealists obliterate distinctions and adopt an attitude of indifference toward the everyday. Finally, Heine's critique of German passivity and somnolence includes numerous ironic jabs at the German Michel, ignorant of problems and passively pushed about by clerics and rulers. Unaware that current inadequacies are contingent, not necessary, the Germans live a life of stasis and false repose.

That Heine's position is not exhausted with an account of this criticism is suggested, first, by Heine's occasionally earnest praise of German depth in dreaming, i.e., philosophical speculation, vis-à-vis French superficiality.[67] Second, despite his frequent admonishment of German „Langsamkeit" (V, 510), Heine does argue in one passage of *Lutetia* that progress requires time; it cannot be rushed. He uses a medical metaphor to suggest that the realization of freedom „bedarf auch der Tausendmischerei des Apothekers, der Sorgfalt der Wärterin, er bedarf der Ruhe, er bedarf der Zeit" (V, 461). Heine, with his complex desire for and fear of revolution equivocates on the central question of how a country, specifically Germany, might best

---

[67] See esp. II, 87; III, 577; IV, 499; and V, 510.

develop.[68] Third, Heine refers, self-ironically, to his own dreaming. In the second book of *Ludwig Börne. Eine Denkschrift* he dreams that he is waking the Germans from their sleep; in this passage, however, Heine too is asleep (IV, 55). While the dream may represent a wish-fulfillment, it also implies an interesting self-critique: Heine, the poet, is an intellectual, a critic, in his own metaphor nothing more than a slumbering dreamer.

Political Quietude and Aesthetic Motion in Heine's *Zeitgedichte*

In 1844 Heine, openly committed to an art that focuses on the everyday and the political, published 24 poems under the rubric *Zeitgedichte* as part of his *Neue Gedichte*. A *Zeitgedicht* generally makes reference to a contemporary figure or event;[69] it can easily become outdated and require editorial commentary. The poems are geared for immediate effect. In his *Zeitgedichte* Heine turns from the abstract and speculative concerns of idealist literature, in which the particular is seen primarily as a moment in the whole,[70] to a concern with the particular in and of itself. The particular and the temporal *(die Zeit)* take on increased importance. For Heine the artist should deal with real, contemporary problems; in this way he can help move history forwards.

Heine's *Zeitgedichte* remain interesting today in part because they shed light on basic attitudes and problems that transcend the Germany of the 1830s and 40s. Heine was not a party politician; he was a poet interested in broad social issues such as emancipation and justice. In addition, Heine adopts an ironic stance that raises his poems above the level of political pamphlet and makes them both aesthetically and intellectually interesting. Instead of offering an emotional plea for a particular cause, Heine awakens thought.

One can divide the themes of the *Zeitgedichte* into three broad categories: the essence of good political poetry; the injustice of Germany's ruling elite; and the servility of the German population.[71] In his *Zeitgedichte* Heine defines the significance of political poetry (1, 23), admonishes those poets who don't meet his standards (8), and attacks the various weaknesses of nature lyricism (8, 13), false optimism (6, 12, 15), and vague generalization (13). In addition, Heine's *Zeitgedichte* contain a critique of the personalities and policies of

---

[68] Cf. Bodi (1971).
[69] Concerning the term „Zeitgedicht" see Wilke (1974). On Heine's *Zeitgedichte* see esp. Hasubeck (1972) and Hinck (1978).
[70] See WL I, 145.
[71] Subsequent numbers in this paragraph refer to the specific *Zeitgedichte*.

Germany's ruling elite. The poems address such topics as Frederick William IV (16, 17), restrictions on freedom in contemporary Prussia (2, 12, 24), implicit and explicit censorship (3, 6, 14), French vs. German forms of justice (6, 7), clerical repression (3, 9), religious persecution (11), and poverty and hunger (11, 22). Finally, the poet admonishes the political quietude of the Germans in the form of interiority or withdrawal (1, 4, 19, 20), resignation (19, 22), and servility (6, 15, 20). Each of the three general themes of the *Zeitgedichte* relates to the overriding topic of political quietude: Heine would negate the tyrannic *Ruhe* of the princes and clerics as well as set for the poet the program of awakening the Germans from their servile and apathetic attitude toward this oppression. We see these themes already in „Doktrin", the poem that introduces Heine's *Zeitgedichte*.

„Doktrin"

Doktrin

Schlage die Trommel und fürchte dich nicht,
und küße die Marketenderin!
Das ist die ganze Wissenschaft,
Das ist der Bücher tiefster Sinn.

Trommle die Leute aus dem Schlaf,
Trommle Reveille mit Jugendkraft,
Marschiere trommelnd immer voran,
Das ist die ganze Wissenschaft.

Das ist die Hegelsche Philosophie,
Das ist der Bücher tiefster Sinn!
Ich hab sie begriffen, weil ich gescheit,
Und weil ich ein guter Tambour bin. (IV, 412)

„Doktrin" consists of three stanzas, each with four lines. All but the final two lines are either imperatives (1, 2, 5, 6, 7) or statements beginning with „Das ist..." (3, 4, 8, 9, 10); the suggestion throughout is that the poet's imperatives capture the essence of Hegelian philosophy. Adding structural unity to the poem, the penultimate line of stanza one recurs in the penultimate stanza, while the first stanza's final line is repeated in the poem's final stanza. It is not clear whether the imperatives are addressed by the poet to himself and thus function as an internal definition of his task in the *Zeitgedichte* or whether, as is frequent in the poems that follow, the poet is addressing someone else, in this case the reader, who should grasp with ease the core of idealist philosophy and thus enjoy sensual delights as well as help awaken the sleeping populace to the call of progress. The programmatic tone of the poem, along with the poet's later definition of himself as a good drummer, supports the first of the two readings.

Sleep and hibernation function here as metaphors for the German indifference that blocks material progress. Drumming and, in the poem

„Wartet nur", thunder should awaken the sleeping Germans to the need for political action and progresss („Marschiere trommelnd immer voran"). The metaphor of drumming for engaged poetry revives the image of drumming from the seventh chapter of *Ideen. Das Buch le Grand* as a demonstration of the ideology of progress, i.e., the French Revolution, and, perhaps even more importantly, suggests, on the symbolic level, an awakening from sleep, slumber, and unawareness.[72] Heine suggests that idealist philosophy, in particular Hegel's, leads not to quietude and resignation, but to activity, even sensual enjoyment. „Doktrin" is a revely of progress, power, and sensualism. As Heine suggests in *Zur Geschichte der Religion und Philosophie in Deutschland* and his *Briefe über Deutschland*, the revolutionary essence of idealist philosophy denies spiritualist otherworldliness and attempts to create a better life in the present. Hegel's dictum „Alles was ist ist vernünftig" becomes for Heine „Alles was vernünftig ist muß sein" (V, 197).[73]

The poet's „Doktrin" suggests that drumming captures the *entire* essence of Hegel's philosophy („die ganze Wissenschaft", „der Bücher tiefsten Sinn"). As such the poem might be read as a criticism of Hegel – to the effect that if his system is exhausted in this simple program, it can't be worth a great deal. Or, one might turn the statement back toward the speaker and suggest that the person is aware of the simplicity of his own advice and, given the speculative depth and encyclopedic breadth of Hegel's system, his naive interpretation of philosophy. In this reading, the poet becomes slightly ironic at the end of the poem. He calls himself „gescheit" and „ein guter Tambour" in an intentionally self-mocking tone.[74] Already in „Doktrin" we see then the primary moments of the *Zeitgedichte*: the critique of German quietude; the self-conscious turn from idealism to action; and the ironic, in part self-ironic, undertone.

„Wartet nur"

> Wartet nur
>
> Weil ich so ganz vorzüglich blitze,
> Glaubt Ihr, daß ich nicht donnern könnt!
> Ihr irrt Euch sehr, denn ich besitze
> Gleichfalls fürs Donnern ein Talent.

---

[72] Heine's appeal to drumming is not without influence. Besides the obvious example of Oskar in Grass' *Die Blechtrommel*, one thinks of Kattrin in Brecht's *Mutter Courage*. For the critic they might be said to represent Heine's ambiguous and heroic-idealistic "voices".

[73] Heine's quote is not exact. The famous passage reads: „Was vernünftig ist, das ist wirklich; / und was wirklich ist, das ist vernünftig" (Hegel 7, 24).

[74] Mayer (1951) and Reeves (1974: 144) read the entire poem without irony. Hinck (1978: 19–21) speaks of unintentional irony.

> Es wird sich grausenhaft bewähren,
> Wenn einst erscheint der rechte Tag;
> Dann sollt Ihr meine Stimme hören,
> Das Donnerwort, den Wetterschlag.
>
> Gar manche Eiche wird zersplittern
> An jenem Tag der wilde Sturm,
> Gar mancher Palast wird erzittern
> und stürzen mancher Kirchenturm! (IV, 431)

In the context of Heine's doctrine of drumming, we can turn briefly to the poem that, with the exception of the biographical „Denk ich an Deutschland in der Nacht", closes Heine's cluster of *Zeitgedichte*, „Wartet nur". No small number of Heine's works have been interpreted as inversions of texts by Goethe;[75] here, too, we see Heine mocking a work of Goethe's, specifically his famous „Wanderers Nachtlied":[76]

> Über allen Gipfeln
> Ist Ruh,
> In allen Wipfeln
> Spürest du
> Kaum einen Hauch;
> Die Vögelein schweigen im Walde.
> Warte nur, balde
> Ruhest du auch. (HA I, 142)

Goethe's poem leads the listener toward an identification with nature marked by tranquillity, perhaps even death. Directed to an individual, the poem invites withdrawal. Heine's poem, on the other hand, is social; his imperative is set in the second person plural. Moreover, the poems differ in their relationships to repose, nature, and poetry. Goethe's nature is idyllic; Heine's is revolutionary. Goethe's poet soothes the reader, lulling him/her to sleep; Heine threatens to disturb the peace, not just with drumming but with thunder and ultimately with the destruction of palace and church tower.

Here too, however, the poem is so bombastic it ironizes itself. Consider in this context a comparison with „Die Tendenz", where Heine parodies the tendentious poetry of his contemporaries.[77] Stanza one is, first, too hymnic in its tone, then, too mechanical in its rhyme:

---

[75] See Hermand (1976) and Spencer (1973).
[76] See Wikoff (1975), 69. Besides the intertextual quote and Heine's pattern of inversion, two additional arguments support this reading: first, Goethe's works are mentioned in another *Zeitgedicht* „Die Tendenz" and are criticized for their idyllic tone („Girre nicht mehr wie ein Werther, / Welcher nur für Lotten glüht – / […] Sei nicht mehr die weiche Flöte, / Das idyllische Gemüt –" IV, 422–23); second, *Ruhe* plays a significant role in not only Goethe's poem but the *Zeitgedichte* as a whole.
[77] IV, 422–23. Wikoff (1975) misreads „Die Tendenz" when he takes it as a serious guide to political poetry and reads it without irony. His suggestion that "poetry

> Deutscher Sänger! sing und preise
> Deutsche Freiheit, daß dein Lied
> Unsrer Seelen sich bemeistre
> Und zu Taten uns begeistre,
> In Marseillerhymnenweise.

The penultimate stanza passes into the final one with these exaggerated and ridiculous lines:

> Sei des Vaterlands Posaune,
> Sei Kanone, sei Kartaune,
> Blase, schmettre, donnre, töte!
> Blase, schmettre, donnre täglich,
> Bis der letzte Dränger flieht –

„Wartet nur" shares with „Die Tendenz" the figure of hyperbole. Both poems show Heine mocking his own role and power as a political poet. While criticizing tendentious poetry, the aristocracy, and the church, he also invites self-criticism. Instead of trying to overpower his readers with propaganda, Heine invites reflection and criticism.

„Bei des Nachtwächters Ankunft zu Paris"

> Bei des Nachtwächters Ankunft zu Paris
>
> „Nachtwächter mit langen Fortschrittsbeinen,
> Du kommst so verstört einhergerannt!
> Wie geht es daheim den lieben Meinen,
> Ist schon befreit das Vaterland!"
>
> Vortrefflich geht es, der stille Segen,
> Er wuchert im sittlich gehüteten Haus,
> Und ruhig und sicher, auf friedlichen Wegen,
> Entwickelt sich Deutschland von innen heraus.
>
> Nicht oberflächlich wie Frankreich blüht es,
> Wo Freiheit das äußere Leben bewegt;
> nur in der Tiefe des Gemütes
> Ein deutscher Mann die Freiheit trägt.
>
> Der Dom zu Cöllen wird vollendet,
> Den Hohenzollern verdanken wir das;
> Habsburg hat auch dazu gespendet,
> Ein Wittelsbach schickt Fensterglas.
>
> Die Konstitution, die Freiheitsgesetze,
> Sie sind uns versprochen, wir haben das Wort,
> Und Königsworte, das sind Schätze,
> Wie tief im Rhein der Niblungshort.

should be kept *somewhat general* to avoid being censored" does not accord with Heine's *ironic* proposal to keep poetry *as general as possible* („so allgemein als möglich") (68, emphasis added).

Der freie Rhein, der Brutus der Flüsse,
Es wird uns nimmermehr geraubt!
Die Holländer binden ihm die Füße,
Die Schwyzer halten fest sein Haupt.

Auch eine Flotte will Gott uns bescheren,
Die patriotische Überkraft
Wird lustig rudern auf deutschen Galeeren;
Die Festungsstrafe wird abgeschafft.

Es blüht der Lenz, es platzen die Schoten,
Wir atmen frei in der freien Natur!
Und wird uns der ganze Verlag verboten,
So schwindet am Ende von selbst die Zensur.

(IV, 415–16)

„Bei des Nachtwächters Ankunft zu Paris" is an ironic poem that deals in unmistakeable ways with political quietude. It begins with a question from the poet, followed by a lengthy response from the night watchman.[78] The poet addresses the night watchman as having a sense for progress („mit langen Fortschrittsbeinen"). While the watchman calls out the hours of the night – in a metaphorical sense the years from 1815 – he also points toward the morning awakening, when a new societal structure should appear. Rather than stressing this preparation for a new morning, Heine emphasizes in the course of the poem the eternal night of Germany. The reference to the night watchman's motion might lead the reader to think that he is full of energy and optimism, but Heine's contemporaries would have noticed the irony in this line. The poet's question concerning the freedom of the fatherland addresses the status of the very country from which the night watchman Dingelstedt is fleeing („verstört einhergerannt") to avoid the consequences of the publication of his verse. In answering the question, the poet adopts the voice of the night watchman; he praises, effusively and ironically, his countrymen's morality, piety, tranquil development, depth, freedom, and promising future.

The poet, employing the rhetorical figure of *simultatio*, assumes the position he would undermine – an ironic act that would help him avoid the censor (Why should anyone prohibit such demonstrative praise of Germany?) and allows him to present an immanent critique of his opponents' position. The poet takes the antithetical position to its extreme and demonstrates its internal inadequacies. We see irony in the diction of the poem. The watchman praises parochial Biedermeier values („der stille Segen / Er

---

[78] The poet Dingelstedt, the person behind the fictive night watchman, came to Paris in the fall of 1841 to avoid the consequences of his politically volatile work, *Lieder eines kosmopolitischen Nachtwächters*, which was just appearing with Hoffmann and Campe. See Bayerdörfer (1976), 78–79 and (1978), 16–17, 69, 228. The first section of Dingelstedt's *Lieder*, „Stilleben", includes a critique of German stillness.

wuchert im sittlich gehüteten Haus"). The verb „wuchern", obviously comical in this context, has essentially three meanings: to grow beyond control or be rampant, as for example weeds;[79] to profiteer or practice usury; and to develop a capacity to the utmost. Obviously, the third meaning is "intended" here, but the two other associations remain in the foreground; indeed, they suggest that the Germans are trying to get more mileage out of their religious stillness than can be had. The idea of a morally guarded house, also a mocking phrase, suggests that the standards of morality are imposed and artificial.

Germany is peaceful and is developing internally but also fully, whereas France's already attained freedom is of a merely superficial sort. Though Heine expresses in his writings a fear of public disorder and revolutionary chaos as well as a view of France as superficial,[80] the praise of German depth in this poem is undercut. In the context of the final two lines („Und wird uns der ganze Verlag verboten, / So schwindet am Ende von selbst die Zensur") external freedom is indeed important. Without it even inner intellectual development becomes impossible. The poet mocks German freedom earlier in the poem as well. Being purely verbal, German freedom is more superficial than the French variety. The Germans salute the mere promise of a constitution and blindly await reform. Like the buried and unattainable treasure of the Nibelungen, the imperial promise of a constitution will not be fulfilled.[81] The poet's praise of German depth („Tiefe des Gemüts") is subverted when likened to the depth of the lost Nibelungen treasure („tief im Rhein"). Finally, the rhyme „blüht es / Gemütes" presents German depth in an ironic light. Similarity in sound contrasts with dissimilarity in meaning. The rhyme is superficial; the levels of discourse are incongruous. As we later recognize, the German spirit will not blossom. The concept of German freedom is undercut, therefore, not only by diction but also by relativizing content (the final 2 lines), undermining parallelism (the repetition of "tief"), and comic rhyme.

---

[79] In figurative use as well the verb is primarily associated with negative objects. Especially frequent according to Grimm are „anwendungen auf unliebsame Verhaltensweisen, die in einer gemeinschaft überhand nehmen" (*Deutsches Wörterbuch*, XIV/2, 1713). Heine uses the verb, as far as I can tell, only with negative connotations. See V, 507; VI/1, 103; and VI/1, 616.
[80] On Heine's fear of revolution see II, 660; III: 172–73, 638–41; IV: 75–79, 595, 639–40; V: 232, 405–07, 457; HSA XXII: 276, 288. On his view of French superficiality see II, 87; III, 577; IV, 499; V, 510.
[81] Promises of a constitution and representative government had been made by Frederick William III during the Wars of Liberation. Many expected Frederick William IV to fulfill his father's pledge after ascending to the throne in 1840. He did not.

The watchman moves within the poem from one variation on freedom and the state of the fatherland to another. In stanza 4 he reports on the Cologne cathedral. From other texts of this period, *Atta Troll* and *Deutschland. Ein Wintermärchen*, we are familiar with the poet's belief – whether genuine or rhetorical – that the cathedral will not be completed.[82] From the external context then, but also from the pattern of ironic undercutting already established, the Cologne cathedral becomes a symbol of Germany's unfinished nature, its development without fruition. Silent blessings may proliferate in Germany but not completed deeds. The references to the various leaders who have contributed to the building effort (Emperor Frederick William IV of Prussia, Emperor Ferdinand I of Austria, and King Ludwig I of Bavaria) underscore the kind of unity Germany enjoys – financial, symbolic, spiritual, not legislative.[83] German unity is on the superficial level of a building. One thinks ahead to the cutting remarks in Caput 2 of the *Wintermärchen* that only the German *Zollverein* and the censor unify Germany.

The poet's reference to the free Rhine plays on Nikolaus Becker's patriotic „Der deutsche Rhein" of 1840. The watchman imitates the patriotic voice in comical fashion with his personification of the Rhine („Füße" and „Haupt") and the silly image that to steal the Rhine means not to change territorial borders but to move the river itself. Moreover, if one does take the image literally, it adds force to the suggestion that the quiet Germans have no control over their fate. If the Rhine stays in German hands, one can thank not the Germans but the Swiss and the Dutch. Finally, the suggestion that the Rhine is being bound inverts a traditional symbol, still prominent in Heine's day, whereby rivers are symbolic of freedom, revolution, and progress.[84] In holding the river fast, the Germans exhibit a stagnant nationalism and inhibit progress. Their chauvanistic nationalism blocks them from cultivating, or even envisaging, progressive, universal values.

The water of the Rhine and the nationalism of Becker's song take the watchman to the next image, a German naval fleet. The fleet is for Heine indicative, like the cathedral, of misplaced energy – Prussia should be building a parliament not a cathedral or a naval fleet – and of the military and commercial nationalism that Heine would like to see replaced with an

---

[82] See the preface to *Atta Troll*, where Heine lists the Cologne cathedral *and* the Prussian Constitution among the great works of the Germans that were never completed (IV, 493). Cf. Caput 4 of *Deutschland. Ein Wintermärchen* (IV, 585–86).
[83] Cf. the variant of this stanza in the flyleaf printed in the spring of 1842: „‚Der Köllner Dom, des Glaubens Freude / Ein edler König baut ihn aus; / Das ist kein moedernes Chartengebäude, / Kein sündiges Deputirtenhaus'" (DHA 2, 704). The cathedral replaces the promise of a parliamentary building.
[84] See Jäger (1971), 20–22.

enlightened internationalism. The call for a navy is not informed by a progressive spirit: moving back in time, the Germans will turn the prisoners into galley slaves. In addition, the nationalists' belief in the development of a German navy as a means toward national unity is indicative of their false hopes.[85] As Heine's later poem „Unsere Marine" suggests, the navy operates only in the imagination of the nationalists, only as they sleep.[86]

In the final stanza Heine ridicules German nature lyricism: „Es blüht der Lenz, es platzen die Schoten, / Wir atmen frei in der freien Natur!" While in stanza 3 „blüht es" refers to *French freedom*, in stanza 8 „Es blüht" refers to the *German spring*. The belief that nature, not ideals or institutions, makes us free is undercut of course by the final reference to the censor. The repetition of „frei" (first as an adverb, then as an adjective) in the same sentence strikes the reader as ironically forced as well. In addition, the rhymes are comical. Similarity in sound once again contrasts with dissimilarity in meaning. The two images of natural freedom („die Schoten", „der freien Natur") are jarringly paired with two words that convey the negation of freedom („verboten", „die Zensur"). Heine's critique can also be seen it its broader perspective. In the late eighteenth and early nineteenth century spring symbolized not only warmth, motion, and new life but revolution, while winter was the coldness and stillness of reactionary force. Hölderlin speaks of „die eiskalte Zone des Despotismus" (StA VI, 92/no. 65); Anastasius Grün writes: „Winter ist ein Erzdespote" (II, 351); Freiligrath refers to the „Winterfrost der Tyrannei" (II, 94); and Herwegh writes: „Frühling nie für den Despot" (35). In spring the frozen ice melts into rivers and streams; it thus becomes transformed into the symbols of progress. For Heine the use of spring as a metaphor for revolution is suspect: first, because the revolution is not as inevitable as the change of seasons; second, because the Germans tend to view the symbols as ends in themselves. In „An Georg Herwegh" Heine criticizes the false optimism and nature lyricism of the German liberals:[87]

---

[85] Cf. Wollstein (1977), 255–65.
[86] „Wir träumten so schön, wir hatten fast / Schon eine Seeschlacht gewonnen – / Doch als die Morgensonne kam, / Ist Traum und Flotte zerronnen" (IV, 464).
[87] In „Entartung", too, the new spring, which has now become routine, is suspect (IV, 418). The speaker refuses to adopt the positive view of nature, yet he fails to invert the pathetic fallacy. Nature is not soulless; it is morally bad. The speaker would seem to be ironized here, especially as one considers Heine's reckoning with the pathetic fallacy in his *Nordsee* poems. It is possible, however, that the sentiments are genuine; as such they would show that Heine's negation of Romanticism is only partial.

> Herwegh, du eiserne Lerche,
> Mit klirrendem Jubel steigst du empor
> Zum heilgen Sonnenlichte!
> Ward wirklich der Winter zu nichte?
> Steht wirklich Deutschland im Frühlingsflor?
>
> Herwegh, du eiserne Lerche,
> Weil du so himmelhoch dich schwingst,
> Hast du die Erde aus dem Gesichte
> Verloren – Nur in deinem Gedichte
> Lebt jener Lenz den du besingst. (IV, 485–86)

Herwegh, like the other poets targeted earlier in „Die Tendenz", is blind to political realities and continues to believe in simple, natural, historical progress.[88] These optimistic heralds of newness („Ist schon befreit das Vaterland?") are left with nothing but the change in seasons. For Heine nature and history or nature and man evolve in different, unrelated spheres. In one revealing passage he speaks of „eine fast ironische Ruhe der Natur, die von den Qualnissen der Menschenseele keine Notiz genommen hat und nach wie vor grünt und blüht" (HSA XXIII, 92). The final line of Heine's poem underscores the German inability to recognize real problems: they could get rid of the censor but don't notice that the price would be the elimination of the condition for the need of a censor, i. e., the freedom of publishing houses to publish.[89]

Heine's poem moves from one theme to the next, but not without preparation. Each strophe introduces the theme for the next:

Stanza	Content
1–2	The question ‚Is Germany *free*?' elicits the response ‚Germany is *internally free*.'
2–3	Germany's *internal* development is associated with *depth*.
3–4	Praise of German *depth* is mocked by the *superficial* unity of the *cathedral*.
4–5	The *cathedral* (misplaced interests), *superficiality* (mere words), and *depth* (the sunken hoard in the *Rhine*, unfulfilled promises) prevent the introduction of a constitution.
5–6	The *Rhine river* is taken as a motto for *nationalism*.

---

[88] Heine's writings were not open to this charge, for his political verse was wholly negative, without a projected utopia. See Sammons (1978).

[89] A historical situation lies behind the final two lines. All the books of the Hoffmann and Campe publishing house were banned by the Prussian government from December 1841 to June 1842. The immediate causes were the publication of Hoffmann's *Unpolitische Lieder* and Dingelstedt's *Lieder eines kosmopolitischen Nachtwächters*. See Galley (1958), 105.

6–7 The Germans express their *nationalism* through *ocean* ships and galley *slaves*.
7–8 *Nature* takes the place of German *freedom*.

Adding a circular structure to the poem, the first and final stanzas discuss the central theme of freedom. This circular structure symbolizes Germany's lack of progress; one speaks incessantly about freedom without ever moving forward.

Like much of Heine „Bei des Nachtwächters Ankunft zu Paris" is negative. No solutions are offered, yet the reader is invited to see the problematic aspects of Biedermeier insularity, nationalist illiberalism, and *Vormärz* optimism, and to question the premises of the German *Innigkeitsideologie*, the obsession with private over public happiness, the praise of tranquillity over conflict, and the overriding blindness to essential issues. The poem, constructed in the form of question and answer, invites the reader to adopt the role of night watchman and reflect on conditions in Germany. The poem, communicative in nature, does not rest in itself; it transcends its own artistic boundaries and turns to its readers.[90]

„Zur Beruhigung"

Zur Beruhigung

Wir schlafen ganz, wie Brutus schlief –
Doch jener erwachte und bohrte tief
In Cäsars Brust das kalte Messer!
Die Römer waren Tyrannenfresser.

Wir sind keine Römer, wir rauchen Tabak.
Ein jedes Volk hat seinen Geschmack.
Ein jedes Volk hat seine Größe;
In Schwaben kocht man die besten Klöße.

Wir sind Germanen, gemütlich und brav,
Wir schlafen gesunden Pflanzenschlaf,
Und wenn wir erwachen, pflegt uns zu dürsten,
Doch nicht nach dem Blute unserer Fürsten.

Wir sind so treu wie Eichenholz,
Auch Lindenholz, drauf sind wir stolz;
Im Land der Eichen und der Linden
Wird niemals sich ein Brutus finden.

Und wenn auch ein Brutus unter uns wär,
Den Cäsar fänd er nimmermehr,
Vergeblich würd er den Cäsar suchen;
Wir haben gute Pfefferkuchen.

---

[90] Cf. Hasubeck (1972), 35.

> Wir haben sechsunddreißig Herrn
> (Ist nicht zu viel!), und einen Stern
> Trägt jeder schützend auf seinem Herzen,
> Und er braucht nicht zu fürchten die Iden des Märzen.
>
> Wir nennen sie Väter, und Vaterland
> Benennen wir dasjenige Land,
> Das erbeigentümlich gehört den Fürsten;
> Wir lieben auch Sauerkraut mit Würsten.
>
> Wenn unser Vater spazieren geht,
> Ziehn wir den Hut mit Pietät;
> Deutschland, die fromme Kinderstube,
> Ist keine römische Mördergrube. (IV, 428–29)

The title of „Zur Beruhigung", another poem focusing on German quietude, is ironic; rather than inducing docile tranquility, the poem activates the reader's critical abilities, awakens him or her to contemporary problems, and encourages – at least indirectly – activist politics.

Heine likes to play with contrasts. In „Bei des Nachtwächters Ankunft zu Paris" the poet compared Germany and France. Here the Germans are likened to the Romans, specifically Brutus;[91] the German lords, meanwhile, are compared with Caesar. Almost as soon as the poet proposes these parallels, however, he undercuts them. The revolutionary Romans were „Tyrannenfresser"; the placid Germans are literal eaters, concerned with filling their bellies. There are, moreover, no German princes as grand as Caesar (stanza 5).

The poet, speaking in the first person plural, identifies with the Germans and praises them for their cordiality, quietude, loyalty, and of course their cooking. A typical Heine technique of irony through association is at work here. By juxtaposing German virtues as well as German sovereigns with the mundane world of tobacco,[92] dumplings, and sauerkraut, the poet undermines his own praise. He adds force to the irony by introducing comical rhymes. The „Größe / Klöße" rhyme (stanza 2) jolts the reader's initial expectation for something exalted.[93] While the Romans' actual thirst for tyrant's blood is expressed in the one compound „Tyrannenfresser", German

---

[91] The allusion in line 1 is to Shakespeare's *Julius Caesar*: "Brutus, thou sleep'st; awake!" (II, i, 48).
[92] „Tabakspfeife" belongs, much like the „Zipfelmütze", to the Philistine image of the German Michel. Heine writes: „Der öftere Regierungswechsel in Frankreich ist nicht bloß eine Nachwirkung der Revolution, sondern auch ein Ergebnis des Nationalcharakters der Franzosen, denen das Handeln, die Tätigkeit, die Bewegung, ein ebenso großes Bedürfnis ist, wie uns Deutschen das Tabaksrauchen, das stille Denken und die Gemütsruhe" (V, 423). See also IV, 589; HSA XXII, 19; and Glaßbrenner, *Unterm Brennglas*, 249.
[93] See also Hinck (1978), 24.

eating habits are linked to their „Fürsten" only by rhyme: „dürsten" and, especially comical and not without influence, „Würsten".[94] This eating imagery shows that Heine's sensualism is not one-sided. Heine tempers his usually enthusiastic affirmation of material well-being wherever material concerns undermine moral development or social justice. True sensualism still recognizes the supremacy of the spirit.[95] Just as the poem's literal extension of the eating imagery indicates irony, so too do further rhymes, especially the intentionally awkward internal rhyme in stanza 4: „Wir sind so treu wie Eichenholz, / Auch Lindenholz, drauf sind wir stolz." The poet behind the mask is obviously all but proud of German loyalty and subservience.

Both the form and content of the poem are comic. The comic content derives from the discrepancy between the ideal (the poet's praise of the Germans) and the real (the reader's awareness, via his/her ironic reading, of Germany's problems). The comic form functions through the incongruity between finite content (two words or concepts that don't accord) and finite form (the forced harmony and connectedness of the rhyme itself).

The first line of the poem refers to German somnolence. The poet extends this motif in stanza 3 when he writes: „Wir sind Germanen gemütlich und brav, / Wir schlafen gesunden Pflanzenschlaf." The ironic image refers in general to German quietude and servility, specifically to the organic metaphor, prominent from Herder to Menzel, of a country that is evolving, slowly but surely, toward a great future. Heine questions the idea of inner evolution. When the Germans awake, they are ready for not democracy but another drink: „Und wenn wir erwachen, pflegt uns zu dürsten, / Doch nicht nach dem Blute unserer Fürsten."

Heine's suggestion that no Caesar exists in Germany has been taken to mean that Germany is without powerful or repressive lords, thus no Brutus is necessary.[96] Since Germany has no dangerous lords, any call for revolution

---

[94] Consider Johannes Scherr's rhyme in „Des armen Michel's Lebenslauf. Teutsches Heldengedicht in sechs Klageliedern" (1845). The passage follows a contrast between Michel, whose faith is in the beyond, and the heroes of other nations, whose development is here on earth: „Ich blieb der Michel und ging nach Haus und legte mich auf den Glauben; / Denn weil mir die irdischen hingen zu hoch, so schielt' ich nach himmlischen Trauben. / So bracht' ich das Mittelalter herum, gehorsam Gott und dem Fürsten, / Den einen Hang verspürend nur, nach Sauerkraut und Würsten." Cited in Wander, III, 654.

[95] In *Zur Geschichte der Religion und Philosophie in Deutschland* Heine writes that sensualism strives for „ein Rehabilitieren der Materie [...] ohne die Rechte des Geistes, ja nicht einmal ohne die Supremacie des Geistes zu leugnen" (III, 556). It would be course be impossible to argue the reverse position coherently, i. e., the supremacy of matter over spirit.

[96] The comment that Germany is without a Caesar surfaces again in IV, 25.

would be foolish.[97] I would read stanza 5, however, to be saying simply that the German princes lack the grandeur of Caesar. There is not one great prince but 36 little ones, all of whom are associated with the mundane world of „Pfefferkuchen". Roman despotism is for Heine monumental. Consider the lines in Caput 11 of *Deutschland. Ein Wintermärchen*, where Germany is again contrasted with Rome: „Wir hätten Einen Nero jetzt / Statt Landesväter drei Dutzend" (IV, 602). What is lacking is not oppression but worldhistorical importance. For Heine Caesar ranks with Moses, Pythagoras, Plato, Christ, and Napoleon as one of the „große Männer" of all time (VI/1, 508). Though a Brutus might still be useful, Germany will never find one; the Germans are, as Heine and his contemporaries never cease to insist, too loyal.

The „Eiche", until the Napoleonic wars symbolic of freedom,[98] is now in Heine's poem the reverse, a symbol of German loyalty passing over into subservience and servility. In another inversion, here combined with a play on words,[99] the poet speaks of his lords as „Väter", then calls the country where they rule „Vaterland", a word that contained at the time opposite connotations: a fatherland was a land in which one was free.[100] In the next line Heine delivers yet another play on words: he writes that the country belongs to the princes „erbeigentümlich". Heine's adverb is composed from „Erbeigentum", meaning inherited property, and „eigentümlich", meaning (with penultimate stress) peculiar, strange, or odd. While feigning praise of the homeland and its monarchical system, the poet lets his critique shine through.

We have seen Heine's irony in his motifs, his internal and forced rhymes, his inversions, and his puns. Heine's diction adds to this irony. The poet praises the Germans for their religious and political holiness. Germany is credited with being a pious nursery home („fromme Kinderstube"), a remarkable and of course subversive image, which further develops Heine's pun on the words „Väter" and „Vaterland". The irony underscores the inadequacies of Germany's pious and naive acceptance of authoritarian rule; nonetheless, the alternative offered in the poem, open revolution, is nowhere explicitly embraced. Indeed, as Walter Hinck (1978) has argued (24), the ideal connotations of revolution are undercut through the literalization of the

---

[97] See Hinck (1978), 25.
[98] See Jäger (1971), 38. Cf. IV, 58: „Werden wir endlich von unseren Eichenwäldern den rechten Gebrauch machen, nämlich zu Barrikaden für die Befreiung der Welt?"
[99] The pun is not unique to Heine. Glaßbrenner writes in „Die Väter": „Mein Vaterland, mein Vaterland. / Du hast zu viele Väter!" (*Verbotene Lieder*, 74–75).
[100] See Bertaux (1974), 20, 52, 125 and Heinrich Mann (1977), 78.

motif of eating, which calls into question the specific concept of „Tyrannenfresser".[101] In addition, a „Mördergrube" is hardly an ideal alternative to a „Kinderstube". The poem ends, negatively, without a suitable solution. The two poems just analyzed present two extremes of German insularity. In „Bei des Nachtwächters Ankunft zu Paris" the Germans are not materialistic enough; they are concerned only with the spiritual, ethereal. In „Zur Beruhigung" the Germans are involved in petty, private, material activities; they are obsessed with good food and show no concern for moral development or social justice.[102] In either case they avoid direct political activity and sink back into a stance of quietude. Jeffrey Sammons (1969) makes an apt criticism of Heine's political poems insofar as they do not move beyond direct insult or "private invective" (217). In fact, not only is the content suspect but so too are the origins. In „Enfant Perdu" the poet speaks of „die frechen Reime eines Spottgedichts" that originate not out of conviction or a sense of cause but rather from „Langweil" and „Furcht" (VI/1, 121). „Bei des Nachtwächters Ankunft zu Paris" and „Zur Beruhigung" transcend this situation. They serve not a private but an overarching purpose, they address general and significant themes, and they seek enlightenment.

Irony and Motion

With the exception of a poem like „Die schlesischen Weber" Heine's political poetry does not aim at manipulation via emotional identification. Instead of overwhelming the readers and inviting them to suspend their critical perspectives, Heine's political poetry is ironic; it appeals to the intellect. The readers, already critical of the text's explicit message, are encouraged to become equally critical observers of political events.

---

[101] Hinck (1978), 24.
[102] Glaßbrenner makes a similar critique of the Austrians in 1836. He criticizes Austria's „absolute Ruhe" and calls the country „ein schlafender Riese", removed in century long sleep from the two revolutions of the age: the political revolution, commencing in 1789, and the social reform of the immediate present. The reason for Austria's lethargy is its overriding materialism: „Das Allgemeine, der Gedanke werden von materiellem Genusse verdrängt [...] Die Fülle des Körpers erstickt das Leben des Geistes; Oesterreich ist ein dicker lustiger Pächter" (*Bilder und Träume aus Wien*, II: 167, 173). Büchner's even earlier analysis is again strikingly similar: „Seht die Östreicher, sie sind wohlgenährt und zufrieden! Fürst Metternich, der geschickteste unter allen, hat allen revolutionären Geist, der jemals unter ihnen aufkommen könnte, für immer in ihrem eigenen Fett erstickt" (*Werke und Briefe*, 463). Finally, even the idealist Schiller knew of the materialism that engenders political stasis. Consider Posa's critique of King Phillip's tactics of suppression in *Don Carlos* (III, 10). For an analysis see Simons (1969). Not only idealism but materialism, too, can lead to a false or deficient stillness.

With its irony, Heine's poems could be said to arouse motion in the reader: first, by inviting the reader to set himself and the work in motion by relating its various parts in an attempt to grasp its irony; second, by moving the reader, however indirectly, to political action. When confronted with an ironic text, the reader's critical faculties are set in motion. A dynamic relationship is awakened between text and reader, for he or she must work to decipher its underlying meaning. The reader relates the text's different parts and levels to one another and eventually moves from an explicit to an implicit meaning.[103] Not only the reader but the text, too, can be said to be in motion, for the meaning of the text is transformed in the reading process. In interpreting the text aesthetically, the reader uses, expands, and erases the immediate statement of the poem, what is said, to reconstruct what is meant. He/She makes connections that the poem suspends but simultaneously invites. In „Bei des Nachtwächters Ankunft zu Paris" and „Zur Beruhigung" the reader, attentive to diction, rhyme, parallelism, and historical allusion, translates praise of the fatherland into implicit criticism. In addition, the ironic text would move the reader to political action by awakening his/her consciousness of inadequacies in present governmental structures. Moreover, the reader becomes attentive to the reigning political psychology, in the case at hand, the passive psychology of acceptance, toleration, and quietude. The reader would discern in the poem a questioning of conventional linguistic and ideological norms, including, for example, the underlying ideal status of *Ruhe*, which Heine's poems attempt to dismantle.

The Critique of German *Ruhe* in *Deutschland. Ein Wintermärchen*

Heine's mock epic *Deutschland. Ein Wintermärchen*, originally published in 1844 together with his *Neue Gedichte* and thus with the *Zeitgedichte* analyzed above,[104] unites a number of themes already introduced in this chapter: aesthetic stillness, religious otherworldliness, somnolence, and German

---

[103] To be more precise, irony is not just the motion between two meanings, the literal and the ironic. It is also the stillness of one spatiotemporal statement that engenders a duplicity of statements and a shift in meaning. Irony represents another instance of dynamic stillness.

[104] While *Deutschland. Ein Wintermärchen* shares many themes with the *Zeitgedichte*, the reason for their publication together was in part external. By combining the texts Heine was able to produce a publication of over twenty signatures, i.e., 320 pages; smaller publications were subject to censorship before they appeared. Cf. Reisner (1975).

quietude.[105] Heine's work, an example of the new poetry with which he would counter aesthetic stillness of the *Kunstperiode*, opens with a battle of songs. Conceived as a kind of lullaby, the old song promises eternal bliss in an otherworldly sphere. The harp girl sings of renunciation, abnegation, and religious stillness: „das alte Entsagungslied, / Das Eiapopeia vom Himmel, / Womit man einlullt, wenn es greint, / Das Volk, den großen Lümmel" (IV, 577). She lulls the people to sleep, such that they lose sight of present problems and focus only on the timeless beyond. She sings of present sacrifice and future bliss, of „Aufopfrung und Wiederfinden / Dort oben, in jener besseren Welt, / Wo alle Leiden schwinden" (IV, 577). With her gaze directed toward the eternal beyond, the singer has a static view of the present. The very form with which the narrator summarizes the song suggests stagnation and tranquillity; he employs anaphora to introduce stanzas 5 through 7:

> Sie sang von Liebe und Liebesgram,
> [...]
> Sie sang vom irdischen Jammertal,
> [...]
> Sie sang das alte Entsagungslied,
> [...]
> (IV, 577)

The identical meter in these lines also suggests stasis. We find the otherwise rare occurrence of metrically identical verses once again in the closing lines of each of the above stanzas:[106]

> [...]
> Wo alle Leiden schwinden.
> [...]
> Verklärt in ewgen Wonnen.
> [...]
> Das Volk, den großen Lümmel.
> (IV, 577)

Instead of being interested in the movement of history, the harp girl, like the Germans, holds to outdated ideas, institutions, and forms. The narrator counters with a new song, the song of progress:

> Ein neues Lied, ein besseres Lied,
> O Freunde, will ich Euch dichten!
> Wir wollen hier auf Erden schon
> Das Himmelreich errichten. (IV, 578)

---

[105] For comprehensive analyses of Heine's *Wintermärchen* see Atkinson (1975); Hannah (1981); Kaufmann (1958); Loeben (1970); Prawer (1961), 103–29; and Sammons (1969), 291–300. Specific points are covered in the following interpretations: Brummack (1979), 166–96; Hermand (1979); Rose (1978); Woesler (1973); and Würffel (1977).
[106] See also Atkinson (1975), 186.

The new song, with its realization of heaven on earth, suggests both a new religion and a new god; in Caput 2 the narrator carries in his head „die Tempelkleinodien des neuen Gotts" (IV, 580). The theme of somnolence surfaces in *Deutschland. Ein Wintermärchen*, specifically in Caput 7, where the narrator discusses German featherbeds and German superiority in the airy realm of dreams.[107] He defines German freedom not as freedom toward a better world but as freedom from the existing world:

> Man schläft sehr gut und träumt auch gut
> In unseren Federbetten.
> Hier fühlt die deutsche Seele sich frei
> Von allen Erdenketten.
>
> Sie fühlt sich frei und schwingt sich empor
> Zu den höchsten Himmelsräumen.
> O deutsche Seele, wie stolz ist dein Flug
> In deinen nächtlichen Träumen! (IV, 592)

While the French and Russians hold the land, and the British rule the seas, the Germans remain peerless in the realm of fancy and flight:

> Franzosen und Russen gehört das Land,
> Das Meer gehört den Briten,
> Wir aber besitzen im Luftreich des Traums
> Die Herrschaft unbestritten. (IV, 592)

In a later draft for a French preface to the *Wintermärchen* Heine stresses the theme of German somnolence. The mock epic represents a counterpart to his „Briefe aus Helgoland", in which Germany momentarily wakes in response to the French Revolution of 1830. In the *Wintermärchen* Germany has once again fallen asleep. The poem portrays the country's lethargy and stagnation:

> Les pages suivantes forment la contre-partie des «Lettres d'Héligoland» où éclate le réveil politique de l'Allemagne à l'époque de la révolution de juillet. Elle s'est endormie de nouveau et la léthargie générale, la stagnation qui régna au delà du Rhin avant la révolution de février est dépeint dans ce poème humoristique que j'ai appelé «Germania, un conte d'hyver», et que je publie ici en prose française. (IV, 645)

---

[107] Heine offers in *Wintermärchen* an interesting variation on the motif of sleeping. After writing that one sleeps easily in Germany because the Germans are experts at sleeping, dreaming, and preparing feather beds (IV, 592), he finds in Caput 18 that he can't fall asleep, for he looks upon *red* damask curtains, a faded *gold* canopy, and a dirty *black* tassle, colors associated with Barbarossa and German nationalism: „Ging schlafen sogleich, doch schlief ich nicht, / Mich drückten so schwer die Decken. // Es war ein breites Federbett, Gardinen von rotem Damaste, / Der Himmel von verblichenem Gold, / Mit einem schmutzigen Quaste. // Verfluchter Quast! der die ganze Nacht / Die liebe Ruhe mir raubte!" (IV, 618). In the face of nationalism Heine cannot sleep, i.e., remain quiet.

Germany relapsed into a deep slumber, where it snores as once before: «Au bruit du tocsin de juillet, l'Allemagne s'était éveillée en sursaut, mais elle ne manqua pas de retomber dans un sommeil profond, et elle ronfla même comme autrefois» (IV, 645). Heine's epic uncovers his country's deficiencies, most of which relate in one way or another to political quietude. By stressing Germany's faults rather than celebrating its national virtues, the *Wintermärchen* inverts the traditional national epic.[108]

A Travelling Narrator in a Stagnant Land

The title of Heine's poem links Germany, indirectly, with stillness.[109] Winter has a literal and figurative meaning. The weather remains a theme throughout the poem. In Caput 8 the musicians „starrten / Vor Kälte" (IV, 597). In Caput 10 „ein seltsames Frösteln" overcomes the poet (IV, 599). In Caput 15 the rain falls „eiskalt" (IV, 610), and in 24 „Das Wetter ist / Schon winterlich geworden" (IV, 633). This association with winter suggests a country where nothing grows, where the land is frozen, where, in the common political metaphor of the day, despotism reigns.

Just as in Caput 1 where the poet announces a new song, so does he at the poem's conclusion speak of a new generation who will hear this song. Because the progressive generation will move history forward, it is associated with warmth. In fact, it is the poet who warms this burgeoning youth (IV, 642). The poet, in whose mind progress exists (IV, 579–80), is directly associated with „Licht", „Feuer", and „Flammen" (IV, 642–43). He is also likened to Prometheus (IV, 619). These associations with fire and light allude to the poet's cognitive task. He is to enlighten the reader and educate him/her to contemporary injustice. This enlightenment will eventually destroy the Prussian regime. Note here the humorous image of revolutionary lightning blasting the Prussians' spiked helmuts as well as the later comparison of the poet's weapons with „Jovis Blitz" (IV, 643).[110] The sun, clearly an optimistic symbol (IV, 606–07), will help Germany overcome its winter. The warmth of the poet's revolutionary flame will likewise assist in erasing the cold of Germany. Heat, which is associated, not least of all scientifically, with motion, will replace coldness, a condition invariably associated with stillness.

---

[108] See Loeben (1970), 271.
[109] Heine makes the natural connection between stillness and winter explicit in another context when he writes: „Hier in Frankreich herrscht gegenwärtig die größte Ruhe. Ein abgematteter, schläfriger, gähnender Friede. Es ist alles still, wie in einer verschneiten Winternacht" (V, 425).
[110] „Nur fürcht ich, wenn ein Gewitter entsteht, / Zieht leicht so eine Spitze / Herab auf Euer romantisches Haupt / Des Himmels modernste Blitze! –" (IV, 582).

The narrator is linked to motion not only by way of fire and light; he is himself physically in motion. *Deutschland. Ein Wintermärchen* is the story of the poet's travels through Germany.[111] While his country has remained stagnant and separate from the world, he has travelled and developed progressive ideas. Finally, the narrator is a figure of Protean proportion; he continually changes roles and positions.[112] He is a poet (1, 2, 27), an Antaeus figure (1), a prophet (1, 26), the organizer of a shooting match (3), a judge (4), the murderer of a king (4), a connoisseuer of food and wine (4, 9, 20, 23), a dreamer (7, 15, 16, 18), the Angel of Death (7), an eyewitness to Napoleon's funeral (8), a wolfish demagogue (12), a cousin of Christ (13), a revolutionary (15, 16, 27), an *Untertan* (17), a new Odysseus (18), another Prometheus (18), a tourist (19), a son (20), the composer of the *Reisebilder* (21), and Germany's greatest poet (24).

Various images and themes convey, in contrast to the traveller's Protean motion, the stagnation in Germany and the stillness of the Germans. In Caput 2 a German passenger claims that Germany has already attained unity through the customs union and the censor. Not only is censorship not a progressive symbol of unity but both – what the passenger calls external and internal unity – are instituted from above. Such unity serves only to preserve the ruling structure. In Caput 3 the narrator notes that Germany has hardly changed. In particular the Prussian military „hat sich nicht sehr verändert" (IV, 581). „Noch" and „noch immer", frequent phrases which help underscore the stagnation of Germany, introduce the next three stanzas:

Es sind die grauen Mäntel noch
[...]
Noch immer das hölzern pedantische Volk,
Noch immer ein rechter Winkel
[...]
Sie stelzen noch immer so steif herum
[...] (IV, 581)

Other themes help capture the stillness and stagnation of Germany: the boredom in Aachen (IV, 581); the wonderful image which suggests that the Prussian soldiers are so stiff because they've swallowed the sticks with which they were once beaten (IV, 581); the unfinished nature of the Cologne cathedral and of the Prussian and Austrian constitutions (IV, 585–86); finally, the many allusions to the overriding significance of the past for the present.

---

[111] In his letter to Campe of February 20, 1844, Heine speaks of „versifizirte Reisebilder" (HSA XXII, 96).
[112] Paranthetic references in this paragraph are to the various *capitis*.

221

The Cologne cathedral houses important symbols of the past that for the narrator no longer deserve reverence. In the narrator's dream one of the Three Wise Men turns to him and demands respect:

> Zuerst weil er ein Toter sei,
> Und zweitens weil er ein König,
> Und drittens weil er ein Heilger sei –
> Das alles rührte mich wenig. (IV, 595)

In Romantic Germany, kings and saints, those relics of the past, still carry weight. For Heine they are without life. In an attempt to link the conservative and hierarchical tradition of the church with unjust government, the narrator suggests that two of the kings promised, but never delivered, constitutions. The contemporary reader thinks, of course, of Prussia and Austria:

> Der Balthasar und der Melchior,
> Das waren vielleicht zwei Gäuche,
> Die in der Not eine Konstitution
> Versprochen ihrem Reiche.
>
> Und später nicht Wort gehalten – (IV, 586)

In the narrator's dream the kings die as a consequence of the poet's thought, but before „die Tat von deinem Gedanken" – to use lictor's phrase – becomes reality, the world may have to wait (IV, 592). The very caput that portrays the kings' demise is introduced by a discussion of German dreams and interiority; again we see the tension between a Germany whose thoughts will eventually lead to political revolution and a sleepy, merely thinking Germany.

In Caput 11 the narrator contemplates what would have happened to Germany if Varus had won the battle of the Teutoburg forest. The Germans would have been Roman slaves: „So gäb es deutsche Freiheit nicht mehr, / Wir wären römisch geworden!" (IV, 601). Yet the Germans are still slaves. The distinction is merely linguistic: the difference between „Esel" and "asinus" (IV, 602). This section, a satire on Germany's current lack of freedom, climaxes in the refrain that the Germans remained German, that is, that Arminius did win the battle, but also that they *remain* backward-looking nationalists.[113] They are not the cosmopolitans Heine praises in his preface, nor are they heroes facing new challenges; instead, they are, as he says of the Westphalians, „fest", „sicher", and „treu" (IV, 600) – mock praise behind which one hears the word stagnant.

---

[113] Note the fourfold repetition of the verb „bleiben" (IV, 602).

Barbarossa: Germany's Hibernating Hero

Heine's *Märchen* or fairy tale takes place decidedly – and in opposition to the tradition of the genre – in the present, but the present is so filled with myths that the poet, in order to capture the present, must invoke these myths, one of which is of Barbarossa's return. The story of Barbarossa is the third of three fairy tales mentioned in Caput 14. Each repeats the same tale: someone waits for salvation from above, much as already the harp girl in Caput 1 had been waiting quietly and passively for heavenly salvation.[114] In the first tale Ottilie finds salvation and retribution, literally, from above. The sun, addressed as „klagende Flamme", reveals her murderer to the Vehmic court (IV, 606–07). In the second tale the royal princess finds enlightenment from the magic of a speaking horse. These two tales prepare the reader for the introduction of the Barbarossa myth. Ottilie and the royal princess, together with the harp girl, might be seen as symbols for the German nation. In the Barbarossa tale the Germans themselves wait quietly for salvation from above, to be more precise, from a dead ruler, a hero in hibernation or, as the Germans would have it, *Winterschlaf*.

The narrator situates his encounter with Barbarossa in the center of the epic. Much of his criticism of present-day Germany comes to a head in these passages. Barbarossa, like the Three Wise Men, is a symbol of the past that the Germans nonetheless continue to worship. According to the legend, Barbarossa sleeps in Mount Kyffhäuser and has been waiting for the right moment to rescue Germany from its troubles. Heine could scarcely have invented a better image for German somnolence and backwardness. In his essay on Börne he writes critically of „das deutsche Volk, das schlummersüchtige, träumende Volk, welches sich auch seinen Messias nur in der Gestalt eines alten Schläfers denken kann" (IV, 120). While Barbarossa awakens momentarily to meet with the narrator, his soldiers continue to sleep:

> Sie sind gerüstet von Kopf bis Fuß,
> Doch alle diese Braven,
> Sie rühren sich nicht, bewegen sich nicht,
> Sie liegen fest und schlafen. (IV, 608)

---

[114] Cf. Tonelli (1975), 175. The tales have more than one common feature. In the first two and in the poet's initial reception of the Barbarossa myth (IV, 609–10), the concepts of avengance and justice are prominent. Depending on emphasis and context, the tales might be said to have positive as well as negative import. The positive reading focuses on the unambiguous need for justice, while the negative stresses the fact that superstitious fairy tales and passive waiting are improper means for achieving this end.

The entire dream presents a picture of stasis: not just the soldiers but the horses sleep;[115] Barbarossa's abode with its stone chair and table is almost statuesque (IV, 610); the King himself initially appears as a „Steinbild", later as an „Antiquar" (IV, 610); the soldiers' weapons are rusty (IV, 611); and dust covers their helmuts (IV, 611). While the narrator encourages Barbarossa to accomplish his deeds now, the King responds that there is no rush, and the reader hears in the background the thesis of a slowly developing fatherland:

> Der Rotbart erwiderte lächelnd: „Es hat
> Mit dem Schlagen gar keine Eile,
> Man baute nicht Rom an einem Tag,
> Gut Ding will haben Weile.
>
> Wer heute nicht kommt, kommt morgen gewiß,
> Nur langsam wächst die Eiche,
> Und chi va piano va sano, so heißt
> Das Sprüchwort im römischen Reiche." (IV, 612)

The narrator decides, eventually, to tell Barbarossa to go back to sleep.[116] Barbarossa's ideas are old and outdated; he is unaware of historic developments, stagnant in his knowledge.[117] By making these bold comments only in a dream, the narrator mocks German quietude and resignation:

> Ich habe mich mit dem Kaiser gezankt
> Im Traum, im Traum versteht sich, –
> Im wachenden Zustand sprechen wir nicht
> Mit Fürsten so widersetzig.
>
> Nur träumend, im idealen Traum,
> Wagt ihnen der Deutsche zu sagen
> Die deutsche Meinung, die er so tief
> Im treuen Herzen getragen. (IV, 616)

Barbarossa, the representative of Old Germany and ideal of German nationalists, is demythologized into an old fool who deserves the poet's criticism, just as earlier the father Rhine, an object of many nationalist hymns, is reinterpreted as a sober old man who wants to side with the French

---

[115] „Sie sind gesattelt und gezäumt, / Jedoch von diesen Rossen / Kein einziges wiehert, kein einziges stampft, / Sind still, wie aus Eisen gossen" (IV, 608).

[116] Three years later Ludwig Pfau suggests, similarly, that Barbarossa continue sleeping. Shifting his focus from the myth of Barbarossa to the present, Pfau addresses his poem „Michel Rotbart" to Michel and writes: „Laß ruhn den Barbarosse doch [...] Und wach du selber auf!" Characteristically, Heine's version is less optimistic. Pfau concludes his first stanza: „Michel! hervor zum Werke! / Aus deiner langen Nacht, / Mit deiner Heldenstärke, / Mit deiner Geistesmacht" (135).

[117] The narrator's comment implies that those who want to restore Barbarossa and the traditions for which he stands are equally unaware of the significance of modern advances.

(IV, 587–88), and the Cologne cathedral, another nationalist image, is praised, mockingly, as a perfect symbol for Germany; it remains unfinished (IV, 585). By placing sacred symbols in new contexts Heine undermines nationalist illusions.

The narrator completes the Barbarossa episode by bringing the focus of his critique back to the present. The real object of his ridicule is not Barbarossa but his present-day worshippers. The narrator concludes: I'd rather live with Barbarossa, the genuine king, than with the present rulers, who are imitative and without grandeur. To say that medieval Germany is preferable to German medievalism with its odd combination of Prussian militarism and Romantic otherworldliness is not to praise feudalism but to make the critique of the present that much firmer.

False promises play a role throughout Heine's critique of German royalty and clergy, but the Germans' naive and obsequious belief in these promises comes under attack as well. In „Bei des Nachtwächters Ankunft zu Paris" Heine mocked the Germans' illusory hope for a constitution. In the *Wintermärchen*, too, he jabs not only Germany's rulers – for using tradition to preserve the status quo – he ironizes the inactive liberals who await reform from above. Ernest Augustus, King of Hannover, is protected less by his own soldiers than by the quietude of his opponents:

> Idyllisch sicher haust er hier,
> Denn besser als alle Trabanten
> Beschützet ihn der mangelnde Mut
> Von unseren lieben Bekannten. (IV, 621)

Waiting for reform from above, even the liberals are locked into Germany's Barbarossa syndrome.[118]

Hammonia's Reading of Germany

The narrator's fictive accounts of his meetings with the Three Wise Men and Barbarossa are the highpoints of the beginning and middle of the epic. At the end of the *Wintermärchen* the poet meets yet another fictive figure, Hammonia, the spirit of Hamburg. A Philistine who extols „den Seelenfrieden" (IV, 635), Hammonia appeals to an odd combination of medieval and Biedermeier values in order to entice the narrator into staying in Germany:

---

[118] In this context see also „Verheißung". After having predicted that German freedom – here personified as a Michel figure – will enjoy a great future, the poet concludes: „Werde nur nicht dreist und dreister! / Setz nicht den Respekt beiseiten / Vor den hohen Obrigkeiten / Und dem Herren Bürgermeister!" (IV, 424).

> Geh nicht zurück und bleib bei uns;
> Hier herrschen noch Zucht und Sitte,
> Und manches stille Vergnügen blüht
> Auch hier, in unserer Mitte. (IV, 635)

After meeting Hammonia, the narrator does recognize changes, though they are hardly progressive; the people look like „wandelnde Ruinen" (IV, 626), and the whores on the Drehbahn are no longer the ones of his youth: „Du findest nicht die alte Zeit / Und die Zeitgenössinnen wieder!" (IV, 631). The changes represent more of the same or a regressive circularity:

> Die mageren sind noch dünner jetzt,
> Noch fetter sind die feisten,
> Die Kinder sind alt, die Alten sind
> Kindisch geworden, die meisten. (IV, 626)

Hammonia invites the narrator to stay and tries to convince him that Germany has progressed:

> Bleib bei uns in Deutschland, es wird dir hier
> Jetzt besser als ehmals munden;
> Wir schreiten fort, du hast gewiß
> Den Fortschritt selbst gefunden. (IV, 635)

Her account of Germany's progressive spirit and of a past that the narrator should see in a new light is humorously self-contradictory. One could avoid servitude by committing suicide; the censor limits only those who want to publish:[119]

> Ja, daß es uns früher so schrecklich ging,
> In Deutschland, ist Übertreibung;
> Man konnte entrinnen der Knechtschaft, wie einst
> In Rom, durch Selbstentleibung.
>
> Gedankenfreiheit genoß das Volk,
> Sie war für die großen Massen,
> Beschränkung traf nur die geringe Zahl
> Derjenigen, die drucken lassen. (IV, 636)

Despite her announcement of a progressive spirit, Hammonia still misses the good old days. Her vision of a pure past contrasts with the narrator's recent mockery of Barbarossa. One might also think, intertextually, of the fate of external freedom in „Bei des Nachtwächters Ankunft zu Paris". Hammonia states:

> Es blühte in der Vergangenheit
> So manche schöne Erscheinung
> Des Glaubens und der Gemütlichkeit;
> Jetzt herrscht nur Zweifel, Verneinung.

---

[119] Similarly, in Caput 13, it is only mockingly progressive that Christ, had he lived today, would not have been crucified; the censor would have eliminated all controversial statements from his published speeches.

> Die praktische äußere Freiheit wird einst
> Das Ideal vertilgen,
> Das wir im Busen getragen – es war
> So rein wie der Traum der Liljen! (IV, 636)

Internal contradiction and surrounding context undercut Hammonia's vision of progress and her interpretation of an ideal past.

The marriage of Europe with freedom, of which the poet sings in his introductory lines (IV, 578–79), is replaced at the poem's conclusion with the proposed marriage of the narrator and Hammonia. The first marriage would have brought many, the latter marriage no future children: the „Zensorschere" – which, significantly enough, rhyme with „Pastöre" (IV, 641) – castrate the poet. If the narrator were to return to the stagnant life of Biedermeier Germany, represented by Hammonia, he would lose his intellectual connection to the spirit of the future.

In his poem Heine offers a complex picture of this future. The new song of Caput 1 promises a good life for all, as does the final suggestion of a new generation in Europe (IV, 642). The alternate vision of a stinking future, the narrator's vision in the chamber pot (IV, 639), is reinforced, however, by the complexities of the earlier scene in the Cologne cathedral. The poet condemns the Three Wise Men, but as the lictor spirit, whose deeds follow the narrator's thoughts, destroys them „ohn Erbarmen" (IV, 595), the poet is horrified to see his own blood flow:

> Es dröhnte der Hiebe Widerhall
> Aus allen Gewölben, entsetzlich, –
> Blutströme schossen aus meiner Brust,
> Und ich erwachte plötzlich. (IV, 595)

The reactionary kings appear to be as much a part of the poet as does the revolutionary lictor spirit. The narrator's patriotism is infused not only with the spirit of the future; he is emotionally attracted to the past as well. The complexity of his stance is reflected in the fact that two images portray the future as happy and just, while two others suggest turmoil and disaster, even as the future adheres to the poet's explicit wishes.

Negativity in the *Wintermärchen*

Heine's stance vis-à-vis contemporary Germany is primarily negative. He ridicules Germany for its backwardness and stagnation, but the poet does not – despite his confident announcement of a new song and a new generation, his view of his own words as weapons (IV, 579–80), and his saber rattling at the conclusion of the poem (IV, 643–44) – offer a constructive alternative. Two passages demonstrate the poem's negativity particularly well: the narrator's discussion with the wolves in Caput 12, in which he pledges his allegiance to them just as he ridicules and mocks them;[120] and his conversation with his mother, in which he avoids all discussion of politics and of position-taking by commenting instead on his fine German meal.[121] While the narrator's optimistic vision of the future, his new song, promises good food and a good time – „Rosen und Myrten, Schönheit und Lust" (IV, 578) – for everyone, the reader is not told how to arrive at this utopia or what sacrifices must be made along the way. It has even been argued – if not convincingly, at least suggestively – that the narrator's new song is ironized for its exaggerated and unrealistic claims; Atkinson cites the lines „Das Miserere ist vorbei, / Die Sterbeglocken schweigen" (IV, 578) and views the „Zuckererbsen" as a mock placebo.[122] While the poet is confident in his negations, in what we should be moving away from, he is less sure of where we should be settling, where we might rest with a new system, and, importantly, how we might get there. The difficulties of enlightenment are associated with not only his quietist audience but his own platform as well,[123] one that is characterized, as is much in Büchner's and Heine's post-synthetic world, by negativity and motion without rest.

One might view Heine's stance as a stubborn attachment to pure ironic destruction and a failing inability or unwillingness to commit himself to a positive program.[124] One might also see it as a safeguard against the kind of utopian thinking of which negative writers like Heine are so critical. Any attachment to a specific, positive program could lessen the utopian spirit of his writing and weaken his ability as an independent thinker to criticize the political goals and tactics of all parties.[125] Either evaluation suggests that Heine remains a primarily negative writer, one who does not express, even though he may at times strive for, synthesis. Heine focuses throughout his writings on a critique of the present and of the various modes for improving

---

[120] The narrator's allegiance to the wolves is without content, purely rhetorical. In addition, after making an ambiguous statement of allegiance and commitment, „Ich bin ein Wolf und werde stets / Auch heulen mit den Wölfen" (IV, 604), the narrator concludes that the wolves should help themselves („helft Euch selbst" IV, 604). Finally, the wolves are presented, symbolically, as nonprogressive; the narrator meets them only as his carriage stops (IV, 603).

[121] One might read the narrator's comment, that he enjoyed the sweet juice of the oranges and left the skins, to mean that he is concerned with only the ideal core not the everyday, external shell of politics. This political reading of the conversation, however, does not alter the conclusion that the narrator is still unwilling to embrace a positive party platform.

[122] See Atkinson (1975), 186–88.

[123] On the difficulties of enlightenment consider the poet's comparison of the sun's daily appearance with the vain efforts of Sisyphus and the Danaides (IV, 605).

[124] See Atkinson (1975).

[125] See Würffel (1977).

upon the present. His perspective never comes to rest in a specific and positive solution.[126] Indeed, the only position into which Heine is locked is that of incessant negativity, and it is this position alone which Heine, paradoxically, never negates.

Heine's Concept of Political Quietude in its Intellectual-Historical Context

Lessing's *Emilia Galotti*

In *Die romantische Schule* Heine calls Lessing his favorite poet: „ich kann nicht umhin zu bemerken, daß er in der ganzen Literaturgeschichte derjenige Schriftsteller ist, den ich am meisten liebe."[127] He adds: „In allen seinen Werken lebt dieselbe große soziale Idee, dieselbe fortschreitende Humanität, dieselbe Vernunftreligion, deren Johannes er war und deren Messias wir noch erwarten" (III, 371). In *Zur Geschichte der Religion und Philosophie in Deutschland* Heine insists: „seit Luther hat Deutschland keinen größeren und besseren Mann hervorgebracht, als Gotthold Ephraim Lessing" (III, 585). Heine sees himself, if not as Germany's third liberator, certainly as part of the tradition begun by Luther and Lessing.

Lessing fits Heine's image of the politically engaged artist; he is „politisch bewegt" (III, 372). Besides being a champion of religious freedom, Lessing is for Heine a critic of despotism: „wir merken jetzt erst was er mit der Schilderung des Duodezdespotismus in ‚Emilia Galotti' gemeint hat" (III, 372). *Emilia Galotti* is not only one of Heine's favorite dramas and the penultimate scene the subject of numerous allusions,[128] it is an important document in the history of the idea of *Ruhe*.

Ruhe is central to the entire play. Already in the first scene the Prince, lost in his passions, laments: „Ich war so ruhig, bild' ich mir ein, so ruhig – Auf einmal muß eine arme Bruneschi, Emilia heißen: – weg ist meine Ruhe, und alles! –" (I, 1). Emilia's encounter with the Prince leaves her, too, in chaos,

---

[126] Heine's position changes only insofar as the objects of his critique become increasingly broader. For accounts of the religious and cosmic dimensions of Heine's poetry see Prawer (1970), Preisendanz (1970), and Sengle (1971–80), III, 514–18. See also Brummack (1967), who shows that the structure of comic contrast between individual experience and desired ideal, which informs Heine's satirical poetry, both political and religious, is already present in his earlier, more subjective poetry – in the form of the contrast between the poet's frustrating experiences and the ideal of traditional love poetry.

[127] III, 372. For an exact account of Heine's knowledge of Lessing see DHA 8/2, 879–81.

[128] I, 309; III, 372; IV, 560; IV, 631.

and her mother tells her to calm herself: „Fasse dich [...] sei ruhig" (II, 6). She also admonishes her not to tell Appiani, lest she make him „unruhig" (II, 6). Odoardo, Emilia's father, strives consistently for *Ruhe* and with it the suppression of protest. He asks Claudia: „Bin ich nicht ruhig? Kann man ruhiger sein, als ich bin? *(sich zwingend)*" (IV, 8). As his anger at the Prince begins to swell, he tries to quiet himself again: „Ruhig, alter Knabe, ruhig" (V, 4).

Additional references to *Ruhe* surface at various points in the text,[129] most significantly in the penultimate scene and climax of the play, Act V, scene 7. Here the *Ruhe* theme is dominant from the very first exchange:

> Emilia. [...] Und Sie so unruhig, mein Vater?
> Odoardo. Und du so ruhig, meine Tochter?

Emilia expects deliverance from her father but finds that he has failed her. He is willing to leave her in the Prince's hands „allein; ohne deine Mutter; ohne mich". Emilia holds her composure. She remains „ruhig", but she defines *Ruhe* to include activity and resistance, the opposite of what one would expect. Just as she acquires inner repose, she becomes active.[130] Emilia does not simply say, let's be *ruhig* because it's an ideal, she says, let's redefine it to include what we take to be ideal. For her this means action and protest:

> Odoardo. Ich meine, du bist ruhig, mein Kind.
> Emilia. Das bin ich. Aber was nennen Sie ruhig sein?
> Die Hände in den Schoß legen? Leiden, was man nicht
> sollte? Dulden, was man nicht dürfte?

Emilia is determined to resist the Prince, but she can do so only by sacrificing herself. In death she would find final security. Throughout the play she has been in motion; on stage we often see her hurrying, running, or looking for some sort of protection.[131] She has found refuge through neither religion, the state, nor her family. After being thwarted in her desire for suicide, Emilia implores her father to take her life – not so much because she wants to preserve morality but because death is the only means of protest open to her in a shattered world. She becomes active (*seeking* death) and passive (seeking *death*) at once.

Odoardo, despite being introduced and idolized as a moral authority throughout the first three acts, is unveiled as a weak embodiment of submissive, middle class *Gelassenheit*.[132] In the face of aristocratic injustice

---

[129] For additional passages not quoted see II, 2; IV, 8; and V, 5.
[130] Lessing notes Emilia's increasing activity in a letter to his brother of February 10, 1772: „Am Ende wird denn auch freylich der Charakter der Emilia interessanter, und sie selbst thätiger" (LM XVIII, 19).
[131] Cf. Angress (1968), 18.
[132] Cf. Brüggemann (1926), 101 and Heitner (1953), 487.

Emilia's father clings to a false idea of *Ruhe*. In the final act he begins to recognize his own passivity and the failings of tranquil composure as an antidote to evil: „Ich lasse mir ja alles gefallen; ich finde ja alles ganz vortrefflich" (V, 5). After he hesitates in the face of Emilia's request, Emilia accuses him „*in einem bitteren Tone*" of surrendering his morals. Finally, he stabs Emilia, killing her and preserving, so it seems, her purity and freedom. In the face of oppression Emilia asserts her will through her father, but the *Ruhe* for which she had been searching throughout the play becomes the *Ruhe* of death – not particularly satisfying for the play or exemplary in the tradition of "live stillness". The viewer's emotions are not purged.[133] He/She senses that if someone was to be murdered, it should have been the prince; but Odoardo is too passive. The audience, unsatisfied with the outcome, is awakened to the evils of both the arbitrary despot and the passive, quietistic, middle class subject.

Although Lessing, in his correspondence, plays down the Virginia story of Livy, a source with direct political import – the father, in killing his daughter, arouses the population to revolution – the drama's political criticism remains implicit.[134] The action of the play is primarily psychological, but the determinants are, as Frank Ryder has suggested, political.[135] The play shows from the first to the last scene the arbitrariness of despotic power; it gives its readers reason to protest tyranny even as the play's characters, falsely holding to passive notions of *Ruhe*, fail. Their failure and false passivity are partly due to social constraints associated with absolutism, but they are also the result of a tradition of morally idealized *Ruhe*.

The play encourages criticism not only of the tyrant's injustice and the passivity with which his subjects respond – the negative political category of oppressive *Ruhe* – it exhibits, however briefly, the opposing political category of pastoral *Ruhe*. In Act II, scene 4 Odoardo paints the picture of an evil city and court filled with machinations and false virtues. He praises the life in the country to which he has retired and where in „Unschuld und Ruhe" he is no one's servant. Away from the court one is no longer a slave to *fortuna*, a figure represented in Lessing's play by the moody and capricious prince. After the wedding with Appiani, Emilia, too, would have retired to an idyllic and autonomous existence in the country; her fiancé in fact had already withdrawn from public life.

These two forms of political *Ruhe*, the pastoral *Ruhe* of an idealized life away from the city and state and the oppressive *Ruhe* of a government that seeks obedient and silent subjects, will be the focus of the next two sections.

---

[133] The contemporary audience was in most cases stirred, not quieted. See Heitner (1953), 489.
[134] See LM XVII, 133; LM XVIII, 21–23.
[135] Ryder (1972), 344.

Pastoral *Ruhe*

The golden age of innocence and bliss is frequently placed in mankind's prehistory, often in childhood; both are traditionally associated with *Ruhe*. Pastoral poetry attempts to recapture this age by turning away from the focus of historical progress, cities and civilization, to the cultivators of simplicity, shepherds and peasants.[136] Pastoral has been divided into bucolic *(Schäferdichtung)* and georgic poetry *(Landlebendichtung)*.[137] Both depict a life in the country away from city and court and characterized by simple, self-sufficient, virtuous, and tranquil existence. While bucolic poetry focuses on the shepherd or herdsman, the georgics portray the life of the farmer or peasant. The primary model for bucolic poetry is Vergil's *Eclogues*. Here the shepherd is portrayed in a state of tranquillity and happiness. Important for this genre and the state it describes is the identification of the poet with the shepherd. The shepherd enjoys his leisure in part by singing. According to the theoreticians of the genre, poetry has its origins in this state as well, for the repose enjoyed by shepherds is also the calm that is prerequisite for creativity.[138] In the bucolic tradition authors spend few words describing the life of the shepherd; they dwell instead on the location and merits of pastoral life. In contrast, georgic poetry – its models being Vergil's *Georgics* and Horace's second epode ("Beatus ille...") – focuses on the daily activities of the farmer. While the shepherd is portrayed in leisure, the farmer is shown at work. Between his chores, however, the pious and virtuous farmer does enjoy repose. The principle moment of bucolic is thus also a moment of georgic poetry. The worker enjoys his leisure reclining under a tree, usually near a brook and with a soft breeze. Horace gives us a model:

> libet iacere modo sub antiqua ilice,
>   modo in tenaci gramine.
> labuntur altis interim ripis aquae,
>   queruntur in silvis aves,

---

[136] It cannot be my task here to trace the development of bucolic and georgic poetry from Theocritus, Vergil, and Horace to the modern period. I will simply draw attention to the pastoral and idyllic as elements in the development of political *Ruhe* and define Heine's relationship to this tradition. While no single work traces the entire complex history of the pastoral tradition, numerous important monographs and articles do sketch significant stages. In general see Böschenstein-Schäfer (1967); Garber (1982); and Mähl (1965). For antiquity see esp. Halperin (1983); O'Loughlin (1978); Rosenmeyer (1969); and Snell (1975), 257–82; for the modern era see Dedner (1972); Garber (1974); Hibberd (1976); Hirsch (1957); Lohmeier (1981); Meyer (1964); Nemoianu (1977); and Sengle (1963; 1965; 1971–80: II, 743–86). A comprehensive bibliography on the subject can be found in Garber (1976), 483–529.

[137] See Garber (1976), xii–xvi and Garber (1974), 82–84, 199–213.

[138] See Garber (1974), 82–83.

fontesque lymphis obstrepunt manantibus,
somnos quod invitet levis.
(Epode 2)

The *locus amoenus* recurs in the German continuation of this tradition. An excerpt from Opitz' „Lob des Feldtlebens", the first georgic poem of seventeenth-century Germany, will serve as an example:

> Ist er vom gehen laß / so kan er sich fein strecken / Bald in den Schatten hin wo ihn die Båume decken / Bald in das grůne Graß / an dem fůrůber fleußt Das wasser und durchhin mit stillem Rauschen scheußt. [...] Nicht weit von dannen kômpt auß einem kůlen Brunnen / Ein Båchlein durch das Graß gleich wie Cristall gerunnen / Drauß schôpfft er mit der Hand / eh er sich schlaffen legt / Worzu der Bach Geråusch' und Murmeln ihn bewegt. (*Weltliche Poemata* I, 241)

Both bucolic and georgic poetry offer a kind of dynamic stillness. The shepherd and poet are active as artists, the farmer as a worker; all enjoy the repose of the *locus amoenus*.

In pastoral landscape repose is often literal; people recline, sit, or stand still. But repose is also abstract, signifying an internal state of mind as well as an external atmosphere. *Otium*, in German „Ruhe", „Muße", or „tatenloses Glück", is a frequent word in Vergil, more frequent in fact than *hēsychia* in Theocritus, for Vergil, like Horace, prefers abstractions; he likes to reflect on what his poems dramatize.[139] The word „otium", a dynamic and positive concept to be distinguished from *desidia* or *inertia*, captures the social and psychological state of the herdsman or farmer. Horace's ode 16 of book II, the most famous ancient poem about *otium*, describes the repose of the individual, not tempted by wealth, who lives a modest life free of fear and greed. The individual content with the present is not concerned with the future; he tempers dismay with an easy laugh:

> laetus in praesens animus quod ultra est
> oderit curare et amara lento
> temperet risu. nihil est ab omni
>   parte beatum.

In *De Otio* Seneca suggests that the solitude and withdrawal of *otium* offers the leisure necessary for philosophical contemplation, through which one can better serve the world. He acknowledges the extent to which *otium* is an ideal for both Epicureans and Stoics, even though their reasons for seeking it differ. For Seneca, like Cicero, *otium* and politics can still be integrated; indeed, *otium* can be justified only insofar as it is useful to the community. In

---

[139] Cf. Rosenmeyer (1969), 67. Curtius (1950) calls *otium* „eines der Schlüsselworte virgilischer Dichtung" (19). On the various dimensions of *otium* see André (1966); Bernert (1949–50); Putnam (1970); Rosenmeyer (1969); Wirszubski (1954); and Woodman (1966).

contrast, for the Epicureans and in the tradition of pastoral poetry, especially as it developed in the German Baroque, *otium* and politics, *Ruhe* and life at the court, are enemies. Individuals who spend their lives in pastoral activities find a kind of utopia. *Otium* grants them the proper conditions for virtuous existence; the *locus amoenus* guarantees the virtuous happy lives. *Ruhe* is both the condition of and the reward for a moral existence. It is a state achieved not at the courts or in the city but far away from conventional politics, on the land:[140]

> Hier merk ich, daß die Ruh' in schlechten Hütten wohnet,
> Wenn Unglück und Verdruß nicht der Paläste schonet;
> Daß es viel besser ist, bey Kohl und Rüben stehn,
> Als in dem Labyrinth des Hofes irre gehn.

Away from the city and court virtue can prosper. The farmer – much like the shepherd or herdsman – leads a modest and content existence. He does not grasp for ephemeral glory. Unlike court heroes he does not desire honor and fame, wealth and power. In the pastoral, one finds an ideal morality which differs from that of the courts but nonetheless has or should have validity beyond the idyllic sphere.

In keeping with the interrelation of pastoral repose and morality many of the moral weeklies from the early eighteenth century encourage their readers to leave the city for the country and seek there both tranquillity and morality.[141] The most famous German moral weekly *Der Patriot* (1724–26) opens with the fictive moral character telling his readers that he is „mit mir selbst in Gelassenheit zu frieden"; he closes with an invitation to tranquillity and peace. The last word of the three volume collection is „Ruhe".[142] The fictive moral personality of *Der Weltbürger* enjoys „das unschuldige Landleben" far from the „Gefahr und Verdruß […] des Hofes".[143] In his weekly messages, he tries to help his readers overcome „Unruhe" and „Verwirrungen" and experience „sanfte Menschlichkeit", which he calls, programmatically, „Mutter des Friedens, der Einigkeit und der Ruhe".[144] The popularity of moral weeklies as well as Salomon Geßner's idylls with their „Gemählde von stiller Ruhe und sanftem ungestöhrtem Glük" attest to the continuing attractiveness of *Ruhe* as an alternate moral and political ideal in the eighteenth century (15). One strain of German literature kept the notion of an ideal pastoral *Ruhe* alive even into the nineteenth century. Hebel, Möricke, Gotthelf, and Stifter play major roles in this development; Heine

---

[140] Canitz, 117. Cited in Dedner (1972), 40.
[141] On Germany's moral weeklies see Martens (1968).
[142] *Der Patriot*, January 5, 1724; December 28, 1726.
[143] *Der Weltbürger*, February 2, 1741.
[144] *Der Weltbürger*, February 9, 1741.

does not, though he is certainly familiar with the major figures and ideas of the pastoral tradition.

Heine and Pastoral *Ruhe*

Heine longed for pastoral repose, as I suggested earlier, but he resisted this temptation as he began to write political poetry. Heine's occasional longing, however, did result in a number of poems in praise of idyllic *Ruhe* – from the ninth poem of his *Lyrisches Intermezzo* (1822/23) to the late fragment „Bimini" (1853).[145] Wolfgang Preisendanz (1981) cites Heine's recurrent evocations of India as a fictive counter-world to historical reality and notes in diverse texts of Heine either the memory of a lost paradise or the prereflection of utopia. Preisendanz' thesis of Heine as an idyllic writer may strike some readers as odd; after all, the stamp of Heine lies not in his visions of Arcadia but in his ironic breaking of these visions. Heine is more likely to rhyme „Ruh" mockingly with „Kuh" than with an idealized image of bliss (I, 130). We already discussed Heine's consistent undercutting of the dream world. Preisendanz acknowledges these breaks even as he stresses the idyllic Heine. These idyllic moments must be granted. In fact they can be integrated into the political Heine insofar as one reflects on the social criticism implicit in the idylls. Nonetheless, the more significant of the two forms of political *Ruhe* for Heine, in terms of both quantity and quality, is the critique of oppressive, not the evocation of pastoral, *Ruhe*.

There are several reasons for this. First, much like Schiller, Heine was sceptical of any return to innocence and naive repose. Though he recognizes the advantages of a quiet childhood spent „im Stilleben" (II, 89), he knows that tranquillity must eventually pass; otherwise, the pastoral becomes a haven for lack of progress, consciousness, and freedom. Consider Heine's accounts of the islanders in *Die Nordsee* (II, 213–16) and the Tyroleans in *Die Reise von München nach Genua* (II, 337–38). Such simplicity does not allow for spirit; *otium* of this kind is static. Second, a return would be not only regressive; in Heine's eyes it would be unrealistic, impossible. Even Hammonia recognizes that the face of Germany is changing: „Zu Ende geht die Idylle."[146] Third, Heine was not a moralist. The simplicity, innocence, and denial of passions associated with the pastoral ideal could not have appealed to this believer in the emancipation of the flesh. Fourth, for Heine idylls are restricted and restricting.[147] Like the works of German *Klassik*, they

---

[145] I, 78; VI/1, 243–66.
[146] IV, 637. Cf. VI/1, 649.
[147] For a general assessment of the restrictiveness of the traditional idyll, see Böschenstein-Schäfer (1981).

shun negativity in order to capture a seemingly perfect but merely private world. Along with the German-French dualism Heine wanted to overcome the country-city opposition. He was, despite his elitist tendencies, a wholist critical of untenable dualisms and exclusive utopian spheres. His cosmopolitanism is clear evidence of this.[148] Finally, Heine was inclined to negate what he didn't like, not promote what he did. This relates to his stress on the current, the everyday, the temporal. He could not leave the present to sketch a new and otherworldly ideal. It is thus not as an invoker of pastoral but as a critic of oppressive *Ruhe* that Heine occupies a position in the history of German conceptions of *Ruhe*.

Oppressive *Ruhe*

Heine shares his critique of political quietude with many writers of the 1830s and 40s. For models Heine and his contemporaries refer back not only to Lessing but also to Schiller. In the same breath with which he criticizes Goethe for his politics, Heine champions Schiller, „den edelsten, wenn auch nicht den größten Dichter der Deutschen" (II, 385). For Heine and his contemporaries Schiller's name becomes synonymous with the critique of oppressive *Ruhe*.[149] Heine's contemporaries frequently cite *Don Carlos*, which contains Marquis Posa's famous attack on the graveyard quietude of Spain and Flanders. Already in 1830 Börne speaks of „die Stille eines Kirchhofs" (II, 826). In 1848 liberals such as Gutzkow and Hartmann again revived Posa's slogan.[150] Heine's work contains numerous allusions to Schiller's play, specifically to the central encounter between King Phillip and Marquis Posa in Act III, scene 10.[151] Graveyard quietude or „Kirchhofsruhe" suggests an atmosphere not only of stasis but of direct oppression. For the unjust state, civic repose is ideal; it eliminates resistance and protest. For many individuals in the state, meanwhile, quietude of this sort guarantees a

---

[148] The one apparent exception to Heine's cosmopolitanism would seem to be his caricatures of England and the English in his *Englische Fragmente* and elsewhere, but Prawer (1984) has recently highlighted the "counter-currents" in Heine's depiction of the English and so emphasized his hidden respect for British values and achievements (26).
[149] By looking back toward Schiller in delineating the tradition of oppressive political *Ruhe*, we see a certain unity among the four writers of this study. An author who praises *Ruhe* for its dynamism will condemn it insofar as it lacks this quality. Schiller, who equates *Ruhe* with „Vollendung", criticizes „die Ruhe eines Kirchhofs". Though only two of the four authors openly support dynamic stillness, all four condemn its contrary, deficient stillness.
[150] See Ladendorf (1906), 168.
[151] See esp. III, 393. Heine takes another, more sceptical view of Posa in connection with his critique of Herwegh's audience with Frederick William IV. See IV, 421–22 and VI/1, 231–33. Like Herwegh, Posa is, after all, ultimately unsuccessful.

life free of immediate disruption even as it requires the individual to turn his/her back on inequities and oppression.

Neither Lessing, Schiller, nor Heine invented the concept of oppressive *Ruhe*; it was part of the structure of German government and society, embedded even into provincial law. The primary historical document for the development of political *Ruhe* in Germany is the *Allgemeines Landrecht für die preußischen Staaten* of 1794, a work of great importance for Germany's political, social, and intellectual history. Here political stabilization is officially associated with *Ruhe*: the citizen is obliged to preserve „Ruhe und Ordnung"; the state in turn guarantees „Ruhe und Sicherheit" (§ 10 II 17).[152] Wolfgang Frühwald (1976) has sketched the importance of these two formulas for the years 1789–1848, i.e., for much of Heine's adulthood.[153] „Ruhe, Sicherheit und Ordnung" became a slogan for reactionaries and a formula for Metternich's policies of repression.[154] The phrase, which signifies the political stability guaranteed by a strong police and pious and obedient subjects,[155] can also be seen as a counter-slogan to the French revolutionary triad of «liberté, égalité, fraternité».[156] After the revolution of 1848 the term „Fanatismus der Ruhe" became especially prominent.[157] Heinrich Hoffmann writes satirically in the voice of those who support political stillness at all costs: „Ja! Ich will Ruhe. Ich schwärme für Ruhe. Ich wühle für Ruhe. Ich bin ein Fanatiker der Ruhe und Ordnung, der Ruhe um jeden Preis" (9).

The two social-political forms of *Ruhe* defined here, the pastoral and oppressive, are, surprisingly, not mutually exclusive. Conrad Wiedemann (1977) has argued that the Baroque principle of sovereignity supports both forms of *Ruhe* in a complementary way.[158] The individual who is mistrustful

---

[152] Cf. Frühwald (1976), 93–94.

[153] Equally important in this context would seem to be a work by Wolfram Siemann, which had not been released before the completion of this study: „*Deutschlands Ruhe, Sicherheit und Ordnung." Die Anfänge der politischen Polizei 1806–1866*.

[154] See Frühwald (1976), 35–36, 71. Contemporaries called Metternich the rock of order («rocher de l'ordre»).

[155] An abstract association of *Ruhe* with political stability is reflected in nineteenth-century literature as well. Kleist, for example, while not necessarily evaluating political *Ruhe*, shows in *Penthesilea* (1586–91) and *Prinz Friedrich von Homburg* (I, 5; II, 2) that a lack of „Ruhe" creates social disorder and instability.

[156] Cf. Schieder (1974), 443.

[157] Ladendorf (1906), 79–80. See also Blum's article on „Ruhe der Staaten" in his *Volksthümliches Handbuch*. Blum writes of the present age as one in which „alles, was eine Stimme hat, nach Ruhe ruft. Ruhe, Ruhe! – um jeden Preis" (II, 214).

[158] Cf. Oestereich (1969), who notes that Lipsius, the prime spokesman for the Neostoic ideal of *constantia*, preached acceptance of political necessity and developed in his *Politicorum seu civilis doctrinae libri sex* the foundations for a moderate absolutism.

of freedom in the hands of those ruled by passions will renounce his own political freedom in favor of a central authority who will secure domestic peace. Tyranny is viewed as preferable to civil war. Those who criticize courtly life will often refrain from attacking the government of the court, for it preserves domestic tranquillity. The ideal life of repose can thus be associated with strong government and antidemocratic tendencies. The question becomes not how can individuals become free but how can they be guaranteed peace.[159] That the individual need no longer care about politics frees him to enjoy his repose in the country. He renounces political responsibility but benefits from domestic peace. Much later, belief in a strong central government will continue to legitimize, however incorrectly, a serene lifestyle free of political concerns.

Heine sensed the collusion of pastoral and oppressive *Ruhe* in its modern variants as Biedermeier tranquillity and the repression of dissent. Consider his poem „Im Oktober 1849". After the revolution of 1848 the political winds in Germany had settled. Not only is the quieting of winds a favorite context for Heine's parodies of relativistic and opportunistic politics,[160] but the phrasing in this poem borrows ironically from Genesis.[161] The poet mockingly compares the revolution of 1848 to the great flood. Germany, a mere child politically speaking, now enjoys the domestic bliss of Christmas and a „Goethefeier" (VI/1, 117):

> Gelegt hat sich der starke Wind,
> Und wieder stille wirds daheime;
> Germania, das große Kind,
> Erfreut sich wieder seiner Weihnachtsbäume.
>
> Wir treiben jetzt Familienglück –
> Was höher lockt, das ist vom Übel –
> Die Friedensschwalbe kehrt zurück,
> Die einst genistet in des Hauses Giebel.
> (VI/1, 116)

The use of the verb „treiben" with the object „Familienglück" is skillfully mocking. With Heine adopting the voice of the reactionaries, this mockery is not unreminiscent of the earlier ironic expression: „Der stille Segen [...]

---

[159] Heine's desire for *both* peace and freedom is a significant reason behind his vacillation between belief in constitutional monarchy, as the safeguard of aristocratic repose (a position most forcefully presented by Tonelli 1975), and revolution (most vociferously defended by Hermand 1975, 1976, and 1979).

[160] See the conclusion of „An den Nachtwächter": „Du fragst mich, wie es uns hier ergeht? / Hier ist es still, kein Windchen weht, / Die Wetterfahnen sind sehr verlegen, / Sie wissen nicht, wohin sich bewegen..." (IV, 428). See also V, 457 and VI/1, 199.

[161] See Rose (1976), 56. The allusion is to Gen. 8, 1–3.

wuchert im sittlich gehüteten Haus." The poem, however, is more than just playfully ironic; it is bitter in its recognition that the return of idyllic peace depends on the violent repression of protest. Biedermeier and oppressive *Ruhe* become one:

> Gemütlich ruhen Wald und Fluß,
> Von sanftem Mondlicht übergossen;
> Nur manchmal knallts – Ist das ein Schuß? –
> Es ist vielleicht ein Freund, den man erschossen.
>
> (VI/1, 116)

For the Young Germans *Ruhe*, in all its manifestations, became an object of critique. While the government and its supporters appealed to „Ruhe", the Young Germans took as a central slogan „Bewegung",[162] a concept that served to counter both the stagnant government (oppressive *Ruhe*) and apolitical, idyllic withdrawal (pastoral *Ruhe*). In desiring not only to watch but also to undermine the existing order, contemporaries appealed to the dynamism of „Bewegung". Just as stillness had assumed political import, so too had motion. Karl von Rotteck writes in *Das Staats-Lexikon*:

> Mit dem Namen Bewegungspartei oder Bewegungsmänner bezeichnet man in der großen Spaltung, welche heutzutage durch alle europäischen, d. h. der europäischen Civilisation angehörigen Völker geht, Diejenigen, die nach Fortschritten – zumal nach andauernden Fortschritten – im Staats- (oder auch im kirchlichen) Leben begehren und daher diejenigen Verbesserungen oder Entwickelungen, deren sie die gesellschaftlichen Einrichtungen für bedürftig oder empfänglich achten, ohne Zeitverlust verwirklicht wissen wollen. Ihnen stehen gegenüber die Männer des Widerstandes oder des Stillstandes, die da entweder überhaupt dem Fortschreiten abgeneigt oder die wenigstens der Meinung sind, daß die bereits gemachten Fortschritte einstweilen genügen, und die daher den – wie sie glauben oder vorgeben – gefährlichen oder verderblichen Bestrebungen der Bewegungsmänner ihren Widerstand entgegensetzen.[163]

When Heine speaks of „Männer der Bewegung" in *Die romantische Schule*, he addresses the ideal contemporary whose tasks span aesthetics, religion, and politics.[164] „Bewegung", as a counterterm to „Ruhe", becomes as expansive as the originally positive term itself. „Ruhe" meanwhile assumes in the political sphere not the ideal associations of the pastoral or of universal peace; it signifies stasis and repression.

---

[162] See Wülfing (1967), 166–77. For a résumé of „bewegliche Strukturen" in Heine see Windfuhr (1976), 287–99.
[163] Article on „Bewegungs- oder Fortschrittspartei" (II, 720). Cf. the similar entry in Blum's *Volksthümliches Handbuch* (I, 146–48). Heine was of course familiar with the concept. See B V, 30.
[164] III, 396. Cf. IV, 87.

Excursus. The Politics of *Ruhe* in the Wake of Heine:
Tucholsky, Brecht, and Handke

Twentieth-century critics of political *Ruhe* must look back to Heine and his contemporaries for models. Tucholsky, with his biting journalistic commentary, Brecht, with his critique of the political heritage of German *Klassik*, and Handke, with his concern for the linguistic dimensions of oppressive *Ruhe*, share elements with Heine in their attempts to shed light on oppressive political *Ruhe* in the twentieth century.[165]

Already in 1913, at the age of 23, Kurt Tucholsky satirized the formula „Ruhe und Ordnung". Tucholsky, a student of law, opens his journalistic commentary on „Verbotene Filme" by citing the *Allgemeines Landrecht*:

> O du gesegnetes Allgemeines Landrecht für die Preußischen Staaten! O du sein gesegneter § 10 II 17:„Die nötigen Anstalten zur Erhaltung der öffentlichen Ruhe, Sicherheit und Ordnung und zur Abwendung der dem Publiko oder einzelnen Mitgliedern desselben bevorstehenden Gefahr zu treffen, ist das Amt der Polizei." Das ist ein Sätzchen! Jeden Bürger, der mit dem Kasernenton kollidiert, jeden verprügelten Streiker, jedes Opfer stiller Polizeiwachstuben – sie alle weist ein dicker Zeigefinger auf jene Vorschrift. Die ist aus Gummi und umfaßt wie eine Zelle die Gehirne unterer und oberer Subalterner. (I, 89)

Tucholsky makes clear his belief in the powerful legacy of the *Allgemeines Landrecht* by arguing: „ER zeugte die Filmzensur" (I, 89).

Twelve years later Tucholsky mocks the passive acceptance of evil in his poem „Ruhe und Ordnung". What is important is not equality and justice but peaceful existence without protest. Organic evolution or dormant regeneration will erase all ills:

> Wenn Millionen arbeiten, ohne zu leben,
> wenn Mütter den Kindern nur Milchwasser geben –
>   das ist Ordnung
> [...]
> Wenn reiche Erben im schweizer Schnee
> jubeln – und sommers am Comer See –
>   dann herrscht Ruhe.
> [...]
> Die Hauptsache ist: Nicht auf Hungernde hören.
> Die Hauptsache ist: Nicht das Straßenbild stören.
>   Nur nicht schrein.
>   Mit der Zeit wird das schon.
>   Alles bringt euch die Evolution. (II, 19)

Tucholsky's poem „Holder Friede" (1929) mockingly celebrates peace („Ruh und Stille") and progress (radios on yachts). Both come at a price. The

---

[165] On Tucholsky's reception of Heine see Schweikert (1969). On similarities between Heine and Brecht, of which there are many, see esp. Hermand (1981).

individual who enjoys peace and progress is forced to overlook problems and forget individuals: „Vergessen sind die Invaliden – / jetzt haben wir Frieden." The poem closes with a gesture to the similarities between Tucholsky's age and Heine's. Both periods find domestic peace via the violent eradication of left wing and liberal elements: „Wir spielen Metternich-Epoche / und haben nichts dazugelernt" (III, 195–96).

While Tucholsky's poems are hardly as complex or aesthetically pleasing as Heine's, they exhibit to a remarkable degree the importance of earlier conceptions of political *Ruhe* for twentieth-century Germany: the *Allgemeines Landrecht*, the slogan „Ruhe und Ordnung", organic evolution, Metternich's peace of repression, and restricted utopian spheres.

Bertolt Brecht, equally aware of the heritage of the eighteenth and nineteenth century as central to twentieth-century conceptions of political *Ruhe*, presents in his „Liturgie vom Hauch" one of the almost countless parodies of Goethe's „Wanderers Nachtlied".[166] What interests both Heine and Brecht in their inversions of Goethe's poem is its political import. For Brecht the poem is emotional rather than reflective; it encourages lethargic behavior rather than action and protest. „Liturgie vom Hauch" takes its refrain from Goethe's work and inverts its seemingly quietist tendencies. Where one might debate the meaning of *Ruhe* in „Wanderers Nachtlied", the *Ruhe* of Brecht's poem is in the first few sentences clearly death. However, it is not an idealized death but the pathetic starvation of a old woman. A doctor – not unlike the „braver / Chirurgus" of Heine's „Jammertal" (VI/1, 305) – acknowledges her right to a death certificate but not a better life. A single individual voices his protest („Der hatte für die Ordnung keinen Sinn"), but as he begins to speak of man's common right to subsistence, a police inspector murders him. The policeman then recites a variation on Goethe's poem:

> Und jetzt schweigen die Vöglein im Walde
> Über allen Wipfeln ist Ruh
> In allen Gipfeln spürest du
> Kaum einen Hauch.

The inspector, who enjoys Goethe's classical lyrics, lacks any consciousness of justice. He even legitimizes his evil acts by citing Goethe's poem: in killing a demonstrator, he preserves *Ruhe und Ordnung*. After increasingly more men protest, they too are shot, eventually with machine guns. At the poem's conclusion a great red bear – whether or not Russian, in any case a symbol of revolution and of the active, dynamic element of nature – devours, not the police but, the little birds in the forest. Only at this point does change seem

---

[166] VIII, 181–86. For examples and analyses of both imitations and parodies of Goethe's poem see Segebrecht (1978).

possible. The silent birds, symbolic of those men whose quietude keeps them from protesting injustice, accept hunger and suppression, in part out of their own inner quietude, in part out of a fear of being slain. Where in Goethe's poem the „du" identifies with the tranquillity of nature, in Brecht's version no such expectation of *Ruhe* exists. The poem concludes:

> Da schwiegen die Vöglein nicht mehr
> Über allen Wipfeln ist Unruh
> In allen Gipfeln spürest du
> Jetzt einen Hauch.

In Goethe's poem one moves progressively from the summits to the treetops to the birds; Brecht reverses this order. Moreover, he focuses not on nature but on man, specifically on man's injustice and on social upheaval. For Brecht, unlike Goethe, *Ruhe* is one of man's worst possible states; it encourages the acceptance of unjust conditions. The „Hauch" of Goethe's poem, which suggests, literally, near silence and, proleptically, eventual repose, is in Brecht's poem an indication of political unrest. The *Ruhe* of Nature should not extend to man; rather, man's unrest should extend to his environment. Brecht accuses the classical tradition, exemplified in Goethe's „Ruhelied" (WA IV/24, 221), of supporting the status quo and inhibiting progress. In Brecht's reading, classical literature lulls our reflective capacities and shows us merely how the world is, not what it should become. Goethe falsely proposes man's quietude as a virtue. The *Ruhe* of Nature with which one might identify in Goethe's poem is dangerous insofar as it leads one to passivity and silence. Before revolution or any meaningful social change is possible, the silent little birds, the men whose ideal or condition is *Ruhe*, must be transformed or removed. As with Heine, progress demands an overcoming of both aesthetic stillness and political quietude.

In his play *Kaspar*, Peter Handke not only advances our understanding of language and linguistic manipulation, he adds a new dimension to the politics of *Ruhe*. To see in *Kaspar* an absolute critique of language would be to misinterpret the play or to reduce its meaning to a set of self-cancelling propositions. *Kaspar* is a play about *specific* forms of education and language that suppress individuality, invite or force conformity, and serve to preserve both the order of the status quo and the individual subject's quietude. For Kaspar language turns out to be a prison, but it is not *a priori* so. In learning language Kaspar gains as much as he loses. With language Kaspar's possibilities are indeed limited, but without language and its limitations he has no possibilities, a point not unrelated to our earlier discussion of Fichte's and Hölderlin's interpretation of the nothingness of the absolute ego. Through language Kaspar gains awareness of his environment and his self; language permits differentiation, individuality, and self-consciousness. In addition, the author of the play, Peter Handke, can express his insights into language only with the aid of language. For this reason as well, the focus of critique in *Kaspar* cannot be language as such.

Kaspar learns language from the prompters, the voices of authority and upholders of society's order. Rather than developing Kaspar's individuality and his capacity for reason, they force him into imitation, repetition, obedience. With their rhythmic and repetitive slogans and their authoritative voices they suppress his questions and manipulate him into adjusting to the given order. They suppress Kaspar's individuality. He becomes like everyone else; the appearance on stage of many Kaspars symbolizes this process, as does the fact that Kaspar himself eventually begins to sound like the prompters. When Kaspar tries to break out, the others employ their files, shaping him, symbolically, into their image of what he should be.

The object of Brecht's critique is the *Ruhe* encouraged by the aesthetic tradition and enforced by the military police. For Handke it is the often more, sometimes less subtle influence of language: political propaganda; advertising; dogmatic, undialectical instruction; truisms of belief. For Handke language is equally violent and equally conducive to quietism and the loss of critical autonomy.[167] As the prompters begin to address Kaspar, he is repeatedly still: „Er ist still" (20); „Kaspar sitzt still" (21); „Kaspar ist still" (34); „Kaspar ist ruhig" (57); „Kaspar ist noch ruhiger" (58). These are more than just stage directions. As Kaspar learns language, he learns order; he becomes conscious and desirous of *Ruhe*: „alles, was still ist, ist friedlich: alles, was auf seinem Platz ist, ist friedlich: alles, was friedlich ist, ist freundlich: alles, was freundlich ist, ist wohnlich" (42). With language Kaspar seems to find repose: „*Ich* beruhige *mich*" (51). The prompters tell him explicitly: „Du kannst dich mit Sätzen beruhigen: du kannst *schön* ruhig sein" (58). The prompters are not without influence. The next stage direction suggests: „Es ist sehr hell. Kaspar ist sehr ruhig" (58). In section 58, Kaspar's first lengthy discourse, Kaspar refers repeatedly to his quiet integration into the status quo:

> Ich bin verantwortungsbewußt. Ich bin fleißig, zurückhaltend und bescheiden [...] Meine Ordnungsliebe und Sauberkeit geben nie zu Tadel Anlaß [...] Ich bin friedliebend und unbescholten [...] Ich bin ruhig, pflichtbewußt und aufnahmefähig [...] Ich habe mich schon an alles gewöhnt. Es geht mir besser. Es geht mir gut. Ich kann in den Tod gehen. (68)

The section culminates with Kaspar's affirmation of order and his desire for stillness: „Ich weiß jetzt, was ich will: / ich will / still / sein" (69–70). The stillness of Kaspar dissolves into the stillness of the many Kaspars, i.e., the society that takes away his identity and preserves general quietude:

---

[167] For the association of language with violence see 19 and 77.

„Alle vier Kaspars sind still" (77).
„Alle fünf Kaspars sind still" (78).
„Alle sechs Kaspars sind still" (79).
„Er ist einige Augenblicke still. Auch die Kaspars auf dem Sofa hinten sind recht still" (81).
„Er ist einige Augenblicke still. Auch die Kaspars auf dem Sofa hinten sind noch still" (83).

The prompters praise this ordered world: „so herrscht Ruhe auf Erden" (79). When Kaspar finally recognizes that his words are hardly his own, his identity nonexistent, he is unable to protest rationally. He must choose between silence, the language imposed upon him, and meaningless utterances. Near the end of section 58 he chooses silence. At the text's conclusion he protests openly, but his dissent ends with a seemingly meaningless gesture to goats and monkeys; he is placed in the context of Othello, another helpless object of rhetoric. Kaspar's *Ruhe* is transformed into restlessness, chaos, and despair. Handke develops, as Heine had before him, the associations between *Ruhe*, language, and power. As with Heine the critique is obvious, the solution unclear.

5. Conclusion

In my chapter on Schiller's *Über naive und sentimentalische Dichtung* I argued for a reevaluation of the idyllic as a synthesis of the naive and sentimental or of stillness and motion, perfection and becoming. I began by suggesting that the naive and sentimental are not exclusively aesthetic categories. I offered two reasons for viewing Schiller's distinction on a more general, philosophical level. First, Schiller himself applies the terms to areas outside of art: psychology, social behavior, politics, morality, and the philosophy of history. Second, Schiller's definition of the naive closely resembles the contemporaneous philosophical concept of intellectual intuition, while his definition of the sentimental parallels contemporary philosophical notions of infinite striving and infinite approximation.

After establishing the philosophical status of Schiller's two categories, I analyzed them for their logical consistency. I showed that the dualism of the two terms breaks down; each category cancels itself and passes into its other. The naive is essentially also sentimental, and the sentimental contains the naive as a moment within itself. The results of this philosophical analysis only appear to subvert Schiller's intentions; in truth, they provide support for his intuitive sense of a unity of the two terms.

In the second part of the chapter I identified this unity with Schiller's concept of the idyllic. Actually, Schiller presents four different definitions of the idyll. After subdividing the sentimental into satire, which is characterized by its vehement negation of reality, and the elegy, which is marked by its longing for a past or future ideal, Schiller suggests that the idyll is a subcategory of the elegy. Second, Schiller tells us that the idyll is a direct subcategory of the sentimental and on an equal level with the elegy and the satire. Third, Schiller defines the idyll as a weak attempt on the part of the sentimental self to return to a naive state. The individual locked into such a false idyll sacrifices the advantages of sentimental consciousness, e.g., an orientation towards the future and a consideration of higher ideals. Finally, Schiller implies that there is a true idyll which contains both naive and sentimental moments without sacrificing the advantages of either. Schiller does not state this position quite so directly, but by analyzing Schiller's diction we could see that his final and lengthiest definition of the idyll allows for not only sentimental moments of motion and becoming but also naive moments of perfection and repose. The "dominant tone" of this idyll is "stillness" but a stillness that does not exclude "striving". The idyllic then is not really a subcategory of the sentimental, but rather the highest term in Schiller's essay; it marks the synthesis of the naive and the sentimental.

In a concluding section I pointed to the importance of an idyllic synthesis of stillness and motion in Schiller's other theoretical works as well as in a selection of his dramas and poems. Discussions of Goethe and Hegel showed that the dynamic stillness uncovered in Schiller's concept of the idyllic is also central to their writings and can be used as a key for an understanding of German *Klassik* as a whole.

In my chapter on Hölderlin I argued that stillness is a central concept in *Hyperion*, indeed, that the hero's development consists in his ability to synthesize in himself the pure stillness he ascribes to his beloved, Diotima, and the one-sided energetic striving he finds in his friend Alabanda. As Hyperion narrates he becomes more and more „ruhig". I analyzed Hyperion's increasing stillness in relationship to the various levels of discourse in the text: quotations from the past, reflections in the present on the past, and reflections on the present act of narrating the past. The more reflective Hyperion becomes, the greater his repose.

As Hyperion becomes more stable and secure in his stillness, he reevaluates his previous ideals. After having projected a seemingly perfect yet also static stillness into Diotima, the gods, Nature, and childhood, Hyperion begins to realize that all beings fulfill themselves not in a state of original oneness or static simplicity but rather in the passage to consciousness and temporality and, ultimately, in the recognition of the unity of oneness and multiplicity, of stillness and motion. That Hyperion calls his synthesis not motion but stillness speaks for the magical associations of the term „Ruhe" during this period of German intellectual and literary history.

My study of stillness in *Hyperion* also led to a new interpretation of the novel's conclusion. Previous interpreters have located the chronologically last significant statement of the narrating narrator as well as the goal of his development in the third to last letter, where Hyperion reaches a state of sovereign consciousness and utter repose. According to my reading, the narrating narrator makes his final statements (not counting the last five words of the novel) in the penultimate letter, specifically in a scathing critique of the historical present. I offer five reasons for this interpretation. First, applying to the fifty-ninth letter the linguistic criteria that distinguish the narrating from the experiencing narrator, I show that this letter is not, as previously believed, a quotation from the past; rather, it is spoken by the narrator in the present. My second argument develops from the concept of dynamic stillness that I elaborate in the course of the chapter. The third argument rests upon a full understanding of Hölderlin's appropriation and development of Schiller's categories from *Über naive und sentimentalische Dichtung*, to which Hölderlin makes both direct and indirect reference in the novel. The fourth argument makes use of the allusion to Sophocles' *Oedipus at Colonus*, with which Hyperion introduces his fifty-ninth letter. The final argument draws upon Hölderlin's dialectics of totality and particularity, identity and difference, and stillness and motion, as he developed them in his philosophical essays of the period. On the basis of my reinterpretation of the novel's conclusion, one can see that Hyperion's development leads to a stillness that does not exclude critical engagement in the historical present.

In my third section I discussed the structure of Hyperion's selfhood and analyzed the aesthetic nature of the novel in relationship to Hyperion's definition of beauty. I could thus show why Hyperion includes reflections from his past life at the novel's conclusion and after he has reached the pinnacle of his development.

In my study of Büchner I focused on the two conceptions of *Ruhe* in *Lenz*: first, a positive stillness that leads toward salvation; second, a negative stillness that signifies lack of direction and, eventually, insanity. The negative concept of stillness, more prominent towards the story's conclusion, inverts the traditional associations of *Ruhe* in aesthetics, religion, psychology, and morality.

In the discourse on art Lenz denounces idealist aesthetics. He condemns not only the idealist's selection of noble figures and unrealistic events, he attacks the concept of selection in general. Preferring the fluidity of existence to the static nature of art, Lenz suggests that one resist the temptation to transform beautiful figures into stone. Instead, one should allow beautiful scenes to disappear and see in this dissolution the even greater beauty of life and motion.

Büchner inverts the traditionally positive associations of *Ruhe* in religion as well. In the beginning of the story Lenz has several religious experiences: he prays, he reads from the Bible, he preaches, and he has mystical experiences. Towards the end of the story he suffers religious torment. Noting God's inability or unwillingness to eliminate suffering, Lenz tries in a moment of hybris to replace Christ and revive a child. After this first reversal of roles, Lenz then pictures himself as Satan; the narrator calls him an atheist, and he is explicitly described as „ruhig". Far from suggesting proximity to God as in the tradition, Lenz's *Ruhe* becomes a mark of emptiness, of distance from God. Evidence indicates that Büchner was aware of this traditional association and that the inversion in *Lenz* was intentional.

Towards the end of the story, as Lenz becomes ever more tranquil, he becomes impassive; eventually he goes insane. This loss of meaning derives in part from Lenz's anti-idealist stance. The inversion of idealist options leads, necessarily, to contradictions, and Lenz's inability to resolve these contradictions threatens his existence. Lenz's insanity can also be situated in the context of the history of the idea of stillness. Lenz's passive indifference inverts a traditional association of *Ruhe* with peace of mind and life in harmony with society. For the Middle and Late Stoics, Spinoza, and the German Classicists *Ruhe* signifies an equanimity of spirit that enables the self to function in harmony with the world. Büchner had encountered this topos through his readings in ancient literature and his intensive study of Spinoza.

By inverting the traditional associations of *Ruhe* Büchner seems to opt for motion over stillness. Büchner models the hero of his story after the Storm and Stress writer Lenz, who argued in his philosophical essay *Versuch über das erste Principium der Moral* that stillness and motion are the two major principles in the world. Lenz argues that motion, not stillness, is the proper condition for man. Büchner's own position is less clear. He has inverted the positive associations of stillness, yet the explicit critique of aesthetic stillness voiced by Lenz cannot be identified with Büchner. One is left with the impression that behind Büchner's reigning antithetical nature the *ideal* of a synthesis of motion *and* stillness remains intact. Indeed Lenz's few moments of happiness and centeredness occur when he is not only active but also in repose.

In the chapter on Heine and the politics of *Ruhe*, I considered, first, the relationship of aesthetic stillness to political quietude. In his criticism of Goethe Heine focuses on the political import of Goethe's art, likening it to cold, marble statues that fail to move the viewer to political action. Though Heine experiences a personal desire for idyllic and artistic repose, he relinquishes this for political engagement. Religious stillness, like its aesthetic counterpart, engenders a spurious political stance. The state desires apolitical and obedient subjects; the religious populace, versed in mysticism, Pietism, and the doctrine of two realms, responds all too willingly. Inverting the traditionally ideal concept of religious stillness, Heine affirms his belief in a God of motion and progress.

In a section on German somnolence I considered the increasingly pejorative association of *Ruhe* with sleep. Heine and his contemporaries attack the idea of dormant regeneration, prominent from Herder to Menzel, as a justification of the status quo and a false excuse for lethargy, blindness, and inactivity. Heine criticizes not only this tradition, he questions the dream world of German Romanticism and the merely theoretical inclinations of the German Idealists. The nineteenth-century concern with Germany's political sleepiness led to a resurgence of the awakening-motif as well as the reverse image of the drowsy German Michel. At moments of political unrest Germany seemed to awaken, but repression and passivity inevitably took the upper hand; Michel, the symbol of Germany, donned his night cap and fell asleep.

The themes of aesthetic and religious stillness, German somnolence, and political quietude played significant roles in my analyses of several of Heine's *Zeitgedichte*, particularly „Bei des Nachtwächters Ankunft zu Paris" and „Zur Beruhigung", and Heine's mock epic *Deutschland. Ein Wintermärchen*. In his *Zeitgedichte* Heine offers detailed ironic commentary on Biedermeier values, Germany's supposed depth, its nationalism, its false vision of its own destiny, and its servile, political quietude. My analysis of the *Wintermärchen* stressed the frozen stillness of Germany's political landscape; the flight into dreams; the passive wish to find salvation from a hibernating hero, Barbarossa; and the overall negativity of Heine's critique.

A final section considered the two competing associations of political *Ruhe*: the pastoral ideal of a moral and political countersphere to the cities and courts that builds upon bucolic, georgic, and idyllic poetry; and the oppressive stillness associated with the slogans „Kirchhofsruhe" and „Ruhe und Ordnung". A final excursus suggested that twentieth-century critics of oppressive *Ruhe*, such as Tucholsky, Brecht, and Handke, develop strains of thought already present in Heine.

Ruhe has proven to be of interest for the continuity and discontinuity of its historical development and the diverse spheres in which it plays a role. As a heuristic category, it has led to new interpretations of important literary works. The significance of *Ruhe*, however, is not exhausted by its wide range and powerful explanatory power. Dynamic stillness, not simply a psychological and an aesthetic ideal, is a metaphor for philosophical truth.[1] Synthesizing a circular and a linear conception of history, it allows for both the stillness of eternally valid logical structures (systematic perfection) and unending motion or progress within particular fields of inquiry and endeavor (material perfection). Under stillness one understands those structures, both logical and ontological, which are valid *a priori* and, which, whenever seemingly swept away, always return to exhibit the self-cancellation of the purely negative. Stillness thus corresponds to the *philosophia perennis*, to the eternal validity of categories such as unity, reason, and intersubjectivity. Under dynamism one understands the *Realien* of truth,

---

[1] I can elaborate on this point only briefly in this context. Any reader of Hösle's brilliant *Wahrheit und Geschichte* will understand to what extent the concept of dynamic stillness mirrors the relationship of philosophical truth to history.

those insights that are developed *a posteriori* and allow us to speak of change and progress. Here one thinks of advances in specific fields of inquiry from psychology to political economy.

Büchner's and Heine's inquiries into the social and political dimensions of art and human consciousness fit this dynamic model, even if their negative and anti-idealist positions led them to a mistaken denial of the need for systematic thought. In order to make their negation of stillness and valorization of dynamism more effective, Büchner, Heine, and other nineteenth-century authors critical of stillness, such as Mundt, tried not only to free themselves from the idealist inheritance and the strains of systematic thought, they consistently misinterpreted their opponents. Their misreadings of Winckelmann, Goethe, and Hegel were partly psychological and arose from the need to clear out a space for their own ideas and spheres of inquiry. But the misreadings were also partly rhetorical: by misquoting their predecessors, these writers hoped to make their case against the seemingly false ideal of stillness that much more convincing.

To make matters more complex, we found in Büchner and Heine genuine longings for *Ruhe*, which they attempted – not always successfully – to deny or resist, and, more importantly, an underlying philosophical ideal of dynamic stillness. Even deficient stillness is, paradoxically, dynamic. First and on the most superficial level, "deficient stillness" alters the previously ideal notion of "dynamic stillness": as the concept „Ruhe" *changes* its meaning through time, the very concept becomes *dynamic*. Second and more importantly, insofar as Büchner, Heine, and others suggest that „Bewegung" is „das dauernde Gesetz", that whatever is in motion, is eternal („was sich bewegt, das ist ewig"), they too embrace the unity of the temporal and the eternal, motion and stillness.[2] To use Schiller's categories, sentimental change – when taken to its absolute level – becomes the permanence of the naive. Finally and most importantly, despite their pronounced rejection of stillness, the nineteenth-century writers who stress motion, restlessness, and history do not deny the stillness of eternal values. History is viewed not as proof of the relativity of ideas and values but as the element in which to recognize their validity and to work to realize them – be they justice, sympathy, freedom, or equality. While Büchner, Heine, and their contemporaries – with their stress on progress and politics – finally subvert the traditionally positive, potentially quietistic connotations of *Ruhe*, the philosophical integrity of a genuinely dynamic stillness remains intact.

Much can be done with the concept of dynamic stillness beyond what I have attempted here. One important area of future research would be the interre-

---

[2] Mundt, „Über Bewegungsparteien..." 1; Mundt, *Madonna*, 5.

lation of aesthetic, religious, psychological-moral, and political conceptions of *Ruhe*. A few generalizations will suffice in the present context to suggest the richness of this field of inquiry. Just as in the religious tradition, where the mystic receives grace in a moment of repose, so does the poet in the Age of Goethe receive divine inspiration or creativity in a moment of stillness. The viewer, too, should be in repose; Wackenroder likens the reception of the aesthetic object to silent prayer (71–75). Concepts such as „ästhetische Kirche" (Hölderlin) or „Kunstreligion" (Wackenroder) provide useful markers for the significance of the interrelation of religious and aesthetic stillness in the late eighteenth and early nineteenth century. The secularization of religious *Ruhe* in German *Klassik* coincides with a revival of the idea of psychological-moral stillness. Whether they developed independently or whether the secularization led to a reawakened interest in Stoicism and Spinoza or whether the revival of psychological-moral stillness helped hasten the process of secularization seem significant questions. One also wonders to what extent the religious concept of *Ruhe* helped generate the extraordinary importance of political inwardness and *Ruhe* in Germany. Schleiermacher, who views *Ruhe* as a predominantly religious category, defines religion in direct opposition to Fichte, who had derived religion from ethics in the socalled fourth critique of Kant.[3] This kind of dichotomy between religious virtue and ethical activity might well have contributed to the valorization of interiority within the German tradition that Nietzsche notes in *Zur Genealogie der Moral* (1887) and Thomas Mann sketches in „Deutschland und die Deutschen" (1945). Heine saw a conflation not only of religious and political stillness; in his view, aesthetic stillness helped contribute to Germany's political interiority and backwardness. Aesthetic and psychological-moral stillness converge in a positive way in the concept of aesthetic education. Schiller's extension of the aesthetic idyll to psychology, ethics, and politics, and Hölderlin's attempt to demonstrate the education of the self through narration or reading or both are only two of many such examples. A study of these and other interesting combinations would surely help clarify the interdisciplinary significance of *Ruhe* and shed new light on the interrelation of semantic and cultural history.

One could relate not only the meanings of *Ruhe* within the individual spheres to one another but also the positive and negative modes of each. We have considered dynamic and deficient aspects of aesthetic, religious, and psychological-moral stillness. Of the two political modes – the pastoral and the oppressive – both are inadequate, the former being restricted, the latter reactionary. There is, however, a positive political *Ruhe*, and it too can be

---

[3] See Fichte's *Versuch einer Kritik aller Offenbarung* (1792) and Schleiermacher's *Über die Religion* (1799).

related to other forms of stillness; I'm thinking of *Ruhe* as peace, or in its influential Roman form, *pax*.[4] Here political and religious forms of stillness overlap in a positive way, beginning already in Neoplatonism. In Book 19 of *De civitate dei*, for example, Augustine discusses levels of peace in a Neoplatonic hierarchy and argues that knowledge of God's peace, the "summum bonum" of heaven,[5] enables one to seek and have peace on earth, to act justly toward one another.[6] Insofar as God is peace, one loves peace and strives to realize it:[7] "For so great a good is peace that even where earthly and mortal affairs are in question no other word is heard with more pleasure, nothing else is desired with greater longing, and finally nothing better can be found."

Ideal political *Ruhe* can be related to other forms of stillness as well. The Stoics sought to achieve tranquillity of mind by acting in harmony with others and with the laws of the cosmos. In their view political peace derives from and generates the concordance of all. Psychological-moral and ideal political *Ruhe* are related in another sense as well: peace extends the Stoic demand for the overcoming of disturbance *(perturbatio)* from the individual's body and soul to the larger communities of city, state, and world. Pastoral *Ruhe*, too, can be related to political *Ruhe*. Pastoral existence normally represents a model harmony; ideal political *Ruhe* would simply extend this harmony to a wider sphere and assure us that development will override the pastoral temptation toward stasis.

Even writers openly critical of stillness, such as the Young Germans, would have to acknowledge that unity and peace are already present among those striving to upset the current order. It is one of Augustine's major arguments in Book 19 that even the disturbers of peace dislike not peace as such, but only its present form:[8] "For even those who prefer that a state of

---

[4] Unlike *otium* or the Greek *eirēnē*, *pax* presupposes at least two subjects, even when only one is named; whenever the word designates an internal condition *(pax animi)*, it still implies the denial of externally disturbing factors. See Fuchs (1926), 40, 182–88, 190. For the important relation between *pax* and *imperium* see Klingner (1979). The different, yet often overlapping, connotations and uses of *Ruhe* and *Frieden* invite further inquiry, especially in their relation to the Roman and Christian traditions.

[5] At the beginning of chapter 20 Augustine calls everlasting and perfect peace ("pax aeterna atque perfecta") the supreme good. Cf. the similar formulation at the conclusion of chapter 27.

[6] Augustine describes the peace of the celestial city as *Ruhe* ("pax omnium rerum") and *Ordnung* ("tranquillitas ordinis"). These terms, which have developed decidedly negative connotations, are not *a priori* regressive, reactionary, or violent.

[7] "Tantum est enim pacis bonum ut etiam in rebus terrenis atque mortalibus nihil gratius soleat audiri, nihil desiderabilius concupisci, nihil postremo possit melius inveniri" (XIX, 11). See also *Confessions*, X, 27.

[8] "Nam et illi qui pacem, in qua sunt, perturbari volunt, non pacem oderunt, sed eam pro arbitrio suo cupiunt commutari" (XIX, 12).

peace should be upset do so not because they hate peace but because they desire a different state of peace that will meet their wishes." The Young Germans, with all their martial metaphors, Heine included, simply seek a more just and equitable peace.[9]

While critics of dynamic stillness do not stress the associations of *Ruhe* with ideal peace, writers who uphold the ideal of dynamic stillness do. Hyperion's dynamic repose has political as well as aesthetic implications. Hyperion's education should serve as a model for the peace of the entire nation. Not surprisingly, attempts to define the conditions for universal and perpetual peace have often arisen during periods when the concept of dynamic stillness was prominent. Consider Pseudo-Dionysius' *Divine Names*, Cusanus' *De pace fidei*, or Kant's *Zum ewigen Frieden*, all three of which recognize peace as a dynamic stillness that allows for both unity and difference.

The overlap of different kinds of stillness within the German tradition has helped make „Ruhe" a uniquely significant concept. Religious, aesthetic, psychological-moral, and political stillness are all frequently conveyed by the one word „Ruhe". While there have been English, French, and American authors interested in the concept of stillness (One thinks of such diverse writers as Wyatt,[10] Rousseau,[11] and Nemerov.),[12] the terms "stillness" and

---

[9] On Heine's martial metaphors see Kurz (1967), 115–17 and Sengle (1971–80), III, 497–98.

[10] Wyatt translated Plutarch's *De tranquillitate animi* in 1527.

[11] Repose plays a prominent role in Rousseau's analysis of culture; it represents one of the three basic goods of savage man that modern man has lost. Towards the end of the *Second Discourse*, in a contrast between savage man and civilized man, Rousseau highlights the ideal aspects of repose: «L'homme Sauvage et l'homme policé différent tellement par le fond du cœur et des inclinations, que ce qui fait le bonheur suprême de l'un, réduiroit l'autre au désespoir. Le premier ne respire que le repos et la liberté, il ne veut que vivre et reŝter oisif, et l'ataraxie même du Stoïcien n'approche pas de sa profonde indifférence pour tout autre objet. Au contraire, le Citoyen toujours actif, suë, s'agite, se tourmente sans cesse pour chercher des occupations encore plus laborieuses: il travaille jusqu'à la mort, il y court même pour se mettre en état de vivre, ou renonce à la vie pour acquerir l'immortalité» (III, 192). Rousseau, however, also knows of a negative repose that he associates with unenlightened servitude and bondage: «Je sais que les premiers [enslaved people] ne font que vanter sans cesse la paix et le repos dont ils joüissent dans leurs fers, et que *miserrimam servitutem pacem appellant*» (III, 181). Servitude assures tranquillity. See also III, 187.

[12] See esp. "Painting a Mountain Stream" (203–04) and "Runes" (211–18). Nemerov's ideas on stillness might well have originated in part from his acquaintance with the German tradition. Nemerov was, after all, in 1939 „der junge Gelehrte der Harvard University" whose Senior Honors Thesis on "The Quester Hero" Thomas Mann cites in his preface to *Der Zauberberg*. See Hatfield (1979), 37.

"repose" lack the highly charged and diverse associations of „Ruhe".[13] The numerous reasons for the special status of *Ruhe* range from the extraordinary impact of Winckelmann's reflections on aesthetic stillness to the conflation of religious and psychological-moral stillness in eighteenth-century Germany and the development of important political slogans such as „Fanatismus der Ruhe" and „Ruhe und Ordnung" that have no equivalent in English or French. A comparative study taking into account both national diversity and cross-cultural influence might shed new light on the intercultural concept of dynamic stillness as well as the specific German concept of „Ruhe".

Another area of future inquiry would be the rhetoric of *Ruhe*, by which I mean the structures, images, and stylistic devices used to convey stillness. In both a religious and philosophical sense *Ruhe* has been associated with totality and perfection. This association is commonly expressed through circular imagery. I opened my discussion of dynamic stillness with Cusanus' description of the spinning circle, which at infinite velocity is both absolutely still and perfectly in motion. The association of dynamic stillness with perfect, circular motion can be found earlier still, in Proclus and Pseudo-Dionysius, who view divine emanation and epistrophe as a singular, circular movement without beginning or end.[14] This relation between dynamic stillness, perfection, and circularity is important throughout Christian thought. God is not only still, he is a circle whose center is everywhere and circumference nowhere.[15] Motion from center to (non-)circumference is thus immediate or still. In Germany the conflation of divine circularity and stillness is secularized with diverse connotations in, for example, Schiller's „Die Worte des Glaubens" (SA I, 164) and Grillparzer's *Ein Bruderzwist in Habsburg* (47). In Romanticism this conflation takes on a magical dimension. For the Romantics time stands still in the center of the earth. The tranquil miner of Novalis' *Heinrich von Ofterdingen* is immersed in the stillness of the earth's depths (I, 245). Here in the center of the earth, where time is still and thus ever present, Heinrich can observe his future development. Poets often use circular imagery to convey the structure of a perfect aesthetic construct.[16]

---

[13] Although Rousseau's use of «repos» represents an exception in this regard, the point remains: the broad significance of repose – for so many authors and with so many connotations – remains unique to the German tradition.

[14] See Proclus, *The Elements of Theology*, props. 33 and 146; Pseudo-Dionysius, *Divine Names*, IV, 8–9 = 704 D–705 B; IV, 14 = 712 D–713 A. On Cusanus' view of the perfect circle see esp. *De docta ignorantia*, I, 21.

[15] See, for example, Suso: „got ist als ein cirkellicher ring, des ringes mitle punct allenthalb ist und sin umbswank niene" (Bihlmeyer 178 = *Seuses Leben*, ch. 51).

[16] Philosophers meanwhile use circular imagery to illustrate the completeness of their systems. See, for example, Hegel 3:23, 36–37, 559, 8:60, 63; 18:46, 400; WL I 56; WL II 504.

We have already discussed the circularity of *Hyperion*, which gives the novel a dimension otherwise reserved only for the visual arts.[17] One might consider in this regard Stifter's *Der Nachsommer*, with its concept of *Vertiefung* and its series of returns. Finally, poems about stillness will often adopt circular structures or directly address the topic of circularity. One thinks, for example, of Goethe's „Wenn im Unendlichen dasselbe" and Möricke's „Die schöne Buche".[18]

Dynamic stillness suggests not just the simple stillness of circularity but the progress of, in Hegel's words, „die sich erreicht habende Linie" (WL I, 138–39). Insofar as stillness indicates either rest or perfection, it is normally reached at the end of a development. The Sabbath, Heine notwithstanding, comes at the end of the week. On a more limited temporal scale, stillness is associated with the evening, after the restlessness of the day has elapsed; „abendliche Stille" and „stille Nacht" are extraordinarily frequent images. On a structural level stillness is often invoked at the end of a text. One can observe this in a number of philosophical works, from the final chapter of Augustine's *City of God* to the fifth book of Spinoza's *Ethics* and the concluding preface of Hegel's *Phänomenologie des Geistes*. In literature the structure frequently serves to highlight *Ruhe* as the pinnacle of edification. What we saw at the conclusion of Hölderlin's *Hyperion*, applies, surprisingly, to such diverse texts as Grimmelshausen's *Simplicissimus* and Fontane's *Effi Briest*.

Another privileged location for stillness, one which relates to the image of the circle, is the center of the text. The Athens-letter in *Hyperion* comes to mind (StA III, 76–90). Still more widespread is the temporal center of noon peace, which is frequently combined with the myth of Pan. Germanists will recognize the motif from Goethe's *Novelle*: „Über die große Weite lag eine heitere Stille, wie es am Mittag zu sein pflegt, wo die Alten sagten, Pan schlafe und alle Natur halte den Atem an, um ihn nicht aufzuwecken" (HA VI, 499–500). Eichendorff and Seeger each wrote a poem on the topic of noon peace.[19] In „Die schöne Buche" Mörike speaks of a midday stillness characterized by „dämonische Stille, / Unergründliche Ruh" (53). Things happen during this midday stillness: it is a time for revelations in both the Greek and Judaeo-Christian traditions.[20] Midday silence is coupled, after all, with the dynamism of the sun's heat.

---

[17] On the stilling of movement through literature's adoption of spatial metaphors see Krieger (1967).
[18] Cf. Brecht's skillful inversion of the conflation of perfect repose and circularity in „Der Radwechsel" (X, 1009).
[19] Eichendorff 22; Seeger I, 116.
[20] See *The Odyssey*, 4: 400, 450; *Phaedrus* 238 c–d, 242 a–d; Gen. 18, 1; Acts 22, 6.

When stillness can't be reached so easily, it is often projected into distant nature, mountain peaks, for example, or the stars. Hölderlin employs both images.[21] Stars often serve as embodiments of dynamic stillness; though they appear to be still, they are really in motion. Hyperion calls them „still und bewegt" (StA III, 48). Novalis addresses them as „Ihr stillen Wandrer" (I, 277). Another natural element to which stillness is ascribed is water. Indeed, writers occasionally combine the heavens and water in order to express the presence of *Ruhe* on earth. In the evening, when lakes and rivers are especially still, water reflects the stillness of the stars and brings to earth what otherwise seems so distant.[22]

The association of tranquillity of mind with the stillness of water is common to several schools of Greek philosophy – the Epicureans, Stoics, and Sceptics – and reaches through the German tradition to Schopenhauer and Nietzsche.[23] Goethe, Eichendorff, and Heine wrote poems entitled „Meeresstille", which tell their readers as much about psychological states as they do about nature. Goethe's poem, which contains an extreme and ominous stillness, a kind of „Todesstille", is complemented in an ultimately harmonic way by its companion poem, „Glückliche Fahrt" (HA I, 242). For Eichendorff the stillness of the sea invites the viewer into a melodious dream world (148–49). The sea of Heine's „Meeresstille", consistent with his breaking of harmonic images, isn't the least bit calm: tension and discord undermine the proposed image of stillness (B II, 182).

Water, which can be still, in motion, or both, is, much like the circle or midday, a perfect image for dynamic stillness. In Winckelmann's analogy between Laocoon and the sea the surface may be full of rage but underneath all is still. The connection in Western philosophy between motion and water is, of course, as old as Heraclitus' fragments, but even here the overriding concern is not restless change but the unity of permanence and flux.[24] Of the many German poems that capture with water imagery the conflation of stillness and motion, let me name just two, C.F. Meyer's „Der römische Brunnen" and Rilke's final sonnett to Orpheus, where the poet closes with the following synthetic image: „Und wenn dich das Irdische vergaß, / zu der stillen Erde sag: Ich rinne. / Zu dem raschen Wasser sprich: Ich bin" (89).

Frozen water is absolutely still, and coldness is a favorite image for the reverse concept of deficient stillness. While sun, heat, and flowing water are

---

[21] StA III: 74 and 318.
[22] Note also Heine's ironic literalization of this image in *Atta Troll* (B IV, 525).
[23] Epicurus, *Letter to Herodotus* (83); Marcus Aurelius, *Meditations*, V, 2; VIII, 28; XII, 22; Sextus Empericus, I, 10; (cf. I, 25–30); Schopenhauer, 2, 507; Schlechta II, 68.
[24] See Hösle (1984/Wahrheit), 187.

images for progress and revolution, winter and ice represent, as we saw in our discussion of the Young Germans, stasis, emptiness, and indifference. The association of deficient stillness with coldness has not only political but also social and psychological significance: occasionally this coldness suggests boredom; more often it implies the *Ruhe* of objectivity and non-involvement, of unsympathetic distance.

At the opposite end of indifference and non-involvement is the ideal repose of love, and there is no shortage of passages in German literature suggesting that peace is found in intersubjectivity, from relatively forgotten poems like Justinus Kerner's „Ruhe bei Ihr" (I/2, 95–96) and Ferdinand Freiligrath's „Ruhe in der Geliebten" (I, 187–88) to Wilhelm Meister's famous *Ruhe* with Mariane.[25] In this study we have noticed the theme both in the Hyperion-Diotima relationship and in Lenz's remembrance of Friederike Brion. Though I didn't stress intersubjective stillness in Heine, he, too, is a master at this theme.[26] Love, which of course shares with dynamic stillness the synthetic unity of difference, is privileged in the literature of dynamic *Ruhe* as far back as Aristotle.[27]

As one might easily imagine, *Ruhe* is often ascribed to childhood and innocence. Mature writers will recognize – as does Goethe – that this initial *Ruhe* is lost as soon as one strives for knowledge (HA IX: 129, 324). *Ruhe* is again achieved either through clarity of insight or with death. The *Ruhe* of death is often perceived as a positive relief from suffering, as for example with Emilia Galotti or with Paul Bäumler at the end of the famous war novel *Im Westen nichts Neues*. Writers from Kleist to Freud speak of the striving of all objects toward *Ruhe*.[28] More interesting perhaps are writers like Büchner who question whether *Ruhe* is to be found in death or like Nestroy who recognize that those who want *Ruhe* might not want it once they get it; what they really want is a form of "live" stillness.[29]

---

[25] HA VII, 64. It is not uncommon in the literature of the eighteenth and early nineteenth century that men search for *Ruhe*, while women are already in repose. Insofar as women represent the *object* of men's desires, their ideal *Ruhe* is often transformed into the *Ruhe* of passivity and silence. A full account of gender differentiation in uses of *Ruhe* would surely bring interesting results.

[26] See BI: 78, 128, 176, and 217.

[27] *Metaphysics*, 1072 b.

[28] See Kleist: „von ganzer Seele sehne ich mich, wonach die ganze Schöpfung und alle immer langsamer und langsamer rollenden Weltkörper streben, nach *Ruhe*!" (II, 643). Freud speaks of the death instinct as „das allgemeinste Streben alles Lebenden, zur Ruhe der anorganischen Welt zurückzukehren" (XIII, 68).

[29] Danton is told: „im Grab sey Ruhe, und Grab und Ruhe seyen eins," but he later senses that there is „keine Hoffnung im Tod" (L I: 9, 61). Cf. *Lenz*: „für ihn war ja keine Ruhe und Hoffnung im Tod" (29). For Nestroy see *Nur Ruhe!* esp. Act III, scene 13.

Besides the various structures and images of *Ruhe* one might consider the stylistics of stillness. I noted in my discussion of Büchner and Heine their use of polysyndeton and anaphora. In the 1920s and early 30s Wilhelm Schneider developed an entire stylistics of stillness and motion, which still has a certain relevance today.[30] Stillness is conveyed primarily through the various figures of repetition and parallelism such as gemination, alliteration, and assonance, but also through verb ellipses, abstract nouns, the passive voice, hypotaxis, and simply the use of more words than may seem necessary. A dynamic effect calls for verbs of motion, prepositions of direction, verbal nouns, antitheses, chiasmi, oxymora, gradation, parataxis, reflexives, incomplete sentences, exclamations, and question marks. Eichendorff's poetry and Nietzsche's prose seem to fit the model of a stylistics of motion particularly well. For writers whose styles often convey stillness, one might think of Stifter or Broch.

Future research may identify other works beyond those in this study for which an understanding of the philosophy and rhetoric of *Ruhe* would lead to new interpretations. Among those that might fit this category: Schlegel's *Lucinde*, which contains both a Romantic „Idylle über den Müßiggang" and an intertwining of „Sehnsucht und Ruhe"; Grillparzer's *Ein Bruderzwist in Habsburg* with its problematic but interesting conflation of religious and political stillness; Stifter's *Der Nachsommer*, which revives eighteenth-century ideas of aesthetic stillness both in content and structure; and Raabe's *Unruhige Gäste* with its integration and variation of the Biblical motif.

There are other texts that come to mind as well; indeed, enough texts that one could imagine an interesting history of the idea of *Ruhe* from the late nineteenth century to the present. The shifting meaning of *Ruhe* in the nineteenth century is nowhere clearer than in Nietzsche's ambivalent stance,[31] which ranges from the critique of Schopenhauer's ideal of „Ruhe"[32] and of „die Ruhesuchenden" and „Winterschläfer"[33] to the jubilant midday hour, Zarathustra's „stillste Stunde", when the world becomes perfect.[34] In the twentieth century major authors such as Freud *(Jenseits des Lustprinzips)*, Kafka („Der Bau"), Thomas Mann („Der kleine Herr Friedemann"), Musil *(Der Mann ohne Eigenschaften)*, Rilke („Sonnetten an Orpheus"), and Heideg-

---

[30] Schneider (1925) and (1931).
[31] The ambivalent attitude continues into the twentieth century where two main camps are discernible: one predominantly affirmative of *Ruhe* and basically mystical, the other critical of *Ruhe* and political.
[32] Schlechta II: 187–88, 244–46. Cf. Schopenhauer, 2:420, 484–85, 490; 4:717; and 4,751, where he speaks of „die unendlich vorzuziehende Ruhe des säligen Nichts".
[33] Schlechta II: 142, 448.
[34] Schlechta II: 399–401, 512–15.

ger *(Sein und Zeit)* continue to show a fascination with the concept of „Ruhe". I have already suggested that Tucholsky, Brecht, and Handke extend into the twentieth century the association of *Ruhe* with oppression. The opposing category of pastoral *Ruhe* has not disappeared in this century. Ernst Bloch, for example, argues for a socialist utopia, characterized by „tätige Muße", and calls it „Ruheland".[35] Various dimensions of the concept „Ruhe" are still prominent in the sixties, seventies, and eighties, as the works of Wolf Biermann („Noch"), Thomas Bernhard *(Die Jagdgesellschaft, Über allen Gipfeln ist Ruh)*, and Joachim Walter *(Ruhe bewahren)* attest. By far the most important twentieth-century author with respect to the topic of *Ruhe* is, however, Gottfried Benn, whose poems „Trunkene Flut", „Wer allein ist", „Statische Gedichte", and „Reisen" are steeped in the traditional rhetoric of *Ruhe*. To unravel the meanings and structures of these poems, one would have to be versed in conceptions of stillness ranging from Aristotle and Epicurus through Eckhart and Cusanus to Schopenhauer and Nietzsche.

---

[35] *Das Prinzip Hoffnung*, 1080. See also 1073–86.

Works Cited

Primary Literature

Schiller

Schiller, Friedrich. *Schillers Briefe*. Kritische Gesamtausgabe. Ed. Fritz Jonas. 7 vols. Stuttgart: Deutsche Verlagsanstalt, 1892–96.
– *Schillers Sämtliche Werke*. Säkular-Ausgabe in 16 Bänden. Stuttgart: Cotta, 1904.
– *Schillers Werke*. Nationalausgabe. Ed. Julius Peterson and Hermann Schneider. Weimar: Böhlhaus, 1943–.

Hölderlin

Hölderlin, Christian Friedrich. *Sämtliche Werke*. Große Stuttgarter Ausgabe. Ed. Friedrich Beißner. 8 vols. Stuttgart: Kohlhammer, 1946–85.

Büchner

Büchner, Georg. *Lenz. Studienausgabe*. Ed. Hubert Gersch. Stuttgart: Reclam, 1984.
– *Sämtliche Werke und Briefe*. Historisch-kritische Ausgabe mit Kommentar. Ed. Werner R. Lehmann. 2 vols. Hamburg: Wegner, 1971–.
– *Werke und Briefe*. Gesamtausgabe. Ed. Fritz Bergemann. Wiesbaden: Insel, 1958.

Heine

Begegnungen mit Heine: Berichte der Zeitgenossen in Fortführung von H. H. Houbens „Gespräche mit Heine". Ed. Michael Werner. 2 vols. Hamburg: Hoffmann, 1973.
Heine, Heinrich. *Historisch-kritische Gesamtausgabe der Werke*. Düsseldorfer Ausgabe. Ed. Manfred Windfuhr et al. Hamburg: Hoffmann, 1973–.
– *Säkularausgabe*. Ed. Nationale Forschungs- und Gedenkstätten der klassischen deutschen Literatur in Weimar and Centre National de la Recherche Scientifique in Paris. Berlin: Akademie; Paris: Editions du CNRS, 1970–.
– *Sämtliche Schriften*. Ed. Klaus Briegleb et al. 6 vols. München: Hanser, 1968–76.

General

Die Achtundvierziger. Ein Lesebuch für unsere Zeit. Ed. Bruno Kaiser. 4th ed. Weimar: Thüringer Volksverlag, 1955.
Allgemeines Landrecht für die preußischen Staaten von 1794. Frankfurt: Metzner, 1970.
Aristotle. *The Basic Works of Aristotle*. Ed. Richard McKeon. New York: Random House, 1941.
Arnold, Gottfried. *Gottfried Arnolds sämmtliche geistliche Lieder mit einer reichen Auswahl aus den freieren Dichtungen und einem Lebens=Abriß desselben, ein Beitrag zur christlichen Hymnologie und Mystik*. Ed. K. C. E. Ehmann. Stuttgart: Steinkopf, 1856.

Auersperg, Anton Alexander. [Anastasius Grün]. *Anastasius Grün's gesammelte Werke.* Ed. Ludwig August Frankel. 5 vols. Berlin: Grote, 1907.
Augustine. *Confessionum libri XIII.* Stuttgart: Teubner, 1969.
- *De civitate dei contra paganos.* 7 vols. The Loeb Classical Library. Cambridge: Harvard UP; London: Heinemann, 1960.
Marcus Aurelius. *MARKOU AURĒLIOU ANTŌNINOU AUTOKRATOROS TŌN EIS EAUTON.* The Loeb Classical Library. Cambridge: Harvard UP; London: Heinemann, 1979.
- *Meditations.* Trans. Maxwell Staniforth. New York: Penguin, 1981.
Bacchylides. *The Poems and Fragments.* Trans. Richard C. Jebb. Cambridge: Cambridge UP, 1905.
Biermann, Wolf. „Noch." In his *Mit Marx- und Engelszungen. Gedichte. Balladen. Lieder.* Berlin: Wagenbach, 1973, 79.
The New Oxford Annotated Bible with the Apocrypha. Revised Standard Version. Ed. Herbert May and Bruce Metzger. New York: Oxford UP, 1973.
Bloch, Ernst. *Das Prinzip Hoffnung.* 2 vols. Frankfurt: Suhrkamp, 1959.
Börne, Ludwig. *Sämtliche Schriften.* Ed. Inge Rippmann and Peter Rippmann. Düsseldorf: Melzer, 1964.
Brecht, Bertolt. *Gesammelte Werke in 20 Bänden.* Frankfurt: Suhrkamp 1967.
Briefe von und an Hegel. Ed. Johannes Hoffmeister. 4 vols. Hamburg: Meiner, 1952.
Canitz, Friedrich von. *Gedichte.* Ed. Johann Ulrich König. Leipzig: Hauden, 1727.
Cicero. *De natura deorum.* The Loeb Classical Library. Cambridge: Harvard UP; London: Heinemann, 1933.
- *De officiis.* The Loeb Classical Library. Cambridge: Harvard UP; London: Heinemann, 1913.
- *Tusculan Disputations.* The Loeb Classical Library. Cambridge: Harvard UP; London: Heinemann, 1971.
Dingelstedt, Franz. *Lieder eines kosmopolitischen Nachtwächters.* Ed. Hans-Peter Bayerdörfer. Deutsche Texte 49. Tübingen: Niemeyer, 1978.
Dio Chrysostom. *Dio Chrysostom.* The Loeb Classical Library. Cambridge: Harvard UP; London; Heinemann, 1934.
Diogenes Laertius. *Leben und Meinungen berühmter Philosophen.* Trans. Otto Apelt. 2nd ed. 2 vols. Philosophische Bibliothek 53–54. Hamburg: Meiner, 1967.
Eckermann, Johann Peter. *Gespräche mit Goethe in den letzten Jahren seines Lebens.* Ed. Ernst Beutler. München: DTV, 1976.
Eckhart, Meister. *Die deutschen und lateinischen Werke.* Hrsg. im Auftrage der deutschen Forschungsgemeinschaft. Stuttgart: Kohlhammer, 1936–,.
Eichendorff, Joseph von. *Gedichte. Eine Auswahl.* Stuttgart: Reclam, 1966.
Epictetus. *The Discourses as Reported by Arrian, The Manual, and Fragments.* 2 vols. The Loeb Classical Library. Cambridge: Harvard UP; London: Heinemann, 1946.
Epicurea. Ed. Hermann Usener. Leipzig: Teubner, 1887.
Epicurus. *The Extant Remains.* Ed. Cyril Bailey. Oxford: Clarendon, 1926.
Euripides. *Euripidis perditarum fabularum fragmenta.* Ed. F.G. Wagner. Paris: Didot, 1846.
Feldmann, Leopold. „Der deutsche Michel, oder Familien-Unruhen. Zeitbild in fünf Aufzügen." In *Der deutsche Michel. Revolutionskomödien der Achtundvierziger.* Ed. Horst Denkler. Stuttgart: Reclam, 1971, 209–89.
Fichte, J. G. *Briefwechsel. Kritische Gesamtausgabe.* 2 vols. Ed. Hans Schulz. Leipzig: Haessel, 1925.
- *Johann Gottlieb Fichtes sämmtliche Werke.* Ed. I.H. Fichte. 8 vols. Berlin: Veit, 1845–46.

Fleming, Paul. *Gedichte*. Ed. Johannes Pfeiffer. Stuttgart: Reclam, 1980.
Freiligrath, Ferdinand. *Freiligraths Werke*. Ed. Julius Schwering. 6 vols. Berlin: Bong, n. d.
Freud, Sigmund. *Gesammelte Werke*. 18 vols. London: Imago, 1940.
Geßner, Salomon. *Idyllen. Kritische Ausgabe*. Ed. Theodor Voss. Stuttgart: Reclam, 1973.
Glaßbrenner, Adolf. *Bilder und Träume aus Wien*. 2 vols. Leipzig: Volckmar, 1836.
– *Unterm Brennglas. Berliner politische Satire, Revolutionsgeist und menschliche Komödie*. Ed. Franz Diederich. Berlin: Singer, 1912.
[–] *Verbotene Lieder. Von einem norddeutschen Poeten*. Bern: Jenni, 1844.
Goethe, Johann Wolfgang von. *Goethes Werke*. Ed. Erich Trunz. 10th ed. 14 vols. München: Beck, 1974.
– *Goethes Werke*. Hrsg. im Auftrage der Großherzogin Sophie von Sachsen. 143 vols. Weimar: Böhlaus, 1887–1919.
Goethes Briefe. Ed. Karl Robert Mandelkow. 4 vols. Hamburg: Wegner, 1967.
Grabbe, Christian Dietrich. *Don Juan und Faust. Eine Tragödie in vier Akten*. Stuttgart: Reclam, 1975.
Gregory of Nyssa. *The Life of Moses*. Trans. Abraham J. Malherbe and Everett Ferguson. New York: Paulist, 1978.
Grillparzer, Franz. *Ein Bruderzwist in Habsburg. Trauerspiel in fünf Aufzügen*. Stuttgart: Reclam, 1977.
Grimmelshausen. *Der abenteuerliche Simplicissimus*. Darmstadt: Wissenschaftliche Buchgesellschaft, 1978.
Großes vollständiges Universal-Lexikon aller Wissenschaften und Künste. Leipzig: Zedler, 1732–54.
Gutzkow, Karl. *Karl Gutzkows ausgewählte Werke in zwölf Bänden*. Ed. Heinrich Hubert Houben. Leipzig: Hesses, n. d.
Handke, Peter. *Kaspar*. Edition Suhrkamp 322. Frankfurt: Suhrkamp, 1977.
Hegel, G. W. F. *Werke in zwanzig Bänden*. Ed. Eva Moldenhauer and Karl Markus Michel. Frankfurt: Suhrkamp, 1970.
– *Wissenschaft der Logik*. Ed. Georg Lasson. 2nd ed. 2 vols. Philosophische Bibliothek 56–57. Hamburg: Meiner, 1932.
[Hengstenberg, Ernst Wilhelm]. Preface. *Evangelische Kirchen-Zeitung*, 8 (1831), 1–36.
Herder, Johann Gottfried von. *Herders sämmtliche Werke*. Ed. Bernhard Suphan. 32 vols. Berlin: Weidmann, 1877–1913.
Herodotus. *Herodotus in 4 volumes*. The Loeb Classical Library. Cambridge: Harvard UP; London: Heinemann, 1975.
Herwegh, Georg. *Herweghs Werke in einem Band*. Ed. Hans-Georg Werner. Berlin: Aufbau, 1967.
Hesiod. *Carmina*. Ed. A. Rzach. Stuttgart: Teubner, 1967.
[Hoffmann, Heinrich]. *Der Heulerspiegel. Mittheilungen aus dem Tagebuche des Herrn Heulalius von Heulenberg*. Leipzig: Mayer, 1849.
[Hoffmann von Fallersleben, August Heinrich]. *Schwefeläther*. Freisingen: Michel, 1857.
Hoffmann von Fallersleben, August Heinrich. *Unpolitische Lieder*. 2 vols. Hamburg: Hoffmann, 1840. Rpt. Hildesheim: Olms, 1976.
Homer. *The Iliad*. 2 vols. The Loeb Classical Library. Cambridge: Harvard UP; London: Heinemann, 1978.
– *The Odyssey*. 2 vols. The Loeb Classical Library. Cambridge: Harvard UP; London: Heinemann, 1953.

Horace: *The Odes and Epodes.* The Loeb Classical Library. Cambridge: Harvard UP; London: Heinemann, 1914.
Kant, Immanuel. *Briefwechsel.* Ed. Otto Schöndörffer. Hamburg: Meiner, 1972.
– *Werke in zwölf Bänden.* Ed. Wilhelm Weischedel. Frankfurt: Suhrkamp, 1968.
Kaprow, Allan. *Assemblage, Environments and Happenings.* New York: Abrams, 1966.
– "The Legacy of Jackson Pollock." *Art News.* October 1958, 24+.
Keller, Gottfried. *Sämtliche Werke und ausgewählte Briefe.* Ed. Clemens Heselhaus. 3 vols. München: Hanser, n.d.
Kerner, Justinus. *Werke.* Ed. Raimund Pissin. 2 vols. Berlin: 1914. Rpt. Hildesheim: Olms, 1974.
Kleist, Heinrich von. *Sämtliche Werke und Briefe.* 6th ed. 2 vols. Ed. Helmut Sembdner. München: Hanser, 1977.
Klopstock, Friedrich Gottlieb. *Oden.* Ed. Karl Ludwig Schneider. Stuttgart: Reclam, 1976.
Lactantius, L.C.F. *De ira dei.* Ed. H. Kraft and A. Wlosok. Darmstadt: Wissenschaftliche Buchgesellschaft, 1971.
Leibniz, Gottfried Wilhelm. *Sämtliche Schriften und Briefe.* Ed. Deutsche Akademie der Wissenschaften zu Berlin. Berlin: Akademie, 1923–.
Lenz, Jakob Michael Reinhold. *Werke und Schriften.* Ed. Britta Titel and Hellmut Haug. 2 vols. Stuttgart: Goverts, 1966.
Lessing, Gotthold Ephraim. *Gotthold Ephraim Lessings sämtliche Schriften.* Ed. Karl Lachmann. 23 vols. Stuttgart: Göschen, 1886–1924.
– *Werke.* 8 vols. München: Hanser, 1970–78.
Liederbuch des deutschen Michel. Ed. Hermann Marggraf. Leipzig: Peter, 1843.
Lipsius, Justus. *Opera omnia.* 4 vols. Wesel 1675.
– *Von der Bestendigkeit. [De Constantia.]* Trans. Andreas Viritius 1601. Rpt. Stuttgart: Metzler, 1965.
Lucretius. *De rerum natura.* The Loeb Classical Library. Cambridge: Harvard UP; London: Heinemann, 1975.
Mann, Thomas. *Doktor Faustus.* Frankfurt: Fischer, 1976.
Mendelssohn, Moses. *Gesammelte Schriften.* Ed. G.B. Mendelssohn. 7 vols. Leipzig: Brockhaus, 1844.
Menzel, Wolfgang. *Die deutsche Literatur.* 2nd ed. 4 vols. Stuttgart: Hallberg, 1836.
Michelet, C.L. *Entwickelungsgeschichte der neuesten deutschen Philosophie mit besonderer Rücksicht auf den gegenwärtigen Kampf Schellings mit der Hegelschen Schule.* Berlin: Duncker, 1843.
Mundt, Theodor. *Madonna. Unterhaltungen mit einer Heiligen.* Leipzig: Reichenbach, 1835.
– „Über Bewegungsparteien in der Literatur."*Literarischer Zodiacus. Journal für Zeit und Leben, Wissenschaft und Kunst,* 1 (1835), 1–20. Rpt. Frankfurt: Athenäum, 1971.
Nemerov, Howard. *The Collected Poems of Howard Nemerov.* Chicago: University of Chicago Press, 1977.
Nestroy, Johann. *Gesammelte Werke.* Ed. Otto Rommel. 6 vols. Vienna: Schroll, 1948–49.
Nietzsche, Friedrich. *Werke.* Ed. Karl Schlechta. 6th ed. 3 vols. München: Hanser, 1969.
Nikolaus von Kues. *Philosophisch-theologische Schriften.* Ed. Leo Gabriel. 3 vols. Vienna: Herder, 1964–67.
Novalis. [Friedrich von Hardenberg]. *Schriften. Die Werke Friedrich von Hardenbergs.* Ed. Paul Kluckhohn and Richard Samuel. 2nd ed. 4 vols. Stuttgart: Kohlhammer, 1960.

Opitz, Martin. *Weltliche Poemata 1644. Erster Teil.* Ed. Erich Trunz. Deutsche Neudrucke. Barock 2. Tübingen: Niemeyer, 1967.
- „Zlatna Oder Getichte Von Ruhe deß Gemûthes." In his *Gedichte. Eine Auswahl.* Ed. Jan-Dirk Müller. Stuttgart: Reclam, 1970, 75–109.
Ottwald, Ernst. *Ruhe und Ordnung. Roman aus dem Leben der nationalgesinnten Jugend.* Berlin: Malik, 1929.
Der Patriot. Neue und verbesserte Ausgabe mit vollständigem Register. 3rd ed. 3 vols. Hamburg 1747.
Pfau, Ludwig. *Ausgewählte Gedichte.* Ed. Ernst Ziel. Stuttgart: Cotta, 1898.
Plato. *The Collected Dialogues including the Letters.* Ed. Edith Hamilton and Huntington Cairns. Bollingen Series 71. Princeton: Princeton UP, 1978.
Plutarch. *Moralia.* 14 vols. The Loeb Classical Library. Cambridge: Harvard UP; London: Heinemann, 1939.
Proclus. *The Elements of Theology. A Revised Text with Translation, Introduction and Commentary.* Trans. E.R. Dodds. 2nd ed. Oxford: Clarendon, 1963.
Pseudo-Dionysius Areopagite. *The Divine Names and Mystical Theology.* Trans. John D. Jones. Mediaeval Philosophical Texts in Translation 21. Milwaukee: Marquette UP, 1980.
Richter, Christian Friedrich. *Christian Friedrich Richters Erbauliche Betrachtungen.* Halle 1718.
Richter, Johann Paul Friedrich. [Jean Paul]. *Werke.* 6 vols. München: Hanser, 1959–73.
Rousseau, Jean-Jacques. *Oeuvres Complètes.* Ed. Bernard Gagnebin and Marcel Raymond. 4 vols. Paris: Pléiade, 1959–69.
Ruge, Arnold. „Wer ist und wer ist nicht Partei." *Deutsche Jahrbücher für Wissenschaft und Kunst,* 5 (1842), 190–92.
Schelling, F.W.J. *Friedrich Wilhelm Joseph von Schellings sämmtliche Werke.* 14 vols. Stuttgart: Cotta, 1856–61.
Schlegel, Friedrich. *Kritische Friedrich-Schlegel-Ausgabe.* Ed. Ernst Behler et al. München: Schöningh, 1958–.
Schleiermacher, Friedrich. *Über die Religion. Reden an die Gebildeten unter ihren Verächtern.* Ed. Hans-Joachim Rothert. Philosophische Bibliothek 255. Hamburg: Meiner, 1958.
Schopenhauer, Arthur. *Zürcher Ausgabe. Werke in zehn Bänden.* Zürich: Diogenes, 1977.
Schwäbisches Wörterbuch. Ed. Hermann Fischer. 6 vols. Tübingen: Laupp, 1920.
Seeger, Ludwig Wilhelm Friedrich. *Ludwig Seeger's Gesammelte Dichtungen.* 2 vols. Stuttgart: Ebner, 1863.
Seneca. *Ad Lucilium Epistolae Morales.* 3 vols. The Loeb Classical Library. Cambridge: Harvard UP; London: Heinemann, 1953.
- *Moral Essays.* 3 vols. The Loeb Classical Library. Cambridge: Harvard UP; London: Heinemann, 1979.
Seuse, Heinrich. *Deutsche Schriften.* Ed. Karl Bihlmeyer. Stuttgart: Kohlhammer, 1907.
Sextus Empiricus. *Outlines of Phyrrhonism.* The Loeb Classical Library. Cambridge: Harvard UP; London: Heinemann, 1955.
Shakespeare, William. *The Riverside Shakespeare.* Ed. G. Blackmore Evans et al. Boston: Mifflin, 1974.
Silesius, Angelus. [Johannes Scheffler]. *Cherubinischer Wandersmann. Kritische Ausgabe.* Ed. Louise Gnädinger. Stuttgart: Reclam, 1984.
Sophocles. *Oedipus at Colonus.* Trans. Robert Fitzgerald. In *The Complete Greek Tragedies. Sophocles I.* Ed. David Greene and Richmond Lattimore. Chicago: The University of Chicago Press, 1954.

Spinoza. *Opera.* Ed. Carl Gebhardt. 4 vols. Heidelberg: Winter, 1925.
- *Works of Spinoza.* Trans. R.H.M. Elwes. 2 vols. New York: Dover, 1955.
Das Staats-Lexikon. Encyklopädie der sämmtlichen Staatswissenschaften für alle Stände. Ed. Karl von Rotteck and Karl Welcker. 3rd. ed. 12 vols. Leipzig: Brockhaus, 1858.
Stifter, Adalbert. *Der Nachsommer.* München: DTV, 1977.
Tauler, Johannes. *Die Predigten Taulers aus der Engelberger und der Freiburger Handschrift sowie aus Schmidts Abschriften der ehemaligen Straßburger Handschriften.* Ed. Ferdinand Vetter. Deutsche Texte des Mittelalters 11. Berlin: Weidmann, 1910.
Tersteegen, Gerhard. *Geistliches Blumen=Gärtlein Inniger Seelen; oder, kurze Schluß= Reimen, Betrachtungen und Lieder, Über allerhand Wahrheiten des Inwendigen Christenthums.* 6th. ed. Frankfurt: Böttiger, 1757.
Theognis. *The Elegies of Theognis and other Elegies included in the Theognidean Sylloge.* Ed. T. Hudson-Williams. London: Bell, 1910.
Thomas Aquinas. *Opera omnia.* 25 vols. Parma 1852–73. Rpt. New York: Musurgia, 1948–50.
Tragicorum Graecorum Fragmenta. Ed. August Nauck. 2nd ed. Leipzig: Teubner, 1889.
Tucholsky, Kurt. *Gesammelte Werke.* Ed. Mary Gerold-Tucholsky and Fritz J. Raddatz. 3 vols. Hamburg: Rowohlt, 1960.
Volkstümliches Handbuch der Staatswissenschaften und Politik. Ein Staatslexikon für das Volk. Ed. Robert Blum. 2 vols. Leipzig: Blum, 1848–51. Rpt. Frankfurt: Wissenschaftliches Antiquariat, 1973.
Wackenroder, Wilhelm Heinrich and Ludwig Tieck. *Herzensergießungen eines kunstliebenden Klosterbruders.* Stuttgart: Reclam, 1979.
Wander, Karl Friedrich Wilhelm. *Deutsches Sprichwörter-Lexikon.* 5 vols. Leipzig, 1873. Rpt. Aalen: Scientia, 1963.
Der Weltbürger. Berlin 1741–42.
Wienbarg, Ludolf. *Wanderungen durch den Thierkreis.* Hamburg: Hoffmann, 1835. Rpt. Frankfurt: Athenäum, 1973.
- *Zur neuesten Literatur.* Mannheim: Löwenthal, 1835. Rpt. Frankfurt: Athenäum, 1973.
Winckelmann, Johann Joachim. *Gedanken über die Nachahmung der griechischen Werke in der Malerei und Bildhauerkunst.* Ed. Ludwig Uhlig. Stuttgart: Reclam, 1977.
Zinzendorf, Nikolaus Ludwig von. *Ergänzungsbände zu den Hauptschriften, II.* Ed. Erich Beyreuther and Gerhard Meyer. Hildesheim: Olms, 1964.

Secondary Literature

Schiller

Anderegg, Johannes Mathias. „Friedrich Schiller. Der Spaziergang. Eine Interpretation." Diss. Zürich 1964.
Bahti, Timothy Howe. "Dialectic and Negativity. Readings in the Rhetoric of Romanticism." Diss. Yale 1980.
Basch, Victor. *La Poétique de Schiller. Essai d'esthétique Littéraire.* Paris: Alcan, 1911.
Bauch, Bruno. „,Naiv' und ,sentimentalisch' – ,klassisch' und ,romantisch'. Eine historisch-kritische Parallele." *Archiv für Geschichte der Philosophie*, 16 (1903), 486–514.
Berghahn, Klaus L. „Ästhetische Reflexion als Utopie des Ästhetischen. Am Beispiel Schillers." In *Utopieforschung. Interdisziplinäre Studien zur neuzeitlichen Utopie.* Ed. Wilhelm Voßkamp. 3 vols. Stuttgart: Metzler, 1982, III, 146–71.

Binder, Wolfgang. „Die Begriffe ‚naiv' und ‚sentimentalisch' und Schillers Drama." *Jahrbuch der deutschen Schiller-Gesellschaft*, 4 (1960), 140–57.

– „Schillers ‚Demetrius'." *Euphorion*, 53 (1959), 252–80.

Böhler, Michael J. „Die Bedeutung Schillers für Hegels Ästhetik." *PMLA*, 87 (1972), 182–91.

Borchmeyer, Dieter. „Über eine ästhetische Aporie in Schillers Theorie der modernen Dichtung. Zu seinen ‚sentimentalischen Forderungen' an Goethes ‚Wilhelm Meister' und ‚Faust'." *Jahrbuch der deutschen Schiller-Gesellschaft*, 22 (1978), 303–54.

Brinkmann, Richard. „Romantische Dichtungstheorie in Friedrich Schlegels Frühschriften und Schillers Begriffe des Naiven und Sentimentalischen." *Deutsche Vierteljahrsschrift für Literaturwissenschaft und Geistesgeschichte*, 32 (1958), 344–71.

Cysarz, Herbert. „Naive und sentimentalische Dichtung." *Reallexikon der deutschen Literaturgeschichte*. Ed. Werner Kohlschmidt and Wolfgang Mohr. 2nd ed. Berlin: Gruyter, 1959.

Dierse, U. „Idylle." *Historisches Wörterbuch der Philosophie*. Ed. Joachim Ritter and Karlfried Gründer. Basel: Schwabe, 1971–.

Düsing, Wolfgang. „Kosmos und Natur in Schillers Lyrik." *Jahrbuch der deutschen Schiller-Gesellschaft*, 13 (1969), 196–220.

Eggli, Edmond. *Schiller et le romantisme français*. Paris: Gamber, 1927.

Eichner, Hans. "The Supposed Influence of Schiller's ‚Über naive und sentimentalische Dichtung' on Friedrich Schlegel's ‚Über das Studium der griechischen Poesie'." *Germanic Review*, 30 (1955), 260–64.

Ellis, John M. *Schiller's Kalliasbriefe and the Study of his Aesthetic Theory*. Anglica Germanica. British Studies in Germanic Languages and Literatures 12. The Hague: Mouton, 1969.

Field, G. W. "Schiller's Theory of the Idyl and Wilhelm Tell." *Monatshefte*, 42 (1950), 13–21.

Frye, Lawrence O. "Schiller, Juggler of Freedoms in ‚Wilhelm Tell'." *Monatshefte*, 76 (1984), 73–88.

Geißler, Rolf. „Versuch über die Idylle." *Wirkendes Wort*, 11 (1961), 271–78.

Gerhard, Melitta. *Schiller*. Bern: Francke, 1950.

Gethmann-Siefert, Annemarie. „Idylle und Utopie. Zur gesellschaftlichen Funktion der Kunst in Schillers Ästhetik." *Jahrbuch der deutschen Schiller-Gesellschaft*, 24 (1980), 32–67.

Grimm, Reinhold. „Festgemauert und noch nicht entbehrlich. Enzensberger als Erbe Schillers." In *Friedrich Schiller. Kunst, Humanität und Politik in der späten Aufklärung. Ein Symposium*. Ed. Wolfgang Wittkowski. Tübingen: Niemeyer, 1982, 310–25.

Habel, Reinhardt. „Schiller und die Tradition des Herakles-Mythos." In *Friedrich Schiller zur Geschichtlichkeit seines Werkes*. Ed. Klaus L. Berghahn. Kronberg/Ts.: Scriptor, 1975, 67–94.

Havenstein, Martin. „Wahrheit und Irrtum in Schillers Unterscheidung von naiver und sentimentalischer Dichtung." *Zeitschrift für Ästhetik und allgemeine Kunstwissenschaft*, 32 (1938), 237–51.

Helmerking, Heinz. „Energische Ruhe. Über Schillers Plan zu einer Idylle."*Neue Zürcher Zeitung*, November 10, 1959.

Hermand, Jost. „Schillers Abhandlung ‚Über naive und sentimentalische Dichtung' im Lichte der deutschen Popularphilosophie des 18. Jahrhunderts." *PMLA*, 79 (1964), 428–41.

Hinderer, Walter. „Jenseits von Eden: Zu Schillers ‚Wilhelm Tell'." In *Deutsche Geschichtsdramen. Interpretationen*. Ed. Walter Hinck. Suhrkamp Taschenbuch 2006. Frankfurt: Suhrkamp, 1981, 133–46.

Hoffheimer, Michael H. "The Influence of Schiller's Theory of Nature on Hegel's Philosophical Development." *Journal of the History of Ideas*, 46 (1985), 231–44.
Homann, Renate. *Erhabenes und Satirisches. Zur Grundlegung einer Theorie ästhetischer Literatur bei Kant und Schiller*. Theorie und Geschichte der Literatur und der schönen Künste. Texte und Abhandlungen 43. München: Fink, 1977.
Jäger, Hella. *Naivität. Eine kritisch-utopische Kategorie in der bürgerlichen Literatur und Ästhetik des 18. Jahrhunderts*. Skripten Literaturwissenschaft 19. Kronberg/Ts.: Scriptor, 1975.
Jauß, Hans Robert. „Schlegels und Schillers Replik auf die ‹Querelle des Anciens et des Modernes›." In his *Literaturgeschichte als Provokation*. 5th ed. Edition Suhrkamp 418. Frankfurt: Suhrkamp, 1974, 67–106.
Jones, Michael T. "Twilight of the Gods: The Greeks in Schiller and Lukács." *Germanic Review*, 59 (1984), 49–56.
Kaiser, Gerhard. *Von Arkadien nach Elysium. Schiller-Studien*. Göttingen: Vandenhoeck, 1978.
– *Wandrer und Idylle. Goethe und die Phänomenologie der Natur in der deutschen Dichtung von Geßner bis Gottfried Keller*. Göttingen: Vandenhoeck, 1977.
Knippel, Richard. *Schillers Verhältnis zur Idylle*. Leipzig: Quelle, 1909.
Koopmann, Helmut. *Schiller Kommentar*. 2 vols. München: Winkler, 1969.
Kraft, Herbert. „Über sentimentalische und idyllische Dichtung." In *Studien zur Goethezeit. Festschrift für Lieselotte Blumenthal*. Ed. Helmut Holtzhauer et al. Weimar: Böhlhaus, 1968, 209–20.
Liepe, Wolfgang. „Rousseau – Kant – Schiller." In his *Beiträge zur Literatur- und Geistesgeschichte*. Neumünster: Wachholtz, 1963, 106–19.
Lovejoy, Arthur O. „Schiller and the Genesis of Romanticism." *Modern Language Notes*, 35 (1920), 1–10, 136–46.
Lukács, Georg. „Schillers Theorie der modernen Literatur." In his *Werke*. 17 vols. Neuwied: Luchterhand, 1964, VII, 125–63.
Mainland, William F. Introduction. *Über naive und sentimentalische Dichtung*. By Friedrich Schiller. Oxford: Blackwell, 1951, vii–xxxviii.
Marleyn, Roland. "The Poetic Ideal in Schiller's ‚Über naive und sentimentalische Dichtung'." *German Life and Letters*, 9 (1955–56), 237–45.
Martini, Fritz. „Wilhelm Tell, der ästhetische Staat und der ästhetische Mensch." In *Schiller. Zur Theorie und Praxis der Dramen*. Ed. Klaus L. Berghahn and Reinhold Grimm. Wege der Forschung 323. Darmstadt: Wissenschaftliche Buchgesellschaft, 1972, 368–406.
Meng, Heinrich. *Schillers Abhandlung über naive und sentimentalische Dichtung. Prolegomena zu einer Typologie des Dichterischen*. Frauenfeld: Huber, 1936.
Meyer, Herman. „Schillers philosophische Rhetorik." In his *Zarte Empirie. Studien zur Literaturgeschichte*. Stuttgart: Metzler, 1963, 337–89.
Middell, Eike. *Friedrich Schiller. Leben und Werk*. Leipzig: Reclam, 1982.
Müller, Joachim. *Das Edle in der Freiheit. Schillerstudien*. Leipzig: Koehler, 1959.
Oellers, Norbert. „Idylle und Politik. Französische Revolution, ästhetische Erziehung und die Freiheit der Urkantone." In *Friedrich Schiller. Kunst, Humanität und Politik in der späten Aufklärung. Ein Symposium*. Ed. Wolfgang Wittkowski. Tübingen: Niemeyer, 1982, 114–37.
Rockwell, Elke Haase. „Funktion und Destruktion des Idyllen-Begriffs bei Jean Paul." Diss. Princeton 1982.
Rohrmoser, Günter. „Zum Problem der ästhetischen Versöhnung. Schiller und Hegel." *Euphorion*, 53 (1959), 351–66.
Rüdiger, Horst. „Schiller und das Pastorale." *Euphorion*, 53 (1959), 229–51.

Sautermeister, Gert. *Idyllik und Dramatik im Werk Friedrich Schillers. Zum geschichtlichen Ort seiner klassischen Dramen.* Studien zur Poetik und Geschichte der Literatur 17. Stuttgart: Kohlhammer, 1971.

Sayce, Olive. „Das Problem der Vieldeutigkeit in Schillers ästhetischer Terminologie." *Jahrbuch der deutschen Schiller-Gesellschaft*, 6 (1962), 149–77.

Seidlin, Oskar. "Schiller: Poet of Politics." In *A Schiller Symposium. In Observance of the Bicentenary of Schiller's Birth.* Ed. A. Leslie Wilson. Austin: University of Texas, 1960, 31–50.

Siekmann, Andreas. *Drama und sentimentalisches Bewußtsein. Zur klassischen Dramatik Schillers.* Pommersfeldener Beiträge 1. Frankfurt: Haag, 1980.

Silz, Walter. "Antithesis in Schiller's Poetry." *Germanic Review*, 34 (1959), 165–84.

Simons, John D. *Friedrich Schiller.* Twayne's World Authors Series 603. Boston: Twayne, 1981.

– "The Nature of Oppression in ‚Don Carlos'." *Modern Language Notes*, 84 (1969), 451–57.

Szondi, Peter. „Das Naive ist das Sentimentalische. Zur Begriffsdialektik in Schillers Abhandlung." *Euphorion*, 66 (1972), 174–206.

Völker, Ludwig. „Tell und der Samariter. Zum Verhältnis von Ästhetik und Geschichte in Schillers Dramen." *Zeitschrift für deutsche Philologie*, 95 (1976), 185–203.

Weigand, Hermann J. "Illustrations to Highlight some Points in Schiller's Essay on Poetry." *Monatshefte*, 46 (1954), 161–69.

Weigand, Paul. "A Study of Schiller's Essay ‚Über naive und sentimentalische Dichtung' and a Consideration of its Influence in the Twentieth Century." Diss. New York University, 1949.

Wells, G. A. "Schiller on Tragedy and Comedy." *German Life and Letters*, 21 (1967–68), 185–89.

– "Schiller's View of Nature in ‚Über naive und sentimentalische Dichtung'." *Journal of English and Germanic Philology*, 65 (1966), 491–510.

Wentzlaff-Eggebert, Friedrich-Wilhelm. *Schillers Weg zu Goethe.* Tübingen: Wunderlich, 1949.

Wertheim, Ursula. „‚Der Menschheit Götterbild'. Bemerkungen zur gesellschaftlichen und ästhetischen Funktion des Herakles-Bildes bei Schiller." *Weimarer Beiträge. Sonderheft*, (1959), 97–149.

Wessell, Leonard P., Jr. "Schiller and the Genesis of German Romanticism." *Studies in Romanticism*, 10 (1971), 176–98.

Wiese, Benno von. Introduction. *Schiller Kommentar.* Ed. Helmut Koopmann. 2 vols. München: Winkler, 1969, I, 5–69.

– *Friedrich Schiller.* Stuttgart: Metzler, 1959.

– „Das Problem der ästhetischen Versöhnung bei Schiller und Hegel." *Jahrbuch der deutschen Schiller-Gesellschaft*, 9 (1965), 167–88.

Witte, William. *Schiller.* Oxford: Blackwell, 1949.

Hölderlin

Alewyn, Richard. „Dominikgesichter." *Hölderlin-Jahrbuch*, 13 (1963–64), 77–78.

Aspetsberger, Friedbert. „Ende und Anfang von Hölderlins Roman ‚Hyperion'." *Jahrbuch des Wiener Goethe-Vereins*, 72 (1968), 20–36.

– *Welteinheit und epische Gestaltung. Studien zur Ichform von Hölderlins Roman* Hyperion. Zur Erkenntnis der Dichtung 10. München: Fink, 1971.

Bachmaier, Helmut. „Theoretische Aporie und tragische Negativität. Zur Genesis der tragischen Reflexion bei Hölderlin." In *Hölderlin. Transzendentale Reflexion der Poesie.* Ed. Helmut Bachmaier et al. Stuttgart: Klett, 1979.

Barnouw, Jeffrey. „‚Der Trieb, bestimmt zu werden.' Hölderlin, Schiller und Schelling als Antwort auf Fichte." *Deutsche Vierteljahrsschrift für Literaturwissenschaft und Geistesgeschichte,* 46 (1972), 248–93.

Beck, Adolf. *Hölderlins Weg zu Deutschland. Fragmente und Thesen.* Stuttgart: Metzler, 1982.

– „Hölderlin und Friedrich Leopold Graf zu Stolberg. Die Anfänge des hymnischen Stiles bei Hölderlin." *Iduna. Jahrbuch der Hölderlin-Gesellschaft,* 1 (1944), 88–113.

Benn, Maurice B. *Hölderlin and Pindar.* Anglica Germanica. British Studies in German Languages and Literatures 4. The Hague: Mouton, 1962.

– „Hölderlin und Sophocles." *German Life and Letters,* 12 (1958–59), 161–73.

Bertaux, Pierre. *Hölderlin und die französische Revolution.* Edition Suhrkamp 344. Frankfurt: Suhrkamp, 1974.

Binder, Wolfgang. „Abschied und Wiederfinden. Hölderlins dichterische Gestaltung des Abschieds von Diotima." In his *Hölderlin-Aufsätze.* Frankfurt: Insel, 1970, 263–93.

– „Hölderlin und Sophocles." *Hölderlin-Jahrbuch,* 16 (1969–70), 19–37.

– „Hölderlins Dichtung im Zeitalter des Idealismus." In his *Hölderlin-Aufsätze.* Frankfurt: Insel, 1970, 9–26.

– „Hölderlins ‚Friedensfeier'." In his *Hölderlin-Aufsätze.* Frankfurt: Insel, 1970, 294–326.

– „Hölderlins Namenssymbolik." In his *Hölderlin-Aufsätze.* Frankfurt: Insel, 1970, 134–260.

Böschenstein, Bernhard. *Konkordanz zu Hölderlins Gedichten nach 1800.* Göttingen: Vandenhoeck, 1964.

Böschenstein-Schäfer, Renate. Rev. of *Einfalt und einfaches Leben. Der Motivbereich des Idyllischen im Werk Friedrich Hölderlins,* by Gregor Thurmair. *Hölderlin-Jahrbuch,* 22 (1980–81), 390–98.

Corssen, Meta. „Der Wechsel der Töne in Hölderlins Lyrik." *Hölderlin-Jahrbuch,* (1951), 19–49.

De Man, Paul. «L'Image de Rousseau dans la Poesie de Hölderlin.» *Deutsche Beiträge zur geistigen Überlieferung,* 5 (1965), 157–83.

Düsing, Klaus. „Ästhetischer Platonismus bei Hölderlin und Hegel." In *Homburg vor der Höhe in der deutschen Geistesgeschichte. Studien zum Freundeskreis um Hegel und Hölderlin.* Ed. Christoph Jamme and Otto Pöggeler. Stuttgart: Klett, 1981, 101–17.

Eppelsheimer, Rudolf Bernhard. „Hyperions ‚Schicksalslied' im Gegensatz zu Hyperions Schicksal. Eine Kontextstudie." *Archiv für das Studium der neueren Sprachen und Literaturen,* 199 (1962), 34–39.

Gaier, Ulrich. „Hölderlins ‚Hyperion': Compendium, Roman, Rede." *Hölderlin-Jahrbuch,* 21 (1978–79), 88–143.

Gaskill, Howard. *Hölderlin's Hyperion.* [Durham]: University of Durham, 1984.

– „‚Ich seh', Ich sehe, wie das enden muß': Observations on a Misunderstood Passage of Hölderlin's ‚Hyperion'."*Modern Language Review,* 76 (1981), 612–18.

Gerlach, Ingeborg. *Natur und Geschichte. Studien zur Geschichtsauffassung in Hölderlins Hyperion und Empedokles.* Frankfurt: Akademische Verlagsgesellschaft, 1973.

Hamlin, Cyrus. "The Poetics of Self-consciousness in European Romanticism. Hölderlin's ‚Hyperion' and Wordsworth's ‚Prelude'." *Genre,* 6 (1973), 142–77.

Harrison, R.B. *Hölderlin and Greek Literature.* Oxford: Clarendon, 1975.

Hauschild, Hans-Ulrich. *Die idealistische Utopie. Untersuchungen zur Entwicklung des utopischen Denkens Friedrich Hölderlins*. Europäische Hochschulschriften. Deutsche Literatur und Germanistik 185. Bern: Lang, 1977.
Henrich, Dieter. „Hegel und Hölderlin." In his *Hegel im Kontext*. 2nd ed. Edition Suhrkamp 510. Frankfurt: Suhrkamp, 1975, 9–40.
Hof, Walter. *Hölderlins Stil als Ausdruck seiner geistigen Welt*. Meisenheim: Hain, 1954.
Kampe, Rudolf. „Christian Friedrich Hölderlins Wortgebrauch im Spiegel seiner Weltanschauung." Diss. Prague 1902.
Konrad, Michael. *Hölderlins Philosophie im Grundriß. Analytisch-kritischer Kommentar zu Hölderlins Aufsatzfragment „Über die Verfahrungsweise des poetischen Geistes."* Abhandlungen zur Philosophie, Psychologie und Pädagogik 37. Bonn: Bouvier, 1967.
Kurz, Gerhard. *Mittelbarkeit und Vereinigung. Zum Verhältnis von Poesie, Reflexion und Revolution bei Hölderlin*. Stuttgart: Metzler, 1975.
Lepper, Gisbert. „Zeitkritik in Hölderlins ‚Hyperion'." In *Literatur und Geistesgeschichte. Festgabe für Heinz Otto Bürger*. Ed. Reinhold Grimm and Conrad Wiedemann. Berlin: Schmidt, 1968, 188–207.
Lüders, Detlev. ‚*Die Welt im verringerten Maßstab.*' *Hölderlin-Studien*. Tübingen: Niemeyer, 1968.
Mason, Eudo C. „Hölderlin und Novalis. Einige Überlegungen." *Hölderlin-Jahrbuch*, 11 (1958–60), 72–119.
– *Hölderlin and Goethe*. Ed. Peter Howard Gaskill. Bern: Lang, 1975.
Mieth, Günther. „Einige Thesen zu Hölderlins Spinoza-Rezeption." *Weimarer Beiträge*, 24 (1978), 175–80.
Miles, David H. "The Past as Future. ‚Pfad' and ‚Bahn' as Images of Temporal Conflict in Hölderlin." *Germanic Review*, 46 (1971), 95–118.
Miller, Drayton Granville. "Schiller and Hölderlin. A Comparative Study." Diss. Washington University, 1970.
Mojašević, Miljan. „Stille und Maß." *Hölderlin-Jahrbuch*, 13 (1963–64), 44–64.
Mommsen, Momme. „Hölderlins Lösung von Schiller. Zu Hölderlins Gedichten ‚An Herkules' und ‚Die Eichbäume' und den Übersetzungen aus Ovid, Vergil und Euripides." *Jahrbuch der deutschen Schiller-Gesellschaft*, 9 (1965), 203–44.
Müller, Ernst. *Hölderlin. Studien zur Geschichte seines Geistes*. Stuttgart: Kohlhammer, 1944.
Neubauer, John. „Intellektuelle, intellektuale und ästhetische Anschauung. Zur Entstehung der romantischen Kunstauffassung." *Deutsche Vierteljahrsschrift für Literaturwissenschaft und Geistesgeschichte*, 46 (1972), 294–319.
Nickel, Peter. „Die Bedeutung von Herders Verjüngungsgedanken und Geschichtsphilosophie für die Werke Hölderlins." Diss. Kiel, 1963.
Pott, Hans-Georg. „Natur als Ideal. Anmerkungen zu einem Zitat aus dem ‚Hyperion'." *Hölderlin-Jahrbuch*, 22 (1980–81), 143–57.
Prignitz, Christoph. *Friedrich Hölderlin. Die Entwicklung seines politischen Denkens unter dem Einfluß der Französischen Revolution*. Hamburger philologische Studien 40. Hamburg: Baske, 1976.
Prill, Meinhard. *Bürgerliche Alltagswelt und pietistisches Denken im Werk Hölderlins. Zur Kritik des Hölderlin-Bildes von Georg Lukács*. Studien und Texte zur Sozialgeschichte der Literatur 10. Tübingen: Niemeyer, 1983.
Requadt, Paul, „Das literarische Urbild von Hölderlins Diotima." *Jahrbuch der deutschen Schiller-Gesellschaft*, 10 (1966), 250–65.
Ryan, Lawrence. „Hölderlins Dichtungsbegriff." *Hölderlin-Jahrbuch*, 12 (1961–62), 20–41.

- „Hölderlins ‚Hyperion': ein ‚romantischer' Roman?" In *Über Hölderlin*. Ed. Jochen Schmidt. Frankfurt: Insel, 1970, 175–212.
- *Hölderlins Hyperion. Exzentrische Bahn und Dichterberuf*. Stuttgart: Metzler, 1965.
- *Hölderlins Lehre vom Wechsel der Töne*. Stuttgart: Kohlhammer, 1960.

Schadewaldt, Wolfgang. „Das Bild der exzentrischen Bahn bei Hölderlin." *Hölderlin-Jahrbuch*, (1952), 1–16.

Scharfschwerdt, Jürgen. „Die pietistisch-kleinbürgerliche Interpretation der Französischen Revolution in Hölderlins Briefen. Erster Versuch zu einer literatursoziologischen Fragestellung." *Jahrbuch der deutschen Schiller-Gesellschaft*, 15 (1971), 174–230.

Schmidt, Jochen. Afterword. *Hyperion*. By Friedrich Hölderlin. Frankfurt: Insel, 1979, 199–229.
- „Die innere Einheit von Hölderlins ‚Friedensfeier'." *Hölderlin-Jahrbuch*, 14 (1965–66), 125–75.
- *Hölderlins letzte Hymnen. „Andenken" und „Mnemosyne."* Untersuchungen zur deutschen Literaturgeschichte 7. Tübingen: Niemeyer, 1970.
- *Hölderlins später Widerruf in den Oden „Chiron", „Blödigkeit" und „Ganymed"*. Studien zur deutschen Literatur 57. Tübingen: Niemeyer, 1978.

Schuffels, Klaus. „Schiksaal und Revolution bei Hölderlin. Die Überwindung des ‚Schiksaals' durch den Befreiungskrieg in ‚Hyperion'." *Recherches Germaniques*, 7 (1977), 90–112.

Silz, Walter. *Hölderlin's Hyperion. A Critical Reading*. Philadelphia: University of Pennsylvania Press, 1969.

Stierle, Karl-Heinz. „Dichtung und Auftrag. Hölderlins ‚Patmos'-Hymne." *Hölderlin-Jahrbuch*, 22 (1980–81), 47–68.

Strack, Friedrich. *Ästhetik und Freiheit. Hölderlins Idee von Schönheit, Sittlichkeit und Geschichte in der Frühzeit*. Tübingen: Niemeyer, 1976.

Szondi, Peter. *Hölderlin-Studien. Mit einem Traktat über philologische Erkenntnis*. 3rd. ed. Edition Suhrkamp 379. Frankfurt: Suhrkamp, 1977.

Thurmair, Gregor. *Einfalt und einfaches Leben. Der Motivbereich des Idyllischen im Werk Friedrich Hölderlins*. Münchner Germanistische Beiträge 28. München: Fink, 1980.

Walser, Jürg Peter. *Hölderlins Archipelagus*. Zürcher Beiträge zur deutschen Literatur und Geistesgeschichte 18. Zürich: Atlantis, 1962.

Wörterbuch zu Friedrich Hölderlin. I. Teil: Die Gedichte. Auf der Textgrundlage der Großen Stuttgarter Ausgabe. Ed. Heinz-Martin Dannhauer et al. Indices zur deutschen Literatur 10/11. Tübingen: Niemeyer, 1983.

Yom, Syng Sup. „Spiel und Harmonie bei Schiller und Hölderlin." Diss. Rice University 1972.

Büchner

Adolph, Winnifred R. "Mythic and Moral Structures in the Works of Georg Büchner." Diss. University of North Carolina at Chapel Hill, 1978.

Anz, Heinrich „‚Leiden sei all mein Gewinnst'. Zur Aufnahme und Kritik christlicher Leidenstheologie bei Georg Büchner." *Georg Büchner Jahrbuch*, 1 (1981), 160–68.

Armstrong, William Bruce. „‚Arbeit' und ‚Muße' in den Werken Georg Büchners." In *Georg Büchner III*. Ed. Heinz Ludwig Arnold. München: Text und Kritik, 1981, 63–98.

Beckers, Gustav. *Georg Büchners Leonce und Lena. Ein Lustspiel der Langeweile*. Heidelberg: Winter, 1961.

Benn, Maurice B. "Anti-Pygmalion. An Apologia for Georg Büchner's Aesthetics." *Modern Language Review*, 64 (1969), 597–604.

- *The Drama of Revolt. A Critical Study of Georg Büchner.* Cambridge: Cambridge UP, 1976.
Buck, Theo. „‚Man muß die Menschheit lieben.' Zum ästhetischen Programm Georg Büchners." In *Georg Büchner III.* Ed. Heinz Ludwig Arnold. München: Text und Kritik, 1981, 15–34.
Fellmann, Herbert. „Georg Büchners ‚Lenz'." *Jahrbuch der Wittheit zu Bremen,* 7 (1963), 7–124.
Gersch, Hubert. „Georg Büchners ‚Lenz'-Entwurf: Textkritik, Edition und Erkenntnisperspektiven. Ein Zwischenbericht." *Georg Büchner Jahrbuch,* 3(1983), 14–25.
Hasubeck, Peter. „‚Ruhe' und ‚Bewegung'. Versuch einer Stilanalyse von Georg Büchners ‚Lenz'." *Germanisch-Romanische Monatsschrift,* 50 (1969), 33–59.
Hauser, Ronald. *Georg Büchner.* Twayne's World Author Series 300. New York: Twayne, 1974.
Hinderer, Walter. *Büchner Kommentar. Zum dichterischen Werk.* München: Winkler, 1977.
- „Georg Büchner: ‚Lenz' (1839)." In *Romane und Erzählungen zwischen Romantik und Realismus. Neue Interpretationen.* Ed. Paul Michael Lützeler. Stuttgart: Reclam, 1983, 268–94.
- „Pathos oder Passion: Die Leiddarstellung in Büchner's ‚Lenz'. In his *Über deutsche Literatur und Rede.* München: Fink, 1981, 168–90.
Holub, Robert C. "The Paradoxes of Realism: An Examination of the ‚Kunstgespräch' in Büchner's ‚Lenz'." *Deutsche Vierteljahrsschrift für Literaturwissenschaft und Geistesgeschichte,* 59 (1985), 102–24.
Horn, Peter. „‚Ich meine für menschliche Dinge müsse man auch menschliche Ausdrücke finden.' Die Sprache der Philosophie und die Sprache der Dichtung bei Georg Büchner." *Georg Büchner Jahrbuch,* 2 (1982), 209–26.
Irle, Gerhard. „Büchners Lenz – eine frühe Schizophrenie." In his *Der psychiatrische Roman.* Stuttgart: Hippokrates, 1965, 73–83.
Jansen, Peter K. "The Structural Function of the ‚Kunstgespräch' in Büchner's ‚Lenz'." *Monatshefte,* 67 (1975), 145–56.
Jancke, Gerhard. *Georg Büchner. Genese und Aktualität seines Werkes. Einführung in das Gesamtwerk.* Scriptor Taschenbücher Literaturwissenschaft 56. Kronberg/Ts.: Scriptor, 1975.
King, Janet K. "Lenz viewed sane." *Germanic Review,* 49 (1974), 146–53.
Knapp, Gerhard P. *Georg Büchner.* Stuttgart: Metzler, 1977.
Kobel, Erwin. *Georg Büchner. Das dichterische Werk.* Berlin: Gruyter, 1974.
Lehmann, Werner R. „Prolegomena zu einer historisch-kritischen Büchner-Ausgabe." In *Gratulatio. Festschrift für Christian Wegner zum 70. Geburtstag am 9. September 1963.* Hamburg: Wegner, 1963, 190–220.
Lindenberger, Herbert. *Georg Büchner.* Carbondale: Southern Illinois UP, 1964.
Mayer, Hans. „Georg Büchners ästhetische Anschauungen." *Zeitschrift für deutsche Philologie,* 73 (1954), 129–60.
Mayer, Thomas Michael. „Büchner und Weidig – Frühkommunismus und revolutionäre Demokratie. Zur Textverteilung des ‚Hessischen Landboten'." In *Georg Büchner I/II.* Ed. Heinz Ludwig Arnold. 2nd. ed. München: Text und Kritik, 1982, 16–298.
Michels, Gerd. „Landschaft in Georg Büchners ‚Lenz'." In his *Textanalyse und Textverstehen.* Uni-Taschenbücher 1044. Heidelberg: Quelle, 1981, 12–33.
Mosler, Peter. *Georg Büchners* Leonce und Lena. *Langeweile als gesellschaftliche Bewußtseinsform.* Abhandlungen zur Kunst-, Musik- und Literaturwissenschaft 145. Bonn: Bouvier, 1974.

Müller-Seidel, Walter. „Natur und Naturwissenschaft im Werk Georg Büchners." In *Festschrift für Klaus Ziegler*. Ed. Eckehard Catholy and Winfried Hellmann. Tübingen: Niemeyer, 1968, 205–32.

Neuse, Erna Kritsch. „Büchners ‚Lenz'. Zur Struktur der Novelle." *German Quarterly*, 43 (1970), 199–209.

Parker, John J. "Some Reflections on Georg Büchner's ‚Lenz' and its Principal Source, the Oberlin Record." *German Life and Letters*, 21 (1967–68), 103–11.

Pascal, Roy. "Büchner's ‚Lenz' – Style and Message." *Oxford German Studies*, 9 (1978), 68–83.

Pütz, Heinz Peter. „Büchner's ‚Lenz' und seine Quelle." *Zeitschrift für deutsche Philologie. Sonderheft*, 84 (1965), 1–22.

Requadt, Paul. „Zu Büchners Kunstanschauung: Das ‚niederländische' und das groteske, Jean Paul und Victor Hugo." In his *Bildlichkeit der Dichtung. Aufsätze zur deutschen Literatur vom 18. bis 20. Jahrhundert*. München: Fink, 1974, 106–38.

Richards, David G. *Georg Büchner and the Birth of the Modern Drama*. Albany: State University of New York Press, 1977.

Schmidt, Henry J. "Structural Parallels in ‚Lenz'." In *Georg Büchner. The Complete Collected Works*. Ed. Henry J. Schmidt. New York: Avon, 1977, 328–31.

Sharp, Francis Michael. "Büchner's ‚Lenz': A Futile Madness." In *Psychoanalytische und Psychopathologische Literaturinterpretation*. Ed. Bernd Urband and Winfried Kudszus. Darmstadt: Wissenschaftliche Buchgesellschaft, 1981, 256–79.

Spieß, Reinhard F. „Büchner's ‚Lenz'. Überlegungen zur Textkritik." *Georg Büchner Jahrbuch*, 3 (1983), 26–36.

Stern, Joseph Peter. "A World of Suffering: Georg Büchner." In his *Reinterpretations*. London: Thames, 1964, 78–155.

Thorn-Prikker, Jan. „‚Ach die Wissenschaft, die Wissenschaft!' Bericht über die Forschungsliteratur zu Büchners ‚Lenz'." In *Georg Büchner III*. Ed. Heinz Ludwig Arnold. München: Text und Kritik, 1981, 180–94.

– *Revolutionär ohne Revolution. Interpretationen der Werke Georg Büchners*. Literaturwissenschaft-Gesellschaftswissenschaft 33. Stuttgart: Klett, 1978.

Ueding, Cornelie. *Denken – Sprechen – Handeln. Aufklärung und Aufklärungskritik im Werk Georg Büchners*. Tübinger Studien zur deutschen Literatur 2. Bern: Lang, 1976.

Wessell, Leonard P., Jr. "Eighteenth-Century Theodicy and the Death of God in Büchner's ‚Dantons Tod'." *Seminar*, 8 (1972), 198–218.

Wittkowski, Wolfgang. „Europäische Literaturrevolution ohne Büchner? Büchners Christlichkeit im Licht der Rezeptionsforschung." *Literaturwissenschaftliches Jahrbuch*, 19 (1978), 257–75.

– *Georg Büchner. Persönlichkeit – Weltbild – Werk*. Reihe Siegen 10. Heidelberg: Winter, 1978.

– „Georg Büchner, die Philosophen und der Pietismus. Umrisse eines neuen Büchnerbildes." *Jahrbuch des freien deutschen Hochstifts* (1976), 352–419.

– „Georg Büchners Ärgernis." *Jahrbuch der deutschen Schiller-Gesellschaft*, 17 (1973), 362–83.

Heine

Atkinson, Ross. "Irony and Commitment in Heine's ‚Deutschland. Ein Wintermärchen'." *Germanic Review*, 50 (1975), 184–202.

Bayerdörfer, Hans-Peter. „Laudatio auf einen Nachtwächter. Marginalien zum Verhältnis von Heine und Dingelstedt." *Heine-Jahrbuch*, 15 (1976), 75–95.

Bodi, Leslie. „Heine und die Revolution." In *Dichtung, Sprache, Gesellschaft. Akten des IV. Internationalen Germanisten-Kongresses 1970 in Princeton*. Ed. Victor Lange and Hans-Gert Roloff. Frankfurt: Athenäum, 1971, 169–77.

Brummack, Jürgen. „Heines Entwicklung zum satirischen Dichter." *Deutsche Vierteljahrsschrift für Literaturwissenschaft und Geistesgeschichte*, 41 (1967), 98–116.

- *Satirische Dichtung: Studien zu Friedrich Schlegel, Tieck, Jean Paul und Heine*. Theorie und Geschichte der Literatur und der schönen Künste 53. München: Fink, 1979.

Calvié, Lucien. „Heine und die Junghegelianer." In *Internationaler Heine-Kongreß Düsseldorf 1972*. Ed. Manfred Windfuhr. Hamburg: Hoffmann, 1973, 307–17.

Clasen, Herbert. *Heinrich Heines Romantikkritik. Tradition – Produktion – Rezeption*. Hamburg: Hoffmann, 1979.

Fingerhut, Karl-Heinz. *Standortbestimmungen. Vier Untersuchungen zu Heinrich Heine*. Heidenheim: Heidenheimer Verlagsanstalt, 1971.

Galley, Eberhard. „Heinrich Heine und der Kölner Dom." *Deutsche Vierteljahrsschrift für Literaturwissenschaft und Geistesgeschichte*, 32 (1958), 99–110.

Hannah, Richard W. "The Broken Heart and the Accusing Flame. The Tensions of Imagery and the Ambivalence of Political Commitment in Heine's ‚Deutschland. Ein Wintermärchen'." *Colloquia Germanica*, 14 (1981), 289–312.

Hasubeck, Peter. „Heinrich Heines Zeitgedichte." *Zeitschrift für deutsche Philologie. Sonderheft*, 91 (1972), 23–46.

Hengst, Heinz. *Idee und Ideologieverdacht. Revolutionäre Implikationen des deutschen Idealismus im Kontext der zeitkritischen Prosa Heinrich Heines*. München: Fink, 1973.

Hermand, Jost. *Der frühe Heine. Ein Kommentar zu den Reisebildern*. München: Winkler, 1976.

- „Heine und Brecht. Über die Vergleichbarkeit des Unvergleichlichen." *Monatshefte*, 73 (1981), 429–41.
- „Heines ‚Wintermärchen'. Zum Topos der ‚deutschen Misere'." In his *Sieben Arten an Deutschland zu leiden*. Königstein: Athenäum, 1979.
- *Streitobjekt Heine. Ein Forschungsbericht 1945–1975*. Frankfurt: Athenäum, 1975.

Hinck, Walter. „Ironie im Zeitgedicht Heines. Rezeptionsprobleme." In his *Von Heine zu Brecht. Lyrik im Geschichtsprozeß*. Edition Suhrkamp 481. Frankfurt: Suhrkamp, 1978, 9–36.

Hohendahl, Peter Uwe. „Geschichte und Modernität. Heines Kritik an der Romantik." *Jahrbuch der deutschen Schiller-Gesellschaft*, 17 (1973), 318–61.

Hooton, Richard Gary. *Heinrich Heine und der Vormärz*. Hochschulschriften Literaturwissenschaft 30. Meisenheim: Hain, 1978.

Iggers, Georg G. "Heine and the Saint-Simonians. A Re-examination." *Comparative Literature*, 10 (1958), 289–308.

Kaufmann, Hans. *Politisches Gedicht und klassische Dichtung. Heine. Deutschland. Ein Wintermärchen*. Berlin: Aufbau, 1958.

Klussmann, Paul Gerhard. „Die Definition des romantischen Traummotivs in Heines früher Lyrik." In *Untersuchungen zur Literatur als Geschichte. Festschrift für Benno von Wiese*. Ed. Vincent J. Günther et al. Berlin: Schmidt, 1973, 259–85.

Koopmann, Helmut. „Heine in Weimar: Zur Problematik seiner Beziehungen zur Kunstperiode." *Zeitschrift für deutsche Philologie. Sonderheft*, 91 (1972), 46–66.

Krüger, Eduard. *Heine und Hegel. Dichtung, Philosophie und Politik bei Heinrich Heine*. Monographien Literaturwissenschaft 33. Kronberg/Ts.: Scriptor, 1977.

Kurz, Paul Konrad. *Künstler, Tribun, Apostel. Heinrich Heines Auffassung vom Beruf des Dichters*. München: Fink, 1967.

Loeben, Maria-Beate von. „‚Deutschland. Ein Wintermärchen.' Politischer Gehalt und poetische Leistung." *Germanisch-Romanische Monatsschrift*, 20 (1970), 265–85.

Lukács, Georg. „Heinrich Heine als nationaler Dichter." In his *Werke*. 17 vols. Neuwied: Luchterhand, 1964, VII, 273–333.
Maier, Willfried. *Leben, Tat und Reflexion. Untersuchungen zu Heinrich Heines Ästhetik*. Literatur und Wirklichkeit 5. Bonn: Bouvier, 1969.
Malsch, Sara Ann. „Die Bedeutung von Goethes Pantheismus und seiner satirischen Brechung für Heines Demokratiebegriff." *Heine-Jahrbuch*, 17 (1978), 35–54.
Mayer, Hans. „Anmerkung zu einem Gedicht von Heinrich Heine." *Sinn und Form*, 3 (1951), 177–84.
Mende, Fritz. „‚Indifferentismus.' Bemerkungen zu Heines ästhetischer Terminologie." *Heine-Jahrbuch*, 15 (1976), 11–22.
Oesterle, Günter. *Integration und Konflikt. Die Prosa Heinrich Heines im Kontext oppositioneller Literatur der Restaurationsepoche*. Stuttgart: Metzler, 1972.
Prawer, S. S. *Coal-smoke and Englishmen. A Study of Verbal Caricature in the Writings of Heinrich Heine. The 1983 Bithell Memorial Lecture*. University of London: Institute of Germanic Studies, 1984.
– *Heine. The Tragic Satirist. A Study of the Later Poetry 1827–1856*. Cambridge: Cambridge UP, 1961.
– „Heines satirische Versdichtung." In *Berliner Germanistentag 1968. Vorträge und Berichte*. Ed. Karl Borck and Rudolf Henss. Heidelberg: Winter, 1970, 179–95.
Preisendanz, Wolfgang. „Glückslandschaften als Gegenwelt. Modalitäten des Idyllischen bei Heine." In *Zu Heinrich Heine*. Ed. Luciano Zagari and Paolo Chiarini. Stuttgart: Klett, 1981, 112–23.
– „Ironie bei Heine." In *Ironie und Dichtung. Sechs Essays*. Ed. Albert Schaefer. München: Beck, 1970, 85–112.
Reeves, Nigel. „Heine and the Young Marx." *Oxford German Studies*, 7 (1972–73), 44–97.
– *Heinrich Heine. Poetry and Politics*. Oxford: Oxford UP, 1974.
– "Heinrich Heine – Politics or Poetry? Hegel or Enfantin? A Review of Some Recent Developments in Research." *Modern Language Review*, 75 (1980), 105–13.
Rose, Margaret A. *Die Parodie. Eine Funktion der biblischen Sprache in Heines Lyrik*. Deutsche Studien 27. Meisenheim: Hain, 1976.
– "The Idea of the ‚Sol Iustitiae' in Heine's ‚Deutschland. Ein Wintermärchen'." *Deutsche Vierteljahrsschrift für Literaturwissenschaft und Geistesgeschichte*, 52 (1978), 604–18.
Sammons, Jeffrey L. *Heinrich Heine. The Elusive Poet*. Yale Germanic Studies 3. New Haven: Yale UP, 1969.
– *Heinrich Heine: A Modern Biography*. Princeton: Princeton UP, 1979.
– *Heinrich Heine: A Selected Critical Bibliography, 1956–1980*. Garland Reference Library of the Humanities 302. New York: Garland, 1982.
– „‚Der prosaisch bombastischen Tendenzpoesie hoffentlich den Todesstoß geben': Heine and the Political Poetry of the ‚Vormärz'." *German Quarterly*, 51 (1978), 150–59.
Sandor, A. I. *The Exile of the Gods. Interpretation of a Theme, a Theory and a Technique in the Works of Heinrich Heine*. Anglica Germanica 9. The Hague: Mouton, 1967.
Saueracker-Ritter, Ruth. *Heinrich Heines Verhältnis zur Philosophie*. München: Dissertationsdruck-Schön, 1974.
Schmidt, Johann Michael. „Thron und Altar. Zum kirchengeschichtlichen Hintergrund von Heines Kritik des preußischen Protestantismus." *Heine-Jahrbuch*, 16 (1977), 96–128.
Schweikert, Alexander. „Notizen zu den Einflüssen Heinrich Heines auf die Lyrik von Kerr, Klabund, Tucholsky und Erich Kästner." *Heine-Jahrbuch*, 8 (1969), 69–107.

Seeba, Hinrich C. „Die Kinder des Pygmalion: Die Bildlichkeit des Kunstbegriffs bei Heine. Beobachtungen zur Tendenzwende der Ästhetik." *Deutsche Vierteljahrsschrift für Literaturwissenschaft und Geistesgeschichte,* 50 (1976), 158–202.
Siegrist, Christoph. „Heines Traumbilder. Versuch einer Gliederung." *Heine-Jahrbuch,* 4 (1965), 17–25.
Spencer, Hanna. "Heine: Between Hegel and Jehovah." In *Heinrich Heine. Dimensionen seines Wirkens. Ein internationales Heine-Symposium.* Ed. Raymond Immerwahr and Hanna Spencer. Studien zur Literatur der Moderne 8. Bonn: Bouvier, 1979, 23–33.
– „Heines Spiel mit Goethes Erbmantel." *Seminar,* 9 (1973), 109–26.
Sternberger, Dolf. *Heinrich Heine und die Abschaffung der Sünde.* Hamburg: Claassen, 1972.
Storz, Gerhard. *Heinrich Heines lyrische Dichtung.* Stuttgart: Klett, 1971.
Tonelli, Giorgio. *Heinrich Heines politische Philosophie (1830–1845).* Trans. Lisel Bisanti-Siebrecht. Studien und Materialien zur Geschichte der Philosophie 9. Hildesheim: Olms, 1975.
Wikoff, Jerold. *Heinrich Heine. A Study of* Neue Gedichte. Stanford German Studies 7. Bern: Lang, 1975.
Windfuhr, Manfred. „Heine und Hegel. Rezeption und Produktion." In *Internationaler Heine Kongreß Düsseldorf 1972.* Ed. Manfred Windfuhr. Hamburg: Hoffmann, 1973, 261–80.
– *Heinrich Heine. Revolution und Reflexion.* 2nd ed. Stuttgart: Metzler, 1976.
– „Heinrich Heine zwischen den progressiven Gruppen seiner Zeit. Von den Altliberalen zu den Kommunisten. Ein Arbeitspapier." *Zeitschrift für deutsche Philologie.* Sonderheft, 10 (1972), 1–23.
Woesler, Winfried. „Das Liebesmotiv in Heines politischer Versdichtung." In *Internationaler Heine Kongreß Düsseldorf 1972.* Ed. Manfred Windfuhr. Hamburg: Hoffmann, 1973, 202–18.
Würffel, Stefan Bodo. „Heinrich Heines negative Dialektik. Zur Barbarossa-Episode des Wintermärchens." *Neophilologus,* 61 (1977), 421–38.

General

Abrams, M. H. *Natural Supernaturalism. Tradition and Revolution in Romantic Literature.* New York: Norton, 1973.
Altmann, Eckhard. *Christian Friedrich Richter (1676–1711). Arzt, Apotheker und Liederdichter des Halleschen Pietismus.* Arbeiten zur Geschichte des Pietismus 7. Witten: Luther, 1972.
André, Jean-Marie. *L'Otium dans la vie morale et intellectuelle romaine des origines à l'époque augustéenne.* Paris: Presses universitaires de France, 1966.
Angress, R[uth] K. "The Generations in ‚Emilia Galotti'." *Germanic Review,* 43 (1968) 15–23.
Barner, Wilfried. „Geheime Lenkung. Zur Turmgesellschaft in Goethe's ‚Wilhelm Meister'." In *Goethe's Narrative Fiction. The Irvine Goethe Symposium.* Ed. William J. Lillyman. Berlin: Gruyter, 1983, 85–109.
Barth, Paul and Albert Goedeckemeyer. *Die Stoa.* 6th ed. Stuttgart: Frommann, 1946.
Bayerdörfer, Hans-Peter. Introduction and Commentary. *Lieder eines kosmopolitischen Nachtwächters. Studienausgabe.* By Franz Dingelstedt. Deutsche Texte 49. Tübingen: Niemeyer, 1978.
Benn, Maurice. "Büchner and Heine." *Seminar,* 13 (1977), 215–26.
Bernert, Ernst. "Otium." *Würzburger Jahrbücher für die Altertumswissenschaft,* 4 (1949–50), 89–99.

Blum, Hans. *Die deutsche Revolution. 1848–49. Eine Jubiläumsausgabe für das deutsche Volk.* Leipzig: Diederichs, 1898.
Boldt, Hans. *Deutsche Staatslehre im Vormärz.* Beiträge zur Geschichte des Parlamentarismus und der politischen Parteien 56. Düsseldorf: Droste, 1975.
Böschenstein-Schäfer, Renate. „Arbeit und Muße in der Idyllendichtung des 18. Jahrhunderts." In *Goethezeit. Studien zur Erkenntnis und Rezeption Goethes und seiner Zeitgenossen. Festschrift für Stuart Atkins.* Ed. Gerhard Hoffmeister. Bern: Francke, 1981, 9–30.
– *Idylle.* Sammlung Metzler 63. Stuttgart: Metzler, 1967.
Bowra, C.M. *Sophoclean Tragedy.* Oxford: Clarendon, 1944.
Brockard, Hans. *Subjekt. Versuch zur Ontologie bei Hegel.* Epimeleia 17. München: Pustet, 1970.
Brown, Marshall. "The Eccentric Path." *Journal of English and Germanic Philology,* 77 (1978), 104–12.
– *The Shape of German Romanticism.* Ithaca: Cornell UP, 1979.
Brüggemann, Fritz. „Lessings Bürgerdramen und der Subjektivismus als Problem. Psychogenetische Untersuchung." *Jahrbuch des freien deutschen Hochstifts,* (1926), 69–109.
Büchmann, Georg. *Geflügelte Worte.* Ed. Hanns Martin Elster. 2nd. ed. Stuttgart: Reclam, 1956.
Butler, E.M. *The Saint-Simonian Religion in Germany. A Study of the Young German Movement.* Cambridge: Cambridge UP, 1926.
– *The Tyranny of Greece over Germany.* New York: Macmillan, 1935.
Caspari, Wilhelm. *Vorstellung und Wort „Friede" im Alten Testamente.* Beiträge zur Förderung christlicher Theologie 14. Gütersloh: Bertelsmann, 1910.
Clark, James M. *The Great German Mystics. Eckhart, Tauler, and Suso.* Oxford: Blackwell, 1949.
Curtius, Ernst Robert. "Virgil." In his *Kritische Essays zur europäischen Literatur.* Bern: Francke, 1950, 13–27.
Daniel-Rops, H. *L'Église des Temps Classiques.* Paris: Fayard, 1958.
Dedner, Burghard. „Vom Schäferleben zur Agrarwissenschaft. Poesie und Ideologie des ‚Landlebens' in der deutschen Literatur des 18. Jahrhunderts." *Jahrbuch der Jean-Paul-Gesellschaft,* 7 (1972), 40–83.
Dietze, Walter. *Junges Deutschland und deutsche Klassik. Zur Ästhetik und Literaturtheorie des Vormärz.* 3rd. ed. Neue Beiträge zur Literaturwissenschaft 6. Berlin: Rütten, 1962.
Dilthey, Wilhelm. *Gesammelte Schriften.* Leipzig: Teubner, 1921.
Doppler, Alfred. *Der Abgrund. Studien zur Bedeutungsgeschichte eines Motivs.* Cologne: Böhlau, 1968.
Egermann, Franz. *Vom attischen Menschenbild.* München: Filser, 1952. Rpt. New York: Arno, 1979.
Fischer, Heinz. „Heinrich Heine und Georg Büchner. Zu Büchners Heine-Rezeption." *Heine-Jahrbuch,* 10 (1971), 43–51.
Freudenthal, J. *Die Lebensgeschichte Spinozas in Quellenschriften, Urkunden und nichtamtlichen Nachrichten.* Leipzig: Vert, 1899.
Frühwald, Wolfgang. „Ruhe und Ordnung." *Literatursprache – Sprache der politischen Werbung. Texte, Materialien, Kommentar.* Reihe Hanser 204. München: Hanser, 1976.
Fuchs, Harald. *Augustin und der antike Friedensgedanke. Untersuchungen zum neunzehnten Buch der Civitas Dei.* Neue philologische Untersuchungen 3. Berlin: Weidmann, 1926.

Garber, Klaus. „Arkadien und Gesellschaft." In *Utopieforschung. Interdisziplinäre Studien zur neuzeitlichen Utopie.* Ed. Wilhelm Voßkamp. 3 vols. Stuttgart: Metzler, 1982, III, 37–81.
- *Der locus amoenus und der locus terribilis. Bild und Funktion der Natur in der deutschen Schäfer- und Landlebendichtung des 17. Jahrhunderts.* Literatur und Leben 16. Cologne: Böhlau, 1974.
- ed. *Europäische Bukolik und Georgik.* Wege der Forschung 355. Darmstadt: Wissenschaftliche Buchgesellschaft, 1976.

Grimm, Jacob and Wilhelm Grimm. *Deutsches Wörterbuch.* 16 vols. Leipzig: Hirzel, 1854–1965.

Grote, Bernd. *Der deutsche Michel. Ein Beitrag zur publizistischen Bedeutung der Nationalfiguren.* Dortmunder Beiträge zur Zeitungsforschung 11. Dortmund: Ruhfus, 1967.

Halperin, David. *Before Pastoral. Theocritus and the Ancient Tradition of Bucolic Poetry.* New Haven: Yale UP, 1983.

Hatfield, Henry. *Aesthetic Paganism in German Literature. From Winckelmann to the Death of Goethe.* Cambridge: Harvard UP, 1964.
- *From the Magic Mountain. Mann's Later Masterpieces.* Ithaca: Cornell UP, 1979.

Hauffen, Adolf. *Geschichte des deutschen Michel.* Prague: Verlag des Vereines, 1918.

Heitner, Robert. „‚Emilia Galotti': An Indictment of Bourgeois Passivity." *Journal of English and Germanic Philology,* 52 (1953), 480–90.

Heppe, Heinrich L. *Geschichte der quietistischen Mystik in der katholischen Kirche.* Berlin: Hertz, 1875.

Hibberd, John. *Salomon Geßner. His Creative Achievement and Influence.* Cambridge: Cambridge UP, 1976.

Hirsch, Arnold. *Bürgertum und Barock im deutschen Roman. Ein Beitrag zur Entstehungsgeschichte des bürgerlichen Weltbildes.* Ed. Herbert Singer. 2nd. ed. Literatur und Leben 1. Cologne: Böhlau, 1957.

Hösle, Vittorio. *Die Vollendung der Tragödie im Spätwerk des Sophokles. Ästhetischhistorische Bemerkungen zur Struktur der attischen Tragödie.* Problemata 105. Stuttgart-Bad Cannstatt: Frommann-Holzboog, 1984.
- *Wahrheit und Geschichte. Studien zur Struktur der Philosophiegeschichte unter paradigmatischer Analyse der Entwicklung von Parmenides bis Platon.* Elea 1. Stuttgart-Bad Cannstatt: Frommann-Holzboog, 1984.

Hösle, Vittorio and Dieter Wandschneider. „Die Entäußerung der Idee zur Natur und ihre zeitliche Entfaltung als Geist bei Hegel." *Hegel-Studien,* 18 (1983), 173–99.

Jäger, Hans-Wolf. *Politische Metaphorik im Jakobinismus und im Vormärz.* Texte Metzler 20. Stuttgart: Metzler, 1971.

James, William. *The Varieties of Religious Experience. A Study in Human Nature. Being the Gifford Lectures on Natural Religion Delivered at Edinburgh in 1901–1902.* New York: New American Library, 1958.

Janke, Wolfgang. *Historische Dialektik. Destruktion dialektischer Grundformen von Kant bis Marx.* Berlin: Gruyter, 1977.

Karrer, Otto. *Meister Eckehart. Das System seiner religiösen Lehre und Lebensweisheit.* München: Müller, 1926.

Kaufmann, Walter. *From Shakespeare to Existentialism.* New York: Doubleday, 1960.

Kirk, Rudolf. Introduction. *Tuuo bookes of constancie in Latine by Iustus Lipsius.* Trans. Sir John Stradling. New Brunswick: Rutgers UP, 1939.

Klingner, Friedrich. „Virgil und die römische Idee des Friedens." In his *Römische Geisteswelt. Essays zur lateinischen Literatur.* Ed. Karl Büchner. Stuttgart: Reclam, 1979, 614–44.

Knox, Bernard M. W. *The Heroic Temper. Studies in Sophoclean Tragedy*. Berkeley: University of California Press, 1964.
Knox, R. A. *Enthusiasm. A Chapter in the History of Religion with Special Reference to the Seventeenth and Eighteenth Centuries*. New York: Oxford UP, 1950.
Korff, H. A. *Geist der Goethezeit. Versuch einer ideellen Entwicklung der klassisch-romantischen Literaturgeschichte*. 5 vols. Leipzig: Weber, 1930.
Krieger, Murray. ",Ekphrasis' and the Still Movement of Poetry; or, ,Laokoön' Revisited." In *The Poet as Critic*. Ed. Frederick P. W. McDowell. Evanston: Northwestern UP, 1967, 3–26.
Kuhn, Reinhard. *The Demon of Noontide. Ennui in Western Literature*. Princeton: Princeton UP, 1976.
Ladendorf, Otto. *Historisches Schlagwörterbuch. Ein Versuch*. Berlin: Trübner, 1906.
Langen, August. „Der Wortschatz des 18. Jahrhunderts." In *Deutsche Wortgeschichte*. Ed. Friedrich Maurer and Friedrich Stroh. 2nd ed. 3 vols. Berlin: Gruyter, 1959, II, 23–222.
– *Der Wortschaftz des deutschen Pietismus*. 2nd. ed. Tübingen: Niemeyer 1968.
– „Zur Geschichte des Spiegelsymbols in der deutschen Dichtung." *Germanisch-Romanische Monatsschrift*, 28 (1940), 269–80.
Lohmeier, Anke-Marie. *Beatus ille. Studien zum ,Lob des Landlebens' in der Literatur des absolutistischen Zeitalters*. Hermaea n. s. 44. Tübingen: Niemeyer, 1981.
Mähl, Hans-Joachim. *Die Idee des goldenen Zeitalters im Werk des Novalis. Studien zur Wesensbestimmung der frühromantischen Utopie und zu ihren ideengeschichtlichen Voraussetzungen*. Probleme der Dichtung. Studien zur deutschen Literaturgeschichte 7. Heidelberg: Winter, 1965.
Mann, Heinrich. *Politische Essays*. Bibliothek Suhrkamp 209. Frankfurt: Suhrkamp, 1977.
Martens, Wolfgang. *Die Botschaft der Tugend. Die Aufklärung im Spiegel der deutschen moralischen Wochenschriften*. Stuttgart: Metzler, 1968.
Mensching, Gustav. *Das heilige Schweigen. Eine religionsgeschichtliche Untersuchung*. Religionsgeschichtliche Versuche und Vorarbeiten 20. Gießen: Töpelmann, 1926.
Merrifield, Doris Fulda. „Senecas moralische Schriften im Spiegel der deutschen Literatur des achtzehnten Jahrhunderts." *Deutsche Vierteljahrsschrift für Literaturwissenschaft und Geistesgeschichte*, 41 (1967), 528–46.
Meyer, Herman. „Hütte und Palast in der Dichtung des 18. Jahrhunderts." In *Formenwandel. Festschrift zum 65. Geburtstag von Paul Böckmann*. Hamburg: Hoffmann, 1964, , 138–55.
Mommsen, Momme. „Spinoza und die deutsche Klassik I." *Carleton Germanic Papers*, 2 (1974), 67–88.
– „Spinoza und die deutsche Klassik II." *Carleton Germanic Papers*, 3 (1975), 220–39.
Nemoianu, Virgil. *Micro-Harmony. The Growth and Uses of the Idyllic Model in Literature*. European University Papers. Comparative Literature 11. Bern: Lang, 1977.
North, Helen. *Sophrosyne. Self-Knowledge and Self-Restraint in Greek Literature*. Ithaca: Cornell UP, 1966.
Oestreich, Gerhard. „Justus Lipsius als Theoretiker des neuzeitlichen Machtstaates." In his *Geist und Gestalt des frühmodernen Staates. Ausgewählte Aufsätze*. Berlin: Dunkker, 1969, 35–79.
Ogilvy, James. "Reflections on the Absolute." *Review of Metaphysics*, 28 (1975), 520–46.
O'Loughlin, Michael. *The Garlands of Repose. The Literary Celebration of Civic and Retired Leisure. The Traditions of Homer and Vergil, Horace and Montaigne*. Chicago: The University of Chicago Press, 1978.

Petzet, Christian. *Die Blütezeit der deutschen politischen Lyrik von 1840 bis 1850. Ein Beitrag zur deutschen Literatur- und Nationalgeschichte.* München: Lehmann, 1903.
Pohlenz, Max. *Die Stoa. Geschichte einer geistigen Bewegung.* 4th ed. 2 vols. Göttingen: Vandenhoeck, 1972.
Poschmann, Henri. „Heine und Büchner. Zwei Strategien revolutionär-demokratischer Literatur im 1835." In *Heinrich Heine und die Zeitgenossen. Geschichtliche und literarische Befunde.* Berlin: Aufbau, 1979, 203–28.
Putnam, Michael C. J. *Vergil's Pastoral Art. Studies in the Eclogues.* Princeton: Princeton UP, 1970.
Quint, Josef. „Mystik und Sprache." *Deutsche Vierteljahrsschrift für Literaturwissenschaft und Geistesgeschichte,* 27 (1953), 48–76.
– „Die Sprache Meister Eckeharts als Ausdruck seiner mystischen Geisteswelt." *Deutsche Vierteljahrsschrift für Literaturwissenschaft und Geistesgeschichte,* 6 (1928), 671–701.
Rehm, Walther. *Gontscharow und Jacobsen oder Langeweile und Schwermut.* Göttingen: Vandenhoeck, 1963.
– *Götterstille und Göttertrauer. Aufsätze zur deutsch-antiken Begegnung.* Bern: Francke, 1951.
Reisner, Hanns-Peter. *Literatur unter der Zensur. Die politische Lyrik des Vormärz.* Literaturwissenschaft-Gesellschaftswissenschaft 14. Stuttgart: Klett, 1975.
Rosen, Stanley. Rev. of *Hegel,* by Charles Taylor. *Hegel-Studien,* 12 (1977), 245–49.
Rosenmeyer, Thomas G. *The Green Cabinet. Theocritus and the European Pastoral Lyric.* Berkeley: University of California Press, 1969.
Ryder, Frank G. „Emilia Galotti." *German Quarterly,* 45 (1972), 329–47.
Sammons, Jeffrey. *Angelus Silesius.* Twayne's World Authors Series 25. New York: Twayne, 1967.
Schieder, Wolfgang. „Kirche und Revolution. Sozialgeschichtliche Aspekte der Trierer Wallfahrt von 1844." *Archiv für Sozialgeschichte,* 14 (1974), 419–54.
Schings, Hans-Jürgen. *Der mitleidigste Mensch ist der beste Mensch. Poetik des Mitleids von Lessing bis Büchner.* München: Beck, 1980.
– *Die patristische und stoische Tradition bei Andreas Gryphius. Untersuchungen zu den Dissertationes funebres und Trauerspielen.* Kölner germanistische Studien 2. Cologne: Böhlau, 1966.
Schmidt, Martin. *Pietismus.* Urban Taschenbücher 145. 2nd ed. Stuttgart: Kohlhammer, 1978.
Schneider, Klaus. *Die schweigenden Götter. Eine Studie zur Gottesvorstellung des religiösen Platonismus.* Spudasmata Studien zur klassischen Philologie und ihren Grenzgebieten 9. Hildesheim: Olms, 1966.
Schneider, Wilhelm. *Ausdruckswerte der deutschen Sprache. Eine Stilkunde.* Leipzig: Teubner, 1931.
– „Nomen und Verbum als Ausdruckswerte für Ruhe und Bewegung." *Zeitschrift für Deutschkunde,* 39 (1925), 705–723.
Schöne, Albrecht. *Emblematik und Drama im Zeitalter des Barock.* München: Beck, 1964.
Schrade, Herbert. *Götter und Menschen Homers.* Stuttgart: Kohlhammer, 1952.
Schulz, Franz. „Die Göttin Freude. Zur Geistes- und Stilgeschichte des 18. Jahrhunderts." *Jahrbuch des freien deutschen Hochstifts,* (1926), 3–38.
Segebrecht, Wulf. *Johann Wolfgang Goethes Gedicht „Über allen Gipfeln ist Ruh" und seine Folgen. Zum Gebrauchswert klassischer Lyrik. Text, Materialien, Kommentar.* Reihe Hanser 258. München: Hanser, 1978.
Sengle, Friedrich. *Biedermeierzeit. Deutsche Literatur im Spannungsfeld zwischen Restauration und Revolution 1815–1848.* 3 vols. Stuttgart: Metzler, 1971–80.

- „Formen des idyllischen Menschenbildes. Ein Vortrag." In his *Arbeiten zur deutschen Literatur. 1750–1850*. Stuttgart: Metzler, 1965, 212–31.
- „Wunschbild Land und Schreckbild Stadt. Zu einem zentralen Thema der neueren deutschen Literatur." *Studium Generale*, 16 (1963), 619–31.

Siemann, Wolfram. *„Deutschlands Ruhe, Sicherheit und Ordnung." Die Anfänge der politischen Polizei 1806–1866*. Studien und Texte zur Sozialgeschichte der Literatur 14. Tübingen: Niemeyer (forthcoming).

Snell, Bruno. „Arkadien. Die Entdeckung einer geistigen Landschaft." In his *Die Entdeckung des Geistes. Studien zur Entstehung des europäischen Denkens bei den Griechen*. 4th ed. Göttingen: Vandenhoeck, 1975, 257–74.

Strich, Fritz. *Deutsche Klassik und Romantik oder Vollendung und Unendlichkeit. Ein Vergleich*. 2nd ed. München: Meyer, 1924.

Stuke, Horst. *Philosophie der Tat. Studien zur „Verwirklichung der Philosophie" bei den Junghegelianern und den Wahren Sozialisten*. Industrielle Welt. Schriftenreihe des Arbeitskreises für moderne Sozialgeschichte 3. Stuttgart: Klett, 1963.

Taylor, Charles. *Hegel*. Cambridge: Cambridge UP, 1975.

Vlastos, Gregory. "Solonian Justice." *Classical Philology*, 41 (1946), 65–83.

Völker, Ludwig. „‚Gelassenheit.' Zur Entstehung des Wortes in der Sprache Meister Eckharts und seiner Überlieferung in der nacheckhartschen Mystik bei Jacob Böhme." In *„getempert und gemischet." Für Wolfgang Mohr zum 65. Geburtstag von seinen Tübinger Schülern*. Ed. Franz Hundsnurscher und Ulrich Müller. Göppingen: Kümmerle, 1972, 281–312.
- *Langeweile. Untersuchungen zur Vorgeschichte eines literarischen Motivs*. München: Fink, 1975.
- „Die Terminologie der mystischen Bereitschaft in Meister Eckharts deutschen Predigten und Traktaten." Diss. Tübingen, 1964.

Welzig, Werner. „Constantia und barocke Beständigkeit." *Deutsche Vierteljahrsschrift für Literaturwissenschaft und Geistesgeschichte*, 35 (1961), 416–32.

Wiedemann, Conrad. „Heroisch – Schäferlich – Geistlich. Zu einem möglichen Systemzusammenhang barocker Rollenhaltung." In *Schäferdichtung. Referate der fünften Arbeitsgruppe beim zweiten Jahrestreffen des internationalen Arbeitskreises für deutsche Barockliteratur vom 28. bis 31. August 1976 in Wolfenbüttel*. Ed. Wilhelm Voßkamp. Dokumente des internationalen Arbeitskreises für deutsche Barockliteratur 4. Hamburg: Hauswedell, 1977, 96–122.

Whitman, Cedric H. *Sophocles. A Study of Heroic Humanism*. Cambridge: Harvard UP, 1951.

Wiese, Benno von. *Zwischen Utopie und Wirklichkeit. Studien zur deutschen Literatur*. Düsseldorf: Bagel, 1963.

Wilke, Jürgen. *Das „Zeitgedicht". Seine Herkunft und frühe Ausbildung*. Deutsche Studien 21. Meisenheim: Hain, 1974.

Wirszubski, Ch. "Cicero's 'cum dignitate otium': A Reconsideration." *Journal of Roman Studies*, 44 (1954), 1–13.

Wollstein, Günter. *Das „Großdeutschland" der Paulskirche. Nationale Ziele in der bürgerlichen Revolution 1848/49*. Düsseldorf: Droste, 1977.

Woodman, A.J. "Some Implications of 'otium' in Catullus 51. 13–16." *Latomus*, 25 (1966), 217–26.

Wülfing, Wulf. „Schlagworte des Jungen Deutschland." *Zeitschrift für deutsche Sprache*, 21 (1965), 42–59, 160–74; 22 (1966), 36–56, 154–78; 23 (1967), 48–82, 166–77; 24 (1968) 60–71, 161–83; 25 (1969), 96–115, 175–79; 26 (1970), 60–83, 162–75.

Index of Names

Abrams, M. H. 110
Adolph, W. 131
Alewyn, R. 115
Altmann, E. 151
Anaxagoras 103
Anderegg, J. 42
André, J.-M. 233
Angress, R. 230
Anselm of Canterbury 143
Aristotle 60, 139, 142, 145, 150, 257, 259
Armstrong, W. 154
Arndt, E. 200
Arnold, G. 145, 147–148
Aspetsberger, F. 65, 85, 96, 108
Atkinson, R. 218, 228
Auersperg, A. (s. Grün, A.)
Augustenburg, Duke 51
Augustine 2, 140, 252, 255
Marcus Aurelius 161, 164–166, 169, 256

Bacchylides 98
Bachmaier, H. 95, 104
Baggesen, J. 13
Bahti, T. 20, 25–26, 42
Barner, W. 59
Barnouw, J. 74
Barth, P. 164
Basch, V. 30
Bauch, B. 29
Bayerdörfer, H.-P. 207
Beck, A. 83, 114
Becker, N. 209
Beckers, G. 160
Benn, G. 259
Benn, M. 96, 107–108, 128–129, 134, 155, 176–178.
Bennett, B. 111
Berghahn, K. 37
Bernert, E. 233
Bernhard, T. 259

Bertaux, P. 81, 215
Biermann, W. 259
Binder, W. 6–7, 43, 65, 70, 74, 78, 89, 96, 100, 105, 116
Bloch, E. 37, 259
Blum, H. 237, 239
Bodi, L. 202
Böhlendorff, C. V. 107
Böhler, M. 60
Böhme, J. 145
Boldt, H. 187
Borchmeyer, D. 59
Börne, L. 123, 180–182, 192, 195–196, 198, 223, 236.
Böschenstein, B. 114
Böschenstein-Schäfer, R. 42, 107, 113, 232, 235.
Bowra, C. 97
Brecht, B. 121, 204, 240–242, 249, 255, 259
Brinkmann, R. 44
Broch, H. 258
Brockard, H. 113
Brown, M. 110
Brüggemann, F. 230
Brummack, J. 218, 229
Büchmann, G. 192
Büchner, G. ix, x, 86, 121–123, ch. 3 *(passim)*, 178, 189, 216, 247–248, 250, 257
Buck, T. 131
Butler, E. M. 7, 30, 58, 186

Caesar 215
Calvié, L. 195
Campe, J. 207, 211, 221
Canitz, F. v. 234
Caspari, W. 141
Chrysippus 164
Cicero 98, 164, 166, 233

283

Clark, J. 144
Clasen, H. 193
Corssen, M. 105
Curtius, E. 233
Cusanus (s. Nicholas of Cusa)
Cysarz, H. 42

Daniel-Rops, H. 147
Dedner, B. 232, 234
De Man, P. 113, 115
Democritus 165
Diderot, D. 4
Dierse, U. 42
Dietze, W. 180
Dilthey, W. 168
Dingelstedt, F. 198, 207, 211
Dio Chrysostom 98
Diogenes Laertius 98, 165
Doppler, A. 110
Düsing, K. 101
Düsing, W. 56

Eckermann, J. 5, 57–58
Eckhart x, 139, 142–145, 259
Egermann, F. 97
Eggli, E. 44
Eichendorff, J. v. 122, 255–56, 258
Eichner, H. 44
Ellis, J. 21
Emerich, F. 107
Enfantin, B. 186
Epictetus 164
Epicurus 98, 139–140, 150, 166, 172, 256, 259
Eppelsheimer, R. 73
Euripides 98

Feldmann, L. 123, 198
Fellmann, H. 124, 136
Fénelon, F. 147
Ferdinand I 209
Fichte, J. 8–9, 13–18, 47–49, 69, 74, 76, 93, 101–104, 106, 111–114, 153, 156–158, 162, 242, 251
Field, G. 41
Fingerhut, K.-H. 181, 183
Fischer, H. 178
Fleming, P. 167
Fontane, T. 255
Forberg, F. 69
Franckenberg, A. v. 145

Frederick William III 208
Frederick William IV 203, 208–209, 236
Freiligrath, F. 210, 257
Freud, S. 257–258
Freudenthal, J. 168
Frühwald, W. 237
Frye, L. 50
Fuchs, H. 252

Gaier, U. 68, 89, 110
Galley, E. 211
Garber, K. 232
Garve, C. 11
Gaskill, H. 68
Geißler, R. 37
Gerhard, M. 40, 42
Gerlach, I. 68
Gersch, H. 124
Geßner, S. 36
Gethmann-Siefert, A. 44
Glaßbrenner, A. 196–198, 214–216
Goethe, J. W. v. 2–3, 5, 25, 31, 57–62, 89, 122, 125, 127, 132–133, 159–161, 168–170, 178–183, 188, 197, 205, 236, 238, 241–242, 246, 248, 250–251, 255–257
Gotthelf, J. 234
Gottsched, J. 36
Grabbe, C. 162
Grass, G. 204
Gregory of Nyssa 141
Grillparzer, F. 254, 258
Grimm, J. 208
Grimm, R. 42
Grimmelshausen, H. J. v. 146, 255
Grote, B. 198, 200
Grün, A. 210
Gryphius, A. 167
Gutzkow, K. 123–124, 236
Guyon, J. 147

Habel, R. 37, 56
Halperin, D. 232
Hamlin, C. 108–109
Handke, P. x, 240, 242–244, 249, 259
Hannah, R. 218
Harrison, R. 80
Hartmann, M. 236
Hasubeck, P. 162, 202, 212
Hatfield, H. 7, 253
Hauffen, A. 198

Hauschild, H.-U. 80
Hauser, R. 126, 129
Havenstein, M. 6, 29
Hebel, J. 234
Hegel, G. W. F. 2, 8–10, 18–19, 21, 23, 26–28, 45, 57, 60–62, 93, 102–103, 110–111, 113–114, 126, 150, 156, 162, 183, 186, 195, 203–204, 246, 250, 254–255.
Heidegger, M. 258–259
Heine, H. ix, x, 97, 118, 121–123, 160, 162, 169, ch. 4 (passim), 248–251, 253, 256
Heinse, J. J. W. 176
Heitner, R. 230–231
Helmerking, H. 38
Hengst, H. 186
Hengstenberg, E. 188
Henrich, D. 102
Heppe, H. 147–148
Heraclitus 256
Herder, J. G. v. 2, 82, 169, 190–192, 201, 214, 248
Hermand, J. 4, 205, 218, 240
Herodotus 98
Herwegh, G. 197, 210–211, 236
Hesiod 98
Heusinger, J. x
Hibberd, J. 232
Hinck, W. 202, 204, 213, 215–216
Hinderer, W. 50, 135, 137, 156–157, 175
Hirsch, A. 232
Hof, W. 115
Hoffheimer, M. 60
Hoffmann, B. 207, 211
Hoffmann, H. 237
Hoffmann von Fallersleben, A. H. 197–198, 211
Hohendahl, P. 193
Hölderlin, F. ix–x, 2–3, 10, 50, 62, ch. 2 (passim), 121, 132–133, 150, 157, 169, 172, 177, 179, 191–193, 210, 242, 246–247, 251, 253, 255–257
Holub, R. 128–130
Homann, R. 42
Homer 30, 71, 78, 98, 255
Hooton, R. 198
Horace 232–233
Horn, P. 131
Hösle, V. 31, 98, 113, 249, 256
Hoven, F. v. 16

Humboldt, W. v. 29, 38, 43, 55–56

Iggers, G. 186
Irle, G. 158

Jacobi, F. 11, 93, 168
Jäger, H.-W. 209, 215
Jäger, H. 4
Jahn, F. 200
James, W. 144
Jancke, G. 160
Janke, W. 37, 42
Jansen, P. 131
Jauß, H. 7, 42, 44
Jean Paul 2, 133
Jones, M. 31

Kafka, F. 129, 258
Kaiser, G. 44–45, 50
Kampe, R. 113
Kant, I. 6–9, 11–15, 18, 24, 26–27, 37, 60, 106, 126, 133, 153, 156–157, 173, 194, 251, 253
Kaprow, A. 129
Karrer, O. 145
Kaufmann, H. 218
Kaufmann, W. 58, 60, 72
Keller, G. 170–171
Kerner, J. 257
King, J. 131, 137, 160
Kinkel, G. 188
Kirk, R. 167
Kleist, E. v. 38
Kleist, H. v. 124, 237
Klingner, F. 252
Klopstock, F. G. 150
Klussmann, P. 194
Knapp, G. 129
Knebel, K. L. v. 57
Knippel, R. 5, 42, 43
Knox, B. 97
Knox, R. 147
Kobel, E. 135, 137
Konrad, M. 103
Koopmann, H. 4, 15, 42, 180
Korff, H. 29
Körner, C. G. 16, 49, 59
Kraft, H. 42
Krieger, M. 255
Krüger, E. 186
Kuhn, R. 160

Kurz, G. 80, 104
Kurz, P. 253

Lactantius 140
Ladendorf, O. 236–237
Langen, A. 133, 155
Lehmann, W. 124, 156
Leibniz, G. W. 103, 157
Lenz, J. M. R. 10, 114, 175–176, 248
Lepper, G. 68
Lessing, G. E. 9–11, 17, 55, 111, 168, 229–231, 236–237, 257
Liepe, W. 7
Lindenberger, H. 137
Lipsius, J. 161, 165, 167, 171, 237
Livy 231
Loeben, M.-B. v. 218, 220
Lohmeier, A.-M. 167, 232
Lovejoy, A. 9, 44
Lucretius 139–140, 142, 150
Lüders, D. 106, 116
Ludwig I 209
Lukács, G. 19, 42, 188
Luther, M. 185, 187, 196, 229

Mähl, H.-J. 232
Maier, W. 193
Mainland, W. 42
Malsch, S. 179
Mann, H. 215
Mann, T. 162, 251, 253
Marleyn, R. 42
Martens, W. 234
Martini, F. 50
Mason, E. 62, 107
Matthison, F. x
Mayer, H. 126, 153, 204
Mayer, T. 178
Meister Eckhart (s. Eckhart)
Mende, F. 179
Mendelssohn, M. 4, 36, 168
Meng, H. 5, 7, 27, 40, 44
Mensching, G. 139
Menzel, W. 192–193, 196, 201, 214, 248
Merrifield, D. 169
Metternich, Prince 169, 237, 241
Meyer, C. F. 256
Meyer, H. 37, 232
Michelet, C. 195
Michels, G. 155
Middell, E. 42

Mieth, G. 95
Miles, D. 45, 73–74, 110
Miller, D. 62, 73
Mojašević, M. 113
Molinos, M. de 147
Mommsen, M. 62, 95, 165
Mörike, E. 234, 255
Moses 215
Mosler, P. 160
Müller, E. 169
Müller, J. 42
Müller-Seidel, W. 137
Mundt, T. 123, 186, 250
Musil, R. 258

Napoleon I 215
Nemerov, H. 253
Nemoianu, V. 232
Nestroy, J. 257
Neubauer, J. 112
Neuffer, C. x, 114, 191
Neuse, E. 124
Nicholas of Cusa 1–2, 253–254, 259
Nickel, P. 82, 95
Niethammer, I. 92
Nietzsche, F. 72, 151, 157, 251, 256, 258–259
North, H. 164
Novalis 20, 123, 133, 150, 193–194, 254, 256

Oellers, N. 43
Oesterle, G. 188
Oestreich, G. 237
Ogilvy, J. 113
O'Loughlin, M. 232
Opitz, M. 167, 233
Ortlepp, E. 197
Ottwald, E. 200

Panaitius 164–165, 171
Parker, J. 137
Pascal, R. 159
Petzet, C. 197
Pfau, L. 197, 224
Pindar 107
Plato 2, 23, 99, 104, 111, 114, 142, 163, 215, 255
Plutarch 98, 171, 253
Pohlenz, M. 164
Pollock, J. 130

286

Porsena 47
Poschmann, H. 178
Posidonius 164
Pott, H.-G. 89
Prawer, S. S. 218, 229, 236
Preisendanz, W. 229, 235
Prignitz, C. 74, 80, 106, 111
Prill, M. 85
Proclus 254
Pseudo-Dionysius Areopagite 2, 253–254
Putman, M. 233
Pütz, H. 159
Pythagoras 215

Quint, J. 144

Raabe, W. 258
Reeves, N. 184, 186, 195, 204
Rehm, W. 160, 163, 176
Reinhold, K. 13
Reisner, H.-P. 217
Remarque, E. 257
Requadt, P. 62, 131
Richards, D. 137, 153
Richter, C. F. 139–140, 147, 149–151, 165
Richter, J. P. F. (s. Jean Paul)
Rilke, R. M. 96, 256, 258
Rockwell, E. 36, 43
Rohrmoser, G. 60
Rose, M. 218, 238
Rosen, S. 28
Rosenmeyer, T. 232–233
Rotteck, K. v. 239
Rousseau, J.-J. 7, 46, 82, 114–115, 175–176, 253–254
Rüdiger, H. 7, 29, 37, 40, 42
Ruge, A. 188
Ryan, L. 73, 80, 84, 89–90, 98–99, 101, 105–106, 108–110, 113, 115
Ryder, F. 231

Sammons, J. 145–146, 183, 186, 211, 216, 218
Sandor, A. 180
Saueracker-Ritter, R. 186
Sautermeister, G. 37, 41, 50
Sayce, O. 33
Scaevola, G. M. 47
Schadewaldt, W. 110

Scharfschwerdt, J. 83
Scheffler, J. (s. Angelus Silesius)
Schelling, F. W. J. 8, 16–18, 28, 57, 112, 128, 168
Scherr, J. 214
Schieder, W. 237
Schiller, F. ix–x, 2–3, ch. 1 *(passim)*, 64, 79–80, 82–83, 87, 89–93, 105, 114–115, 126, 131–133, 150, 153, 156–157, 162, 164, 169, 171, 178, 183, 216, 235–237, 245–247, 250–251, 254
Schings, H.-J. 127, 167
Schlegel, F. 28, 44, 122, 133, 150, 162, 169, 258
Schleiermacher, F. 8, 169, 251
Schmidt, H. 124
Schmidt, Jochen 89, 113, 116–118, 165, 169
Schmidt, Johann 187
Schmidt, M. 148
Schneider, K. 139
Schneider, W. 258
Schöne, A. 71
Schopenhauer, A. 127, 151, 173, 256, 258–259
Schrade, H. 71
Schuffels, K. 73, 81
von der Schulenburg, F. W. 192
Schulz, F. 165
Schweikert, A. 240
Seeba, H. 180
Seeger, L. 255
Segebrecht, W. 241
Seidlin, O. 50
Seneca ix, 161, 164–169, 171, 233
Sengle, F. 122, 229, 232, 253
Seuse, H. 144–145, 254
Sextus Empiricus 98, 256
Shakespeare, W. 213
Sharp, F. 158
Siegrist, C. 194
Siekmann, A. 37, 40, 42, 50
Siemann, W. 237
Angelus Silesius 139, 145, 149
Silz, W. 55, 89, 110
Simons, J. 5, 40, 42, 216
Sinclair, I. v. 103
Snell, B. 232
Socrates 30, 99, 196
Sophocles x, 81, 96–98, 160, 247

287

Spencer, H. 188, 205
Spieß, R. 124
Spinoza, B. de ix, 2, 73, 76, 93–95, 102, 104, 108, 112, 150, 163, 165, 167–172, 179, 248, 251, 255
Stäudlin, G. x
Stern, J. P. 135
Sternberger, D. 186
Stierle, K.-H. 82
Stifter, A. 234, 255, 258
Stöber, A. 171, 175
Stolberg, F. x, 114
Strack, F. 62, 110
Strich, F. 60
Stuke, H. 195
Sulzer, J. 4
Szondi, P. 5, 11, 25, 42, 57, 105, 116

Tauler, J. 143–145
Taylor, C. 28
Tennemann, W. G. 139
Tersteegen, G. 147–149
Theocritus 36, 41, 232–233
Thomas Aquinas 142
Theognis 98
Thorn-Prikker, J. 128, 135, 161–162
Thurmair, G. 80, 87, 113, 118
Tieck, L. 122
Tonelli, G. 223, 237
Tucholsky, K. 240–241, 249, 259

Ueding, C. 137

Vergil 36, 232–233
Vlastos, G. 171
Völker, L. 50, 143, 145, 160

Wackenroder, W. H. 133, 251
Walser, J. 116
Walter, J. 259
Wander, K. 200, 214
Wandschneider, D. 113
Weigand, H. 5, 40, 90
Weigand, P. 40
Wells, G. A. 26
Welzig, W. 167
Wentzlaff-Eggebert, F.-W. 5
Wertheim, U. 37, 42–43, 56
Wessell, L. 42, 44, 173
Whitman, C. 97
Wiedemann, C. 237–238
Wieland, C. M. 4
Wienbarg, L. 123, 196, 198
Wiese, B. v. 29, 37, 42–43, 60, 131
Wikoff, J. 205
Wilke, J. 202
Winckelmann, J. J. ix, 2, 49, 126–128, 131–134, 163, 176, 180, 250, 254, 256
Windfuhr, M. 179, 186, 195, 239
Wirszubski, C. 233
Witte, W. 5
Wittkowski, W. 135, 156
Woesler, W. 218
Wollstein, G. 210
Woodman, A. 233
Wülfing, W. 239
Würffel, S. 218, 228
Wyatt, T. 253

Yom, S. 62

Zedler, J. 165, 198
Zelter, C. F. 57
Zenge, W. v. 124
Zeno of Citium 164
Zinzendorf, N. L. v. 147

Index of Subjects

absolute ego 8, 14–15, 102–104, 242
aesthetic education 92, 251
anaphora 218, 258
anti-idealism 153–158, 160, 248, 250
antinomies of pure reason 11–13, 26–27
apathy 50, 55, 76, 87, 125–126, 138, 161–164, 166, 173–175
atheism 69, 122, 124–125, 137–139, 145, 151, 156, 181, 247
Athens 63–64, 75–76, 78, 90, 96
Aufhebung 45
Austria 216, 221–222
autonomous art 181–184

Baroque 145–146, 167, 234, 237
beauty 72, 87, 99–101, 109, 111, 127–129, 132, 134, 247
Bewegung (s. motion)
Bewegungsmänner 123, 239
Bewegungspartei 239
Biedermeier 207, 212, 225, 227, 238–239, 249
boredom 11, 17, 126, 138, 151, 160–161, 173, 221, 257

Catholicism 147, 186
center, centeredness 64, 110, 254–255
childhood 3, 63–64, 68, 75–77, 88, 90, 108, 118, 152, 232, 235, 246, 257
Christ 116, 131, 136, 138, 140–142, 146–148, 184–185, 215, 221, 226, 247
Christianity 2, 167, 180, 184–188, 190, 252, 254
circles, circularity 1–2, 45, 110–111, 182–183, 226, 249, 254–256
coincidentia oppositorum 45
cold 78, 127–128, 131, 135, 162–163, 180–181, 210, 220, 248–249, 256–257
Cologne cathedral 209, 221, 225

complacency 83, 88–89
consciousness 9, 47, 50, 60, 75–76, 79, 81, 91–93, 98–104, 107–108, 111–113, 116–117, 156–157, 162–163, 173–175, 235–242, 245–246
constantia 167
contentment 39, 47, 56, 123, 125, 137, 155, 163, 167, 179
contradiction 3, 11, 13, 25–28, 36, 57, 111, 130, 155–156, 162, 181, 226, 248
cosmological proof 12, 19
cosmos 56, 163–164, 166, 170, 252

death 44, 72, 76–78, 80, 88, 97, 116, 122, 126, 136, 162, 173, 193, 205, 230–231, 241, 257
deconstruction 25–26, 68–69
departure 67, 69, 72, 79–80, 88, 163
differentiation 21, 104, 108–109, 111, 116, 242
dissonance 91
divine right of kings 187
dreaming 157, 190, 193–196, 201–202, 222, 249
drumming 203–205
duty (s. responsibility)
dynamism (s. also stillness, dynamic) 38, 55, 75, 81, 91, 114–115, 121, 132, 144, 177, 179, 198, 217, 239, 249–250, 258

ego/non ego 14–15, 17, 48–49, 102, 157, 162
elegiac 9, 25, 33–39, 44, 89–92, 98
emptiness 122, 124–125, 127, 138, 151, 160–163, 173–174, 247, 257
Epicurean 139–140, 166, 233–234, 256
Eternal Jew 137–139, 160
eternity 123, 130, 137, 160, 169, 173, 193, 218, 249–250
euthymia (s. also happiness) 123, 165

289

evolution 122, 190–191, 214, 240–241
exzentrische Bahn 110

Fanatismus der Ruhe 237, 254
finitude 11–15, 19, 22, 24–25, 27, 46, 61, 74, 83, 90, 101, 133, 144
fire 77–78, 199, 220
France, French (s. also French revolution, revolution of 1830) 179–180, 188, 190, 193–194, 201, 203, 208, 210, 213, 219, 224, 253
freedom 6, 12–13, 22–24, 50, 55, 94, 104, 185, 196, 207–212, 215, 219, 222, 225–227, 229, 235, 237–238, 250
French revolution 23, 173, 182, 194, 200, 204, 237

Gelassenheit 145, 230
Gemütsruhe 94, 163, 165, 167, 179
gender 257
God 2, 10, 12–13, 16, 18, 60, 69, 75–76, 94–95, 122, 125, 128, 134–151, 155, 160, 163, 165, 175, 179, 184–189, 193, 247–248, 252, 254
Godhead 142, 144–145
gods 3, 68, 71–76, 95–96, 98, 100–101, 104–106, 111, 113, 118, 140, 180, 189, 191, 193, 246
Greece 19, 25, 31, 41, 99–100, 110, 133, 163, 180, 256

happening 130
happiness (s. also euthymia) 157, 165–166, 168, 170, 175–177, 185, 234, 248
harmony 64, 68, 74, 79, 82, 89, 93, 111, 116–118, 121, 152, 163–164, 166, 174–175, 180, 248, 252
hen diapheron eauto 75, 103
hēsychia 171, 233
hibernation 203, 223, 249
history 3, 19, 43, 61, 76–77, 81, 85, 92–93, 99, 104, 106–107, 113, 118, 123, 179, 182–184, 186, 194, 202, 211, 249–250

idealism 5, 20, 29–30, 46, 49, 59, 62, 91, 122, 126–127, 153, 155–158, 172, 185–186, 194–195, 201, 204, 247–248
idyllic x, 3, 13, 25, 32–47, 81, 87, 89–92, 98, 172, 245–246, 251
indifference 122, 124–126, 138, 146, 152, 161–164, 171, 179–182, 184, 188, 201, 203, 257
infinite approximation 8–19, 44–45, 106–107, 245
infinitude, infinity 9–19, 23–25, 27–28, 46, 60, 83, 90, 133, 184
insanity 131, 134, 156, 158, 172, 247–248
inspiration 112–113, 132–133, 251
intellectual intuition 7–8, 101–102, 112, 245
intersubjectivity 86, 98, 249, 257
irony 181, 202, 204–210, 213–217, 228, 238, 249
is/ought 9, 15, 47, 127, 153, 155–156

Kirchhofsruhe 249
Klassik 2, 47–50, 60, 151, 163, 165, 171, 235, 240, 246

language 85, 112, 159–160, 242–244
light 72, 125, 152–153, 220
limit 9, 12–17, 24–25, 27, 90
locus amoenus 163, 233–234
locus terribilis 163
love 52–54, 78, 95, 101, 123, 257

materialism 216
der deutsche Michel 123, 198–202, 213–214, 225, 248
misreading 26, 250
moral weeklies 234
motion 2, 22, 38–39, 42–45, 55, 57–58, 60, 71, 73–75, 78, 87, 89, 91, 96, 118, 121–123, 128, 132, 134, 138, 142, 144, 162, 173, 176–177, 179, 184–186, 189, 216–217, 221, 230, 239, 245–248, 250, 254, 256, 258
mysticism 133–136, 141–147, 150, 248, 258

naive x, 3–9, 11, 14, 17, 19–25, 28–32, 38, 45–46, 55, 88, 91, 112, 245–246, 250
narration 64–70, 84–85, 96, 99, 107, 251
narrator
  experiencing 64–70, 76, 84–85, 107–111, 246
  narrating 64–77, 80–81, 84–85, 107–111, 246
narrowmindedness 82–83, 92, 99
National Socialism 200

nationalism 209–210, 219, 222, 224–225, 249
nature 3, 7–8, 17–18, 21, 61, 63–64, 67–68, 75–76, 80, 89–91, 107–113, 127–128, 151, 155, 163, 179, 205, 210–211, 241–242, 246
necessity 23–24, 104
negation 7, 95, 156, 158
negativity 57, 70, 88, 93, 95–98, 100, 121, 177, 227–229, 236, 249
Neoplatonism 252
night 193, 207, 255–256
nihilism 87
nonclosure 43–44, 47, 106–107
nondifferentiation 21, 101, 103, 106, 108–109, 116, 193
noon 255–256, 258
nothingness 15, 26, 44, 47, 65, 73, 87, 104, 108, 144, 151, 162, 242

obedience 186–188, 200, 243
oneness with God 124, 146, 163
ontological proof 19, 73
oppression 50, 55, 231, 235–244, 249, 251, 259
otherness 9, 21–22, 27–28, 49, 95, 144, 151
otium 233–235, 252
oxymoron 115, 258

pain (s. suffering)
pantheism 168, 179
particularity 105–106, 117–119, 121–123, 172–173, 177, 202, 247
pastoral 53, 231–236, 238–239, 249, 251–252, 259
peace 141, 143, 237–238, 240, 251–253, 255
peace of mind 122, 143, 163–168, 171, 248
Pietism 2, 89, 140, 145, 147, 149–150, 165, 248
perfection 2, 4, 7, 13, 16–17, 22, 32–33, 36, 38, 42–48, 61, 88–90, 94, 107, 110, 121, 172, 175–176, 245–246, 249, 254–255, 258
philosophia perennis 249
polysyndeton 162, 258
progress 178, 181, 184–186, 195, 201–204, 207–208, 212, 218, 226, 232, 235, 240, 242, 248–250, 257

Prussia 220, 222, 225
Pythagorean 56

Quietism 92, 147
quietude (s. *Ruhe*, political)

reader 98–100, 194, 212, 217, 251
realism 5, 20, 29, 36, 46, 59, 62
reception 132–134, 143, 251
reflection 64–66, 68, 70, 80, 84, 97, 104, 109, 111–112, 133, 165, 206, 246
Reformation 184, 186
regulative idea 12
responsibility 53–54, 116–117, 164, 166, 171, 238
revolution (s. also French revolution, revolution of 1830, revolution of 1848) 78, 182, 187, 190, 192, 195–196, 205, 208–210, 215, 222, 231, 237, 241, 257
revolution of 1830 183, 219, 237
revolution of 1848 199–200, 238
rhetoric (of *Ruhe*) 254–258
rhyme 205, 208, 210, 213–214
Romanticism 44, 60, 110, 122–123, 129–130, 133, 150–151, 184, 193–194, 201, 210, 225, 248, 254
Ruhe (s. also stillness)
　aesthetic ix–x, 2, 126–134, 161, 163, 178–181, 184, 198, 218, 242, 247–248, 250–251, 254, 258
　political ix–x, 122, ch. 4 *(passim)*, 250–252, 258
　psychological-moral ix–x, 2, 163–173, 248, 250–252, 254
　religious ix–x, 2, 134–152, 161, 163, 186–189, 208, 218, 247–248, 250–251, 254, 258
Ruhe und Ordnung ix, 200, 237, 240–241, 249, 252, 254

Sabbath 187, 189, 255
Saint-Simonism 185–186
satiric 9, 33–35, 39, 81, 89–93, 98, 172, 181, 197, 222, 245
Scheltrede 80–84, 90, 103, 106, 119
Schiksaalslied 70–75
sculpture 123, 128–129, 131–133, 163, 178–181, 224, 247
selection 127–129, 247
self-cancellation 21–27, 30, 69, 103, 130, 154, 242

selfhood 102, 109, 247
self-reflection 30, 69
self-sufficiency 7, 21, 76–77, 232
sensualism 204, 214
sentimental x, 3, ch. 1 *(passim)*, 89, 112, 183, 245–246, 250
silence 80, 85, 136, 145–148, 160, 191, 200, 242, 244, 257
sleep 37, 51, 108, 122, 125–126, 138, 155–156, 189–203, 205, 210, 218–219, 223–224, 248–249
spiritualism 185
spring 210
stars 88, 256
stasis 10, 43, 46–48, 57, 87–88, 107, 161, 173, 179, 201, 218, 224, 235–236, 239, 252, 257
stillness (s. also *Ruhe*)
  deficient x, 53, 75, 86, 114, 121–123, 160, 198, 216, 236, 250, 256
  dynamic ix–x, 1–3, 47–50, 81, 88, 90, 111, 114–115, 121, 125–132, 160, 169, 177, 181, 192, 217, 233, 247, 249–250, 253–257
Stoicism ix, 2, 108, 146, 149, 161, 163–172, 233, 248, 251–252, 256,
Storm and Stress 176, 248
striving 4, 9–10, 14–17, 24, 38, 44–46, 48, 56, 58, 60, 67, 76–77, 83, 87–88, 142, 157, 162, 245–246, 257
sublime 132–133
suffering 46–50, 55, 66–67, 72–75, 77, 85, 93–96, 106–108, 110, 131–138, 140, 155–157, 162–163, 171–175, 185, 188, 247
sun 78, 110, 220, 223, 228, 255–257
sympathy 127–128, 135, 137, 152, 162, 164, 166, 168, 173, 175, 250
synthesis 2–3, 9, 13, 21–22, 24, 27, 29, 31–33, 36–39, 41, 44–48, 56, 61–62, 74, 80, 107, 113, 115–119, 121, 174, 177, 228, 245–246, 256

teleological proof 19
teleology 153–155, 158, 173
temporality 76–77, 88, 115, 123, 202, 246, 250
thunder 204–205
totality 7–8, 81, 92, 95, 100, 103–106, 111, 170, 247, 254
tragedy 103, 105, 179–180
travel 123, 161, 221
truth 10, 75, 249

unity 2–4, 7–8, 14, 16–17, 19–20, 27–32, 64, 73–74, 82, 87–89, 95, 99, 103–122, 135, 142, 209–210, 221, 245–246, 249–253, 256–257
unmoved mover 60, 139, 142, 145

vitality 127, 161–162

water 71–73, 94, 105, 133, 155, 180, 209–210, 256–257
winter 220, 257
withdrawal 51–55, 78, 86, 118–119, 134, 143, 164–165, 171, 182, 184, 203, 205, 231, 239
writing 65–66, 70, 79, 84–85

Young Germany 186, 190, 196, 239, 252–253, 257

Zeitgedicht 202–203